Y0-CCT-601

MEANING AND VALUE IN WESTERN THOUGHT

MEANING AND VALUE IN WESTERN THOUGHT

A History of Ideas in Western Culture
Volume II: The Medieval and Modern Development

J. William Angell
Robert M. Helm

Lanham • New York • London

4720 Boston Way
Lanham, MD 20706

3 Henrietta Street
London WC2E 8LU England

Printed in the United States of America

British Cataloging in Publication Information Available

ISBN 0–8191–6844–0 (pbk. : alk. paper)
ISBN 0–8191–6843–2 (alk. paper)

All University Press of America books are produced on acid-free paper which exceeds the minimum standards set by the National Historical Publications and Records Commission.

To
Alma Jones Helm
and
Marjorie Sutterlin Angell
for
Encouragement, Patience, and Love

ACKNOWLEDGEMENTS

The text that follows adequately demonstrates our indebtedness to numerous authors, books, and articles. Many of them are cited and sometimes briefly quoted. We are grateful for all of them and for the contributions they have made not only to our knowledge and thought but also to the record of human development.

We are happy to express again, as in the first volume of this work, our deep gratitude to those who have assisted us in the writing and publishing of this second volume. We give special thanks to Wake Forest University for financial support and to Provost Edwin G. Wilson and Dean Thomas E. Mullen for making research time available to us. Again, we could not have completed the task without the encouragement and support of our colleagues in the Departments of Religion and Philosophy.

Finally, we are especially grateful to Mrs. Ann F. Francis and Ms. Helen Gilmore for their typing and editorial assistance in the long process of manuscript preparation; and to Dr. Watson E. Mills of Mercer University for his help in setting the type for publication.

CONTENTS

PREFACE

This is the second and final part of a two-volume work that seeks to describe the major ideas of Western cultural history. The first volume, published in 1981, dealt with the ancient foundations, tracing the roots of Western thought from their beginnings in the ancient Near East to the time of the rise of Christianity in the Roman Empire. This volume, appearing later than we intended, carries the development from the fusion of cultures in the Roman Empire to the expansion of Western culture during medieval and modern times.

Each volume may stand alone but together they tell the continuous story of the growth of the major ideas of Western civilization. They are by no means complete; rather, they propose to identify creative ideas and principles, especially in terms of philosophy and religion, that have provided the assumptions and directions of the West. We have been intentionally selective in our choice of thinkers, ideas, and books. It has also been our decision to avoid a discussion of the other great civilizations of world history, as significant as they are. Instead, we have focused on the West and its culture, recognizing that our audience is composed primarily of Western readers and, at the same time, being aware of the fact that Western culture has become pervasive in all the other societies and cultures of the earth.

We have led hundreds of students through this exciting historical journey. Their response has always been encouraging and enthusiastic. Now we are happy that the material will be in print so that many outside our classroom may participate in the cultivation of our cultural roots.

J. William Angell and Robert M. Helm

I.
MERGING STREAMS OF CULTURE IN ANTIQUITY

Chapter 1

The Roman Synthesis

While Jesus was engaged in his ministry in Palestine, Tiberius, master of the Roman Empire, was spending the last years of his life in a clifftop eyrie on Capri, surveying the world with an increasingly jaundiced eye and cultivating exotic vices. To his credit, he had, in the course of his reign, presided with admirable efficiency and some concern for justice over the heterogeneous collection of peoples bequeathed him by Augustus. Thanks to Roman law, Roman legions, Roman seaways, and Roman roads, the world known to classical geographers at last achieved, under the Julio-Claudian emperors, the unity of which Alexander had dreamed.

In no area of individual and civic life was the growing receptivity of the Romans to foreign influences more evident than in that of religion. The early Latin settlers had worshiped a variety of indigenous spirits, or *numina,* who were believed to be resident in sacred places or associated with specific human activities. These beings, while more or less personal, were so imprecisely defined that prayers to them often contained the words *sive mas, sive femina,* "whether male or female." Their functions, however, were in many instances clear enough to Roman householders and farmers. Every aspect of indoor and outdoor life was influenced by the presence of the spirits, and it was, therefore, a matter of practical self-interest to see to it that they were treated with the sort of courtesy which might be calculated to incline them to benevolence toward the human beings who shared their domain.

Domestic worship was under the control of the *paterfamilias,* who determined the roles to be played by other members of the family. Traditionally, the worship of Janus, god of the doorway, was the province of the men, while the women concerned themselves with ministry to Vesta, the spirit who inhabited the flames of the hearth. The numina of the storeroom were the *penates,* to whom offerings of a small quantity of food were made at meals and more substantial sacrifices on special festive occasions. The *lares* originally inhabited the fields, but later apparently became associated in an important way with the household. The *lar familiaris* may have had his origin in the worship of ancestors, but more probably he was a migrant from the fields who took over the spiritual management of the farmer's home. Each man had a *genius* and each woman a *juno*. The entire household showed proper reverence for the *genius* of the *paterfamilias,* who presumably ruled over the other domestic spirits as the father ruled over his family.

Out of doors, the early Roman lived in the presence of an even greater assortment of *numina* than he encountered under his roof. Some of them were reasonably well defined and could be addressed by name, while others were felt only as vague presences inhabiting some stream or tree or sacred spot. Worship of these beings was governed by agricultural concerns. Spring festivals, held in March at the beginning of the Roman year, were designed to win the favorable attention of the spirits to the planting of crops. Late summer and autumn celebrations were held to honor the divinities responsible for the storing of the crops and the transforming of the grape harvest into wine. Winter festivities, such as the Saturnalia, were retrospective or anticipatory in character, acknowledging anew the last successful harvest or looking forward to the sowing of seed in the coming spring.

Civic Religion

With the development of urban life under the Tarquin kings, many of the earlier forms of agrarian religion underwent a transformation as the city-state recognized the need for communal religious practices. The *lares* and *penates* of the rural cultures gave rise to the *Lares Praestites* and the *Di Penates populi Romani Quiritium,* who had important functions in the life of the state. The *genius* of the *paterfamilias* found his glorified counterpart in the *Genius* of Rome itself. The spirit of the domestic hearth inspired the elaborate cult of the Vesta of the City, whose virgin servitors, originally known as the "king's daughters" were held in public reverence and accorded special privileges throughout the history of the monarchial, republican, and imperial eras. Janus, in assuming a broader role as a civic deity, acquired two faces, reflecting his character as god of doors, which are used for coming in or going out. Symbolically, he came to represent the doorway to new periods of time—the first hour of the day, the calends of the months, and, at last, with changes in the calendar, the first month of the year, named in his honor. Even more significantly, foreign gods began to find welcome in Rome, and many of the native deities of Etruscan and Latin origin, incorporated into the state religion during the period of Tarquin domination, ultimately came to be identified with the gods and goddesses of the Greeks. The initial impetus to this development came from Roman association with the Hellenic cities of Magna Graecia to the south. The highly regarded Sibylline Books, brought to Rome from Cumae and consulted in times of crisis, sanctioned the occasional importation of cults from abroad, and the Romans responded by introducing the worship of such deities as Dionysus, Demeter, Persephone, Apollo, and Hermes, some of whom found ready identification with native divinities while others were simply recognized as having been appropriated from the Greek world.

Jupiter, a prominent sky god in the rural religion, became a god of war and justice in the greater life of the state, and from there it was only a short step to his identification with the Greek Zeus. Mars, originally an agricultural divinity, moved from cornfield to battlefield and, in his new character, was at last recognized as Ares, the Greek god of war, whose mythology he appropriated. In similar fashion, Diana was identified with Artemis, Juventa with Hebe, and Juno with Hera.

The introduction of Greek cultic practices under Sibylline guidance was accelerated by the near-disaster of the second Punic War and its aftermath. The efficacy of the old ways of worship in the defense of the state came under serious question, and the people became receptive to innovations which might give promise of restoring the peace, even if the new practices had a foreign flavor.

Mystery Religions

In 206 B.C., the Romans, acting on a command of the Sibylline books, imported the worship of Cybele, the *Magna Mater,* the Great Mother of the gods, from the principal seat of her worship, Pessinus, in Galatia. Long incorporated into Greek religion and variously identified with Rhea, Ge, and Demeter, she nevertheless had a distinctively Oriental flavor which would ordinarily have made it more difficult for her to secure a foothold in Rome than was the case with the more definitely Greek divinities. With Hannibal in Italy though, the situation called for desperate measures, and the Sibylline prophecy that a foreign invader could be expelled from Italy if the Idean Mother were to be brought to the city was readily heeded. Arriving in the form of a small meteorite, the goddess was given a temple on the Palatine and diplomatically identified with several Roman and Graeco-Roman deities.

The introduction of the Great Mother was to have far-reaching effects, not only in the civic religion but in meeting religious needs of a more personal nature. The goddess, according to one story popular in Phrygia, was in love with a beautiful youth named Attis. He emasculated himself, and when he died of the injury beneath a pine tree, flowers grew where his blood had fallen to the ground. Cybele raised him from the dead, and, in the sort of association of the rebirth of nature in the spring with the renewal of life in the individual worshipper common to the mystery religions, the Great Goddess and her lover became the principal figures of a cult which involved practices offensive to conservative sensibilities in Rome but which had a strong emotional appeal to many of the people. In time, the city accepted the presence of priests who, in emulation of Attis, had emasculated themselves, and the religion became a part of the established culture of the city.

During the first half of the second century of the Christian era, the *taurobolium,* another practice associated with the worship of the Great Mother, was established in Rome. The initiate, ceremonially garbed, went down into a trench covered by a wooden grating. A bull was slaughtered on the grating, and its blood ran down over the neophyte, who, by virtue of the ceremony, was *renatus in aeternum,* reborn into eternity. The *taurobolium* also became a public ceremony, often being performed on March 24, the *Dies Sanguinis* of the annual spring festival of the Great Mother and Attis, as a means of securing the well-being of the Emperor or the state.

Mithraism, a mystery cult from Persia, reflected the dualism of the Zoroastrian religion, in which the god Mithras, slayer of the primeval bull which was the first created being, made an early appearance as a heavenly power fighting on the side of Ahura-Mazda,the god of light. The world, according to Mithraism, is a battleground between good and evil, on which the human soul, exiled from its heavenly home, strives to avoid the power of the demons who seek its damnation. Through right action, it can return to its heavenly source. As the central figure of a mystery involving ceremonies of initiation and purification, Mithras appeared as savior and, in the belief of his followers, he was the judge of the soul after death.

Imported to Rome in the first century B.C., the cult acquired a wide following throughout the Empire by the latter part of the second century of the Christian era. Mithras, identified with the sun, *Sol Invictus,* was ultimately to be regarded as the donor of authority to the imperial house, and so the religion enjoyed official encouragement. It was especially favored by officers and men of the legions, to whom Mithras, as a fighter for good against evil, seemed a proper patron for military men who hoped, through the exercise of soldierly virtues, to rise through seven stages of development, corresponding to the spheres of the seven planets recognized by astrology, to a state of beatitude.

Devotees, of the cult of Mithras were apparently all male. They honored the god three times daily, at dawn, midday, and sunset. The seventh day of the week was a day of special worship. The principal feast day was the twenty-fifth of December, celebrating the rebirth of the sun after the winter solstice. With many similarities to Christianity in matters of ritual, Mithraism would remain antagonistic to the newer religion, but after its decline in the third and fourth centuries, many of its tenets were to make their way into Manicheism.

Like the other mystery religions, the cult of Isis and Osiris, imported from Egypt, promised spiritual regeneration and eternal life to those who identified themselves with the death and resurrection of a god. The god in question was Osiris, a good and generous monarch. He was killed by his evil brother Set, who then put his body into a chest and threw it into the Nile. Isis, sister and wife of Osiris, lamented his death and wandered over the face of the earth searching for his body. Coming at last to Byblos, she found it, but Set regained possession of it and cut it into pieces, scattering its members around Egypt. Isis gave birth to Horus, the posthumous son of Osiris, brought the child up in secrecy, and again searched for her husband's body. She succeeded at last in recovering its members, and Osiris, brought back to life, became lord of the dead. Horus took vengeance on Set and assumed his father's former office.

The mystery religion centering around these popular Egyptian divinities spread into Greece in the third century before Christ, and a temple devoted to the worship of Isis was established in Rome about 80 B.C. The consuls opposed the importation, and legislation enacted to discourage or suppress the cult was in effect until the time of Caligula, when it attained legitimacy and prominence in public worship.

Herodotus had identified Isis with Demeter, and Osiris had been hailed by the Greek world as the Egyptian Dionysus. In Rome, Isis was recognized as Demeter's Italian counterpart, Ceres, and at times, with other native goddesses. The ritual of the cult involved morning and afternoon services and dramatic representations of the death and resurrection of Osiris.

Emperor Worship

In many of the areas dominated by Imperial Rome, political legitimacy had been maintained in earlier days by the assertion of some sort of identification between the ruler of a nation and the gods who protected it. If a king was seen as an incarnation of a god or as enjoying a special relationship with the celestial hierarchy, his claim to authority rested on grounds difficult to challenge without impiety. Although rulers of Greek states had made no such claims in the days when the city-states were dominant, the practice of asserting the divinity of living and dead rulers had been adopted by the Seleucids and the Ptolemies in Syria and Egypt, after Alexander's conquest of those countries, as a way of strengthening the control of the Grecian dynasties on native populations. As for Alexander himself, his mother had persistently claimed divine paternity for him, and he had done nothing to discourage the attribution of more than human status to him by the peoples of his short-lived empire.

It was, perhaps, inevitable that Rome would in time discover the political utility of such a religious claim. When Julius Caesar died, he was made a god, and an official cult was established to honor *Divus Julius*. Augustus, who enjoyed genuine popularity throughout the Empire, was worshipped as a god in some Eastern countries, and although he forbade his official deification during his lifetime, he saw the usefulness of establishing a divine sanction for imperial rule and permitted the worship of the genius of the Emperor along with that of the old *lares*. On his death, in A.D. 14, he was officially declared to be a god by the Roman Senate. Although successors to Augustus were accorded similar honors, official deification of living rulers was never permitted in Rome. However, the practice of erecting temples and conducting religious services in their honor remained widespread outside of Italy, and the idea that the Emperor ruled by divine right was a powerful force in holding the Empire together. The mystique thus established about the living symbol of Roman authority was destined to play an important part in Western history long after the collapse of the political authority of the Roman state.

In this connection, it is important to note that the prosecution of Christians in the Roman Empire was a political rather than a religious matter. If the adherents of the new faith had been content to enjoy the toleration which almost any cult could claim under the law, Christ might have been honored in Rome along with Cybele and Mithras. In refusing to recognize the divinity of the Emperor, however, the Christians were thought guilty of a political crime, and so subject to legal penalties.

Epicureanism and Stoicism

With the transformation of Rome from city-state into empire, Epicurean and Stoic philosophy, which had established a foothold in the city through the writings of Lucretius and Cicero, among others, won a growing number of converts. Many Romans who felt uprooted in the changed political environment found in the *ataraxia* sought by the Epicureans the best possible refuge from complexity. The increasing prosperity of the patrician and merchant classes provided the means for acquiring and maintaining the walled gardens and pleasant houses which were the proper stages for the enactment of the Epicurean way of life. If we read little of the practitioners of that day, aside from those who contributed to the literature of the school, it is because their philosophy discouraged the participation in the affairs of state which brought the names of more active men to the pages of history.

The situation is quite different with respect to the Stoics. The sort of modified Stoicism which formed an important part of Cicero's philosophy furnished a suitable framework for the thought of those Romans who were engaged in the attempt to fuse the known world into a single civilization which, while preserving cultural diversity, would be attractive to many patriotic citizens of the Empire who might find it difficult to give more than lip-service to the divinity of the Emperor. The Cosmopolis of Stoic doctrine provided the pattern for their political philosophy.

On the other hand, the ever-growing emphasis on individualism, which in Rome, as in Greece, had followed the radical internationalization of the social structure of the Mediterranean world, found appropriate expression in Stoicism. The concept of a universal city grounded in natural law, with every individual of supreme value under that law, had as its corollary the duty of each toward all. If slave and emperor were brothers in the Universal City, it was equally true that the moral development of each was of primary importance.

One of the greatest of the Roman Stoics began life, in fact, as a slave. Born about A.D. 60, probably at Hierapolis, in Phrygia, Epictetus was a resident of Rome while Nero was Emperor, and at some time in his life he became a freedman. Near the end of the century, Domitian expelled him from Rome along with the rest of the philosophers responsible for opposition to the openly tyrannical form of government which had by then replaced the semblance of the historic Roman institutions preserved during the first century of imperial rule. He emigrated to Nicopolis in the southern part of Epirus and spent the rest of his life there imparting his philosophy to a circle of students. He put none of his thoughts into writing, and we are dependent for a knowledge of his teaching on two works of his pupil Flavius Arrianus: the *Encheiridion* and the *Discourses of Epictetus*. The former work and four volumes of the latter survive.

Epictetus stressed the personal rather than the public elements of the Stoic philosophy. Like Immanuel Kant, almost two millenia after his time, he maintained that the only thing in the world which can truly be called good is the good will. There are two sorts of things which surround a human being. "Some," Epictetus said, "are free from hindrance and in the power of the will. Others are subject to hindrance, and depend on the will of other men. If then he place his own good, his own best interest, only in that which is free from hindrance and in his own power, he will be free, tranquil, happy, unharmed, noble-hearted and pious; giving thanks for all things unto God, finding fault with nothing that comes to pass, laying no charge against anything. Whereas if he place his good in outward things, depending not on the will, he must perforce be subject to hindrance and restraint, the slave of those that have power over the things he desires and fears."

The world has a governor, God, who is responsible for everything that is and from whom nothing can be concealed, not even the innermost thoughts of men. He is the great artist who has made us, implanting something of himself in us, and we dishonor him if we act in such a way as to violate the rational nature with which he has endowed us. One's own self-interest is inextricably bound up with the well-being of one's fellows, and so one can find fulfillment only in the commonwealth of which he is a part and in that larger city which ideally is the model for all human social institutions.

This awareness of the political nature of man provided the rationale for the usual Stoic advocacy of participation in the affairs of state. Epictetus, however, preferred a different way of life and justified it by emphasizing his primary identity as a citizen of Cosmopolis. The daily duties of farmers and merchants or the public activities of politicians are, he thought, too trivial to command the concern of one who has experienced the larger vision. Such a man will be concerned "not about revenue, not about peace and war, but about Happiness and Misery, Prosperity and Adversity, Slavery and Freedom." In his attention to his own good and evil, he is participating in the "administration of the World" and this is the greatest possible act of government.

A more active side of Roman Stoicism came to the fore in the person of Marcus Aurelius (121-180). Originally named Marcus Annius Verus, he was the son of Annius Verus, a Roman patrician of Spanish stock. An uncle, Titus Antonius Pius, was adopted by the childless emperor Hadrian as his successor, on condition that Antoninus, in turn, adopt the seventeen-year-old Marcus, who had been fatherless since infancy. In his new role as a member of the imperial family, he acquired the name of Marcus Aelius Aurelius Antoninus and embarked on a career of study and public service, becoming consul in 140. He acquired his philosophical leanings from one of his tutors named Rusticus and, throughout his life, was guided by a sort of Roman Stoicism which left him free to give expression to the sentiments which dominated his character and to participate fully in the life of the state.

Antonius succeeded Hadrian as Emperor, and when he died in 161, Aurelius and Lucius Verus, another adopted son of Antonius, shared the imperial sovereignty. Verus died in 169, and Aurelius became sole Emperor. A good soldier and able administrator, he was one of the finest men ever to hold the office. It is a regrettable though understandable circumstance that a man who possessed so many of the virtues prized by Christians remained an uncompromising foe of Christianity, reviving, in some measure, the persecutions of an earlier day. Even if he had been better versed in Christian teachings than was probably the case, however, he might have had difficulty in reconciling Jesus' conception of the Kingdom of God with his own vision of the Universal City, of which he, in common with other Stoics, presumably saw the Roman Empire as the highest earthly expression. The Christians, with their implacable hostility to emperor worship, were a menace to the order of the state, and no similarities between Christianity and Stoicism could have been expected to gain sympathy for revolutionaries from a man who thought himself ordained by God to maintain and extend the sway of Roman law.

Marcus Aurelius' greatest philosophical work, to which he gave the name *Ta eis eauton,* survived under the title *Meditations*. The thoughts expressed in his writing were drawn from his own experience and set down in the course of his day-to-day activities as soldier and ruler. As a record of his inner life, the *Meditations* were not designed for publication or the instruction of others, but they have had enduring value as an expression of the highest sort of character to which a man of the classical world could aspire.

The Stoics derived their conception of the Logos from Heraclitus. More than most of the school, Marcus Aurelius emphasized the Heraclitian idea of the impermanence of all earthly things. "Some things," he wrote, "are hastening to be, others to be no more, while of those that haste into being some part is already extinct. Fluxes and changes perpetually rule the world, just as the unbroken march of time makes ever new the infinity of ages. In this view of change, which of the things which swirl past him whereon no firm foothold is possible, should a man prize so highly? As well fall in love with a sparrow that flits past and in a moment is gone from our eyes."

Like all the rest of the world of things, human life and association with family and friends are evanescent. But the universe is not chaotic.

Behind the flux lies "one God immanent in all things, and one substance, and one Law, one Reason common to all intelligent creatures, and one Truth, if indeed there is also one perfecting of living creatures that have the same origin and share the same reason." Since every part of the cosmos is intertwined with every other part, and since all men share in the life and divinity of God and possess reason in common, they are divinely ordained to care for one another and are even under obligation to treat the lower animals with consideration.

It is, in Aurelius' view, useless and impious to rail against fate. What is must be, and it is the duty of a human being to cultivate the attitude of *apatheia,* which will make him indifferent to suffering. Observed from a lofty perspective, the things most valued by acquisitive men are seen to be indifferent in value. Only a sense of duty, stemming from the "inner cause" and prompting benevolent action, is a trustworthy guide for a rational being. For the rest, the cultivation of that which makes a man "just, temperate, manly, free" is the worthwhile course. One who sees things in the proper perspective will not fear death, but will welcome it as a natural event. Like an actor who plays in only three acts of a five-act play, one who faces a death he thinks premature may protest "but in life, three acts count as a full play. For he that is responsible for thy composition originally and thy dissolution now, decides when it is complete. But thou art responsible for neither. Depart then with a good grace, for he that dismisses thee is gracious."

In advocating and living a philosophy based on the idea that the primary end of life is service to one's fellows and the cultivation of personal virtue, Aurelius gave expression to the best side of the Roman character. The emphasis on a world ruled by a law transcending the laws of states, coming from a man wielding the greatest power possible for a ruler, was a significant contribution to the development of the medieval and modern formulations of the concept of natural law and its application to political institutions. In the earlier days of Roman expansion, only *jus civile*—law for Romans, and *jus gentium*—law for other peoples—had been recognized. Natural law provided a yardstick by which the degree of justice embodied in human laws could be measured, with the result that the gap between *jus civile* and *jus gentium* was progressively narrowed and, as Rome extended the rights of citizenship to more and more of her subject peoples, all but disappeared.

The *jus civile* itself, which had in many ways emphasized justice at the expense of humanity, became softened in response to the new ideas. The *patria potestas*—the absolute power of the head of a family over his household—became increasingly subject to restriction, and even slaves, whose lot in Rome had been far worse than in most of the Greek states, were gradually accorded rights undreamed of in republican days. The softening influences of humane philosophy were similarly evident in the emergence of a concern for public and private works of charity, which led to the establishment of recreational facilities, libraries, schools, and foundations for the support of the poor. These civilizing influences spread throughout the Roman world, and despite the growing corruption and political disintegration of the centers of power, the Empire endured long enough for the leavening to do its work.

Chapter 2

Hellenistic Judaism

Judaism is the religion that initially resulted from the survival and development of ancient Hebrew religion after the conquest and devastation of the Kingdom of Judah by the Babylonians in the sixth century B.C. It has maintained its remarkable vitality for more than twenty-five hundred years. Like all living things, Judaism has been formed and nourished both from its own inner resources and in relation to its history and environment.

Hellenism was probably the most significant single external factor that contributed to the character of early Judaism. Hellenism is the familiar term denoting the rich and broad culture created by the Greek-speaking peoples who lived in the region of the Aegean Sea during the first millenium B.C. That culture was spread eastward into Asia and southward into Africa by the armies of Alexander the Great (332-323 B.C.), and it became the dominant culture in the Mediterranean world and in the Levant until the fall of the Roman Empire and the rise of Islam.

Since the Jews lived in the so-called Greco-Roman world during the precise centuries when their religion was in the stage of its essential formation, it was inevitable that Hellenism would contribute to that formation. Hence it is useful to speak of Hellenistic Judaism as the religion of most of the Jews in the Roman world. However, we should also note that the Jews were more prone to reject Hellenism than to accept it. The effect of Hellenism was probably more negative than positive. As we shall see, some Jews were thoroughly Hellenized and few were able to escape the influences of the pervasive culture; but the essential character and content of Jewish faith and practice were derived from another distinctive source: the traditions and writings of the People of Yahweh.

We shall proceed in this chapter, then, by first reviewing the ancient Hebrew faith which Judaism carried forward as its central core. That background has been presented in some detail in the first volume of this work. Then we shall investigate the nature of Hellenistic Judaism, noting especially its contributions to the composite culture of the Greco-Roman world which was to provide the foundation for Western civilization. And, finally, we shall observe the literary products of Hellenistic Judaism, particularly the Septuagint, the extant works of Josephus, and the writings of Philo.

The Hebraic Heritage

The *sine qua non* of Judaism is its conception that the Jews are the Covenant People of God. Without the cohesive power of that conviction, Judaism would be meaningless and would cease to exist. The people of the Kingdom of Judah, apparently first called "Jews" in Babylonian times, were scattered among the nations for all time to come, but they have maintained their self-conscious identity and a continuing sense of community by loyalty to a covenant among themselves and with God, making them historically and culturally the children of Abraham, Isaac and Jacob—the Israelites. Whenever, through the centuries, Jews have become apostate, denying or straying from this identifying center and adopting either secularism or other faiths, they have ceased to be Jews.

The idea of covenant did not originate with the ancient Hebrews, for it is known to have been used as a legal and social instrument in the civilizations of the Near East before the Hebrews appeared in history. However, the descendants of Abraham, as they believed themselves to be, adopted the concept and used it as the center around which to cluster all other aspects of their ethnic existence and, especially, their religious faith and practice. "The Children of Israel" and the "Covenant People of God" were and remain synonymous. They believed and believe that God made a covenant with Abraham (cf. Genesis 12-15) and that the covenant was renewed after the Exodus from Egypt, at Sinai (Exodus 19). That covenant was the context of the Torah, first given by Moses, and it was the fixed point in the preaching of the prophets. It has often been broken by Israel and as often renewed by repentance; but because it issues from the eternal grace and purpose of God, it cannot finally be abrogated. Thus Israel lived and lives in and by the Covenant, and Judaism is the beneficiary and custodian of that sustaining promise. That profound conviction was the centripetal force which created Judaism, its primary legacy from Hebrew religion.

A second, closely allied, aspect of the Hebrew heritage of Judaism is its theological insistence upon universal monotheism. Israel's covenant is with the one and only God, revealed and worshipped by his covenant name Yahweh. Judaism's confession of faith states it unequivocally: "Hear, O Israel: The Lord our God is one Lord; and you shall love the Lord your God with all your heart, and with all your soul, and with all your might" (Deuteronomy 6:4-5). Much of the tragic history of Judaism may be understood in the light of its stubborn and uncompromising adherence to that credo. The history of the Hebrews from the Exodus to the Exile is the record of the gradual development and clarification of that fundamental insight, and the subsequent story of Judaism may be read as the keeping and sharing of that light.

A demanding personal and social morality was a third part of the legacy Judaism received from its forebearers. No people in antiquity could match the Jews in their stern morality. Truth, justice, compassion, and personal integrity were required of every Jew, not by the structures of society alone, or even primarily, but by God. The Ten Commandments were a moral mandate, and religion was not a thing apart from other areas of life but, rather, directly related to every detail of existence. The Jews were constantly reminded that God, as distinguished from all the false gods of human creation, is not nearly as concerned with ceremony, ritual, and the religious words of men, as with justice, mercy, and love. It is small wonder that the Greeks and Romans, while looking with scorn and skepticism on the religion of the Jews, frequently admired their ethical teachings.

A fourth, perhaps less obvious but highly significant characteristic of Hebrew religion which was carried over and developed in Judaism is a unique assumption regarding the nature and meaning of history. The typical Hellenistic view of history, shared by most religions and philosophies, ancient and modern, was that it is empty and meaningless, a cycle of unreality and despair. The only possible meaning and value are to be found beyond the transient realm inhabited by man; hence the nearly-universal yearning for escape from destiny and mortality. But the Jews avoided such destabilizing relativity by assuming the stance of faith: beyond the ever-changing realm of history and nature, yet caring for it, involved in it, and even directing it, there is its source and creator, ineffable and self-giving, indescribable and personal, the One Who Is, Yahweh, the covenant-making God of Abraham, Isaac, Jacob-Israel, Moses, and the prophets. Because history is the creation of a personal and purposive Being, it has meaning and value. History began and it will end. The process which is evolving between those two extremes is where man came into existence and where God is at work in his mysterious judgment and redemption. But because man has, by the grace of God, the unique gift of spirit (*ruach*), which is likeness to God, he may actually transcend the temporal and attain a continuing status with God. That is the Creator's intention and goal, but understanding it is beyond human capacity. Informed by such faith, Judaism has always been characterized by joy and hope, but it has also been wary of eschatology.

Finally, Judaism in the Hellenistic age developed a system of piety which sprang from the religious beliefs and practices of the pre-exilic Hebrews. The nature of that piety has been described in some detail in the first volume of this work, in chapters 31 and 32. It is needful here merely to indicate several elements of the religious practice of Hellenistic Judaism which are directly related to the source in Hebrew religion. Obviously, for example, the Mosaic Torah, containing the essential traditions, received its final form and was canonized in the Hellenistic Age. The Torah has remained at the heart of Judaism ever since. Again, the holy days, which became fixed in their order and meaning during this period, were for the most part designed as annual commemorations of events in Hebrew history so that their celebration would bring past experiences into the present. Further, the memory of the Land of the Fathers was urgently kept alive among the Jews wherever they were scattered, maintaining among the People of Israel an imperishable sense of community and spiritual continuity (cf. Psalm 137; Nehemiah 1ff.; Acts 2:5ff.). This characteristic of early Judaism is unquestionably the seed-bed of modern Zionism. And, finally, the cultic practice of Hebrew religion was transformed but not abandoned. For example, the Temple was repeatedly destroyed and finally given up, but the synagogue arose as a substitute center for worship wherever there were Jews in the ages to come. And the ancient system of priestly sacrifices was necessarily replaced by the regular prayers of pious Jews.

Jews Among Greeks and Romans

The term *Diaspora* is used to denote the people of Israel who were scattered among the nations of antiquity and increasingly into modern times. In fact, the twelve tribes of Israel were unified in their own land and kingdom for only a relatively short time, during the reigns of Saul, David, and Solomon, until a permanent division occurred in 922 B.C.; and the larger kingdom, Israel, disappeared from history after the Assyrian conquest in 722 B.C. Judah, the small kingdom around Jerusalem, maintained a tentative existence until it was destroyed by the Babylonians in 586 B.C. During the twenty-five centuries since that first holocaust, a majority of the Covenant People have been dispersed, retaining their unity through a common memory, a common faith, and a common hope.

During the Hellenistic Age, therefore, the most obvious characteristic of Judaism was that it was the religion of a dispersed people. In the imagery of the book of Jonah, the Jews were swallowed up and carried into the overwhelming seas of paganism. There were large communities of Jews in Mesopotamia and Persia as well as in every area of the Greco-Roman world, from Syria and Egypt to the valley of the Rhine. Alexandria, which followed Athens as the intellectual center of the ancient world, counted two-fifths of its population as Jewish, and it was in Egypt, in the second century B.C., that the so-called "Temple of Onias" was built, the only Temple established by Jews outside of Jerusalem (cf. II Maccabees and Josephus, *Wars,* chapter VII).

A second characteristic of Hellenistic Judaism was its cultural distinctiveness. The Jews were monotheists in a polytheistic world filled with a vast array of gods, goddesses, idols, mythologies, and superstitions. They lived by their own lunar calendar, emphasizing a seven-day week which culminated in the strictly-observed Sabbath. They celebrated many other holy days annually, most of them related to special events in their own accepted history. They tended to be religiously intolerant and socially separate, and they insisted on certain rituals and dietary restrictions which marked them as different from all their neighbors. Clearly, in their own eyes as well as in the view of the Greeks and Romans, they were a "holy" (separate) people, and that fact became increasingly the cause of suspicion and hatred.

Paradoxically, there is considerable evidence that the Jews were admired for their superior moral teachings and behavior among their pagan neighbors. We have noted above that the Jews of the Diaspora preserved and lived by the ancient traditions of righteousness, justice, and compassion which they inherited from Moses and the prophets. Hence a high morality was another distinctive mark of Hellenistic Judaism. Western civilization subsequently built upon that heritage as its primary foundation for ethical principles.

A fourth feature of Hellenistic Judaism, indicated by the phrase itself, was an inevitable cultural syncretism. The Jews who lived among the *goyim* (nations) were markedly different, as described above, and they continued to protect their identity by resistance to paganism, intermarriage, and many kinds of social assimilation. Nevertheless, physical proximity and the passing of the generations continually eroded all lines of distinction. Language was probably the most powerful force for cultural unity. Numerous languages and dialects were spoken throughout the Greco-Roman world, but Greek was the chief vehicle for international communication and literature. All who spoke Greek, including the Jews of the Diaspora, thereby shared the elements of Hellenistic culture. Hence, a widening gap developed between the growing communities of Jews throughout the Diaspora, on the one hand, and the poor and shrinking community which remained in the ancient homeland, on the other.

Finally, a consequent feature of Hellenistic Judaism was its creation of a significant body of Jewish literature in the Greek language. That fact may have influenced the final editing and canonization of the Scriptures (the *Tenakh*), along with the growth of the vast body of interpretive material finally comprising the Palestinian and Babylonian Talmuds, all in Hebrew. Nevertheless, the Scriptures were themselves translated into Greek, especially in the version called the Septuagint, and numerous other Jewish writings were composed, such as the books familiarly known as the *Apocrypha* and the *Pseudepigrapha,* as well as the works attributed to Josephus and Philo of Alexandria. These writings, especially the latter, contain most of what is known about the thought of Hellenistic Judaism. Because of that significance, therefore, the remainder of this chapter will be devoted to a brief discussion of that ancient Jewish Greek-language literature.

Hellenistic Jewish Literature

"Septuagint" is the traditional name for the earliest known translation of the Hebrew Scriptures. The term means "by seventy" (hence the symbol LXX), and is derived from the propagandistic account of its origin which is recorded in the pseudepigraphical *Letter of Aristeas,* a much-debated document probably written in Alexandria in the second century B.C. According to that legend, Demetrios, the royal librarian during the reign of Ptolemy II Philadelphus, persuaded the monarch to sponsor the translation of the Jewish holy books into Greek. Accordingly, Eleazar, the High Priest in Jerusalem, sent seventy-two priests who were equally familiar with Hebrew and Greek to Alexandria where they accomplished the task in a miraculous manner, all producing identical translations in seventy-two days. Essentially the same story is found in Philo's *On the Life of Moses* and in Josephus' *Antiquities* and *Against Apion,* all three written in the first century after Christ.

The *Letter of Aristeas* praises this translation because of its superiority over earlier Greek translations, thus attesting the existence of such although nothing more is known about them. The Greek translation was begun around 250 B.C. and was originally limited to the Torah. The Prophets (Nebi'im) and the remaining books (Kethubim) which also were ultimately included in the canon were translated during the following century, and all of them together have come to be known as the Septuagint. However, modern scholars have raised serious questions about the historicity of this legend recorded in the *Letter of Aristeas,* and many believe it is incorrect even to speak of the Septuagint as though it is a single version. Critical research has shown not only that the translation was done over at least a century and by many hands, but also that it is based on a variety of Hebrew texts, with varying degrees of literalness, and in several recensions. Hence we probably have several Septuagintal types rather than *the* Septuagint.

Whatever the precise facts may be, however, there is no doubt that the Hebrew Scriptures were translated into Greek, beginning as early as the third century B.C., and that the result is one of the most significant literary products of Hellenistic Judaism. There are at least three reasons that this is true. First, the translation of the holy books into Greek made the theological and moral teachings of Judaism available to a wider audience in the ancient world. Hebrew was no longer a living language, even among the Jews. Now the teachings of Moses and the prophets were open for universal appeal. Second, an interchange of ideas between Judaism and Hellenism was carried forward. Every translation is necessarily a commentary, and the choice of word, phrase, or idiom by the translators sometimes produced a radically new meaning in the Septuagint as compared with the Hebrew. Two important examples may be cited in the use of the Greek *nomos* (custom, law) for *Torah* (divine teaching), and the Greek *hilaskesthai* (propitiation, appeasement) for the Hebrew *kippur* (God's annulment of sin). Third, the Septuagint was the primary version of the Scriptures used by the early Christians, rather than the Hebrew; and it was probably largely for that reason that the rabbis, and Judaism in general, rejected it in favor of the original Hebrew text. Many central Christian teachings were derived from the interpretations of the Septuagint rather than from the Hebrew. It is worth noting that the Septuagint was in the *koine* Greek, rather than the classical Attic, just as was the New Testament.

At least three other important translations of the Hebrew Scriptures into Greek are known to have been made during the Hellenistic Age. That of Aquila was made about A.D. 130 by a Christian who became converted to Judaism. It was apparently a literal translation designed to deny the interpretations of the Septuagint being used by Christians. A second was by Theodotion, but very little is known about him or his work, though they are usually dated in the second century after Christ. The third version was done by Symmachus, apparently an Ebionite Christian of the late second century, and it may have used the earlier translations of Aquila and Theodotion. Only fragments and a few quotations in the early Church Fathers remain of the three versions, though, as we shall see, they were used in the great *Hexapla* by Origen in the third century, making them important for the origins of the modern Bible.

Another literary product of Hellenistic Judaism is the collection of fifteen books known as the *Apocrypha*. The term is Greek, meaning "hidden, of unknown origin." The books were given canonical status in the Septuagint but were ultimately rejected in Judaism, probably because of their Hellenistic origin. They represent several distinct types of literature, including history, novel, wisdom, epistle, and apocalyptic. The books supply support for certain doctrines of the Roman Catholic and Orthodox Churches, but they are not accepted as canonical by Protestants. Furthermore, their influence has been widespread in subsequent Western culture, especially in literature, music, and art. A passage from the Apocryphal book of Second Esdras even played an important part in the discovery of the New World by Christopher Columbus. Second Esdras 6:42, about the Creation, was believed to imply that the ocean to the west of Spain could not be very wide, and on that assumption Ferdinand and Isabella sponsored the voyage of Columbus.

The term *Pseudepigrapha* is ambiguous and probably should be abandoned in favor of the more accurate phrase "outside books," used in Rabbinic literature to describe certain writings excluded from the canon. Literally, the term means, "false writings" and indicates pseudonymity. The limits of the collection have never been defined. It usually includes such writing as the *Apocalypse of Baruch,* the *Ascension of Isaiah,* the *Assumption of Moses,* I and II *Enoch,* the *Letter of Aristeas,* the *Sybilline Oracles,* the *Testaments of the Twelve Patriarchs,* and at least a dozen other such writings. They are of interest here primarily because they were, at least for the most part, literary products of Hellenistic Judaism and therefore preserve some of the thought of Judaism in the Hellenistic Age. Taken as a whole, the books classified as *Pseudepigrapha* reveal a stage in Judaism between that of the latest Scripture (second century B.C.) and that of the Rabbis and the Talmud (second to fifth centuries after Christ). The material focuses on the future, usually in apocalyptic imagery, whereas the later Rabbinic literature is almost entirely concerned with the meaning and application of the Torah.

Josephus was a Jewish historian and apologist who was born in Judea about A.D. 37 and died in Rome near the end of the century. His Jewish name was Joseph ben Mattathias, later Latinized to Josephus Flavius, the latter from the Flavian emperors who befriended him. He was from a prominent family, related to the Hasmoneans, and was a leader in the rebellion against Rome in A.D. 66. But when he was captured by the general, later emperor, Vespasian, he became a loyal servant of the Romans, spending the last part of his life as an honored scholar in Rome. His voluminous writings which have survived make him one of the most important, if often suspected, sources available concerning the Jews in the Hellenistic Age. Though his native language was Aramaic, his works are all in Greek, and they reveal a man well educated, widely travelled, and acquainted with most of the Hebrew, Greek, and Roman literature of earlier times.

The three major works of Josephus are *The Jewish War, The Jewish Antiquities,* and *Against Apion*. The first was admittedly written by Josephus in order to justify himself to the Romans for his part in the Jewish rebellion as well as to explain the nobility of the Jews in their stubborn defense of their religious beliefs and practices. It is an invaluable source for historical information in spite of Josephus' habit of exaggeration, but it does not provide sufficient details about the Judaism of the time. *The Jewish Antiquities,* given the title *The Archaeology of the Jews* in its original Greek, is a mine of facts and tales about the history of the Jews from the creation to the rebellion against Rome. Like the earlier writing, *The Antiquities* had an explanatory and apologetic purpose. The Scriptures were its main source, but Josephus often supplemented the Biblical account by reference to other histories. He frequently recorded narrative and commentary which later appear in Rabbinical literature, thus demonstrating the devclopment of Jewish theology prior to the Talmud.

In his treatise *Against Apion,* Josephus made his strongest defense of Judaism. The occasion was the persecution of the Jews in Alexandria by Flaccus, the Roman governor, in A.D. 38, when the mad Caligula was Emperor. The Jews had refused to worship Caligula and to allow his statue to be raised in the synogogues; and when the Roman puppet-king of Judea, Agrippa I, the grandson of the despised Herod the Great, visited Flaccus in Alexandria, the Jews had risen in rebellion. In order to settle the matter, delegations from the Jews and the pagans were sent to Rome to appeal to Caligula. Among the Jews was Philo, whose work will be discussed below; and among the pagans was Apion, a mortal enemy of the Jews. Flaccus was recalled to Rome and later executed. Caligula was soon assassinated. And Apion died in A.D. 48.

Against Apion is a fascinating refutation of the calumnies against the Jews by Apion and all other pagans. In it Josephus surveyed the histories of the Greeks, the Egyptians, the Babylonians, the Phoenicians, and others, arguing the greater antiquity and superior morality of the Hebrew people. He claimed that the greatest of the Greek philosophers, including Pythagoras, Plato, and the Stoics, received their wisdom from Moses, and that Clearchus, a disciple of Aristotle, wrote that his master met, admired, and learned from Jews in Syria. The treatise is a splendid example of the ambivalent attitude of Hellenistic Judaism toward Greek culture: while rejecting the polytheistic idolatry and gross immorality of the Greeks and Romans, admiring and adopting the wisdom and general culture of the best of Hellenism. The result was cultural fusion.

Philo and Jewish-Alexandrian Philosophy

Philo, the scholarly and irenic Jew of Alexandria, was born about 20 B.C. and lived until after A.D. 40, when, as mentioned above, he was part of the Jewish delegation to Rome on behalf of the persecuted Jews of Alexandria. Thus he was a contemporary of Hillel, Herod the Great, Augustus, Jesus, and Paul. He represents the essence of Hellenistic Judaism—the synthesis of loyal Jewish piety and idealistic Greek philosophy—and his thought has been generously preserved in the thirteen modern volumes of his surviving writings.

The writings of Philo are usually divided into four categories. First is a group of treatises on various subjects, including history (*Against Glaccus* and *The Legation to Caius*) and ethics (*That Every Good Man Is Free* and *On the Contemplative Life*). Second is *Questions and Answers,* composed of commentaries on Genesis and Exodus in a fashion anticipating medieval scholasticism. Third is *The Allegory of the Torah,* comprising a series of essays based on selected passages from the Scriptures. *The Allegory* was clearly intended for Jews who were familiar with the Torah, but the fourth category, *The Exposition of the Torah,* was apparently designed for pagan readers who might desire to understand the holy books of the Jews.

This arrangement of Philo's writings should not be understood as his, however, but rather as that of modern scholars who have attempted to clarify and systematize his thought. He did not develop a unified system of doctrines. Nevertheless, his central purpose and the method he chose to achieve it are clear throughout, and we may conclude this discussion of Hellenistic Judaism by describing briefly his method and its results.

Philo's purpose was to expound the profound truths of Judaism, especially as found in the Torah, in terms of both Jewish and Greek thought, so as to lead all men along the road to virtue and truth, toward the ultimate goal of communion with God. He wished to bring together Jew and Greek, revelation and reason, grace and moral effort. And the method he chose was allegorical interpretation, evidently learned from the Stoic philosophers, who used it in their interpretation of Homer. By that method Philo read the Scriptures as more than records of ancient persons and events, though he believed they were that also; he saw them as symbolic truths about meaning and value for everyman which are found also, in different terms, in the best of Greek philosophy, especially in Plato and the Stoics.

Philo interpreted the two accounts of creation in Genesis 1 and 2 as concerned primarily with the dual nature of man. The first account describes the creation of man in the abstract, as an idea (cf. Plato's "forms"); the second tells how God made man (Adam) of the dust, as a part of the material world, but also gave him spirit, which is the God-like quality. Adam therefore is body and mind (or soul, or spirit). The mind is incomplete until it is joined to the perceiving senses (Eve). Adam and Eve were in Eden, a state of virtue (the four rivers of Eden represent the four cardinal virtues) until they succumbed to the inclination toward self-satisfaction in pleasure (temptation and fall). Expelled from Eden (virtue), man still retains hope because he is partially spirit. Hope leads to repentance (Enoch) which is followed by peace of mind (Noah). Now lost man is on the royal road to restoration, and the stories of the Patriarchs (Genesis 12-50) symbolize the stages in man's approach to God. Abraham depicts the process of learning by leaving error (Ur) and migrating to Haran (which means introspection, turning from perception to conception). Isaac is intuition, the proper means for apprehending reality by the higher mind. Jacob-Israel exemplified the realization of virtue by practice.

This is a mere sample of the detailed theology derived from the Scriptures through the method of allegorical interpretation by Philo. He worked primarily in terms of theology and etymology. The truths he believed and sought to teach were evidently drawn from his Jewish faith and from his wide and sympathetic reading of Greek philosophy, especially Plato and the Stoics; but he was convinced that their ultimate source was the Torah, in which he found them clearly manifest in the names of persons and places as well as in the spiritual meaning of the ancient narratives.

It is possible here merely to mention only three of the foundational principles of Philo's philosophy. First, he was a consistent dualist, but not in the same way the Plato and Zoroaster were. His dualism was not between spirit and matter or between two transcendent forces, the one good and the other evil; rather, in Hebraic fashion, he saw an absolute distinction between God and the world, between the transcendent and the immanent. Borrowing from Plato, but with an echo from the Torah (cf. Exodus 6), Philo called God *To On,* "the Being," or *To Ontos On,* "the Being that Is;" and God in that sense is wholly other, unknowable, indescribable, and unapproachable. There can be no direct relation between such a God and the physical, created realm below.

Nevertheless, Philo taught that there is a bridge between God and the world, a way from man to God. That is the *Logos,* a term familiar to the Hellenistic mind from Heraclitus, Pythagoras, Plato, and Stoicism; but the same concept, Philo believed, may be seen in the Hebrew teaching about *Hokma,* the revealed Wisdom of God (cf. Proverbs 8). The Logos is the Divine in his self-projected relatedness. The Logos creates, sustains, and permeates the whole creation so that man, through learning, spiritual apprehension, and virtue, may rise above the sensible world to approach and know God as he is revealed. Thus the ineffable God speaks to man by his Words (*Logoi*) and man may return to God, the Source of all Being.

Philo frequently wrote of that return to God as the royal road. It is clearly illustrated in the story of Jacob-Israel at Bethel (Genesis 28:10-22) where the Patriarch in a dream saw a ladder set up on the earth and reaching to heaven, with angels ascending and descending. Philo insisted that the capacity of man for ascending is not due to any power or virtue of man but rather is a gift of grace, the creative and revealing power of God through his Logos. Using that gift, man may recognize not only that God *is* (*theos*) but that he is *ruler* (*kyrios*), and man may come to know God in his fulness (*pleroma*), thus living in virtue according to "the unwritten law of nature," (cf. Stoicism and the Noachian laws) and the law of Moses (*Torah*).

In conclusion, we should observe at this point that Philo's synthesis of Judaism and Hellenism was not accepted by his fellow Jews in the future. He was almost totally ignored by the magisterial rabbis of the Talmud. The Judaism that survived the Roman wars rejected Hellenistic Judaism and developed instead the piety of the oral and written Torah in the traditions of the Pharisees. Nevertheless, Hellenistic Judaism, and Philo in particular, exerted powerful influence on the rising new religion, Christianity, which began among the Jews of Palestine with many affinities with the Pharisees but soon spread from that birthplace and became the dominant religion of the Greco-Roman World.

II.
THE BEGINNINGS OF CHRISTIAN THOUGHT

Chapter 3

Apostolic Christianity: Paul

The Apostle Paul is the primary source for Christianity. The term "primary" here may be understood to mean both first in time and first in importance. That is to say, Paul's writings remain the earliest testimony available concerning Christian origins, since the Gospels and all other parts of the New Testament were written later than Paul's letters. And Paul's theology, which is rather fully sketched in his writings, has continued ever since to be the foundation and norm of all Christian teachings. Thus it is impossible to exaggerate the significance of Paul for the history of Christianity. He is by far the most influential person in all Christian history. And, further, since the Christian religion has in so many ways supplied the structure and determined the course of subsequent Western culture, we may even claim that Paul is the most influential figure in world history in the last two thousand years!

Saul the Jew and Paul the Christian

The life of Paul is better known than that of most famous persons in antiquity, though scholars still find many uncertain details about which to debate. The two main sources of information are the letters attributed to him in the New Testament and the Book of the Acts, the second half of which is composed of an account of the activities of Paul after his conversion. However, serious differences are apparent between the letters and Acts, and some desirable information is simply not recorded. Possibly the most fascinating lacuna is that of his last years. He was taken as a prisoner from Jerusalem via Caesarea to Rome, where he remained for two years awaiting a hearing before Caesar. Was he then released or executed? We can only surmise.

While granting variations in date and detail, we may assume that Paul was born near the beginning of the Christian era and that he died, probably as a martyr under Nero, around A.D. 64. He was a loyal Jew of the Diaspora, born in the great city of Tarsus in Cilicia. He claimed to be of the tribe of Benjamin and thus was given the name of that tribe's greatest hero, the first Israelite king, Saul. He grew up in Tarsus, apparently in an orthodox Jewish home, though his father enjoyed the unusual status of being a Roman citizen and seems to have been rather well-to-do. There is some evidence that during the previous century the family had migrated from upper Galilee. Saul had a married sister and a nephew who lived in Jerusalem.

Tarsus was strategically located at the southern entrance to the Cilician Gates, a focal point for land and sea travel between east and west. The city boasted of its advanced culture (cf. Strabo) and it was a center of Stoic philosophy. The young Saul could hardly have escaped a broad acquaintance with Hellenism and Hellenistic Judaism as well as the strict Phariseeism to which he adhered. And he obviously grew up in a polyglot milieu, speaking Greek, Latin, and Aramaic as well as the Hebrew of the Scriptures.

Saul of Tarsus was a young man, probably in his teens, when he went to Jerusalem in order to study under the famous Rabbi Gamaliel II. He remained there during the time of the ministry of Jesus, and the record suggests that he strongly opposed the new Christian movement from its inception. Most of the priests and rabbis considered the teachings of Jesus to be a dangerous heresy. It is a moot question as to whether Saul the Pharisee ever saw Jesus, but it is at least possible; and it is certain that he became familiar with the earliest disciples and their teachings. He abhorred the followers of Jesus and persecuted them strenuously, even participating in the execution by stoning of at least one of the leaders (Acts 8:1).

One of the most decisive and familiar stories in history is that of the sudden conversion of Saul of Tarsus as he travelled from Jerusalem to Damascus seeking to crush the new faith. That event occurred soon after the death of Jesus, not long after A.D. 30. The radically shaken young man, henceforth known as the Christian Paul instead of the Jew Saul, remained for three years in and around Damascus. He obviously had much to learn and more to assimilate. Around A.D. 34/35 he spent two weeks in Jerusalem, in the company of the Apostles Peter and James, the brother of Jesus. Then he returned to his native Tarsus, where he remained for about eight years, no doubt thinking through his new faith and giving witness to it.

Paul's great ministry as the Apostle to the Gentiles began around A.D. 43/44 when he went to live and work in Antioch with the Christian leader Joseph of Cyprus, a Hellenistic Jew now called Barnabas. The Christian community of Antioch, strengthened by the arrival of many who fled the recent persecutions in Judea, soon commissioned Paul and Barnabas to carry their faith to the Jews of Cyprus and the territories to the west. They went, taking with them John Mark of Jerusalem, a nephew of Barnabas, going first to Cyprus and then to the provinces of south-central Asia Minor. When they were refused a hearing in the synagogues, they turned to Gentiles and gained many converts among them.

The admission of Gentiles to the churches, without requiring them to abide by the ceremonial requirements of Judaism, led to a crisis among the Christians, especially in Jerusalem. A major conference was held in Jerusalem, probably in A.D. 47 or 48, attended by Paul, Barnabas, Silas, Peter, James, and other "pillars" of the Church. The result was the so-called "apostolic decree" (cf. Acts 15) which permitted the acceptance of Gentiles who had not first become converted to Judaism but who were required, in addition to accepting the Gospel, to live by the so-called Noachian Laws of fundamental morality (cf. Genesis 9:9-19). The decision marked a momentous event in the history of Christianity.

Subsequently, Paul made another missionary journey from Antioch, this time accompanied by Silas. The work lasted four or five years, and for the first time the Christian Gospel was preached in Europe. The missioners worked in the Greek homeland, encircling the Aegean and establishing churches in such cities as Thessaloniki, Corinth, and Ephesus. After visiting Jerusalem again, they returned to Antioch.

Soon a third missionary journey began, probably around A.D. 54. The itinerary was similar to that of the second round, except that this time the center of activity appears to have been Ephesus. Paul finally returned again to Jerusalem, obviously still his spiritual home, about A.D. 59. There serious trouble arose because of the opposition of the orthodox Jews, and Paul was arrested and imprisoned. He was confined for safekeeping in the coastal city of Caesarea, the headquarters of the Roman procurator. When no decision in his case was forthcoming, Paul exercised his citizen's right of appeal to Caesar, and he was taken under guard to Rome. The account of the journey (Acts 27-28) is one of the masterful sea stories in ancient literature.

Paul arrived in Rome as an imperial prisoner around A.D. 62. The record indicates that he remained there for two years, enjoying considerable freedom and awaiting his trial. That is where the account ends. The scholars disagree as to the result of his trial, but most believe that even if he were temporarily given his freedom he was soon imprisoned again and finally beheaded outside the walls of the city, probably about A.D. 64, when the infamous Nero was polluting the world with his crimes.

The Writings of Paul

We began this chapter by claiming that Paul's primary significance is due in part to the fact that his writings supply the earliest witness to

Christianity that is available to us. He probably wrote many letters to individuals and churches during and after his missionary journeys. If that is true, most of them have been lost, but, fortunately, several have survived. The extant letters are filled with his interpretations of the faith and his counsel to the young churches. They were collected and preserved by the churches not long after Paul's death (cf. II Peter 3:15-16), and ten of his letters, along with the Gospel of Luke and the Book of the Acts, were designated, by Marcion and his followers in Rome before the middle of the second century, as the Christian canon of Scriptures.

Fourteen of the twenty-seven books in the New Testament have been attributed to the Apostle during the course of Christian history. They are as follows: Romans, I and II Corinthians, Galatians, Ephesians, Philippians, Colossians, I and II Thessalonians, I and II Timothy, Titus, Philemon, and Hebrews.

The Pauline authorship of the Letter to the Hebrews has been seriously questioned since patristic times, and few now accept it as such. It does not claim to be by Paul and the arguments against it are convincing. Further, most modern scholars reject the claim that Paul wrote the so-called Pastorals, I and II Timothy and Titus, largely because they represent an ecclesiology of a later period. There remain questions about the authenticity of II Thessalonians, Ephesians, and Colossians. Some insist that they were written by the Apostle and few would doubt that they reflect a "Pauline circle." That leaves seven which are almost certainly genuine products of Paul's hand. The significant fact may be that those remaining without serious question contain the core of Paul's thought and contributions. We may be confident that we know his mind well.

Interpreting Paul

What are the ideological sources of Paul's thought? This is a key question in the light of his significance. It has been widely debated and variously answered, especially during the past century, when the most stringent research has been pursued into every aspect of Christian origins. Individuals and schools of thought have claimed with strong conviction that they have marshalled the evidence and then clearly delineated the particular controlling source which alone explains the total theology of the Apostle. But a measure of the failure of each of the claims to be completely satisfactory may be seen in the fact that there is considerable evidence to support all views. It becomes increasingly certain that Paul was too eclectic and comprehensive in his experience and thought to be placed in a narrow category.

Nevertheless, it is useful to identify three distinctive types of culture which were available to Paul and which seem to have contributed to his thought. Each has been argued to have been dominant by many modern interpreters of the Apostle. First, there was the Judaism of Palestine, particularly the religion of the synagogues, which was being developed by the great rabbis and which was often permeated by the apocalyptic coloring of the ages. Second, there was the Hellenistic paganism of the Greco-Roman world, dominated in Paul's day by a synthesis of redemption motifs derived from moral philosophy and the popular mystery cults. And, third, there was the broad piety of Hellenistic Judaism, best represented by Philo, which attempted to preserve the essence of the Torah and the Prophets while acknowledging other ways of God in a wider world.

1. Paul himself testified to his religious origins and training in Palestinian Judaism. The author of the Acts recorded that when Paul was arrested on his last visit to Jerusalem, he asked the Roman tribune, in Greek, for the privilege of addressing the violent mob which opposed him. "I am a Jew, from Tarsus in Cilicia, a citizen of no mean city," he said, identifying himself to the confused official. Given permission, he spoke to the crowd in Aramaic, saying, "I am a Jew, born in Tarsus in Cilicia, but brought up in this city at the feet of Gamaliel, educated according to the strict manner of the law of our fathers, being zealous for God as you all are this day" (Acts 22:3).

Later, when Paul was imprisoned in Caesarea awaiting transport to Rome for his appeal to Caesar, he defended himself before the puppet king, Agrippa, claiming that "my manner of life from my youth, spent from the beginning among my own nation and at Jerusalem, is known to all the Jews. They have known for a long time, if they are willing to testify, that according to the strictest party of our religion I have lived as a Pharisee" (Acts 26:4-5).

In his letter to the Philippians, Paul recorded that he was "circumcised on the eighth day, of the people of Israel, of the tribe of Benjamin, a Hebrew born of Hebrews; as to the law a Pharisee, as to zeal a persecutor of the church, as to righteousness under the law blameless" (Phil. 3:5-6). And he wrote to the Galatians: "For you have heard of my former life in Judaism, how I persecuted the church of God violently and tried to destroy it; and I advanced in Judaism beyond many of my own age among my people, so extremely zealous was I for the traditions of my fathers" (Gal. 1:13-14).

There is no reason to question the accuracy of any of those claims. But aside from such direct testimony, there is much evidence in the writings and teachings of the Apostle to support the assumption that Palestinian Judaism was a major source of his Christian theology. Two examples will be sufficient here. First, Paul often used the method of exegesis which was common to the rabbinical schools of first-century Palestine. He frequently supported his teachings by citing scriptural references, revealing a careful awareness of the priority of Torah over Nebi'im and Kethubim. He developed his ideas in the form of Midrash. His writings are filled with both Halachah and Haggadah, similar to those found in the Talmud. He never ceased to be a rabbi, albeit a Christian rabbi.

A second factor derived from Palestinian Judaism in the theology of Paul is his apocalyptic eschatology. The apocalyptic genre was a primary mode of expression among the Jews, especially during the three centuries from the Maccabean War to the Bar Cochba Revolt—precisely at the time of the rise of Christianity (cf. Volume I, chapter 25). Paul's letters are filled with conceptions from that milieu, such as frequent references to the two aeons separated by the appearance of the heavenly Messiah (Jesus); the imminent second parousia, resurrection of the dead, and final judgment; and the cosmic struggle between the forces of God and the powers of evil. Such language was incomprehensible in the Gentile world until it was heard from Paul and the other Jewish Christians.

2. Nevertheless, it has been quite popular in this century to find the fundamental source of Paul's theology in the pagan Hellenism of his world rather than in his native Judaism. According to this interpretation, Paul is best understood as the creator of a new mystery religion, centered in a concern for salvation through sacramental union with a dying and rising god, the achievement of immortality, and apotheosis. Major proponents of this approach are the so-called "History of Religion" school (especially Bousset and Reitzenstein) and, in a different manner, Bultmann and his followers.

Support for this point of view again may be found both in the testimony we have from and about Paul and in the structure and concepts of his theology. He was born and lived as a youth in Tarsus, the "Athens of Asia Minor," a city famous not only for its Stoic philosophers but also for its cult of Sandan-Heracles, a fertility god like Adonis, Osiris, and Tammuz. The young Saul could no more have escaped familiarity with the cult, in spite of his orthodox Jewish upbringing, than a Jew in America today can fail to know about Christmas and Easter.

Furthermore, except for his few years in Jerusalem before his conversion, most of Paul's life was spent in the context of Gentile, Hellenistic culture. He would therefore not only be acquainted with its religious ideas and practices; he would be expected to present his Gospel to the Gentiles in concepts familiar to them.

Two of the predominant motifs in Hellenistic mystery religions were the desire for saving knowledge and for escape from control by superhuman powers and the finality of death. *Gnosis* (revealed, delivering knowledge) and *athanasia* (immortality, the conquest of death) were the universal craving. They were precisely what the cults promised. And much of Paul's language may be understood in the same vein.

Paul's theology is based upon the proclamation (*kerygma*) of a mystery (*mysterion*): that the Lord (*kurios*), who is the Son of God (*huios theou*), has died and been raised from the dead, thereby providing salvation (*soteria*) for those who sacramentally unite with his body (*soma Christou*). The very words and concepts seem parallel to the familiar mystery religions of the Greco-Roman world. However, those who refuse to accept such an interpretation of Paul argue that there are vast differences between the content of his Gospel and the cultic mysteries, not the least being the fact that he speaks of the historical man, Jesus, who was his contemporary rather than of a legendary figure from ancient mythology. Further, the most gnostic teachings are found in Ephesians and Colossians, which may represent the thought of later "Paulinists" who were more influenced by Hellenistic ideas. Whatever the claim, Paul's assimilation of Hellenistic terms and ways of thought can hardly be denied.

3. Since Saul of Tarsus was a Jew of the Diaspora, it would appear to be natural that the primary sources of his thought would be Hellenistic Judaism. It is true that he was trained as a rabbi in Jerusalem in the religion of the Torah and the Prophets, and it is also true that most of his life was spent in close proximity to Hellenistic culture. Yet he remained a loyal Jew, and later a Christian, whose language of thought and communication was the vernacular (*koine*) Greek, and he lived on the boundary between Athens and Jerusalem.

Although there is no evidence that the Apostle knew anything of the work of Philo of Alexandria or even that he was familiar with the Septuagint as such, there are striking parallels between the teachings of Philo and the so-called "piety of the Septuagint," on the one hand, and the theology of Paul on the other. It is likely that the similarities are not due to Paul's acquaintance with Philo or the Alexandrian Scriptures but rather that they all three grew out of the same soil, Hellenistic Judaism, with a common culture and language.

Paul used the allegorical method on occasion, but much less so than Philo. Philo's understanding of the Patriarchs of Israel as both historic figures and eponyms may be seen in Paul; and Paul's Christology may be somewhat parallel to the Moses of Philo—a unique figure, a "man of God," whose mediation by ascent, descent, and death brings salvation to the people. Furthermore, linguistic and conceptual harmonies abound between the Septuagint and Paul. H. J. Schoeps, for example, has enumerated five features common to Paul and the "piety of the Septuagint": (1) the missionary emphasis, (2) the moralizing and legalizing of the Torah, (3) the understanding of sin as essentially *hamartia,* arrogant rebellion, (4) the shifting of meaning for atonement from expiation to annulment, and (5) the view of the Torah as *paideia,* moral pedagogy.

We may conclude, therefore, that evidence may be presented to support the arguments that Paul's theology had its source in Hellenistic religion and philosophy, or in Palestinian Judaism with its mix of rabbinic interpretation and apocalyptic, or in the Hellenistic Judaism of the Diaspora. All three views have been vigorously promoted. However, a compromise opinion may be closer to the truth.

Since all three cultural sources were available to the Apostle, and since elements of all three may be found in his theology, it is probable that he consciously used terminology, concepts, and methods from the whole of his knowledge and experience, willingly being "all things to all men, that I might by all means save some" (I Corinthians 9:22). We should not overlook the fundamental claim of Paul, however, that all things were new for him after his conversion to Christianity. His experience on the road to Damascus became henceforth the basis for his apostleship and the key to his gospel. If any one ingredient of his life and thought is to be emphasized and isolated, that was it—the vision of the crucified and risen Christ. He admitted that he learned from Peter, James, and the other earlier "pillars" of the Church; and he passed on to the churches the tradition (*paradosis;* cf. I Cor.15:3) which he had received. Yet he insisted that the message he delivered was essentially his, based on experience with God in Christ (Galatians 1:11-20). In that way he used the traditions of the Christians who were before him and the traditions of men in the various cultures of his world.

Elements of Paul's Theology

In the light of the inestimable significance of the thought of the Apostle Paul, so that he has, indeed, been designated the creator of

Christianity, we shall conclude this chapter with a brief sketch of his theology as it is found in the New Testament.

1. Paul's teaching, like subsequent Christianity in general, began with history rather than with ideas. The early Christians, including Paul, first announced an event (*kerygma*) and only then proceeded to the continuing task of teaching (*didache*) the meaning of what had occurred. There was, of course, a long history to recount, the story of God's purpose in creation and redemption which is recorded and interpreted as "holy history" (*heilsgeschichte*) in the Hebrew Scriptures and brought to fulfillment in the work of Jesus the Christ. The Apostles considered themselves commissioned as witnesses to what God had done in Jesus in their presence and time. They did not initially teach ideas about truth and righteousness; rather they urgently announced that in Jesus Christ God had defeated sin and death, and they called upon all men, and first of all the people of Israel, to repent and submit to the new reign of God.

The centrality of historical event was just as characteristic of Paul's gospel as for the writers of the canonical Gospels and other books of the New Testament. Certainly his letters are filled with specific counsel and broad interpretations, and his profound and well-developed ideas have never been exhausted in the long life of the Church. He went far beyond mere proclamation to thorough teaching and practical application. Nevertheless, he insisted that everything was necessarily based on the once-for-all events of the cross and the resurrection. He went so far as to claim that the authenticity of his apostleship and message depended upon the specific, historic encounter he had experienced on the road to Damascus.

This unique consideration of a specific history as the basis for religion is the source of several permanent characteristics of Western culture. For example, it meant that the Church in its earliest days rejected claims that salvation may be achieved by receiving an esoteric knowledge (*gnosis*), by escapist asceticism, by man's own moral effort, or by various forms of mystical endeavour. Dependence on God's self-initiated revelation through historical events and persons led to the increasing recognition by Christian thinkers that redemption is grounded in grace. Further, emphasis on the centrality of history caused the Church to refuse the narrow antinomianism of Marcion and assured a Christian foundation in the Hebrew Scriptures. Finally, we may see in broader terms that the Western conception of history as progressive and meaningful has its roots in the Hebraic view which was continued in the thought of Paul.

2. The teaching of Paul concerning who and what Jesus was has been a controlling factor in the subsequent development of Christianity and

hence of formative significance for Western culture. The Apostle brought to his conversion, and to his later Christian reflection, an uncompromising Jewish monotheism and a variety of Messianic expectations. He remained totally loyal to Yahweh, the covenant God of his forefathers; yet he bequeathed to his fellow-Christians in all succeeding generations a commitment to and an understanding of Jesus of Nazareth as Lord, described by many titles and concepts that have proved to be both definitive and problematic.

In the extant and authentic Pauline literature of the New Testament, the Apostle referred to Jesus as Lord more than 200 times. He used the Greek word *kurios,* which he certainly knew had been used to translate the Hebrew sacred name Yahweh in the Greek versions of the Scriptures. He frequently spoke of Jesus both as the Son of God and as Savior, and he regularly attributed to Jesus the title Christos, the Greek translation of the Hebrew term Messiah, the Anointed One. Perhaps significantly, Paul did not use the designation Son of Man, the title so prominent in the early Christian tradition about Jesus which later appeared in the Synoptic Gospels, and which carried important meaning in contemporary Judaism; however, he did employ the name Adam, from Genesis, as a key concept in his interpretation of the nature and role of Jesus, indicating thereby the historically influential idea that Jesus is a new Adam who restores fallen mankind by recapitulation.

By using these and other designations for Jesus, Paul clearly showed that he intended to teach what has been known in the later Church as a "high Christology," holding to the uniqueness, heavenly origin, and even deity of Jesus. At the same time, however, Paul emphasized the humanity and historicity of Jesus, insisting, for example, that he was "born of woman, born under the law" (Galatians 4:4), and "descended from David according to the flesh" (Romans 1:3). There are numerous references in the letters of Paul that speak of Jesus as a man, a Jew, being obedient, being betrayed, suffering, dying on a cross, being buried, and appearing to his followers after his resurrection. Paul left unexplained and unresolved the resultant problem of the "two natures" for reflections and debates of later Christian theologians.

Two particular passages from Paul have received special emphasis as well as various interpretations. One of them is Philippians 2:5-11:

> Have this mind among yourselves, which you have in Christ Jesus, who, though he was in the form of God, did not count equality with God a thing to be grasped, but emptied himself, taking the form of a servant, being born in the likeness of men. And being found in human form he humbled himself and became obedient unto death, even death on a cross.

> Therefore God has highly exalted him, and bestowed on him the name which is above every name, that at the name of Jesus every knee should bow, in heaven and on earth and under the earth, and every tongue confess that Jesus Christ is Lord, to the glory of God the Father.

Many modern scholars have claimed that this passage was borrowed by the Apostle from a pre-Pauline Christian hymn. If that is the case, and it is by no means certain, it is still true, of course, that Paul used it to express his own thought and the result remains essentially the same. Did Paul here teach that Christ was pre-existent deity (see Proverbs 8:25-31, and the *Wisdom of Solomon* 7:22-8:1)? Did Paul claim a divine self-emptying (*kenosis*) in the Incarnation? Did he suggest a subsequent exaltation into heaven of the man Jesus? We shall observe the later struggles with these and similar questions.

A second passage is Colossians 1:15-20:

> He is the image of the invisible God, the first-born of all creation; for in him all things were created, in heaven and on earth, visible and invisible, whether thrones or dominions or principalities or authorities—all things were created through him and for him. He is before all things, and in him all things hold together. He is the head of the body, the church; he is the beginning, the first-born from the dead, that in everything he might be preeminent. For in him all the fulness of God was pleased to dwell, and through him to reconcile to himself all things, whether on earth or in heaven, making peace by the blood of his cross.

That is extravagant language indeed. Such claims not only show the high Christology of Paul and his followers (if Colossians was not written by Paul it came at least from a Pauline circle) but prepared the ground for the coming centuries of Trinitarian and Christological debate in the Church.

3. Paul's understanding of the nature, condition, and potential of man must be gathered from his incidental statements in the course of his passionate arguments against legalism, his missionary appeal for faith in Christ, and his demand for righteous living through the transforming power of the Spirit of God. He did not write abstractly about man but his views are nonetheless clear and definite. The principles of anthropology that he assumed and expressed have remained at the center of subsequent Christian belief, especially in the tradition of such creative teachers as Irenaeus, Augustine, Calvin, and Barth. Those principles may be conveniently summarized in the following four statements.

First, man is part of the creation of God and thus remains dependent, frail, and subject to death and decay. The Greek terms Paul used to signify this condition are *sarx,* flesh, and *sarkikoi,* fleshly. They apparently meant the same as the Hebrew *basar,* which Paul certainly knew. However, it is important to note that Paul did not consider flesh to be intrinsically evil, an unfortunate view which was to lead to attempts to attain salvation by asceticism and other-worldlincss. For Paul the flesh is weak and dependent, the opportunity for sin, but it was created by the one God who is altogether good, and it may be the Temple of the Holy Spirit, an instrument of righteousness. Jesus was in the flesh, yet without sin. Human beings may be made holy—sanctified—while in the flesh. Hence food, work, and sex, or the desire for them, are not evil in and of themselves.

Second, man is spirit, which is the quality of God-likeness, the potential to become a loving and obedient child of God. The Greek word Paul used for this is *pneuma,* parallel to the Hebrew term *ruach*. It is the power of self-transcendence, the ability to choose or refuse, to obey or rebel. This element of man's nature is both his opportunity and his peril. If the spirit is led by the flesh it chooses self, evil, and death; but if the spirit is led by the Spirit of God, it finds love, joy, and peace—all gifts of "life in Christ." The spirit, then, is the seat of the will, bound in its natural state by the sinful condition of historic mankind, but still capable of receiving the creative power of God's grace so that deliverance from bondage may result in the righteous freedom of the children of God. The Gospel, for Paul, is the announcement of that possibility because of what God has done in the life, death, and resurrection of Jesus the Christ.

Third, man is sinful individually, historically, and universally. For Paul, sin is not an act but a condition which results in evil acts. It springs from the power of choice, the freedom of the will which is God's unique gift to man. The flesh is not its cause, but because man is flesh, dependent creatureliness, he is unable to know and do the will of God without the concomitant power of God's grace. A created self always chooses its own center unless it is drawn by a greater power outside itself. But when the created self thus becomes selfish, it turns away from its source and hence inevitably experiences weakness, decay, and death. Paul described these insights with rhetorical brilliance, using numerous figures and examples. Perhaps his most memorable statements are in terms of his empirical self-analysis (Romans 6-8) and in his use of the symbolic figure of Adam (Romans 5:12-21).

Fourth, man is redeemable in spite of himself because of the invincible purpose, power, and love of God. It is a mistake to think that because Paul emphasized the universality and fatal tragedy of human sinfulness that he therefore taught a pessimistic view of man. Rather, his letters ring with hope and assurance that nothing in "all creation will be able to separate us from the love of God in Christ Jesus our Lord" (Romans 8:39). To proclaim that truth was his consuming passion. He believed that sin, which at the core is alienation from God the giver of life, has brought spiritual death to every man and all men; but the gift of God's grace through faith in Jesus Christ is life in place of death. "For this perishable nature must put on the imperishable, and this mortal nature must put on immortality. When the perishable puts on the imperishable, and the mortal puts on immortality, then shall come to pass the saying that is written: 'Death is swallowed up in victory' " (I Corinthians 15:53-54).

4. There can be no doubt that the foundation of Paul's gospel was the redeeming event of the death and resurrection of Jesus the Christ. He constantly referred to that event in all of his letters, as, for example, near the beginning of I Corinthians: "For Christ did not send me to baptize but to preach the gospel, and not with eloquent wisdom, lest the cross of Christ be emptied of its power. . . . For I decided to know nothing among you except Jesus Christ and him crucified" (1:17;2:2). He kept to that intention in everything that he wrote, as though he were erecting a great tent (tabernacle), with the cross as the center pole.

Perhaps it was due to the centrality of the cross that Paul expressed its meaning so frequently and variously. The subject was simply too inclusive to be explained in one way. He found it necessary to resort to several models in order to convince his hearers and readers that God's eternal work of redeeming man was accomplished, once and for all, in the crucifixion and resurrection of his Son. What remains, according to Paul, is every person's response to that deed of God by turning, receiving, and obeying. He said it in many ways so as to make the message clear.

As would be expected, in the light of his rabbinic training in the Torah, Paul often conceived of the efficacy of the cross of Jesus according to a legal model. He taught that all men have broken God's law and hence stand condemned to death. But Jesus died in fulfillment of all consequences of sin, though he was not sinful, so that all who have faith in him thereby gain his standing of innocence and are counted as righteous. That is justification by grace through faith, made possible by the death of Jesus and the identification of the sinner with him. Clearly the model is borrowed directly from legal practice, known to both Jew and Roman. It provides a rationale for acquittal of the guilty and justification of the unrighteous. Especially relevant passages are Romans 3:21-26; 4:9-12; 5:18-21; Galatians 2:20-21; 3:13-14; Colossians 1:19-20.

A second model natural to Paul and well understood by both Jews and pagans was expiatory sacrifice. Hebrew religion and post-exilic Judaism had developed elaborate systems of worship by the shedding of the blood of animals, especially lambs, and by the offering of various gifts in thanksgiving to Yahweh. Most other peoples of the ancient world regularly depended upon priestly sacrifices as means of atoning for sins, gaining the favor of the gods, and even for attaining immortality. Thus Paul made familiar contact with the minds of his readers when he spoke of the blood of Jesus as the supreme and eternally adequate sacrifice for all sinners who sought atonement with God. He specifically used the term *hilasterion* with reference to the cross because it unmistakably pointed to the "mercy seat" of the ancient Ark of the Covenant, the precise place of atonement for the people. (Cf. Romans 3:25). Further, the Apostle suggested a profound relationship between Judaism and the new faith by his allusion to the offered sacrifice of Isaac by Abraham (the *aqedah,* binding of Isaac) in comparison with the giving of Jesus (also the only Son) by God the Father: "He who did not spare his own Son but gave him up for us all, will he not also give us all things with him?" (Romans 8:32).

Again, Paul frequently described the death of Jesus and his subsequent resurrection as the means of deliverance from the powers of evil. Wars, conquests, enslavement, imprisonment and all kinds of defeat were as commonplace in the ancient world as in the modern. The idea was especially appropriate to those whose thoughts were saturated by apocalyptic imagery, which was the case with both Jews and Christians in the first century. Paul believed and taught that the world is the scene of a mighty struggle between God and his forces of righteousness, on the one hand, and Satan and the powers of evil, on the other. He declared that the battle has been won by Christ's defeat of death in his resurrection from the dead, and he announced that this age is approaching a catastrophic conclusion which will be marked by the final triumph of righteousness. The death of Jesus thus assures the deliverance from sin, death, and the demonic powers, of those who have faith in Christ and share in his sufferings. That message of hope and joy because of the cross was often repeated in the writings of Paul, most memorably in passages such as Romans 5-8, I Corinthians 15, and II Thessalonians 2:1-12.

Finally, Paul sometimes chose to explain the death of Jesus as the means by which he most fully shared in the nature and status of man as creature, and therefore also as the symbol of man's possible identification with the second, obedient Adam in whom may be found reconciliation with the Creator/Father. On the cross the old Adam died but the new Adam gives life. This is a model taken up with great power and imagination by many Fathers of the Church, beginning with Irenaeus and his doctrine of recapitulation. Its classic statement is in Romans 5:17-20: "If, because of one man's trespass, death reigned through that one man, much more will those who receive the abundance of grace and the free gift of righteousness reign in life through the one man Jesus Christ. Then as one man's trespass led to condemnation for all men, so one man's act of righteousness leads to acquittal and life for all men. For as by one man's disobedience many were made sinners, so by one man's obedience many will be made righteous." See also II Corinthians 5:14-15 and Philippians 2:5-11.

5. The final element of Paul's theology that we may list here concerns the nature and work of the Church. It is significant that this aspect of Christianity received such clear definition and emphasis so early in the history of the faith, and the insights and directions of the Apostle have remained determinative through subsequent centuries. Paul believed that the Church is not accidental and incidental but rather is divinely ordained and essential for the saving work of Christ in history.

Paul frequently used the Greek word *ekklesia,* a common term for an assembly of persons. The word literally means "those called out," denoting a group of people who have come together for a regular or special purpose. As Paul and his readers were aware, the term had been used in the Greek versions of the Hebrew Scriptures to translate the word *qahal,* a term also meaning "those called" but carrying specific reference to Israel as the People of God. Thus Paul and the early Christians by the very use of the word suggested the basic continuity between the faith and community of Israel and those who followed the Way of Christ. The kinship is obvious between the Greek *ekklesia* and the Latin *ecclesia,* the English *ecclesiastical,* and the French *eglise*. The corresponding English word *Church,* German *Kirche* and Scottish *Kirk* are derived from the Greek *kyriakon,* an adjective describing that which belongs to the Lord, *kurios*.

When Paul thought and spoke of the Church, therefore, he meant the corporate body of believers who respond in their faith to the saving grace of God. They form a community of persons who share a commitment to Jesus Christ as Lord, signified by their baptism and renewed by the breaking of bread and the drinking of wine in fellowship as a memorial to his sacrificial death (Romans 6:4 and I Corinthians 11:23-26). They also share their possessions with those in need, they share frequent sufferings for their faith, and they share a common hope for ultimate victory over all the enemies of God and man, including evil and death. The Church for Paul is composed of all the People of God, without distinction as to race, class, sex, or nation; yet he specified his concern for local groups (Antioch, Jerusalem, Philippi, Corinth, Rome, for example) and for many beloved individuals (see Romans 16 and Colossians 4). He taught that the sure marks of the Church arc faithfulness, hope, and loving service.

Paul's conception of the Church probably received its most profound and manifold expression in his metaphor "the Body of Christ." This figure depicts the Church as a living organism rather than as an organization. It specifies the various and valuable roles of the individual members, each with a necessary relation to the whole body. And it gives emphasis to the vital place of Christ as the directing head, without whom there is no life or useful function (I Corinthians 12-14 and Ephesians 4). In this phrase, then, Paul contributed to the future generations of Christians their primary understanding of the Church as the means of Christ's continuing spiritual presence and work in the world.

This sketch of the life, writings, and teachings of the great Apostle is sufficient to show his permanent and formative influence on the development of Western, and world, thought and civilization. As we said at the beginning of this chapter, it is impossible to exaggerate the significance of Paul. Nevertheless, we need to see that there were other voices in the earliest chorus of Christian proclamation, and they also have exerted lasting influence. The next chapter is intended to give them a hearing.

Chapter 4

Apostolic Christianity: Other Varieties

One of the remarkable characteristics of the New Testament is the variety of its witness to Christian origins. The twenty-seven little books which compose the canon, some extremely brief and limited in scope, represent a wide spectrum of experience and thought by a number of persons from scattered locations and in differing circumstances. However, they also contain a persuasive consistency in purpose and teaching, springing from a clear unity in faith. It was no doubt due to their common teaching that they were brought together to form the Christian Scriptures, along with the Old Testament, by the leaders of the early Church. It is the good fortune of all later believers to have such unified yet varied testimony from the pens of many witnesses.

We have observed the work of Paul,noting that his proclamation and interpretation of the Gospel is the earliest available to us. It comes from the first generation immediately following the time of Jesus himself. Now we shall look at the other material in the New Testament, made up of at least fourteen and as many as seventeen separate compositions, depending upon how many we attribute to Paul. All of them were written probably during the remaining years of the first century following the death of Paul.

For the sake of convenience, and following usual practice, we may list these non-Pauline books in five categories:

The Synoptic Gospels and Acts—Matthew, Mark, Luke-Acts
The Pastoral Letters—I, II Timothy, Titus
The General Letters—I, II, III John, James, Jude, II Peter
The Conflict Writings—Hebrews, I Peter, Revelation
The Fourth Gospel—John

The books vary greatly in size, literary type,grammatical quality, subject matter, and theological depth. Some, such as the Gospels, have stood alongside the writings of Paul in Christian usage and influence, whereas others were barely included in the canon and have received relatively less notice in liturgy or doctrine. However, the fact that they have all been preserved in the canon requires that they be taken into account for their distinctive contributions to Apostolic Christianity, whether great or small.

The Story of Christian Beginnings

The content and relationship of the three Synoptic Gospels have been discussed in Chapter 25 of the first volume of this work. There we described the three Gospels as intended to be much more than mere biographical accounts to the life of Jesus. On the contrary, modern scholarship has shown that they are theological documents composed by early Christians out of the many available traditions about the life and teachings of Jesus. Their selected materials and intricate structure preserve for all future ages both the Church's memories of Jesus and meaningful reflections which came to form the foundations of Christian teaching. Except for the sparse but theologically profound accounts of the infancy of Jesus, contained only in Matthew and Luke, the Synoptics present similar series of pericopes from the short ministry of Jesus, beginning with his baptism and concluding with his resurrection.

The Acts of the Apostles is in fact a second-volume continuation of the Gospel of Luke, apparently by the same author, the faithful Gentile companion of Paul. It presents most that is known about the days and years of Christian beginnings and development, first in Judea and ultimately, in the story of Paul, throughout the eastern Mediterranean and as far west as Rome. The reader should be cautious in interpreting Acts, as in the case of the Synoptics, keeping in mind the author's purpose in the selectivity and use of the materials. The anti-Gnostic perspective of the author, for example, appears to have been a controlling element in his composition, and the portrait of Paul in Acts is frequently dissimilar from that drawn from his letters, as many have clearly shown.

The Acts records a decisive juncture in Western history, marking a watershed which has determined the direction of subsequent world civilization. The book describes the tragic separation of official Judaism from the teachings and followers of Jesus, giving rise to what has become the dominant religion of the West. The breach began with the Jewish rejection of Jesus and the eventual persecution of his disciples in Jerusalem by the priests and the Sanhedrin. Then the leadership passed to Hellenistic Jews, such as Joseph of Cyprus (Barnabas) and Saul of Tarsus, and in a short time the new sect had been established among both Jews and Gentiles in Cilicia and Syria, in Cyprus, and in the provinces of Anatolia. Soon the seeds of the Gospel were planted in North Africa and in Europe as far as Italy, Spain, and Gaul. The story begins with a tiny, confused group of disciples in Jerusalem and it rapidly narrates the growth of the Christian faith in one generation, concluding with the Apostle Paul in Rome, a prisoner in chains but laying the foundations for the conquest and transformation of that Eternal City and its ancient culture. We may only surmise what the result would have been if there had been acceptance instead of rejection in Jerusalem; or if Gentile converts had been required to obey the ceremonial Torah; or if Paul had turned back eastward from ancient Troy, as he originally intended, and thus had not carried the Gospel to Europe. That first century indeed determined the direction of all those to follow.

Letters of Pastoral Counsel

Nine of the shortest books in the New Testament are concerned with specific problems in the young and rapidly forming institutionalized churches. Three of them, the Pastoral Letters, have been attributed by tradition to Paul, though most modern scholars have concluded, on grammatical and theological grounds, that they were written pseudonymously after Paul's death by someone well acquainted with his thought. The other six letters of this type are the so-called "general letters," three by "John" plus James, Jude, and II Peter. Usually, Hebrews and I Peter are also regarded as general letters, but we are excluding them here so as to discuss them below, along with Revelation, in the light of the increasing challenge of persecution.

One of the valuable lessons of history is that spiritual and moral movements tend to become organized, institutionalized, and controlled. They thus become increasingly concerned with authority, orthodoxy, and power, rather than with their intial purpose and charismatic spirit. The tendency may be clearly seen at work in the cares and emphases of the general and pastoral letters. The Pastorals, for example, stress the qualifications for a proper ministry (I Timothy 3, Titus 1), the necessity of holding strictly to traditional belief (I Timothy 4, II Timothy 3-4, Titus 2), and the Christian demand for impeccable moral behavior (I Timothy 5-6, II Timothy 3-4, Titus 3). In these early writings there are the unmistakable beginnings of problems that would beset the Church for centuries, leading to divisions, exclusions, self-righteousness, and primary concern for position and power.

The six general letters, noted above, arose out of interests similar to the Pastorals. The three brief letters attributed to John bear many resemblances in language and style to the Fourth Gospel, leading to the traditional belief that they all came from the same author, the Apostle, who calls himself "the elder" in II and III John. The first letter is an appealing sermon in epistolary form. It is a blend of theology and ethics, attempting to deepen the spiritual life and understanding of its recipients while also warning them against false teachers who deny the reality of the incarnation of God in Christ. The letter is memorable for its epigrammatic statement that "God is love" (4:8,16).

II John contains essentially the same ideas as the first letter, though in much briefer form, and it was apparently written to a single church rather than to a larger audience. The third letter is more specific still, addressed to an individual church leader, Gaius, for the purpose of praising him for respecting a certain Demetrius, who had been sent by the elder. The letter condemns another churchman, Diotrephes, who had rejected both Demetrius and the elder, thus raising the question of Christian hospitality and apostolic authority.

James is a sermonic exhortation filled with imperatives, calling for the highest personal morality and responsible social ethics. Its teachings have been compared with the Sermon on the Mount (Matthew 5-7) and with the hortatory parts of Paul's letters as well as with I Peter. Some in Christian history, notably Luther, have criticized James for its apparent legalism and singular emphasis on good works, but it has been more often praised because of its strong demand for the moral practice of faith. The author was apparently acquainted with I Peter and some of the letters of Paul.

Jude is a very short letter containing a stern warning against false teachers. Like James, it has been attributed to a brother of Jesus, but that remains a moot question. It is perhaps best known for the words dear to all defenders of orthodoxy: "contend for the faith which was once for all delivered to the saints" (1:3). II Peter is dependent on Jude (compare 2:1-8 with Jude 4-16) and also shows a knowledge of "all" the letters of Paul (3:16). It joins the chorus of the general letters in warning against heresy, and it also seeks to sustain the expectation of the imminent return of Christ, in spite of the delay which apparently was causing questions and doubts. II Peter was itself held in doubt by many leaders of the early Church.It is the New Testament book which came closest to being omitted from the canon.

The Conflict Writings

Christianity was born in conflict. Its founder was involved in dangerous controversy from the beginning of his short public career; and the cross, the Roman instrument of his torturous death, has remained the challenging symbol of the faith. The disciples of Jesus experienced rejection and persecution immediately after his death, and before a century had passed the imperial government adopted a policy of scorn and attempted extermination against all followers of the Way. The ancient traditions of the Church tell of the martyrdom of all of the Apostles along with many thousands of other saints. It is not suprising, then, that the New Testament records the beginnings of the persecution, and that some of the books in the canon were written in special reaction to the problem of such suffering.

Hebrews,I Peter, and Revelation especially deal with issues raised by faith in the presence of pain and death. How important is it that a Christian remain steadfast when forced to choose apostasy and life or faithfulness and death? How should a Christian react to those who cause suffering for the righteous? If God is good and powerful, why do his faithful ones suffer? What will be the outcome of the continuing struggle against the mighty forces of evil? Questions such as these were first asked with increasing urgency in the closing decades of the first century, and they were addressed by much of the literature.

Hebrews is a unique book in the New Testament. It is an anonymous essay with an exceptional unity of argument. The author's purpose was to persuade believers to hold on to their faith in spite of the temptation to become apostate in the face of imminent suffering. The writer is unknown, though a strong argument may be made that he or she composed the treatise before the destruction of the Jerusalem Temple in A.D. 70. The intended readers were either converted Jews or others well versed in Hebrew history and the cultic practices of Judaism. There are frequent references to the Old Testament, and a knowledge of Jewish theology and practice is assumed by the writer.

The theme of Hebrews is that the Christian revelation is higher than the incomplete and partial truth in Judaism. Therefore, to deny the faith would be to fall from the saving truth God has revealed in his Son, Jesus Christ. The superiority of the Christian revelation may be demonstrated by three examples. First, the revelation in Jesus Christ is greater than that given by the prophets, by angels, or by Moses (1-3:6). They were all good servants, but Christ is the Son. Second, the priesthood of Christ is greater than that of Aaron, the source of the Levitical priesthood of Judaism (4:14-7:28). Christ, the Son of God, is demonstrably qualified to be a priest because he became human, experiencing the human condition even to death; but he is superior to the Levitical priests because he was made by God to be a priest after the order of Melchizedek, the mysterious priest-king of Jerusalem to whom Abraham paid homage (Genesis 14), thus making all the descendants of Abraham inferior to Melchizedek and his order. Third, the atoning sacrifice of Christ is infinitely greater than the sacrifices of the early altar (8:1-10:39). The

Temple in Jerusalem is a mere copy or shadow of the eternal Tabernacle in heaven, and the repeated sacrifices of animals on earth are no match for the once-for-all self-offering of Christ, the eternal High Priest, in the Holy of Holies in heaven.

> But when Christ had offered for all time a single sacrifice for his sins, he sat down at the right hand of God, then to wait until his enemies should be made a stool for his feet. For by a single offering he has perfected for all time those who are sanctified (10:12-14).

The powerful and sustained argument of Hebrews concludes with a grand review of the ancient faithful. Then it appeals for a similar tenacity, in spite of the shaking of all foundations.

> Therefore let us all be grateful for receiving a kingdom that cannot be shaken, and thus let us offer to God acceptable worship, with reverence and awe; for our God is a consuming fire (12:28-29).

Such faith is to bear fruit in stability and morality (13:1-21).

First Peter is similar to Hebrews in several ways. It was written to Christians who were being persecuted because of their faith, either during the reign of the infamous Nero, around A.D. 64, or in the time of Domitian (A.D. 81-96). It appealed to the faithful to stand fast in spite of their trials, and it emphasized the example of the redemptive suffering of Christ. However, unlike Hebrews, I Peter appears to have been directed to Gentile Christians, especially those in northwest Asia Minor, and it is more concerned with righteous conduct than with steadfast belief. The letter purports to have been written by the Apostle Peter himself, though most modern scholars think that is unlikely. It is possible that there is a Petrine background and that the real author was Silas, a companion of Paul (see 5:12).

Three aspects of I Peter should be given special notice. First, the writer preserves in several instances the method of early Christian interpretation of the Old Testament. Several key passages from the older Scriptures are either quoted or alluded to and applied directly to the work, especially the death, of Jesus Christ. (Note, for example 1:16 and Leviticus 11:44; 1:24 and Isaiah 40:6-9; 2:6-10 and Isaiah 28:16, Psalms 118:22, Isaiah 8:14-15, Exodus 19:6, and Hosea 2:23; 3:10-12 and Psalms 34:12-16; 4:18 and Proverbs 11:31). Second, influential and problematic teachings about the duties of citizenship and the responsibilities of servants, wives, and husbands, are contained 2:11-3:7. The Christians of the later first century and all those who followed have found the simple exhortation to social obedience less than realistic in a world of power politics and moral ambiguities. Frequently it has been impossible at the same time to "fear God" and "honor the emperor" (2:17). Third the difficult passage (3:18-22) about Noah, about the activity of the dead Christ before the resurrection, and about the meaning of baptism, has given rise to many varied traditions and practices among Christians of later ages. The apocryphal *Gospel of Nicodemus,* from the second century, and the subsequent accounts of the "harrowing of Hell" may have their source in this passage.

The third book of the New Testament written specifically in response to persecution is Revelation. Its Greek title,Apocalypse, is preferable because it makes clear the literary genre of the book, thus aiding in its proper interpretation. Apocalypticism was a prominent means for the encouragement of the faithful in the midst of suffering and despair in both Judaism and Christianity (cf. Vol.I, chapter 25). Using that way of kindling hope, this book was clearly intended to strengthen the Christian cause by emphasizing the certainty of victory over all the forces of evil at the end of the age and beyond. It is a powerful drama, set in heaven at the dawning of the new age, and it is filled with the sights and sounds that depict the glorious rewards awaiting God's faithful people.

This Christian apocalypse was apparently written near the end of the first century, during the reign of the Emperor Domitian (A.D. 81-96). Its author, whose name was John (1:1, 4, 9; 22:8), was a prisoner on the rocky Aegean island of Patmos, not far from Ephesus. Tradition has identified him as the "beloved disciple," the brother of James and a son of Zebedee; but that opinion has been disputed by careful scholars since the earliest days of the Church and there is no good evidence to support that claim. Further, the bizarre language of the book caused it to be accepted into the canon with much hesitation. The Orthodox Churches, though including it, have remained so cautious as not to use it in the liturgy.

Nevertheless, the Apocalypse has contributed many elements to subsequent civilization, so much so that its influence cannot be overlooked. Outstanding examples of that influence may be seen in the art, music, literature, and common assumptions of medieval and modern times. One thinks immediately of the awesome painting, "The Last Judgment," by Michelangelo, on a wall of the Sistine Chapel in Rome, or of the familiar painting by Holman Hunt, "The Light of the World." Many of the stirring passages in Handel's "Messiah" are taken from the mighty choruses of the Apocalypse, and most of the moving "spirituals" from the American South were derived from its imagery. It would be difficult to understand the poetry of Dante, Milton, or Blake apart from their dependence on the book. And the notion of the final consummation of all history, initiated by a titanic Armageddon and climaxing in a final Judgment with appropriate rewards and punishments, is engraved so deeply in the culture that even the modern secular age operates on the assumptions while scarcely aware of their source.

The Apocalypse is divided into two major parts in addition to a brief, explanatory prologue (1:1-20) and an epilogue of warning and exhortation (22:6-21). The first division (2:1-3:22) contains messages from the Almighty to seven churches in the Roman province of Asia; Ephesus, Smyrna, Pergamum, Thyatira, Sardis, Philadelphia, and Laodicea. All of the brief letters are similar in structure; however, each carries a specific message of praise or condemnation to suit the life and character of the congregation. Laodicea, for example, was a rich and powerful city, and the Christian community there had, not surprisingly, became comfortable and indifferent. The message to that church, therefore, was a sharp chastening, demanding repentance. Laodicea has been synonymous with indifference ever since.

The second part of the book (4:1-22:5) contains the major portion and is the apocalypse proper. The author, John the Seer, accomplished his purpose of reassuring the saints by using all the imagination and artistry at his command. He painted a series of scenes with brilliant colors. The language was designed to threaten, to shock, to inspire, to strengthen, and above all to persuade the readers that those who remain faithful, no matter what the cost, will participate in a final victory and an eternal bliss which defy the most exaggerated description. The awesome visions are filled with the elaborate symbolism that had become familiar in Jewish apocalypticism: cryptic numbers, angels and demons, unearthly beasts, cosmic battles, unconsumed lakes of fire and brimstone, series of millenia, double deaths and resurrections, and especially a finally transformed new universe for the perpetual habitation of the surviving saints of God.

There are seven visions. The first (4:1-5:14) begins the unveiling (*apocalyptein,* in Greek) by providing a view through the door of heaven, where God sits on his throne in preparation for the final judgment of all history. The record is contained in a scroll sealed with seven seals which can be opened only by the Lamb who has been slain. The second vision (6:1-8:1) discloses the fearful results of the opening of the seven seals by the Lamb. The third vision (8:2-11:19) shows seven angels blowing seven trumpets, each announcing devastating calamities, plagues, and woes upon nature and mankind. The fourth vision (12:1-14:20) depicts a mighty struggle between a woman (the old and new Israel), her child (the Christ), and the dragon (Satan). The fifth vision (15:1-16:21) continues the terrible judgment as seven angels empty seven bowls of plagues upon the wicked. The sixth vision (17:1-19:10), in barely hidden symbolism, describes the defeat and fall of Babylon (Rome), ending with joyful "Hallelujah Chorus" at the victory of God's people over their tormentor. And the climactic seventh vision (19:11-22:5) discloses the Christ in universal victory, reigning as the conquering Lamb over a new heaven and a new earth.

Hebrews, I Peter, and Revelation may best be understood as early Christian responses to the often painful opposition encountered by the faithful in the world. They were warned against apostasy and urged to stand fast at all costs in confident hope that theirs was the highest truth and the greatest value. They were taught that a Christian attempts to live by the standard of righteousness, even if that results in suffering. And they were assured that the rewards of faithfulness and righteousness are worth any cost since they are the gracious gifts of the eternal and omnipotent God.

The Fourth Gospel

The final variety of Apostolic Christianity in the New Testament to be described here is that of the Fourth Gospel. It is quite different from the witness of Paul, the Synoptic Gospels, and the other segments of the New Testament. Nevertheless, we must not emphasize the differences to the point of overlooking the basic truth that all deal with the same historical figure, Jesus of Nazareth, and all are clearly derived from the same body of tradition. The Gospel of John, as it has been called since the second century, provides an apparently simple account of the life and teachings of Jesus, so charmingly simple that it may easily be read and understood by an unsophisticated child. Yet, this "spiritual gospel," as it was called by Clement of Alexandria, has been praised by many for its unsurpassed literary beauty and philosophical depth. The Apostolic witness would be seriously diminished without this voice in the choral proclamation.

It is unnecessary to repeat here what was said in the first volume (pages 397-400) concerning the structure and content of the Fourth Gospel. There we noted the radical differences in the use of the traditions about Jesus in John when compared with Matthew, Mark, and Luke; but we also observed the important fact that most of the material is similar and often identical in spite of the variation in arrangement and interpretation. The Fourth Gospel, we suggested, may be understood as an appeal for faith in the divine Logos who was made flesh in Jesus of

Nazareth and who provides light and life by his words, deeds, and sacrificial death as the Lamb who takes away the sins of the world.

Certain key concepts from this Gospel have remained indelibly and creatively in the religious thought and expression of Western culture. Perhaps most prominent is the ancient idea of the Logos. Many modern scholars have debated the source of this concept for the writer of the Gospel, but the appropriateness of its use is beyond dispute. The term was familiar in the Hellenized Roman world before the rise and spread of Christianity. We have taken account of its use and meaning in Heraclitus, Pythagoras, Plato, Stoicism, and in the works of Philo. It had carried a variety of meanings, but at the core was the idea of a permanent, creative rationality prior to and yet permeating all existence, thus making possible the power of self-transcendence and understanding in man precisely because he is a unique mixture of spirit and matter. John seized that familiar term and used it to explain the Christian belief concerning the pre-existent Son of God who had entered the creation he had made in order to redeem it. Prospective believers who knew nothing of Jewish messianic expectations could understand and build on this idea of the Logos. Hence the author of this Gospel introduced the concept at the beginning and composed the entire book as an account of the earthly, temporal appearance and saving work of the Logos, the giver of light and life who was full of grace and truth.

Another major theme of John's Gospel, closely related to the first, is the emphasis on the reality, necessity, and significance of the incarnation. "The Logos became flesh and dwelt among us" (1:14a). The eternal became temporal, the Creator entered the creation. (The Greek *sarx,* like the Hebrew *basar,* translated "flesh," refers to the frail, dependent realm of creation rather than to materiality as such.) Whereas the Synoptic Gospels contain a mass of evidence that Jesus was born, that he grew, suffered, and died—that, in short, he was fully human, John begins with that truth as his central principle and then constructs his Gospel to dramatize the historical manifestation and accomplishment of the incarnate Logos. In that way this Gospel not only begins and ends with the active grace of God working in Jesus for the defeat of evil and the redemption of the estranged creation; it also everywhere discloses a fundamental assumption that the creation is not inherently evil (the Logos was the creator and was not corrupted by becoming flesh) and that salvation is wrought by God's descent to man rather than by man's vain attempts to ascend to God. Three centuries later, St. Augustine pointed to this teaching of John as the distinctive truth of the Christian faith which is opposed to the noblest Greek idealism and, indeed, to the universal human desire to ascend to God by ways of asceticism, meditation, and merit.

A third central concept in the Fourth Gospel is its teaching concerning love, specifically the *agape* of God. Probably the most familiar verse in John is 3:16: "For God so loved the world that he gave his only Son, that whoever believes in him should not perish but have eternal life." This little summary of the Gospel chooses the specific Greek term, *agape* for love in place of other possibilities (e.g. *philia* or *eros*) in order to describe the nature of God as self-giving, gracious, and transforming. *Agape* is the characteristic of God which motivates him to give his utmost in the sacrifice of his only Son for the rescue of the endangered creation. The concept may be found in other books of the New Testament, of course, but nowhere more prominently than in John. As a result, love of the *agape* type has remained the controlling motif of authentic Christian teaching through the centuries. (See the influential study by Anders Nygren, *Agape and Eros,* S.P.C.K.,1932.)

A fourth leading theme of the Fourth Gospel concerns the Holy Spirit of God. A careful examination of the teaching of this Gospel will reveal why Clement of Alexandria correctly named it "the spiritual Gospel." The concept appears regularly from the beginning to the end, and the development of the idea parallels the unfolding of the incarnate life of the eternal Logos. At the beginning John the Baptist bears witness to the true identity of Jesus of Nazareth by saying, "I saw the spirit descend as a dove from heaven, and it remained on him. I myself did not know him; but he who sent me to baptize with water said to me, 'He on whom you see the Spirit descend and remain, this is he who baptizes with the Holy Spirit' " (1:32, 33). Following that beginning, the Gospel increasingly relates the work of Jesus to the presence and power of the Spirit (3:5,6,34; 4:23,24; 6:63; 7:39; 14:15-31; 15:26; 16:12-15; 20:22). Due to John's Gospel more than to any other segment of Apostolic teaching, the Church has subsequently found its most adequate theological explanation of the relation between the Father and the Son by appealing to the work of the Holy Spirit. Furthermore,this Gospel has been a constant reminder that true religion is the life of the Spirit—nothing more, nothing less.

Finally, the powerful idea of the Lamb of God runs through the Gospel, and indeed through all the Johannine literature, like the theme of a Bach fugue. The writer appeals to the Hellenistic mind by identifying the subject of his Gospel with the well-known eternal Logos; but he also appeals to those acquainted with the teachings, practices, and expectations of Judaism by having John the Baptist, the Announcer, to proclaim that Jesus is "the Lamb of God, who takes away the sins of the world" (1:29). That title involves sacrifice, redemptive suffering, the covenant, and the requirements of participation. The first half of John (1-12) presents the seven signs, telling the story of the ministry of Jesus as the disclosure of his nature and purpose. The second half (13-20) describes the Passion, the historical sacrifice of the Lamb on the cross for the reconciliation of sinners to the Father. The result has been the Church's vision of the conquering Lamb, unforgettably enthroned in the Apocalypse as the Judge of History who is also the gentle Lamb who is to reign eternally in the new heaven and earth.

Chapter 5

The Reaction to Persecution and Heresy

One of the valuable lessons to be learned from both nature and history is that struggle is more likely to produce physical strength and moral advancement than are conditions of ease. More specifically, bad times have usually been good times and good times have usually been bad times for the development of thought and morality throughout the course of Western cultural history.

The accuracy of that general claim was clearly illustrated in the experience of Christianity during its first three centuries. The faithful were constantly beset by multitudes of dangers. The fledgling Church appeared destined for infant mortality as it was frequently threatened from within by weakening aberrations and from without by attractive alternatives. However, the challenges were always overcome and each difficulty seems to have left greater strength and broader acceptance. The Christian way was like scattered fire, burning ever more brightly and in widening circles. At the beginning of the Christian missionary enterprise, the Apostle Paul had said that "we rejoice in our sufferings, knowing that suffering produces endurance, and endurance produces character, and character produces hope, and hope does not disappoint us" (Romans 5:3-5). That hope bore fruit in the growth and flowering of the Christian cause so that indeed the blood of the martyrs was the seed of the Church. Struggle was the source of strength.

This section of our study will now proceed to describe the particular opponents which challenged the faith and thought of the young Church. Five major threats may be identified: Judaism, Marcionism, classical paganism, Gnosticism, and Montanism. There were other problems, of course, and there were many varieties especially of paganism and Gnosticism. However, these five distinct opponents, as we shall see, exercised permanent influence on the nature and structure of Christianity as the faithful reacted against them.

Rejection by Judaism

Christianity began as a movement for reform and fulfillment within Judaism. All of the early records, especially the New Testament, show that origin and character. Jesus himself, his disciples, and all of the original Christians were Jews and apparently considered themselves legitimate followers of Moses and the Prophets. The beliefs and practices of Judaism, along with its scriptures, were adopted, or retained, almost totally by the members of the new sect, though many of the practices of Judaism were modified according to what was believed to be God's new work in Jesus the Messiah.

Nevertheless, most of the religious leaders of Judaism, both priests and rabbis, vigorously rejected the new movement from its inception because they believed it to be religiously blasphemous and politically dangerous. The result was an immediate separation of synagogue and church, leading further to frequent opposition and tragic hostility on both sides. The situation made it necessary for Christian thinkers to examine the historic roots of their faith and to listen with care to the claims of their Jewish antagonists. In the process, of course, Christian belief was clarified and Christian practice was developed. Thus reaction to the challenge of Judaism was the earliest factor in the Christian formulation of self-understanding.

The oldest account available to us of the theological debate between Judaism and Christianity is contained in Paul's letters to the Galatians and to the Romans. There, as we have seen above in chapter 3, the question is essentially that of the requirements of God for salvation: is it necessary for Christians to keep the Law, especially the ceremonial regulations of Judaism? Paul argued that it is not, since salvation is the free gift of God's grace received by faith. Other segments of the New Testament, written soon after Paul, deal with the same problem in a variety of ways. The Gospel of Matthew clearly reflects the belief that Jesus superseded Moses and that a New Israel has replaced the Old Israel. Hebrews interprets the person and work of Jesus the Christ as a fuller revelation and a higher fulfillment of the previous work of God in the former covenant. Acts 15 deals specifically with the decision of the Apostles that Gentile converts are not required to keep the ceremonial Torah but rather only the universal moral laws of humanity, the so-called Noachian laws.

The Romans crushed the Jewish revolts of A.D. 70 and 135, destroying Jerusalem with its Temple, dispersing the Jews again, and bringing Jewish national existence to an end. The catastrophes so weakened Judaism that it had difficulty surviving. Further serious opposition to Christianity was out of the question. As Christianity became stronger and more widespread in the Roman world and beyond, the debate with Judaism continued for the most part among Christians themselves when they carried on the inevitable task of apologetics and theological construction.

One of the first post-Apostolic examples of the Christian dialogue with Judaism is the *Epistle of Barnabas*, an anonymous tract written in the first half of the second century and rediscovered in the late nineteenth century. It interprets the Old Testament as preparatory for the coming of Christ and his establishment of the New Israel. Justin Martyr, a native of Palestine living around the middle of the second century, composed the *Dialogue with Trypho the Jew* in order to compare, with all courtesy and fairness, the claims of Judaism and Christianity. Irenaeus, in the late second century, dealt extensively with the issue in both his *Against Heresies* and *Demonstration of the Apostolic Preaching*. In the third century, Cyprian argued the Christian case against the adequacy of Judaism in *To Quirinus: Three Books of Testimonies Against the Jews*. In fact, almost all of the Christian writers of the first five centuries took part in the dialogue in one way or another.

The original and essential disagreement between Jews and Christians was concerned, of course, with the person and teachings of Jesus. The Jews did not accept him as the Messiah, and certainly not as the Son of God or the Savior; and they condemned most of his reputed teachings as contrary to the Torah and therefore blasphemous. From the beginning the quarrel expanded to include questions about the nature of God, the way of salvation, the finality of Moses and the Prophets, the necessity of the ceremonial laws and rituals, the acceptance of Gentile converts, the identity of the true Israel, the shape of eschatology, and so on. Unfortunately the debate became increasingly polemical and bitter. The Christians' treatment of Jews in the Middle Ages did not follow Christianity's professed ethics of justice and love, and Judaism became both resentful and defensive. Only during the twentieth century has the dialogue became tolerant and friendly so that progress might be made toward fairness, understanding, and mutual acceptance.

Marcionism: The Rejection of Judaism

The quarrel between Judaism and Christianity was within the family until the daughter was forced to leave home. Then she became assimilated among the *goyim* and achieved an identity of her own, though she has never completely lost the family resemblance. Some Christians, however, have sought to deny the former relationship. They have been determined to make the separation complete. One of the earliest and most famous of these separatists was Marcion of Pontus.

Nearly everything known to us about Marcion is derived from the writings of his opponents, particularly Irenaeus and Tertullian, about whom we shall hear more presently. The same is true, unfortunately, concerning most of the other so-called heretics and schismatics of the early Church. Hence it is only fair that we exercise caution in our interpretation of them, since hostile witnesses may at least exaggerate. Nevertheless, the main outlines of Marcionism seem to be reasonably clear. He was a native of Sinope, a prominent city in the Roman province of Pontus, on the south shore of the Black Sea. His father was a bishop there, and it may be that Marcion was excommunicated for false beliefs, around A.D.140. Tertullian claimed that he was a student of Cerdo, the Gnostic. He went to Rome and used his wealth as a means of gaining a place of leadership in the Christian community there. By A.D. 144 he was condemned by the church at Rome, though he retained a large following. We do not know anything about his later life, but it is certain that the Marcionite churches were numerous and widespread in the empire, some surviving in the East as late as the sixth century.

Marcion rejected Judaism just as thoroughly as mainline Judaism rejected Christianity. He believed that the message of Jesus was a heady new wine, so new that it could not be put in the old wineskins of the Law and the Prophets. Jesus was the emissary of the previously unknown "alien God" of love and grace, not the evil Jewish God of creation, law, and judgment. The Gospel had already been corrupted by the leaders of the early Church who worshipped the God of the Jews, retained their Scriptures, and talked of continuity and fulfillment. Only Paul had kept the true faith, and even his writings, along with those of his followers such as Luke, had been tainted by Jewish errors. The true Gospel is the new Gospel, which rejects the creation in all its parts and provides in Christ the means for the rescue of the souls of the faithful from the perishing world to the transcendent realm of the spirit.

Marcion wrote a book, *The Antitheses,* which placed the teachings of Law and Gospel in sharp opposition. The book did not survive, as was the case with many condemned works, but it can be fairly well restored from references by Tertullian and others. More importantly, Marcion gathered the ten known letters of Paul, excluding the Pastorals, and added to them the Gospel of Luke and Acts. These he purged of all favorable references to the Old Testament, which he believed to be false emendations. These writings he proposed as the authentic Christian Scriptures. Thus Marcion, in spite of his views, must be credited with the first known step in the process which ultimately resulted in the canon of the New Testament.

Most Christians almost immediately refused to follow the teachings of Marcion, as we have seen. Tertullian's *Against Marcion* is one of the most vituperative works in Christian literature, famous for calling Marcion the ''Pontic mouse'' who gnawed away the Scriptures. Without yet formulating its reasons, the Church refused to divide the Creator from the Redeemer, to separate Law and Gospel, or deny the genuine humanity and passibilty of its Christ. Marcion thus made a significant contribution, even if in a negative way, by forcing the Christian community to think more creatively about its spiritual roots and its theology; and, perhaps more notably, Marcion aided in the necessary establishment of a source of Apostolic authority which would serve as a firm anchor in the many storms to come.

Montanism: The Presence and Power of Spirit

The glow of excitement associated with great events inevitably fades with the passing of time into dullness and disappointment. This universal experience occurred no less in the Christian communities of the Roman world during the second century. By then the original Apostles had passed into vague memories and their voices had been replaced by oral traditions and various old records. Their successors, the bishops, elders and deacons, were weaker in power and inspiration, sometimes lacking in certainty and unity. Those who had promised an imminent return of the Lord and the triumph of his people were clearly mistaken, as the postponement of the parousia made manifest. The leadership of God's Spirit seemed to be increasingly absent.

Montanism arose as a reaction to that development. Unlike Marcinonism and Gnosticism, it was not a heresy, an aberration in teaching, so much as it was a schism, a division within the fellowship. The sparse evidence that has survived concerning the movement indicates that it was an effort toward revitalization in terms of the presence and power of the Holy Spirit of God, both in the life of the individual believer and in the Church. It was not entirely a new phenomenon, as may be seen, for example, in the problem of spiritual gifts discussed by Paul in First Corinthians 12-14.

Montanus was a Christian presbyter in Phrygia who began his work of spiritual reform around the middle of the second century. There have been uncertain claims that he was a convert form the orgiastic cult of Cybele, the mother goddess, and that his teachings and practices were carried over from that pagan soil. Others have contended that his movement may be better understood as a protest against the developing authoritarian hierarchy, the relaxing moral demands of the Church, and the diminishing eschatological hope. It is at least clear that the major thrust of his work was an attempt to restore the prominence of prophecy and other charismatic gifts, and to revive the apocalyptic visions and expectations of the Christian communities.

Montanus claimed that the promises of Jesus (John 14-16) concerning the Paraclete were realized in him. He taught that the long-expected last days had come and that his task was to announce the impending second coming of Christ and to lead the people in rigorous spiritual preparation through repentance, moral discipline and fasting. Two of his numerous followers were the women Priscilla and Maximilla, both of whom were believed to be special instruments through whom the Spirit spoke. They prophesied, spoke in ecstatic tongues, and proclaimed the revelations they had received by the Spirit in dreams and visions. One of their characteristic emphases was related to the imminent parousia, the events associated with the return of Christ, the final Judgment, and the end of the age. They believed that the New Jerusalem was about to descend from heaven upon the little town of Pepuza, in Phrygia, and that the millenial reign of Christ upon the earth would be centered there. Their rigorous moral demands, including celibacy and fasting, were preparation for that glorious final event.

The movement spread rapidly in Asia Minor and then throughout the Empire. It became especially popular in Southern Gaul and North Africa, and at one point it almost received the support of Bishop Eleutherus of Rome. Its most famous convert was Tertullian of Carthage, one of the most significant and creative theologians among the early Fathers. However, it also met strong and increasing opposition from the official leaders of the Church and from such teachers as Hippolytus, Epiphanius, and Eusebius. The movement gradually faded from view during the third century; nevertheless, its teachings and practices have occasionally reappeared throughout the course of Christian history.

The permanent results of the Montanist movement have been both positive and negative. Positively it contributed to the specifically trinitarian doctrine of God which was formulated during the third and fourth centuries; it left its mark as the apocalyptic eschatology and dispensationalism which have frequently reappeared in Christian theology; and it provided justification for the structural institutionalizing and hierarchial authority of the Church. Negatively, Montanism caused suspicion to be cast subsequently on all forms of spiritual enthusiasm. The primitive charismatic gifts were discredited and prophecy was thereafter believed to have ceased with the revelation to John on Patmos. And, finally, a double standard of morality became the norm in the Church, with the rigors of saintliness reserved for the celibate monks and clerics while increasing worldliness was allowed for the laity.

Gnosticism, an Insidious Revision

It has become convenient and customary for modern scholars to speak of "Gnosticism" as though it were a distinct religious philosophy that was especially prominent, and threatening to Christianity, in the Roman world of the second century. Careful investigation reveals, to the contrary, that the term is merely a modern designation for a variety of systems of salvation that reached their apex of development and influence around the middle of the second century. They were often quite different from one another, named for the independent teachers who constructed them. Gnosticism *per se* did not exist. There were indeed cults led by such gurus as Cerinthus, Basilides, Saturninus, Ptolemy, and others, the greatest probably being Valentinus. A common feature apparently shared by all was the belief that redemption may be attained through *gnosis,* one of several Greek words meaning "knowledge," but designating specifically a revealed, esoteric knowledge.

Although the "Gnostic" cults differed from one another, it is possible to discover several characteristics that are more or less common among them. First, they were eclectic in their sources and content. They were not so much new philosophies or religions as they were syntheses of older teachings and practices. They usually borrowed elements from pre-Socratic and Platonic ontologies, Iranian astrologies and cosmologies, the Hellenistic myths and mysteries, and some aspects of Judaism. In the first and second centuries they appeared to be eager to absorb many elements of the Christian Gospel, though usually in highly selective and distorted forms.

Again, these cultic systems displayed a marked tendency toward ontological and ethical dualism. They emphasized a sharp distinction between soul (or spirit) and flesh. Following the lead of Platonism, they sought the salvation of the immortal, human soul by its release and separation from the material world. This, of course, led to a thorough-going asceticism and mystical otherworldliness. Third, most Gnostics developed complicated mythologies designed to explain the creation of the evil, unreal world and the primeval entrapment of immortal spirits within that world of appearances. In these constructions they borrowed heavily from ancient Oriental and Hellenistic theogonies, often adding materials from Judaism and Christianity. The architect of this world was, in their view, a lower being, a demiurge, whose creation was the result of either ignorance or rebellion against the Supreme God. This conception of the created order led to a fourth characteristic of most Gnostic teaching, usually designated a "docetic" Christology. When they attempted to assume a Christian stance, they usually found it necessary because of their dualism to interpret the Christ of the Gospels in one of two ways: either he was a natural man, Jesus, who was temporarily adopted and used by the true, spiritual Christ; or he only appeared (*dokeo,* to appear) to be born, to suffer and die, whereas in reality he was pure spirit, a phantom. In a word, they denied the incarnation. Finally, a fifth usual characteristic of the systems was their mystical method of salvation. They taught that the imprisoned, blinded human soul may be released and enlightened by the edifying vision of revealed truth and by a constant turning away from this world. The ways to those goals took various forms but always they were essentially a way of self-righteousness and self-salvation through moral effort and spiritual insight.

The Gnostic systems thus were judged as a threat to the faith because they proposed an insidious revision of that faith. While appearing to continue the teachings and practices of Jesus and his Apostles, the Gnostic teachers were vigorously opposed even in the first century by the writers of what came to be known as the New Testament (cf. Colossians, I John, the Pastoral Epistles) and, later, by many who were accepted as authentic interpreters of the Apostles, the early Fathers. The opposition focused on three major points in the Gnostic systems: they were unable to demonstrate a legitimate continuity with the Apostles and their Gospel; they usually separated the God of creation from the God of redemption; and they distorted the Gospel by denying that the Word was made flesh.

Classical Paganism: Opposition and Opportunity

When the Apostles and their successors were expelled from the familiar milieu of Judaism and began to carry their Gospel into the wide expanses of the Roman world, they increasingly encountered multitudes of religions, divinities, and cults. Paul's experiences in Asia, and especially in Athens, are the clearest record of that fact (cf.Acts 17:16 ff.). We have already observed the varieties of Roman religions, in chapter two, above. In addition, the far-flung borders of the Empire contained all the beliefs and practices of innumerable conquered peoples, often the remnants of the cultures of a greater antiquity. Beyond the Roman world—behind the Rhine and the Danube in Europe, the great desert of northern Africa, and the unending mountains and seas of Asia—lay a largely unknown world that only gradually became an open field for missions. This vast, so-called pagan world provided both opposition and opportunity for the Christian enterprise.

The most obvious distinction between Christianity (and Judaism) and the other religions of the ancient world was its monotheism and their polytheism. A host of gods and goddesses was recognized and revered everywhere. Frequently the same deities were called by different names, though every ethnic community and political entity gave special homage to its peculiar gods, as symbols of separateness and distinction. The popular mystery religions were expressed in terms of the theogonies and myths of early Hellenism or, in some cases, the polytheistic mythologies that had been inherited from ancient Egypt and the Fertile Crescent. In addition to that source of inevitable conflict, the cult of emperor worship came to its fullest development at precisely the same time that Christianity began to spread throughout the Empire. Thus the pervasive paganism of the Gentile world provided a possible rich harvest of converts. However, the paganism of the classical age was often very strong in its appeal and sophisticated in its intellectual challenge when compared with the intolerant new sect from Palestine that worshipped a crucified man and claimed that he was the only Son of God, raised from the dead, and now reigning in heaven.

The aggressiveness, intolerance, and irrationality of the Christians were enough to cause the populace to despise and ostracize them, but their refusal to engage in the various forms of emperor worship only compounded the rejection and opened them to charges of treason and sedition. When the Roman officials discovered that the followers of Jesus were not merely another sect among the Jews, who were legally exempted from the cult of the emperor, but that they claimed to give absolute devotion to another king, legal action was initiated and continued intermittently and ever more severely until the conversion of Constantine in the fourth century. Untold thousands of Christians suffered imprisonment, banishment, and martyrdom, even though they steadfastly protested their desire to be good citizens if allowed to worship only their one God. That conflict has continued in various forms and circumstances throughout the subsequent centuries with the struggle between state and church, law and conscience.

Polythesim and persecution were but two overt aspects of pagan challenge to the new faith. More subtle and dangerous was the pretended cultural superiority displayed by sophisticated opponents. Christians were ridiculed and condemned as ignorant, credulous, and uncivilized. They were frequently accused of atheism, because they abhorred idols; immorality and magic, because they met in secret and believed in miracles; cannibalism and ritual murder, because of their celebrations in the Eucharist; and of crimes against the state because of their rejection of the emperor cult. One of the most famous intellectual critics of the Christian faith was the Platonist Celsus (c. A.D. 177) who was strongly refuted by the great Alexandrian theologian, Origen, in his *Contra Celsum,* written about A.D.248. Origen quoted Celsus as saying that Christianity is "a barbarous and absurd doctrine, suitable for people without culture," and that Christians "separate themselves from other men, despise the law, customs, and culture of the society in which they live."

However, the Christian Church was not without powerful defenders.The New Testament itself contains challenging arguments in defense of the faith by Paul and other Apostles, and the exant Christian writings of the first half of the second century, known collectively as the Apostolic Fathers, exhibit a growing need to develop intellectual and moral support for what they usually called "the new law" or "the new philosophy." Beginning with Justin Martyr's *Apology* and *Dialogue with Trypho,* around A.D. 150, and continuing for the next two centuries, an impressive list of apologetic works appeared in both East and West. Among them are the earlier writings of men such as Tatian, a Syrian Christian, and Athenagoras, an Athenian philosopher; but later many more profound apologies were composed by Irenaeus, Hippolytus, Tertullian, Clement of Alexandria, Origen, Eusebius, and others, including the massive *City of God* by Augustine.

The Christian Reaction

Having made a brief survey of five major challenges to Christianity during its early years, we must now investigate the Christian reaction. That reaction produced both positive and negative results, and, as always in this book, we are especially interested in determining the results that were permanent, that made lasting contributions to subsequent Western culture.

At first glance, the reply of thoughtful Christians to their opponents would appear to have been complete rejection. That would certainly seem to be the case regarding Judaism, Gnosticism, and paganism. On the contrary, however, we have already noticed that Christians from the beginning displayed a spiritual and historical kinship with Judaism, adopting the Hebrew Scriptures as their own, adapting many Jewish principles and practices to Christian belief, and claiming to follow the essential teachings of Moses and the prophets. Marcion's rejection of both the Jewish God and Jewish theology was itself repudiated by the Church, and constant attempts were made by Christian theologians to demonstrate that their faith was in unity and continuity with that of Israel. Although the various Gnostic systems were repudiated by many of the Fathers, especially Irenaeus, the Gnostic way of salvation by receiving and accepting a revealed *gnosis* has left its legacy, for example, in the constantly recurring equation of faith with assent to creedal propositions, or in the view that enlightenment is humanity's greatest need. And, as we shall see later in greater detail, classical paganism provided much of the structure and many of the ideas that were used in the development of Christian dogma. The use of the ancient concept of the universal *logos* as a major Christological theme is a striking illustration of that.

The multiform challenges, perversions, and alternatives to the Christian faith were also sources of growth and strength, as we suggested at the beginning of this chapter. That may be seen, in the first place, in the early and continuing appeal to the original apostolic witness as the final criterion of judgment regarding every question of faith and practice. That is to say, the teachers and leaders of the churches, especially the bishops, acknowledged that they were the inheritors of an earlier, original tradition, the Gospel of Jesus himself, which was to be the permanent guideline and standard. How was that original tradition to be recognized and kept unchanged through the passing centuries? It is to be found, they said, in the preserved writings of the Apostles and their immediate associates: Peter and Paul, James and John, Matthew, and their friends and disciples, Mark and Luke. Whenever, throughout all future time, the question is asked: what is the faith?—the answer may be found, direct or implied, in the authentic apostolic witness. Thus the *canon* of the New Testament was formed and, added to the Jewish Scriptures, became the Christian Bible, the Word of God. A line was drawn between the age of the apostles and the age of the bishops, between Bible and Church, so that bishops and Church could always be judged and corrected, if needed, by reference to the original apostolic witness.

Second, the Church began, at least by early in the second century, to compose a normative theology in creedal form, a required confession of faith. That process has never ended, of course, because every age must restate the faith in its own language and for its own cultural conditions. The early Church met its needs for the work of conversion, nurture, and interpretation by reducing the essentials of the faith to brief baptismal creeds and short catechisms that could be understood and memorized by the uncultured masses. The best known result of that inevitable process is the Apostles' Creed. Many creeds and much theology have been composed during the following centuries in response to growth, historical circumstances, changing world views, and frequent controversies. Challenge has produced reflection, and reflection often results in theology.

Many theological historians have interpreted the Apostles' Creed as a specific antidote to Gnostic teachings. For example, Anders Nygren, in his seminal study, *Agape and Eros,* describes in a convincing way what he calls "the three fundamental dogmas of the early church"—belief in God as Creator of heaven and earth, belief in the Incarnation of Jesus Christ, and belief in the Resurrection of the flesh. Then he discusses at considerable length the Gnostic rejection of those three dogmas and demonstrates how the articles of the Creed are a conscious and concise rebuttal (op. cit., Part II, Vol. I, pp.60-97).

Finally, the growing Christian community found it natural and necessary to develop itself into an organization, an institution, in response to the persecution and challenge. The living voice of Jesus and the Apostles had to be replaced by the written record and witness. The authentic Gospel was preserved and summarized in the creeds and confessions. Both canon and the creed required a visible, historical guarantor that would complete the three-fold, triadic apostolic authority which could transmit the true faith into the ages and against the threats which were to come. The Montanist movement, especially, showed the dangerous, uncontrolled possibilities of depending on the experience of the Spirit alone. Thus the community of the New Covenant was divided between *clericos,* the rulers, and *laos,* the ruled. The clergy, especially the bishops, claimed to be the appointed successors of the apostles and therefore the creators and custodians of the creeds as well as the rightful interpreters of the canon.

The Christian reaction to presecution and heresy prepared the way for the development of doctrine and the growth of a powerful and, unfortunately, corruptible institution. The struggle of the beginnings determined the directions of the future, not only for Christianity but for Western culture as a whole.

III.
TOWARD A CHRISTIAN PHILOSOPHY

Chapter 6

The Challenge of Neoplatonism

One of the most important of the philosophical influences on Christian doctrine was Neoplatonism, a fusion of Platonic ideas with a number of other forms of thought popular during the third and fourth centuries.

Plotinus (c. 204-270) is regarded as the principal author of the synthesis. He was born in Egypt and, although his ancestry is uncertain, he had a Roman name. After attending elementary school in his home town, he went to Alexandria for further study. There he went from philosopher to philosopher until his twenty-ninth year, searching for a key to the truth about the universe. At last, on the advice of a friend, he sought instruction from Ammonius Saccas, called "The Porter," who had once been a Christian but who had returned to the Greek religion. Ammonius's teaching was of such high quality that Plotinus stayed with him for eleven years.

Interested in learning something about Oriental philosophy, Plotinus went with the army of the Emperor Gordian III in a campaign against King Sapor of Persia, hoping to be able to have consultation with the Persian Magi and perhaps even the Indian sages. Gordian was murdered in Mesopotamia, and Plotinus, on his way home, got back as far as Antioch. Instead of returning to his native Egypt, however, he went to Rome in 244. There he established a school and spent the rest of his life as a teacher. He was a favorite of the Emperor Gallienus and his wife. Gallienus once gave him permission to found a city named Platonopolis, to be based on the principles of the *Republic,* but the Emperor apparently had second thoughts about the project, for he withdrew his consent before it could be gotten under way.

Like his master, Ammonius Saccas, who never committed his thoughts to writing, Plotinus confined himself to oral teaching until he was fifty years of age. Then he began writing down his thoughts in the work we know as the *Enneads,* so called because of the arrangement of its chapters in groups of nine. The modesty which probably delayed his literary activity also showed itself in his refusal to permit his portrait to be painted. "Is it not enough," he asked, "to have to bear the image (*eidolon*) in which nature has wrapped me, without consenting to perpetuate the image of an image, as if it were worth contemplating?'' An artist who attended his lectures painted his portrait from memory. Though Plotinus exercised a profound influence on Christian Platonism, he himself never became a Christian. The strongly religious character of his philosophy was evident in his mysticism—a mysticism which led to no claims of spectacular private revelation, although he did think that on several occasions he had experienced the beatific vision.

On a visit to Campania, he realized that he was about to die of an illness from which he had suffered for a long time. A friend of his, the physician Eustochius, was sent for from nearby Puteoli. He did not arrive in time to administer medical assistance, but heard Plotinus's last words: ''I was waiting for you, before that which is divine in me departs to unite itself with the Divine in the Universe.'' Porphyry, one of his pupils and himself a celebrated Neoplatonist, wrote his master's biography and used it as an introduction to the *Enneads,* which he edited and published.

For Plotinus, the Platonic philosophy was not simply a way to know about the universe through rational speculation. It was a way of life by which he sought to ascend through the stages of reality to the source of his own being through intellectual and moral self-discipline. It thus had for him a distinctly religious quality, and it was seen by his followers as an alternative to Christianity and the other cults which commanded the allegiance of people of the Empire. It thus represented the last stand of enlightened Paganism against the onslaught of Eastern religious thought. In making that stand, though, Plotinus and his followers, while recognizing the role of reason as it had been defined in classical philosophy, went beyond the merely rational and advocated a way of knowing which is essentially mystical in nature. The reason for this step lay in his conception of the ultimate ground of reality.

The One

Relying on Plato's identification of that ground as ''the Good,'' or ''Beauty,'' or ''the One,'' Plotinus gave preference to the third term because the dialectic, which is the path to truth, shows that the intelligible world, which Plotinus called the spiritual world, *must be,* by proving that one cannot have the idea of plurality without the idea of unity any more than one can have the idea of imperfection without that of perfection. ''The One,'' however, is not a term with merely numerical significance. It does not point to an impossible abstraction of absolute unity, but rather to the supreme Unity which is the ultimate source of the distinction between unity and plurality. Through dialectic we learn that all progress toward reality proceeds from lower to higher unities. The final reality must, therefore, be a reality which transcends all differentiation.

The One is "beyond existence," and so, in view of the fact that our intellectual life is based on the making of distinctions about existent categories, the ultimate nature of reality is unknown to us. Through the mystical intuition which represents the final stage of the ascent of the soul, we can, however, attain a revelation of that which has no form and cannot be described. It can best be dealt with intellectually by the *via negativa*—the denial of attributes—rather than by positive definition. We must, nevertheless, acknowledge that behind the world of sense, and even beyond the knowable world of the ideas, there lies the infinite and ineffable source about which the negative statements are made.

The negations in terms of which Plotinus described the One, however, are countered by other predicates which seem to involve a paradox. The Absolute does not will and yet is all will, does not think and yet knows everything, is not conscious and yet is supremely awake. It is the ground of will, as of everything else, but cannot be said to will, for it lacks nothing. It has a discernment of its own being in which the subject-object relationship is transcended. It enjoys a superconscious state of wakefulness beyond anything which we can imagine as consciousness. In permitting himself characterizations of this sort, Plotinus laid himself open to the criticism that after telling us that the One cannot be described,he gave us so much information about it as to make it almost necessary to postulate something yet more ultimate.

Plotinus undoubtedly recognized this difficulty. "The One," he said, "is in truth beyond all statement; whatever you say would limit it; the All-Transcending, transcending even the most august Mind, which alone of all things has true being, has no name. We can but try to indicate, if possible, something concerning it. If we do not grasp it by knowledge, that does not mean that we do not seize it at all. We can state what it is not while we are silent as to what it is." In the last analysis, anything that we may say about the One is designed not to define or describe it, but rather to provide a sort of guidepost to suggest the goal toward which we ascend when we set our feet on the path that leads us to the mystical vision.

From such a being, how can the imperfect world of things be derived? For what reason would the One dissipate its own perfect reality? Plotinus suggested that though it has no need of the created world, creativity is a part of its nature, and so the inferior world must be created—or rather, in Plotinus's formulation, emanated. As the One, the Absolute is first cause; as the Good, it is the final cause of everything.

Emanation

The way in which the One produces the world is analogous to the way in which a candle produces light, or perhaps that in which an artesian well emits water, which then falls on the ground and makes its way back to its source so that the source is not diminished. The idea of emanation differs from that of creation in that the latter term suggests a making something out of nothing, whereas the former, as posited by Plotinus, refers to a process in which what is produced is essentially of the same substance as that which produces it, though without diminution of the original sources. Since the One is the totality of Being, its emanation of the world is a projection of itself into nothingness, and as that projection proceeds farther and farther from its source—although, of course, the spatial analogy must not be taken literally—there is a corresponding diminution of the degree of reality which can be claimed by any particular feature of the universe, until at last, on the outer fringes, those objects farthest from the center have hardly any existence at all. Plotinus thus posited a hierarchy of being, descending from the One, which is absolutely real, down through the material world, which borders on nothingness.

First emanation from the One and closest to the source of light is *Nous,* Divine Mind or Spirit, which, recognizing its distinction from its source, longs to turn back to it. *Nous* is the highest category of being accessible to human thought. Different from the One, it nevertheless reflects its origin as completely as its derivative nature permits. In *Nous* there is awareness of differentiation, but the Divine Mind sees subjects and objects as included in the higher unity. "The perceiving Spirit," Plotinus said, "must be one and two, simple and not simple." Related to *Nous* are the concepts of *noesis* and *noeta*. *Noesis* is the activity of *Nous,* and the *noeta,* the Platonic archetypes, share a common origin with *Nous* in the One and are, in a sense, identical with *Nous*.

"What, then," Plotinus said, "is the activity of Spirit (*Nous*) in virtue of which we may say that it is the things which it knows? Plainly, since Spirit has real existence, it knows and posits reality. Spirit therefore *is* all that really exists . . . The objects of spiritual knowledge cannot be in the world of sense, for sensible objects are only derivative. The *noeta* existed before the world; they are the archetypes of sensible things, and they constitute the true being or reality of Spirit . . . Spirit is the first lawgiver, or rather it is itself the law of being. This is the meaning of the saying 'To know is the same as to be'; and the *knowledge of* immaterial things is identical with the things known . . . Thus Spirit and the real world are one."

The world of Spirit is perfect, permanent, and unchanging. It is, indeed, not in the stream of time at all. When we move another step from the center, we find ourselves in the category of Soul, or *Psyche,* the world of the senses, in which spatial extension and temporal succession make their appearances. Here too, sharp distinctions between subjects and objects occur, and the plurality of the everyday world comes into existence. Soul itself partakes of the dichotomy of the One and the Many. As the World Soul, it retains its unity, reflecting the oneness of *Nous,* from which it proceeds. As individual souls, its consciousness is fragmented. Like the World Soul, individual souls are immortal and not merely temporary emanations, destined one day to be swallowed up into a featureless Absolute, for the creative activity of the One is timeless, and all beings have their place in the eternal order.

Just as Spirit turns toward the One with Longing, so Soul, recognizing its separation from Spirit, yearns to return to its source. However, its principle is movement, and it is caught up in the web of space and time, discursive logic and sensation. It finds itself in a position between a higher principle, the Spirit from which it proceeds, and a lower. This lower is the next and final emanation. Soul is impelled to generate something other than itself, and it does this by producing the physical universe, which operates according to laws imposed upon it by the higher categories of reality. As a part of this process, individual souls become incarnate in particular bodies, through which they relate themselves to the world of things. Those things cannot, in turn, look downward and continue the creative process. They exist on the outer fringes of reality, and to try to go beyond matter in that direction would be to encounter nothing but the darkness of non-being. Nature, then, could have no existence apart from the Soul, which must animate it. At its higher level, Soul looks up, contemplates Spirit, and seeks to become one with it. At the lower, it produces the processes of life and growth in the organic world and, in its lowest form of activity, is responsible for the forms of those non-contemplative bodies which exist at the edge of non-being.

It is in this connection that Plotinus dealt with the difficult problem of "matter." Objects, properly speaking, are not "material" in the popular sense. They are projections of soul. From the classical point of view, "matter" is a relative term, in that the same aspect of the world may be form with reference to that which is below it and matter with respect to that which is above it. At the lowest level, then, it must be that which has nothing at all below it, and that, for the Neoplatonist, would be whatever would remain if one began with an object and stripped away all its predicates. Such a process would leave one with no ponderable and extended stuff, but only with a bare abstraction. Matter, Plotinus decided, is "no thing," but it is not "nothing." It is "incorporeal, because Body only exists after it." It rightly should be called Not-being rather than Being. It is "an image and phantom of extension, an aspiration to exist." So powerless is it that if the forms provided by Soul did not act upon it, it would not exist at all. Where the activity of Soul ends, then, we have the outer limits of Being.

This conception of matter has important implications for the Neoplatonic treatment of the problem of evil. Evil has its origin in matter, but in view of the fact that matter is nothing more than a deprivation of reality, evil has no positive ontological status. In human life, it comes through the turning of the soul outward—or downward—away from the cause of Being. It is a movement toward nothingness.

At this point, Plotinus had some difficulty in formulating his philosophy in such a way as to avoid contradiction. It is clear enough that what appears superficially to be a dualism asserting the existence of two principles—Spirit, which is good, and matter, which is evil—is really a monism in which the latter has no claim to independent existence. The activity of the One, Spirit,and Soul in emanating a hierarchy of existent categories is a natural and necessary process and is, indeed, the function which justifies our application of the name "The Good" to the Absolute. However, the generative activity is the source of evil, and life in the Soul World, while essential to the fullness of Being, is actually a fall from the Good.

If Plotinus can be said to have solved the problem at all, he did so by placing the whole meaning of moral conflict within the life of the Soul in time. Moral goodness is a step in the ascent to a perfection which transcends the antithesis between good and evil. When a soul confines itself to looking downward and becomes absolved in concern with the lesser reality of things, it is, in depriving itself of the upward—or inward—movement which is an essential aspect of the outgoing and return of the creative life of the One, acting wrongly. When, on the other hand, it looks upward and recognizes its essential identity with Spirit and finally with the One, it is engaging in right action. Although Plotinus may have been influenced in some measure by the Manichaeans, his essential monism would not permit him to regard the physical world as evil in itself, for whatever reality it has comes ultimately from the One.

The One is the center of everything. We constantly move around it, but we do not always attend to it. When we do turn our attention fully toward it, we achieve the end of our existence. Life in the world is a falling away from the center, and our ethical aim must be to detach ourselves in as great a measure as possible from the body, to see ourselves as Spirit, and ultimately to have the sort of ineffable mystical vision which reveals to us our own divinity. The soul which falls comes to the evil of not-being, though never to absolute non-being. But if it moves toward its origin, it arrives at itself alone and rises above the world of Being to communion with the One. When a man sees himself as united with the One, he knows himself a likeness to the One, and when he descends from the vision, he can make the journey again through Spirit and back to the One. "Such is the life of gods and godlike men," Plotinus said, "liberation from all earthly bonds, a life that takes no pleasure in earthly things, a flight of the alone to the alone."

The universe is like a great dance, a dance in which all things play their parts, going out from a radiant center and then returning to their source, reasserting their oneness with the Absolute, while somehow retaining their identity. Plotinus held the Orphic and Platonic view that souls are reincarnated again and again until at last they find salvation through union with the One.

The process by which a human being moves toward that salvation is a long and difficult one, for the soul's attachment to its spatial and temporal world is strong. It involves first the attainment of self-mastery through the cultivation of indifference to pleasure and pain and dutiful attention to the obligations which one incurs as a member of society. At this stage of development, the contemplation of nature is useful. Like Plato, Plotinus thought that the calm and dispassionate admiration of the order and harmony of the physical world could lead to an appreciation of its archetype, the intelligible world.

Farther along the *scala perfectionis* is the turning of attention from the lesser reality of the physical world to the greater reality of the eternal ideas of which the items of sense experience are only limitations. In this phase of the ascent, reason is the guide and philosophy the discipline which purify the soul and fit it for the last stage of the ascent. That final stage comes when the mind, free at last of the bondage of sense and reason alike experiences the beatific vision in a way that can neither be imagined or described because in it one transcends all duality and knows the fullness of life in the One, which is beyond all categories.

Other Neoplatonists

Plotinus's two most distinguished pupils were Amelius and Porphyry. Both men modified the teachings of their master to some extent, and Porphyry especially was responsible for some alterations that won greater popularity for Neoplatonism in the Roman world. A native of Syria, he was originally named Malchus, which means "king" but his tutor jokingly called him Porphyrius—"dressed in purple"—and he adopted the name. In the year 262, he went to Rome to study under Plotinus and stayed there for six years. Suffering from ill health brought about by overwork, he spent five years in Sicily, after which he returned to Rome and devoted himself to the teaching of philosophy. He married a scholarly widow named Marcella, who gave him a ready-made family of seven children. He died at some time around the beginning of the next century, possibly about the year 304. In addition to his *Life of Plotinus,* he produced a number of other philosophical and literary works.

An uncompromising opponent of Christianity, Porphyry advocated Neoplatonic discipline as a better way to attain virtue and assure the salvation of the soul. Although he was in agreement with Plotinus that the body in itself is not evil, he saw the desires of the soul for the pleasures of the body as so dangerous that he advocated a rigorous form of asceticism that prohibited sexual intercourse, the drinking of wine, and the eating of meat. His opposition to Christianity was based not on an aversion to the person or the teaching of Jesus, but rather on his distaste for the practices of the Christian Church of his day, which he believed to be based on the writings of ignorant and deceptive men. When the Empire became Christian, his works were condemned and destroyed, but much of his writing was preserved in books written by other authors.

Iamblichus (c.250-c.330), a native of Chalcis, was a student of Porphyry and later became the founder of a school in Syria which emphasized the theological rather than the philosophical aspects of Neoplatonism. The combination of classical paganism and Eastern religion popular in his time provided him with materials which he combined in such a way as to appeal to large segments of the population of the Roman world who were more at home with myth and ritual than with the rational mysticism of Plotinus. He appears to have been in no small measure responsible for the introduction into Neoplatonism of the sort of theurgy which sought to conjure up beneficent spirits through magical practices. His major philosophical works have been lost, but from references to his thought by later writers, he seems to have drawn a picture of the universe as a complex hierarchical structure involving many levels of being, each of which mirrors those above and below it according to the "law of mean terms," which holds that two aspects of being which are unlike each other must be related by a third which resembles one of them in one way and the other in another. He also posited a generation of effects by causes and turning back of those effects to their sources according to an order of "remaining," "possession," and "return." Apparently seeing the One of Plotinus as insufficiently ineffable because of its identification with the Good, Iamblichus suggested the necessity of recognizing a higher One, beyond all possible qualification.

The Neoplatonism of Iamblichus was a suitable vehicle for polytheism, for it provided a world view in which gods, as well as the souls of men, are emanations from the One. Defenders of the old religions saw in his teaching a rallying point for their fight against Christianity, and a number of his followers, while contributing little of significance to philosophy, worked diligently as Neoplatonic missionaries. Under their influence, the followers of a number of diverse sects, all of whom could find some grounds for enlisting under the banner of Neoplatonism, joined together in the fourth century for a last-ditch battle against Christianity.

Their opposition to the Christian religion was attributable not to any spirit of intolerance on their part, but rather to a refusal of the Christians to accept a position as worshippers of one god among many in a comfortably broad-minded culture. They insisted that Christ was the way, truth, and life. The Church owed allegiance to him alone and could not accommodate itself to the syncretism advocated by the Neoplatonists.

On the other hand, Christianity had shown a remarkable ability to absorb into its own doctrine and practice an astonishing variety of materials from the very religions with which it refused to share the stage with equal billing. The Greek philosophies which, from the early days of the Church, had provided a framework for Christian thought had been joined with elements of Gnosticism and other popular religious movements in such a way as to enable converts with diverse backgrounds to accept the theological tenets of their new faith without having to repudiate all their past. Repression had served only to strengthen and unify the growing Church, which now threatened to dominate the religious life of the Empire.

Pagan Neoplatonism did not succumb to its adversary without a struggle. Around the beginning of the fourth century, it had an ally in the Emperor Diocletian, who launched a campaign of persecution against the Christians. On his retirement in 305, however, the repressive activities subsided as six claimants to the throne tried to strengthen their positions.

On July 25, 306, the eighteen-year-old son of the Emperor Constantius I was proclaimed Augustus by the army. Of illegitimate birth and with no clear right to imperial authority, the young Constantine was slow in establishing his claim, but, through patience and persistence, he gradually gained ascendancy over his adversaries. In the spring of 312, he crossed the Alps from the north to attack Maxentius, his principal rival in the West. The enterprise was a bold one for a man given to caution, but Constantine was given confidence by a vision of a flaming cross in the sky, bearing the legend "In this sign conquer." He adopted the device and had it borne into battle on the "labarum," a jeweled purple cloth suspended from a bar fastened across the top of a gilded spear. Victorious over Maxentius, he became undisputed ruler in the West. In 313, the Edict of Milan granted absolute freedom of conscience to Christians in that part of the Empire over which he had established control. In 323, having vanquished the last of the rival claimants to the imperial throne, Constantine became sole master of East and West, and Christianity enjoyed protected status throughout the Empire.

In Constantine's view, the future of Rome depended upon an alliance between the state and the religion responsible for his triumph. He took an active interest in ecclesiastical and theological matters and had the Christian monogram stamped on the coinage. Wanting to bring about the sort of unity in the Church that he desired for the Empire, he called the Council of Nicaea in 325 to settle the Arian controversy. He also established a new seat for what was to become the Eastern Church when he founded a new seat of government, the "City of Constantine," on the Bosporus.

On Constantine's death, in 337, his three sons plunged the Empire into another series of civil wars. It was reunited in 353 by Constantine's sole surviving son, Constantius. In 353, Constantius gave the subordinate title of Caesar to his cousin Julian to deal with a disturbance in Gaul. Trouble broke out between the two, Julian was declared Emperor by the Legions, and only Constantius's death in 361 forestalled a new outbreak of civil strife.

At the time of his accession, Julian, like his cousins, professed Christianity, which had been declared the official religion of the Empire. A young man of high character and serious purpose, the new Emperor disliked the intolerance of the Christian Church, however, and deplored the lack of brotherly love on the part of adherents of a faith which publicly held that virtue in such high esteem. Influenced by such followers of Iamblichus and Maximus of Smyrna and finding intellectual stimulation only in the company of pagans, Julian, in his early youth, had become secretly committed to the sort of syncretistic Neoplatonism which was now making a final militant stand against Christianity. On becoming Emperor, he publicly professed his allegiance to the ancient

Greek religion and decreed tolerance for all faiths, while forbidding the teaching of Christianity in the schools. With himself as *pontifex maximus,* he made Neoplatonic Hellenism a sort of official creed.

But if the Neoplatonists seemed to have gained the upper hand, their triumph was short-lived. Two years after he became Emperor, Julian was mortally wounded in a battle against the Persians. He became known in the history of the Christian West as "Julian the Apostate." Neoplatonic paganism was not dead, and in the next century it had an able exponent in Proclus (410-485), head of the Academy of Athens. The vigorous and well-organized Christian Church, however, continued to show a superior ability to adopt all that was best in the systems of thought which had been its chief rivals, and the final act of the drama which had pitted the two movements against each other was to be the absorption into Christian theology and philosophy of Neoplatonism itself.

Chapter 7

The Augustinian Synthesis

No one is likely to dispute the claim that Augustine of Hippo was the most influential Christian since New Testament times. He was the creator of a synthesis, composed of a variety of elements from antiquity, that has endured at the center of Western Christianity and, indeed, of Western culture as a whole. The strength and breadth of that synthesis may be observed in the fact that the division of Western Christendom resulting from the Reformation did not appreciably disturb the allegiance of both sides to the theology of Augustine. To a remarkable degree, Western Christianity remains Augustinian Christianity.

The Man Between the Ages

The life of Augustine coincided with a major juncture in history. Antiquity was drawing to its conclusion and a new age was dawning. Western civilization, having originated in western Asia and northern Africa, had already shifted its center of creativity toward the west, from the Levant and Greece to Italy and the northern Mediterranean basin; and now, with the incursion into Europe of the barbarians from the north and east and the imminent demise of the Western Empire, the light and power of antiquity were beginning to move farther north and west, across the Alps, to be absorbed and transformed by the vital new peoples who were to dominate the future. Augustine revealed an awareness that he was witnessing a transition of epoch-making proportions, as though he stood at the epicenter of an earthquake and could only imagine the shape of the future after the seismic convulsions subsided. He recorded his view of the past, in terms of self and God, in his *Confessions;* he similarly described his vision of the future, in the language of faith and hope, in the *City of God.*

Aurelius Augustinus was born in the year 354, a short generation after the conversion of Constantine and the official establishment of Christianity. He died in 430 as the Vandals, one of the barbarian peoples who were conquering and replacing the Empire, held his episcopal city of Hippo under siege.

During the half-century prior to his birth the old order had begun to suffer its death throes with the abdication in 305 of the Emperor Diocletian, who had permanently divided the empire (and the Christendom to be). Diocletian had ruled with coercive social control and had decreed the last ruthless attempt to exterminate Christianity by official persecution. His retirement initiated a rapid series of decisive events. The young Constantine, son of the "Caesar of the West," Constantius Chlorus, under Diocletian and Maximian, was declared the new Augustus by his troops at York, in England. That audacious action led finally, after many maneuvers and battles, to Constantine's acquisition of power over the whole Empire in 323/25 with the defeat of Licinius. Eager to enlist the unifying strength and blessing of the growing Christian population, Constantine and his cohorts issued the so-called Edict of Milan in 313, which guaranteed religious freedom and granted Christianity the status of a *religio licita,* a licensed cult. In 325, the new Christian Emperor sponsored and presided over the theologically decisive Council of Nicea, the first in a long line of ecumenical councils of the Church. The seat of government was moved to Byzantium on the Bosporus in 330, and the "new Rome" was called Constantinople, the city of Constantine. Thus, when Augustine was born, the Church had already achieved position and power, and the process of radical cultural change had irrevocably begun.

During the half-century following the death of Augustine, the newly powerful Church held its third and fourth ecumenical councils, at Ephesus in 431 and at Chalcedon in 451, setting forth the permanent dogmas concerning the Trinity and Jesus Christ, the former dogma especially having been influenced by Augustine's teaching. The Empire had undergone a brief pagan revival in 361 when Julian the "apostate" ascended the throne upon the death of his hated cousin, Constantius, son and successor of Constantine. However, Julian's efforts to undermine Christianity by re-establishing the classical tradition were aborted by his early death in battle against the Persians in 362. Politically and socially, the Western Empire continued its dying agonies. The barbarian peoples, some of whom were now Arian Christians and some of whom were still pagan, gradually decimated the imperial territory in central Europe, North Africa, and finally in Italy. Alaric, the Visigoth chieftain, captured Rome itself in 410, and the "eternal city" was sacked again by the Vandals in 455. The last of the Roman emperors was the pitiful Romulus Augustulus, son of a temporary leader of the tattered army, who was deposed and succeeded in 476 by the Germanic general, Odoacer. Thus the civilization (*civitas terrena*) that Augustine knew in all its vaunted glory came to its death soon after his.

Because he lived at such a time of historic change, Augustine was able to serve as a bridge between antiquity and the Middle Ages. He obviously possessed an unusual mind, capable of retaining great learning while flashing with insight and synthesizing new ideas; and he was fortunate to receive a splendid education, made possible by the policies of both Julian and Valentinian, which provided him with a thorough knowledge of both classical literature and Christian teaching. Augustine mastered the Latin classics and the Greek and Roman philosophic systems, especially that of the Platonists, and he combined what he chose from those traditions with the biblical theology of the Church, and with his own reflections, to create the synthesis that was passed into the Middle Ages, and, indeed, to modern times, as the dominant form of Christianity.

Divine Guidance

Augustine recorded the experiences of his early life in his *Confessions,* not so much as an autobiography as an example of the divine guidance that he believed might be perceived, through faith, in every life and in the whole course of human history. His mature theology was a consistent expression of his conviction that the sovereignty of God is manifested as creative and redeeming grace. He composed his *Confessions* in the form of a lengthy prayer that glorifies and praises God for the evidences of the grace which he believed could be clearly seen, in retrospect, throughout his life and times. The result is one of the primary classics of Western literature.

He was born on November 13, 354, in the small Numidian village of Thagaste (the modern Souk-Ahras), near the eastern border of what is now Algeria. He was the first child of Patricius and Monica, the father being a local official who was still a pagan, and the mother a youthful, respected and pious Christian. There followed a brother, Navigius, and a sister, Perpetua, both of whom later devoted themselves to religious vocations. Augustine showed promise as a scholar even as a lad and was sent away to school in nearby Madaura when he was only eleven. In 370 he was assisted by a wealthy neighbor to enter the more advanced rhetoric schools of Carthage, and within a year his father died, having just been baptized into the Church. He admits to a typically profligate life while he was a student in Carthage, occupied by ambition for fame and fortune, succumbing to youthful immoralities, and enamored with the theatre and the games, but avoiding the urgent religious interests of his clinging mother. He took a concubine and became the father of a son in 371, when he was only seventeen. Significantly the child was named Adeodatus, "given by God."

Completing his formal education in 373, Augustine began his anticipated career by teaching rhetoric in Thagaste and Carthage until 383. During that decade he also began the intellectual and moral struggles that were to bring him finally to the precipice of despair, and hence to faith and vocational dedication. He later described the ordeal with penetrating psychological and spiritual insight as well as literary brilliance. The fires of consuming philosophical passion were lighted by his reading Cicero's *Hortensius,* a high-minded work of Stoic philosophy modeled after Aristotle's *Protreptikos,* which, unfortunately, did not survive the dark ages that followed. He also spent nine years as an auditor of the Manichean sect, a pseudo-Christian religious philosophy that had originated during the previous century in Persia and had spread with considerable success in the West, especially in North Africa. He finally grew weary of his unruly pupils and became disenchanted with the arrogant emptiness of the Manichees. Even their leading light, Faustus the Bishop, failed to supply the theological and moral answers which Augustine so desperately sought.

He later interpreted it to be the hand of Providence that led him to flee to Rome, where he taught for a year but also learned both the useful method of the Skeptics and the grand idealism of the Academics and the New Platonism. He also began to gather a company of loyal friends who were to contribute to his maturing life and thought. Prominent among these was Alypius, a native also of Thagaste and a former student of Augustine in both their home town and in Carthage. Alypius, of wealthy and noble parentage, had gone to Rome before Augustine in order to study law and, when Augustine arrived in the capital, their companionship was renewed. Another member of the closely-knit group was Nebridius of Carthage, whose cogent questioning of Manichean doctrine and astrology was to contribute to the development of Augustine's mind.

The establishment of a new system of state-controlled education, initiated as a part of the reforms begun by the Emperor Valentinian I led to the appointment of Augustine in 384 as professor of rhetoric in the great city of Milan, seat of the royal court. Augustine later interpreted the event as an act of God. It did indeed determine his future and therefore was of inestimable significance for the development of Western thought and history. By going to Milan he met Ambrose the Bishop who, in turn, led him to become an orthodox Catholic Christian and, eventually, the most influential teacher of Western Christendom.

> To Milan I came, to Ambrose the Bishop, known to the whole world as among the best of men. Thy devout servant; whose eloquent discourse did then plentifully dispense unto Thy people the flour of thy

> wheat, the gladness of Thy oil, and the sober inebriation of Thy wine. To him was I unknowingly led by Thee, that by him I might knowingly be led to Thee. That man of God received me as a father, and showed me an Episcopal kindness on my coming. . . . I determined therefore so long to be a Catechumen in the Catholic Church . . . (*Confessions,* V, 23, 25).

Ambrose and Simplicianus, a presbyter, gently guided him toward decision and commitment. His pious mother, Monica, who had followed him with prayer and presence from Thagaste to Milan, and his band of intellectual friends, led by Alypius, also contributed to his increasing agony and final ecstasy. Unlike Faustus the Manichee Bishop, whose promising words brought no fulfillment, Ambrose the Catholic Bishop attracted his young auditor with both eloquent speech and convincing truth. A factor of permanent significance was the method of biblical hermeneutics that Augustine learned from Ambrose. By practice and counsel, the preacher opened the deeper meanings of the Scriptures, especially the Old Testament, which Augustine had long disdained as inferior to the Greek and Latin classics, by the use of the allegorical method borrowed from the Alexandrian school of Clement and Origen and made prominent earlier by the Stoic philosophers in their interpretation of the myths of Homer. By rejecting the literal meaning of the biblical literature as its sole or even primary meaning, Augustine was able to discover the profound moral and spiritual truths of the Gospel preached and taught by Origen, Ambrose, and the other leaders of the early Church. Simplicianus helped him to see that the philosophy of the Platonists, which Augustine had recently found most satisfying, could be retained and was no impediment for a Christian.

The *Confessions* record the agonizing trauma of Augustine's time of decision during his three years of residence in Milan. He struggled like a game fish that has struck the fly and is hooked, yet runs hither and thither as though free, all the time being drawn in by the angler and soon to be brought into the boat. He came to believe that God is the angler and the boat is the Church, the Ark of Salvation.

The climax came in August, 386, at his borrowed villa in Milan. He had been struggling for more than a decade with personal and intellectual problems, especially the problem of evil. He had been unable to accept the solution of Manichean dualism; yet Christian monotheism, teaching that the one God is both omnipotent and perfect in goodness, seemed to be reasonably unacceptable in the light of the reality of evil. How could a perfect God create or permit the ever-present evil in the world? But more pressing for Augustine than this apparently insoluble question was the moral issue in his own life: how could he find the strength of will to do what he believed to be right and cease doing what he believed to be wrong? He hated his proud immoralities, yet he found himself enslaved by them.

In great anguish and at the brink of despair, Augustine sat weeping and alone, except for Alypius, in the garden of his villa. Suddenly he heard a neighboring child chanting, as in a game, "Take up and read; take up and read." He interpreted it to be a command from God. Opening the volume of Paul's Epistles, which he had been reading, his eyes fell on Romans 13:13, 14: "not in reveling and drunkenness, not in debauchery and licentiousness, not in quarreling and jealousy; but put on the Lord Jesus Christ, and make no provision for the flesh, to gratify its desires." He later wrote: "No further would I read; nor needed I: for instantly at the end of this sentence, by a light as it were of serenity infused into my heart, all the darkness of doubt vanished away" (*Confessions,* VIII, 29). The following spring, at Easter, he was baptized by Ambrose in Milan. As he prepared to return to Thagaste, intending to devote himself to monastic prayer and teaching, his mother died, full of joy that her own prayers were answered.

The hand of Providence was not yet finished. The quiet life at Thagaste lasted only about a year before he was called to the priesthood in nearby Hippo Regius by the aged Bishop Valerius. Augustine himself succeeded Valerius as the Bishop in 395, and he spent the remaining thirty-five years of his life in that office, preaching, teaching, and writing with expanding influence. Death came to him on August 28, 430, just before the Vandals were to capture Hippo and not long before all the barbarians were to conquer the whole Western Empire. That had been anticipated and described by the old Bishop, though without regret, since he believed that, by the grace of God, he would escape into the City of God with all the elect.

The Writings of Augustine

Many have said that Augustine is more fully and intimately known to us than any other person of antiquity. The chief reason is that so many of his writings have survived and are available in various languages. Although he carried a heavy burden of pastoral and administrative duties, the Bishop maintained a regular correspondence with great and small throughout the Roman world, and he was constantly at work on major volumes concerning biblical interpretation, doctrinal issues, and apologetic challenges. His extant treatises number 118, and more than 200 of his letters remain. All may be found in the standard edition, *Patrol-*

ogia cursus completus, series latina, edited by the Abbé J. P. Migne, where they occupy sixteen large volumes, each containing around twelve hundred double-columned pages. Hence the famous saying: "He lies who says that he has read all his works."

Three of the treatises are perhaps best known and permanently influential: the *Confessions,* the *City of God,* and *On the Trinity.* As we shall observe in the next chapter, Augustine also gave much thought during his years as a bishop to combatting what he considered to be dangerous heresies and schisms, and he wrote a large number of books, letters, and sermons concerning them, sometimes in gentle persuasion and often in sharp debate. Against the Manicheans, the pseudo-Christian sect to which he had belonged for a decade, he composed *On the Book of Genesis Against the Manicheans, On the Morals of the Catholic Church and the Morals of the Manicheans,* and *Against Faustus the Manichean.* Many writings challenged the teachings of Pelagius and his supporters, among them *On Nature and Grace* and *On Grace and Free Will.* A third major group of his works carried on the long struggle between the Catholic Church, of which he became the strongest defender, and the powerful Donatist Church, which was the dominant form of Christianity in much of North Africa. One of the most influential of the anti-Donatist essays is *On Baptism Against the Donatists.*

In addition to these writings of Augustine, we must note three others that have exerted enormous influence: the *Soliloquies,* the *Enchiridion,* and *On Christian Doctrine.* The latter, though a comparatively small book, became fundamental in structure and content for many medieval scholars such as Rabanus Maurus, Hugh of St. Victor, and Peter Lombard. It was highly praised later by Erasmus. Finally, we must not forget that Augustine often changed his mind, after thought and perspective had cooled the passions of debate. In his last years he composed the *Retractions,* in which he attempted to review the earlier works in order to correct their errors and perfect their claims.

Elements of the Synthesis

We began this sketch of Augustine's pilgrimage and works by stating that his continuing dominance in Western thought is due, in large measure, to the broad and profound synthesis he created. It is crucial for the understanding and appreciation of Augustine that one see clearly the components of that synthesis and how they were used, consciously and unconsciously, in his teachings. What are the elements of the synthesis? In general terms it may be said simply that they are reason and revelation, or the major traditions of Greek and Roman philosophy wedded to the ideas and claims of the Christian Scriptures. More specifically, Augustine wove the fabric of Western theology from the threads of Neoplatonism and New Testament religion, particularly the Pauline writings. The pattern that emerged has remained visible in spite of wear and stain during the course of subsequent cultural history.

We have reviewed the major teachings of the New Testament in chapters three and four and of Neoplatonism in chapter six. It is sufficient here merely to specify the radical differences between the two approaches to life and reality and then to show by brief illustrations how they appear together in the thought of Augustine.

Neoplatonism was developed by Plotinus and his disciples as an all-encompassing philosophy. It assumed the power of reason to grasp and describe, at least metaphorically, the whole of reality—Being, non-being, and the ambiguous process of existence between them. The purpose of that system of thought and life was far more important than a mere academic exercise for the stretching of the mind. Rather it attempted to construct a vision so true and so appealing that it would bring light and deliverance to those who see and follow it. Combining the noble idealism of Plato and the continuing Academy with the rational morality of Stoic cosmology, Neoplatonism directed the benighted and enslaved souls of human beings to the upward way, toward beauty, goodness, and truth. It disdained the flesh but complimented the mind and encouraged the will. One of its central convictions was that the human soul is essentially good and immortal by nature, needing only enlightenment and liberation. Thus Neoplatonism was both a descriptive philosophy and an edifying religion.

More than seven centuries before the days of Augustine, Plato had given classic expression to the way of salvation:

> The right way of love (*eros*), whether one goes alone or is led by another, is to begin with the beautiful things that are here and ascend ever upwards aiming at the beauty that is above, climbing, as it were, on a ladder from one beautiful body to two, and from two to all the others, and from beautiful bodies to beautiful actions and from beauty of actions to beautiful forms of knowledge, till at length from these one reaches that knowledge which is the knowledge of nothing other than beauty itself (*Symposium*).

The mainstream of Apostolic Christianity, available in its original and unadulterated form in the New Testament and still confessed and taught in the universal Church, was fundamentally at odds with Neoplatonism. As we have seen, Christianity held that revelation is the source of its saving truth, not reason. The universal sinfulness of mankind has perverted both the reason and the will. The eye of the mind is incapable of beholding the proffered vision described by the philosophers because blindness requires healing before vision is possible. The moral law, no matter how noble, is a teasing mockery when the will is unable to obey it. What is required is not mere enlightenment but a radical transformation of the soul, a change in its moral and spiritual disposition by the power of God's creative grace. The upward way is impossible for the soul precisely because it is both crippled and weighted down by its own self-centered gravity. But God in Christ has descended in the Incarnation to bring healing—forgiveness and justification—so that all the powers of sin, death, and evil have been defeated by his death and resurrection.

Augustine perceived the similarities and differences between the two ways even before he became a professing Christian. While a student in Carthage he had read Cicero's *Hortensius,* which, he said, "altered my affections, and turned my prayers to thyself, O Lord. . . . and I longed with an incredibly burning desire for an immortality of wisdom, and began now to arise, that I might return to Thee" (*Confessions* III, 7). Later in Rome and Milan, he had procured "certain books of the Platonists" and read them with increasing agreement, yet without full satisfaction. He recorded in detail how he found in those books much of the truth, in different words, that he later read in the Christian Scriptures. But the Christian teaching that the transcendent God had humbled himself, "was made flesh, and dwelt among" men, and even suffered death for their redemption, "I read not there." He found it necessary and possible to add the healing power of the Gospel to the high idealism of the Platonists. Doing so he formed the synthesis that has persevered.

One example of that combination of disparate approaches may be seen in Augustine's bipolar views of God. Following the biblical model and usage, he spoke of and to God in a most intimate way, as to a loving father. He addressed God as Person, one who loves, seeks, and saves. His writings abound in the attitude of personal relationship and, as we have seen, his *Confessions* is *one* continuous prayer of thanksgiving and praise to the Father who had providentially guided him through life. On the other hand, especially when he was writing *about* God rather than speaking *to* him, Augustine used the objective language of philosophy. One of his favorite expressions is that God is the *summum bonum,* the highest good which is also the Absolute Being. God is the source and goal of all that is, the perfect love that we must love because he is lovely. Augustine saw God first with one eye and then with the other, as active

Person and as immutable Being, and the different angles of vision focus into a composite perception that has endured in theology and piety.

A second example of an apparently unconscious ambiguity in his thought may be seen in his understanding of evil. We have noted that he struggled for many years with this most difficult question in philosophy and theology. It was also an inescapable reality in his own experience in that he found himself to be addicted to the sin he abhorred. The more he tried to rise, the more he sank into perdition. The Manichees offered the rational solution of an ontological dualism, with the two ultimates of good and evil reflected in the nature of man as spirit and flesh. The Neoplatonic and biblical insistence upon the ultimate unity of Being was sufficient ground for rejecting the Manichean option. But, he repeatedly asked, if all is One and that One is both supreme and good, whence is evil? He could not accept the suggestion that the perfect God is also the creator of evil. Further, even if a satisfactory theory of the nature and origin of evil were somehow constructed, there remained the personal problem of one's own sinfulness: how can the will overcome the weight of habit and desire, those of the individual and of the race of mankind, so as to choose the good and refuse the evil? The problem was both intellectual and moral.

Augustine discovered a compelling solution to the problem of theodicy in Neoplatonism. Evil is *privatio boni,* a lack of good. It belongs to the non-being which lies around and beyond Being, posing both a threat and a challenge. It is not created; it is the power of the discreative, of corruption, decay, and death. It is no thing, but it is a cruel and devastating enemy of nature, man, and God. It cannot be removed by effort since it is intangible, a choice instead of a thing to be chosen. Therefore God made all things good and needs no justification; but man has made evil a reality by turning toward self and away from God, the Creator and Sustainer.

Implicit in this much-discussed understanding is the ambiguity that evil is both the threatening non-being that endangers the whole creation and, at the same time, a moral condition of every human being made real by the rejection of God and resulting in the crushing burden of guilt. The further question of why we make such a foolish and destructive choice, and what the remedy may be, Augustine was to work out in the theological controversies that occupied his thought during most of his years as a bishop.

Chapter 8

The Augustinian Legacy

The legacy of ideas that Augustine bequeathed to the Western Church is without parallel in terms of lasting, formative influence. At one time or another during his career as a Christian leader he found it useful or necessary to examine with care most of the major areas of Christian doctrine. The orthodox teachings about God and Christ had already largely received their dogmatic formulation before his time and, except for the final agreements at Chalcedon in 451, which his *On the Trinity* contributed to, he readily accepted the definitions as they had become fixed in the tradition. However, Christian teachings about man, sin, grace, the death of Christ, the Church and the sacraments, and eschatology were all unsettled. There was no orthodoxy on these matters—and, it must be said, there remains none.

Many of the major ideas that composed his legacy to the Church received their formulation in the heat of controversy. Such circumstances frequently result in exaggeration and one-sidedness, as was certainly the case with Augustine; yet, on the other hand, critical dialogue can be the occasion for development and clarification that would not otherwise occur. Such was the situation confronting the Bishop of Hippo during all of his thirty-five years of service. Three powerful sources of opposition required his attention for the defense of his faith and his people as well as for the hoped-for correction of those he deemed in error. All three were a clear and present danger in North Africa at the time. They were Manicheism, Donatism, and Pelagianism. If we are to understand the thoughts and contributions of Augustine, we must first know the essential beliefs of each of these and then see the content of the theology he developed against them.

Against the Manichees

Manicheism was a highly developed, eclectic religion of salvation that arose in southern Babylonia in the third century. Its founder was Mani (c. 215-274), son of Patek, who himself had joined a religious community that may have been influenced by Judaism or early Christianity as well as other religions. The family also had connections with the Parthian royalty of the time. Mani claimed to have seen visions from which he learned new truths and during which he was commissioned to be the "seal of the prophets," the bearer of a universal message that had been revealed previously only in a local and distorted form by earlier prophets, among them Adam, Enoch, the Buddha, Zoroaster, and Jesus. He proclaimed his message in many portions of the Sassanian empire and even in India, making a host of converts who carried on his missionary efforts. He was usually opposed by Zoroastrian priests and, finally, he was imprisoned, tortured, and executed. However, he had assured the survival of his ideas by writing seven major works which he claimed had been inspired by a spirit who was his "Twin."

The religion spread for several centuries in Asia, Africa, and Europe, eventually claiming adherents from the Atlantic to the Pacific. It had reached its height of influence in the Roman world during the years of Augustine's life and we have already noted his affiliation for nine years with the sect in Carthage. Nevertheless, several epoch-making movements in world history eventually caused its decline and ultimate disappearance. The most powerful of these was the rise and rapid expansion of Islam in the seventh century and later. All the territory that had been the heartland of Manicheism was overrun by the soldiers of the Prophet of Mecca. Although Islam tolerated other religions, Manicheism was eventually restricted and finally crushed. In like manner, the rising dominance of Christianity, both Eastern and Western, finally overcame the influence of the Manichees through theological and institutional power. In this Augustine was a major factor, as we shall see. Further, the Manichean outreach into central Asia, beyond the Oxus and even into China, was eclipsed by the Mongol invasions and official persecution. The faith gradually dwindled away, leaving its lasting mark in the medieval dualistic sects such as the Paulicians, the Bogomils, the Cathars, and the Albigenses. It may also be identified as a source of Christian dualism, asceticism, and celibacy.

The teachings of Manicheism were based on an exceedingly complex mythology about gods and goddesses, cosmic origins and principles, genealogies and theogonies, angels, aeons, and devils. Its fundamental conviction was that there is an ontological dualism between light and darkness, good and evil, spirit and flesh. The affinity with earlier Gnosticism and Marcionism is obvious. Its revealed message provided the means for the redemption of imprisoned and corrupted human souls by first providing truth about reality and then prescribing liturgies and moral practices for the initiated. The faithful were of two varieties: the "elect," who knew the mysteries as well as taught and practiced them; and the "hearers," who supported and served the elect while striving to attain the higher status. The true Manichees believed that the physical cosmos is corrupt because it is the result of the aggressions of darkness. Marriage and procreation were forbidden because they were the means of enslaving more spirits in the flesh. The eating of meat by the elect was prohibited. The secrets of one's destiny could be discovered and controlled by a correct study of astrology as well as by other esoteric procedures. The Jewish Scriptures were scorned both because of their teaching of monotheism and a good creation and because they were filled with references to wicked acts by God and his people. The Manichees held to a strict ethic and claimed to follow a rigorous rationality. In the West they sought to represent a superior, purified Christianity while in the East they adapted their teachings to Buddhism or Chinese religions.

As we observed in the last chapter, Augustine remained a hearer of the Manichean doctrine during the decade of his twenties. He hoped to find the answer to his persistent intellectual problems, especially regarding the source and nature of evil, and he admired both its moral teachings and its rationalistic disdain for the apparent simplicities of the Old Testament. However, he eventually was disenchanted with the lack of depth and finality in the theology, especially when glibly presented by Faustus the Bishop, and he later wrote devastatingly against the whole system.

Augustine finally rejected and opposed Manicheism on at least four grounds. First, he learned to define God in terms of the Neoplatonic conception of the ultimate unity of Being and, increasingly, in terms of the biblical requirements of a personalistic monotheism. Second, he developed the doctrine of *creatio ex nihilo,* which, while contrary to the Neoplatonic notion of emanation, provided from that source a satisfactory answer to the problem of evil. Further, the doctrine of creation by the will of God alone out of nothing served as a basis for his views of the essential goodness of all that is created and of creation as a continuing exercise of the providential, sustaining will of God. Third, he rejected the vaunted rationalism of the Manichees by observing the distorted function of reason in depraved humanity; and he learned to accept the authority of the Scriptures and the Church, thereby to begin with faith and to proceed from there to understanding. Hence his famous motto: *credo ut intelligam*. Finally, instructed primarily by Ambrose, he adopted the allegorical method of interpreting the Scriptures, thereby finding moral and spiritual truths that the Manichean literalness overlooked. This hermeneutic unfortunately became grossly exaggerated in the exegesis of Augustine and more so in subsequent centuries by those who followed him.

Against the Donatists

Precisely defined, Donatism was more of a schism than a heresy, although it approached heresy by its exclusivist doctrine of the Church and the sacraments. It posed a dangerous threat to the unity and strength of the Christian communities especially in North Africa, the home of Augustine. The Church had only recently escaped the fires of persecution and it now faced the continuing task of converting the pagans and developing its faith and structure. However, many areas of Numidia and the adjoining provinces counted more Donatists than Catholics (as the traditionally orthodox were now denominated). Division could not provide strength to the Church for its arduous enterprise. It was a perplexing problem for the Bishop of Hippo.

The schism was a recent development. There had been antecedents, of course, even in the New Testament debate over requirements for Jewish and Gentile converts, and, more recently, in the question concerning the readmission of lapsed Christians after the Decian persecution in the middle of the third century. However, the most widespread and costly of all the persecutions was the last one, that under Diocletian in 303-305. This time there was the official intent to exterminate the despised cult of the Christians, to root it out of the court, the army, and from the Empire as a whole. Christian worship was prohibited, churches and sacred writings were burned, thousands of the faithful were martyred while others fled or were banished, and large numbers gave up the faith in order to survive. Included among the lapsed were priests and bishops as well as lay people. Some, however, only pretended to abandon the faith, dishonestly purchasing fraudulent certificates (*libelli*) from corrupt officers, giving them credit for performing the required pagan rituals. When the persecution had ceased, these weak Christians sought forgiveness and restitution in the churches.

The problem was complicated by both political and religious factors. In his struggle to succeed Diocletian, Constantine had become a Christian and then, by the Edict of Milan in 313 and later decrees, first tolerated and then established Christianity as the official religion of the Empire. He built great basilicas, gave gifts to religious leaders, and took part in the administration of church affairs. It was the beginning of the Constantinian Era, with its long history of growth, power, and corruption in the Church. Constantine quickly moved into ecclesiastical disputes with the power of the Empire at his command in an attempt to unify the Empire by unifying the Church. He claimed to be both supreme ruler and *pontifex maximus,* chief priest.

Donatism arose in Carthage in 311 when, upon the death of the Bishop Mensurius, three neighboring bishops elected and consecrated Caecilian, the archdeacon, as his successor, without regard to the rights of their Numidian colleagues. To make matters worse, one of the bishops who consecrated Caecilian, Felix of Aptunga, had been accused of acting as a traitor (*traditor*) during the persecution; and Caecilian himself was charged with unsympathetic behavior toward the martyrs. Therefore, when the Numidian bishops arrived in Carthage, they held a council that deposed Caecilian and elected Majorinus, a prominent deacon from Carthage. Majorinus was soon succeeded by Donatus of Numidia, who gave his name to the puritan, separatist movement. Constantine attempted to heal the schism by arbitration, choosing Miltiades, Bishop of Rome, who was himself an African, with four bishops from Gaul, as the mediators. After investigation, they decided for Caecilian. When the dissenters refused to accept the decision and appealed, a council was held in 314 at Arles in Gaul, attended by thirty-three bishops, including three from Britain. It was the first interprovincial council held in the West and the first sponsored by the imperial government. Again, the council fathers supported Caecilian against the Donatists. When the schismatics refused again to accept the findings of the council, Constantine took severe action in 317 by outlawing them. Nevertheless, the Donatist Church survived and thrived in North Africa for another century, led first by Donatus the Great and then by Parmenian (362-392). By the end of the century, Jerome could say that "nearly all Africa" had become Donatist.

Beneath the surface issue of the choice of a bishop, determined by the worthiness of the candidates, lay several more important and permanent principles. Is unity necessary for the Church to be authentic? Can salvation be found outside the Church? Are the grace-giving sacraments valid if received from unworthy hands, even from schismatics or traitors? Must not the Church as the Body and Bride of Christ, remain pure and undefiled, especially in the presence of the cleansing blood of so many martyrs? It had only been a few years since Cyprian, the sainted Bishop of Carthage, had taught that there is no salvation outside the church: *salus extra ecclesiam non est.* North African Christians, more than any others, were always concerned with grace and purity in contrast to sin and guilt.

Augustine thus began his work as a bishop with the Church divided all around him and with his side in the minority. He began at once to remedy the situation, first by debate and persuasion and then by the stronger means of official coercion. He argued that the Church on earth cannot be perfectly pure but must remain "a mixed body." The validity of the sacraments is based on the grace of God in Christ, not on the character of the priest or bishop who administers them. The holiness of the Church is by virtue of the holiness of God, not its own accomplishment. And it ought to be obvious that, because God is one and the Gospel is one, the one Church that lives throughout the world and has remained since Christ and the Apostles is the true Church rather than a new, schismatic group in a local or limited area, no matter how pure it may claim to be.

As Augustine continued the debate, for nearly twenty years, he developed a view of the Church and its sacraments that was to become standard in Western ecclesiology. He described the true Church as marked by four essential characteristics: unity, holiness, universality, and apostolicity. The People of God are one because as such they are in communion with their Father and with one another. The Church is holy because it is made so by virtue of the grace of God and the sanctifying presence of the Spirit. The blood of Christ makes it spotless, cleansing it of sin and guilt. The Church is universal (*catholic*) both in time and space, one Body wherever the faithful are found, and in fellowship with all the saints and martyrs, "a great cloud of witnesses." And the true Church is apostolic because it traces its foundations to the work of the Apostles and remains the faithful depository of their teachings.

When the Donatists refused to accept these arguments, Augustine turned to the secular power of Rome and encouraged coercion. Did not Jesus command to "compel them to come in" (Luke 14:23)? In 411 edicts were issued that severely punished the Donatists, though, at the insistence of Augustine, there were no Donatist martyrs. Finally the schism was crippled and crushed, so that most of the puritans joined the Catholic Church. Some remained separate, however, rejoicing in their suffering, and the movement survived until the conquest by Islam in the seventh century.

Against the Pelagians

The controversy between Augustine and the Pelagians bore fruit in the formulation of the views of human nature, sin, grace, and freedom which have remained dominant in Western Christianity ever since. There were radical modifications, of course, even immediately after the death of Augustine; and the temper of modern thought, especially following the Enlightenment, has reacted in the opposite direction. It remains true, nonetheless, that Augustine's teaching concerning these matters has supplied much of the motivation for what the Church has done in its preaching, teaching, mission, and liturgy.

The Pelagian debate arose almost accidentally, a product of the shocking conquest of Rome in 410 by the Visigoth chief, Alaric. Many leading citizens of the crumbling empire fled to Sicily and North Africa in the vain hope of escape. Among those who sought refuge were Pelagius and his companion, Coelestius, both of whom were pious and intelligent laymen dedicated to the strictest form of Christian living. There is uncertainty in the record about the background of Pelagius but tradition suggests that he was from Britain, born around 360, the son of a Roman civil official. It is known that he was in Rome in the early 380's where he served many years as the chaplain of a noble family and also became embroiled in a controversy with the irascible Jerome.

While in Rome, Pelagius read some of the writings of Augustine, with which he generally agreed. However, he became disturbed by Augustine's famous prayer: "give what you command, and command what you will" (*Confessions,* 10, 40). During those years also he wrote commentaries on the Pauline Epistles and a treatise entitled, *On Nature*. His primary aim was to encourage the ascetic life, in holy imitation or the example of Jesus. He had been appalled at the laxity of morals he observed among many Christians at Rome and he wished to emphasize the necessity of obedience to the commandments of Christ. Augustine's words upset him because he perceived them to suggest that human beings are unable as moral agents to choose the good unless God through the power of grace does it for them. That, Pelagius believed, takes away responsibility.

Pelagius and Coelestius sailed in 411 from Sicily to Hippo, hoping to meet the famous bishop there and perhaps to discuss their differences. Unfortunately, Augustine was away from the city and the two visitors travelled on to Carthage. Soon afterwards Pelagius departed for Palestine, leaving Coelestius in Carthage. When Coelestius asked Bishop Aurelius, a friend of Augustine, for ordination, his examination revealed ideas considered heretical and he was first refused and then excommunicated. Pelagius also found himself suspect in Palestine. His old adversary, Jerome, now lived in Bethlehem and, encouraged by messages from Augustine, charged him with heresy. However, Pelagius had found favor with Bishop John of Jerusalem and other Eastern leaders so that synods at Jerusalem and Diospolis (Lydda) acquitted him and accepted him to full communion.

Although Augustine did not meet Pelagius in Hippo, he had heard of Pelagius, had read some of his works, and admired him. He called

Pelagius "a holy man" who "has made no small progress in the Christian life." Nevertheless, by 415 the relationship had changed and Augustine later wrote in his *Retractions* that "the necessity arose which compelled me to write against the Pelagian heresy" (2, 58).

What were the specific teachings of Pelagius and his friends that brought so strong a reaction? He believed that the commandments of God are to be obeyed, and the righteousness of God would not allow him to require man to do the impossible. Man retains the moral nature that God created in him so that he remains able both to hear and to obey the Word of God, in spite of sin. The problem is in habit, not nature. Man, especially because of sin, is weak and self-centered, but God has provided sufficient help to enable man to do what he ought. There are the Scriptures for instruction, the example of Jesus to follow, and the added assistance of God's grace. Grace is not the power of God doing for man what he cannot do for himself; rather, grace is *adjutorium,* an assistance enabling obedience.

Based on this conception of man's nature and God's grace, Pelagius proceeded to develop the following arguments: (1) Adam died because he was mortal, not because he sinned; (2) Adam's sin was his alone and was not inherited by his offspring; (3) sin and guilt are not transmitted by procreation; (4) infants are born in the same moral state as that in which Adam was created so that baptism does not remove an "original sin;" (5) there were men without sin before the coming of Christ; (6) the Law leads to the Kingdom as well as the Gospel; (7) the rich must give up all that they have if they are to enter the Kingdom of God.

Augustine believed that these views constitute dangerous heresy, destroying the faith and undercutting the life and work of the Church. He agreed with Pelagius that God is perfect and that the whole creation, including mankind, was good when God brought it into being; but God's greatest gift to man was moral freedom, the possibility of knowing and doing the good. Both Scripture and experience show that mankind, always and everywhere, has chosen to disobey God, corrupting not only himself but the whole creation. Death is the result. More than that, the will is corrupted also by sin so that since Adam mankind is bound in "a mass of perdition." He is curved in upon himself so that he cannot love either God or his neighbor, as he is commanded to do. All the children of Adam and Eve inherit their chosen condition. Concupiscence, the clearest example of which is sexual lust, has become characteristic of all human beings, the means even of procreation and the continuation of the sinful human race. The condition of all mankind, therefore, is total helplessness, hopelessness, and despair.

The Gospel reveals that God is infinitely powerful and gracious. He has descended in humility to redeem mankind in Christ. All are justly condemned, of course, but God in his wisdom and love gives his transforming grace to those whom he has chosen to complete the Kingdom. Augustine suggested that the number of the elect will replace the fallen angels. It is unreasonable and unjust to find fault with God because he has not chosen to save all, since all are guilty of sin and deserve its wages, death. The freedom of will that human beings lost by choosing the enslavement of sin is revitalized by the prevenient (coming before) grace of God, the gift of faith, and now a greater freedom, like that of God, is the possession of the redeemed.

Perhaps the clearest exposition that Augustine gave of the condition of man is the three-fold statement included in several of his writings. He said that man was created with *posse non peccare, posse non mori* (ability not to sin, ability not to die). This freedom obviously carried with it the opposite choice, to sin and to die. In Adam that choice was made and remains the status of all. Thus man's present condition is *non posse non peccare, non posse non mori* (unable not to sin, unable not to die). The grace of God that is given in Christ and through the Church bestows a new condition on the faithful: *non posse peccare, non posse mori* (not able to sin, not able to die). That is not instantly realized, of course, but it is the final result of God's sanctifying work by the power of his Spirit in the life of the Church.

This is a mere summary of the teachings of Augustine about the nature of mankind, sin, grace, and freedom, which he developed in detail in many writings during the last fifteen years of his life. As may be seen, his thought prepared the way for the subsequent emphasis in the West upon sin and guilt, with all the means provided by the Church to alleviáte them: all the sacraments, as well as celibacy, mortification of the flesh, and a primary concern with escape from this corrupting world.

Continuation and Modification

In addition to these major views formulated by Augustine against the Manichees, the Donatists, and the Pelagians, he also dealt extensively with other aspects of Christian theology in a more positive way. One primary example of his influential contributions may be found in the massive *City of God*. There, in answer to the charge by sophisticated Romans that Christianity was the cause of the troubles besetting the empire, by leading to the abandonment of the gods who had made Rome great, Augustine composed a complicated philosophy of history. He believed that not only Rome is passing into decay but also the whole *civ-*

itas terrena, the civilized world of man. Rome is falling and the Kingdom of God is rising. The Church in the world gathers the elect to bring them finally into the *civitas dei,* the City of God that is truly eternal.

Augustine's teachings were passed on, often in adulterated form, into the Middle Ages. Gregory the Great, Bishop of Rome (590-609), was one of the early conduits. The ideas appeared in much of the work of the schoolmen and among the mystics of the following millenium. Even the great reformer, Martin Luther, began his career as an Augustinian monk and never departed far from the teachings of his master; and it may be said that John Calvin appears as a darker carbon copy of Augustine.

All did not agree with the Bishop of Hippo, however. Augustine had won his case (*"causa est finita"*) when the council of 214 bishops, meeting at Carthage in 416, followed the wishes of the Emperor Honorius against even Zosimus, Bishop of Rome, and condemned Pelagianism. Julian of Eclanum and 18 other bishops of southern Italy were forced to resign because they remained loyal to the position of Pelagius and Coelestius, who was now a presbyter at ancient Ephesus. The final victory was sealed the year following the death of Augustine when, at the third Ecumenical Council at Ephesus, in 431, Pelagianism was anathematized along with Nestorianism and other Christological heresies. Opposition to some aspects of Augustine's theology, especially predestination and irresistible grace, grew among the monks of southern Gaul. John Cassian of Marseilles, Vincent of Lérins, and Faustus, abbot of Lérins, all modified Augustine's views in the direction of Pelagianism. The result was the general teaching of the medieval Church known as "semi-Pelagianism."

It was Vincent of Lérins who gave classic definition to the orthodox faith. In his *Commonitorium,* which opposed Augustine indirectly as an innovator, Vincent argued that the Church should "follow universality, antiquity, and consent." The truth is "that which has been believed everywhere, always, and by all" (*quod ubique, quod semper, quod ad omnibus*).

Chapter 9

The Growth of Christian Dogma

Vincent of Lérins defined orthodox Christian faith as that which is believed everywhere, always, and by all. Is there any Christian teaching that meets that restrictive standard? A careful search of the whole history of Christian thought shows that there is none. We have noted that there were varieties of theology even in the New Testament—not contradictions so much as differences of view and statement; and we have reviewed a number of the heresies and schisms that constantly arose among Christians from the first century onwards. There never has been a constant, universal consensus.

This undeniable fact may be made tolerable by giving attention to the difference between experience on the one hand and theology on the other. It is also necessary to distinguish between doctrine and dogma.

It is true of all religions and ideologies, indeed of human life itself, that many adherents, perhaps most, do not possess the desire or ability to engage in studied analyses or logical construction so as to understand, criticize, and build systems of descriptive theory, either philosophical or theological. Most simply accept (or reject) the beliefs and practices that are given in their culture or advocated by trusted leaders. They are too occupied by the grinding tasks of labor, by the constant demands of family and society, and often by illiteracy and ignorance, to have any concern with searching questions, abstract theories, and logical systems. They simply want to accept their beliefs, if any, on the basis of authority, and to fulfill the moral and liturgical prescriptions, more or less faithfully, without question or complaint. Thus experience precedes theory and may be continued and found adequately satisfying to the masses without ever becoming, to any meaningful degree, the object of thought.

The recognition of this manifest condition should convince us that religious experience is primary and that theology is secondary. Though probably inevitable and certainly useful, doctrines follow experience and therefore can hardly be said to be necessary for experience. For example, every human being began breathing at birth and has continued to live by doing so; but few have considered the intricate details of respiration with its related particulars of chemistry, circulation, and health.

By the same token, the Christian religion is grounded in the essentially personal and relational factors that are described as grace, repentance, faithfulness, forgiveness, joy, regeneration, sanctification . . . and so forth. But the relation described is prior to its description. The reality and validity of the experience does not depend upon the precision and accuracy of its definition. It is possible that the relation may be initiated and continued for a life-time without ever being well understood and described; and it is possible that many may enjoy essentially the same experiences without being able to agree on any objective statements about them. That is why the fact of a variety of theologies, in New Testament times and since, is to be not only tolerated but expected.

Doctrine and Dogma

As for the distinction between doctrine and dogma, it should be noted in the beginning that the two are commonly interchangeable terms, and in ordinary parlance that is acceptable. However, there is an important difference between the two in Christian theological, ecclesiastical usage. Doctrines are teachings that may be only opinions or that may be changeable and provincial. They are frequently held with strong conviction, of course, and they may have serious or formative significance. But they have not yet attained the standing of consensus and necessity. They are still to be debated, corrected, and modified if further examination requires it. Dogma, on the other hand, is doctrine that has received final definition, is considered the statement of necessary truth, and is supported by the authority of its promulgators. Dogma requires acceptance and thus has the status of *sine qua non*. To reject a dogma is to exclude oneself from the community of the faithful who support it.

This distinction between doctrines and dogma leads us to see why Christianity has produced very few true dogmas. In fact, there are only two, at least in the light of the canon of Vincent of Lérins. Official consensus has been increasingly impossible to attain because, among other things, the Church has been effectively divided since its early days and officially since the division between East and West in 1054 and the later Protestant Reformation. The Orthodox Churches of the East are correct in holding that no truly ecumenical council has been held since the Second Council of Nicaea in 787.

The Dogma of God as Trinity

The New Testament itself shows that there was from the beginning both a variety of perceptions and a lack of uniformity in statement concerning the relation between God and Jesus as the Christ, not to speak of the relation between the Father, the Son, and the Spirit. According to the Gospels, Jesus spoke of God as did all pious Jews, though he seems also to have claimed a unique relation to the Father. The variety of perceptions in the New Testament may be seen in the large number of titles assigned to Jesus, some of the main ones being the Christ (Messiah), Savior, Lord (*kurios,* the word used in the Septuagint to refer to Yahweh), Word (*logos*), Son of Man, Son of God, Prophet, Priest, and King. Further, the powers and functions of deity were attributed to him, including the creation of all things, the control of nature, the forgiveness of sin, and the final judgment at the end of history.

At the same time, all of the New Testament writers retained an uncompromising loyalty to the Jewish Scriptures and to the central affirmations of Judaism. They rejected idolatry, polytheism, and all the attendant elements of paganism. They believed in one and only one God. They apparently were not conscious of any real inconsistency between their faith in the God of Moses and the Prophets on the one hand and their commitment to Jesus as Lord on the other.

As the Apostolic Age passed and as Christianity became predominantly a Gentile faith, the largely unconscious ambiguity continued. The growing number of Christians, most from pagan backgrounds, not only accepted Jewish monotheism but also added to that the conviction of the strongest philosophies that an ontological unity lies behind and beneath all reality. The Church of the Roman world inherited both a theological monotheism and a philosophical monism; but it was also founded on a faith in Jesus Christ as Savior and Lord. It worshipped and served one God, the God of the Patriarchs and the Prophets; but it also worshipped Jesus of Nazareth, who had lived in recent history—born under Herod and crucified under Pontius Pilate. As if that were not apparently contradictory enough, the Church believed itself vitalized and guided by the Holy Spirit, who had been promised by Jesus and given by the Father.

It was inevitable, therefore, that Christians would be forced to ask and answer the question: What is the relation between the Father and the Son? As they struggled with that problem they could not avoid an accompanying issue: What is the relation between Father, Son, and Holy Spirit? More than three centuries of debate, rejection, and clarification were required before the Church constructed its permanent answer in terms of the dogma of the Trinity. That solution was composed from biblical material in philosophical form. It both is and is not a biblical doctrine, but it remains the fundamental dogma of Christianity, the understanding of God based on revelation and most satisfying to reason.

We should take note that the Church experienced God as Father, Son, and Holy Spirit before it ever expressed the terms of the dogma.

As would be expected, one of the earliest assessments of the relation between Father and Son is that of the Jewish Christian party known as the "Ebionites," from the Hebrew word for "the poor." According to Irenaeus, they held to a strict monotheism, observed the Torah, and emphasized the expectations of the Prophets; but they also accepted Jesus as the promised Messiah, believing that he had been adopted by God because of his moral perfection. They disappeared soon after the Jewish War against Rome (66-70). The Ebionite Christology was dismissed as unsatisfactory primarily because it did not take into account the essential unity of Father and Son.

In chapter 5, above, we noted another suggested Christology, the "docetic" view of the Gnostics. Because of their belief in a way of cosmic redemption through *gnosis* (esoteric knowledge), the Gnostics interpreted Christ as the spiritual agent of the Unborn Father who appeared in history in order to rescue the souls of men from their entrapment in the flesh. Christ was pure spirit, however, and was not really born, did not suffer, and certainly did not die. The various masters of this heresy, according to Irenaeus, proposed different explanations of how the Christ appeared and accomplished his work, but all avoided the Gospel teaching of incarnation and death. Some taught that he was "a man in appearance only" while others maintained that he used the man Jesus as a temporary instrument. We have seen above how the Church rejected this Christology by emphasizing, as in the Apostles' Creed, the doctrines of creation, incarnation, and resurrection. Before the end of the second century it was clear that Christianity would not accept any solution that compromised either the deity or the humanity of Jesus.

Another way of expressing the relationship between the Father and the Son had been available from the beginning of the Church's theological endeavors. Conveniently, it lay at hand in the ancient concept of the Logos, a concept well known in the writings of Heraclitus, Plato, Stoicism, Philo, and in the Gospel of John. It had affinities also with the teaching about the creative Wisdom of God in Proverbs as well as the explication of that idea in rabbinical commentary. Just as the Logos was said to have been the means of mediation between the Creator and the creation and between Hellenistic philosophy and Jewish theology, so now the eternal, divine principle might provide the key for understanding the ontological distinction-in-unity between the Father and the Son. The Logos had been variously interpreted but always carried the characteristics of pre-existence, mediation, and universality. In early Christian thought, as in the Gospel of John, the concept had been joined with the theology of incarnation. Hence the Logos Christology provided a useful means of expressing the relation between the Father and the Son as well as the relation, in both creation and redemption, between God and the world.

Justin Martyr was one of the earliest Church Fathers to develop a Logos Christology after New Testament times. He was a Hellenistic philosopher born in Palestine near the beginning of the second century. Following a career as a teacher of philosophy, he lived in Rome around A.D. 153. He is known as a leading early apologist for the new Christian faith and two of his writings have survived: *Apology* (with an appendix) and *Dialogue with Trypho the Jew*. He claimed to have found in the new faith the "true philosophy," and he taught that Jesus was the incarnate Logos, "the first-born of God," "the Spirit and the Power from God," who "was born as a human being of a virgin, and given the name Jesus, and was crucified and died and rose and ascended into heaven." Justin even went so far as to claim that "those who live according to the Logos are Christians, even though they are accounted atheists. . . . Such were Socrates and Heraclitus among the Greeks" (*Apology,* 33, 46).

Irenaeus (c. 135-200), a native of Asia Minor but Bishop of Lyons in Gaul, took up the concept of the eternal Logos and made it a central element in his influential theology. He found it necessary to defend the Christian faith against numerous perversions, especially Marcionism and Gnosticism, and in so doing he gave new depth and structure to Christian teaching. Irenaeus identified the three-fold nature of Apostolic authority—creed, canon, and Church—and emphasized the incarnational Christology by which God seeks to redeem his creation by "recapitulation," recreating the fallen Adam in Jesus as the Second Adam. He taught that Christians are disciples of "the only true and steadfast teacher, the Logos of God, our Lord Jesus Christ, who did through his transcendent love become what we are, that he might bring us to be even what he is himself" (*Against Heresies,* 5).

Slightly later than Irenaeus, Tertullian of Carthage, "the father of Latin theology," contributed to Christian thought both the language and the formulas that have remained ever since as characteristic features of Western theology. Very little is known about the details of his life, which apparently began about 160 and ended about 225. He was the first known Christian to write theology in Latin, thereby choosing both the terms and the tendencies of ideas that had been expressed in the words and nuances of Greek. The significance of that fact is difficult to exaggerate. However, we are here primarily concerned with his adoption of the Greek idea of the Logos as a means of understanding the nature of Jesus Christ. Tertullian spoke of God as ''trinity'' (*trinitas*), the first to do so, and he argued that God is one ''substance'' but three ''persons,'' who are Father, Son, and Holy Spirit. The Son is the Logos who was in the flesh as Jesus Christ, the union of two distinct ''substances,'' divine and human.

Tertullian strongly opposed many heresies, one of which he called ''monarchian,'' an emphasis upon the unity of the deity that tended to exclude a genuine threeness. There were two completely different kinds of Monarchianism. The first, usually designated ''dynamic'' or ''adoptionist'' Monarchianism, was taught in Rome c. 190 by Theodotus, a tanner from Byzantium, and his disciples, and later in Syria by Paul of Samosata, who was condemned by a synod at Antioch in 268. This theory held that Christ was only a man but that he was adopted by the power (*dunamis*) of God at his baptism and raised to heaven after the resurrection. Similar as it is to some Gnostic Christologies, this teaching was rejected for the same reasons. A second form of Monarchianism is known as ''modalistic.'' Its earliest proponent seems to have been Noëtus of Smyrna, who arrived in Rome around 200 and soon enlisted the support of Praxeas and Sabellius ''the Libyan.'' This solution held that God is indivisibly one in substance but that he is related to time and the world in three energies (*energeiai*) or modes. As father he appears as Creator; as Son he appears as Savior; as Holy Spirit he appears as Sanctifier. Tertullian, in his *Against Praxeas,* and Novatian of Rome, in his *On the Trinity,* immediately attacked this view. They called it ''Patripassianism,'' pointing out that if the Father and the Son are the same substance without distinction, then when the Son was crucified, God himself would have suffered and died. But God is the giver and source of life, incapable of death (immortal).

A further complexity to the yet-unsolved puzzle of the relation of the Father and Son (and Spirit) was contributed by the great Alexandrian scholar and teacher, Origen (C. 185-254). Born in a Christian family (his father, Leonidas, died as a martyr), Origen was well educated both in Christian teachings and in classical culture. He dedicated his life to the study and teaching of the Scriptures, but he insisted on developing the revelation found there with the tools and insights of philosophy, especially Platonism. Two of his primary works resulting from that effort were the *Hexapla,* a massive instrument for the comparative study of available texts of the Old Testament, and *On First Principles (Peri archōn)*, the first systematic theology in Christian history. His total writings were said to number about 6,000! Origen succeeded Clement of Alexandria as leader of the great catechetical school around 202 and spent nearly thirty years there. Then he went to Caesarea in Palestine, where he remained until his death. He probably was the most influential teacher in the Church before Augustine, though some of his ideas were later condemned and, like Tertullian, who became a Montanist in his last years, Origen is not counted among the saints.

Origen's Christology is exceedingly complex and may easily be misinterpreted, as has frequently been the case. It is intricately related to his total theology and cannot be understood apart from the whole. It also employs both biblical and philosophical elements. He believed that the Scriptures teach (cf. Genesis 1, 2) that God first created the spiritual realm and only later the material cosmos. The original creation was composed of spiritual beings, reflections of God's own image, which is the eternal Logos. These spirits were finite because they were created, but they were rational and free because they were like the Logos. However, many of the spiritual beings turned away from their divine source toward self and alienation, some becoming demons, some fallen angels, some human beings. God's way of restoring the fallen spirits is by the incarnation of the pre-existent Logos, who took on the perfect self of Jesus. The Logos is the eternally generated Son of the Father, partaking of the nature of the Father and thus not temporal. He is not the same as the Father because he was begotten or generated and therefore in a sense subordinate to the Unborn Father; but neither is he a creature since he was begotten by the Father rather than created out of nothing, as are all creatures. The teachings, example, death and resurrection of the incarnate Logos provide the necessary tutelage to restore the fallen spirits, and that restoration (*apokatastasis*) will ultimately be complete.

By the middle of the third century the Church had gone a long way toward solving its problem of God; it had constructed its Christology to the point of confessing that Jesus Christ is both divine and human and also the pre-existent, eternal, only begotten (*monogenes*) Son or Logos of the Father. However, even Origen had left room for debate and confusion. No satisfactory answer had yet been proposed to the fundamental question: how can there be one and only one God who is both eternally Father and Son? And if the Holy Spirit is somehow brought into consideration, are we not forced to admit an unacceptable tritheism?

When Constantine became sole sovereign over the reunified Roman Empire, became a Christian, and established Christianity as the official religion, he was disappointed to find acrimonious divisions within the Church itself. We have noted earlier how he attempted to heal the Donatist schism by turning to the bishops for mediation and decision, as in the council of Arles (314). It was natural, therefore, for him to use the same procedure when debate flared anew concerning the nature of the Son of God, the Christ.

The controversy began in Alexandria around 318 between the Bishop, Alexander, and one of his presbyters, Arius. Arius had studied under Lucian of Antioch, whose school used the method of historical and grammatical interpretation of the Scriptures rather than the allegorical method preferred in Alexandria. Following that usage, Arius argued that the Scriptures clearly teach that the Son, or Logos, "is the image of the invisible God, the first-born of all creation" (Colossians 1:15) as well as "the only-begotten from the Father" (John 1:14). Such words could only mean that the Son is distinct from the Father, derived from the Father, and subordinate to the Father. Though eternally generated, as Origen had taught, yet "there was when he was not."

Alexander, perceiving that both monotheism and redemption are threatened by the Arian separation of the Father and the Son, first opposed Arius and then called a council of Egyptian bishops, in 320, that condemned Arius and all of his supporters. Arius fled to Palestine and finally to Nicomedia, the temporary capital of the East, whose Bishop, Eusebius, agreed with his interpretation. When the exacerbated argument came to the attention of Constantine, he followed the advice of his spiritual advisor, Hosius of Cordoba, and called a council of all the bishops of the empire, both East and West, to gather at government expense at Nicaea, near the capital. This was the first Ecumenical Council of the Church, assembled in May, 325.

Three groups composed the Council. First, there were the Arians, led by their champion and strongly supported by Eusebius of Nicomedia. Second, there was the party of Alexander, now led by the Bishop's secretary and deacon, Athanasius of Alexandria. The third group, probably a large majority, were led by Eusebius of Caesaria in Palestine, later to become the great historian of the early Church. The majority were apparently not fully aware of the fine points in the debate and thought the whole matter could be easily solved by adopting a neutral baptismal creed, perhaps the one Eusebius used at Caesaria. However, when the issues were fully revealed, the majority were shocked at the implications of the Arian language. They came to agree with Athanasius that the Son and the Father are the same God, the same Being, though different Persons (*prosopoi* in Greek, *persona* in Latin); otherwise, they believed, Christianity is in danger of reverting to theistic dualism, and, worse, the Savior/Son cannot save since only God creates and gives life.

The result was the adoption of the historic Nicene Creed, which contains such decisive phrases as "true God from true God," "begotten not made," "of one substance (*homoousios*), with the Father." The term *homoousios* became henceforth the touchstone of orthodox Christology, guaranteeing belief in one God and in the full deity of the Son.

Of course the official decision did not settle the debate, as no forced agreement ever does. Arianism was condemned, but Arius and his supporters remained of the same opinions. The controversy continued in many forms and places during the rule of Constantine's successors, and it is especially significant that the Arians carried the Gospel, according to their interpretation, in a vast mission to the barbarian peoples north and east of the Empire, just as the same barbarians were poised to invade and conquer the Western Empire.

We must take note also of the final development of the dogma of the Trinity in the century following Nicaea. Attention had been devoted almost exclusively to the question of the relation of the Father and the Son; now the place of the Holy Spirit demanded clarification. That involved discussion during the next five decades, led by the three great Cappadocian theologians: Basil of Cappadocia; his brother, Gregory of Nyssa; and Basil's lifetime friend, Gregory of Nazianzus, who became Patriarch of Constantinople. They continued the struggle against the Arians and also against several groups that did not believe in the equal deity of the Holy Spirit. One of the formative writings that helped to settle the issue was Basil's *On the Holy Spirit*. The second Ecumenical Council, meeting in Constantinople in 381, agreed that the Holy Spirit is the same Being (*ousia*) as the Father and the Son. The distinction is between activities, energies, or persons, not in *ousia* or *substantia*. That definition was further refined and ratified by the third Council (Ephesus, 431) and at the fourth Ecumenical Council (Chalcedon, 451).

The fundamental dogma of the Christian faith thus was fixed and remains: God is one Being in three Persons, Father, Son, and Holy Spirit. The Son is begotten before all ages of the Father, and the Spirit proceeds from the Father (the Western Church later added "and from the Son").

The Christological Dogma

The Nicene settlement of the question concerning the relation of the Father and the Son immediately led to the central Christological problem: what is the relation between the divine nature and the human nature in Jesus Christ? We have observed how the Church had gone through extended and difficult struggles for three centuries following the life of Jesus so as finally to affirm the full deity of the Son. Now, following

Nicaea, the Church found itself considering how this definitive dogma could be retained in the light of the Gospels' plain teachings that Jesus was a human being, subject to all the conditions of humanity and, in terms of Carlyle's famous characterization of Richard the Lionhearted, "a man living upon victuals."

Athanasius, the victor in the debates at Nicaea, was believed by some to have supplied the basis for a solution. He had become Bishop of Alexandria in 328 and then had been deposed and reinstated four times, as the political winds changed, before finally dying in office in 373. He had continued, in and out of office, to defend the full deity of the Son (*homoousios*) and, in 339, published his treatise, *On the Incarnation,* which remains one of the primary classics of Christian theology. Athanasius stressed the idea of incarnation, that the eternal Logos had entered into union with humanity in Jesus Christ so as to make possible the deification of humanity. But he always carefully distinguished between the divine nature, the Logos, and the human nature, the "body" of the man Jesus. It was the human nature only that was described in the Gospels as growing, weeping, hungering, disclaiming omniscience, suffering, and dying. Jesus Christ achieved the redemption of mankind by combining divine nature and human nature in one person.

Apollinaris, Bishop of Laodicea in Syria, a loyal friend and disciple of Athanasius, sought to restate the views of his master so as to make explicit the precise way in which the two natures were related in Jesus Christ. He explained that there are constituent elements that compose a normal human being. These are variously designated, but one common description is to say that a person has spirit, soul, and body. These may be called intellect, animal soul, and physical body. It is the intellect, or spirit, that knows, thinks, and wills, controlling the soul and body even though also influenced by them. In Jesus Christ, therefore, it may be said that the divine Logos took the place of the normal human spirit or intellect, thus assuring a complete person able to withstand temptation and to accomplish the perfect union of God and man. The two natures, divine and human, that had been alienated since the fall of Adam and Eve, now dwelt together in complete unity.

On the face of it, Apollinaris' solution seemed to be simple and accurate enough to please everyone. It is probable that something like that has been the unexamined assumption of most Christians down through the centuries. Nevertheless, probing thinkers began at once to find serious flaws in the theory. The Cappadocian theologians led the attack upon it. Gregory of Nyssa wrote a treatise entitled *Against Apollinaris,* and Gregory of Nazianzus argued that it would not do for the divine nature merely to exist alongside the human nature in one person. A partial incarnation would not suffice; the incarnation must be complete; God must become fully man for man to become fully like God. "For that which he has not assumed he has not healed, but that which is united to his Godhead is also saved" (*On the Union,* 4). Such arguments exposed the insufficiency of the theory offered by Apollinaris and he was condemned in synods at Alexandria (362), Rome (377), Antioch (379), and finally at the second Ecumenical Council at Constantinople (381).

The strongest opposition to Apollinaris and the whole Alexandrian way of thinking came from the school of Antioch. We should recall that the different controlling assumptions of these two theological centers was evident in the contrary views of Arius, who had studied under Lucian of Antioch, and of Anthanasius, the hero of Alexandria. Thus Diodore, Bishop of Tarsus (378-394), a former presbyter in Antioch, contended against the Apollinarian view that the two natures in Christ had been unified, in effect making one nature of two parts as two halves make a whole. The two natures must remain distinct, he argued. Diodore's thought was developed more explicitly by his pupil, Theodore, Bishop of Mopsuestia in Cilicia, a monk of Antioch who has been called the greatest exegete in the early Church. Theodore taught what has been known as the doctrine of "the prosopic union," according to which Jesus Christ was "the Man," the second Adam, and in his one person (*prosopon*) there dwelt a complete human nature and a complete divine nature, the Logos. The Gospel statements about Jesus must be attributed to which ever nature is appropriate, but not to both. The human being who suffered and died was born of the Virgin Mary, but not the divine nature, which is pre-existent and eternal. Because of this distinction, Theodore objected to calling the Virgin "*theotokos*," bearer of God, since she gave birth to Jesus but obviously not to God.

The views of Diodore and Theodore were further refined and given more official status by their follower the Antiochene monk, Nestorius, who became Patriarch of Constantinople in 428. His name has been used ever since to designate the views of all three. Nestorius insisted upon the separation of the two natures in Jesus Christ, abstractly before the incarnation and actually in the incarnation. He proclaimed in sermons in Constantinople that "that which is formed in the womb is not God," though "God was within the one who was assumed," and "the one who was assumed is styled God because of the One who assumed him" (*First Sermon Against the Theotokos*). Though he was willing to use the term *theotokos* with reference to Mary, Nestorius contended that it would be more accurate to say *Christokos,* bearer of Christ, since the one she bore was the Man, Jesus of Nazareth, the Christ.

The Alexandrians, led by their proud and acerbic bishop, Cyril, were incensed by the Nestorian doctrine. They accused Nestorius of reverting to the heresy of Arius by opposing the use of *theotokos,* which they sensed to be a subtle way of denying the Nicene doctrine of the full deity of Christ. Further, they claimed that Nestorius was guilty of "worshipping an assumed man" by his characterization of Jesus as the Man indwelt and therefore redeemed by the Logos. A careful analysis of the positions taken by the two sides reveals not only unbecoming jealousy between two powerful Patriarchates but also a fundamentally different conception of Christianity: Alexandria sought salvation by deification through the mystical union of God and man in Jesus Christ whereas Antioch (now associated with Constantinople, "new Rome") sought salvation by moral change in human nature as accomplished in and by Jesus Christ.

Nestorianism was condemned at the third Ecumenical Council at Ephesus in 431. The shameful intrigues by both sides prior to the settlement are a black mark on the history of Christianity. Each side met independently and condemned the other. Finally, Nestorius was deposed and banished, first to Syria and then to Upper Egypt, where he died in 450, still defending his views. His followers fled beyond the reaches of the Empire, establishing churches in Persia, China, India, and northern Africa, where their minority views remain extant to the present.

The current Emperor, Valentinian II, forced the Alexandrians, led by Cyril, and the Antiochenes, led by Bishop John of Antioch, to compromise their positions in a *Formula of Reunion* in 433. But the agreement was not substantive, and the quarrel broke out again over the claims of Eutyches, an aged archimandrite of a monastery in Constantinople that was allied with the Alexandrians. Eutyches insisted on following the teachings of Cyril, now dead, to the effect that there was one divine-human nature in Jesus Christ even though the one nature was derived from two natures: "I follow the doctrine of the blessed Cyril and the holy fathers and the holy Athanasius. They speak of two natures before the union, but after the union and incarnation they speak of one nature not two."

Flavian, now the Patriarch of Constantinople, called a synod that condemned Eutyches. That angered Dioscorus, successor of Cyril in Alexandria, and he asked the Emperor to assemble a general council. Both Flavian and Dioscorus also appealed for support from Leo, Bishop of Rome. Leo responded in a long letter, known as Leo's *Tome,* which condemned Eutyches, calling him "ignorant." It also reviewed the whole controversy and agreed with the view, essentially Nestorian, that the two natures remain distinct in the incarnation: "thus the properties of each nature and substance were preserved entire, and came together to form one person." The council met in Chalcedon, near Constantinople, in the autumn of 451. Taking rank as the fourth Ecumenical Council, Chalcedon reaffirmed the first three and give the final solution to the Christological problem:

> Therefore, following the holy Fathers, we all with one accord teach men to acknowledge one and the same Son, our Lord Jesus Christ, at once complete in Godhead and complete in manhood, truly God and truly man, consisting also of a reasonable soul and body; of one substance (*homoousios*) with the Father as regards his Godhead, and at the same time of one substance with us as regards his manhood; like us in all respects, apart from sin; as regards his Godhead, begotten of the Father before all ages, but yet as regards his manhood begotten, for us men and for our salvation, of Mary the Virgin, the God-bearer (*theotokos*); one and the same Christ, Son, Lord, Only-begotten, recognized in two natures, without confusion, without change, without division, without separation; the distinction of natures being in no way annulled by the union, but rather the characteristics of each nature preserved and coming together to form one person and subsistence (*hypostasis*), not as parted or separated into two persons, but one and the same Son and Only-begotten God the Word, Lord Jesus Christ; . . .

That creed of Chalcedon has remained for more than a thousand years as the accepted answer to the Christological question. A careful reading of it reveals that it both condemns the prior misdirections and exaggerations and gives emphasis to the concerns of all. Of course, there were those relatively small groups that disagreed, and their remnants have been perpetuated until the present. The Nestorians survived, as we have noted, and other dissidents against Chalcedon are known as Monophysites (one nature) and Monothelites (one will). Further, modern thought has challenged every aspect of the ancient creeds. Nevertheless, an effective consensus has remained in the churches of East and West regarding both the dogma of God as Trinity and the dogma of Christology defined at Chalcedon.

IV.
THE CHURCH IN SCHISM AND STRUGGLE

Chapter 10

The Challenge of Islam

The Arabian city of Mecca lies in a valley devoid of rich vegetation, but in the seventh century it was important for two reasons. It was, in the first place, an important center of trade, a point of convergence of the great desert caravan routes. In the second place, it enjoyed an exalted status as a holy place in the center of the Haram, an inviolable region where an assortment of fairs having religious significance were held annually. The Meccans, fully appreciating the value of both their claims to distinction, made their city the foremost international trade mart on the Arabian peninsula.

In the Kaaba, at the center of Mecca, were a number of images of gods of the region, together, in all probability, with those of foreign deities worshipped by the merchants whose caravans passed through the city. It is even reputed to have held an image of the Virgin Mary and the infant Jesus. An atmosphere of tolerance for diverse religious practices apparently fostered the development of a sort of synthetic religion in which all the divinities represented there were regarded with respect. This religious syncretism was treasured by the businessmen of the city because it was good for trade.

There, in the holy city, about the year 570, a son was born to a woman named Aminah, whose husband, Abdullah, is said to have died before the child's birth. The boy, whose original name is given in the Koran both as Kotham and as Halabi, was to become the Prophet Mohammed, founder of the third of the three great religions stemming from the faith of Abraham. His mother died in his early childhood, and he was brought up by his grandfather, Abd al-Mottalib, and his uncle, Abu Talib. From the Bedouins of the region, he learned the ways of the desert tribes, and as a conductor of caravans, he had an opportunity to visit other countries and learn their ways.

When he was about twenty-five years of age, he married Khadija, a rich forty-year-old widow, and seems for a time to have been a partner in a business enterprise in Mecca. The tradition that he was illiterate, to which appeal has been made in support of the claim that the Koran was miraculously inspired, may have stemmed from the mistranslation of an adjective describing him as a native of Mecca. In view of his upbringing in reasonably affluent circumstances, it is likely that he had at least a modicum of learning, but it is clear that nothing in his early career suggests the possession of scholarly attainments of any note.

Some time after his marriage, he experienced a series of revelations which convinced him that he had been commissioned to communicate to men the Word of God, the Koran, the original text of which exists eternally in heaven. The intermediary through whom the material was made available to the Prophet is variously called an angel, the Spirit, the holy Spirit, and Gabriel.

According to tradition, the Prophet was originally given written communications which he could read "by the grace of God" and which he was to reveal at first only to his nearest relatives. He converted his wife, his cousin Ali, and a man named Abu Bekr, who was destined to succeed Mohammed as leader of the movement. The written communications came to an end before long, and the Prophet began to deliver the messages orally in a state of trance, induced by wrapping himself in a blanket in a manner prescribed by the Koran. His words were then written down by his followers, and it is probable that the whole body of the work was put into writing during his lifetime. In its present form, it consists of a hundred and fourteen chapters, or *suras,* arranged with the exception of the *Fatiha,* or "opening," in quite arbitrary fashion, in order of length, proceeding from longest to shortest.

The contents of the Koran cover a wide range of religious and moral doctrine. It is uncompromisingly monotheistic. The God who is represented as its author, called Allah, (*al Ilah*, "the God") by Mohammed, is the one who spoke to Abraham, Moses, the Hebrew prophets, and Jesus, all of whom are recognized as authentic revealers of his will for men. It is denied that the divine nature can be divided in such a way as to permit Jesus to be regarded as the Son of God, but he has an honored place in the Moslem tradition. God, according to that tradition, gave Moses the Law (*taurat*), Jesus the Gospel (*injil*), and Mohammed the Koran, which is the final revelation.

Many of the materials in the Koran show a close connection with Old and New Testament sources, while others bear a relation to non-canonical Jewish and Christian writings. Like the Hebrew Scriptures, the Koran expresses implacable opposition to the making of idols or the worship of any created thing. God, described as a moral judge, will reward the faithful and punish the wicked after death with pleasures and torments, which are described with vivid imagery. As in the Torah, civil, moral, and religious laws are set out in considerable detail, and in many instances, specific penalties are prescribed for violation of those laws.

Although Mohammed clearly saw his religion as historically continuous with Judaism and Christianity, there are a number of discrepancies between the Koran and the sacred writings of the earlier faiths. The critical study of the work is complicated by the fact that Mohammed did not hesitate to "abrogate or cause to be forgotten" whole verses and to substitute others for them.

By about the year 616, Mohammed already had a substantial number of followers, and his militant monotheism was beginning to disturb the rulers of Mecca. His claim to a special revelation which would, if believed, discredit the tolerant polytheism of the Meccans, threatened their commerce as well as their religion. A theocracy of the sort sanctioned by the Koran and advocated by the Prophet would inevitably lessen the hospitality traditionally shown the merchants whose gods shared lodging in the Kaaba in substantial amity with one another. Conflict broke out between Mohammed and his fellow citizens, and the Prophet was forced to find refuge for some of his less influential followers in Abyssinia. The Abyssinian king took the side of the exiles when the Meccans demanded their extradition, and the enraged Meccan leaders, prohibited from shedding blood by the status of the city as a sanctuary, prevented the Prophet and his followers from leaving their quarter of the city and cut off their supply of food. Rather than starve to death, Mohammed listened attentively to a new revelation, which assured him that the deities of Mecca were entitled to reverence along with Allah. This acknowledgement was, of course, all his opponents needed, and they dissolved their blockade of the Prophet's quarters. Word was sent to his exiled followers in Abyssinia that the way was open to them to come home, and they began the return journey. Mohammed, in the meantime, had issued a new proclamation. The tolerant revelation, he said, had come not from God, but from the Devil. The controversy broke out again, and the exiles thought it expedient to go back to Abyssinia. Mohammed's wife and his uncle, Abu Talib, both died, and the Prophet prudently retired to the oasis of Taif. Later he returned under the terms of a promise that he would not be molested.

The situation in Mecca was, of course, too tense for comfort, and Mohammed was ready to try a new center of operations. A little more than two hundred miles to the north lay the city of Yathrib, afterwards called Medina, Al-Madinah, or Madinat Rasul Allah, "the city of the apostle of God." The people of Yathrib sent word to Mohammed that his presence in their city as dictator would be welcome, and secret negotiations were initiated on the proposal.

The Meccans somehow found out about the plan and reacted with extreme alarm to the prospect of having their old enemy securely lodged in a strategically located post on the northern route of their caravans. Setting aside their prohibition against bloodshed, they planned to kill the Prophet, involving in the plot every local tribe except that of Mohammed himself, in order that the guilt might be shared. The delegated assassins set out for Mohammed's home, only to find his bed occupied by his cousin Ali. The Prophet had fled.

His departure, on July 16, 622, marked the beginning of the Islamic era. Since that time, dates in the Moslem world have been designated by the initials A.H. for *Anno Hegairae,* from the Arabic word *hejaira,* meaning "flight." In inaugurating the new age, Mohammed imposed on his followers a strictly lunar calendar, which, being about eleven days shorter than the solar calendar employed by most of the rest of the world, causes annual Moslem festivals to come at different seasons of the year.

On his flight, accompanied by his friend Abu Bekr, the Prophet took refuge in a cave on Mount Thaur. The story is told that, with his pursuers hot on his heels, he was saved by three miraculous events. An acacia tree laden with leaves suddenly sprang up at the mouth of the cave. In its branches was a woodpigeon, provided with a fully finished nest, and between the cave and the tree was a spider web. No one, the hunters concluded, could have gone into the cave without disturbing the nest and the web, and so they passed it by. Whether his evasion of the Meccans was effected by miracle or more prosaic means, Mohammed reached Kuba, on the outskirts of Yathrib on September 20, 622.

In Yathrib, or Medina, he devoted himself to the propagation of the new faith, developing formidable skills as an advocate of his cause. One of the stories about his teaching is responsible for a popular saying known throughout most of the Western world. Challenged to produce miraculous proofs in support of his claims, the Prophet promptly commanded Mount Safa to come to him. The mountain remained in its place.

"God is merciful," the Prophet said. "Had it obeyed my words, it would have fallen on us to our destruction. I will therefore go to the mountain, and thank God that he has had mercy on a stiffnecked generation."

It was during his residence at Medina that the Prophet changed the custom of bowing in the direction of Jerusalem for prayer to the one which Moslems have observed since his time of bowing toward Mecca. His edict may have been due to difficulties in gaining Jewish support in his fight against polytheism. Having closed the book on revelation centuries earlier, the Jews were not in the least disposed to acknowledge the claims of a prophet not of their people, whose references to their history seemed to them to be shot through with inaccuracies and who incorporated in his theology a place of great honor for a Messiah long since rejected by the Jewish community. Mohammed never ceased to regard his own faith as a continuation of the tradition of revelation embodied in the Old Testament, but now, rebuffed by those who, it seemed to him, should be his natural allies, he modified the Jewish elements in his system in such a way as to make it clear that the distinctive identity of the new way was not to be compromised.

Similarly he freely adopted practices and beliefs from Christianity, while at the same time declining to permit his own religion to be considered a version of the older faith. His dietary laws were a combination of Jewish and early Christian prohibitions, with the addition of a commandment against the drinking of wine, brought about, it is said, by the behavior of one of his followers who had dipped too deeply into his cups.

For Mohammed, as for Jews and Christians, Israel was the chosen people of God. From obscure sources, many of them apocryphal, he formed a version of the life and mission of Jesus which was, by Christian standards, highly unorthodox. He accepted the doctrine of the Virgin birth without question, as well as the stories of the healing of the sick and the raising of the dead. He did not, however, believe in the crucifixion and the resurrection. Jesus, he held, was spirited away, and a substitute took his place on the cross. Returning to the Christian version, however, the Prophet accepted the story of the ascension as true.

During the formative years of Islam, relations between Moslems and Christians were often strained and sometimes involved open hostility. Gradually, however, they ameliorated to the point where members of the older sects were granted tolerance and protection on condition that they pay tribute to their new rulers.

To support the newly formed Moslem community at the expense of the Meccans, Mohammed started raiding caravans coming from his native city, even going so far as to launch one of his attacks during the sacred month of Rajab, a time of supposedly inviolable peace. The assaults led to a battle between Moslems and Meccans in 624, in which the Meccans were defeated. This encounter at Badr is celebrated in the Koran as the "Day of Deliverance."

The Meccans were by now becoming alarmed at the growing power of a declared enemy who threatened to dominate the whole western coast of Arabia. A year later, Abu Sofian led an army against the Medinans and at last succeeded in defeating the Prophet's forces at Mt. Uhud to the northwest of Medina. He did not follow up his victory, however, and Mohammed, by military strategy and the work of secret agents, succeeded in so disorganizing the Meccan confederacy that it was unable to pursue the war further.

Mohammed made a truce with the Meccan authorities, according to the terms of which his followers were free to make pilgrimage to the holy city. His success in the negotiations won him popular support, and his cause was further advanced by the conversion of some of the important Meccans who had been his enemies. The Prophet pressed his advantage, and at this time, seems to have formed the vision of a Moslem world united under his leadership in the worship of Allah.

He sent letters to all the rulers of the region, including those of the Byzantine and Persian empires, who controlled substantial portions of the Arabian Peninsula, urging them to convert to Islam and promising them protection if they would do so. As an earnest of his seemingly grandiose design, he mounted a campaign against Mecca, and, some seven years after the Hegira, found himself master of the city.

Conducting the annual pilgrimage the following year, he proclaimed the completion by God of the true religion. Mecca retained its status as a holy city, dedicated now to Islam, but Medina remained the political capital. All Arabs were commanded to become Moslems within four months under threat of the use of force against them if they should prove recalcitrant. Some tribes did challenge Mohammed's authority, but he crushed them with armed force and accelerated his efforts to stamp out every vestige of idolatry.

The flood of pilgrims to the Kaaba and the merchants who came with their caravans to Mecca listened to the teachings of the new religion and were converted. They, in turn, carried these teachings back to their own people and Islam spread like wildfire, until, by the end of Mohammed's life, in about 632 A.D., he was, in effect, the ruler of an enormous new nation. His identification of the secular with the sacred set a pattern for Islamic thought which persists to this day.

The reverence in which Moslems hold the Prophet is reflected in a characterization of him given in the Mishkat, where it is said of him that at the peak of his power, "he visited the sick, followed any bier he met, accepted the invitation of the lowliest, mended his own clothes, milked his goats and waited upon himself. He never first withdrew his hand out of another's clasp and turned not before the other had turned. His hand was the most generous, his breast the most courageous, his tongue the most truthful; those who saw him were filled with reverence, those who came near him loved him. Modesty and kindness, patience, self-denial, and generosity pervaded his conduct and riveted the affection of all around him. With the bereaved and afflicted he sympathized tenderly . . . he would stop in the streets listening to the sorrows of the humblest. He would go to the houses of the lowliest to console the stricken and comfort the heartbroken."

The Koran is the final authority for Islam. It is regarded by Moslems as the final and perfect revelation of God. It is independent of time and space, contains no contradictions, and has been protected by God from any corruption of its text since it was first revealed to the Prophet. It is, however, possible for error to arise through misinterpretation, and the divergencies of opinion regarding the true meaning of the text, together with jurisdictional disputes, have, since the early days of the religion, divided its followers into factions.

On certain fundamentals, however, there has been general agreement. The first of the so-called "five pillars of Islam" is the *kalimah,* the creed: "There is no God but Allah, and Mohammed is the messenger of God." God is one and undivided, and no creature may be identified with him. The second is divine worship, *salat*. From the turrets of the mosques of Islam, the call to prayer is made five times every day. The believer, on hearing the call, turns his face toward Mecca, and, in the course of his worship, assumes the prescribed twelve poses expressing adoration, supplication, submission, and humility.

The third pillar is fasting, which is held to discipline and purify the soul. During the month of Ramadan, no food or drink may be consumed from first light until darkness, in order that the believer may be brought to closer communion with God. The fourth is almsgiving, legal, and voluntary. Once a year, the Prophet and his assistants originally collected a fortieth of the possessions of those subject to Moslem rule to be distributed among the poor. Voluntary almsgiving includes all gifts not included in this "poor rate."

Last of the five pillars is the pilgrimage to Mecca. In Islam, the Kaaba has continued to hold special significance, though its association with idolatry has long since been repudiated. Only Moslems may visit Mecca, and it is the general goal of the faithful to make the sacred pilgrimage at least once in a lifetime.

The Spread of Islam

After Mohammed's death, Abu Bekr succeeded him as Caliph and ruled for about two years. He, in turn, was succeeded by Oman, who held the office from about 634 to 644. Under these two men, Moslem rule over the Arabian Peninsula became consolidated, and a nation of seasoned warriors, fired with religious passion, faced Byzantium and Persia to the north. Both of these formerly powerful empires had become weakened by internal and external strife, and in a surprisingly short time, Moslem armies were in control of Egypt, Palestine, Syria, Iraq, and Persia.

True to Mohammed's teaching, the new rulers tolerated Jews, Christians, and Zoroastrians, recognizing them, by virtue of their monotheism, as "Peoples of the Book." Their taxes were essential to the support of the growing Islamic empire, and the Moslem conquerors, being in the minority, needed their good will and their administrative skills.

With power and access to luxury, the adherents of the growing faith began to develop schismatic disputes. The descendants of Mohammed's son-in-law, Ali, who had been killed in 661, founded the Shiite sect. In 680, Ali's second son, Hussein, who was living in Mecca, was invited to Baghdad by the Shiites to be their leader. While on his way to accept the call, he was captured by supporters of Yazid, Caliph (*Khalifah,* "Successor") of the dominant (Sunni) sect. Hussein and the members of his escort taken with him were deprived of food and water for two days and then hacked to pieces. The breach between Sunni and Shiite Moslems has never been healed.

Unlike the Sunnites, who elect their caliphs, the Shiites hold that the right to the office is divinely bestowed and that it can properly be held only by a descendant of Ali. While agreeing on this point, the Shiite sect itself split into several factions. The *Ithna'ashariyya,* or "Twelvers" regard a dozen descendants of Ali as *imams* and heirs to the prophetic and interpretative powers of the Prophet. One of these twelve historic figures, named Mohammed, after his ancestor, disappeared in the ninth century and is held to be still alive and waiting to return to establish the Shiite faith throughout the world. The Ismailis, or followers of Ismail, whom they regard as the seventh imam, include the Fatimites, the Carmathians, the Assassins, and the Druses. Shiites are the dominant sect in modern Iran.

In addition to the Sunnites and the Shiites, there is a third major Islamic group known as the Khawarij, who hold that anyone selected by the faithful, even a slave, may be caliph. Greatly reduced in number in modern times, they survive in eastern Arabia and North Africa.

A number of sects have sprung up over the centuries, some of which have ceased to exist and others of which have followers to the present day. There is an old tradition that the Prophet predicted that Islam would be divided into seventy-three sects. Seventy-two of these would die, and one would be saved. Technically, then, the hundreds of divergent heretical groups must of necessity be classified by Arabic writers under seventy-two headings, thus presenting a problem of nomenclature which has not always been easy to solve.

Early divisions within the Islamic ranks did not diminish their enthusiasm or capacity for conquest. In the years between 661 and 750, the Ummayad caliphs conquered North Africa and carried the banners of Islam into southern Spain. Envisaging a Moslem Europe, the Arabs advanced as far into the heart of the Continent as Tours, where, in 732, they were brought to a halt by Charles Martel, King of the Franks.

Islamic Philosophy

With the establishment of the Moslem Empire, a renaissance of classical culture began to flourish in the Near East which was not to have its counterpart in the West for several centuries. Acquaintance with the Greek language had declined almost to the vanishing point in the West with the triumph of Latin as the universal language of the Church of Rome. It was much more widespread in the East, especially among the Syrian Christians, who had translated many Greek works into Syriac. In the court of the Persian capital, Baghdad, many of the ancient writings were translated by Syrian scholars into Arabic, with the result that the achievements of the Greeks of the classical age in mathematics, the physical sciences, medicine, literature, and philosophy were far more readily available to Islamic thinkers than they were to Western scholastics. For those unversed in Greek, there was a plentiful supply of Arabic translations of Greek writings. Among these could be found almost all the principal works of Aristotle, who, for various reasons, exercised an especially strong influence on Moslem thinkers.

By the end of the first third of the ninth century, a school for translation and original scholarship was active in Baghdad, and in the following century, the creative forces set in motion there shaped the thought of the first of the great Islamic Aristotelian philosophers.

Ibn Sina, better known in the West as Avicenna (980-1037), was a versatile man in the true Aristotelian tradition. In addition to the study of the Koran and Islamic theology, he studied logic, physics, geometry, jurisprudence, and medicine. He became a physician at the age of sixteen, but later devoted himself to setting down a philosophy which owed most of its character to Aristotelian sources. There were, to be sure, evidences of some Neoplatonic influence, due in part, no doubt, to the fact that Arabian scholars of the period erroneously attributed a portion of Plotinus' *Enneads* to Aristotle.

In reflecting on the nature of the universe, Avicenna noted that for everything which requires a cause, it can be concluded that it might or might not have come to be. It is therefore a possible, rather than a necessary one. There cannot, however, be an infinite chain of possible beings. The entire series must, rather, be grounded in a first cause which is not within the series, and which could not not-be. It is this necessary Being whom we call God.

God's creation of the universe does not begin at some point in time. Creation is essential to his nature and is, therefore, eternal. It does, however, perpetually proceed downward through a series of "Intelligences." The first Intelligence, created by God himself, is the highest angel. He, in turn, creates a subordinate Intelligence, who, in turn, creates the next. The Ninth Intelligence in the series creates the Tenth, which is the Agent Intellect. The Agent Intellect, in turn, is responsible for the creation of the four elements of which the physical world is composed and the individual souls of human beings.

The individual intellect is, of course, only a possible being, and this is equally true of any knowledge it may possess, It is, of course, the essence of any intellect to know, but the existence of actual knowledge requires certain conditions. The mind must, in the first place, have access to sense data and images. In the second place, it must have the power to apprehend and abstract from experience the universals that provide the structures for rational thought. The individual soul cannot, however, perform this second function merely on the basis of sensation and imagery. It is dependent, rather, on the Agent Intellect, which, in radiating forms to individual minds, makes it possible for them to know rather than merely to experience and thus to add existence to the essence of the soul. There is, then, only one active intellect, and lesser intellects are dependent on it for their knowledge.

With the Moslem conquest of southern Spain, the groundwork was laid for the reintroduction of Aristotelian thought into Western Europe, if not immediately into Christendom. Cordoba, in particular, became a prominent center of Islamic thought, and it was there that Ibn-Rushd, or Averroës, one of the greatest of the Moslem philosophers, was born in the year 1126. Like Avicenna, he had an encyclopaedic mind and became expert in theology, mathematics, medicine, jurisprudence, and philosophy. Active as a physician and a judge, he became best known as "the Commentator," in recognition of his writings on a variety of subjects. He died in Morocco in 1198.

In Averroës' judgment, Aristotle was the greatest of all philosophers and a model of human perfection. Indebted to Avicenna for some of his ideas, he nevertheless disagreed with him on several points which were of considerable significance in subsequent European philosophical disputation. Like Aristotle, he denied the possibility of creation in time. That idea, he maintained, is only a teaching of religion and has no place in philosophy.

There is, he maintained, no real difference between essence and existence, although it is convenient to posit a logical distinction in order to facilitate analysis. The form of man, is, as Aristotle said, the soul, and Averroës held the soul to be material rather than spiritual. It perishes with the body and nothing in the human personality survives death. Man, however, unlike the lower animals, is united with the Agent Intellect. It is the Agent Intellect which is the repository for all knowledge, and human beings do not even have possible intellects distinguishable from the Agent Intellect.

Averroës made a sharp distinction between philosophy and theology, with philosophy occupying a much higher position. The two disciplines, he thought, serve different sorts of people. An uncritical acceptance of religious notions guides the mass of people, who, living by imagination rather than reason, are easily ruled through fear. At a somewhat higher level are the theologians, who seek to provide intellectual foundations for their systems, but whose reasoning starts from a set of inflexible assumptions which prejudice the outcome of their thinking. Highest of all in the hierarchy are the philosophers, the small segment of humanity who, unhampered by preconceived notions, can come to know truth directly.

Another important thinker within the framework of the Islamic culture was not himself a Moslem. A contemporary and fellow townsman of Averroës, Moses ben Maimon, or Maimonides, was a Jew, born in Cordoba in 1135. Forced to leave Spain, he traveled to Morocco and then to Egypt, acquiring such fame in the practice of medicine that he became court physician to the Sultan Saladin, whose generous treatment of Jews and Christians was as notable as his military prowess. Ben Maimon died in 1204.

In his celebrated work, *Guide of the Perplexed,* this greatest of medieval Jewish philosophers was concerned to try to prove that there are no fundamental contradictions between sound philosophy and the teachings of Judaism. The Scriptures, however, are of unique value in providing truths which are inaccessible to the unaided reason. The reason can assess these revelations and coordinate them with data from other disciplines, so that faith and reason together can provide the framework for a coherent structure embracing philosophy, science, and theology.

Like Averroës, he saw the doctrine of creation as religiously grounded, but it is not disprovable by philosophy and thus may be accepted on faith. The apparent conflicts between faith and reason are, he held, due to the use of anthropomorphic language in religion. To discover the true meanings which lie behind that language, he maintained, training in philosophy is desirable.

Anticipating Thomas Aquinas, whom he was to influence, Maimonides saw the various forms of the cosmological argument as powerful instruments for supporting belief in God. He himself used the argument for a Prime Mover responsible for all motion, together with the argument from contingent to necessary being and the proof of the necessity for the existence of a primary cause. His views on the nature of man were, for the most part, derived from Avicenna. Individual souls acquire an active intellect from the Agent Intellect, and it is this intellectual ingredient which is immortal.

The preservation of the classical writings of antiquity by Islamic and Jewish scholars in the Arab world were later to prove of the utmost importance to Christian thinkers in Europe, and their emphasis on those works of Aristotle that had been lost to the West for centuries was to provide the spark that would light the fire of the revival of learning and ultimately result in the birth of the great universities of the West.

Chapter 11

The Divorce of Greek and Latin Christianity

If the proverbial man from Mars, or even a devotee of some non-Christian religion, were to make an objective observation of Christendom in the modern world, he would certainly be bewildered if not repelled. He would probably wonder how this vast throng of professed believers in one God and one Lord, claiming to follow love and peace, can be so diverse in faith and practice. For that matter, most Christians would admit to hurt and shame because of the lack of unity, though the admission would be followed by all kinds of explanations and excuses.

One explanation too often given in the Western world is that the varying reforming movements of the sixteenth century brought about the continuing divisions among Christians, no matter which side is blamed. It cannot be denied that the Reformation resulted in a splintering of the Western Church, which had maintained remarkable unity for many centuries. However, it is not accurate or fair to hold Luther, Calvin, Henry VIII, and their fellow reformers responsible for dividing a hitherto unified Christendom. There had been a permanent schism in the Church five centuries before the rise of Protestantism. The Eastern churches (Orthodox) and the Western Church (Roman) were officially separated in 1054. In fact, the separation had been partial and growing for centuries before that, reaching back even to the second century. Roman Catholics and Protestants alike need to recognize, more than has been their habit, that they are too often guilty of ignoring the existence of their Orthodox fellow Christians, resulting in great loss to both East and West.

The Beginning of the Separation

How did the unfortunate separation occur between Christians of the East and West? It is a long and complex history, but at least half a dozen especially significant events and factors may be considered that together caused the hostility on both sides that led finally to divorce.

One of the earliest breaches in fellowship occurred during the last half of the second century. By that time Christianity had been widely established around the whole Mediterranean basin, from Gaul in the northwest to Persia and Egypt in the east. However, the Christian communities were small and weak, largely urban, and subject to constant opposition and persecution. Rome, the capital of the Empire, began to achieve special leadership among all of the churches because of its strategic location, its claim to a special relation to both the Apostles Peter and Paul, and because of the weakness of Jerusalem, the site of Christian beginnings. Nevertheless, the heartland of the Christian movement was still Asia Minor, where numerous churches had thrived since their establishment by Paul and other New Testament leaders.

Polycarp, Bishop of Smyrna, who as a boy is said to have seen the aged Apostle John, visited Anicetus, Bishop of Rome, in 154/155, perhaps because so many Roman Christians had come there from Asia Minor. The two bishops discussed their differing ways of celebrating Easter, in commemoration of the resurrection of Jesus. Rome and the other Western churches observed Easter on the first day of the week, "the Lord's Day," following the Jewish Passover. The churches of the East, on the other hand, celebrated Easter during the night before the Passover, regardless of the day of the week. The issue was rooted in the diverse accounts of the Passion found in the Synoptic Gospels as distinct from the Gospel of John. Polycarp and Anicetus acknowledged their differences but allowed each side to continue its own custom without rancor. However, the variation soon grew into a dispute and, when Victor was Bishop of Rome (189-198), synods in Rome and in Palestine confirmed the Roman practice. When the churches of Asia Minor, led by Polycrates of Ephesus, refused to conform, Victor excommunicated them. Irenaeus, a native of Asia Minor but now Bishop of Lyons in Gaul, questioned the Roman action, to no avail. The customs have remained divergent ever since.

About the time of the Easter controversy, another development began in Carthage that seemed of little consequence but actually was to contribute a great deal to the ultimate separation of East and West. That factor was the use of Latin as the language of the Church in the West in place of the Greek that had been the primary language of Christianity since the days of the Apostles. As we have observed earlier, Tertullian was the first Christian writer of any note to use Latin, the language that was soon to become and remain the vernacular of all Western Christendom. The result was far more than simple translation. Every translation is a commentary, carrying different nuances and often changing the original meaning. The cultural context of the words goes along with the words themselves, frequently introducing new assumptions and directions. So it came about that Tertullian chose many central words in

Western theology and thereby contributed to the emphases and content of that theology. Significant examples are such Latin-derived words as trinity, person, satisfaction, essence, and substance. To illustrate the factor from a different angle, how were such key Greek terms as *ousia, hypostasis,* and *prosopon* to be understood in Latin? When Western Christians began to speak a language different from that of Eastern Christians, misunderstandings, quarrels, and separation were bound to be the result.

Political Division

After a generation of invasion and defeat for the Roman Empire, the great emperors Aurelian (270-275) and Diocletian (284-305) were able to reestablish the power and unity of the Empire. Diocletian immediately began a series of reforms that were to result in lasting consequences. One of those reforms involved the administration and defense of the Empire. Recognizing the cumbersome size of the Empire and the frequent necessity for defending its borders in several places at once, Diocletian decided to divide the administrative and military responsibilities by appointing a colleague, Maximian, who would serve as "Augustus" in the West while he ruled as "Augustus" in the East, at Nicomedia in Asia Minor. Each of the Augusti then appointed an heir apparent, with the title "Caesar," to share in the administration of his half of the Empire. Constantius I was Caesar of the West and Galerius was Caesar of the East. Further, Diocletian modified the boundaries of the ancient provinces so as to double their number and then grouped them in units called "dioceses," each diocese in charge of a "vicar," or governor general. The dioceses in turn formed four prefectures.

Beset by declining health and discouraged because of the cost and ineffectiveness of his persecution of the troubling Christian sect, Diocletian retired in 305. The succession did not proceed as smoothly as he had planned and during the next twenty years there were several changes in leadership in both West and East. Constantine, son and successor of Constantius I, soon became sole ruler of the West by defeating Maxentius, in 312, at the famous battle of the Mulvian Bridge on the Tiber near Rome. The following year a similar struggle in the East left Licinius the sole ruler there. Then, after a dozen years of tension, Constantine invaded the East in 324 and defeated Licinius, thereby reuniting the whole Empire under one sovereign.

Although the administrative division of the Roman world was short-lived, its results have been visible ever since. If a line is drawn down the middle of the Adriatic Sea, between Italy and the Balkans, and then is extended north into central Europe and south into northern Africa, the political, cultural, and religious differences are still evident. The division was approximately between the Greek-speaking and the Latin-speaking Christians, with all the historic cultural consequences noted above. In addition that line in Europe was later to become, with small exceptions, the unseen barrier that stopped the Moslem invasions of Christendom. It has also become, in the twentieth century, the location of Winston Churchill's "Iron Curtain," still separating East and West.

Eastern Schisms After Chalcedon

Another major factor that contributed to the separation of the East and the West was the continuing quarrels concerning the acceptance and interpretation of the Definition of Chalcedon. That dogma was adopted in the West without serious question. After all, it had been based upon the *Tome* of Leo, Bishop of Rome and Patriarch of the West. However, the East was racked by constant debate over the issue for more than a century, and then permanently divided. We noted at the end of chapter 9, above, that the Nestorians and Monophysites (followers of Cyril) have survived as autonomous Christian bodies until the present day.

The Nestorians, condemned at Ephesus in 431, had fled eastward from the Empire and successfully carried their interpretation of the faith first to eastern Syria and then to Persia, India, and China. On the other hand, the Monophysites, outvoted at Chalcedon in 451, continued their struggle within the Empire. They frequently gave lip-service to the dogma but insisted upon a Cyrillian interpretation. Even at Chalcedon they had claimed that "Leo agrees with Cyril." They believed that to confess "two natures" *in* the incarnate Christ could only mean that there were two Persons, two Sons. That in turn would indicate (God forbid!) a denial of the unity of the divine and the human natures in Christ which they insisted provides the basis of human salvation. Refusing to compromise on a matter so fundamental, they fought at every opportunity to take over the whole Empire for the "true faith"—Monophysitism.

On several occasions during the late fifth and early sixth centuries the Monophysites came close to success. They drove Juvenal, Patriarch of Jerusalem, from his see, and they lynched Proterius, successor of Dioscorus in Alexandria, replacing him with Timothy "Wobble Cap" (*Salafaciolus*), a Monophysite leader. They temporarily replaced Martyrius of Antioch with Peter the Fuller, another Monophysite. When Emperor Leo died in 475, his successor, Zeno, was briefly usurped by Basiliscus, who supported Timothy and Peter and rejected the decisions of Chalcedon. Zeno was restored the following year, however, through the support of Acacius, Patriarch of Constantinople. Together they attempted to settle the quarrel by compromise. Zeno issued the famous *Henotikon,* a letter to Eastern Christians intended to please the dissidents by affirming the Christological formulas of Nicaea, Constantinople, and Ephesus but pointedly omitting the authority of Chalcedon. The strategy was successful in the East, but only temporarily.

During the reign of Zeno's successor, Anastasius (491-518), the Monophysite party made another attempt to win the East. The leading figure in the fateful struggle was the monk and presbyter, Severus (c. 465-538), who became for a while Patriarch of Antioch (512-518) and, when later exiled in Alexandria, reluctantly contributed to the permanent division, in 530, of Eastern Christendom between Chalcedonians and Monophysites. During the reign of Anastasius, Severus and his supporters in Constantinople gained the favor of the Emperor who then officially condemned Chalcedon and Leo's *Tome*. Nevertheless, their victory was brief because, on the death of Anastasius, a Latin-speaking Chalcedonian, Justin I, became emperor. He reestablished the Chalcedonians and exiled Severus.

These bitter struggles in the East not only weakened and divided the churches there; they also added to the increasing separation of the East and the West. Of the five Patriarchates—Jerusalem, Antioch, Alexandria, Rome, and Constantinople—four were in the East, where they were jealous of each other, competing for leadership, and theologically divided. Rome remained faithful to Chalcedon and unchallenged in ecclesiastical preeminence in the West. Monophysite attacks on the *Tome* of Leo and the Definitions of Chalcedon were perceived as attacks on Rome, the see of Peter, and its growing authority. Thus, when Acacius, Patriarch of Constantinople, joined Zeno, the Emperor, in issuing the compromising *Henotikon,* which discounted Chalcedon, Simplicius, Bishop of Rome, excommunicated Acacius, leading to a schism that lasted until 519, when the Emperor Justin restored the faith of Chalcedon. Again, the weak Vigilius, Bishop of Rome from 537 to 555, visited Constantinople in 548 and found himself excommunicated by a synod of African bishops because he approved the attempt by the Emperor Justinian to mollify the Monophysites by condemning the Nestorian "Three Chapters." Vigilius, strengthened by such action from his own domain, reversed himself and excommunicated the Patriarch of Constantinople and other advisors of the Emperor. In addition we should be reminded that the West had long ago been lost to the Empire now centered in Constantinople, "New Rome," because the various barbarian invaders had defeated and occupied all of the West except southern Italy (Calabria) and Sicily. The West after 476 was a different world from the ancient East.

The Monophysites were also increasingly estranged from Emperor and Patriarch in Constantinople, especially by the strong actions of the great Justinian (527-565). In spite of the Monophysite sympathies of his wife, Theodora, he accepted the orthodoxy of the Four Councils, including Chalcedon. He also outlawed paganism, required the baptism of all of his subjects, closed the ancient Academy of Plato, condemned the remaining heresies, and even persecuted Samaritans and Jews. The result was that the Monophysites established separate, national churches in Syria (the Jacobites), in Egypt (the Copts), and in Armenia—the non-Chalcedonian Christians who remain vital in the twentieth century.

The East Isolated by Islam

In the last chapter we took note of the rapid rise of the faith of Islam, based on the teachings of the Prophet Mohammed and the Koran. One of the most remarkable religious developments in all history may be observed in the spread of that faith during the brief career and following the death of Mohammed. The movement began with the flight (*Hejaira*) of the Prophet and his small band of followers from Mecca to Medina in 622. Before he died in 632 an Islamic state had been established in the southern and eastern half of the Arabian peninsula. Under his successors (*caliphs*), the faithful captured most of Palestine, Syria, Egypt, and the Persian Empire, all within a decade. The long and bitter struggles between the Chalcedonians and the Monophysites, as well as the debilitating wars between the Eastern Roman Empire and the Persians, no doubt contributed to the ease of the Moslem success. The tide of conquest continued unabated during the following century, inundating all the lands from Spain eastward along the southern rim of the Mediterranean and on to Afghanistan and India. It is one of the commonplaces of history that the expansion of Islam was finally halted only after it had crossed the Pyrenees and reached central France, at the battle of Tours in 732, precisely one century after the death of Mohammed.

Our interest at this point is to recognize the permanent result of this religious movement in the further separation of Eastern and Western Christendom. Nearly all of the original territory of Christianity became the homeland of the Moslems. The Monophysite national groups found themselves further isolated from the Orthodox churches of the East and, evidently, frequently preferred the relative tolerance of their Islamic masters to the persecution of the Chalcedonians. The Eastern Roman Empire faced a long struggle with successive Moslem powers until the final fall of Constantinople itself in 1453. The Balkan peninsula was overrun to the extent that henceforth, until the twentieth century, all eastern Orthodox Christians have managed to survive only as a minority within lands dominated by Islamic religion and political control. The only exception has been the Orthodox who lived in the Russian Empire and the Slavic communities of eastern Europe or those who fled to the New World of the Americas.

Eastern Christianity, therefore, has managed to survive under constant difficulty, largely isolated from the West. A siege mentality was inevitable, characterized by ethnic self-consciousness and a static devotion to continuity in theology, organization, and ritual. It is remarkable that the Orthodox churches have been able to retain their identities under such severe restrictions and in the face of the powerful and dogmatic, albeit usually tolerant, majority as the Moslems have continued to be. The possibilities of reunion with Western Christendom have remained few, in spite of occasional efforts. The modern bitter fratricide between Christians and various Moslem sects, as well as the wars between the State of Israel and her Arab neighbors, may be traced ultimately to the Moslem conquest of the Eastern Christian homelands in the seventh century.

The Iconoclastic Controversy

Another factor that helped to widen the gulf between East and West was the controversy over ikons—painted or sculpted images of Christ, the Virgin Mary, angels, and the saints, which were commonly used in worship. Just as in the case of the Monophysites earlier, this quarrel was mainly in the East; yet it led to estrangement with the West.

Emperor Leo III began his reign in 717 and thereby established a dynasty known as Isaurian, from their homeland in central Asia Minor then on the boundary between the Empire and the Moslems. For reasons that remain obscure, in 726 Leo forbade the further use of ikons and ordered their destruction. He demonstrated his opposition by destroying an image of Christ that stood over the entrance to his palace in Constantinople. Both the policy and the action were violently rejected by the Patriarch, Germanus, as well as by the monks and most of the people. Nevertheless, supported by the army, Leo remained firm and secured the backing of a synod he called in 730. Germanus was deposed and replaced by the weaker Anastasius. The Emperor then attempted to enforce his iconoclasm in the western parts of his domain, in Sicily, Calabria, and the regions around Ravenna, the imperial headquarters in Italy. However, most Christians in Italy and throughout the West, whether ruled by Visigoths, Lombards, or Byzantines, looked to the Bishop of Rome for spiritual leadership and authority. Gregory II, the incumbent at Rome, condemned Leo's iconoclasm on the grounds that his was an improper secular intrusion into spiritual affairs and that his views appeared to be a denial of the Incarnation, understood as the assumption of the flesh by the divine for the achievement of human salvation.

The dispute soon reached divisive proportions in the East. Two of the major theologians of the Orthodox churches, John of Damascus and Theodore of Studios, led the struggle on behalf of the use of ikons against the Isaurian emperors. John wrote several major treatises on the subject that were to exert lasting influence. He defended ikons against the charge of idolatry by making a distinction between veneration (*proskunesis*), which he argued is proper for images as symbols of the angels and saints they represent, and worship (*latreia*), which is permissible only to God. He claimed, further, that iconoclasm is at bottom a denial of the orthodox dogma of the two natures in Christ; it is a tendency toward Monophysitism and hence heresy. Theodore developed the same defense of ikons, emphasizing their presentation of the salvific entrance into the created order by the divine.

During the reign of the Isaurians, many of the monks fled to Italy and the protection of the Pope. Eastern emperors became the enemies of the Western Patriarch. Thus East and West were further separated. Finally, the Empress Irene, after blinding and murdering her son, the Isaurian Constantine VI, summoned a council in 787 at Nicaea, the Seventh (and last) Ecumenical Council, which approved the use of images and restored the monastic lands confiscated by former emperors. The controversy was effectively resolved, though occasional iconoclasm appeared in imperial policy until 843, when the Empress Theodora made the canons of Nicaea official policy.

The Great Schism

The movements and events that we have sketched above, along with many other minor irritations, were like wedges driven into the trunk of a large tree. Each wedge brought serious damage, and the accumulated pressure of all of them finally caused a complete split that has not been healed to this day. The Church as the Body of Christ remains divided between East and West, and, more tragically, each half has suffered further splintering. If "only God can make a tree," then surely only God can heal one so grievously wounded.

The final and official divorce between East and West occurred in the eleventh, twelfth, and early thirteenth centuries. Two major causes may be identified: the quarrel over the addition of the *filioque* clause to the ancient Creed by the Western Church, cluminating in the excommunications and anathemas of 1054; and the fratricidal sack of Constantinople by the crude brigands of the West in the Fourth Crusade in 1204. After those events, Eastern Christians became convinced that their Western brothers had departed from the true faith and, further, that the Orthodox Churches would fare better as a minority in a Moslem world than in communion with subversive, destructive, uncivilized heretics.

The Latin term *filioque* means "and from the Son" and refers to the procession of the Holy Spirit in relation to God. The issue first came to the fore in the trinitarian debates of the fourth century, especially in the thought of the Cappadocian theologians after Nicaea. Basil of Cappadocia, as noted in chapter 9, wrote the seminal treatise, *On the Holy Spirit,* which helped to establish belief in the full deity of the Holy Spirit as affirmed at the Second Ecumenical Council, at Constantinople, in 381. His younger brother, Gregory of Nyssa, clarified the teaching of Basil by explaining that the Spirit is derived from the Father and is also "of the Son" in that he proceeds from the Father through the Son as a light may be kindled from another light through the medium of a second light. The Spirit therefore proceeds from the Father but also is sent by the Son. A few years later, Augustine, in his *On the Trinity,* wrote that "God the Father alone is he from whom the Word is born, and from whom the Holy Spirit principally proceeds. And therefore I have added the word principally, because we find that the Holy Spirit proceeds from the Son also."

So far no great question was raised. However, in 589, at a council in Toledo, in Spain, when the Visigoth king, Riccared, and his Arian bishops were received into the orthodox Church, the term *filioque* was added to the Nicene-Constantinopolitan Creed which they were required to profess. Later, in 809, a synod at Aachen, Charlemagne's capital, approved the addition of the clause to the Creed without even the approval of the Bishop of Rome. Not long afterwards, Photius, the Patriarch of Constantinople (858-867 and 877-886), accused the West of heresy for adding the *filioque* to the Creed. Photius and Nicholas I, Bishop of Rome, went so far as to excommunicate each other, partially because of the issue but primarily because of papal attempts to intervene in the affairs of the Eastern patriarchates and because of Eastern and Western maneuvers to capture control of the newly-converted Bulgarians. That schism, fortunately, was soon healed by both sides upon the death of the antagonists.

The issue finally brought a breach that was to remain permanent when Cardinal Humbert, a papal legate, laid a bull of excommunication with anathemas on the altar of St. Sophia, the great cathedral of Constantinople, against the Patriarch Michael Cerularius. That hostile action of 1054, though of limited application and questionable legality, remained as a mark of separation until it was revoked on December 7, 1965, in the aftermath of the Second Vatican Council and as a part of the modern attempts at reconciliation between Rome and Constantinople.

The Crusades, which began in 1095 and continued through nine successes and failures until 1291, were initially attempts by Western Christians to liberate the holy places of Palestine from Moslem control. Unfortunately, they frequently deteriorated into wild orgies of murderous pillage and conquest, motivated by greed and savagery. One of their worst results was the destructive occupation of Constantinople in 1204 by the marauders of the Fourth Crusade. Encouraged by the imperial designs of Venice, the crusaders, mostly from France and Flanders, turned aside from their goal and raided the Dalmatian coast. Then, invited to capture Constantinople by Alexius Angelus, ambitious son of the deposed Emperor Isaac II, the army accepted the opportunity and plundered the city, making Baldwin of Flanders the Latin emperor of the defeated city and installing a Latin patriarch who was subject to Rome. The success did not last, however, partially because the terror was opposed even by Pope Innocent III himself and also because the legitimate Eastern Empire was able to recapture the capital in 1261. Nevertheless, the experience caused permanent hatred of Rome in the East, adding to all the cumulative causes of division that had developed since the second century.

Constantinople was finally captured by the Ottoman Turks in 1453. The Eastern Empire ceased to exist and the Eastern Church has continued barely to survive, under Moslems, Tsars, and Soviet commissars. The West, meantime, has tended to ignore and even to forget the churches of the East. Going her separate way, Rome allied itself with Western sovereigns, first the Franks and then the Holy Roman Empire. In modern times, the churches of the West, both Roman and Protestant, have usually thought of themselves collectively as Christendom, with all the rest of the earth, including the East, a field for missions.

Chapter 12

The Struggle of Church and State

In the political confusion occasioned by the collapse of the Western Roman Empire and the instability of the Germanic kingdoms that succeeded it, the Church was the one institution capable of maintaining some semblance of order and purpose in society. Christianity had triumphed in the West, and the Catholic faith as interpreted by the bishops of Rome was gradually becoming recognized as the rule by which societies should be governed. The popes, as the Roman bishops were known, maintained that their authority in matters of faith and morals came from St. Peter himself, who had received it from Jesus when he said, "Thou art Peter, and upon this rock I will build my church; and the gates of hell shall not prevail against it. And I will give unto thee the keys of the kingdom of heaven; and whatsoever thou shalt bind on earth shall be bound in heaven: and whatsoever thou shalt loose on earth shall be loosed in heaven." (Matthew 16:18-19) The Apostle, according to Petrine theory, had been martyred in Rome and his authority had been passed on in unbroken fashion to the bishops who succeeded him.

The Catholic bishops in such important centers of civilization as Bordeaux, Lyons, and Milan were forced by the decline of the Roman administrative machinery to take over a number of secular duties, and the barbarian rulers found that they could not rule effectively in Roman lands without the cooperation of the clerics. The bishops, for their part, needed the military power of the kings to protect the property of the Church. The result was an uneasy alliance between Church and state in which the lines between sacred and secular authority were sometimes difficult to define. As early as 452, Pope Leo I, called "The Great," headed the embassy that met the invading Attila the Hun at the Mincio River and persuaded him to turn back from his march on Rome, and when the Vandal King Gaiseric occupied Rome, it was Leo who persuaded him not to sack the city.

When Odoacer deposed young Romulus Augustus in 476 and sent the imperial insignia to the Eastern Emperor in Constantinople, one effect of his action was the strengthening of the prestige of the papal office in the West. The new importance of the position was not lost on Odoacer, who, on the death of Pope Simplicius, sent word to the assembly of Roman senators and clergymen that he expected to be consulted concerning the election of Simplicius' successor and that the new pontiff would be required to give his word that he would not alienate any of the wealth of the Church, of which he was to be the administrator.

That wealth included at the time a considerable amount of real property, and in succeeding generations, the Church's holdings in land were to grow to enormous size, as the feudal system began to develop.

As civil authority became increasingly incapable of providing protection for the inhabitants of the Western lands, it became necessary for them to make private arrangements for their security through a complex pattern of institutions drawn from Roman and barbarian law. The relationship between patron and client known as *patrocinium* was deeply embedded in Roman life and had been adopted by the barbarian heirs of the Western Empire. Another institution, dealing with land, was known as *precarium,* from the prayer that initiated the relationship. It involved a holding granted by a landowner to a tenant as a matter of favor and kindness rather than for profit.

With the partial collapse of the Roman economy in the latter days of the Empire, taxes rose until many farmers who could not meet their assessments found it expedient to escape punishment for delinquency by deeding their property to great landholders, who then permitted the former owners to work the land as tenants. A similar practice was followed by smaller farmers in turbulent areas who, unable to defend their property, signed it over to powerful neighbors whose men-at-arms could defend them against the attacks of roving bandits. This transaction came to be known as the commendation of lands, or *patrocinium fundorum.* The original owner became a *precarium* tenant, holding his land for life, but without the right to pass it on to his descendants.

When the Franks conquered Gaul, they found these Roman practices compatible with their own institution of the *comitatus,* which contributed greatly to the rise of the feudal spirit in its governing idea that the relationship between lord and vassal is an honorable one, demanding personal loyalty and equal service on both sides. This conception of the bond ultimately made it possible for great nobles to enter into feudal pacts with one another that had formerly been limited to persons of unequal rank. At last, the ownership of property became a maze of interlocking obligations, in which Lord A might have the status of vassal to Lord B for some of his holdings, while Lord B stood in a like relationship to Lord A for some of his. In the mature feudal system, these pacts came to be binding on the heirs of those who had originally contracted them.

The Church found itself at the center of these developments. It was increasingly the recipient of large gifts and gradually became the greatest landholder in Europe. It was easy for the clergy to theorize that God was, after all, the only actual owner of real estate, that everyone actually held property under his control in precarium as a fief, and that the Church, as God's agent, had the right to dispose of any area of the world as it saw fit. Christian kings were held to be no less subject to the pope than Christian bishops.

Augustine had, to be sure, made a distinction between ecclesiastical and secular authority which made prelates and princes independent in their proper spheres, and an echo of his view could be heard in the doctrine promulgated by Gelasius I, pope from 492 to 496. Christ, according to Gelasius, had "separated the kingly duties and powers from the priestly, according to the different functions and dignity proper to each." Kings, however, were dependent upon priests for the means of their salvation, and Gelasius had no hesitancy in reminding the Emperor that "although you are placed in rank above all the race of men, nevertheless you bow your neck in devoted submission to those who are set in charge in matters of religion." The question as to which matters are secular and which religious is, of course, not always beyond dispute, but it is unlikely that Gelasius would have recognized the right of the Emperor or any other secular ruler to make the determination.

In 554 a "pragmatic sanction" of the Emperor Justinian recognized and indeed increased the pope's secular role by stipulating that he would in the future have a part to play in the nomination of governors of the Italian provinces and in the control of their finances.

Pelagius I, pope from 555 to 561 made enthusiastic use of his newly acquired rights to organize the territories under his control and establish the papacy as a genuine political power.

Gregory I, "the Great," pope from 590 to 604, confessed puzzlement about the nature and limits of the power of the papacy. "I should like to know," he mused, "whether the pope, in this world, is a spiritual leader or a temporal king." His confusion was understandable, for at the time, the situation was so critical that he was forced to concern himself more with the protection of the Italian people against the barbarians than with the conduct of the spiritual life of the Church. It was this same Gregory who sent Augustine—not the Bishop of Hippo, but the prelate known to history as St. Augustine of Canterbury—on the mission to England after seeing some handsome fair-haired captives from that island on the slave block in Rome. According to an often-told story, he had asked who they were and upon being told that they were "Angli,'' had remarked, ''Non Angli sed angeli.'' During Gregory's tenure as pope, the Roman Church turned increasingly away from Constantinople and toward the West, and the two cultures began the long process of separation which would, at last, culminate in the schism between the Eastern and Western churches. It was inevitable, under the circumstances, that in the West the resident pope would become increasingly more influential than the distant emperor.

By Gregory's time, the schism between the Catholics of Rome and Arians among the barbarian conquerors was no longer the problem it had once been. During the reign of Gregory's predecessor, Pelagius II, the Visigothic rulers of Spain had been converted to Catholicism, and the Franks, who were becoming a major power in Gaul, had been Catholic Christians since the conversion and baptism of their young king Clovis in 496. During the early years of Gregory's reign, a new and somewhat surprising Christian influence was being felt among the Germanic peoples who now controlled the political life of the former Western Empire. The Irish, converted to Christianity by St. Patrick a century and a half earlier, had developed a healthy monastic system and were now busily engaged in spreading it on the European Continent, where their monks displayed a scholarship which did much to restore and preserve the light of learning throughout the turbulent age between the fall of the Empire and the maturing of the feudal culture.

Like the energetic Irish Church, the ecclesiastical establishment founded by Augustine in England educated Anglo-Saxon monks and sent them as missionaries to the Continent. One of these was Winfrith of Wessex, better known as Boniface, the name by which he was later canonized. He began his missionary career in 716 and, in response to an appeal on his part, the English Church sent him a veritable army of Benedictines, who, in effect, completed the work of making loyal Catholic Christians of the eastern Franks. The most powerful leader of the Franks, a man named Charles Martel (''The Hammer'') found that there were numerous areas in which Boniface's superb talent as a organizer suited his purposes very well. Charles was not much interested in Rome and the papal claim to power, but the idea of a unified Christendom seemed to him to be a powerful rallying point in his struggles against Moslem raiders from Spain who, by 730, had reached the banks of the Loire.

Exercising secular authority to the full, even to the extent of confiscating Church properties to pay off Franks in his armies, Charles forged a strong fighting force and, in 732, won a victory over the Moslems near Tours and Poitiers which, if it did not prevent another twenty years or so of raids north of the Pyrenees, established Charles as a personage of great importance in the Christian West.

He could not declare himself King of the Franks. Nobody but a Merovingian—a descendant of Clovis, grandson of Merovech—could hold that august title. Clovis's successors were an ineffectual lot, however, and Charles held the kingly power if not the title. His son, Pepin, known as *Le Bref* ("The Short"), who in time inherited all his father's authority, thought it unreasonable that one who ruled in fact should not also rule in law. He had worked closely with Boniface in the reform of the Frankish Church, and in 751, he took advantage of his excellent relations with the ecclesiastical establishment to ask Pope Zacharias whether he agreed with him. The Pope, seeing an excellent chance to strengthen his claim that secular authority rested on papal sanction, replied, "It is better that he who possesses power be called king than he who has none." Pepin promptly called together an assembly of nobles at Soissons and had himself elected King of the Franks. Childeric, the hapless Merovingian incumbent, was shorn of his royal locks and sent to a monastery. The triumphant Pepin was crowned and anointed with holy oil by Boniface in the first such ceremony in Frankish history. Pope Stephen II, the successor of Zacharias, later visited him, declared him "Patrician of the Romans," and recrowned him *Gratia Dei Rex Francorum*. As an anointed sovereign, ruling "by the Grace of God," he now had the full support of the Church, which promptly forbade the Franks, under threat of excommunication, to name as king anyone who was not a member of Charles' family, the Carolingians. It was understood that the king, for his part, was to rule justly, defend the Church and uphold Christian teaching. The alliance between king and pope was seen to be beneficial to both parties. The power of the sovereign was given a legitimacy it had never before enjoyed in the barbarian kingdoms, and the Church had a strong champion to defend its interests.

About 756, Pepin had a golden opportunity to show his gratitude to the Church in concrete form. In two expeditions into Italy, he had captured the exarchate of Ravenna from Aistulf, King of the Lombards, and now he ceded the enormous tract of land to the Church, declaring Pope Stephen II—or III, according to one way of counting Stephen's place in the line of succession—its temporal administrator, thus in effect, creating a papal state with the Roman pontiff as sovereign. This recognition of the temporal powers of the pope may have been prompted in part by the so-called *Donatio Constantini*, the Donation of Constantine, one of the most influential forgeries in history. It had allegedly been made by the Emperor in the Fourth Century as an expression of his gratitude for his baptism and his recovery from leprosy. It granted Sylvester, the pope at that time, imperial power and dignity, and all the garments and insignia of imperial power except the crown. In matters of faith and worship, it gave Sylvester and his successors forever spiritual authority over the entire Church as well as temporal dominion over Rome, and "the provinces, places, and *civitates* of Italy or of the western regions." It even ceded to the pope the Emperor's Lateran Palace. Subsequent popes used the *Donatio* freely in making their claims to temporal power, and it was not until 1440 that Laurentius Valla declared the document to be a forgery, initiating a controversy that was to last until the late eighteen hundreds, when the last claim to its genuineness was abandoned. Whether or not the Donation was a prime factor in Stephen's attainment of secular authority, he and his successors greatly expanded the powers of the papacy, and by the end of the eighth century, popes were issuing their own coinage and performing other functions formerly reserved for temporal sovereigns.

Charlemagne

In 768, Pepin's son Charles, known in history as Charlemagne, succeeded his father on the Frankish throne and set out to introduce a new dimension of temporal authority into the turbulent world of Western politics. It was under his reign that the concept of a united Europe became a living force that is still very much in evidence today. In sixty well-planned campaigns, he established boundaries which effectively marked off the West as an entity distinct from the domain of Constantinople on one side and that of the Moorish conquerors of Spain on the other.

When the Lombards broke the treaties they had made with Pepin and seized papal lands, Charlemagne marched on them. By 774, they were defeated and Charles, though he treated first Pope Adrian and then Pope Leo III with the deference due their exalted ecclesiastical position, made it clear that he thought little of their claim to secular supremacy by declining to return the recovered lands to them.

In a series of successful military operations, Charles expanded the Frankish rule in every direction and in time doubled the size of the territories with which he had started. With the exception of the British Isles and Spain, virtually the whole of Western Europe was under his control.

The dream of a revival in the West of the glories of imperial Rome was very much alive in Charlemagne, and it led him to press his power to its logical conclusion. On Christmas day of the year 800, he went to mass in Saint Peter's basilica, and Pope Leo III placed an imperial crown on his head. The congregation burst into a triumphant chant, "To Charles the most pious Augustus, crowned by God, the great and peace-giving Emperor, life and victory." At the close of the third rendition of the choral acknowledgment, the Pope prostrated himself before Charles.

Charlemagne was a deeply religious man and a devoted son of the Roman Church. His loyalty was not lost on Leo, who saw his coronation as a claim that sovereignty of the whole Roman Empire resided in the West. If that claim could be supported, the claim of the Pope to be the spiritual, and perhaps even the temporal, overlord of Christendom might be strengthened. Charlemagne, a shrewd politician, and unready for the conflict with Byzantium that would inevitably result from such a sweeping claim to authority, preferred to think of himself as Emperor of the Roman Christians and limited his ambitions to the West.

The Carolingian Empire, nevertheless, provided the papacy with a welcome rationale for asserting the supremacy allegedly given the popes by the Donation of Constantine. Despite the papal prostration before Charlemagne at his coronation, the fact remained that the legitimacy of the Emperor's reign rested on his coronation by Leo. As the Church saw the situation, then, the Empire was an instrument for forwarding the secular aims of the pope.

When Charlemagne died in 816, his son, Louis I, became Emperor. Pope Stephen IV (or V by one calculation) placed on the head of the new sovereign a crown which he said had belonged to Constantine and declared Louis sole Roman Emperor. The message he was conveying was unmistakable. Emperors were made by popes. Constantinople, of course, did not agree. In Eastern theory, the imperial throne was established and maintained directly by God. Popes were no more than churchmen of high standing, and their authority was limited to such matters as ecclesiastical administration, clerical discipline, and determination of doctrine.

The papal claims were, as a matter of fact, disturbing to the Western Emperors. Uncomfortably aware that their claim to imperial power had become dependent on the theory that only a pope could confer it, they still had to maintain that a crowned emperor was not subordinate to the man who had crowned him. The resultant ill-defined lines of authority were to lead to centuries of tension between church and state in the West.

Growing Conflict

Political instability in the Frankish states in the ninth century weakened the imperial government and encouraged the papal claims. A succession of popes defined their authority in terms reminiscent of the Donation of Constantine. The whole body of Christians, Eastern and

Western, was declared to be subject to the Pope as Vicar of Saint Peter. Clerics were asserted to have immunity from secular law. Even more daringly, the claim was made that the primacy of the Holy See over the government in Constantinople must be recognized—a contention unenforceable from the West and ignored by the East.

Unlike the Franks, who regarded the Empire as a sort of extension of their own kingdom, the authorities of the Church saw no necessary connection between the imperial office and the Carolingian house. If they had the authority to bestow the crown, the popes reasoned, they had the right to determine who should wear it. When the descendants of Charlemagne were unable to agree on an occupant for the imperial throne in 875, Pope John VIII selected Charles the Bald, and later showed sufficient confidence to declare that "he who is ordained by us to the Empire must be by us first and foremost invited and elected." It was, in fact, through the papacy that the idea of empire was able to survive the dissolution of the Frankish kingdom and find a new seat in Germany. After a period of confusion, during which the imperial office was for a time without an occupant, Pope John XII crowned the German King Otto emperor on Candlemas day in 962, thus inaugurating the Holy Roman Empire, which would endure for eight and a half centuries.

It was not long, however, before the secular structure preserved by the Church began to flex its muscle and become a threat to papal ascendancy. The symbols of subordination, to be sure, remained intact. The ceremony of imperial coronations still clearly acknowledged papal supremacy. The emperor had to take an oath of allegiance to the pope, kiss his feet, and receive the emblems of office from him. The pope, as "father," adopted the emperor as a "son" of the Roman Church. In fact, however, throughout the first half of the eleventh century, it was the occupants of the imperial throne who determined who would sit in the chair of Saint Peter.

From the imperial viewpoint, it may be argued that they performed that function too well. The appointment of cosmopolitan and highly intelligent popes by Henry III (1039-1056) led to a resurgence of papal power, and in 1059, the Church began crowning its popes, whereas it had, prior to that time, been content merely to consecrate them.

In 1054, the long-seething controversies between the Eastern and Western branches of Christendom at last resulted in their separation. Subsequent claims to papal authority could be advanced without regard for what the reaction might be in Byzantium, although those claims invariably asserted the primacy of the Pope over the whole of Christendom. In 1075, some two years after his coronation, Pope Gregory VII, issued his famous *Dictatus Papae,* defining with new vigor what his predecessors had held as their ideal for centuries. Any matter related to the well-being of the commonwealth of Christians is, he said, one which is subject to final adjudication by the pope, while the pope himself is not subject to judgment by anyone (*papa a nemine judicatur*). In order for a council to be ecumenical, the pope must have summoned it or must authorize its decrees. No one but the pope may wear the imperial emblems, and he alone may require the kissing of his feet (*osculatio pedum*). The pope, Gregory VII, maintained, in perhaps the most sweeping of the twenty-seven "sentences" of the *Dictatus,* may depose kings, emperors, and princes, and he may create new kingdoms.

Had he been less ambitious and more cautious, Gregory might have foreseen that a manifesto of that magnitude would not remain unchallenged. The matter came to a head in the same year the *Dictatus* was published, when Gregory suspended some German bishops and published an investiture decree that forbade the receipt of any spiritual office from a layman.

Henry IV, King of Germany and a claimant to the imperial crown, ignored a papal nomination to the archbishopric of Milan and nominated a cleric named Tedald. Gregory ordered him to withdraw the nomination. Henry countered by calling a national assembly to meet at Worms on January 24, 1076, to include twenty-four German bishops and two archbishops. Loyal to their sovereign, they declared Gregory to be deposed, and their decision was echoed by a synod of Lombard bishops at Piacenza.

The acts of deposition were delivered to Gregory in the Lenten Synod of 1076, and when they were made known to the assembly, they aroused such fury that Roland of Parma, the messenger who had brought the decrees, would have lost his life if Gregory himself had not saved him. The Pope's response was prompt. He, in turn, deposed Henry, excommunicated him, and declared that all his subjects were released from their oaths of fealty to their former king.

Henry's bishops broke ranks at news of the papal action, and a number of his powerful vassals, taking advantage of an opportunity to diminish imperial power, met at Tribur in October of 1076, listened to suggestions that another sovereign be chosen to supplant Henry, and decided to invite the Pope to Augsburg to confront Henry.

At this point, the King realized that the game was going against him. He crossed the Alps in secret, and on January 25, 1077, he arrived at the castle of Canossa, where he had learned the Pope was staying, and sought an audience. Gregory, savoring his triumph, refused to see him, and the King, seeing no alternative, took off his shoes and stood outside the castle gate barefoot in the snow for three days, at the end of which time Gregory magnanimously let him come inside and lifted the ban of excommunication.

Henry returned to Germany in the good graces of the Church, but the dissident princes, having burned their bridges behind them in their attempt to depose him, elected Rudolph of Swabia as king in March of 1077. In the resulting civil war, both claimants sought Gregory's support, and, in time, both agreed to a papally involved assembly to examine the legitimacy of their respective claims. Before it could convene, however, Henry got the upper hand in the war and withdrew his approval of the proceeding. Gregory excommunicated Henry again in 1080 and recognized his rival's claim, but Rudolph was fatally injured in battle later that year.

Henry called another council of imperial bishops, deposed Gregory once more and elected as pope the Archbishop of Ravenna, who selected the name Clement III as the one under which he would reign. Open war now broke out between Henry's and Gregory's forces, and Henry marched on Rome, finally capturing the city after two unsuccessful attempts. Clement was enthroned in March of 1084, and promptly crowned Henry as Holy Roman Emperor. Gregory escaped with the aid of Norman allies and went to Salerno. He died there in 1085.

Although Henry had achieved his aims, the investiture contest, as the struggle came to be called, ultimately worked to the advantage of the Church in a Europe dominated by the enormous authority of an institution which claimed the power to withhold from sovereigns and subjects alike the instruments of salvation for their immortal souls. In the long run, the Church refused to recognize Clement III as anything more than antipope and hailed Gregory as one of its greatest rulers, worthy to be honored as a saint.

It was, in fact, during the next century that the Church made its greatest advances toward the attainment of universal authority in the West. It is true that Pope Calixtus II, a Bergundian of noble birth, made some concessions to imperial claims in the Concordat of Worms (1122), which brought a formal end to the investiture controversy, but the Roman hierarchy, realizing that excommunication and interdict were more powerful weapons than any instruments of war the princes of Europe could mobilize, was in no mood to concede that administration of secular affairs could be conducted without ecclesiastical sanction. Temporal rulers invoked the Gelasian doctrine in support of their contention that their authority in their sphere was as absolute as that of the spiritual lords in theirs, but the Church would have none of that. Christ, the papacy maintained, had exercised the dual office of Priest and King, and, significantly, the popes dropped their traditional title of "Vicar of Saint Peter," and started calling themselves "Vicar of Christ." This appeal to divine authority proved to be a much firmer ground on which to stand than the Donation of Constantine with its suggestion that the papal power had been derived from an earthly ruler, and that controversial document lost most of its potency centuries before it was finally shown to be a forgery.

Innocent III

About 1160, the wife of the Count of Segni gave birth to a son in the Italian city of Anagni. The child was christened Lotario and brought up with all the advantages considered proper for a boy of his rank. He attended the University of Paris and went on to Bologna for the study of law. Choosing a career in the Church, he was admitted to the lowest of the three clerical orders and was still a cardinal deacon when Pope Celestine III died in 1198. Despite his youth and modest position, Lotario found himself elected to fill the highest office of the Church. He was promptly ordained as a priest and the next day was consecrated as a bishop. His text for the latter occasion, taken from the book of Jeremiah, was indicative of his conception of the papacy: "I have set thee this day over nations and over kingdoms" (Isaiah 1:10). In an early letter, he maintained that the relationship between the *sacerdotum* and the *regnum* is comparable to that between the sun and the moon. This was followed by an even more sweeping declaration: "The Lord left to Peter the governance not of the Church only but of the whole world." He took the name Innocent III.

Innocent's first task was the restoration of the secular power of the papacy in Italy, eroded by the successes of the Emperor Henry VI, and thrown into confusion after his death in quarrels between claimants to the imperial throne. Innocent was so successful in re-establishing control that Henry's widow, Constance, recognized him as overlord of the Kingdom of Sicily and, in 1198, just before her death, named the Pope as guardian of her little son Frederick.

Philip of Swabia and Otto of Brunswick were asserting their rival claims to be emperor, and Innocent, consistently with his theory of papal authority, studied their cases and awarded the throne to Otto in 1201, on condition that Otto take an oath to respect the papal claims to temporal power in Italy. Nine years later, when Otto broke his oath, Innocent deposed him and awarded the Empire to his young ward Frederick, King of Sicily.

Using the established instruments of the feudal structure, Innocent acted decisively on occasion to reduce sovereign states to the condition of papal vassalage. Peter II of Aragon gave his kingdom to the Pope in 1204 and received it back in an arrangement based on the *patrocinium fundorum*. Innocent's most significant venture of this sort, though, occurred during his dispute with King John of England over the appointment of an Archbishop of Canterbury. From 1208 to 1213, England lay under a papal interdict, and John, in order to forestall an invasion from France, was at last compelled to recognize the Pope as his overlord.

While extending his authority in secular matters, Innocent was also occupied with reorganizing the machinery of the Church to make it more effective and with enforcing orthodoxy in Christendom. More than a century before his time, a heretical sect known in history as the Albigenses or Cathari had found a foothold in the south of France. With a dualistic creed, holding the created world to be evil, the Cathari enjoined an ascetic way of life to turn the soul away from material concerns. The movement was antisacerdotal, and Innocent regarded it as dangerous to the Church. When his efforts to convert the Cathari to Catholicism by peaceful methods failed, he began a crusade against them which resulted in a prolonged and bloody war between the nobles of northern France and the titled supporters of the heretics in the south. In the course of the conflict, the brilliant culture which had taken root in Provence was destroyed. Many of the Albigensians survived, however, and the sect was not effectively suppressed until after Innocent's death.

When Innocent died in 1216, the papacy had attained a position of power that subsequent popes were eager to claim but that few were able to maintain. The Empire had not yet abandoned its claim to supremacy in secular matters, and Innocent's own protégé, Frederick, on more than one occasion challenged his one-time guardian's successors, gaining many military victories and much popular support. By the time of his death in 1250, however, he had lost much of his power, and the papal cause seemed in the ascendancy.

The conflict between the Church and the Empire gave rise to two persistent factions in Germany and Italy. The parties had their origin in Germany and took their names from two prominent German families. In 1140, at the battle of Weinsburg, the war cry of Conrad, Duke of Franconia, was *Hie Waiblingen,* Waiblingen being a family estate. Henry the Lion, Duke of Saxony, used *Hie Welfe,* from the old personal name *Hwelp,* which, in the altered form *Welf,* was borne by a Duke of

Bavaria in the eleventh century. *Welf* became transformed into *Guelph,* and *Waiblingen* to *Ghibelline,* and the parties bearing these names played a great part in German and Italian history in the twelfth, thirteenth, and fourteenth centuries. The Guelphs, originally opponents of Frederick I in the dynastic disputes in Germany, became the supporters of the papacy while the Ghibellines were the imperial party.

The question of the scope of secular and ecclesiastical authority was not settled during the Middle Ages, and though it later took different forms and involved a variety of advocates representing governments and religious organizations undreamed of before the Renaissance and the Reformation, it has to this day remained a perennial subject of political controversy.

Chapter 13

The Church and the Means of Grace

One of the most pervasive and productive ideas in Western cultural history is that humanity may be redeemed from sin and death through gracious acceptance and transformation by transcendent power, mediated through a moral and spiritual community and resulting in a new status of incorporation. The inescapable need for such redemption has been acknowledged everywhere and always. The human propensity toward self-centeredness, the condition of finitude, and the universality of death have all persisted like a cancer of despair at the center of consciousness in every age. And yet, just as a caged lion ceaselessly paces back and forth, seeking escape, so the human spirit remains hopeful, searching for redemption through wisdom, righteousness, and corporate participation.

The Covenantal Community

In the first volume of this work we noted the significance of the idea of covenant in the earliest stages of Hebrew religion. The people of the Exodus believed that they could trace their corporate existence to a single forefather, Abraham, who became the "father of the faithful" by responding to the invitation of Almighty God (El Shaddai) to enter into covenant with him (Genesis 15-17). The Israelites were constituted as a community both after the Exodus, at Sinai, (Exodus 19) and as they made their way into the Promised Land (Joshua 24). They were bound together across tribal and linguistic lines in a covenant of faith with their gracious, commanding God, Yahweh.

We have observed also, in the first volume, the long and tragic history of the Hebrews, from the time of Moses and Joshua to the time of Jeremiah and Ezekiel, as they were divided and finally disintegrated because, in the repeated words of the prophets, they broke the covenant and disobeyed their God. Among the prophets, Isaiah especially mitigated the impending disaster by calling the faithful remnant into the Qahal, the assembly of God's people. They would find redemption in the future, he taught, by responding to the call of Yahweh to be his people beyond the tragedies that would surely come. The apocalyptic visions of Ezekiel portrayed the ideal community of the faithful that would perpetuate the covenant (Ezekiel 37; 40-48). Jeremiah also envisioned the future formation of a New Covenant of the spirit (Jeremiah 31).

Even though the Jews were scattered abroad by Babylonian power and have remained primarily in the Diaspora ever since, they have maintained their identity through innumerable trials by holding tenaciously to the commandments and practices of the covenant. The Qahal has been made local and visible in synagogues. These institutions have appeared for more than two millenia wherever there were even small communities of Jews to facilitate unity, worship, and learning. The synagogues are empirical manifestations of the universal, self-conscious people of God.

This institutional expression of redemption by grace continued in Christianity from the beginning. The new faith arose, of course, within Judaism, and it was natural that the followers of Jesus should develop communities of worship and witness after the pattern of the familiar synagogues. Thus the Qahal became the synagogue which in turn became for Christians the *ekklesia* (assembly, congregation, or church), each both local and universal, visible and invisible.

The earliest Christian theologians, however, began to think of the Church as more than the ideal community expressed visibly by local groups of Christians in their churches. Paul, for example, taught that the Church is the body of Christ, the real presence of the resurrected and transcendent Jesus, alive and active redemptively in the world. In less than thirty years after the death of Jesus, Paul was teaching, in Asia Minor, Greece, and Rome, that Christians, both Jews and Gentiles, were members (eyes and ears, hands and feet) of the body of Christ, carrying his message and doing his work of redemption everywhere. The same interpretation, though variously stated, is found in other writings of the New Testament, notably in the Letter to the Hebrews. The Church as the people of God in Christ was believed to be not only the carrier of the Gospel of salvation but also the instrument of God's grace.

That powerful and influential conception of the Church as the means of grace has been transmitted and developed through the centuries. However, it should be noted that the Church, so conceived and described in the time of the Apostles, was more a personal and spiritual fellowship than an organization or institution. The churches knew little if anything of uniformity or control; they were bound rather by a common faith in Jesus, hope for a glorious future, and love for God and one another. As we have observed (chapter 5, above), the rise of heresies and schisms during the second century was the major cause for the transformation of the New Testament *ekklesia* into the structured institution that the Church has been ever since. Whether that historical development has been fortunate or unfortunate, it may at least be judged as inevitable and probably necessary. (An outstanding modern discussion of this question may be found in Emil Brunner's *The Misunderstanding of the Church,* 1952.)

The growth of the idea of the Church as an organized institution, with clearly defined officers and lines of authority and bearing the message and means of redemption, may be distinctly seen even in the scarce extant writings of the early Fathers. Ignatius of Antioch (c. 115) and Irenaeus (c. 185) are primary examples of that development, and the struggles with the Montanists and Gnostics were the evident causative occasions (cf. chapter 5). Further, Cyprian, Bishop of Carthage from 248 to 258, added authority to the teaching. In the midst of deadly persecution and bitter controversy, Cyprian argued persuasively for the unity of the Church and the power of the bishop. He claimed that the bishop owes his position to God alone and possesses his priestly powers by succession from the Apostles. He is the sole ruler of the church over which he presides; the priests who serve under him derive their powers from his delegation. In his most famous work. *On the Unity of the Catholic Church,* Cyprian claimed that the Church is the ark of salvation outside of which no one can be saved. "If anyone could escape who is outside the ark of Noah he also may escape who is ouside the church." "Outside the church there is no salvation." "He cannot have God as father who has not the church as mother."

The Church had already achieved, among believers, the status of the ark of salvation, the divine institution on earth that possessed the keys to the Kingdom of Heaven, guarded and guided by the bishops who claimed to be successors of the Apostles, even while it remained a minority community in the hostile Roman world. That status became rather suddenly legitimized and greatly enhanced when, early in the fourth century, Christianity was legalized and finally adopted as the official religion of the Empire. While the Roman government depended upon its legions and law for its stability, the Church represented the eternal power of God on earth. The meek and lowly Galilean had become more powerful than Caesar. So the Church claimed!

Augustine of Hippo added immeasurably to the power of the Church as the means of grace. We have seen in chapter 8, above, how Augustine broke new ground in his teachings against the Donatists concerning the Church and the sacraments. We noted also that against both the Pelagians and the Donatists he argued for the absolute necessity of grace as God's gift for the salvation of humanity. That grace he believed is to be found in the one, holy, catholic and apostolic Church, which is the means God has provided through Christ. The Church possesses the holy sacraments, which Augustine called "sacred signs" and "visible signs of divine things;" but they are more than signs, he believed, because in and through them saving grace is actually given and received. Without that sacramental grace no one can be saved.

By the end of antiquity, therefore, marked by the fall of the Western Roman Empire and the barbarian incursions, the Church had been established both by claim and by status as the essential dispenser of that saving favor and power of God without which there can be no hope.

Day of Wrath, Day of Mourning

The political and cultural upheavals in the West that brought about the conditions characterizing the Dark Ages made possible the further realization of the Church's claim to be the ark of salvation. The Empire began to collapse from within during the fourth and fifth centuries and finally came to an official end in 476 with the deposing of the last emperor. Romulus Augustulus was succeeded by the German general, Odoacer. The centuries that followed, until the revival of learning under Charlemagne at the beginning of the ninth century, were dark indeed, at least in terms of political stability, social control, and cultural advancement. The successive barbarian peoples who moved across central and western Europe—Goths, Vandals and Lombards, among others—required time to assimilate the civilization of ancient Greece and Rome as well as the orthodox faith of the Church. Life was precarious, learning was limited, and there was little cause for joy or hope in this world.

Those very conditions of suffering and despair provided an opportunity for the Church to call the multitudes to a vision of otherworldly bliss, attainable by way of withdrawal from the world of pain and evil. Asceticism, the more severe the better, was highly recommended and often required. Monasticism became increasingly popular for both men and women. Celibacy was considered morally superior to marriage and was required for the clergy and those who chose religious vocations. Who should desire to bring children into such a dark and dreary place of hunger, toil, sickness, and death? Plato, the philosopher *par excellence* of the early Church, had taught that birth is the entombment of wayward spirits from the realm of light. The living were cautioned not to be overly concerned with the things of the world, even the thought and literature of the classical age. The only learning needed was that provided by the Scriptures and the teachers of the Church. Even Gregory the Great, Bishop of Rome (590-604), rebuked the Bishop of Vienne in Gaul for studying secular literature: "the praises of Christ do not belong in the same mouth with the praises of Jove."

The Sacramental System

The Church's teachings about the number, meaning, and efficacy of the sacraments were not taken fully and directly from the New Testament. Rather, the theory and practice were developed over more than a thousand years, culminating in the work of Peter Lombard and Thomas Aquinas in the twelfth and thirteenth centuries. However, it is evident that the idea had its foundations in the teachings and practice of Jesus and the Apostles. We should note, further, that the beginnings of sacramental practice may be traced to pre-Christian Jewish worship as well as to the cults of Greece and Rome, especially the great Mysteries. In fact, the use of ceremonies and objects for the purpose of pleasing the gods and gaining their favor may be discovered in the earliest records of civilization.

A variety of rites was used by early Christians for such differing purposes as initiation into the Church, portrayal of significant acts of Jesus, symbolizing Christ-like humility, transmitting spiritual blessing, healing the sick and comforting the dying, facilitating unity and worship, and conveying redeeming grace. Baptism and the eucharist, unquestionably having their origins in the ministry of Jesus, were always central and have been practically universal among Christians from the beginning. Eventually, however, the variety was reduced to seven, and they have remained standard in the Western Church since the Middle Ages. Some have suggested that the number was fixed at seven because that had been looked upon as a holy and perfect number at least since Old Testament days; after all, there were also seven deadly sins and seven cardinal virtues. The seven are as follows: baptism, confirmation, penance, eucharist, anointing of the sick and dying, marriage, and ordination. The same person would not ordinarily receive both of the last two since celibacy is required for the clergy and the religious (monks and nuns).

Christian baptism was taken directly from the Jewish practice of dipping and washing in water to symbolize cleansing from sin, paganism, and impurity. It was required by the prophet John the Baptist as a sign of prior repentance in preparation for participation in the imminent Kingdom of God (Matthew 3:1-10). Jesus began his ministry by receiving the baptism of John in the Jordan River (Mark 1, Matthew 3, Luke 3). There is no evidence that Jesus baptized his followers; however, immediately following his death and resurrection the Apostles began to initiate new believers into the Church by baptism (Acts 2). The extant writings of Paul testify that he both taught and practiced baptism among his converts, both Jews and Gentiles (cf. I Corinthians 1:14-16). Further, Paul was probably the original source of the permanent Christian theological interpretation of baptism as more than a symbol of repentance and cleansing; he emphasized that it is also participation in the death and resurrection of Jesus Christ, a burial of the past sinful nature and a rising to newness of life. It is an initiation into the Body of Christ that looks backward to the conquest of death and forward, proleptically, to the resurrection of the believer at the last day (Romans 6:1-11; Colossians 3:1-5). From the second century onward baptism has been understood as not only a sign of repentance and cleansing but also particularly as the means of washing away the original sin that burdens every human soul.

Confirmation is the sacrament of the responsible acceptance of one's prior baptism (in the case of infant baptism) and membership in the Church as the Body of Christ. It also involves the giving of spiritual blessing by the administering clergy. There are obvious parallels to the Jewish solemn ceremonies for the *bar mitzvah* and *bat mitzvah* in which a young man or woman, having reached the age of puberty and maturity, is included formally into the covenant community, the People of God.

Penance is the return to the renewal experienced in baptism. It is the means by which the believer continually repents throughout life, receiving pardon for all sins that have followed baptism. Baptism is given only once, just as birth occurs only once. In modern times in the Roman Church penance is required of every believer at least once a year. The sacrament had its beginning in constant demand for repentance in both the Old and New Testaments. The original call was for a return (*teshubah*) to God and his commandments and a change of direction and attitude (*metanoia*) by the sinner. However, a subtle and extremely significant change in the concept occurred during the Middle Ages, apparently as a result of Jerome's new Latin translation of the Scriptures, the Vulgate, at the beginning of the fifth century. Now "repent" became "do penance," implying that the sinner must not only change direction and attitude but also *do* something to compensate for sin. With this interpretation there developed in the Middle Ages the powerful control by the Church of the means of forgiveness and restoration to righteousness. Penance came to be defined as involving four necessary steps: contrition, confession, satisfaction, and absolution. Satisfaction requires obedience to the priestly mandate for forgiveness. That was the ecclesiastical ground out of which the whole system of indulgences grew, with historic results in the Protestant Reformation, as we shall see.

The Lord's Supper, or Eucharist, is a clear example of the borrowing and transformation of earlier Jewish usage by Christian reinterpretation. Its historical nexus is the Passover, which Jesus and his Apostles were celebrating in the customary manner when Jesus commanded them to continue the breaking of bread and the drinking of wine as memorials of his impending sacrificial death. The earliest account of that event is recorded in I Corinthians 11:23-26:

> For I received from the Lord what I also delivered to you, that the Lord Jesus Christ on the night when he was betrayed took bread, and when he had given thanks, he broke it, and said, 'This is my body which is for you. Do this in remembrance of me.' In this same way also the cup, after supper, saying, 'This cup is the new covenant in my blood. Do this, as often as you drink it, in remembrance of me.' For as often as you eat this bread and drink the cup, you proclaim the Lord's death until he comes.

The event is described in all four Gospels: Matthew 26, Mark 14, Luke 22, and John 13. Thus the ancient Passover, the annual celebration of God's deliverance of his people from their bondage in Egypt, was changed by Jesus and his followers into the celebration of the deliverance of all the faithful from sin and death by his sacrifice.

Since Christianity from its inception has been pre-eminently concerned with the redemption of humanity, and that redemption has been grounded in the death of Jesus Christ, the Church has perforce made the eucharistic celebration of his death central in its life and worship. The long history of the interpretation of the Supper is much too complex to be reviewed in any detail here. The New Testament itself clearly shows that there were problems with respect to practice and understanding from the earliest days (cf. I Corinthians 11). By the early second century, Christian leaders were already teaching that taking the bread and wine of communion bestowed objective, life-giving grace. For example, Ignatius, Bishop of Antioch before A.D. 115, wrote that the elements are "the medicine of immortality, the antidote that we should not die but live forever in Jesus Christ" (*Epistle to the Ephesians,* 20). Pope Gregory the Great, in the early sixth century, interpreted the eucharist as a repetition of Christ's sacrifice for sin and as providing nourishment for the spirit of the recipient.

There were two especially significant controversies in the early Middle Ages regarding the nature of the presence of Christ in the consecrated bread and wine. The first occurred in the ninth century when Paschasius Radbertus, abbot of the monastery at Corbie in Picardy, emphasized the miraculous, physical presence of Jesus Christ on the altar. He was opposed by Ratramnus, his fellow monk at Corbie, as well as by the German theologians Rabanus Maurus and Gottschalk, who interpreted the presence as real but in a mystical and spiritual sense. The sccond debate came two centuries later when the same ground was coverdd more thoroughly by Berengarius, who took the general position of Ratramnus, and Lanfranc, the famous abbot at Bec in Normandy, who defined in precise terms the change of the substance of the bread and wine into the essence of Christ's body even though the appearance (*species*) remains the same. The view of Lanfranc was given the highest sanction of orthodoxy by Pope Innocent III (1198-1216) and the Fourth Lateran Council (1215), and soon afterwards Thomas Aquinas gave full expression to the doctrine of transubstantiation, using the philosophical categories of Aristotelian metaphysics.

The sacrament of the anointing of the sick and dying, or extreme unction, is based upon the common scriptural practice of spiritual anointing and healing, especially the specific mandate of James 5:14, 15: "Is any among you sick? Let him call for the elders of the church, and let them pray over him, anointing him with the oil in the name of the Lord; and the prayer of faith will save the sick man, and the Lord will raise him up; and if he has committed sins, he will be forgiven."

The sacrament of marriage follows biblical usage also. The Church has always considered marriage a holy estate, ordained by God and commended by Jesus of Nazareth. It has been looked upon as the creation of a new being—"the two shall become one flesh"—and indissoluble, except by sin. Marriage is to be monogamous, based on mutual love, and binding until the death of one of the union. It achieved sacramental status primarily because of the Augustinian teaching that sex is inherently evil, though necessary for procreation. The evil of the flesh may be annulled by the grace of the sacrament so that procreation may occur within marriage.

Finally, the sacrament of ordination, or holy orders, is a continuation of the anointing of priests and kings in ancient Israel as well as the giving of special gifts for leadership in the early Church. "Christos" is the Greek translation of the Hebrew "Messiah," or anointed one, and Jesus himself, according to the Scriptures, was conceived by the Spirit, anointed by the Spirit,and raised by the Spirit. In like manner the Apostles were directed by the Spirit in their teaching and mission. They gave instructions concerning the choice and qualifications of their assistants and successors (cf. I Timothy 3 and Titus 1). Thus the Church chose leaders and set them apart for special holiness and purpose. The increasing separation of the clergy and the laity from the second century on gave special legitimacy to the sacrament of ordination as a means of grace.

The Source of Grace

After a thousand years of experience and reflection, the Church had developed a powerful and efficient system of dispensing the saving grace of God to the faithful. The whole Gospel was founded on the joyful conviction that the one true God, the God of Moses and the prophets and of Jesus and the Apostles, is full of mercy, seeking to redeem all nations by his graciousness. "His mercy endures forever." It was also the central belief of Christians that the grace of God was somehow brought near and made available through the death of the Son of God, Jesus Christ. The cross has been the symbol of Christianity since its beginning. However, there was no well-articulated consensus regarding *how* the death of Jesus effected human redemption. There was certainly no dogma of the cross.

The record indicates that most of the thinkers and teachers of the Church interpreted the death of Jesus in terms of conquest and ransom. In Christ, they said, God defeated his enemies and those of mankind—Satan and the demons; or sin, death, and the devil. Human beings were rescued from the bondage in which they had been held since the fall of Adam and Eve. A favorite biblical text for the concept is Mark 10:45, which quotes Jesus himself as saying, "For the Son of Man also came not to be served but to serve, and to give his life as a ransom for many." The same teaching is expressed in other passages in the New Testament, as, for example, I Peter 1:18, 19: "You know that you were ransomed from the futile ways inherited from your fathers, not with perishable things such as silver and gold, but with the precious blood of Christ, like that of a lamb without blemish of spot." Expanding the interpretation is the suggestive passage in the same Epistle, 3:18-20: "For Christ also died for sins once for all, the righteous for the unrighteous, that he might bring us to God, being put to death in the flesh but made alive in the spirit; in which he went and preached to the spirits in prison, who formerly did not obey, when God's patience waited in the days of Noah, during the building of the ark, in which a few, that is, eight persons, were saved through water."

This understanding of Christ the conqueror of sin and death gave rise to a variety of dramatic expressions in the early Church and among the Fathers. The apocryphal *Gospel of Nicodemus,* in the second century, took up the theme in the second passage quoted above from I Peter and described "the harrowing of hell" by the crucified Christ. Leaving the cross and the tomb, he descended into Hades, the abode of the dead, where he bound Satan and opened the prison doors for those who finally believed. Others preferred to see the saving work of Christ as a "deceiving of the deceiver" in which the Lord used the veil of human flesh to trick Satan into dragging him down to death as he had all other human beings; but hidden beneath the flesh was the deity himself, who shared his immortality with the dead. Thus Satan was deceived and defeated, losing his power over all mankind. This theory was frequently described in terms of the baiting of a fishhook or a mouse trap. In all cases, however, the concept was the same: in the man Jesus Christ God assumed both flesh and death in order to overcome the power of evil.

As appealing and persuasive as it is, this "conquest theory of atonement" presents certain difficulties. Perhaps most seriously, it suggests to some an ontological dualism—that there are two opposing forces and moral principles, God and Satan, beyond the created order. That threatens monotheism. And, again, the theory has been seen as suggesting that man is essentially innocent. Sin is not his fault, finally, but the work of evil spirits who have influenced him. If Satan and the demons were eliminated, human beings would be both free and good. As a result, the rationalism of the medieval scholastics sought a better explanation of the saving effect of the death of Jesus. The search was fulfilled in the impeccable logic of Anselm of Canterbury (1033-1109) who followed his mentor, Augustine, in seeking understanding for his faith (*credo ut intelligam*). He wrote a treatise entitled *Cur deus-homo*? (*Why Did God Become Man?*), which propounded a new theory of the atonement and supplied a satisfying rationale for the whole sacramental system.

Without using the concrete language of the Bible and Christian theology, Anselm described the hopeless condition of mankind and the consequent necessity of the incarnation and death of Jesus Christ both to satisfy the justice of God and to provide the merit required for human redemption. Logic, law, and feudalism were the controlling principles of his argument. Man, he said, has sinned by failing to render to God his due, which is absolute righteousness. The just penalty is death unless satisfaction can be made. Satisfaction is impossible by serf-like man, who is and has nothing that is not already the property of his liege lord, the sovereign God. The only possible remedy would be for satisfaction to be paid by a third party, one who is both the man who must make satisfaction and the God who alone is able to do so. However, even such a possible God-man would have to go beyond the perfect obedience which even he would owe; the God-man would have to accept death, the penalty for sin which was not due him. By dying voluntarily the God-man, being infinite in nature, could be justly given an infinite reward by God. The God-man could then give ample grace to his fellow men, having satisfied the required justice of God. That, taught Anselm, is precisely why God joined himself to mankind in Jesus Christ and then died undeservedly on the cross.

The "satisfaction theory" met the need for a rational explanation of the efficacy of the death of Jesus Christ. It demonstrated the source of the grace conveyed to the believer through the sacraments. An inexhaustable reservoir of grace is available, added to constantly by the blood of the saints and martyrs as well as by the repetition of the sacrifice of Christ in the eucharist. That grace, like life-giving water from mountain sources, flows through the aqueduct of the Gospel to the Church. The Church in turn dispenses the grace through the seven sacraments to the faithful.

The Power of the Church

Anselm's theory received widespread acceptance and soon became the dominant explanation for the necessity of the cross and the basis of the sacrament throughout Western Christendom. Even the rise of Protestantism, with its rejection of the sacramental system, did not disturb the concept except that the Reformers insisted that the grace provided by Christ's death is received by faith rather than through sacramental mediation.

The claim that the Church is "the ark of salvation" now stood on more secure conceptual grounds. What greater power on earth could be imagined than that this institution, by the will and gift of God, possesses indeed the means of redemption from sin and death, holding in the mortal hands of its hierarchy of priests the very keys of the Kingdom of Heaven? Earthly kingdoms and empires paled into insignificance in comparison. In the famous words of Pope Innocent III, God has set royal power and pontifical authority on the earth just as he created the moon and the sun in the heavens. "The moon derives her light from the sun, and is in truth inferior to the sun in both size and quality, in position as well as effect. In the same way the royal power derives its dignity from the pontifical authority . . . . "

That power was regularly exercised in the Middle Ages and since, frequently with devastating consequences. The people, from royalty to peasant, were forced to accept the direction and succor of the clergy, from the cradle to the grave. The Church developed two especially effective means of personal and social control. First there was excommunication. If anyone dared to defy or avoid the mandates of the clergy, he could be cut off from the sacraments and thereby left potentially to suffer the unimaginable pangs of eternal punishment. That condition was graphically portrayed in the sermons, dramas, and art of the Middle Ages. In addition, the Church sometimes threatened to use the interdict, the legal instrument that permitted a whole city, province, or nation to be denied the benefits of grace. Such power could foment revolt by a frightened people or destroy the legitimacy of king or emperor.

Few scenes in history depict more graphically the power of the medieval Church as the ark of salvation than the penitent submission of the Emperor Henry IV in the snows of Canossa in January, 1077. Henry had defied Pope Gregory VII, known as Hildebrand, over the question of lay investiture—whether kings could appoint church officials without the approval of the papacy. Hildebrand excommunicated Henry and in effect laid the Empire under the interdict. Facing deposition, Henry went humbly to meet the Pope at a castle in Tuscany, begging as a barefooted penitent in the snow for three days before receiving forgiveness and restoration.

V.
VARIETIES OF MEDIEVAL PHILOSOPHY AND THEOLOGY

Chapter 14

The Rise of Scholasticism

In the year 640, the great library at Alexandria was burned, and much of the stored-up knowledge painstakingly acquired during the classical age was irretrievably lost. The fire was a fitting symbol of the greater conflagration that was engulfing the West. Invaded and occupied by barbarians, confronted in the south and west by a powerful and hostile Islamic culture, and at odds with the Eastern Empire over religious and political matters, the inhabitants of Europe all but lost the classical culture which had been born in Greece and spread over much of the known world by Rome.

Throughout the centuries that followed the fall of Rome, the Church was, as we have seen, the most important source of stability, and the remnants of ancient learning that had survived were channeled through her institutions. Those remnants were few enough. Plato was known directly only through the *Timaeus,* and Aristotle through works on logic. The influence of Platonic and Neoplatonic thought on the early fathers of the Church, and especially on Augustine, had, however, been profound, and so it is not surprising that Plato's philosophy almost completely eclipsed Aristotle's as a foundation for the development of Christian theology and philosophy.

Several works produced during the death struggles of the old Western Empire assumed an importance in the cultural drought of the so-called "dark ages" that, thoughtful as they were, they might not have achieved in another age. The writings of the Pseudo Dionysius and Boethius, which will be discussed in the next chapter, were widely read, and when scholarly activity began to get a new foothold in Europe, they were favored materials for study and commentary.

Between the fall of Rome and the establishment of the Frankish Empire, popular education declined almost to the vanishing point. Literacy became increasingly rare, and the few schools that survived the centuries of barbarian invasion and social and economic upheaval taught little more than a smattering of reading, writing, religion, and Latin.

With the consolidation of Charlemagne's power, however, there grew up a sufficiently peaceful and well-ordered society to permit the Emperor to turn his attention to the cultivation of long neglected arts.

He saw clearly that the grand scheme he envisioned for a new age of learning would require the establishment of schools. Unfortunately, he could not find in all the length and breadth of the kingdom of the Franks the sort of educated men he needed for his purpose. Undaunted, he set about to import them. Two of his most successful pioneers in the enterprise came from Italy. Peter of Pisa, a well-known scholar, came to the capital at Aix-la-Chapelle, and Charlemagne himself studied Latin grammar with him. Paulus Diaconus (Paul Warnefridi) was an unusual prize for another reason. He knew some Greek. His attachment to the court came about through a chance encounter with the Emperor. At the age of about sixty, Paul was at the Benedictine house of Monte Cassino. When Charles visited Rome in 782, the Deacon interceded with him on behalf of his brother Arichis, who had been carried off to France a few years earlier as a prisoner of war. The Emperor arranged for him to be set free and, impressed with Paul's scholarly attainments, offered him employment. Paul accepted and was installed as a teacher of Greek in the Palace School.

That school was an older Merovingian institution, but it was in the process of reorganization by a talented English educator named Alcuin. A native of York (Eboracum), he had acquired an education that it would have been almost impossible for him to get on the Continent. English scholarship had taken a turn for the better as early as 669, when a Greek Monk called Theodore of Tarsus had arrived to take office as Archbishop of Canterbury. Together with a cleric named Hadrian, he had contributed heavily to the development of the cathedral school and added extensively to the holdings of its library. One Aldhelm, who studied under Theodore and Hadrian, carried on their work as abbot of the monastery of Malmesbury, in Wiltshire, of which he was the founder. Similar institutions were founded at Wearmouth and Jarrow by Benedict Biscop. That intellectual climate had produced men like "The Venerable Bede" (c. 673-735). Wearmouth and Jarrow were actually a single monastery, though they were five or six miles apart, and Bede, with his principal quarters at Jarrow, spent his entire life, from the age of seven on, in the establishment, with the exception of brief visits to other localities. His most important work, the *Ecclesiastical History of the English Nation,* was made possible by the fine library developed by Biscop. A student of Bede's, Egbert, became Archbishop of York, and made the cathedral school there the finest in England. It was there, in his native city, that Alcuin got his early education.

On a trip to Rome with his master Aelbert in search of manuscripts, he met Charlemagne and apparently made a favorable impression on him. Certainly his scholarship had earned him a good reputation with his teachers, for when Aelbert became Archbishop of York in 766 or 767, Alcuin was made head of the episcopal school.

In 780 or 781, Alcuin, on an errand to Rome at the behest of Aelbert, met Charlemagne again at Parma, and the Emperor asked him to enter his service. After obtaining the permission of his ecclesiastical superiors and the English King, Alcuin accepted the invitation. He was given two abbeys to govern, but Charles' real interest in him was as an educator. About a year after his arrival, he was made head of the Palace School. The institution had previously been used for training aristocratic youngsters of the court in knightly pursuits. Charles wanted to draw from a broader circle both secular and clerical, and to emphasize the kind of scholarly activity that was so much in need of revival. Alcuin proved to be the best possible man he could have selected for the task. He was not an original thinker but he was familiar with a wide range of Latin literature, and he was a great teacher.

In a letter to Charles from the abbey of St. Martin of Tours, to which he retired in his latter years, he described the sort of teaching he had given to the young people who had been in his charge. Centuries later Henry Wadsworth Longfellow in his narrative poem "Emma and Eginhard" would use Alcuin's own metaphors faithfully in describing the range of education in the Palace School and the other institutions established by Charlemagne:

> When Alcuin taught the sons of Charlemagne,
> In the free schools of Aix, how kings should reign,
> And with them taught the children of the poor
> How subjects should be patient and endure,
> He touched the lips of some, as best befit,
> With honey from the hives of holy writ;
> Others intoxicated with the wine
> Of ancient history, sweet but less divine,
> Some with the wholesome fruits of grammar fed;
> Others with mysteries of the stars o'erhead,
> That hang suspended in the vaulted sky,
> Like lamps in some fair palace vast and high.

The Palace or Palatine School remained at Charlemagne's capital, Aix-la-Chapelle, until the reign of Charles the Bald, when it was removed to Paris, where it became one of several establishments which later resulted in the founding of the University of Paris. As for Alcuin, his usefulness did not end with his semi-retirement. At Tours, he worked to build up the library of the abbey by importing manuscripts from York and was active in efforts to improve the techniques used in copying literary works. His name is associated with the production of the version of the Vulgate Scriptures known as the "Alcuinian Revision."

The Carolingian revival saw the establishment of other schools which were to play an important role in the history of Western thought. Most of these were associated with cathedrals or monasteries and accepted both clerical and lay students. The curriculum, especially for priestly scholars, was demanding. In addition to theology and exegesis, it covered the seven liberal arts, encompassing the Trivium composed of grammar (which included literature), rhetoric, and dialectic—and the Quadrivium—comprising arithmetic, geometry, astronomy, and music.

The instruction was not calculated to cultivate highly original thought, but it did serve to rekindle the love of learning in its recipients, and it produced some noteworthy scholars. One of these, Rabanus Maurus, a pupil of Alcuin, taught at the monastery of Fulda and became its abbot in 822. A quarter of a century later, he was made Archbishop of Mainz. A strong advocate of an educated clergy, he wrote a three-volume work entitled *De Institutione Clericorum* and an encyclopedia, *De rerum naturis,* based on a similar work by Isidore of Seville, written more than two centuries earlier.

One happy result of the scholarly activity of the Carolingian schools was the polishing of the Latin language as a literary instrument to a point of excellence it had lacked since the decline of the classical culture. Already the universal language of the Church in the West, it became, by common consent, the prescribed medium for the transmission of culture. If most of the savants who used it contributed little that was new to the world's store of knowledge, they at least wrote with elegance and discipline.

John Scotus Eriugena

One really original thinker came out of the scholarly activity of the period, interestingly enough, not as a product of the educational system founded by Charles, or even of the English cathedral schools, but rather of a monastic system that had brought the light of classical learning to the last island outpost of European culture.

In 432, a British-born priest named Patricius, or Patrick, who had in his youth been a slave in Ireland, had returned to that country and, in a remarkably short time, transformed in a tiny Christian community into an ecclesiastical structure which was to make Ireland one of the most staunchly Catholic countries in the West. Central to the organization of the Irish church was a network of monasteries where Celtic scholars, drawing on the talents their pagan forbears had displayed as druids, *filid,* and bards, applied those abilities to Christian educational activity. John Scotus Eriugena (c. 810-877) was one of those Irishmen. The word "Scotus" does not suggest any connection with Scotland, for it was a term originally applied to the Irish, and "Eriugena" clearly indicated his origin among the people of Eriu, a patron goddess of Ireland.

Greek had been preserved in the Irish monasteries to a far greater extent than was the case in the other western lands, and John Scotus probably owed his unusual mastery of the language to an early education in one of those institutions. Some time before the year 850, Charles the Bald, who became King of the Western Franks in 843, invited him to France to teach at the Palatine School. It is not certain whether he was an ordained clergyman, and, indeed, the details of his career are remarkably obscure.

It is known that Hincmar, Bishop of Reims, asked for his services in the arbitration of a dispute about predestination. His resultant work, *De praedestinatione,* was an attempt to establish a position that, while acknowledging the absolute sovereignty of God, would allow a real place for freedom of the human will. He went so far in the latter direction as to come under suspicion of Pelagianism, and he ran into further difficulties with his views concerning the Eucharist. His work maintaining that the body and blood of Christ are not really present in the consecrated bread and wine was burned, and no copy of it is known to exist.

Frustrated by his foray into theology, John Scotus turned to other activities. Some years earlier, Louis the Fair had acquired a copy of the works of the Pseudo-Dionysius, but, as they were in Greek, the scholars of Paris were unable to read them. In 858, Charles the Bald asked John Scotus to translate them into Latin. John complied with his request, provided commentaries on the writings, and translated and commented on a number of works of other authors.

Between 862 and 870 or thereabouts, he wrote his greatest work, *De divisione naturae,* expounding a philosophy which sought to synthesize the Neoplatonic world view of many of the writers whose works he had been translating with the Christian faith in which he had been reared. The work took the form of five books, written in the form of a dialogue between a *Magister* and a *Discipulus* concerning Nature, which he defined as the totality of "things that are" and "things that are not." The "things that are not" are not absolute nothingness. They may be distinguished from the "things that are" by any of several criteria. Those which transcend the intellect, those which are merely potential as opposed to actual, and those which are subject to change and dissolution "are not," and the same may be said of sinful human nature. The "things that are" include regenerate human beings and things which are comprehended by the intellect alone.

Nature, as comprising both these categories of reality, may be considered in four categories: Nature that creates and is not created, Nature that is created and creates, Nature that is created and does not create, and Nature that neither creates nor is created.

Nature that creates and is not created is the uncaused cause, God. As such, he is "beyond being" and must be described both affirmatively and negatively. He may, for instance, be called "goodness," but properly he is not goodness, for evil is opposed to goodness; therefore, he is supergood, more than good." In the same way essence, truth, wisdom, eternity, and the like are countered by their denials and the affirmative and negative propositions resolved dialectically by adding the prefix "super" to each term. Words applicable to creatures are, then, applied to God *metaphorice* or *translative*. Though propositions like "God is super-wisdom" have an affirmative character, their negativity is also preserved in the fact that "super" in this connotation has no idea in our minds corresponding to it. God is, as John Scotus was at pains to point out, not less than any of these predicates as they would be applied to creatures, but more. Moreover all the categories applicable to material objects, such as quantity, are to be ruled out in attempts to describe God, and even such terms as "substance" and "relation" can only be used in the figurative manner prescribed by John's dialectic.

How, then, if categories such as motion must be denied of God, can he be the creator of the world? Is not the concept of "creating" unintelligible apart from motion? We cannot say that God *was* before he made all things, for if that were the case, "he would have been subject to the accident of making all things," in which case, "we would understand motion and time in him. God and his making, then, are not two things, but one, and when we speak of God as the maker of things, we mean 'that God is in all things, that is, subsists as the essence of all things.' "

But how does God perform this eternal act of creation? John's answer may be found in his treatment of the second division, "Nature that creates and is created." This designates the "primordial causes," the archetypes, the *rationes,* the "ideas" or "forms" of Greek philosophy. These archetypes exist eternally in the Logos, and the eternal begetting of the Son by the Father in some sense "creates" the ideas which are eternally in the Word. The primordial causes, in turn, are creative in that they provide the essences that particular objects imitate or in which they participate. As seen by us, the archetypes constitute a plurality, but, as existing in the Logos, they are one.

The third division, "Nature that is created and does not create," comprises the particular items that constitute the world of nature. In defining the way in which it is "created", John found himself torn between his Neoplatonic leaning toward a theory of emanation and the Christian affirmation that the world was made *ex nihilo.* Somewhat shakily from a standpoint of Christian orthodoxy, he reasoned that God as revealed by the negative way is beyond all categories and is therefore the "nothing" out of which all things are created. In view of the fact that the creative process—the *Theophania,* the manifestation of God in the world—is eternal, the account of the creation in the Book of Genesis must be seen as allegorical. As the whole of nature is really a manifestation of God, it may be said that he is perpetually creating himself, becoming self-conscious in the *rationes* and producing things in the world of nature which have no effects beyond themselves and so do not create.

Finally, "Nature that neither creates nor is created" refers to that aspect of Neoplatonism under which all things return to God. According to John Scotus, "the end of the whole movement is in its beginning, since it is terminated by no other end than by its principle, from which its movement begins and to which it constantly desires to return, that it may attain rest therein." Though all appearances in the natural world are mutable and in time disappear, substance is eternal and substantially the world finds its end "by its return to the *rationes* from which it proceeds."

To avoid any suspicion that he might be harboring the heretical notion that individual human identities are finally annihilated by being absorbed into the divine nature, John Scotus sought to make it clear that on this point his Neoplatonic world view was not incompatible with Christian orthodoxy. Though ultimately the fourth stage posits a condition in which "nothing will exist but God alone" the return of human nature to the divine is actually a glorification of that nature rather than a loss of it. John Scotus maintained that all human beings will ultimately reunite with God, though some attain a higher degree of union than others through the *deificatio* bestowed upon them by God through grace. He had some difficulty in accounting for the Christian view of eternal punishment. It cannot be administered to human beings or to fallen angels, for all Nature must return to God. But the perverse will of a created being is not, strictly speaking, a part of Nature and if God prevents the will from attaching itself to those things which it has perversely desired, that is, in Scotus' view, sufficiently punitive to preserve orthodoxy while allowing a universalist view of salvation.

The Question of Universals

The great days of the Carolingian Revival may have led many scholars of the period to embrace an ill-founded optimism. The Dark Ages were not at an end. The success of Charlemagne's educational enterprise was intimately linked with his ability to maintain a centralized government bearing some resemblance to that of the Roman Empire, and his successors were unable to match his political and military prowess. The promise of a united Western Christendom was lost in the division of Europe among princes and nobles to whom the institutions of feudalism were more congenial than those of empire. Racked by civil wars and threatened from without by Norsemen. Mongols, and Saracens, Charlemagne's former domain fell apart. The political disorder of the period was accompanied by a decline in the quality of clerical and monastic life, and the flowering of scholarship, begun so auspiciously in the ninth century, was brought to a halt. A partial revival was begun in 910, with the establishment of the Monastery of Cluny by William the Pious, Count of Auvergne and Duke of Guienne, but the effects of the Cluniac reforms were not initially widespread enough to overcome the counterforces of decay.

The ensuing centuries were not, however, entirely sterile. If the questions dealt with by the philosophically-minded clergy were not comprehensive, they were, nevertheless, significant, the most absorbing by far being the problem of universals.

Porphyry had succinctly set the stage for the discussion. As quoted by Boethius in his commentary on the *Isagoge,* he had said, "At present I shall refuse to say concerning genera and species whether they subsist or whether they are placed in the naked understandings alone or whether subsisting they are corporeal or incorporeal, and whether they are separated from sensibles or placed in sensibles and in accord with them."

Boethius had himself suggested a solution to the problem. We may, he said, put two ideas together in the mind to form a third one that has no counterpart in external reality. Thus, we may by composition create in imagination a variety of fanciful objects synthesized from existing elements. Such constructions, if not imitative of objects found in nature, are "false." On the other hand, we may by abstraction arrive at an idea such as "line" or "circle" which has no counterpart in nature but is nevertheless "true." Ideas of genera and species, he held, are of this sort. They are abstracted from individual objects. They "are in individuals, but, as thought, are universals."

Though this suggestion, having its origins in Aristotle, was one which would ultimately gain wide acceptance, the initial reaction to the question when it became the central preoccupation of European scholarship was far more Platonic. Known to history as "exaggerated realists" because of their insistence that universals have a greater degree of reality than particulars, a number of thinkers maintained that individual objects—men, stars, or tables—are no more than accidental modifications of universal substances that exist outside the mind precisely as they are thought. Odo of Tournai (died 1113), for instance, said that no new substance is created when a baby is conceived and born. God simply introduces a new property in a substance already existent. Logically and temporally, then, the universal is prior to the particular thing—*universalia ante rem.* This view proved to be convenient for him and for other realists in providing a rational ground for a number of doctrines of the Church. If, for instance, the sin of Adam and Eve infected an entire substance of humanity of which all men and women are merely manifestations, the Christian account of original sin is not difficult to understand. St. Anselm (1033-1109)—about whom more will be said in Chapter 15—though the evidence is inconclusive that he could properly be considered an exaggerated realist, was clearly appealing for a recognition of the reality of universals when he said, "He who does not understand how many men are specifically only one man cannot understand that several persons, each one of which is God, are only one God."

William of Champeaux (1079-1120) carried the realists' position to its logical limit when he taught at the Cathedral School of Paris that the *whole* of the essential nature involved in a universal is at the same time present in each of the particulars that are accidental modifications of that universal. Peter Abelard (1079-1142), who heard William's Paris lectures, objected that if the whole of the human species is present in Socrates when Socrates is in Rome and at the same time in Plato when Plato is in Athens, then Socrates must be Plato and simultaneously be in Rome and in Athens. This, Abelard maintained, is nonsense, and even worse, it leads inevitably to pantheism, in which all individual identities are swallowed up in the one divine substance. On considering such objections, William dropped his identity theory in favor of one of "indifferentism." The essence of two members of a species, he said, is not the same, but is "like." Socrates and Plato are, thus, the same thing not essentially, but "indifferently."

At the opposite pole from the exaggerated realists were the nominalists, who denied that universals have any reality other than as words. Roscellinus (1050-1125), a native of Compiegne, taught in his native city, in Taches, and in Besançon, and he traveled in France, England, and Italy. We have none of his writings except for a letter to Abelard, but from reports of other writers, he maintained that a universal term like "man" is nothing more than a name *(nomen)* or an "emission of the voice" *(flatus vocis)*. All discussions about universals are, then, discussions about words.

The extent to which Roscellinus was a thoroughgoing nominalist is open to question in view of the secondary nature of our sources of information about his thought, but it is a matter of record that he was sufficiently opposed to the realists' position to suggest that the three persons of the Trinity could properly be called three gods, in view of the fact that their unity is only by virtue of a word. This position led to his condemnation in 1092 by a council at Soissons and to his retraction of the tritheistic statement to avoid excommunication.

It was evident that the nominalists' position if carried to its limit, would threaten not only the doctrine of the Trinity but a number of other concepts which were central to the faith of the medieval Church. The fall of the human race in Adam, its redemption in Christ, the real presence of Christ in the elements of the Eucharist and the idea of the Church as his body, all of these would lose much of their force and, perhaps, even their intelligibility if particular things were thought to be the only reality and universals merely names existing after things *(post rem)*.

The need for a position which would avoid the pitfalls both of exaggerated realism and of extreme nominalism seemed evident not merely on theological grounds, but for more general reasons. After all, most human discourse depends on the recognition of real resemblances among objects given common names, and so the words used to classify them, while more or less arbitrarily selected, emphasize some qualities at the expense of others in pointing to those real resemblances. For instance, the attributes which are shared by dogs and cats are ignored in determining which animals shall be called dogs and which cats. They come into play only as they relate to larger groups, mammals, for instance, to which both dogs and cats must be assigned. It would seem somewhat strained to maintain that the process of classification is wholly arbitrary—that is, that it is the result of the application of names by something like random pointing. Real resemblance, in short, must be taken into account, and it appeared to some critics that neither the realists nor the nominalists had provided a satisfactory account of the way in which universals can account for real resemblance and at the same time allow for the uniqueness of individual objects.

Peter Abelard

Perhaps the most influential attempt to provide a solution to the problem was that suggested by the theologian and philosopher Peter

Abelard, a man whose personal history has been a subject of as much interest as his thought. He was born in Brittany, near Nantes, in 1079, the son of a nobleman. His father wanted him to become a soldier, but the son preferred a scholarly career. He studied logic at Loches and then went to Paris, where he acquired a good perspective on the dispute over universals by studying with both Roscellinus and William of Champeaux. He taught logic for one or two years in Brittany, but the lure of disputation brought him back to Paris, where he devoted some effort to challenging William's views. "By the most patent arguments," he recounted later, "I compelled him to change his opinion; indeed to abandon it," a claim well attested by William's relinquishment of the identity theory in favor of indifferentism. Abelard suspected, perhaps not altogether fairly, that the new position was no more than a subterfuge to enable William to maintain that Plato and Socrates are not the same thing, while still maintaining that they really are. At any rate, William was probably not amused, and he had even less cause to be when Abelard after another absence from Paris, in the course of which he got embroiled in a dispute with the masters at the theological school at Laon, returned to Paris and challenged William's influence with his students by setting up his own classes at Notre Dame.

In Paris, he was retained by Fulbert, a canon of Notre Dame, to instruct his niece, an accomplished young woman named Héloïse, and one of the celebrated love stories in history was under way. Their affair produced a child, and Fulbert insisted on their marriage. A wedding did take place, but Héloïse, fearful that her husband's career would be impeded by their union, insisted that it be kept secret. Fulbert, his desire for proper appearances thwarted, hired a gang of ruffians to set on Abelard and emasculate him. Héloïse entered a convent, and Abelard went to the monastery of St. Denis, where his disputatious nature got him into further trouble. His first theological book, *De Unitate et Trinitate divina,* was condemned by the council of Soissons in 1121, and he was ordered to retire to St. Médard. On his return to St. Denis, he plunged into another dispute. "Denis" is the French version of the name "Dionysius," and the monks at the monastery claimed as their patron Dionysus the Areopagite. That claim, Abelard assured them, would not hold water. The "St. Denis" of their devotion could not be the convert of St. Paul.

Leaving St. Denis, he founded the school of Le Paraclet, near Nogent-sur-Seine, but left there to become Abbot of St. Gildas de Ruys in Brittany. There he attempted to bring under control a community of wayward monks, who responded to his efforts by trying to murder him.

For some thirteen years after 1136, he taught at Ste. Genevieve in Paris, but this relatively peaceful interlude was brought to an end by St. Bernard of Clairvaux, who accused him of heresy. In 1141, the Council of Sens condemned his views, and he was enjoined not to lecture any more. He set out for Rome to appeal to Pope Innocent II, but was dissuaded from the effort by Peter of Cluny. His stormy life came to an end at the Priory of St. Marcel, near Chalon-sur-Saone, on April 21, 1142.

Abelard's position on universals differed so sharply from that of the exaggerated realists that John of Salisbury called him a nominalist. Actually, he was proposing a position that has come to be known as "conceptualism" or "moderate realism." The feature of his philosophy responsible for the charge of nominalism is his contention that the term "universal" is applicable not to things but to words, a position that would seem to place him in the *post rem* camp. Things, he maintained, "can not be called universals, taken either singly or collectively, because they are not predicated of many."

"Just as, therefore, certain words are called appellative by grammarians and certain nouns proper," he said, "so certain simple words are called by dialecticians *universals,* certain words *particulars,* that is, individuals. A *universal* word, however, is one which is apt by its invention to be predicated singly of many, as this noun *man* which is conjoinable with the particular names of men according to the nature of the subject things on which it is imposed. A *particular word* is one which is predicable of only one, as *Socrates* when it is taken as the name of only one."

Abelard took pains to make it clear, however, that he was considering a word not merely as a *flatus vocis* but as something having logical significance. It is the meaning and not the sound or the appearance of the word which is important. In the case of a universal word, the meaning lies in a likeness in certain individuals which induces the mind to conceive "a common and confused image of many things," a "certain figure" arising in the mind so related to the particular objects "that it is common to all and proper to none."

These "confused images" are not arbitrarily formed. They are concepts formed by abstracting from individuals those properties by virtue of which we can classify those individuals under a common name. The conception of an individual such as "Socrates" is clear. That of a universal such as "man" is "confused" which is not to say that we do not know what we mean by it, but only that the process of abstraction robs it of the clarity of particularity.

Universals as conceptions, then, exist in the mind *post rem,* but if we apply the universal term "man" to Socrates or Plato or John Smith, we are referring to properties really present in each of these individuals by virtue of which they resemble one another. Abelard's formula, then, turns out to be not one of mere nominalism, but one which closely resembles the position taken centuries earlier by Aristotle. The universal is not a thing in itself. It is rather *in* a thing which can be thought of as a member of a class—*universalia in re*.

Other Scholastics

Abelard's view of universals found an echo in the thought of some of his contemporaries, an indication that although Aristotle's works were not generally accessible to scholars in the West, enough of his ideas had filtered down through the dominant Platonism to provide a leaven for the great changes that would come with the rediscovery of the main body of his philosophy. When Aristotle's *Analytics, Topics,* and *Fallacies* first became available in Latin translations in 1128, they excited keen interest in the School of Chartres, where they modified the dominant Platonism. The Abbey School of St. Victor, near Paris, acquired William of Champeaux after he was beaten in disputation by Abelard and it is probable that the doctrine he taught there was the one to which he had been forced to retreat when his exaggerated realism became untenable. The view of universals taken by Hugh of St. Victor (1096-1141) was very close to that advanced by Abelard. Peter Lombard (died 1164), educated at the School, achieved lasting fame, not so much for any contribution he may have made to the discussion of universals as for his *Sentences,* the *Libri quatro sententiarum,* which provided the basis for theological education for the remainder of the Middle Ages. The work appeared in four books, the first dealing with God, the second creatures, the third the Incarnation and Redemption and the virtues, and the fourth the seven sacraments of the Church and final things.

John of Salisbury (ca. 1115-1180) was an Englishman who heard Abelard's lectures in Paris and became a stout critic of the Scholasticism of his day. He served as secretary to Archbishop Theobald of Canterbury and later to St. Thomas à Becket. In 1166, he became Bishop of Chartres. He deplored the amount of time that had been wasted in discussion of the problem of universals. It is clear, he maintained, that the position of the exaggerated realists is wrong, and it is a waste of time to try to find species and genera outside of particulars insofar as their concrete existence is concerned. To be sure, they exist as universals in the mind, but only as abstractions from things.

John also made an important contribution to political theory in his *Polycraticus*. In it, he advocated the independence of the Church from the state, expressing a conviction no doubt strengthened by his association with Becket. Going farther, though, he maintained that princes are subject to natural law and that the question as to whether a ruler is truly a prince or a tyrant is dependent on whether the positive laws he promulgates are or are not in accordance with natural law and natural justice. In this, he was echoing the classical tradition appealed to a century earlier by one Manegold of Lautenbach, who regarded the rightful authority of a prince as the result of a pact with his people and affirmed the right of the people to depose a ruler who becomes a tyrant. Both of these writers were among those who, in their searching criticism of the thought of the day, acting within a framework that set limits on the permissible range of thought, laid the groundwork for a later expansion of that range and ultimately for the tradition of intellectual freedom which was to become the most characteristic feature of Western culture.

Chapter 15

The Dominance of Platonism

The rise of Scholasticism demonstrated with unusual clarity the necessary symbiosis of religion and philosophy. The two represent quite different approaches to reality, of course, and the distinctions should not be denied or confused. Religion is essentially relation and practice, based on an assumed revelation. Philosophy is essentially reflection and judgment, based on assumptive reason. However, without reflection and judgment, relation and practice remain individual and passing experiences, devoid of evaluation, result, or continuity; and, without relation and practice, reflection and judgment remain groundless and diverse, failing to provide stability and morality. Thus, as we have attempted to show earlier and frequently, theology is the product of the application of reason to revelation, or the understanding and codification of religious experience. That is the work of scholars, and in the Middle Ages it is called Scholasticism.

Having filled the vacuum created by the collapse of Roman power and culture in the West, the Church faced the awesome task of preserving and transmitting the light and learning of antiquity, now in a distinctly Christian form. But Christian culture could hardly be preserved, much less successfully conveyed, without both institutional means and conceptual forms. The means were available, as we have seen, in the organizational structures that the Church had developed, especially in the hierarchy of priests and the communities of monks. The two were felicitously combined in the cathedral schools and, later, in the universities. The development of theology, and education in general, had been accomplished in the ancient Church mainly by bishops; now the task was carried forward for the most part by monastics.

However, the necessary conceptual forms needed to be brought to the surface, carefully examined, and constantly acknowledged. Ideology, perhaps especially as philosophy and theology, always has its assumptions, its fundamental and determinative substructures. As the Church began its educational work in the medieval period, bringing to an end the Dark Ages, many leaders recognized the prior necessity for clarity concerning those substructures or conceptual forms. They began to recognize that one set of assumptions, or underlying philosophy, had been serving the thought of the Church, at least in most cases, throughout its history. That philosophy was Platonism.

Platonism in the Early Church

The philosophy of Plato was prevalent in the theology of Christianity, especially in the West, from the first century until at least the thirteenth. We have seen its influencc, for example, in the logos theme of the Gospel of John; in the Christology of Irenaeus; in the theology of the Alexandrians, Clement and Origen; and, supremely, in the unparalleled synthesis provided by Augustine. However, one must keep in mind that Platonism constantly underwent change. Plato himself had a variety of antecedents in Socrates and several of the pre-Socratics. He modified his thought considerably during his long career, so much so that it is customary to speak of the early Plato and the late Plato. He died at about eighty years of age, in 347 B.C., and, fortunately, the full corpus of his writings was preserved. His school, the Academy, underwent a number of transformations as the centuries passed, surviving until it was closed, as a bastion of paganism, by the Emperor Justinian in A.D. 529. The last major form of Plato's thought in antiquity was Neoplatonism, based on the teachings of Plotinus and carried forward by Porphyry, Iamblicus, and Proclus, among others (cf. Chapter 6, above). Nevertheless, there was a continuity at the core so that the whole tradition may properly be called Platonism.

The question should be raised as to why Platonism was the overwhelming choice among the several philosophies available to the Fathers. Several reasons may be suggested. First, Platonic metaphysics appeared to be compatible with the biblical view that God is the eternal source of reality and virtue, dwelling in the realm of light and life far removed from the transitory world of shadows and decay. Second, the Platonic epistemology of recollection appealed to the Christian emphasis on meditation, prayer, and visions as both edifying to the spirit and enlightening to the mind. Again, the early Christian glorification of asceticism received strong support in Platonic otherworldliness. There is a fervent tendency toward ontological and moral dualism in both the philosophy and the religion, though it may be argued that dualism is ultimately incompatible with either. And, finally, the complex hierarchy of reality and virtue in Plato's philosophy provided an adaptable model for the organization of the Church as well as for a divine path for living.

Proclus and Boethius

Proclus was one of the last great Neoplatonic philosophiers of antiquity. Although he was not a Christian, his teachings show the modification of Platonic philosophy that had already begun in the presence of Christian theology. Furthermore, his ideas were literally borrowed to the point of plagiarism by the mysterious Dionysius, whose writings were to become very influential in the Christian theology of Maximus the Confessor, in the East, and, through John Scotus Erigena, in the West.

Proclus was born in 410, at Constantinople. He studied first at Alexandria and then at Athens under Plutarch and Syrianus, the *diodochi* (successors) of Plato in the ancient Academy. Later, Proclus himself became the *diadochus,* a position he maintained until his death in 485. It should be noted, therefore, that he was born twenty years before the death of Augustine of Hippo, the greatest of the Western Christian theologians, and that he died soon after the fall of the Western Empire, which itself marked the beginning of the Dark Ages in the West. However, Proclus lived in the East, at Constantinople and Athens, thereby escaping the epoch-making traumas of the West. He carried on the sophisticated thought of classical antiquity, disdaining the crude myths and narrow particularities of specific religions, including Christianity.

Proclus was primarily a systematizer, expositor, and commentator rather than an originator of new ideas. His major writings were commentaries on Plato's dialogues and on the scientific works of Aristotle; various treatises on mathematics and grammar; and an historically influential work entitled *Elements of Theology*. Through this literature he became the source of the Neoplatonism that was later diffused in Byzantine and Islamic cultures, and, through Latin translations, in the Scholastic theology of the West.

Although Proclus professed to teach no new ideas of his own but only to interpret those of Plato and Plotinus, he added significant analyses and direction to the philosophy of his mentors. Those very additions of interpretation were the factors that contributed decisively to later Christian theology, both in the East and in the West. Proclus was a convinced Platonist in that he believed that the real is the ideal, permanent realm of truth, beauty, and goodness, whereas the lower realm of flesh and time is unreal, transitory, and evil. Moreover, like Plato, he taught that human souls are native to the ideal world, temporarily imprisoned in the flesh but capable of ultimate elevation to their ethereal source. Following Plotinus and his sucessors in Neoplatonism, Proclus accepted the doctrine of ontological unity, encompassing the apparent dualism of Plato in a larger wholeness of Being that included, by emanation, the procession of the One to the Many and the return of the Many to the One. Whereas Plato had seen the function of love (Eros) as the yearning of the lower for the higher, Plotinus had interpreted love as both the upward desire of the lower for the higher and the downward care of the higher for the lower. Proclus accepted both insights and went further. He taught that the upward desire and the downward care are intrinsic aspects of the whole, unified reality, "an eros chain" (*erotike seira*) that links the One to the Many even as the One goes out to the other and returns to itself.

Proclus discussed this suggestive ontology in great detail especially as it is related to the human condition and the way of salvation. The soul may return to its source, he taught, by first following the dictum of Socrates: "Know thyself." To know the soul is to know God. That goal is reached by three steps: purification, illumination, and union (*katharsis, ellampsis, enosis*). Thus Proclus supplied the philosophical foundation for medieval Christian mysticism.

Anicius Manlius Severinus Boethius was born in Rome in 480, five years before the death of Proclus in Athens and immediately after the deposition of the last Western Roman Emperor and the beginning of the barbarian hegemony in the West. He belonged to a prominent Christian family, the Anicii, one of whose members had served as Emperor in 472. His father, who was consul in 487, died while Boethius was very young, but the youth was adopted by a leading senator, Symmachus, whose daughter, Rusticiana, later became his wife. Boethius was a favorite of Theodoric, the Ostrogoth king who ruled from Ravenna, and he served in several high administrative positions, including that of *magister ovviciorum* (head of all civil services). However, in 522 he was accused of conspiracy with the Emperor Justin I against Theodoric, who was actually *exarch* in the West under the aegis of the old empire now centered in Constantinople, the "new Rome." Boethius was imprisoned in Pavia, where he was finally tortured and executed in 524.

Boethius was a remarkable scholar as well as a leading statesman. He knew both Latin and Greek and thus was able to help transmit the culture of antiquity into the vernacular of the West during the Middle Ages. His subtle theological treatises included treatments of the dogma of the Trinity and against the heresies of Nestorius and Eutyches. He contributed to later medieval education by writings on the Quadrivium: arithmetic, geometry, music, and astonomy. He composed a large number of works on logic, most notably a Latin translation of Porphyry's *Isagoge,* an introduction to Artistotle's *Categories*. His philosophical writings reveal the strong influence of Aristotle and Cicero as well as the Neoplatonism of Plotinus and Porphyry, an influence that was to leave its mark on the Scholasticism to come.

Nevertheless, the book of Boethius that was to achieve the most permanent place in the history of culture is *The Consolation of Philosophy*.

It was composed during his final days in prison as he endured suffering and faced death. Strangely, the book does not appeal to the Christian faith for courage and hope, even though Boethius was a Christian. Rather, *The Consolation* reveals a calm and rational resignation, supplied by the inspiration of Lady Philosophy. Boethius found peace and consolation by the ministrations of inward wisdom and spiritual strength. He did not reject the life of power and fame and he did not abandon his faith in the Christian God; but he turned inward for a vision of meaning and value that sustained him in spite of the vicissitudes of passing circumstances.

Thus Proclus and Boethius, the one a sophisticated pagan of the East and the other a scholarly Christian of the West, preserved and developed the highest wisdom to be found in ancient classical culture. Their influence was to be decisive in the new age, the Middle Ages, that was about to dawn in the West.

The Pseudo-Dionysius

Near the beginning of the sixth century there appeared in the East a group of writings that claimed to have been written by Dionysius the Areopagite, a convert of the Apostle Paul in Athens near the middle of the first century (cf. Acts 17:34). There were four treatises and ten letters. The treatises are entitled *On the Heavenly Hierarchy, On the Ecclesiastical Heirarchy, On the Divine Names,* and *On the Mystical Theology*. The letters were addressed to various early Christians, including Timothy and the Apostle John. The earliest known reference to the writings was by the Monophysite Severus, Patriarch of Antioch from 512 to 518. They were also quoted by Monophysites at a council in Constantinople in 533, where some questioned their authenticity. Nevertheless, they were soon widely accepted and, in the following century, Maximus the Confessor wrote a commentary on them. After that they were revered as practically canonical, having been composed, it was believed, by a disciple of the great Apostle Paul.

The later fate of the Dionysian documents illustrates the development and significance of the literary criticism that arose during the Renaissance and has continued to serve such a useful function ever since. The great humanist scholar, Lorenzo Valla (1407-1457) of Rome and Florence, demonstrated the dependence of the documents upon the earlier works of Proclus. (It should be remembered that Valla also exposed the fraudulent claims of the famous *Donation of Constantine*. See chapter 13.) His opinion was later supported by Erasmus. Furthermore, nineteenth century scholars produced conclusive evidence that large sections of the treatises were lifted almost verbatim from Proclus. J. Stiglmayr even argued that Dionysius was in fact the Patriarch of Antioch, Severus himself; and only recently it has been noted that Dionysius anachronistically quoted from "the divine Ignatius," Bishop of Antioch in the second century. Hence, one now speaks of the Pseudo-Dionysius.

In spite of their false attribution, however, the Pseudo-Dionysian materials have exerted immense significance in subsequent theology. They were a primary channel for the flow of the Neoplatonism of Plotinus and Proclus into the religious ideas and practices of the West, especially through the Latin translation by John Scotus Eriugina during the Carolingian revival. After that they helped to establish the predominance of Plato in medieval theology until the thirteenth century.

Like Plato, Dionysius believed that this world is only a pale, passing reflection of the glorious and eternal world above. Like Plotinus, he viewed all things as flowing forth from the infinite source of all being, emanating from the One and returning to the One. And, like Proclus, he emphasized both the power of the love (Eros) that caused the downward reach of Being and the upward return of multiplicity, binding all reality into a unity. However Dionysius adapted this Platonic ontology to Christian nomenclature and interpretation, merging philosophical speculation and theological revelation. His underlying concern was the saving return of fallen humanity to God and he conceived that return in terms of the final goal of deification (*theosis*).

The two treatises, *On the Heavenly Hierarchy* and *On the Ecclesiastical Hierarchy,* form a kind of mirror image of each other, together comprising a Christian "great chain of being." The categories of heaven are the archetypes of the Church. God is totally unknowable and indescribable, but the Scriptures reveal that with God in heaven there are three triads of created servants: seraphim, cherubim, thrones; dominions, powers, authorities; principalities, archangels, angels. In like manner, the Church is composed of three orders of clergy: bishops, priests, deacons. It has three types of laity: monks, baptized Christians, catechumens. And it possesses and dispenses three visible means of grace: baptism, eucharist, chrism. Dionysius went to great lengths to declare the absolute otherness of God. He developed what has been called a negative theology (*via negativa*), denying the possibility of any adequate definition or description of God. Yet he gloried in God's provision of a way up, a way of union: the linear way of observing the world; the spiral way of dialectic and discursive reasoning; and the circular way of turning within for mystical deification. Borrowing the terminology of Proclus, Dionysius believed that the human spirit is able to achieve fellowship with God on his own level through the stages of purification, illumination, and union.

Rationalism and Mysticism

The dominance of Platonism in the Middle Ages was largely the result of the synthesis of Neoplatonic philosophy and biblical religion in the theology of Augustine merged with the mystical tradition of the East received through such writings as those of Dionysius. That dominance reached its apex during the eleventh and twelfth centuries. Moreover, just as Plato's philosophy from the beginning was motivated as much by religious as by speculative interests, so the same dual characteristics may be noted in the philosophy and theology of the Christian Scholastics of the early Middle Ages.

Many outstanding scholars and churchmen contributed to the thought of that creative period. Their names may be found in any good work on the history of the Church or the history of Christian thought. However, in order to illustrate the central place of the Platonic tradition it will be sufficient here to discuss only two of the most significant: Anselm of Canterbury (1033-1109) as a master of speculative theology, and Bernard of Clairvaux (1091-1153) as one of the greatest of the mystical theologians.

We have already noted, in chapter 13, the persuasive power of Anselm's *Cur deus-homo?* in changing the Church's understanding of the death of Christ and in supplying the rationale for the whole system of sacraments. He was a conscious follower of Augustine in both the method and content of his theology, a fact that indicates his allegiance also to Platonism. Anselm was born at Aosta in the Piedmont, near the border between Italy and Francc. While still a youth he travelled to Normandy, in northwestern France, and joined the Benedictine monastic community at Bec, where his fellow countryman, the famous Lanfranc, was prior. He studied philosophy and theology at Bec with recognized brilliance and, when Lanfranc left Bec to lead another monastery, Anselm succeeded him as abbot. Following the Norman conquest of England, however, Anselm joined Lanfranc at Canterbury, where the master was now Archbishop and Primate of England. Again, in 1093, Anselm succeeded his mentor, serving as Archbishop until his death in 1109. He achieved fame as a theologian while still at Bec but added political activity at Canterbury by being involved in controversy with King Henry I over the question of investiture. That issue was settled peacefully by compromise.

Anselm was a pious and orthodox churchman but he was also a searching philosopher. He began by accepting the faith that had been handed down in the Scriptures and traditions of the Church and then he insisted that the believer must go on to understand that faith. Although he was opposed to much of the theology of his younger contemporary, Abelard, he agreed completely with the sardonic epigram of Abelard that "he who believes quickly is light minded." For that reason he adopted a motto from Augustine: *credo ut intelligam,* "I believe that I may understand." He was convinced that there is ultimately only one truth, whether it is known through revelation or reason. Those things that may be known by experience and reason, such as mathematics, science, and grammar, should be analyzed, tested, and taught. That is the task of philosophy and the schools. Those things that may be known only by revelation, such as the doctrine of the Trinity, should be accepted on the authority of the Church; but the believer should be encouraged to examine his faith in order to understand it and to be convinced of its rational truth. That is the task of scholastic theology.

There was a practical motivation behind this method of Anselm and many other medieval scholars. It was the recognized need for education and missions. Most of the older barbarian peoples who now populated northern Europe, the inheritors of the Western Roman Empire, had been converted to orthodox Christianity, but they had not adequately absorbed the culture of classical antiquity and their faith was often primitive, semi-pagan, and uninformed. Beyond that, the Church was challenged by unbelievers and culture. Paris, London, and even Rome were cultural backwaters compared to Constantinople, Baghdad, and Cordoba. It did not suffice for the Christian to simply preach the Gospel to the unconverted; he must persuade them by convincing arguments. The only common ground for debate is that universal basis of communication between all rational being, which is reason itself. Thus Anselm wrote theological treatises that were intended to penetrate and expand the major elements of theology for the edification of simple believers. He also wrote works designed to demonstrate the rationality of Christian belief. His treatise on the Trinity is a good example of the first; his *Proslogium* and *Cur deus-homo?* are primary examples of the latter.

Without using normal Christian terminology, the *Cur deus-homo?* attempts to make rationally cogent, in abstract language, the Christian teaching that the incarnation of God as man was necessary so that a God-man might die an undeserved death, thus satisfying the justice of God in the face of sin and at the same time providing an infinite reservoir of merit that might be dispensed through the sacraments. The essay is a model of logical argument. For many it has continued to supply convincing rational support for Christian soteriology.

The *Proslogium* (Discourse) is a brief composition, modeled after Augustine's *Confessions* as a prayer. It followed Anselm's earlier, longer work, the *Monologium* (Soliloquy), which had restated the well-known arguments for the existence of God based primarily on casuality. The *Proslogium* sets forth an essentially new argument, one that, according to Anselm, only a fool would deny. It is the famous ontological argument, considered undeniably cogent by many subsequent theologians and philosophers but rejected by many others, especially Immanuel Kant. It may be summarized in Anselm's words. He referred to Psalm 14:1, which quotes the fool as saying in his heart that there is no God. Then Anselm commented:

> even the fool is convinced that something exists in the understanding, at least, than which nothing greater can be conceived. For when he hears this he understands it. And whatever is understood exists in the understanding. And assuredly that than which nothing greater can be conceived cannot exist in the understanding alone. For suppose it exists in the understanding alone: then it can be conceived to exist in reality, which is greater. Therefore, if that than which nothing greater can be exists in the understanding alone, the very being than which nothing greater can be conceived is one than which a greater can be conceived. But obviously this is impossible. Hence, there is no doubt that there exists a being than which nothing greater can be conceived, and it exists both in the understanding and in reality.

These treatises adequately demonstrate the use of reason by Anselm and his fellow Scholastics. They also show the underlying Platonic suppositions on which they were constructed. The *Cur deus-homo?* presumes the prior reality of universals, just as Plato did. "The problem is, how can God forgive man's sin?" It is not the sins of individual human beings but the sin of mankind that requires forgiveness. The problem can be solved, according to Anselm, only when God and man are joined—by incarnation, in orthodox terms—to make one who is both the God who can make satisfaction and the man who ought to make satisfaction. And when this is accomplished through the undeserved death of the God-man, the resulting merit is made over to man. Further, the Platonic ontology is even more explicit in the *Proslogium*. It assumes that being precedes thought. An idea must exist in reality before it can appear in the mind. There is a necessary relation between *ontos* (being) and *logos* (logic, reflection). Hence Anselm's argument is called the ontological argument. It is founded on the Platonic doctrine of ideal forms, and if that foundation is not assumed the argument falls to the ground.

If Anselm was the greatest theologian of the twelfth century, his younger contemporary, Bernard of Clairvaux, was certainly the greatest ecclesiastical statesman and mystic. Both were thorough-going Platonists in their assumptions. Bernard was born into a family of the Burgundian nobility, near Dijon in eastern France. Torn between a secular and a monastic life, he suddenly entered the nearby monastery at Citeaux when he was twenty-two, persuading about thirty friends and relatives to join the order with him. His obvious gift of leadership soon caused the abbot, Stephen Harding, to direct him to take twelve monks and found a new Cistercian monastery at Clairvaux (Clara Vallis) in Champagne. Bernard spent the remainder of his life as abbot there, although he travelled extensively and exerted strong influence in the political and ecclesiastical affairs of western Europe. He decided between the claims of counter popes and often counselled them with authority. He carried on a wide correspondence with many leaders of his time, and more than four hundred of his letters survive. He led in the strengthening and growth of the Cistercian order, leaving more than three hundred and thirty strong monasteries at his death. He is recognized as one of the outstanding preachers and biblical interpreters of the medieval period, and his powerful voice helped to generate the epoch-making Crusades.

Bernard strongly opposed the rationalistic method of Abelard. He thought it impious if not heretical to seek understanding and certainty beyond faith. Faith itself is not opinion or credulity, he believed, but certitude. The greater certainty that should be sought comes not from reason but from progressive experience, the spiritual knowledge of God in Christ that accompanies the exaltation of the soul following its true humility. Bernard tirelessly expounded his view of the mystical way of final union with God in many of his letters, in the eighty-six sermons he composed on the Song of Songs, in several brief treatises, and, most fully, in his major work *The Steps of Humility*.

Bernard's affinity with Platonism is most clearly seen in his constant emphasis on the upward struggle of the soul, empowered by love, as it rises from purification through humility, to illumination by the imitation of Christ, and finally to ecstatic union with God. His is the same *ordo salutis* that may be traced backwards to the Neoplatonized Christianity of Augustine and Dionysius. However, an important distinction should not be overlooked. The union sought by Bernard and most Western mystics is not a union of absorption of identity (*theosis*), characteristic of the East; rather it climbs toward a union of wills between the human and the divine, a beatific vision of the Holy Creator by the sanctified creature.

The "Imitatio-Christi" theme is a controlling principle in the writings of Bernard. He interpreted the Song of Songs as an allegory of Christ's love for the Church and of the soul's reciprocal love for God in Christ. He believed that the answer to the question, why God became man, must be answered so as to emphasize the humiliation of Christ that led to his exaltation. In like manner, just as Christ ascended into heaven, having descended to the condition of humanity, partaking even of death, so the faithful must share his humility so as to ascend to the Father with him. Bernard gave an extensive commentary on the Beatitudes (Matthew 5:3-12), describing them as eight rungs on the mystical ladder that reaches to heaven. The figure of the ladder had already become common in mystical theology, having its inspiration in the great work, *The Ladder of Paradise* (*klimax tou paradaisou*), by the sixth-century Greek monk, Johannes Climacus of St. Catherine's monastery at Sinai.

The Christ-centered mysticism of Bernard of Clairvaux is of immense historical significance. It turned aside from the previous centuries of concern with the Christological dogmas toward a renewed interest in the historical, human Jesus of Nazareth. That led to a desire of the faithful to make pilgrimages to the Holy Land, now occupied by followers of Mohammed. It led also to greater emphasis on sacred places and sacred objects, causing a widespread search for relics. The results were the Crusades, those devastating wars between Western Christendom and Islam, intended to liberate Jerusalem and all of Palestine from the control of nonbelievers. From the experiences of those horrors eventually came the knowledge of a wider world, a new infusion of ancient culture into the West, the Renaissance, and the ages of exploration, discovery, and invention. Although by no means the only factor, the Christian mysticism of Bernard of Clairvaux contributed to the birth of modern times.

The Problem of Universals

We have seen that various forms of Platonism supplied the philosophical substructure for most Christian thought and practice in the West until the thirteenth century. The Moslem conquest of the seventh century and later, claiming most of Asia Minor, North Africa, and the Iberian peninsula as well as the Holy Land, made inevitable the gradual spread of alternative philosophies, especially Aristotelianism, into Western culture. The result was nothing short of culture shock in the

West, producing profound debates in the Church and the universities. Were not medieval Judaism and aggressive Islam to be opposed as infidelities? Was not Aristotle a source of heresy?

The debates, in philosophic terms, took one basic form, often referred to as the problem of universals. That problem, as we have seen in chapter 14, was raised in Porphyry's *Isagoge,* an introduction to Aristotle's *Categories* which was later translated from Greek to Latin by Boethius. The essential question is: what is the relation between being and thought? Which is prior, universals or things? It is clear that Plato's ontology holds that universals are prior. The familiar Latin expression of that position is: *universalia sunt realia ante rem* (universals are real before things). The Aristotelian answer to the problem suggests that universals are found in things, things at all levels being combinations of form and matter. The Latin expression for that view is: *universalia sunt realia in re* (universals are real in things). A third alternative, most commonly associated with Roscellinus of Compiegne and William of Ockham, argues that only specific things are real and that universals are mere names given to categories and groups of similar things. That view is ordinarily called Nominalism and its Latin expression is: *universalia sunt realia post rem* (universals are real after things).

The three ontologies were, generally speaking, successively dominant in the philosophies and theologies of the West during the Middle Ages. Platonism (*ante rem*) was dominant until the thirteenth century. Then, largely through the influence of Jewish and Moslem scholars, Aristotelianism (*in re*) gained partial but not total ascendancy in the West, especially in France and Germany. Neither of those positions has ever been completely abandoned, but the mood and method of modern times since the Renaissance have been largely nominalistic (*post rem*). The next two chapters will describe those significant changes in the development of Western culture.

Chapter 16

The Rediscovery of Aristotle

Little of Aristotle's thought was directly accessible to the European scholastics of the ninth and tenth centuries. His logical works, together with Porphyry's book on the *Categories*, were highly regarded, but his copious writings on other subjects were quite unknown to even the best Christian scholars. The Crusades, however, brought Europeans from all walks of life into contact with a Moslem culture, which was clearly, in many ways, more highly advanced than their own. From Latin translations of Arabic translations of Syrian translations of Greek writings, European scholars learned of the existence of a vast storehouse of Aristotle's material, and the wider European travel which was the product of the greater mobility developed during the Crusades opened up the treasures of Cordovan scholarship to inquisitive travelers, who introduced the lost works into the monasteries and cathedral schools of their own countries.

Their dissemination was given further impetus by the development during the twelfth century of the great European universities—corporations, or guilds of scholars operating under papal, imperial, or royal charter and enjoying such important privileges as the right of internal jurisdiction, the authority to award degrees, and exemption of their students from military service. In southern countries, the government of the universities was often democratic, whereas in England and the north of Europe, the professors were firmly in control. Students matriculated at an early age—sometimes when they were only twelve or thirteen years old. The course in arts lasted four and a half to seven years, after which a student could proceed to theology and attend lectures for four years on the *Sentences* of Peter Lombard. He was then eligible to lecture for two years on two books of the Bible, follow that with lectures on the *Sentences,* and devote several more years to study and disputation. A man who survived all this was, at the age of thirty-four, eligible for a doctorate. The three greatest European universities during the later Middle Ages were at Paris, Bologna, and Oxford.

The history of the medieval universities was, in great measure, destined to be shaped by the so-called "new learning" resulting from the rediscovery of Aristotle. The acceptance of Aristotle's concepts was by no means immediate or enthusiastic, however, even after translations of the major treatises were readily available to interested scholars. As late as the latter part of the twelfth and early part of the thirteenth centuries, scarcely any Peripatetic influences were evident in the writings of the most important scholastics. The works of Aristotle which had, for centuries, been the common property of educated clerics were occasionally mentioned in their discourses, but those which were to give birth to the Aristotelian revolution seem to have been virtually ignored. The first medieval mention of the *Metaphysics* of which we have any knowledge appeared in the *Glossae super Sententias,* somewhat shakily attributed to Peter of Poitiers and written before 1175. Peter, later Chancellor of the University of Paris, in his brief reference to the *Metaphysics*—assuming, of course, that he was the author of the *Glossae* in question—appears not to have been personally acquainted with the *Metaphysics,* but he did imply that it was at that time available in Paris.

By the first years of the next century, the *Libri Naturales* and the *Metaphysics* were subjects of study in the Faculty of Arts at Paris, and conservative scholars began to react to their growing influence with alarm. David of Dinant read Aristotle's writings avidly, if, perhaps, a trifle hastily, and saw his *Quaternuli* condemned to the fire by a decree of 1210, together with some of the Aristotelian treatises which had inspired his work. The ban was reaffirmed in 1215, but by that time the flood tide of the new learning was too full to be stemmed by ecclesiastical prohibition. The ink was scarcely dry on the second prohibition when William of Auxerre began working on his *Summa Aurea,* in which Artistotelian principles were clearly evident. Philip the Chancellor, a member of the Paris faculty, made clear use of the new scholarship in his *Summa de Bono,* written between 1231 and 1236, as did his contemporary and fellow Paris master, Roland of Cremona. From that time on, the triumph of Aristotelianism was all but inevitable.

Thomas Aquinas

In 1225, the Norman wife of a Lombard nobleman, the Count of Aquino, a nephew of the Emperor Frederick Barbarossa, bore a son. The child, born at the family's fortress castle of Roccasecca, near Naples, was christened Thomas. At the age of five. he was sent to the neighboring Benedictine abbey of Monte Cassino to begin his formal education. When he was fourteen or fifteen years old, he was sent to Naples for further schooling, and there he encountered some members of the recently formed Dominican Order. Like the Franciscans, the Dominicans were committed to a simpler way of life than that of the older monastic orders. The idealistic boy saw in their regimen a proper approach to Christian devotion and promptly committed himself to a career as a friar. His outraged family argued against his decision and even solicited the help of the pope to turn the boy from his course. All appeals to young Thomas fell on deaf ears. In desperation, his family locked him up at Roccasecca for a year or two and, it is said, tried to dissuade him from his chosen career by bringing an attractive girl to his bedroom. Thomas promptly drove her away with a burning brand and then used it to scorch the sign of the cross on his door. An attempt to induce him to accept the office of abbot of the "respectable" abbey Monte Cassino was equally unsuccessful.

At last, he managed to make his way to Paris, where he studied with one of the greatest Aristotelian scholars of his day, Albertus Magnus, the "Universal Teacher," some twenty-seven years his senior. Albert, imbued with the "new learning," was well acquainted with the thought of Christian, Jewish, and Arab writers. Christian scholars should, he believed, master philosophical and scientific learning of all sorts. He had a great desire to bring Aristotle's philosophy to prominence in Europe by making Latin translations of all his works available to scholars. Albert proved a good friend to his young pupil and eventually took him with him on a journey to Cologne, after which Thomas returned to Paris at the age of twenty-seven to teach in the University.

He gained great prominence as a teacher and writer and, despite his rational nature, was no stranger to mystical experience. His noble lineage, no less than his academic distinction, put him in a position to become the friend and confidant of King Louis IX of France, himself later declared a saint of the Church. Once, while Thomas was busy with the writing of the *Summa Theologica,* he was dining with the King and became absorbed in his thoughts. Suddenly, while the rest of the guests were engaged in conversation, he struck the table with his hand and exclaimed, "Ha! That settles the Manichees!" The breach of court etiquette caused alarm among the guests, but the King called for a secretary to take down Thomas's thought before it could escape him.

From 1259 to 1265, Thomas taught under the auspices of the Papal Court. He then returned to Paris, where he engaged in controversy with a group of Christian theologians who had been strongly influenced by the philosophy of Averroës in a manner which Thomas, Aristotelian though he was, saw as incompatible with Christian doctrine. In 1274, he was summoned to Lyons to take part in a council. He died on the way, at the age of forty-nine.

Thomas produced a large number of writings on a variety of subjects ranging from theology to mechanical engineering. His two most famous works are the *Summa Theologica* and the *Summa contra Gentiles*. In the *Summa Theologica,* he dealt with the Christian doctrine of salvation and developed a massive and detailed treatment of Christian ethics. In the *Summa contra Gentiles,* he attempted to show that, far from threatening the Christian faith as some held, the Aristotelian learning was thoroughly compatible with the revealed teachings of the Church.

In the development of his philosophy, Thomas did not hesitate to use Platonic and Augustinian ideas where he thought them appropriate, but his major source was Aristotle, to whom he habitually referred as "the Philosopher." When he encountered some apparent discrepancy between an Aristotelian idea and one accepted by the Church, he tried, whenever possible, to avoid a repudiation of Aristotle by attributing the troublesome notion not to Aristotle but rather to a later Aristotelian like Averroës. In cases where this was impossible, he tried to show that what Aristotle had said could be interpreted in such a way as to conform to Christian doctrine. If this method sometimes did violence to Aristotle's original meaning, it nevertheless enabled him to effect a remarkably comprehensive synthesis between the dominant religion of the West and the second of its two most important philosophical systems.

That synthesis seemed infinitely preferable to the invocation of the doctrine of the "twofold truth," according to which one proposition can be true in philosophy and its contradictory in theology. This expedient, suspect, to be sure, in the eyes of the Church, had been adopted by a number of scholars captivated by Aristotelianism or Averroism but committed to the teachings of the Church. Thomas's tidy mind would not permit him to entertain such an illogical solution to the problems posed by the rediscovered Peripatetic philosophy. He recognized a distinction between philosophy on the one hand, which takes its data from the world and uses reason to ascend to God, and theology on the other, which begins with revelation and faith and uses reason to put their data into proper order. He did not, however, consider the two kinds of knowledge as incompatible, regarding them rather as two sources of one species of the truth which is grounded in God.

Thomas did not hold that all the articles of the Christian religion can be demonstrated rationally. Within the scope of Theology, there are two ways of arriving at truth. The first is *natural* theology, essentially a philosophical discipline, which, relying on reason alone, can prove the existence of God, the immortality of the soul, and other matters which are also presuppositions of faith. *Revealed* theology, relying on faith, assures the believer who acquaints himself with the miraculous history of the origin and growth of the Church that God has spoken to men through Christ, the head of the Church. The two support each other, and neither is complete in itself. Together, they constitute the way through which we may know about God while we are yet in the world. After death, however, we may come to know him directly through the *beatific vision*.

Thomas' conception of philosophic knowledge is, in the first instance, empirical. "*Nihil in intellectu quod prius non fuerit in sensu,*" he said. "Nothing in the intellect which was not first in the senses."

But of what can the intellect, acting on sense data, assure us? According to Thomas, it can guarantee a great deal—most importantly, the existence of God. We cannot, he held, rely on any innate knowledge, for no such knowledge exists. Nor can we accept Anselm's ontological argument, which guarantees only the existence of the idea of God rather than of God himself.

The senses, however, give us evidence of a world, and that world provides us with five proofs, which Thomas proceeded to elaborate, of its author.

First, the senses show us that motion exists, and motion, as Aristotle held, is nothing other than the transformation of something from potentiality to actuality. But a thing cannot, in the same respect, be both potential and actual at the same time, and only what is actual can move something from potentiality to actuality. A thing then cannot be both mover and moved. It must be moved by something else and that something else in turn by something still other. But since an infinite regress is impossible, we must arrive at a first mover unmoved, "and this everyone understands to be God."

Second, the senses also show us an order of sufficient causes. In order for a thing to be its own efficient cause, it would have to be prior to itself, and that is impossible. The chain of efficient causation cannot be infinite, and it is necessary to posit a first efficient cause, "to which everyone gives the name of God."

Third, nature shows us things which could either be or not be: such things cannot always exist, for what can not-be is at some time non-existent. So, if everything is capable of non-existence, there was a time when nothing existed. If this were the case, however, nothing would exist now, for there would have been nothing which could bring about existence. Therefore, there must be something the existence of which is not merely possible, but necessary. Such a thing must have its necessity caused by another or be necessary in its own right. An infinite series of things having their necessity caused by others is impossible, and so a being "having of itself its own necessity and not receiving it from another, but rather causing in others their necessity must exist." This all men speak of as God.

Fourth, we find gradations of qualities in things. Some things are more or less good, or true, or noble. But all these gradations derive their meaning from reference to something which has the maximum degree of the quality, and "the maximum in any genus is the cause of all in that genus," and so there must be something which is the cause of every perfection which is found in any being, "and this we call God."

Fifth, we observe that things without knowledge nevertheless act for an end, obeying laws which achieve the best result. Something without knowledge, however, cannot act toward an end unless it is directed by a knowing and intelligent being. So an intelligent being must exist by whom the end of all natural things is determined, "and this being we call God."

The first four arguments are cosmological in character, accounting for the existence of some aspect of nature which cannot be explained by reference to something within the universe by attributing it to something transcending the universe. The fifth is teleological, moving from evidences of design in nature to the necessary existence of a designer.

God's Nature

If we can know of God's existence by reasoning about our experience, can we in similar fashion arrive at knowledge of his nature? Thomas's answer is a cautious affirmative. Our knowledge of God is in many respects negative. We can say what he is not. Affirmatively, we cannot apply predicates to him in univocal fashion—that is to say, in the same way that we would apply them to ourselves or to other created beings. Nor, on the other hand, should they be thought to be equivocal, or totally different from their common meanings. They are, rather, analogical, expressing a real resemblance without being identical in meaning in the two applications.

Through reason, it can be demonstrated that, as unmoved mover and pure form, God cannot be a body and that he cannot be a compound being. Unlike created things, which require reference to something beyond themselves to determine their essence, God is his own essence, unconditioned by anything else. He is pure actuality and so must possess all perfections, "for a thing is said to be perfection in proportion to its actuality." Since the essence of goodness lies in the fact that it is desirable, and since perfection is what is really desired, it follows that God, possessing all perfection, must be supremely desirable and supremely good. By somewhat similar chains of reasoning, Thomas proved to his satisfaction that God must be intelligent, and that, indeed, he possesses perfect knowledge. Going beyond his mentor Aristotle, however, Thomas proceeded from that point to a demonstrating that God's perfect knowledge, rather than being limited to an awareness of the perfect being, which would, of course, be knowledge of himself alone, involves his knowing things other than himself as effects caused by him. To justify the Christian conception of divine providence, however, it was necessary for Thomas to go further and show that the knowledge of other things must encompass the contemplation not only of universals but of singulars as well, which are also effects of which he is the cause.

"If God knows not singulars, which even men know," Thomas said, "this would involve the absurdity which the philosopher urges against Empedocles, namely that *God is most foolish.*" As will is necessary for the providential governance of the world, Thomas was at pains to show that every intellectual being must be one who wills and that will is, therefore, an aspect of God's nature. Moreover, although his own essence cannot be increased or multiplied, he can desire increase and multiplication of essence in his creatures. "Now God wills and loves his own being in itself and for its own sake . . . And all other being is a participation, by likeness, of His being. Therefore, from the very fact that God wills and loves Himself, it follows that He wills and and loves other things."

Thomas tried to reconcile Aristotle's denial that creation out of nothing can occur with the Christian conception of God as creator of the world by drawing a distinction between "the emanation of particular effects from particular causes," in which, of course, the notion of creation from nothing is absurd, and the quite different idea of "the first emanation from the universal principle of things."

The concept of *creatio ex nihilo* in the context of this first emanation simply entails the assertion that nothing exists which does not owe its being, truth, and goodness to God. As to why God should choose to create, we cannot say, Thomas held, but we can note that good tends to be outgoing, and if this tendency is a part of God's nature, it is only to be expected that he would create a world of many diverse things to reflect the divine goodness insofar as that can be done in creatures, which must, by their very nature, reflect that goodness imperfectly.

God's providence is of such a nature that he foresees and causes all events. But Thomas, in order to try to include in his system the human freedom essential to moral responsibility, distinguished between "necessary causes," provided for those things which "happen of necessity," and "contingent causes," provided in order that some things "may happen by contingency, according to the disposition of their proximate causes."

The Created World

God has designed the world according to the best arrangement possible. If it is asked, then, why there is evil, it can only be asserted that evil has no real positive existence. It is, rather, privative in character, a lack of something. Specifically, moral evil stems from man's freedom to move toward the source of his good or away from it.

In the great hierarchy of being, God, of course, is at the summit. Below him are angels, pure intelligences ordered according to rank in a manner which Thomas explored in some detail. Below them, in descending order, are men, animals, plants, and the four elements which constitute the world of matter.

Unlike the angels, man is a unity of soul and body. Thomas shared this view with Aristotle, but his Christian faith required him to provide a reasoned defense of the idea of personal immortality. Far from being inconsistent with Aristotle's position, the notion of the survival of the total personality was justified, in Thomas's view, by Aristotle's characterization of the rational principle, which is immortal, as that which distinguishes the souls of men from those of lesser forms of life. Thomas insisted that the rational soul of a human being includes in its function the operation of the vegetative and sensory processes along with the intellectual. The soul, bearing all the traits of personality, survives the death of the body, for as Plato contended, it is a unity rather than being made up of parts. God, of course, could cause it to cease to be if he chose, but being good, he will not do so. A disembodied soul, however, is an incomplete human being, for the soul can exercise its functions properly only through a body. Fortunately, Thomas maintained, turning to revelation, we are assured that at the resurrection, the soul will once again be united with a body which is spiritual and incorruptible.

In dealing with the problem of universals, Thomas tried to synthesize the three positions which had figured in the debate on the subject throughout the Middle Ages. God eternally has in mind the perfect ideas of things which are represented in the particulars of the world. In those ideas or archetypes can be found the *ante rem* status of universals. But the particulars modeled on God's ideas have real resemblances to those ideas and to one another. Thus, universals exist in *in re* as well. Finally, the discursive mind sees and abstracts the common elements which recur in the varied classes of natural objects and forms universal terms which exist *post rem* in the mind itself.

Man's aim in life is the attainment of happiness, and, in Thomas's philosophy, the ultimate end of human endeavor lies in the vision of God. Happiness is attained through the cultivation of two sorts of virtues—the natural and the supernatural. The natural virtues are those which the Greeks valued: temperance, courage, wisdom, or prudence, and justice. These are attainable by our own strength and can give us a measure of happiness. Perfect felicity, however, can be attained only through the addition of the supernatural or theological virtues, of which we can be made capable only through the grace of God. These virtues, as laid out by St. Paul in the thirteenth chapter of First Corinthians, are faith, hope, and charity or love. With regard to the third of these, Thomas held, in accordance with Christ's injunction, that we must love God for his own sake, and our neighbors and ourselves for God's sake.

Church and State

In his theory of social organization, Thomas did not acknowledge the existence of an unbridgeable chasm between the city of man and the city of God. A good Aristotelian in this, as in other areas of his philosophy, he saw man as a political animal and the state as a natural institution serving basic human needs. He justified his view by elaborating a theory in which human law, as it is promulgated in particular communities, is dependent on natural law, which is the divine law in its application to the human condition. The function of a ruler, who derives his just authority from God, is to make and enforce laws appropriate to the region and the situation in which his authority is exercised. The role of the state is twofold. It provides sanctions to compel obedience to natural law from those not disposed to obey it of their own accord, and it seeks to produce virtue in the persons subject to its laws.

The state, then, is not, as some earlier Christians held, an institution inflicted on humanity by God as a punishment for sin. It is essentially good, and exists because man's nature, unlike that of the lower animals, which can rely on instinct, necessitates the formation of political institutions through which the good of human communities can be sought. "If it is natural for man to live in the society of many," Thomas held, "it is necessary that there exist among men some means by which the group may be governed. For where there are many men together, and each one is looking after his own interest, the group would be broken up and scattered unless there were also someone to take care of what appertains to the common weal." Like Aristotle, Thomas recognized that a state may be ruled by one, few, or many. Sharing Aristotle's view too that ideally monarchy should be the best form of government, he was more optimistic than his mentor about the practical possibility of achieving a decent government by a single man.

That such a rule is the worst when it is perverted, however, was as clear to Thomas as to Aristotle, and so he never proposed that a monarch should exercise the sort of absolute sovereign power that later political theory was to accord to governments. The authority of a temporal ruler is, in the first place, properly limited to the natural man, and since his spiritual end transcends the natural, the royal power must be limited by the priestly. In the second place, the monarch operates even in the secular realm only as an agent of the political community. Ultimate political power, Thomas stated categorically, lies in the people themselves. It follows that what the people may give, they may take away. A ruler who does not exercise his authority in accordance with natural law is, in law, no longer ruler, and the people have the right to remove him from office and substitute another in his place. Revolution is, however, to be resorted to as a remedy for tyranny only as a last resort, after other less dangerous expedients, not the least of which is prayer to God for succor, coupled with moral reform, have been tried.

Similarly, Thomas held that specific laws not conforming to natural law should be disobeyed unless it can be reasoned that disobedience would produce a greater evil than conformity. "We ought to obey God rather than men," he said in justifying his sanctions of civil disobedience. The importance of his conception of governmental authority as resting on something beyond human law and his contention that it may, under certain circumstances be taken away or ignored by the people was to play an important part in the development of subsequent European political philosophy.

The New Learning in England

On the Continent, the Aristotelian revival, dominated by the powerful personality of Thomas Aquinas, achieved authoritative status in every aspect of philosophical and theological thought. In England, where Platonism was perhaps less easy to dislodge and where the Franciscans at Oxford were not overly inclined to follow the lead of the Dominicans, the rediscovery of Aristotle had effects which were no less revolutionary but which had a somewhat different character. There, the Aristotelian passion for direct examination resulted in a true renaissance in scientific inquiry, which led directly to the creation and development of attitudes usually referred to as modern.

As early as the twelfth century, a number of English scholars were showing this enthusiasm for the rediscovered learning. Alexander de

Sancto Albano, for instance, better known by his nickname, Alexander Neckham, meaning "Alexander the Wicked," was calling Aristotle "philosophus noster" and "Doctor Athenarum, dux, caput, orbis honos," and, like Aristotle, he was interested in everything. He looked forward to the liberation of men through the advance of science. "What craftiness of the foe is there," he wrote, "that does not yield to the precise knowledge of those who have tracked down the elusive subtleties of things hidden in the very bosom of nature?" He encouraged the sort of progress he envisioned by painting glowing pictures of an idealized past when, as he imagined, "the greatest princes were diligent and industrious in aiding the investigation of nature."

The two most important names in the life of Oxford during the thirteenth century belong to Franciscans, Robert Grosseteste (1175-1253) and Roger Bacon (c.1220-c.1292) Grosseteste, a professor and chancellor of Oxford and later Bishop of Lincoln, achieved historical distinction for his militant defense of the English Church against royal and papal domination alike. His role as a champion of the new learning is well established in his commentaries on Aristotle, the Pseudo-Dionysius, and Boethius, as well as advice on farming, pastoral and devotional writings in Anglo-Norman and Latin, and a miscellany of translations from the Greek, French poems, and theological, philosophical, and biblical writings.

It was in this profound influence on the development of science, however, that Grosseteste towered above other scholars of his time. For all his interest in the recovery of classical learning, he recognized that the true task of natural philosophers was to forward the development of new and independent methods of inquiry. His own specific incursions into scientific research were impressive. He investigated the properties of lenses and suggested that appropriately designed and ground objectives could correct visual defects, thus laying the foundation for the invention of spectacles at the end of the thirteenth century. He studied rainbows and suggested an explanation for them. A competent mathematician, he explored the question of the summation of infinite aggregates of numbers. His treatises proposing a reform of the Julian calendar were based on sound astronomical observation.

More important than his particular observations, however, was his basic analysis of the methods of scientific inquiry and the nature of scientific explanation. Unlike some of the less critical scholars of the period, he did not become simply a captive of the rediscovered Aristotelian world view. His psychology and epistemology were essentially Augustinian, and his theory of matter, while couched in Peripatetic language, was by no means Aristotelian in content. To him must be ascribed credit for a working synthesis of philosophical and scientific ideas derived directly or indirectly from the two greatest masters of ancient thought, and he was, as well, the author of ideas that brought him to the very threshold of modern philosophy.

Roger Bacon

The work begun at Oxford by Grosseteste was carried on with single-minded devotion by Roger Bacon. A member of an English family of good repute, he probably studied at Oxford and Paris, and it is known that he lectured there in the faculty of arts, apparently with such distinction that he came to be known as *doctor admirablis.* Back in England, he came under the direct influence of Grosseteste and other scholars of note. Now his interest in the more commonly recognized aspects of the new learning burst into a blaze of original research in mathematics, alchemy, optics, language, and astronomy.

At some time in his career, Bacon joined the Franciscan Order and on occasion found himself in difficulty with his superiors for his unorthodox investigations and his openly expressed contempt for colleagues who did share his own point of view. In 1257, he was sent to Paris and committed to the supervision of Giovanni Fidanza, later to become St. Bonaventure, who kept him under restraint for ten years. He was forbidden to write, his instruments and books were taken away, and communication with the outer world was denied him.

In 1265, Guy de Foulques was elected pope, assuming the name Clement IV. While still residing in England, where he had been papal legate since 1263, he privately communicated with Bacon, asking him to write a general treatise on the sciences. Bacon, still in confinement, was unable to reply, and the Pope, unwilling for some reason to deal with him openly, sent secret word to him, asking for writings on certain subjects of importance to the Church and the universities. No such works existed at the time, and Bacon, bound to secrecy by the Pope, had to circumvent his suspicious superiors in order to produce them.

In an astonishingly short time he wrote the *Opus Majus, Opus Secundus,* and *Opus Minus,* in which he elaborated his theory that the sciences constitute a unity and his general view of the way in which the various parts of human knowledge are interrelated. Upon being released from most of the restraints under which he had suffered, he followed those works with a seventy-five chapter *Opus Tertium* an expanded version of the *Opus Majus,* in which he developed more fully his charter for the future of science. Openly contemptuous of the "puerilities" of the orthodox education of the schools, he boldly advocated the penetration of the secrets of nature through positive study and experimentation.

Shortly after Bacon's return to England in 1268, Clement IV died, but Bacon, undaunted by the difficulties under which he worked, continued his writing. Some time near the end of the eighth decade of the century, the Franciscans, disturbed again, less, possibly, by the novelty of Bacon's thought than by irritation at his continued attacks on established educational method, condemned him to prison. How long a term he served is not known, but the last of his written work was produced in 1292, and it is supposed that he died in that year.

Bacon was a man of unusual versatility and catholic taste in learning. Genuinely interested in Christian theology and Greek philosophy, he was equally fascinated by such unorthodox disciplines as alchemy and astrology. As a philosopher, he was primarily an Aristotelian, though with some admixture of Neoplatonic thought.

It was in his treatment of science that he demonstrated the full power of his highly disciplined and original mind. In this regard, his reputation has suffered at the hands of his detractors and from the tendency of his admirers to praise him for the wrong things. The Baconian legend represents Bacon as a wizard, in league with the devil, and as the creator of a brazen head which would guarantee him success if he heard it speak. According to the story, while he slept, the head declaimed at half-hour intervals, "Time is," "Time was," and "Time's past," following which it fell and was shattered.

Bacon may not have been a wizard, but he was an indefatigable experimenter. He left detailed descriptions of many of his empirical investigations, but in themselves they were not sufficiently original or productive of significant results to justify the full measure of esteem which is his due. Their importance lies in the fact that they were painstaking attempts to provide verification or disproof of genuinely scientific hypotheses.

"Neither the voice of authority, nor the weight of reason and argument are as significant as experiment,"he wrote, "for thence comes quiet to the mind."

It is ironic that he has enjoyed a lesser reputation in later times than Francis Bacon. He anticipated much of Sir Francis's thought, and it can be persuasively argued that the later Bacon fell short of Friar Roger in his understanding of the ways in which scientific knowledge is acquired and scientific theories formulated. As the earlier bearer of the name has come to be better understood in our time, it has become evident that, in addition to the widespread influence which his observations exercised on the treatment of particular scientific questions prior to the Renaissance, he must be credited with an uncanny ability to project his mind into realms of speculative thought with such genius that the prophetic nature of some of his ideas was unrecognized by orthodox science for seven centuries after his time.

Opposition to the New Learning

On the Continent, as well as in England, the revival of the Aristotelian point of view met with stout opposition. Thomas Aquinas came under attack for his supposed softness toward the thought of Averroës, which, heretical as it was to Catholic minds, had advocates in Paris. Much of the controversy was initiated by Franciscans, but even among Thomas's fellow Dominicans there were some hostile reactions to the growing popularity of his philosophy.

The questions involved in the dispute were quite technical, with one of the major issues centering around Thomas's theory of the unicity of the substantial form. According to him, the soul is the only substantial form in the human substance. When the soul leaves the body at death, it cannot, then, be said that the body which is left is precisely the same body its owner had when he was alive. This notion frightened some leaders of the Church who saw in it a challenge to the practice of veneration of the bodies of saints or portions thereof. If the skull of St. Lazarus is not really quite the same one he had in life, the cathedral at Autun is a rather expensive shrine in which to house it. Thomas himself excluded the dead body of Christ from his theory, but this concession was not enough to mollify his critics. His claim that matter is pure passivity was another hotly disputed point, as was his contention that the angels are simple, each angel constituting an unique species.

In 1277, the Bishop of Paris condemned two hundred and nineteen propositions, most of them of Averroist origin. In view of Thomas's advocacy of some of them, his followers were indirectly affected by the condemnation.

Robert Kilwardby, Archbishop of Canterbury, straightway forbade the teaching at Oxford of a number of Thomistic propositions, including the doctrine of the unicity of the substantial form, which had not been mentioned in the Paris interdict. The Oxford ban was repeated in 1284 by John Peckham, Kilwardby's successor in the archepiscopal seat. Peckham's prohibition went further than Kilwardby's in declaring the rejected propositions to be not merely dangerous, but also heretical.

During the last two decades of the thirteenth century, Thomism gradually gained ascendancy on the Continent, the victory being in no small measure attributable to the vigorous advocacy of the Dominicans. In 1323, Thomas was canonized, and in 1325, the Bishop of Paris withdrew the censure of 1277. Though the attacks of the Franciscans diminished in intensity, the ban at Oxford was never officially lifted.

It would, of course, be an exaggeration to say that the events of the period produced a philosophical schism between English and Continental Catholicism, but it is evident that they did establish trends in learning in England of some importance to subsequent Western thought. The Platonic tradition, which was, in some measure, eclipsed by the triumph of Thomism throughout most of the Church, remained strong in English philosophy, and the important introduction of Aristotelian elements was confirmed in the Oxford tradition in a form which permitted more intellectual flexibility than could be easily accommodated by official Thomism.

During the latter part of the thirteenth century, Walter Merton founded the Oxford College which bears his name, to train members of the clergy for learned professions and civil services. Under the influence of Thomas Bradwardine, who lectured there from 1325 to 1335, the college became the center of English science. Nearly every notable scientific figure in the country during the fourteenth century was in some way associated at one time or another with Merton. There astronomical instruments of considerable sophistication were constructed, complex mathematical systems were devised for dealing with motion, and the theoretical foundations of many of the accomplishments in physics usually attributed to the sixteenth and seventeenth centuries were laid.

In other areas of learning, the directions taken by the New Learning during the twelfth, thirteenth, and fourteenth centuries affected the later development of Western thought. The empirically oriented philosophical systems of the seventeenth, eighteenth, and nineteenth centuries had specific antecedents in the medieval period, as did the equally important thread of quasi-mystical Platonism in English philosophy and literature. An exploration of the ways in which later European and American ideas of secular and ecclesiastical government had their seeds in medieval thought provides further confirmation of the debt owed by the modern world to the scholars of the Aristotelian revival.

Chapter 17

The End of an Age

Thomas Aquinas had performed a *tour de force* of almost unparalleled magnitude in effecting a synthesis of Peripatetic philosophy and Christian teaching. If the operations which he had to perform on each were on occasion a bit Procrustean, they were nevertheless performed with great skill and a profound respect for the materials with which he worked. A strong testimony to his success is to be found in the fact that Thomism, as his philosophy is called, has officially or unofficially served as the authoritative basis for most Roman Catholic theological instruction since his time.

Given the turbulence of the intellectual life of the thirteenth and fourteenth centuries, however, even a synthesis as artfully constructed as that of Thomas could not have been expected to gain the undivided allegiance of the scholars of the Church, and it was not long before telling criticisms were being leveled against his system.

The Franciscan Order, an old rival of Thomas's own Dominicans, was the source of many of the ideas which threatened the Thomistic system. Significantly, it was from Britain, where the Franciscan enthusiasm for the Peripatetic attitude toward science had not been accompanied by any great diminution of enthusiasm for Augustinian Platonism that two of the most powerful of the rival modes of thought emerged.

John Duns Scotus

The author of the first of the major challenges to Thomism remains a somewhat shadowy figure, not only because the facts of his life are a matter of considerable uncertainty, but also because of the disputes over the authorship of works attributed to him and the intricacies of his thought. Although his work was interpreted as unfavorable to Thomism, it is not improbable that he intended his complex deliberations to supplement and complete the Thomistic system rather than to endanger its authoritative status.

He may have been born about 1265, and as the name "Scotus" applied to him suggests, probably was a Scot, although at an earlier period the word might have suggested Irish origin. It is believed that he was born at Maxton, in the county of Roxburgh, that he became a Franciscan about 1278, and that he held a teaching appointment at Oxford. It is also said that he taught in Paris and died in Cologne about the year 1308. Of the many works attributed to him for several centuries, only five are now generally accepted as authentically his. *On the First Principle, Questions on the Metaphysics,* the *Oxford Work, Parisian Reportata,* and *Quodlibetal Questions.* The sloughing away of spurious sourccs has, in some measure, simplified the modern understanding of the Scotan philosophy, but the intricacies really present in the authenticated works are sufficient to make it evident why he was known as *Doctor Subtilis*.

Unlike Thomas, who looked to Aristotle for the principal foundations of his system, Duns Scotus may be seen as having used Aristotelian and Thomistic apologetic to support positions which, in far more instances than is the case with Thomas, have their origins in Augustinian thought.

Like Aristotle and Thomas, he held that knowledge begins with particulars and proceeds to universals through abstraction. Unlike Thomas, who regarded the human mind as essentially different from the divine mind in its reliance on sense experience, Scotus contended that in its natural condition the human mind is capable of direct knowledge of form. Its present limitations are a result of man's fallen state. This modification of the Thomistic position provided a rationale for the argument that the many truths which the mind can discover can lead to a direct knowledge of eternal truths which Thomas had held to be impossible in this life.

This contention led to the assertion that predicates, since we can be led through our experience of things to apprehend their nature directly, can be applied univocally to created beings and to God in those respects in which likenesses exist in the two natures. To begin with, Being, the primary object of the intellect, is similar in finite and infinite natures, in that for both, it is not nothing.

Another doctrine which, for Scotus, had considerable significance for natural theology—the doctrine of the formal distinction—was not original with him, but was, rather, well known among Franciscan scholars. However, Scotus adopted it and gave it an important role in his philosophy. It defines three kinds of distinction. The first, a "real" distinction, is that which holds between two distinct things or between the form and the matter of a physical object. The second, a "mental" distinction, is one that the mind makes in the absence of an objective distinction corresponding to it, such as that made between "man" and "rational animal," assuming that the two terms are coextensive. Scotus and the other Franciscans posited a third, a "formal" distinction, which is made when two or more *formalitates* are apprehended in an object which, though objectively distinct, cannot be separated from one another. One example is provided by the sensitive and the rational soul in man. Another is found in the distinction between such divine attributes as mercy and justice, which are identical with the divine essence, and thus inseparable.

Scotus used the notion of the "formal" distinction in suggesting another resemblance between the being of God and the being of created things. In both, he suggested, in apparent opposition to the Thomistic position, essence and existence are inseparable. In the case of a finite being, however, they can be thought of separately. That is, there is a "formal" distinction between them, whereas this is not true in God's case. Essence and existence, he said, however, are inseparable in both.

This breaking down of the gulf between the Creator and his creation seemed necessary to Scotus if it is to be maintained that it is possible to have any metaphysical knowledge of God. Concepts based on sense perception represent material quiddites or essence. God, however, being immaterial, cannot be conceived in terms of a material quiddity. Therefore, only through a univocity between infinite and finite being could we have true knowledge of God, and religious agnosticism would be inevitable. He did not really reject Thomas's concept of analogy, for he held that analogy itself is impossible without an underlying univocity of those respects in which two subjects are held to be alike.

As to the identity of essence and existence in creature as well as Creator, Scotus was explicit, stating that "it is simply false that existence is something different from essence." Here, he was opposing the view advanced by Henry of Ghent that there is a distinction between *esse essentia,* the essence of a thing as known by God, and *esse existentiae,* the essence of a thing after its creation. According to Henry, nothing positive was added to the essence by its creation. In Scotus' view such a view was fatal to the idea of *Creatio ex nihilo,* for if something had real essence before its creation, it would not have been created from nothing. Scotus recognized that a possible object may have an *esse cognitum* in the divine mind, but he insisted that in a created object, essence and existence, while "formally" distinguishable, are inseparable.

The concepts of "formal" distinction proved useful to Scotus in steering a middle course between nominalism and extreme realism. Between an object and the genus to which it belongs there is neither a "real" distinction nor merely a "verbal" distinction, but rather a "formal" distinction. He also found the idea convenient in defining the relationship existing among the three persons of the Trinity.

Scotus sought a middle ground on another question of considerable concern to Medieval philosophy. The Augustinians, basing their position on their identification of the Platonic Good with God, had maintained that our knowledge of natural objects is dependent on divine illumination for its adequacy. Thomas, relying on the Aristotelian view, had held that natural knowledge of particulars is adequate without such divine illumination, though he had conceded that knowledge of God may "perfect" it.

Scotus, despite his Franciscan background, was driven by his concept of univocity to a position closer to Thomas's than to Augustine's. Citing an impressive array of arguments for the necessity for divine illumination, he preferred to rely rather on a statement of St. Paul in his letter to the Romans: "The invisible things of God, understood by means of those things which have been made, are clearly comprehended from the creation of the world (*a creatura mundi*)." He then proceeded to set forth an intricate web of arguments to show that the Augustinian position had been misinterpreted by the "academics" and that "infallible certitude can be had naturally of . . . three kinds of knowables . . . , namely, of *principles* known *through themselves* and of *conclusions,* secondly of *things known by experience,* thirdly, of *our actions.*"

As for the validation of principles, Scotus said that they "have such an *identity,* that one term known *evidently* includes the other necessarily." "The Philosopher," he said, referring to Aristotle, "confirms this reasoning by likeness in book IV of the *Metaphysics,* where he insists that the opposite of a first principle such as, *it is impossible that the same thing be and not be* can not come into the understanding of any one, because then there would be contrary opinions in the mind at the same time." Certitude can be had of first principles such as the law of contradiction and of conclusions inferred from them by syllogistic reasoning.

Things known by experience present a greater problem, but the validation of induction as well as deduction was important to Scotus as a ground for science. A difficulty arises from the fact that "experience is not had of all singulars." Inductive conclusions, however, can be certainly drawn from observations of a large number of cases on the basis of the proposition that "*whatever occurs as in a great many things from some cause which is not free, is the natural effect* of that cause." That proposition, which may seem to be more a statement of scientific faith than a self-evident axiom, was justified by Scotus as being "known to the understanding" on the basis of the apprehension that "*a cause which is not free* can not produce *as in a great many things* an effect to the opposite of which it is ordered, or to which it is not ordered by its form."

As for knowledge of our actions, he held, "I say there is certitude concerning many of them just as of principles known through themselves, as is obvious from book IV of the Metaphysics, where the Philosopher says of the reasons of those who say that all appearances are true, that these reasons inquire whether we are now dreaming or awake. *All these doubts, however, amount to the same, for they all think that there is a reason in all things*. And he adds, *They seek the reason for things of which there is no reason, for there is no demonstration of a principle of demonstration*. Therefore, according to the same Philosopher in the same place, that we are awake is known through itself as a principle of demonstration." Many other actions such as seeing and hearing are subject to the same certitude.

Aristotle had held that prime matter is the principle of individuation, and Thomas, with some cautious reservation, had followed his lead. In opposition to this view, Scotus maintained that what is known is form, and so, if the individuality of particular objects can be known at all, it must be through form. Every individual, he said, exhibits "contracted" form, which is that which determines its specific nature, as a particular man or a particular horse, along with the "horseness" and "manness" and other properties which determine the genera to which they belong. The distinction between the two is neither "real" nor "verbal" in Scotus' classification, but "formal." Universals are divisible into "parts" of which they may be predicated. Such a division is no longer possible when the process of contraction has resulted in its final stage—the *haecceitas,* or "thisness" of the individual as opposed to the *quidditas* or "whatness" which determines its class membership.

Intellect and Will

Probably the most important dispute between Thomas and Scotus came in Scotus's rejection of the Thomistic insistence on the primacy of the intellect in the divine and human natures. Scotus's view, derived from Augustinian sources, was that the will is primary in both.

The human will, of course, is limited in its operation to possibilities presented by what is known, but cognition does not cause willing except "accidentally," whereas willing actually causes cognition. One can, that is, will to think or not to think about something one knows. The will, however, is undetermined by anything other than itself, and is thus absolutely free in a much more radical sense than Thomas would have admitted.

The will also has primacy over the intellect in God's nature. If God's activity is determined by eternal archetypes, Scotus thought, even if those archetypes are ideas in the divine mind, God is not absolutely free and is is not all-powerful. On the other hand, if his will is totally arbitrary, good is good not because God knows it to be good, but simply because he wills it to be for no reason at all. Ethics, in that case, cannot be a science, but must consist only in attempts to divine God's commands. Human sacrifice, cannibalism, and genocide could become right if God willed them to be, and the law of love might be replaced by a law of hatred.

Scotus, though still maintaining the primacy of the will, sought to show by an intricate process of rational demonstration that his position did not necessitate the conclusion that God's ethical dictates are wholly capricious. There is, he argued, no real distinction between God's will and his intellect. His perfect intellect provides reasons why his will should act in a certain way, and his will acts in conformity to those reasons, though not *because* of them. The perfect will wills perfectly. It must be remembered, however, that there are not two separate faculties in God. The "formal" distinction between his will and his intellect does not admit any causality between them, though they are in complete harmony.

The Ten Commandments, Scotus held, are willed by God in this way because their goodness is of such a nature that a denial of them would violate the law of contradiction, to which even God is subject, not as a limitation on his freedom, but because the assertion of two contradictory propositions would simply be nonsense. Lesser laws are, he thought, in much greater measure, of such nature that their denial could have been willed if God had so chosen.

Scotus had other differences with Thomas, not the least of which was his reformulation of the scope of natural theology—the discipline in which theology and philosophy overlap to provide knowledge of God through natural reason. His doctrine of univocity, of course, provided a firmer ground for such a discipline than was the case with Thomas's system. However, the access to knowledge of the divine nature, is flawed as a result of the fall, and Scotus, insisting on stricter standards for proof than those employed by Thomas, held that Thomas had claimed more for his natural theology than could be justified by his arguments.

He questioned the finality of Thomas's proofs for the existence of God. The argument from contingent being he thought better than the argument for a prime mover. Certain things, such as the unity, perfection, and goodness of God can be proved, he thought, whereas omnipotence, omnipresence, immensity, providence, justice and mercy cannot. Because God is free and his will is primary, we must, in the last analysis, rely on his revelation rather than on our reason for an account of his nature. God gives us what we need to know of him to turn our wills to good. It is, therefore, better to call theology "wisdom" rather than to refer to it as "science." The Church is the authority to which we must turn for enlightenment on theological matters. Scotus, driven by a passion for intellectual honesty, thus drove a wedge between faith and reason which, more than he probably intended, threatened the exquisitely harmonious structure that Thomas had so painstakingly built.

William of Ockham

That wedge was driven in farther by William of Ockham (c.1300-1349), an Englishman who may have come from the village of Ockham not far from London. Like Roger Bacon and John Duns Scotus, he had an Oxford education, became a Franciscan, and lived for a time in Paris. He became entangled in conflict with ecclesiastical authorities, some of the disputes being occasioned by his philosophical and theological views and others by institutional questions within the Franciscan Order. In 1323, he was charged with teaching heresy, and while his case was in process, he opposed the Pope in a controversy over the degree of poverty which should be required of members of the Franciscan Order. Ockham maintained that St. Francis' vow of literal poverty should be the standard for his followers. The Pope and many influential Franciscans thought that the Order should be organized along more conventional lines so far as the possession of property was concerned. The debate became acrimonious, and in 1328 Ockham, along with others of his persuasion, were excommunicated. The Empire and the Church were again at odds, and when Ockham fled to the Emperor Louis IV in Bavaria, the Emperor gave him sanctuary. "Do you defend me with your sword," Ockham charged him. "I will defend you with my pen." Becoming increasingly involved in political questions, Ockham devoted much of his time during his latter years to the production of political writings.

His theological and philosophical works may, in some respects, be considered a continuation of Scotist thought, but its effects on the grand synthesis of Thomas Aquinas were far more devastating. In effect, he destroyed all possibility of the natural theology that his predecessors had been at such pains to justify. Human reason, he held, is limited to the world of particular things and so God's existence cannot be proved by reason, nor can anything be demonstrated concerning his nature. Faith and reason are totally distinct, and certain dogmas may prove to be contrary to reason which we are nevertheless required to accept on faith.

It is folly, then, to try to provide a rational structure to undergird the teaching of the Church. If we hold, on the basis of revelation that God is omnipotent, it follows that he cannot be bound by the sort of restrictions our reason would attribute to him.

Moreover, if God is all-powerful, we cannot have reliable knowledge about the real nature of other things. If one experiences a physical object, one assumes that there is something in the outer world which is the cause of the experience. But suppose that God were to destroy the object and still, by an act of his will, sustain the experience with no perceptible change. It would follow that, in view of the fact that God could at any time produce exactly the same effect in an observer by any one of a variety of ways, our knowledge of the world is so limited that we are justified in an almost complete skepticism about it.

Ockham did not draw out the full implications of a position that might have led him into a radical skepticism. He was more concerned to try to provide a sound basis for natural science by freeing it from theological considerations. He did this by anticipating in some measure the positivistic approach of later centuries. Rejecting the usual Franciscan advocacy of the Augustianian and Platonic point of view, Ockham thought that even Thomas Aquinas and Duns Scotus were too Platonic in their treatment of universals. If knowledge of the "real" world is knowledge of universals, and if the world of sense is mere appearance, then ultimately, knowledge must be of precisely the sort of reality which, for Ockham, was inaccessible to the reason and can only be validated by revelation. Ockham wanted to start at the other end of the scale, the empirical end, which, he believed, was the point from which Aristotelian thought had originated. Universals, which Thomist and Scotist alike thought to be necessary for the general character of science, were, Ockham decided, unnecessary baggage, even in their somewhat attenuated character in Scotist thought as "formal" rather than "real" in character.

Everything about which we think, Ockham said, is a particular, revealed by sense perception. Universals are nothing outside the mind, and so, we do not think about them except in the science of logic. We think *with* them. The "real" sciences are those which deal with things. Logic, however, is a "rational" science dealing with "signs." A sign is that by means of which something comes into the mind and which stands for that thing. A term "stands for" something. That for which it stands is "stood for."

Signs may be natural or conventional. A natural sign is the concept formed by the mind when it perceives or understands something. A conventional sign is a written or spoken term. Signs may be predicable of a number of things, but they are not the essence of anything. Their being consists entirely in their being known (*esse eorum est eorum cognosci*). Terms can be of "first intention" or "second intention." "First intention" terms are signs of individual existent things which are not signs of anything else. Thus, "man," "animal," and "substance," used to denote actual objects so named, are terms of first intention. "Second intention" terms are signs of other terms. Terms may be used "significantly" or "nonsignificantly." The second intention term "species," in the sentence "A species includes a number of individual objects," is used significantly. When it refers not to what is meant by the term but to the term itself, as in the sentence " 'Species' is a word of Latin origin," it is used nonsignificantly.

Logic deals with terms of second intention used significantly. Universals may thus be considered logically, though they are in themselves nothing but tools with which we think. "Socrates," "Plato," and "Aristotle" signify individuals, whereas the term "man" refers to a class. If we say, "Man is a rational animal," however, to what does the word "man" refer? To nothing, according to Ockham, other than to Socrates, Plato, Aristotle, and all other individuals who comprise the class. Our natural knowledge is of individuals, but science needs universal terms because it is concerned with general knowledge. The term, however, does not designate a thing or an object of thought in the way that Socrates can be an object of thought. It is merely an instrument for scientific use. Universals, then, are only terms, and Ockham's philosophy came to be known as "terminism."

Is there, however, in addition to the conventional sign—the word "man" as spoken or written—something else, a natural sign which exists in the soul as a universal?

Ockham thought that there is and considered three opinions which had been advanced to explain its nature. Some, he said, thought it to be a "fiction produced by the soul." Others held that it is "a certain quality existing subjectively in the soul, distinct from the act of understanding." Still others maintained that it is simply the act of understanding. In arriving at his own answer, Ockham appealed to the principle of parsimony. "What can be explained on fewer principles," he said, "is explained needlessly by more. Everything, however, which is explained through positing something distinct from the act of understanding can be explained without positing such a distinct thing. For to stand for something and to signify something can belong just as well to the act of understanding as to this fictive entity; therefore, one ought not to posit anything else beyond the act of understanding."

The maxim of parsimony, under the form "*Entia non sunt multiplicanda praeter necessitatem*," has come to be known as "Ockham's Razor." It has been pointed out on the one hand, however, that Duns Scotus and other Medieval philosophers appealed to it and on the other, that the "*Entia non sunt multiplicanda*" formulation, attributed to Ockham by Sir William Hamilton, in fact did not come into being until John Ponce of Cork enunciated it some three centuries later. Be that as it may, Ockham's use of the principle came at a time when it was of the utmost importance for the development of the philosophical matrix in which the science of the coming age would be born. Certainly, however, his own application of the rule, as well as his distinction between the spheres of knowledge and faith, was far less radical than that of many of his successors who thought themselves to be following in his footsteps. His impact on the downfall of the Scholastic synthesis was undoubtedly much greater than he could have anticipated.

There were, of course, men of the Church who were able to adjust their outlook to an intellectual climate in which reason can deal only with phenomena and God can be apprehended only through faith, but for others, the destruction of the Scholastic synthesis was intolerable. The realists joined ranks against Ockham's brand of nominalism and a bitter fight broke out in the European universities. At Paris, his books were banned in 1339, and in the following year, nominalism was formally rejected. In the fifteenth century, the faculty of the University was bound by oath to adhere to realism. Meanwhile, however, new universities were established at Prague, Vienna, Heidelberg, and Cologne, at which nominalists were free to present their case.

There, and elsewhere in Europe, it met with sympathetic reception. Some devotees of science were happy to have the option of an intellectual pursuit of a positivistic science which need not be accommodated to scholastic philosophy. The doctrine of twofold truth became popular, according to which reason leads to one sort of truth and faith another. The two varieties were regarded as completely independent of each other, to such an extent, in fact, that it was impossible for one to contradict the other. It was maintained by the Averroists, for instance, that it is true in theology but false in philosophy that man is immortal. With such assaults on the very foundational principles of Aristotelian logic, the stage was set for intellectual anarchy.

Fourteenth-Century Mysticism

Throughout the Middle Ages, the rational theology of the Scholastics was tempered by a mysticism through which the believer could be assured that he not only had knowledge about God, but could know him in a more direct and intimate way. The Church sanctioned and, indeed, encouraged mystical experience so long as it was clearly understood that it was subject to evaluation by ecclesiastical authority. In the fourteenth century, however, a Germanic school of mystics laid claim to a more independent attitude toward the Church.

Prominent in this movement were Johannes Tauler (1300-1361), Johannes Eckhart (ca. 1260-1327) and an assortment of Dutch mystics, among them Jan van Ruysbroek (1293-1381) and Thomas à Kempis (1380-1471), author of the *Imitation of Christ*.

Eckhart, known as "Meister Eckhart," was the most celebrated figure in the movement. A native of Hockheim, near Gotha, he became a member of the Dominican order and successively held the posts of Master of Theology at Paris, Provincial for his order in Saxony, and Vicar-General for Bohemia. In 1311, he returned to Paris and taught there until 1314, when he was assigned to Strasbourg. He later went to Cologne, and in 1326, the Archbishop there took action to suppress his doctrines. He made a public defense of his orthodoxy and appealed to Pope John XXII. Some three years after his death, the Vatican condemned twenty-eight of his propositions.

Far from embarking on an open rebellion against Thomistic Scholasticism, Eckhart constructed his system on the framework provided by Thomas. He was, however, well grounded in the sort of Neoplatonic thought embodied in the writings of the Pseudo-Dionysus, and it was this coloring which, in the minds of his critics, gave his views a heretical cast.

For Eckhart, God is "above being," and in view of the fact that being and knowledge are one, the divine nature is also beyond knowledge. God cannot, then, be defined in terms of human concepts. The eternal Godhead is a "darkness" that even the Godhead cannot know. In one sense, the absolute and infinite being can legitimately be called "nothing," for no predicates applicable to "things" can be ascribed to him. His essence and existence, if indeed, the terms can be used in thinking of him, are identical. He is the "I am that I am" of the Mosaic revelation.

To become manifest to himself and to human beings, God must think himself, and in order to do this, he must think the Trinity and the world, which, in true Neoplatonic fashion, eternally flow from the Godhead and return to it. Nothing exists apart from God, though each creature has its own essence. Eckhart's insistence on the eternal creation of the world was one of the reasons for his troubles with the champions of orthodoxy. It appears that he thought of the "in the beginning" of Genesis in terms of the "eternal now" in which God sees all things as one and all events as present.

Eckhart sought to avoid the stigma of pantheism by making a distinction between the ideal world and the created world of our experience, which, though necessarily of the essence of God, is sufficiently differentiable from the divine nature to make it unnecessary to attribute to that nature the imperfections of the world of time and space.

The human soul has in it an "uncreated spark" which motivates it to seek union with God. This is accomplished through knowledge, which is, in its highest form, beyond reason. The mystical union is attained by freeing oneself from concern with the particulars of experience and accepting the progressive illumination that will ultimately enable one to know immediately his identity with the divine nature. At that point, one can enter "the silent desert into which no difference has ever penetrated, which is immovable and supreme over all oppositions and divisions."

For Eckhart, morality is inseparably bound up with the sort of knowledge which leads human beings to God. "Whoever would see God," he wrote, "must be dead to himself and buried in God, in the unrevealed desert Godhead, to become again what he was before he was." Morality is not composed of outward acts, but upon the character of the agent. It "consists not in doing, but in being." Love of God, however, is at the core of the moral life and if one truly loves God, he will, as a natural result, perform right actions.

The philosophy of Eckhart, stressing, as it did, the direct access of the individual to God, posed an implicit challenge to the role of the Church as a channel of grace, and his Neoplatonic metaphysics, verging on pantheism, ran counter to the carefully crafted Thomistic world view. Together with the voluntarism of Duns Scotus and the nominalism of Ockham, the mysticism for which he was a principal spokesman helped set the stage for the Renaissance and the Reformation.

VI.
THE DISCOVERY OF NEW WORLDS

Chapter 18

Birth and Rebirth

The forces unleashed by the experiences of Europeans in the Crusades did not exhaust themselves in the Aristotelian revolution. The contacts made in the twelfth and thirteenth centuries with the thought of Moslem scholars and the appropriation of Moslem science by thinkers like Roger Bacon had opened up the West to winds of change which could not be stilled.

The causes of the further ferment which erupted in Europe about the middle of the fourteenth century were varied. The rediscovery of classical writings which had been forgotten in the West stimulated interest in the civilizations which had given birth to them and ultimately led to a desire to revive some of the glory associated with Greece and Rome. Coming as it did at a time when the foundations of medieval thought were being shaken by internal dissension, the new vision of antiquity provided an alternative model for Western culture which was irresistible to many Europeans who found the Scholastic pattern too confining.

George Bernard Shaw saw the spirit of the fifteenth century summed up in the person of Joan of Arc, who, in her attitudes, anticipated the two movements which would later dominate the Renaissance—nationalism and Protestantism. She was, he suggested, a nationalist because she thought in terms of nation-states of a sort which had not existed as genuinely unified political entities since antiquity. France was, for her, far more real then the feudal domains which had formerly claimed the allegiance of French-speaking people. She was, albeit unknowingly, a Protestant because she placed the authority of her private voices above that of the Church.

Certainly the economic and political forces which were abroad in Joan's day were drastically altering the face of Europe, and the coalition of churchmen and politicians who burned her were not blind to the danger she symbolized. What they could not admit was that the marvelously intricate system which had held Christendom together since the fall of Rome had already unraveled to such a point that the new order was inevitable.

The fiefdoms of medieval Europe had relied on an economy based on barter. The widening geographical horizons of the late Middle Ages suggested the need for a more flexible mode of exchange, and the age of exploration which followed made such a system an absolute necessity. The solution to the problem was found in a return to the economy of the classical age—an economy based on money and banking.

Money, to be sure, had existed in the Middle Ages, primarily for trade with the Orient, and princes were obliged on occasion to borrow money from bankers, using various subterfuges to evade the laws against usury. With the discovery of America, however, followed by a flow of goods from the New World the attention of merchants was turned from the East to the West, and commerce began to replace agriculture as the principal influence on the economic life of Europe. The result was an enormous increase in the supply of money. The emergence of a class of rich merchants and financiers, engaging in international transactions, made the old feudal system, with its multiple centers of authority, impractical, and power became more and more centered in kings who could bring order into the movement of goods and the minting and exchange of money. The new nationalism was, at least in part, brought about by the economic revolution. On the other hand, the monarchs themselves, aware of the extent to which the new commercial order provided a favorable environment for the growth of their power, worked zealously to foster trade. The Church itself became involved in the changing attitude toward financial transactions. The definition of usury, which had been broad enough to include all lending of money for interest was gradually changed so as to prohibit only those rates of interest which were considered exorbitant. Investment became increasingly profitable and, as a class of rich and powerful merchants began to emerge, the old guilds declined, and the ideals of chivalry, rooted as they were in the dying feudal system, survived mainly as honored anachronisms in the courts of Europe.

The new age was marked by a profound change in the way in which people thought about themselves. The parochialism of the feudal system gradually gave way to the sort of national feeling, based on geographical, historical, and linguistic association which had been a living force in some of the nation states of antiquity but which had existed only nominally in the Middle Ages.

To Europeans emerging from the cocoon of a feudal structure into the broader national life, the experience was exhilarating. Bur nationalism was, paradoxically, a narrowing as well as a broadening influence. The feudal structure, decentralized as it had been politically and economically, had nevertheless fostered a genuine cultural internationalism.

The pervasive ideas of Church and Empire as unifying forces had been strengthened by the universal use of Latin in the West as the language of scholarship and literature. One symptom of the decline of the Medieval spirit was the emergence of literature in the native languages of the writers. Dante Alighieri (1265-1321) wrote his *Divine Comedy* in Italian, and Geoffrey Chaucer (ca. 1343-1400) his *Canterbury Tales* in English. If the production of works in the vernacular narrowed the range of scholarly perusal, it opened the way to wider readership among newly literate inhabitants of the towns and cities who were unversed in Latin. One salutary result was the development of English, Italian, French, German, and other languages of Europe as vehicles for literary expression. The growth of popular literature representative of regional and national culture was made possible on an unprecedented scale by the invention, during the first half of the fifteenth century, of printing, an art known for centuries in the Orient, but new to the West.

All these events, together with other circumstances unfavorable to the continuation of feudal life, came at a time when the Church and the Empire were less capable than ever before of providing the sort of unifying cultural influences which had given a real significance to the idea of Western Christendom. The removal of the papacy to Avignon during the fourteenth century had signaled the emergence of a powerful French monarchy. When the "Babylonian Captivity of the Church," as it was called, resulted in 1378 in a schism in which one pope reigned in Avignon and another in Rome, the impotence of the Church to govern the life of Europe was visible for all to see. The dispute was finally settled in 1417, but by that time, the Renaissance was well under way. As for the Empire, it had become all too evident not only that its claim to be holy and Roman were questionable but that it had lost any ability it might once have had to wield imperial authority in the face of the growing power of secular princes busily forging a new political order. Typical of those princes were Louis XI of France and Henry VII of England, both men who saw their countries as nations in the ancient sense and who were able to rally their subjects to the cause of national unity by trimming their sails to the winds of change. These men and their heirs presided over a flowering of national feeling in their countries which sounded the death knell of feudalism.

In some respects, however, their conception of government was not radically different from that held by their predecessors. The concept of natural law was still honored in French and English political thought, and both Louis and Henry thought of themselves as devout sons of the Church. Even Henry's successor, Henry VIII, who successfully asserted his claim to be the earthly head of the Church of England had no thought of substituting a wholly secular rationale for political authority for one based on divine sanction. Henry, a versatile man who could write passable music, was also something of a theologian, and his attack on Martin Luther, written in 1521, gained for him the title "Defender of the Faith," still claimed by British monarchs in the twentieth century. His practical contribution to the development of the modern world lay in his nationalism. He was not at heart a Protestant.

The new conception of political authority in France was articulated by Jean Bodin (1530-1596), an attorney and philosopher who enjoyed the favor of King Henry III.

Bodin's *Six Livres de la Republique* was published in 1576, significantly in French. It was nine years later that he himself had his own Latin translation published. In that work, he developed his conception of the ideal state, but he used the ideal as a standard by which the government of France could be evaluated and reformed. The book was notable for the concept of sovereignty expressed in it. A state, Bodin maintained, acquires its legitimacy through its utility in providing government in accordance with natural law. "A state," he says, "is a lawful government of many families and of what is common to them, together with a supreme sovereignty . . . We [say] that it is a '*lawful* government,' in order to distinguish it from a gang of robbers or pirates . . . However much such a gang may seem to form a society, and its members to live in amity among themselves, we ought not to call it a 'society' or 'state' . . . because it lacks the principal mark of a peaceful society, namely, a lawful government according to the laws of nature."

While maintaining that legitimate law conforms to natural law, Bodin tried at the same time, with some inconsistency, to accommodate in his philosophy the idea which had gained currency by his time that power is the ultimate source of rightful political authority.

That idea had come to full flower in Italy before Bodin's time in the climate of a political situation in which no king had arisen to unify the land. The Empire still technically exercised the power of the temporal sword, but the Emperor was far away in Germany and held in check by the Church. The Pope, however, while powerful enough to keep anyone else from unifying Italy, was unable to do it himself. The growing dominance of urban life during the Renaissance encouraged the development of city states on the Italian peninsula, and these in turn, produced secular princes whose political philosophy owed little to the concepts that had traditionally dominated European thought during the Middle Ages. For these men, the idea of natural law was, in great measure, replaced by that of power as the chief end of statecraft.

Machiavelli

The new trend in Italy was perceptively described by Niccolo Machiavelli (1469-1527). A native of Florence, Machiavelli served in the government of the city and, on a number of occasions was sent on diplomatic missions to other Italian states. In 1500, he went to France to conduct some negotiations with Louis XII, and two years after that, shortly after his marriage, he reluctantly obeyed an order to proceed as an envoy to the camp of Cesare Borgia in Romagna. Cesare, the illegitimate son of the worldly and unscrupulous Pope Alexander VI, had a burning ambition to unify a quarrelsome assortment of Italian states and was willing to go to any length, including political assassination, to accomplish his ends. Machiavelli became captivated by Cesare's vision, and concluded that under the condition of moral decadence which prevailed in Italy, the Borgia conception of statecraft was the only one appropriate to the times. In no small measure, Cesare was the model for the ideal statesman portrayed in Machiavelli's best known work, *The Prince (Il Principe),* which he completed in 1513.

Machiavelli, seeing man as essentially a political animal, divorced his theory of the state from all considerations of theology and natural law. Men, he thought, are dominated by passions rather than by reason. In view of the fact that these passions are insatiable, strife is the natural condition among men. It follows that the only sort of government which can be successful is the rule of a single, strong individual. Ideally, to be sure, "Governments of the people are better than of princes," but such governments, though possible in the great days of the Roman Republic, had ceased to be a live option in Italy. The virtue of the Romans was attributable to their pagan religion, whereas the tenets of Christianity cultivated a talent for suffering rather than for the achievement of greatness. "These principles," he wrote in *Discourses on the First Ten Books of Titus Livius* "seem to me to have made men feeble, and caused them to become an easy prey to evil-minded men, who can control them more securely, seeing that the great body of men, for the sake of gaining Paradise, are more disposed to endure injuries than to avenge them." This being the case, "It is necessary to establish some superior power which, with a royal hand, and with full and absolute powers, may put a curb upon the excessive ambition and corruption of the powerful."

Private virtue is essential for the well-being of any society, and it is good for a prince to be virtuous, but princely virtue, in Machiavelli's view is that which facilitates the acquisition and retention of power. Vice is that which has the opposite effect. The virtuous prince, then, will manipulate the passions of the people in such a way as to convince them that it is in their best interests to have him as their ruler. While such a program will, at times, dictate benevolent actions, it will at others, necessitate the ruthless use of force and the shameless employment of deception. "Injuries," he suggested, "should be done all together, so that being less tasted, they will give less offense. Benefits should be granted little by little, so that they may be better enjoyed."

It is well, he held, for a ruler to be both feared and loved, but if a choice must be made between the two, it is better to be feared than loved. The reason is that men "have less scruple in offending one who makes himself loved than one who makes himself feared; for love is held by a chain of obligation which, men being selfish, is broken whenever it serves their purpose; but fear is maintained by a dread of punishment which never fails."

A prince is not morally bound to keep his word when it is no longer to his advantage to do so. Nor is he obligated to tell the truth. To make the people believe what it is to the ruler's advantage to have them believe is secondary in importance only to the possession of sufficient instruments of power to compel obedience. Religion, whether true or false, will be used as a powerful sanction by the wise ruler. "In truth," Machiavelli said, "there never was any remarkable lawgiver amongst any people who did not resort to divine authority, as otherwise his laws would not have been accepted by the people; for there are many good laws, the importance of which is known to the sagacious lawgiver, but the reasons for which are not sufficiently evident to enable him to persuade others to submit to them; and therefore do wise men, for the purpose of removing this difficulty, resort to divine authority. Thus did Lycurgus and Solon and many others who aimed at the same thing."

In Machiavelli's philosophy, then, we have the development of a thoroughly secular view of politics. The ends sought by government are purely natural and those ends are not subordinate to any supernatural claim. The idea of justice has reverted to the Thrasymachan conception which Plato was at such pains to refute. It is the will of the stronger, and the wise prince will use force and fraud whenever necessary to achieve his ends. To Machiavelli's credit, it may be acknowledged that he described with complete and merciless accuracy the methods by which political power has, throughout the history of mankind, been gained and exercised, but the view that political philosophy can be reduced to a description of those methods, with no reference to any sort of transempirical standards by which they can be judged, has never been able in the West to overthrow entirely the concept of natural law.

The Rise of Humanism

Throughout the Middle Ages, the respect for classical antiquity had been profound, but it was an antiquity filtered through a churchly scholarship which imparted its own color to the images of Greece and Rome. Dante Aligheiri had such profound respect for Vergil that he made him his guide for the initial stages of the journey described in the *Divine Comedy*. That journey, of course, is through no earthly landscape, but rather through those regions of the spirit with which the Medieval mind was most concerned. The interest in Greece and Rome which had been rekindled in the twelfth and thirteenth centuries, however, was too strong to be contained by the traditional structure of learning, and in the fourteenth and fifteenth centuries it produced a new sort of scholar—one who devoted himself to the study of the *litterae humaniores* and so was called a humanist.

Francesco de Petracco (Petrarch) was a pioneer of the new scholarship. Born at Arezzo in 1304, he was, in 1313, taken to Avignon to live. He studied the humanities at Carpentras and law at Montpellier and Bologna. On April 26, 1327, in the Church of Santa Clara at Avignon, he saw for the first time the "Laura" who figures prominently in his poetry. The identity of the lady remains a mystery. In 1336, on his first visit to Rome, he was struck by the stark contrast between the magnificence of the ancient ruins and the wretchedness of the medieval city. That exposure to the greatness of the past undoubtedly strengthened a passionate devotion he had developed at an early age to classical culture.

Hand in hand with that devotion went an interest in nature not unlike that which emerged centuries later in the Romantic movement. Few of his contemporaries would ever have dreamed of climbing a mountain for other than practical reasons. Petrarch for many years wanted to climb Mount Ventoux, the "Windy Peak" near Avignon, for no other reason than "the desire to see its conspicuous height." The final incentive to make the ascent came when, in reading Livy, he found the account of the ascent of Mount Haemus by Philip of Macedon.

Persisting in the enterprise in the face of advice to turn back from "an aged shepherd in the folds of the mountain," Petrarch and his brother at last reached the summit. "At first," he wrote later, "I stood there almost benumbed by a gale such as I had never felt before and by the unusually open and wide view. I looked around me: clouds were gathering below my feet, and Athos and Olympus grew less incredible, since I saw on a mountain of lesser fame what I had heard and read about them." He could see the Alps, "frozen stiff and covered with snow."

The mountains of the Province of Lyons, the Rhone river, and "the sea near Marseilles as well as the waves that break against Aigues Montes, although it takes several days to travel to this city."

But he was still a child of the fourteenth century. "I admired every detail, now relishing earthly enjoyment, now lifting up my mind to higher spheres after the example of my body." Then, looking into a copy of Augustine's *Confessions* which he always carried with him, he saw the passage, "And men go to admire the high mountains, the vast floods of the sea, the huge streams of the rivers, the circumference of the ocean, and the revolutions of the stars—and desert themselves." He closed the book, he said, "angry with myself that I still admired earthly things. Long since I ought to have learned, even from pagan philosophers, that nothing is admirable besides the mind; compared to its greatness, nothing is great."

Petrarch's humanism was exhibited in his contempt for mere commentary of the sort favored by many Scholastics, as well as for the mere accumulation of facts about the external world. "What is the use—I beseech you—of knowing the nature of quadrapeds, fowls, fishes, and serpents, and not knowing or even neglecting man's nature, the purpose for which we are born, and whence and whereto we travel?" He explored that nature through serious study of the Greek and Roman classics—a study reflected in his own writings and in his participation in public affairs. He was, among his other achievements, responsible for the prolonged popularity of the sonnet-sequence in praise of a beloved who is beyond the reach of the lover—the unattainable mistress being, in his case, the mysterious Madonna Laura, whose death from the plague in 1348, followed by the death of a number of Petrarch's best friends, brought about a crisis in his life which resulted in the introduction of an increasingly religious tone in his writing.

Giovanni Boccaccio, a friend of Petrarch's, brought a more obviously secular emphasis to the early Renaissance with his romances and long poems. The illegitimate child of an Italian father and a French mother, Boccaccio was born in Paris in 1313, but was brought up near Florence. In the most famous of his works, the *Decameron,* he put together a collection of stories which influenced other writers of the period, notably Geoffrey Chaucer (ca. 1343-1400), who used two of the narratives in his own *Canterbury Tales* after a trip to Italy in which he became acquainted with Italian literature. Boccaccio repudiated the *Decameron* in the latter years of his life for the bawdiness of some of the stories and, under the influence of Petrarch, devoted himself to encyclopedic works written in Latin. By the time of Petrarch's death in 1374 and his own a year later, however, the influences which they had brought to bear on Italian literature had set a pattern for Humanism in Italy and elsewhere in Europe for the next two centuries.

Fifteenth and Sixteenth Century Humanism

After the fall of Constantinople in 1453 to the Ottoman Turks, large numbers of Greek manuscripts found their way from the former capital of the Eastern Empire to the universities of Italy. Greek, a language long neglected in the West, even by scholars such as Petrarch, became popular with humanist scholars. Lectures were given in the language, and in Florence a Platonic Academy was established by the Medici for the study of the classics. What was seen as the proper goal of learning—the understanding of man—replaced the other-worldliness which had dominated the curricula of many educational institutions. The concern for other-worldly religion began to give way to an emphasis on the ideal of human excellence and the enhancement of the values of earthly life.

To be sure, most of the great figures of the Renaissance had no thought of repudiating their Christian faith, but their interpretation of the relationship between God and his creation was undergoing a radical transformation. The rekindled interest in pagan antiquity produced a ferment of the spirit which manifested itself in every aspect of human life. The medieval cities, dominated by great Gothic churches drawing the eye toward heaven, retained its dominance in much of Europe, but a new pattern was beginning to emerge in the residences of the well-to-do, as well as in churches and public buildings planned for metropolitan areas sufficiently uncluttered to accommodate the greater horizontality of classical architecture. From Italy to England, the turreted fortresses which had housed the great feudal lords gave place to elegant country residences, with wide windows admitting light and air and affording a view of pleasant gardens.

In painting and sculpture, the changes were equally profound. In medieval art, the human form had been seen primarily as a vehicle for spiritual instruction, and in general, had been attuned to the vertical character of Gothic architecture. Now, in the hands of masters like Leonardo da Vinci, Raphael, Michelangelo, and Ghiberti, it was still seen as expressing the glory of God, but in the context of a natural world valued for its own sake. The typical medieval madonna was visibly the Queen of Heaven, enthroned in stiff hieratic dignity, holding a stylized and equally dignified child in her arms. A Raphael madonna, on the other hand, was a genuine young Italian matron in simple blue, red, and white garments, and the Christ child was a real, wriggling little boy of flesh and blood. The effect of the new art, however, was not to demean the divine but rather to elevate the human as the Greeks had done. The beauty of the figures and the radiance of the surroundings in which they were placed suggested the presence of God in his creation, but the setting was unmistakably the world.

Increasingly too the conduct of life itself was viewed as a sort of exercise of art rather than merely as the preparation for heaven. Pietro Pompanazzi (1462-1525) neatly summed up the new attitude toward morality when he said, "The reward of virtue is virtue itself, while the punishment of the vicious is vice." While William Shakespeare's dramas contain many references to religion, their dominant tone is secular, and the playwright's own attitude, difficult as it is to distinguish from the views of his characters, may have been well expressed in the declaration, "All the world's a stage, and all the men and women merely players. They have their exits and their entrances, and one man in his time plays many parts." Probably the worldliest of all the writers of the period was François Rabelais (1494-1543), the French author of *Pantagruel* and *Gargantua,* works in which a delight in obscenity goes hand in hand with a detestation of a decadent clergy.

Giovanni Pico della Mirandola (1462-1494), an Italian count, received an excellent education in humanistic subjects. Applying the fruits of his studies with Hebrew teachers, he attempted to support Christian theology by reference to the Jewish Kabbalah, and he tried to harmonize the works of Plato and Aristotle. He saw Greek philosophy and the Jewish and Christian Scriptures not merely as being in harmony but as actually forming a complete and unitary revelation of sacred truth. His chief significance for the development of Western thought, however, lay in his philosophy of man, which was not derived directly from classical thought or from the mainstream of Renaissance humanism.

Like his fellow humanists, he stressed the importance of the study of man's nature, but the place he assigned to man in the universe is unique in that unlike all other created things, man makes his own nature. In his best known work, *On the Dignity of Man,* he told how God, "the best of workmen," took up man, "a work of indeterminate form," set him "at the midpoint of the world," and said to him:

> "We have given to thee, Adam, no fixed seat, no form of thy very own, no gift peculiarly thine, that thou mayest feel as thine own, have as thine own, possess as thine own the seat, the form, the gifts which thou thyself shall desire. A limited nature in other creatures is confined within the laws written down by us. In conformity with thy free judgment, in whose hands I have placed thee, thou art confined by no bounds;

> and thou wilt fix limits of nature for thyself. I have placed thee at the center of the world, that from there thou mayest more conveniently look around and see whatsoever is in the world. Neither heavenly nor earthly, neither mortal nor immortal have we made thee. Thou, like a judge appointed for being honorable, art the molder and maker of thyself; thou mayest sculpt thyself into whatever shape thou dost prefer. Thou canst grow downward into the lower natures which are brutes. Thou canst again grow upward from thy soul's reason into the higher natures which are divine.''

His plan to present nine hundred theses in Rome, drawn from various sources, got him into trouble when thirteen of the theses were declared heretical. He lived to see himself exonerated in 1493, however, when Pope Alexander VI lifted the ban of heresy.

Erasmus

No one expressed the values of Humanism better than Desiderius Erasmus (1466?-1536). A priest, and a loyal son of the Church, he nevertheless had an independence of spirit which has made him an important figure in the history of the Reformation as well as the Renaissance. A native of the Netherlands, the illegitimate son of a pair of lovers whose story is told in Charles Reade's novel, *The Cloister and the Hearth,* he became a citizen of the world, at home over the expanse of Europe from Italy to England, where he was a friend of John Colet, lived as a member of Thomas More's household, and later taught at Cambridge.

Erasmus was critical of a great deal of the machinery, ceremony, and dogma of the Church. Rather than trying to overthrow it and substitute other equally questionable theology and praxis, however, he sought to reform it from within. In his *Enchiridion,* he insisted on the worthlessness of ceremonial religion without those inward spiritual qualities which ought to characterize Christians. A true rationalist, he was confident that proper education could eliminate the evils that afflicted the Church and restore it to purity. The original word of God, he thought, was so simple and direct that if it could be made available to the peoples of Europe in their own language, they would have a comprehension of it which would exercise salvific effect.

``Other philosophies,'' he said, ``by the very difficulty of their precepts, are removed out of the range of most minds. [But] no age, no sex, no condition of life is excluded from [an understanding of Christian thought]. The sun itself is not more common and open to all than is the teaching of Christ. For I utterly dissent from those who are unwilling that the sacred Scriptures should be read by the unlearned and translated into their vulgar tongues . . . I long that the husbandman should sing portions of them to himself as he follows the plow, that the weaver should hum them to the tune of his shuttle, that the traveller should beguile with their story the tedium of the journey.''

He assailed the clergy with trenchant, if usually good-natured, satire. In *Julius Exclusius,* a work generally attributed to him, the gate keeper of heaven, Saint Peter, refuses admission to the recently-deceased soldier pope, Julius II, because of the excesses of the papal court. His *Praise of Folly (Encomium Moriae)*, while extolling the simple folly of the sincere believer, assailed the clerics for the foolishness of their attention to the trivialities of theological disputation and monastic discipline. He imagined a priest who boasts of ''so many bushels of prayers'' while trying to get into heaven. Another, he said, ''brags of not having touched a penny without at least two pairs of gloves on.'' Christ, in answering them, says, ''I left you but one precept, of loving one another, which I do not hear anyone plead that he has faithfully discharged.'' All the excess paraphernalia of the Church, Erasmus thought, could be replaced by a universal religion and a simple morality based on the Christian Gospels and Greek philosophy.

Erasmus, in addition to being a brilliant writer and such a witty and charming conversationalist that he was once told, ''You must be Erasmus or the Devil,'' was a classical scholar of considerable ability. He had the true Humanist's love of the Greek language and, with the collaboration of others, produced a new Latin translation of the New Testament, which, published alongside an edited version of the Greek New Testament, brought to light a number of textual inaccuracies of the Vulgate.

Fruits of the Renaissance

The humanistic Renaissance spirit had fruits other than literary achievements. It produced much of the greatest art the Western world has seen, justifying Petrarch's contention that free individual development and social interaction of fine minds are essential to the development of the highest conditions of culture. That individualism, however, was responsible not only for great art but for increasingly bizarre fashions. In Italy, especially , a time came when the whole idea of conventional dress gave way to the design of unique and spectacular clothing for each aristocratic man or woman.

The new freedom was, in great measure, responsible for the age of discovery, when the boundaries of the known world expanded beyond the imagination of previous ages. Christopher Columbus explored the fringes of the New World. Vasco de Gama sailed around the Cape of Good Hope. Ferdinand Magellan sailed as far west as the Philippines, and one of his ships, the *Concepción*, commanded by Juan Sebastián del Caro completed the circumnavigation of the globe. Other explorers and *conquistadores* laid the groundwork for future colonization and brought riches from the newly discovered lands to the courts of Europe.

The influence of the Humanists on Western Civilization has been enduring and, on the whole, beneficent. It is, of course, true that some of their number were less than enthusiastic about science, thinking that it turned the attention of scholars away from such humane disciplines as ethics, but one of the most inquisitive scientific minds of all time belonged to Leonardo da Vinci, who was at the same time, one of the foremost Humanists. It may also be the case that the emphasis on antiquity and the study of languages fostered a sort of classical pedantry in education, but that very emphasis, stressing as it did the well-rounded discipline of the mind, laid the foundation for subsequent European and American educational theory and practice.

Chapter 19

New Visions of Man and the Cosmos

From earliest antiquity, men had watched the heavenly bodies and formed theories to explain their movement. Common sense and everyday experience were sufficient to convince most of mankind that the earth is the stable center of the universe. In the case of the so-called fixed stars, there was little problem. They were supposed to revolve around the earth every day, with the pole star, or a point quite near it, defining the axis. The movement of the sun and the moon were explained with equal ease.

A problem arose, however, in the case of the planets of our sun, the "wanderers." If their progress is observed over an extended period, they generally appear to move forward, but at intervals they seem to reverse direction for a time before resuming their customary course.

The explanation generally accepted during the Middle Ages was that of the second-century Alexandrian astronomer Ptolemy, who provided an ingenious account of the retrograde movement, in the framework of a geocentric system. In that system, based on early Greek theories like the one formulated by Aristotle, the earth is surrounded by a series of crystalline spheres, each of which supports one or more of the heavenly bodies: the moon, Mercury, Venus, the sun, Mars, Jupiter, Saturn, and finally the fixed stars. Beyond these was the ninth crystalline sphere, the *primum mobile*. This was, in essence, the conception of the universe adopted by Dante for his *Divine Comedy*. Like Ptolemy and the better educated scholars of the medieval period, he posited a spherical earth, and the poet added the interesting information that the Devil resides in the exact center of the earth, so that a traveler, after climbing down the body of his Satanic Majesty as far as the waist, would be compelled to climb up his nether extremities on the way to the opposite side of the earth.

Ptolemy had, however, made a mistake about the size of the earth, and that mistake had been perpetuated by his followers. Following Hipparchus, an astronomer and mathematician of the second century B.C., he had divided the equatorial circle into 180 parts or degrees and used the points thus established to determine lines of longitude to the poles. Unfortunately for his system, the points were not far enough apart, for he had ignored Eratosthenes' reasonably accurate measurement of the circumference of the earth and, for some reason, subscribed to a much smaller figure suggested by Posidonius (c.135-150 B.C.).

The Ptolemaic and medieval explanation for the movement of the planets involved the use of epicycles. The nature of the concept can be understood by imagining a spot on the rim of a small wheel mounted through its hub on the rim of a larger one. As both wheels revolve, the spot is carried forward by the movement of the larger, and its velocity is accelerated by the rotation of the smaller through half of its cycle. But in the other half of the cycle, the apparent movement of the spot, as seen from a point at the hub of the larger wheel might, for a time, be retrograde.

Ptolemy had accepted the usual view of his time that the movements of the heavenly bodies had to describe perfect circles, and so even with the admission of his epicycles into the system, it had been necessary to provide an extremely complex calculation in order to provide an explanation of observed astronomical phenomena. In addition to adding the smaller circular orbits of the planets, Ptolemy had been forced to treat the Greek spheres as hypothetical and to posit the existence of additional spheres, some of which moved in a direction opposite to the ones included in the earlier systems. The system was further refined by astronomers after Ptolemy, notably those of the Arab world, until some seventy-nine epicycles were required to account for the observed movements in the sky.

It should be emphasized that there is no scientific reason why the earth cannot be regarded as the center of the universe if one is willing to assume a sufficiently complex pattern in the movements of other astronomical bodies. The Ptolemaic system worked and could still be made to work in our day if we were to proceed from a dogmatically geocentric position while making the further assumption that a circular path is the only possible one for a planet to follow. Such a system, however, involves incredibly complex calculations, and the complexity was already becoming cumbersome in the 15th century.

This, then, was the state of the orthodox cosmology in Europe in the year 1473, when a son was born in Thorn, in Prussian Poland, to the wife of a wholesale trader named Koppernigk, or its Latin equivalent *Copernicus*. The boy was taken under the wing of his uncle, a prominent clergyman named Lucas Watzelrode, who in 1489 became Bishop of Ermeland. As a student at the University of Cracow, he became proficient in mathematics and painting. Later, at Bologna, he studied canon law and attended lectures on astronomy by Domenico Maria Novara. He was in his second year of medical school at Padua, in 1503, when he received his doctorate in canon law at Ferrara.

After completing the study of medicine in 1505, he returned to Poland and lived with his uncle as his physician at the episcopal palace at Heilsburg. After the uncle's death in 1512, Copernicus moved to Frauenburg, where he engaged in a variety of political, religious, administrative and medical activities. It was at this time that he elaborated the theory, already conceived at Heilsburg, on which his fame was to rest.

For a long time, he had been dissatisfied with the Ptolemaic doctrine. In Italy, he had been exposed to the Pythagorean theory of a moving earth, and he was probably familiar with Aristarchus' contention that the earth rotates on its axis and revolves around the sun. Novara, his teacher in Bologna, had exercised a strong influence on him in his criticism of the geocentric theory, based on Platonic-Pythagorean considerations.

Copernicus' Platonism assured him that the universe, created by a God who is an omniscient mathematician, is orderly and that its order is simple and mathematical in character. He was as convinced as his predecessors that the heavenly bodies must move in perfect circles, but he saw that by assuming the sun to be the center of planetary motion, he could get rid of all but thirty-four of the epicycles required to explain the astronomical data of his day in accordance with the Ptolemaic theory. The earth, he declared, following in Aristarchus' footsteps, rotates on its axis every twenty-four hours and circles the sun each year.

A *Commentariolus,* or short account of the theory, written by Copernicus in 1530, was circulated in manuscript form. Johann Albrecht Widmanstadt lectured on its contents in Rome, where it gained the approval of Pope Clement VII, a member of the house of the Medici, who fought vigorously against Reformation theology but was receptive to Renaissance philosophy. Cardinal Schönberg communicated to Copernicus a demand that his treatise be formally published. The author was reluctant to comply, and it was not until 1540 that he yielded to the pressure of friends and allowed one of them, George Joachim Rheticus, to publish an account of the theory in the *Narratio Prima.* Rheticus also sent Copernicus' complete treatise, *De revolutionibus orbium coelestium,* to the press in Nuremburg.

In 1542, Copernicus suffered a stroke and, as he lay dying, a copy of the first printing of the work reached Frauenberg just in time to be presented to him. He died unaware that one Andreas Osiander, a German reformer with a reputation for crudity and arrogance, had appended to the work on anonymous preface declaring Copernicus' reasoning to be purely hypothetical.

The Copernican Controversy

Hypothetical or not, it is certainly true that Copernicus' scheme was based more on philosophical considerations than on direct astronomical observation. It represented a radical shift from the prevailing Aristotelian model of the universe to a Pythagorean-Platonic one. Understandably, it did not meet with ready acceptance. There were, in fact, plausible objections which could be made to the contention that the earth moves. One was that an object shot straight up into the air ought, if the theory were correct, to fall at some distance to the west of where it started. No good response could be given to this criticism until Galileo's work in physics provided a ground for its refutation. A second was that given the enormous velocity of the rotation of the earth if, indeed, its motion were to be admitted, objects would be hurled from its surface. To this objection, Copernicus and Gilbert of Colchester, a supporter of the new theory, replied that the alternative view—that it is the enormous sphere of the fixed stars which revolves around the earth—involved even more rapid movement and should endanger the integrity of the sphere. This defense of the Copernican cosmology was especially significant in that it asserted, by implication, that the same set of laws governs earthly and heavenly bodies, in contrast to the more commonly accepted view of the day that remote celestial bodies are made of different and finer stuff. A third charge, that in the course of the supposed journey of the earth around the sun, no parallax is revealed in the positions of the fixed stars, was not answered until the year 1838, when such a parallax was detected. That the discovery could not be made earlier was, of course, due to the fact that the astronomical distances involved are so great as to have been incredible to Copernicus' critics.

These and similar considerations, combined with the powerful hold which the Aristotelian cosmology had on the minds of European scholars, account for the lack of ready acceptance of a theory which, in addition to flying in the face of common sense, failed to provide an explanation of planetary motions which could not be accounted for with equal accuracy, even if with somewhat greater complexity, by the Ptolemaic model. Some time elapsed after the publication of Copernicus' treatise before it was taken seriously enough for a controversy to develop over matters which from an ecclesiastical point of view were of greater moment. The initial readiness of the Pope and other high Vatican authorities to entertain the heliocentric theory was not unexpected. The intellectual climate of the Renaissance had prepared men of scholarly attainments to look with favor on ideas derived from classical thought, and the heliocentric theory had impeccable credentials in antiquity. Nor were all the holders of high office in the Church believers in a small and tidy universe. Even the great thinkers of the Middle Ages were quite at home with the notion of infinite spatial extension. It was only when the Copernican ideas began to gain wide enough circulation to be seen as a threat to the popular faith that significant opposition developed.

The Ptolemaic model was a comfortable one for human beings in that it permitted them to think of themselves as living in a cosmos in which the importance of the drama of the fall and redemption of man was underscored by the centrality of the earth on which the play was being enacted. To suggest that Adam and his descendants might have been playing their parts in the wings rather than at center-stage seemed, somehow, to diminish the importance of man. Then too, there was the popular cosmography, according to which God's throne was situated in the heavens directly above Jerusalem. A rotating and orbiting earth would place the Creator in a somewhat unstable and, indeed, undignified situation. Even clerics who were not themselves victims of anthropomorphic literalism began to worry about the effect the imagery fostered by the new cosmology might have on the less well educated laity.

Churchmen who might have been able to provide leadership in the transition of Catholic Christendom from one cosmology to another, succumbed to their fears and paved the way for a schism between religion and science which has continued to have serious consequences in Western thought. The Roman Church and the newly emerging Protestant churches alike assailed the Copernican theory as heretical. After all, the devout argued, it was the sun rather than the earth which Joshua had commanded to stand still. And, as John Calvin pointed out, the ninety-third Psalm declares that "the world is established; it shall never be moved." If the hardening of clerical hearts precipitated the crisis, the doubts or fears of scientifically minded scholars did little to diminish its effects. Francis Bacon, who was in the forefront of the revolution in science, advanced the weak argument that the weight of the earth is so great that it must be the center of the universe.

Giordano Bruno (c.1548-1600) became the most celebrated martyr of the new cosmology. An Italian Dominican, he was, while still a young man, compelled to leave Italy because of his expression of some unorthodox views about transubstantiation and the Immaculate Conception. He traveled over a good portion of the Continent, lecturing and writing, but finding little sympathy for his theories among Roman Catholics or Protestants. In 1583, he went to England, where, in spite of an openly-expressed distaste for the manners of the people, he wrote his best works, including his *Cena de la Ceneri,* in which he gave a favorable account of the Copernican theory. Heliocentrism, to be sure, was only one facet of his elaborate and radical model of the universe, which he developed in his most famous work, *Spaccio della Bestia Trionfante*.

Bruno's religious views were indeed unorthodox enough to incur the suspicion of the religious authorities of the day. He posited a God who is thc universal substance from which everything comes into being of necessity. He denied the efficacy of prayer, the particular providential activity of God, and the possibility of arriving at true knowledge of the ultimate nature of God through a study of the world. Every created thing is a *monas,* he said, a self-contained universe, and the human soul is a thinking and immortal monad, which has the power to contemplate the divine unity, which is God, the *monas monadum*.

Many aspects of his thought were a part of the Neoplatonism which was responsible for the Copernican revolution. It is indicative of the alarm which that revolution had produced in the Church that the disfavor into which Bruno's writings brought him with the ecclesiastical authorities was occasioned no more by his unorthodox theology than by his advocacy of the heliocentric theory. When, after two years in England, he resumed his wanderings on the Continent, he found no greater favor than before. Invited to Venice, and hoping, no doubt, that the invitation meant that his views were gaining greater acceptance, he fell into the hands of the Inquisition in 1593. He was taken to Rome, imprisoned for seven years, and, at last, excommunicated and burned at the stake in the Campo dei Fiori. Forty years later, Galileo was to escape the same fate only by agreeing to recant his heretical conviction that the earth orbits the sun.

Triumph of Copernicanism

The heliocentric theory, however, had too many strong supporters in high places and too many arguments in its favor to be entirely suppressed. Even authorities on astronomy who were not convinced of its correctness began to accumulate evidence which was to lead to its acceptance by another generation of thinkers.

Pre-eminent among these transitional figures was Tycho Brahe (1546-1601), a native of Denmark who enjoyed the patronage of a Danish monarch and a Holy Roman Emperor. A true Renaissance savant, he was, in addition to being the foremost astronomer of his day, skilled in chemistry, medicine, glassmaking, and printing. He was also a lover of luxury and highly successful in acquiring the means to enjoy it.

Unlike Copernicus, Tycho was proficient in actual astronomical observation and used instruments of his own design to acquire highly accurate data that provided the foundation for the further development of the heliocentric theory. Tycho, however, would only travel a part of the distance between Ptolemy and Copernicus. With Ptolemy, he assumed the earth to be the center of the universe and the sun, the moon, and the fixed stars to be in orbit around it. He held, however, that Mercury, Venus, Mars, Jupiter, and Saturn travel about the sun in epicyclic paths subsidiary to the orbit of the sun about the earth.

It remained for Johannes Kepler (1571-1630), a German astronomer, to put Tycho's observations to use in a coherent model that provided the simplest possible explanations of planetary movement. Kepler served as Tycho's assistant at his laboratory near Prague during the last years of the Danish astronomer's life, and in 1601 he succeeded Tycho as imperial mathematician at the court of Rudolph II. Kepler lacked Tycho's proficiency in observation, possibly due in part to crippled hands and deficient eyesight, the result of a case of smallpox in childhood. His conceptual ability, however, was of a higher order than Tycho's and ultimately enabled him to place the Copernican theory, to which he had become a convert as a student at the University of Tübingen, on a solid theoretical footing.

Kepler spent months poring over Tycho's observations of the planet Mars and trying to fit them into a circular orbit. His confidence in Tycho's accuracy was to great that he could not force himself to do Procrustean violence to the recorded data, and so he was forced to entertain the notion of a non-circular path for the planet.

Like his predecessors, Kepler was essentially a Pythagorean and a Platonist. It bothered him greatly to discover that celestial movements could not be accommodated to circular patterns, but his faith remained unshaken that God had provided inviolable geometric laws for the governance of the universe. His own religious commitment to the Supreme Mathematician was derived from a Lutheran upbringing. "I am a Lutheran," he said, "attached to the Confession of Augsburg by a thorough examination of doctrine, not less than by the instruction of my parents. That is my faith; I have already suffered for it, and know not the art of dissembling. Religion is for me a serious affair, which I cannot treat with levity."

Christian faith, classical confidence in the mathematical regularity of nature, and Copernican conviction combined to keep Kepler working to find a figure which would accommodate Tycho's observations of Mars, while fitting it into an exclusively solar orbit. He found it at last in the ellipse, and the generalization to the other planets of the solar system of his conclusions about Mars provided the basis for his first law. A planet, he declared, revolves around the sun in an elliptic orbit, with the sun as one of the two foci of the ellipse.

Tycho's observations had confirmed Copernicus' attack on another dogma of the older astronomy that was in error. A planet does not travel at uniform speed. It moves morc rapidly when it is nearer the sun than when it is farther away from it. Kepler, as determined as Copernicus had been to show that nature obeys immutable mathematical laws, was disturbed by the unresolved problem. He made seventy different calculations of the orbit and velocity of Mars and, to his unmitigated delight, discovered that in the elliptical orbit of a planet, a line drawn from the planet to the sun sweeps over equal areas in equal times. This observation became his second law of planetary motion.

In the *De Harmonice Mundi,* published in 1619, Kepler developed his version of the Pythagorean notion of the "music of the spheres." Kepler, to be sure, did not maintain that the planets emit tones audible to human ears, but he did hold that their activity involves mathematical relationships analagous to those which define the physical properties of music. Of greater fruitfulness for the development of modern astronomy was his third law of planetary motion, which appeared in the course of his discussion of the celestial harmonies. It too resulted from his passion for a mathematical explanation of the divine economy. He was looking for a formula which would describe the times taken by the planets to complete their orbits as related to their distance from the sun. He arrived at the conclusion that the square of the period of each planet's revolution around the sun is proportional to the cube of the mean distance of the planet from the sun.

Kepler's science was not pure in the modern sense. His Pythagorean prejudices intruded themselves into his work as when, in the *Mysterium Cosmographicum* of 1597, he published what he thought to be his most significant achievement—the discovery of a relationship between the distances separating the orbits of the six planets known at the time and the shapes of the five regular solids. "The intense pleasure I have received from this discovery," he wrote, "can never be told in words." His enthusiasm, alas, was premature. Further astronomical investigation did not support the hypothesis. He dabbled in astrology and had a mystical reverence for the sun, Plato's "lord and giver of life," which virtually amounted to worship.

When all this has been admitted, however, his status as one of the outstanding pioneers of modern science is secured. His faith in mathematics as the discipline by which cosmic processes can be understood, combined with his respect for precise observation of the empirical data on which scientific laws must be based were significant characteristics of the scientific spirit of the age—a spirit which reached its greatest heights in the person of Kepler's contemporary, Galileo.

Galileo

Galileo Galilei was born at Pisa on February 16, 1564, the son of a poor Florentine nobleman. After early studies at the monastery of Vallambrosa, near Florence, he was sent to the University of Pisa in 1581 to study medicine. In that same year, while watching a lamp swinging to and fro in the cathedral of Pisa, he noted that as the amplitude of its swing diminished, it took precisely as long for the completion of a complete cycle as when the distance of its travel had been greater. His excitement over the resultant formulation of a law of pendular motion led him to the study of mathematics and science, disciplines in which he attained such proficiency that his fame soon spread throughout Italy. In 1589, he became a professor at Pisa and, while there, is said to have conducted the demonstrations with falling balls dropped from the Leaning Tower to prove that bodies of different weights fall with the same velocity. His outspoken rejection of dogmatic Aristotelianism and his criticism of an important personage quickly cost him his chair. In 1592, he was appointed Professor of Mathematics at Padua, and found more freedom there.

In 1609, during a visit to Venice, he learned of a new instrument that would make distant objects appear nearer. On returning to Padua, he conducted some experiments and within a few days had constructed a telescope good enough to be presented to the Doge Leonardo Donato. The Venetian Senate confirmed his Padua lectureship for life and doubled his salary. He worked at the improvement of his instruments until he had one of thirty-three diameters magnification, with which he made the spectacular discovery of four moons orbiting the planet Jupiter. He published an account of his observations in a work entitled *The Sidereal Messenger*. Kepler, when he heard the news, wrote Galileo, telling him, "I am so far from disbelieving the existence of the four circumjovial planets, that I long for a telescope, to anticipate you, if possible, in discovering two round Mars, as the proportion seems to require, six or eight round Saturn, and perhaps one each round Mercury and Venus." Much of the reaction to Galileo's discovery, however, was hostile. Aristotle had not posited the existence of any moons about Jupiter, and therefore, by a truly staggering *argumentum ad ignorantiam,* it was held that they could not exist. Moreover, as the Professor of Philosophy at Padua pointed out in refusing to look through the new telescope, to increase the number of planets would violate the privileged position which God had given the number seven in the economy of the universe—seven windows to the head, seven metals and the like. He further pointed out that in view of the fact that the alleged planets could not be seen with the naked eye, they "therefore would be useless, and therefore do not exist."

A number of the clergy were quite ready to accept Galileo's telescopic observations and, indeed, the whole of the heliocentric cosmology. He had friends in high places in the Church, and, indeed, for many years enjoyed the friendship and protection of two popes, who declined to endorse propagation of the Copernican theory as truth, but admired Galileo for his many scientific achievements.

In 1610, Galileo returned to his native Florence as court mathematician and philosopher to the Grand Duke of Tuscany. In 1611, he visited Rome and demonstrated the results of his researches to members of the papal court. In a work printed at Rome in 1613, he defended the Copernican theory, and before long he began to draw the fire of conservative theologians, who claimed that fidelity to Scripture required adherence to a geocentric cosmology. Galileo boldly responded with arguments to try to show that Copernicus' theory conformed to the Bible with greater fidelity than Ptolemy's. In 1615,he was warned by high churchmen that his advocacy of the theory was likely to bring him into conflict with the Church, and the following year the consulting theologians of the Inquisition declared the heliocentric theory and the diurnal rotation of the earth to be heretical.

For the next sixteen years, Galileo, now popular and famous all over Europe, attempted to get the decree of 1616 revoked, but without success. Nevertheless, in 1632, he published his famous *Dialogo dei due massimi sistemi del mondo,* in which he clearly demonstrated the superiority of the Copernican system.

Sale of the book was prohibited, and Galileo, in spite of increasingly infirm health, was brought before the Inquisition. Fearful of torture and execution, he abandoned his support of the heliocentric theory, and, indeed, declared under oath that despite his apparent advocacy of it, he had never, after the Church's decision, believed it. He was sentenced to imprisonment at the pleasure of the Holy Office and instructed to repeat the seven penitential psalms every week for three years. After a brief time spent in the custody of the Inquisition in Rome, he was permitted to leave for Siena. He spent several months there as the guest of a good friend, Archbishop Ascanio Piccolomini, a member of a powerful and distinguished family. At last, he was permitted to return to his villa at Arcetri, near Florence, and lived there in seclusion, continuing his scientific research and writing with undiminished enthusiasm until his death in 1642.

Though his name and the dramatic story of his conflict with the Church are inextricably associated with the Copernican controversy, Galileo's achievements as a pioneer in the world-view which we call "modern" went far beyond astronomy and cosmology. He improved on the microscope invented by Drebbel and applied himself to the examination of small objects with the same interest with which he had looked at the stars. He made immeasurable contributions to the development of the science of mechanics, giving space, time, and motion interpretations quite different from those accepted by the Aristotelians. He thus laid the groundwork for the work of Isaac Newton, born in the year Galileo died.

Chapter 20

New Visions of Man and Nature

The controversy over the Copernican theory served to obscure in some measure the other aspects of the revolution which Galileo and some of his contemporaries were accomplishing in the physical sciences. His experiments with pendular movement and falling bodies and his views on the propagation of light suggested that nature in general obeyed laws which conformed more closely to a Pythagorean-Platonic picture of reality than to the prevailing Aristotelian model.

That picture had never been wholly eradicated from European scholarship, and this was especially true in England, where the Aristotelian revival had served mainly to cultivate an interest in scientific research without imposing on it the authority of a dogmatically Aristotelian world view. The English church, freed by Henry VIII from papal control, had no Inquisition to inhibit the exploration of nature, and an impressive array of Englishmen arose as contributors to the new science.

To their Platonic faith in the mathematical order of the natural world, they added the English passion for careful attention to empirical data. A devotee of the sciences, in the characteristic English view, must ask questions of Nature, and only when he is in possession of the facts which she reveals to him is he at liberty to fit those facts into a conceptual framework which will demonstrate the rational pattern which lies behind them.

William Gilbert (1544-1603), was an outstanding exponent of the spirit of the new science. After an excellent education in England and extensive travel in Italy, he devoted himself to the practice of medicine and finally became President of the Royal College of Physicians and Surgeons and personal physician to Queen Elizabeth I. His fame, however, rests primarily on his work *On the Lodestone and magnetic Bodies,* published in 1600. He began it with a declaration of his conviction that "in the discovery of hidden causes, stronger reasons are obtained from sure experiments and demonstrated arguments than from probable conjectures and the opinions of philosophical speculators of the common sort." He then proceeded to apply that maxim to an examination of the properties of the lodestone, which had been discussed by a number of writers since the time of ancient Greece but, to Gilbert's mind, had been given such careless treatment that the knowledge of magnetic phenomena current in his day amounted to little more than a collection of old wives' tales.

In contrast to such superstitious nonsense, Gilbert set out scientific procedures by which the poles of a magnet could be established and the north pole distinguished from the south. He then conducted a series of carefully designed experiments to demonstrate that the earth itself is a great magnet, a fact which explains the direction in which a magnetic needle points and its dipping in the direction of one of the earth's poles. Born a year after Copernicus' death, Gilbert was also the first supporter among English savants of the heliocentric theory and a proponent of the view that the fixed stars differ among themselves in their distance from the earth.

Francis Bacon

The empirical method found one of its ablest advocates in Francis Bacon, who, in spite of his failure to understand fully the requirements of a proper scientific procedure, provided some of the important stepping stones which led from the medieval to the modern view.

Bacon was born on January 22, 1561, the youngest son of Sir Nicholas Bacon, a high state official, and his second wife, Ann Cook, the sister-in-law of Sir William Cecil, Lord Burghley, the most powerful lord in England. A Cambridge student at the age of twelve, Francis became disillusioned with Aristotelianism. At sixteen, he was on the staff of the English Ambassador seeking to rise to high positions in public service. A tolerant man, he advocated a lessening of the severity with which Puritans and Roman Catholics were treated during Elizabeth's reign. One of his most prominent patrons was Robert Devereux, Earl of Essex, whose efforts in his behalf had only modest success, in spite of Bacon's exceptional ability. He did, however, with help from Essex and Burghley, succeed in getting an appointment as one of the Queen's learned council, and, in this capacity, aided in the prosecution of Essex for treason when the Earl, despite Bacon's good advice, became involved in an abortive plot against the Queen's person.

In 1607, some four years after the accession of James I to the throne, Bacon became Solicitor General and in 1612,he was made Attorney General. He secured the favor of James's favorite, George Villiers, later Duke of Buckingham, and, due in great measure to Villiers' influence, was, in 1618, appointed Lord Chancellor and made Baron Verulam. In 1621, he was created Viscount St. Albans, but in that same year, his laboriously built career collapsed when he was convicted of bribery and corruption in chancery suits. Bacon admitted that he had accepted gifts but claimed to be "the justest chancellor that hath been in the five changes since Sir Nicholas Bacon's time," on the ground that his judgments had never been affected by anything given him. The House of Lords, which heard his case, imposed a fine of £40,000, sentenced him to imprisonment in the Tower during the king's pleasure, and decreed that he could never again come within the verge of the Court. However, the fine was remitted by King James, he spent only four days in the Tower, and he was given a general pardon after a few months. He lived for five more years, during which his most valuable work was accomplished. In March, 1626, while driving near Highgate, he became curious as to whether snow could preserve meat. He bought a fowl, and, while stuffing it with snow, he suffered a sudden chill. He was carried to Lord Arundel's house, and died of complications on April 9, 1626.

A true man of the Renaissance, Bacon was as concerned with the exercise of power as any of the most ambitious figures of the age, but he saw that knowledge had become essential to the acquisition of the sorts of power which would be accessible to humanity in the world which was rapidly emerging from the ashes of the medieval culture. In *The Advancement of Learning,* published in 1605, and *The New Atlantis,* published in 1624, he looked forward to a day in which careful observation and clear-sighted science would liberate man from the bondage of ignorance through a "total reconstruction of the sciences, arts, and all human knowledge." The human mind, he held, is capable of understanding nature, but because it has in the past proceeded on the wrong assumptions, his "great instauration," as he called his proposed reconstruction, is necessary to rid it of those assumptions and start out afresh.

In his *Novum Organum,* the title of which indicates his ambition to supplant Aristotle, he described four kinds of "idols" which, in his judgment, impede the advancement of learning.

The Idols of the Tribe are those which afflict the race of men generally, due to the fact that "the human understanding is like a false mirror, which, receiving rays irregularly, distorts and discolors the nature of things by mingling its own nature with it." That understanding, for instance, seeks to read more order and regularity into nature than actually exists there and so comes up with fictions such as the notion that the celestial bodies must move in perfect circles. It is "no day light," but is influenced by what it wishes to be true. Moreover, it pays undue attention to the data of the senses, which are dull and incompetent.

The Idols of the Cave are those of the individual man, which stem from his peculiar heredity and environment. One who has cultivated a special interest in some particular subject will, if he seeks to develop a more general philosophy, color it with his own preconceived notions, "a thing especially to be noticed in Aristotle, who made his natural philosophy a mere bond-servant to his logic, thereby rendering it contentious and well nigh useless."

The Idols of the Market-place come from the language by which men converse with one another. Words are not simply products of thought. They shape the understanding, and when a new idea is presented, the words which one is accustomed to use "stand in the way and resist the change." Many disputes which are thought to be about matters of fact are, in actuality, only verbal disputes. Prudence would dictate that the disputants begin with definitions, but even the definitions would not solve the problem, for they themselves consist of words. The Idols of the Market-place involve the names of nonexistent things or of things which do exist but are poorly defined.

The Idols of the Theatre are those "which have immigrated into men's minds from the various dogmas of philosophies, and also from wrong laws of demonstration." The philosophical systems which have captured the human imagination, whether rationalistic like Aristotle's, empirical like those of the alchemists and William Gilbert (for whom Bacon had scant regard), or superstitiously theological like those of Pythagoras and Plato are "but so many stage plays, representing worlds of their own creation after an unreal and scenic fashion."

To correct the sort of thinking that is dominated by these "Idols," Bacon proposed an inductive method that would ask questions of nature by devising experiments to discover the "forms" of phenomena. He gave an inquiry into the cause of heat as an example of his method.

First, he held, a list of instances of the occurrence of heat should be drawn up. This is his "Table of Essence and Presence." Second, a list should be prepared of cases that resemble the items on first list, but in which heat is absent. This is the "Table of Deviation, or Absence in Proximity." Third, there should be a list of instances in which different degrees of heat are found in the same sort of phenomena. This is the "Table of Degrees, or the Table of Comparison."

The fourth step is the "Process of Exclusion." One uses the inductive procedure to try to find from an examination of the three tables something which is always present when heat is present, always absent when heat is absent, and always varying directly or inversely with the degree of heat present in the object being examined.

The "Process of Exclusion", in its complete form, is often impractical, due to the variety and complexity of the phenomena under investigation. Recognizing its limitations for actual scientific procedure, Bacon suggested the abstraction from the mass of accumulated data of certain "Shining or Striking Instances" to arrive at something which he called "the *Indulgence of the Understanding,* or the *Commencement of Interpretation,* or the *First vintage.*" When such conspicuous instances of heat are isolated and examined, the three tables will reveal the likelihood that the "essence and quiddity" of heat is motion. Bacon was careful to indicate, however, that in asserting this identity, he was not referring to "sensible heat," which is psychologically determined, or to the heating of one body by another.

Bacon's concern for a careful and systematic examination of natural phenomena was in the spirit of the age of science of which he was a pioneer. Nevertheless, his carefully crafted inductive method was not sufficient for thc demands of the newly developing disciplines, for it failed to prescribe the testing of hypotheses by crucial experiments in the manner that has subsequently proved to be essential for empirical investigation.

Thomas Hobbes

The concern for careful examination of sense data led to a concentration on the material world quite at variance with the other-worldliness of medieval thought. It is not suprising that an overemphasis on the physical produced a revival of the sort of materialism posited in antiquity by Leucippus, Democritus, and Lucretius. Foremost among the philosophers responsible for that development was an Englishman, Thomas Hobbes (1588-1679).

Hobbes was the second son of the vicar of Westport and Charlton, in Wiltshire. His father is said to have aroused the suspicions of his flock, one Sunday morning while an associatc was reading the lesson, by starting up from a sound sleep shouting, "Clubs is trumps!" Later he lost his position by engaging in a fight at the church door. He disappeared, leaving three children to be brought up by his brother in Malmesbury. Thomas was given a good education, and after his graduation from Oxford, where he paid as little attention as possible to the Scholastic philosophy of his instructors, he began a lifelong connection with the Cavendish family by accepting a position as tutor to William Cavendish, who would later become Earl of Devonshire. In his travels with his pupil, who was almost as old as Hobbes himself, and in subsequent trips to the Continent in the company of the son of Sir Gervase Clinton and later of another Lord Devonshire, the son of his first student, he became well acquainted with the best scholarship of that age. During his lifetime, he was, at one time or another, acquainted with Galileo, Bacon, Descartes, and Gassendi.

One day, at the age of forty, he came upon a copy of Euclid's *Elements* open at the forty-seventh proposition of the first book. He read it and exclaimed, "By God, this is impossible!" Convinced by Euclid's demonstration of the truth of the proposition, he found himself "in love with geometry," and, although he himself was an indifferent mathematician, his studies in the subject proved useful when he became interested in problems of motion.

Everything that exists as an object of philosophical inquiry, Hobbes maintained, is matter, and all change is motion. An alternative name for matter is body, defined as "that which having no dependence upon our thought, is co-extended with some part of space." His contention that reality is a plenum, with no empty space between its parts did not lead him to deal to a denial of the possibility of motion. For him, it was evident, an object may move into a space previously occupied by another body which it displaces.

As for human beings, they are only bodies in motion. In saying this, Hobbes immediately laid himself open to the criticisms which pose the greatest problems for any materialist. In the first place, if everything is material, and if the material world itself has none of the sense properties by which we know it, what is the status of these properties? Hobbes held that they are "phantoms" but in so naming them merely clouded the issue. If matter and motion are the only existent realities, how can moving objects be the sources of such vastly different sensations in other moving objects as red, sweet, hard, flowery, and noisy? Hobbes was forced to assert that sensations are the source of all our knowledge of the world. That admission, however, only led him into confrontation with the second problem, for the senses do not reveal the world as it is. "Whatsoever accidents or qualities our senses make us think there be in the *world,* they be *not* there, but are *seeming* and *apparations* only: the things that really *are* in the world without us, are those *motions* by which things are caused. And this is the *great deception of sense.*" If all our knowledge is illusory then, can we really know that such is the case and that the real nature of the world is what the materialist asserts it to be? Reflection can hardly provoke an answer to the question, for it is dependent on imagination, and imagination is nothing more than "decaying sense," and so, even farther removed from the real world than the original sensations that made it possible. Moreover, thoughts succeed one another in a way which must be due to the mechanical processes occurring in the brain, rather than to any conformity of the thoughts to the true state of affairs in the outer world.

The third great problem faced by materialists has always been the question of value, and here too, Hobbes had as much difficulty as his predecessors. Value judgments had to be reduced to desire and aversion, and even these ultimately had to be stripped of their psychological character and reduced to movements within the brain. Like most materialists, Hobbes saved himself from the worst consequences of a consistent application of his theory by smuggling into it whatever concepts he found necessary to keep its inadequacies from being too obvious.

This felicitous inconsistency is nowhere better illustrated than in his theory of the state. To be sure, he approached the subject of politics with the initial assertion that a commonwealth is nothing other than a human artifact composed of material parts—"an artificial animal," moving in accordance with the same mechanical principles which govern works of nature. But the very assertion that the state—"that great Leviathan" as he called it—is a work of art set him on a course of reasoning in which human motivation rather than the laws of motion determines the nature of human societies.

In a state of nature, Hobbes declared, there is no law. There is only the natural right—*jus naturale* of every man to take any action deemed necessary to preserve his own life. But in such a condition of anarchy, no one is safe, and human life is "solitary, poor, nasty, brutish, and short." Faced with this situation, men are driven by reason to formulate ways in which their lives can best be preserved. Here Hobbes introduced his notion of natural law. "A law of nature, *lex naturalis,*" he wrote in *The Leviathan,* "is a precept or general rule, found out by reason, by which a man is forbidden to do that which is destructive of his life, or taketh away the means of preserving the same; and to omit that, by which he thinketh it may best be preserved."

The first law of nature is "to seek peace and follow it," for the "war of everyone against everyone" which is the natural state of humanity offers no security to the strongest or wisest men.

The second law, which is derived from the first, is "that a man be willing, when others are so too, as far-forth as for peace, and defense of himself he shall think it necessary, to lay down this right to all things; and be contented with so much liberty against other men, as he would allow other men against himself." The transference of right reciprocally among human beings is, Hobbes says, what is called contract.

The third law of nature, which follows from the second, is "that men perform their covenants made," for if the transference of right is not actual, but merely verbal, humanity is still in a condition of war. The idea of injustice, defined simply as "the not performance of covenant" stems from this third law.

Men are driven by these laws to form some sort of society in which injustices can be prevented or punished. They thereupon agree with one another to place themselves under a sovereign whose authority is supreme in both secular and ecclesiastical matters. This action, the formation of a commonwealth, inaugurates the reign of law.

In every matter except that of self-preservation, a citizen of a commonwealth is obliged to give absolute obedience to the state. "Law," Hobbes said, "is the public conscience." In view of the fact that any state of law is better than a state of nature, all revolutions are wrong—wrong, that is, until they succeed, after which the revolutionaries, having become the sovereign power, are in the right.

This contention, that any *de facto* government is a government *de jure,* was one which served Hobbes well during the Cromwellian Rebellion. When *The Leviathan* was published in 1651, Charles I had died under the headsman's ax, and Hobbes's conclusion that submission to the Roundhead government could be justified was consistent with his whole theory of sovereignty. A monarchist and an Anglican churchman by preference, however, he went to France with the royalist exiles and saw no incongruity in presenting a manuscript copy of his new work to Charles II, whom he had instructed in mathematics. Charles's advisors, however, barred him from court, and Hobbes, under suspicion by the French government for a verbal attack on the Roman Church, returned to England and lived as peaceably under Cromwellian rule as was possible to a man whose contentious nature kept him in frequent literary battles with an astonishingly large number of eminent scholars on a variety of subjects.

Charles II was restored to the throne in 1660. Encountering Hobbes in the street shortly after his return to London, he greeted him in friendly fashion, and for the rest of his life, the old philosopher enjoyed royal favor. "Here comes the bear to be baited," the monarch used to say, enjoying to the full Hobbes's wit and his boldness in argument—a boldness inconsistent with a personal timidity in everyday life which is reputed to have included an inordinate fear of ghosts.

Until his death, at the age of ninety, he remained something of a stormy petrel, finding himself at one time in danger of prosecution on charges of heresy, in spite of the King's friendship. In Continental Europe, however, he enjoyed a higher reputation than any of his English contemporaries, and the subsequent importance of his work far transcended the materialism on which it was ostensibly based.

Isaac Newton

The vision of a universe governed by universal mechanical laws expressable in mathematical terms found an exponent of unsurpassed ability in the person of Isaac Newton (1642-1727), born at the family's home, Woolsthorpe, in Lincolnshire, on Christmas day in the year Galileo died. In 1661, he entered Trinity College, Cambridge, where he came under the influence of Isaac Barrow, one of the finest mathematicians of his day. Barrow encouraged the young man to pursue mathematical studies and interested him in optics, a subject in which some of Newton's greatest scientific contributions were to be made.

In 1665, the year Newton took his bachelor's degree, the Great Plague broke out in London, and the authorities at Cambridge, fearful that it might spread there, closed the University. Newton went back to Woolsthorpe, for a stay which proved to be of great significance for his later work. In describing the way in which many of his ideas developed, he later wrote, "All this was in the two plague years of 1665 and 1666, for in those days I was in the prime of my age for invention, and minded mathematics and philosophy more than at any time since."

It was during this period that he developed the mathematical discipline known as the differential and integral calculus, though, characteristically, he waited many years before publishing the results of his reflections. It was at that time too that he is said to have been inspired by watching the fall of an apple to reflect on the nature of gravitational attraction—an incident which led Lord Byron to refer to him as

> "The sole man who could grapple
> Since Adam, with a fall, or with an apple."

However much, or little, the celebrated fruit may have had to do with Newton's cosmology, it may have been the immediate occasion for his reflection on the forces which keep the moon in orbit around the earth. At the time, there was no general understanding that bodies having mass have reciprocal gravitational influence on one another. Even the great Galileo had been able to entertain the notion of something thrown "down" to the earth from the moon. Newton, at Woolsthorpe, was looking for a universal law governing every physical body in the universe, from apples to suns. He found this in his formula for gravitation, according to which every object attracts every other body with a force proportional to the product of their masses divided by the square of the distance between them. If the moon were not in forward motion in such a way that the centrifugal force just counters the gravitational attraction, moon and earth would fly apart or fall toward each other and collide. The same law, applied generally, accounts for the positions of every body in the universe insofar as those positions are determined by gravitational attraction.

Newton's interests, however, took him far beyond the formulation of the law defining the effects of one sort of force. Gravitation is, to be sure, one source of motion, but Newton was determined to arrive at a comprehensive mathematical account of every sort of terrestrial and celestial movement. While at Woolsthorpe, he may have arrived at the "Laws of Motion" published years later.

According to the First Law, a body at rest will remain so unless an unbalanced force acts on it, and a body moving at constant velocity in a straight line will continue to do so unless acted on by an unbalanced force. Newton thus rejected the old view that the constant application of a force is necessary to keep a body in motion. The Second Law states that a body acted upon by an unbalanced force will accelerate in the direction of the force with an acceleration proportional to the unbalanced force and inversely proportional to the mass of the body. The Third Law is that for every action, there is an equal and opposite reaction, a fact of nature which has made possible the science of rocketry.

In the preface to the *Principia,* Newton remarked that "all the difficulty of philosophy seems to consist in this—from the phenomena of motions to investigate the forces in nature, and then from these forces to demonstrate the other phenomena." Like Copernicus, Kepler, and Galileo, he hoped that ultimately all the science of nature could be reduced to mathematical terms. He carried his mathematical faith into his study of optics recommending that the science be handled "not only by teaching those things that tend to the perfection of vision, but also by determining mathematically all kinds of phenomena of colors which could be produced by refractions."

Newton was, however, equally committed to the empirical method and declined to assume that the universe can be fully understood by abstract reasoning. Experimental verification is required for the unlocking of nature's secrets. In this treatment of scientific questions, Newton proposed to avoid the preoccupation with causes which, in his view, infected Aristotelian thought. "These principles," he wrote, "(mass, gravity, cohesion, etc.) I consider not as occult qualities, supposed to result from the specific forms of things, but as general laws of nature, by which the things themselves are formed; their truth appearing to us by phenomena, though their causes be not yet discovered. For these are manifest qualities, and their causes only are occult." It was this insistence that science was concerned only with empirical investigation and the mathematically expressed laws which can be derived from that observation that caused him, in discussing gravitational phenomena, to remark, "But hitherto I have been unable to discover the cause of these properties of gravity from phenomena, and I frame no hypotheses."

This disinclination to regard speculation as truly scientific did not in the least prevent Newton from indulging in a good bit of speculative thought about the nature of the world. For him, the material universe was an aggregate of hard, indestructible atoms, having properties which can be mathematically described but none of what had by his time come to be regarded as the secondary qualities—color, taste, smell, and the like. Man's soul, or mind, is located in the *sensorium* of his brain, and thus his contact with the external world is an indirect one, contingent on the excitation of nerve fibers which conduct impulses to the brain, where somehow they result in sense qualities quite unlike the "real" colorless, silent, odorless objects posited by the physicist. Every body in nature possesses a *vis inertiae,* which can be precisely measured by the amount of external force which must be applied to it to accelerate it—that is to cause it to depart from a state of rest or uniform motion.

Space, time, and motion have an absolute existence independent of any of the processes of observation or measurement that define their "relative" properties. "Absolute, true, and mathematical time, of itself, and from its own nature, flows equably without regard to anything external, and by another name is called duration," he said. Measurement into such units as hours, days, years, and the like, is a relative matter. Similarly, "absolute space, in its own nature, without regard to anything external, remains always similar and immovable." Relative space, defined by the senses, is mutable. "Absolute motion is the translation of a body from one absolute place into another; and relative motion, the translation from one relative place into another." Thus, if a sailor is on a ship and the ship moves over the surface of the sea and the earth moves in space, the absolute motion of the sailor arises from the relative motions.

The concepts of absolute space and time, Newton held, though not immediately verifiable by the senses, can be justified as presuppositions of certain properties of motion which are experimentally verifiable. Space and time as so conceived are not only uniform and homogeneous, but infinite as well. It has been argued with some justice, however, that the spatio-temporal characteristics of the universe as he conceived it were derived not so much from scientific observation as from Newton's religious convictions. In the *General Scholium* added to the second edition of the *Principia,* he wrote, "From his true dominion it follows that the true God is a living, intelligent, and powerful being; and from his other perfections that he is supreme, or most perfect. He is eternal and infinite, omnipotent and omniscient; that is, his duration reaches from eternity to eternity; his presence from infinity to infinity; he governs all things, and knows all things that are or can be done. He is not eternity or infinity, but eternal and infinite. He endures forever, and is everywhere present; and by existing always and everywhere, he constitutes duration and space." In the *Opticks,* we find the further suggestion that infinite space is the *sensorium* of God who, "being in all places is more able by his will to move the bodies within his boundless uniform sensorium, and thereby to form and reform the parts of the universe, than we are by our will to move the parts of our own bodies."

Newton, however, was no more a pantheist than Saint Paul. The world is not the body of God and he is not composed of its parts. He is, however, omnipresent, and the frame of reference which determines absolute motion exists in his consciousness.

This theological justification for the principal concepts underlying Newton's natural philosophy removes his own conception of the universe from the category into which it was placed by those of his followers who dispensed with God and saw Newton's infinite, mathematically describable continuum as the stage for a "world-machine" in which bodies move according to inexorable mechanical law without reference to any spiritual source.

That Newton's religious convictions were sincerely held, and not merely introduced into his scientific writings to satisfy the authorities is amply proved by the existence of a number of theological treatises from his hand which, if in certain places they are suggestive of an Arian bias, nevertheless place him firmly within the framework of a Christian world view. It is, however, a Christian view so intimately allied with his science that God appears above all as the supreme architect of the universe and its preserver from disorder. It would be left to later theorists to attempt to uproot the intricate structure of the Newtonian cosmos from the soil of the Judaeo-Christian world view from which it grew.

By the time of Newton's death in 1727, his genius was widely recognized, and his model of the universe had become so widely accepted in his lifetime by men of reason that his contemporary, the poet Alexander Pope, seemed to his readers hardly to be exaggerating when he wrote:

> Nature and Nature's Laws lay hid in night:
> God said, Let Newton be! and all was light.

Chapter 21

New Visions of Man and God

We have seen how the Renaissance in western Europe brought new perceptions of the place of mankind in the astronomical universe and in relation to the natural world. Astronomers opened new worlds to view in the heavens, explorers discovered new worlds on the earth, and scientists began to find new ways to understand and control nature itself. Along with these fundamental changes in the human vision of the total environment, it was inevitable that similar modifications should occur in the realm of the spirit. Serious questions arose in many quarters with respect to traditional beliefs and practices in religion.

The new vision of the character and capacity of mankind was marked by paradox. It has remained so ever since, giving rise to increasing perplexity. The paradox had been eloquently stated in ancient times by a Hebrew poet:

> When I look at thy heavens, the work of thy fingers, the moon and the stars which thou hast established; what is man that thou art mindful of him, and the son of man that thou dost care for him? Yet thou hast made him little less than God, and dost crown him with glory and honor. Thou givest him dominion over the works of thy hands; thou hast put all things under his feet, . . . (Psalm 8:3-6)

The modern vision of man, beginning with the thinkers of the Renaissance and oscillating in religion, philosophy, and science, has continued to conform to that paradox of simultaneous misery and glory.

The Necessity of Reform

The new vision of man in relation to God grew largely out of the conditions of the late Middle Ages. The need for religious reform had become painfully obvious to all. There had always been intermittent attempts to correct mistaken developments in doctrine and practice, but some of the most blatant instances of corruption and abuse of power occurred during the fourteenth and fifteenth centuries. The consciences of many sensitive Christians, both clergy and laity, were offended by the great disparity between the biblical ideal and the prevalent condition of the Church. The papal claim of absolute temporal and spiritual power and the frequently obscene opulence of the clergy in the midst of the oppressive poverty of the people were enough to bring revolt. Added to that, however, was the infamous "Babylonian Captivity" of the Church, in which the Roman popes were forced by superior political power to reside in Avignon, France; and that scandal was immediately made worse by the spectacle of two and sometimes three lines of pontiffs, all claiming to be the sole legitimate rulers of Christendom.

The papal residence of Avignon, on the Rhone river in southern France, was first called the "Babylonian Captivity" by the contemporary scholar, Petrarch, because it lasted for about 70 years, the traditional length of the ancient Jewish exile in Babylonia. It began with the struggle between King Philip IV of France (1285-1314) and Pope Boniface VIII (1294-1303) over the taxation of clergy. During that controversy, Boniface issued the famous bull *Unam sanctam,* a grandiose papal claim to temporal power. The document proclaimed that "there is one Holy Catholic and Apostolic Church, and that outside this Church there is neither salvation nor remission of sins." The Church is the ark of salvation and the pope is the new Noah, the vicar of Christ on earth. "There is one fold and one shepherd," said Boniface, and "God has set popes over kings and kingdoms." Nevertheless, Philip successfully challenged the power of Boniface, arranging to have him imprisoned and probably causing his early death. Following that tragic episode, the French kings determined to control the papacy by seeing to it that Frenchmen were elected as popes as well as cardinals so that the Church would be ruled from France. That arrangement continued until 1377, when Pope Gregory XI (1370-1378) returned to Rome.

The exile was ended by the return of the papacy to Rome but a worse calamity was soon created. When Gregory died in 1378, the sixteen cardinals, eleven of whom were Frenchmen, assembled in Rome and elected the archbishop of Bari as Pope Urban VI. However, four months later the eleven French cardinals, supported by a Spanish cardinal, met again at Anagni and declared the choice of Urban invalid because coerced by the Roman populace. They then proceeded to elect another Frenchman, the Bishop of Cambrai, as Pope Clement VII. Clement forthwith reestablished the papal residence at Avignon, and the Church now had two popes, both elected by a majority of the same college of cardinals. The scandal of captivity was intensified by schism. When the Council of Pisa (1409) attempted to heal the division by deposing both the Roman and Avignon popes and electing a new one, Alexander V (1409-1410), the action was called illegal and the Church found itself with three popes. Serious Christians everywhere became convinced of the necessity of reform.

The Conciliar Movement

How could reform be achieved? The question was made extremely difficult by the papal claim to absolute and final authority, both sacred and secular. Since there were two or three who claimed that authority, who could judge among them? The question was not new, but it became crucial because of the great schism. Since the popes could not or would not settle the issue among themselves, there were three possible solutions that had already been proposed at various points during the Middle Ages: (1) the Church could devise a means of settlement within itself; (2) the royal power could force a decision; or (3) a parallel responsibility could be established that would make possible autonomy for the secular and the sacred spheres. Clearly, the problem had been a possibility since Constantine because of the continuing contests between royal and papal claims. Now a solution had become necessary.

Two of the greatest proponents of papal supremacy were Giles of Rome (c. 1245-1316), who was said to be the ghost-writer of the bull *Unam sanctam,* and James of Viterbo (c. 1255-1308), both Augustinian monks. In his *De potestate ecclesiastica,* Giles argued that "the temporal sword, as being inferior, is led by the spiritual sword, as being superior, and the one is set below the other as inferior to a superior." James proposed that the secular, being the realm of fallen mankind, needs the perfect kingship of the spiritual power to redeem it just as, according to Aquinas, grace perfects nature.

On the other hand, three of the most influential supporters of the secular supremacy were John of Paris (d. 1306), Dante Alighieri (1265-1321), and Marsilius of Padua (c. 1290-1343). In his treatise *On Royal and Papal Power,* John wrote that the state is supreme in its own realm, where the ultimate purpose is the establishment of justice, and the Church is supreme in its sphere, where the purpose is the healing of souls. Both are of divine origin and mandate, possessing different worldly powers. Dante supported a similar doctrine of "parallelism" in his *De monarchia* (1311).

Marsilius, who was trained in medicine rather than theology, wrote the *Defensor Pacis* (1324), which has been praised as the most significant treatise on politics from the Middle Ages. In that treatise Marsilius argued that the purpose of earthly power is to establish and maintain peace or tranquility, which in turn would lead to salvation both in civil life and for eternity. That fundamental earthly authority has its legitimate source in the will and consent of the people, not in the "head-bishop" of Rome and not in king or emperor. Power flows from the members to the head, not the reverse. The citizens as a whole (*univer-*

sitas civium) express their will and consent through representatives, as in assemblies; and the whole body of the faithful (*universitas fidelium*) express their will and consent through representatives in a council. Thus the people are the ultimate source of all power and authority. The Church is properly concerned with moral and spiritual matters; it possesses no rights of coercion, and its sovereignty is in a kingdom not of this world. Marsilius appealed to thc example of Jesus and the Apostles, who lived humble lives of service and poverty, subjecting themselves to the civil authorities. He believed that the Church experienced a fall from its original mission and status when it attained wealth and power, especially during the fifth and sixth centuries. The practice of excommunication and papal interdiction, he said, "must be checked forthwith; and the procedure whereby such interdicts and excommunications are inflicted must be controlled and left only to the general council of Christians, whose judgment, under the guidance of the Holy Spirit, cannot be perverted by ignorance or malice."

Such radical ideas were strongly opposed by the ecclesiastical authorities, of course, and Marsilius and his assistant, John of Jandun, were forced to flee for protection to the court of Louis of Bavaria, the emperor-elect who was also involved in a struggle with the papacy. Though out of reach, they were condemned by Pope John XXII in 1327. Nevertheless, the teachings of Marsilius were to exert strong influence during the ensuing century as attempts were made to reform the Church through the conciliar movement. Further, the *Defensor Pacis* supplied basic concepts that grew in the Reformation and in the later rise of representative civil government.

A large number of scholars from various parts of Europe took up the suggestion that the Church could best be reformed by the deliberations and actions of a general council. After all, that was the method used by the early Church in the formation of the Trinitarian and Christological dogmas, and councils had been effective in other crises as well. Two of the leaders of the movement were Pierre d'Ailly (1350-1420) and Jean Gerson (1363-1429). They proceeded with caution, being loyal and orthodox churchmen, and they wished to establish the full legality of the counciliar method. They appealed to the canon law, which set limits to papal power, and they cited the basic principle of the constitutive rights of the people in ancient Roman law. They argued that even a pope may be deposed for major sins and willful heresy; and they claimed that the "Universal Church," headed by Christ alone, is superior to the Roman Church, headed by the pope. They further drew an important distinction between the law of the letter and the law of the spirit with its higher intentions of establishing "the good." Finally, they appealed to the law of "equity," as taught by Aristotle. Gerson wrote:

> The pope can be removed by a general council celebrating without his consent and against his will. Normally a council is not legally . . . celebrated without papal calling and approval. . . . But, as in grammar and in morals, general rules have exceptions—and especially when the infinite number of special circumstances surrounding a particular case are taken into account. Because of these exceptions superior law has been ordained to interpret the law. That is what Aristotle called equity.

Under pressure from the Emperor Sigismund, the second pope in the Pisan line, John XXIII, convened a council at Constance in Switzerland on November, 1414. After several months of confused quarreling, the council took decisive action by adopting the famous decree *Sacrosancta* on April 15, 1415, which asserted:

> This holy Council of Constance . . . declares, first, that it is lawfully assembled in the Holy Spirit, that it constitutes a General Council, representing the Catholic Church, and that therefore it has authority immediately from Christ; and that all men, of every rank and condition, including the Pope himself, is bound to obey it in matters concerning the Faith, the abolition of the schism, and the reformation of the Church of God in its head and its members.

The Council proceeded the next month to depose John XXIII, the pope who had convoked it. Recognizing the threat, the Roman pope, Gregory XII, abdicated on July 4, but only after he had refused to recognize the previous sessions and reconvened the council on his own authority, thereby causing *Sacrosancta* to have dubious legality. Nonetheless, the council ended the schism by deposing the Avignon pope, Benedict XIII, and finally electing a new pope, Martin V, on November 11. Thus within a year the conciliar movement appeared to have achieved remarkable success.

Wyclif and Hus

Another problem that disturbed the Church remained unresolved. There were those who believed that the reform required more radical surgery—not only in head but also in members. Equity and unity were desirable, they agreed, but the real need was for radical change in the hearts and lives of all the people according to the teachings of the Scriptures. The two outstanding proponents of this view were the Englishman, John Wyclif (c. 1325-1384) and the Bohemian, John Hus (c. 1372-1415).

Wyclif spent most of his life as a scholar and rector in and near the University of Oxford, where he supported the Platonic realism espoused earlier in England by Robert Grosseteste and Thomas Bradwardine. He first attained prominence by publishing two treatises on "Lordship," in which he developed views of the Church similar to those of John of Paris and Marsilius of Padua. All powers and possessions are the gracious gifts of God, he claimed, but their retention depends upon the righteousness of the recipient. When churchmen live in sin and misuse their positions, they may be disendowed by the civil authorities. Wyclif called for purity of living and "apostolic poverty" against powerful and greedy clericalism. Going further, he found support for his radical views in the Scriptures, which, he wrote, are "the highest authority for every Christian and the standard of faith and of all human perfection." Judged by that standard, he said, the pope is only the head of the visible Roman Church and, if he is unrighteous, may not even be among the elect. The papacy is of human origin, having been founded by Constantine rather than Christ, and its jurisdiction is limited to spiritual concerns.

Wyclif's teaching concerning the Eucharist may have been most responsible for his condemnation and posthumous burning. He wrote that the doctrine of transubstantiation is illogical, unscriptural, and contrary to the original traditions of the Church. The bread and wine are only "efficacious signs" of Christ's body and blood; the real presence of Christ in the Supper is not material and carnal but symbolic and sacramental. Moreover, preaching is more important than any sacramental celebration.

These views led Wyclif to sponsor a host of "poor priests" who travelled throughout England, teaching and preaching the Scriptures. They were given the derisive name "Lollards," a term of Dutch origin that meant "mumblers." Their aim was to evangelize and to lead people into a simple, Christ-like way of religious living. In order to facilitate their work, Wyclif gave leadership to the translation of the Latin Bible into English, thus contributing to the reading of the Scriptures in the vernacular.

Wyclif suffered a series of strokes after 1382 and died in 1384 at Lutterworth, where he had served as rector. His ideas continued to influence English church life, however, and, strangely, soon achieved important results in distant Bohemia. Movements toward reform had already begun there, encouraged by the Emperor Charles IV, who was also king of Bohemia and a strong patriot. When the Bohemian princess Anne married Richard II of England in 1382, Czech students began to attend the University of Oxford, where they imbibed the radical teachings of Wyclif and carried them home to Prague. One of the young scholars there who became enamored with Wyclif's ideas was the fiery preacher, John Hus (c. 1372-1415).

Hus was a native of Bohemia who studied and later taught at the University of Prague. A careful student of the Scriptures, he was ordained to the priesthood in 1400 and soon thereafter was appointed the popular preacher at the famous Bethlehem Chapel in Prague. He became a follower of Wyclif's ideas through the influence of his intimate friend, Jerome of Prague, who had recently taken the master's degree at Oxford. Hus was also a leader of the Czech masters at the University of Prague who opposed the large number of German scholars there, and in this patriotism he was supported by both the archbishop, Zbynek, and Wenceslas IV, the King of Bohemia.

Following the Scriptures, as had Wyclif, Hus began to emphasize personal piety and righteousness. He believed that the true Church is composed only of the elect and that its head is Christ rather than the pope. The Christian should live in Christlike purity, simplicity, and poverty, following the law of the Bible. He did not question the doctrine of transubstantiation, as Wyclif had done, but he did insist that the faithful should partake of both the bread and the wine in the Eucharist rather than of the bread alone, as had become the practice during the Middle Ages. Further, he became strongly opposed to the system of indulgences, which had become more popular with recent popes as a means of raising money. He argued that indulgences are superfluous since God freely forgives sin in those who are truly repentant.

The radical teachings of Hus and his friends become more popular because they were associated with Czech nationalism; but the same factor also brought stronger notice and opposition. The German scholars withdrew from Prague in 1409 and established their own university in Leipzig. Hus was elected rector of the University of Prague but soon was excommunicated for heresy by the archbishop who had previously supported him. The populace became divided, a great tumult arose, and the city of Prague was put under the interdict. In 1412 Hus found it expedient to flee into exile to the countryside of Bohemia from which he had come. However, there he kept up his writing, appealing to God alone for vindication.

When the Council of Constance convened in 1414, the Hussite issue had become a painful *cause célèbre* for the Church, already burdened by the scandal of schism. Hus was commanded to appear before the council to answer the charge of heresy, a capital crime. He was warned against going, but he agreed to go when promised safe conduct by the Emperor Sigismund, the brother of the Bohemian King Wenceslas. Nevertheless, when Hus appeared and was found guilty of heresy, the council sentenced him to death by burning on the ground that heretics have no rights, safe conduct notwithstanding. His death at Constance on July 6, 1415, was a lasting testimony to courage and conscience, destined to leave its mark on the future of Western Christendom.

The Council of Constance not only condemned John Hus to death; it also condemned the long-dead John Wyclif and ordered his body exhumed and burned. Then, two years after the execution of Hus, the council condemned his friend, Jerome of Prague, to the same fate. The result was a furious revolt in Bohemia. The followers of Hus become known as Utraquists (from the Latin *sub utraque,* under both kinds, bread *and* wine) or as Calixtines (from the Latin *calix,* chalice). A more radical group took the name Taborites, from the Tabor, their main fortress. They continued the struggle until the Reformation, finding their ultimate identity in the *Unitas Fratrum,* the ancestors of the modern Moravians.

The End of Conciliar Reform

The Council of Constance had been called with great expectations and some of its purposes were fulfilled. It had written its own charter in *Sacrosancta,* temporarily establishing the principle of superior conciliar authority. It intended to bring needed reform to the Church by dealing with heresy and schism (*causa fidei, unionis et reformationis*). It responded to heresy, as in the cases of Wyclif and Hus, and it rid the Church of the three competing popes and elected another as the sole, legitimate pontiff. Finally, the council determined to perpetuate its work and authority by adopting the decree *Frequens,* which required future popes to call frequent councils to deal with any issues that might arise. In effect, Constance transformed the Church into a constitutional monarchy.

As required by *Frequens,* Pope Martin V called a new council to meet at Pavia in 1423. Unfortunately, a plague in the city prevented all but a few from attending and the sessions were transferred to Siena. Accomplishing nothing of significance, the council was dissolved in 1424. However, the Hussite Wars caused increasing concern throughout Europe and many moral and administrative issues remained to be addressed, making it necessary for Martin to call another council, this time to meet in Basel in 1431. Martin died soon thereafter and was succeeded by Eugenius IV, who ordered the council's adjournment soon after it opened. The council refused, reasserting the principle of *Sacrosancta* that an ecumenical council is superior to the pope. The council then proceeded to enact a large number of reforms regarding both the structure and practices of the Church, especially limiting the power of the papacy. It even made temporary peace with the Hussites and achieved formal recognition of its authority by Eugenius himself.

In the meantime a new issue of major proportions arose which, as it turned out, led to the end of the conciliar movement. The Turks were pressing against Constantinople, causing both the Eastern Church and Empire to be in mortal danger. In desperation, the Emperor of the Byzantines, the Patriarch of Constantinople, and the great Orthodox theologian of Nicea, John Bessarion, agreed to meet with their Latin brothers for the purpose of negotiating a reunion of Christendom. The council at Basel agreed and invited the Orthodox to come there or to Avignon. However, Pope Eugenius seized the opportunity to overpower the Council and proposed a new meeting at Ferrar. The fathers at Basel were divided by that strategem and a minority obeyed the Pope, leading to a schism between the councils of Basel and Ferrar. Basel continued independently for a while, even electing a counter pope, Felix V, before dissolving itself in 1449. The Council of Ferrara, later transferred to Florence, also remaining in session until 1449, temporarily achieving in 1439 a surface reunion of the Latin and Greek churches, including even the Armenians, Nestorians, and Monophysites. It was a hollow accomplishment, however, made meaningless by the fall of Constantinople in 1453. The conciliar movement was dead and the papacy was again supreme. The bull *Execrabilis* was the funeral oration.

A Turn to Popular Piety

We have seen how the new vision of mankind's relation to God that developed during the fourteenth and fifteenth centuries brought widespread revulsion because of the corruption, immorality,and abuse of power in the Church. There was a new emphasis on the study of Scripture as well as the ancient classics, resulting in a sharpening of conscience and an urgent demand for reform. However, the efforts to cleanse the Church through administrative structures did not succeed. The moral condition of the Church continued to decline. In addition, the great famines and devastating plagues that occurred throughout western Europe in the fourteenth century only increased the misery and spiritual anxiety of the populace. The result was a turning to personal piety, a seeking within the self or in a small community of devoted believers for the healing and assurance required for salvation. Institutions and ceremonies could be largely ignored, many thought, if one could discover communion with God through personal devotion or by participation in a like-minded community of the faithful.

The foundation for the new devotion had been prepared throughout the long history of Christianity by the sporadic revivals of personal mysticism. We are reminded especially of the rise of the monastic movement, the teachings of the Pseudo-Dionysius, and the work of the great mystics such as Bernard of Clairvaux, Bonaventure, and Francis of Assisi. The Eastern Church had always been more concerned than the West with mystery and the mystical way that leads to union (*theosis*) with the ineffable God, and that subtle difference became better known in the West because of the increasing contacts after the Crusades. It was inevitable, therefore, that clergy and laity alike should turn to private experience when they witnessed the frequent failure of institutionalized religion.

Three of the primary heralds of the new piety were Johannes "Meister" Eckhart (c. 1260-1328), Johannes Tauler (c. 1300-1361), and Heinrich Suso (c. 1295-1360). We noted the work of Eckhart in chapter 17, above. They were all German Dominican monks and Eckhart was the mentor of the other two. He studied at Cologne and Paris, becoming a follower, as would be expected, of Albert the Great and Thomas Aquinas, also Dominicans who taught in those cities during the previous century. Eckhart spent most of his career as a high official of the order and as a preacher in Paris, Strasburg, and Cologne. He inclined more to the Neoplatonic than the Aristotelian line in Aquinas and carried that fundamental conception of ultimate unity almost to the point of pantheism and heresy, although he confessed that such was not his real intention. He taught that the human soul has a unique spiritual nature, a *Grund,* that gives it an essential godlikeness (*Gottheit*), a capacity for actual union with God that goes beyond the voluntary mysticism of most of the great Christian mystics. He spoke of "the interior birth of the Son," a turning within the self to find salvation by union with God in a Christ who is in the soul rather than externally in history. Accused of heresy, Eckhart admitted exaggeration but insisted that he was only saying what could be found in Augustine and Aquinas.

Tauler and Suso did not go as far toward the philosophical language of ontological unity as Eckhart had done, but they accepted his main affirmation of personal, internal piety. Tauler was famous as a preacher and spiritual director. He insisted that the soul's return to God is dependent upon grace and that the unity sought in salvation is one of will and not substance. Suso proclaimed essentially the same message. He was the author of a popular treatise, *The Little Book of Truth,* which set forth Christ's passion as the supreme model of devotion. All three of these great German mystics contributed to a new flowering of personal religion in the Rhineland and the Low Countries, from which it spread throughout western Europe.

A host of individuals and groups carried on and developed the new manner of religious devotion. Jan van Ruysbroeck (1293-1381) in Flanders, Julian of Norwich (1342-1416) in England, Catherine of Siena (1347-1380) in Italy, and Gerard Groote (1340-1384) in the Netherlands are outstanding examples. There were many communities of the pious, composed of both monastics and laity, such as the Beguines and the Beghards, the Free Spirits, the Sisters and Brothers of the Common Life, and the Modern Devotionalists. From these came a mass of such popular literature as *The Cloud of Unknowing, The Imitation of Christ,* and *The German Theology*.

All of this spiritual ferment represented a deep dissatisfaction with the established Church. It prepared the ground for the coming Reformation of the sixteenth century, insistently calling attention to the increasing waywardness of the Church and at the same time stressing the guidance of Scripture and the competence of the individual before God.

The New Vision of Humanism

Probably the dominant characteristic of the Renaissance was the new "humanism" (*studia humanitatis*), the study of the humane or liberal arts. The focus of vision turned from dogmatic theology and a world-denying faith to the more optimistic assessment of human nature to be found in the ancient classics of Greece and Rome. We have noticed this rebirth of joy and hope in chapter 18, above, and it is necessary here only to be reminded of the major change brought about by the thinkers and writers of the new age regarding the relation between mankind and God. The change of view was radical and epoch-making. It prepared the way for the Reformation, the Enlightenment, and the Modern Age.

The Renaissance is said to have originated in the work of the Italian scholar, Francesco Petrarch (1304-1374). An avid student of ancient Latin literature, especially that of Cicero and Seneca, he rejected most of the work of the Scholastics and turned back instead to Platonic Augustinianism. Petrarch taught that mankind should be the center of study and concern. He and his friend, Giovanni Boccaccio (1313-1375), author of the famous *Decameron,* initiated the new study of the classics, both Latin and Greek, in the schools of Italy, leading ultimately to the reestablishment in 1462 of the Platonic Academy in Florence. Marsilio

Ficino (1433-1499) became the strong director of that school and developed there a new combination of Christianity and Platonism, known as the "pious philosophy." Ficino's influence later spread to France and England where, through the humanist John Colet, it blossomed in the work of Erasmus. The whole spirit of the Italian Renaissance is summarized in the great treatise *Oration on the Dignity on Man* by Pico della Mirandola (1463-1494).

No figure better depicts the character of Renaissance humanism than Desiderius Erasmus (c. 1466-1536). (See chapter 18.) The illegitimate son of a priest, he was born near Rotterdam and received his early training at Deventer, a Dutch city that had long been a center of the new piety. Educated later at Paris and Cambridge, he became the greatest scholar of the day, well known by such leaders of the new age as John Colet and Thomas More in England and Martin Luther in Germany. He never broke with the Church, as Luther did, but he effectively satirized its hypocricy in such works as the *Praise of Folly* and *Familiar Colloquies*. One of his most significant accomplishments was the publication in 1516 of the Greek New Testament, a landmark of textual criticism that opened the way for modern biblical study.

When changing attitudes toward the institutionalized Church met simultaneously with personal piety, man-centered scholarships, and such technological advancements as the printing press, the opening of a new world in the West was inevitable. The ambiguous results have continued as a flood-tide of both good and evil in the Modern Age.

VII.
NEW FORMS OF WESTERN CHRISTIANITY

Chapter 22

The Causes, Varieties, and Principles of Reform

This chapter and the next three discuss the epochal revolution commonly called the Reformation that occurred in western Europe during the first half of the sixteenth century. We begin the discussion in this chapter by examining the movement as a whole, reviewing its causes, taking notes of its differing forms, and analyzing the unifying principles that provide unity to all forms of Protestantism. Then we proceed in the next three chapters by giving a somewhat fuller description of each of the major types of Protestantism. The purpose is not so much to review the historical and biographical details as to emphasize the distinctive ideas of each type and, especially, to discover the elements of each that have contributed to various aspects of modern experience and culture.

The Factors Behind the Reform

It has long been customary to say that the Reformation began when Martin Luther posted his Ninety-five Theses on the castle church door at Wittenberg on October 31, 1517. There is truth in the statement, of course, but it is more accurate to say that the Reformation was without beginning and is without end. Contemporaries of Luther arrived more or less independently at much the same religious conclusions that he did and at around the same time, so that it is safe to surmise that the Reformation would probably have occurred even if Luther had never been born. He pulled the trigger but the gun was already loaded and cocked, and if he had not done so other fingers were in motion. Furthermore, it is even more difficult to specify an end to the Reformation. The process of reform and restructuring has continued even into the twentieth century and the results of the initial explosion will remain as long as the Church lives.

The Reformation in some form was inevitable, given the conditions that we observed in the previous chapters. The factors leading to change and revolt were many and increasingly urgent. It may be useful here to describe them in five major categories: moral, religious, political, scientific, and cultural.

1. The high moral standards of social justice and personal rectitude rooted in the Bible have always stood in objective judgment over the institutional life and leaders of the Church. As a result there have been frequent efforts to reform the Church throughout its history. Already in the New Testament itself there were condemnations of immorality and fervent calls for repentance and renewal, as seen, for example, in I Corinthians 5-6, James 5, and Revelation 2, among many other passages. In the second century the Montanist schism was in large measure caused by the decline in moral purity and expectant spirituality. Later, the monastic movement arose as a reaction against the easy grace and growing worldliness of most Christians. Again, the great abbey of Cluny, founded in 910 in Burgundy, became the center of a powerful movement of moral reform throughout western Europe that lasted for two centuries. And we have noted in the last chapter how the gross corruptions even in the papacy itself during the Renaissance led to such moral revulsion that radical attempts to reform the Church "in head and members" were recognized as necessary.

That unabashed immorality reached its zenith during the fourteenth and fifteenth centuries. In addition to unprecedented claims of absolute political power and shameless displays of obscene opulence without regard for the grinding drudgery and miserable poverty of the people, the popes and the higher clergy frequently ignored their vows of chastity and indulged in the forbidden practices of nepotism and simony. Moral depravity in the papacy reached its worst extreme during the half-century that began with the reign of Sixtus IV (1471-1484). He was a patron of the arts, leaving the Sistine Chapel as a legacy; but he also enriched his relatives, warred against Florence, and extended the Papal States as a secular kingdom, bringing the Church to a condition of bankruptcy. He was succeeded by Innocent VIII (1484-1492), the father of sixteen children, who was notorious for selling ecclesiastical positions in order to support his family in extravagance. The next pope, Alexander VI (1492-1503), is judged as the most immoral of them all. He obtained the pontificate through bribery and spent most of his energies attempting to promote his bastard children, especially his infamous daughter, Lucrezia Borgia, and his conniving and murderous son, Cesare Borgia. His policies not only brought shame to the Church but also opened the door to French and Spanish conquests of Italy.

Julius II (1503-1513), a nephew of Sixtus IV, followed Alexander. Like his uncle, Julius was ambitious to enlarge the papal territories and he personally led his troops in warfare, riding a horse into battle as if he were a secular potentate rather than a holy priest. To his credit, however, Julius was also a lover of sculpture, painting, and architecture. He began the construction of the new basilica of St. Peter which stands today as a symbol of both Christendom and the Renaissance, and he commissioned many of the most famous works of Raphael and Michelangelo. The next pope, Leo X (11513-1521), saw the beginning of the Reformation, though he obviously failed to understand either its necessity or its potential consequences. Leo was a proud member of the rich and powerful Medici family of Florence. He was apparently free from the personal vices of his predecessors, but he was equally guilty of their political ambitions and financial manipulations.

Thus nepotism and simony were common sins among those who were supposed to be examples of holiness. Nepotism is official favoritism toward one's relatives. Simony is buying and selling ecclesiastical power and position, named after the infamous Simon Magus (Acts 8:9-24) who attempted to purchase miraculous power from the Apostles. As it turned out, the related evil of selling indulgences provided the spark that finally lighted the great purging conflagration of reform begun by Luther.

The practice of granting indulgences appeared prominently for the first time when Pope Urban II (1088-1099) proclaimed special privileges to those who participated in the First Crusade to liberate the Holy Land from the Moslems. The idea and practice grew in subsequent crises and received theological explication by Thomas Aquinas. An indulgence is the granting of forgiveness for sin and exemption from punishment as as result of some act of merit, based upon the infinite grace already attained by Christ and the saints. It is theoretically an extension of the sacrament of penance, the reward for contrition, confession, and satisfaction. Renaissance popes and bishops quickly saw the financial possibilities involved in the system and soon a vast machinery for the promotion and sale of "plenary indulgences" was invented for the salvation of souls and the enrichment of ecclesiastical coffers. The flagrant abuse of the system brought widespread abhorrence, not least to Luther, the Saxon professor and preacher of Wittenberg. The long history of moral corruption had brought a surfeit to the pious, making reform inevitable.

2. We refer to a second category of causes of the Reformation as religious, meaning those changes in the religious attitudes and practices of the people that enabled them to break with tradition. Negatively, there was a widespread loss of respect for the institutional Church resulting from the political intrigues, the Great Schism with its multiple lines of popes, the moral scandals, and the insatiable avarice of the clergy. Fur-

ther, the severe famines and plagues that ravaged most of western Europe during the fourteenth century brought new spiritual anxiety accompanied by doubt as to the protective, saving power of the Church. Added to these, the rediscovery of ancient texts and classical learning revealed a wide gap between the simple Gospel of Jesus and the Apostles on the one hand and the complicated systems of medieval Scholasticism on the other hand. To read the Gospels was an edifying pleasure but to study Aquinas and Scotus was a burden to the flesh as well as the spirit.

Positively, both the common people and many scholars were prepared for radical reform by the development of alternate ways to God through private piety and voluntary community. We have noted earlier the simultaneous appearance in many areas of devotional groups that found peace and fellowship through prayer, Christian service, Bible study, and the sharing of a common experience. These simple yet powerful groups came to the conclusion that ritual and dogma were really incidental and expendable, since they could receive the saving grace of God within and among themselves without benefit of clergy or sacrament. Informed by a new reading of the Scriptures and led toward inward spirituality by the great mystics, these reformers and reformed before the Reformation appeared here and there in such groups as the Lollards, the Hussites, the Brothers and Sisters of the Common Life, and the Unitas Fratrum.

3. The political causes of the Reformation are numerous and, in some cases, accidents of history. The rise of nationalism during the late Middle Ages was a central political factor, giving rise to group identification and loyalty outside the Church as well as competition and strife between people who were at the same time united within the Church. We have earlier taken note of the proto-Protestant tendencies of Joan of Arc, who was condemned as heretic because of her ultimate dependence upon her private "voices" and because of her uncompromising French patriotism. Thus, with the breakdown of the feudal system and the expansion of travel and commerce beyond the local community, a new loyalty of national identity began to characterize the populace of western Europe.

Nation states appear when the people of a larger area combine their smaller loyalties of family, tribe, town, and city into a unity based on geography, language, economic and military interests, and traditions, for the social and political benefit of all. In that way France and Spain became unified nations. Britain, though often invaded, had from ancient times considered itself separate and distinct from the Continent because of its insular geography. Though slow in political unification, the numerous jurisdictions of Germany and Italy did not prevent their people from claiming a kind of national loyalty long before their nations achieved political unity.

When patriotism became consciously combined with many grievances against a foreign papacy that was increasingly dominated by Italians and playing the divisive game of international politics, it became inevitable that Germans and English, among others, would rebel against the Church represented by that papacy. Luther, as we shall see, used with great effect a call to the German nobility to stand together against the Roman Church as an avaricious foreign power. And with different motivations, King Henry VIII used English separatist sensibilities to establish a national church independent of Rome. Fortunately for the rebels, political circumstances sometimes contributed to the success of their revolts, as when the struggles between Francis I of France and the Emperor Charles V saved Luther and his colleagues on several occasions from the fate of Joan of Arc or John Hus. Without the support of the Elector Frederick, Luther would probably have been remembered only as a pitiful German martyr who was executed for heresy by the Imperial Diet.

4. The scientific causes of the Reformation are indirect but no less obvious and powerful. The method of inquiry exemplified by such scholars as Roger Bacon encouraged an untrammeled search for truth in spite of received opinion. In addition, the philosophical approach of nominalism led to a primary concern with individual realities in order to discover universal principles, rather than the other way around. Such attitudes toward learning and experimentation could not fail to plant seeds of doubt in thinking minds, giving rise to demands for freedom of inquiry and expression as well as stubborn rejection of all restricting authority.

When the Crusades brought into view a larger and different world, when the increased contacts with Moslem and Jewish Aristotelians in Spain resulted in revolutionary changes in philosophical method and content, and when the fall of Constantinople caused a flood of scholars to flee to the West with their manuscripts and classical learning, the preparations were in place for a great surge of discovery and invention. Soon a whole new universe was unveiled by the revolution of Copernicus and those who followed him. In like manner, a new world was opened to Europe by the voyages of discovery by Vasco da Gama, Christopher Columbus, Ferdinand Magellan, and the armadas of those who sailed in their wake. Rapidly, invention followed upon discovery.

The printing press of Gutenberg and others was perhaps the most creative of them all, making possible the quick and widespread dissemination of new ideas and opinions.

The medieval traditions about nature, man, and God were both challenged and undermined by all the scientific advances. Accepted dogmas about the nature of the earth and the location of heaven, purgatory, and hell were questioned, ridiculed, and rejected out of hand. The perception grew that human beings are more properly concerned with this world than with another and that mankind is both dwarfed by the vast universe and able to understand and, to a degree, control and use it. New ideas begat more of the same. The questioning of old opinions and doctrines generated a quest for additional new truths in the realm of nature. New worlds now seen in the heavens and on earth led inexorably to visions of new worlds of the spirit. Thus revolution in science was accompanied by revolution in religion.

5. A final category of causes bringing about the Reformation may be designated as cultural. Of course the causes we have already discussed are also cultural in the broad sense, but here we refer to the more narrow meaning of culture as the conditions of social life. The Renaissance brought not only a rebirth of ancient learning and an explosion of art, literature, and architecture; it also gave impetus to the rise of cities, expanded commerce, the growth of the middle class, and undeniable demands for freedom and tolerance.

These conditions and desires were the seedbed for hope and optimism. The medieval spirit of fear, obedience, and otherworldliness began to give way to daring, audacity, and appreciation of the beauty and joy of life in this world. As the feudal system began to decay, the poor and oppressed began to question the necessity of accepting their station. Social arrangements may not be fixed by inexorable laws, they thought, but rather it might be possible that the lowly could share in comfort, wealth, and enjoyment.

The new attitudes spilled over from social conditions to religion. All could see the low moral and spiritual state of the Church and its clergy. Why not demand change? Why be subject to higher powers when those powers appear unworthy of respect? If so many ancient truths have been demonstrably false, could it be that the required dogmas and practices of the Church are also in need of correction? If many are finding the peace of salvation through relations to God, without the mediation of sacrament or clergy, why should not all achieve the same results? Such questions, asked in the light of moral earnestness and careful Bible study, began to be answered by those who therefore became the great Reformers.

The Varieties of Reform

The following three chapters discuss in greater detail the varieties of reformed tradition that developed somewhat simultaneously during the second quarter of the sixteenth century. Here we need only to specify the individual varieties, noting enough about each to distinguish its separate origin and character. All together they are usually referred to as Protestantism, a term that is both useful and somewhat technically inaccurate. Nevertheless, the designation is too well established to be dropped.

The four forms of Protestantism are Lutheranism, Calvinism,Radical Protestantism (Anabaptist or Sectarian), and Anglicanism. They have much in common, as we shall see, but they are also quite distinct from each other in history, emphases, structure, and secondary doctrines.

1. More than any of the others, Lutheranism began and remains as a reflection of the personality and teachings of its primary founder, Martin Luther. It was the original form of Protestantism, providing that name for the whole movement, and its intention was to bring about a genuine reform of the Church by the standard of the New Testament while carefully seeking to avoid radical innovation or departure from the essentials of the true faith. Luther himself was a fervent and faithful son of the Church, a priest, monk, preacher, and theologian. He belonged to the Augustinian Order and there were many affinities between him and his fifth-century mentor. He was deeply offended by what he perceived as the moral depravity of the Church in his time, and he tried desperately to instigate correction and cleansing. He also came to believe that most of the scholastic theology and sacramental development of the Middle Ages had gone astray, needing to be rejected in favor of a return to thc teachings and practices of the early Church.

Lutheranism therefore chose a conservative position. It attempted to preserve the essentials of Christianity undisturbed but rather renewed and purified. It sought to avoid extremes of interpretation or practice and it made a special effort to keep within the realm of religion as much as possible rather than to foment revolutionary social and political change. Luther himself stressed both the pervasive sinfulness of mankind and the saving grace of God. He focused so centrally on those convictions that he urged the Church to be involved primarily in the worship of God and the preaching of the Word rather than to allow itself to expend its energies in human efforts at social and political improvements.

2. Calvinism has more than one source. Though it has always been associated with the character and teachings of John Calvin, it also owes

much to William Farel, Ulrich Zwingli, Martin Bucer, Heinrich Bullinger, Theodore Beza, and John Knox, to name only the best known. Therefore it is perhaps better to speak of this type of Protestantism as the Reformed Tradition.

This form of Protestantism arose for the most part out of the concerns of humanism as they were applied to religion. Those concerns, as we have seen earlier, were focused on the power of human rationality; the rediscovery, interpretation, and transmission of ancient literature, including the Scriptures; the high moral idealism of classical philosophy and theology; the intrinsic value and natural capacity for progress of human beings; and the promotion of the virtues of autonomy, freedom, and tolerance. Proceeding with such motivating principles, Calvin and his colleagues believed that the medieval theology and Church that they had inherited stood in dire need of reform. With more reason than passion, they set about the task of examining the teachings and practices of the Church in the light of the Scriptures, respecting tradition without feeling bound by it. They were intent on knowing, describing, and defending God and his will so as to shape individuals and society by those standards.

The reformed Tradition had its original base in Switzerland, the Rhineland, and the Netherlands. It soon spread for a variety of reasons and with different degrees of success into France, Scotland, England, and Hungary. The great migrations from western Europe to the New World, especially to North America, included many with at least a partial dedication to this type of Protestantism, where they were a major force in the formation of a burgeoning new culture.

3. The Radical Protestants were not a unified group, though they may be classified together because of their many similarities. Their very nature made them sectarian; that is, they emphasized local, usually autonomous churches composed of volunteer members, often different not only from the mainline Protestants but also among themselves from area to area. Many of them were also derisively called "Anabaptists," a name they accepted as a badge of honor because or their strong insistence on rejecting the baptism of infants in favor of baptizing believers only. Thus they usually rebaptized new members who had already been initiated as infants into the Catholic or other churches. They were radical in the view of both Protestants and Catholics because they carried the reform to what they believed to be its logical and Scriptural ends, not being satisfied with any compromises or partial solutions. They were particularly eager to break away from the control and service of the state, choosing to serve a higher loyalty and thereby suffering frequent persecution and forced emigration.

The Radical Protestants clearly reflect a formative heritage from many dissenting groups that may be identified during the long history of the Church, but they especially represent the Bible-centered piety and separateness we have noted in various groups that immediately preceded the Reformation. Though not always consciously, they carried on the tradition of the Cathari, the Waldensians, the Lollards, the Hussites, the Joachimites, and the Brothers and Sisters of the Common Life, to list the most prominent ones. Their leaders in the early days of the Reformation were such as George Blaurock, Felix Manz, and Conrad Grebel of Zurich; Balthasar Hubmaier, Thomas Muntzer, Hans Denck, Michael Sattler, Melchoir Hofmann, and Pilgram Marpeck in Germany; Menno Simons in the Netherlands; and Jacob Hutter in Austria.

4. The Anglican type of Protestantism stands distinctly apart from the other three types in several important ways, primarily because its origin is to be found more in nationalism and insularity than in essentially theological factors. It was and remains the branch of the universal Church that belongs specifically to England (and later to English-speaking people throughout the world). It has always desired and claimed to be in true succession from the Apostolic Church, holding the true and essential faith and attempting to maintain Christian fellowship with all other branches of the world Church. However, it is also historically a result of the broader Reformation and it was strongly influenced in its separate formation by all three of the other reformed types.

The Anglican communion shares the major theological principles of Protestantism that give unity to all four types. At the same time, it has attempted more than the others to retain the traditions, forms, and liturgies of the ancient and medieval Church. This effort has been the basis of its claim to be "a bridge," a *via media,* between Protestantism and Roman Catholicism; but the effort has also been the cause of a continuing struggle within the church between those who would become more Roman, on the one hand, and those who would become more reformed, on the other. That struggle has led to a return to Rome by some and the final separation into new denominations by others.

Basic Protestant Principles

We have stressed the fact that all four types of Protestantism are united by a common affirmation of certain fundamental principles. Though a number might be identified, there are three that are unquestionably basic and held unanimously: (1) salvation by grace through faith alone; (2) the sole ultimate authority of Scripture; and (3) the priesthood of every believer. These principles are not always interpreted in the same way in differing Protestant communions, but they were all instrumental in the formation of each group and they have all received strong affirmation in the confessions of faith that all have developed.

Salvation by grace means that sinful human beings may be forgiven and restored to divine favor by the redeeming power of a God of love and mercy. Christianity has always taught that the grace of God was fully revealed and made available through Jesus Christ, especially in his death and resurrection. There has been a variety of opinion about how those beliefs should be confessed and taught, but they have always been at the heart of the Gospel in every type of theology.

The major point of disagreement between Roman Catholics and Protestants does not concern whether salvation is by God's grace; all believe that it is. Rather, the two sides disagree as to the nature of that grace and as to the means by which it may be efficaciously received. For centuries, as we have seen, the Roman Church at least implied, even if it did not always mean, that saving grace is in some manner an objective commodity, a divine power that may be dispensed, received, refused, and withheld. It could, moreover, be transmitted by physical means and through human hands and institutions, even unworthy ones. Often, practice suggested that God's grace could be bought and sold. The Reformers rejected that view in favor of an interpretation that grace is essentially God's unmerited, loving favor, a spiritual graciousness or loving kindness toward persons. That understanding of grace led to the conviction that it cannot be transmitted by sacramental means or any third agency, even God's holy Church; it cannot and need not be merited by any act or attitude, since it is God's free gift. All that is required to receive it, said the Reformers, is repentance (a turning from sin and self, a returning to God) and faith (the acceptance of God's love in Christ in trust and obedience). The fundamental disagreement was clearly perceived by Martin Luther at the very beginning of the Reformation. It became the detonator of the explosion within the Church that led to the separation by all of the Reformers, and it remains one of the basic distinctions between Protestants and Catholics.

Belief in the ultimate authority of the Scriptures alone came to be defined more slowly and with less precision and unanimity. We should note that the early Church accepted the authority of the Hebrew Scriptures and added the writings of the Apostles, the New Testament, beginning as early as the second century (see Chapter 5, above). However, as the centuries passed, the teachings of the Fathers and the doctrines of the councils, especially the first four, began to form a body of tradition that was increasingly acknowledged as authoritative. Gradually this *consensus fidelium* became the basis of authority for the Church in its teaching function, the *magisterium*. Nevertheless, as we have seen, many theories and practices of the Church became the subject of debate, especially in Renaissance times. A critical example was the challenge of the sacramental system, especially the sale of indulgences, by Martin Luther. Many scholars before Luther, such as the humanists, began to doubt the dependability of tradition. Abelard, as early as the twelfth century, had demonstrated the inconsistency of the Fathers.

The result was that Luther and his fellow Reformers found it necessary to judge the beliefs and practices of the whole Church by the standard Scriptures, especially the New Testament. They drew a sharp line of distinction between the age of the Apostles and the subsequent history of the Church. Everything must be regarded as true or false, right or wrong, according to whether it is in line with the teachings of Jesus and the Apostles. The Lutheran and Reformed Tradition thus adopted the doctrine of *sola Scriptura*.

The Church of England demurred to some degree. It did not accept the necessity of abandoning tradition as a guide in theology any more than in form and practice. Thus, somewhat ambiguously, it retained a place for tradition as authoritative while granting the primary place to Scripture. That has served well in the Anglican Church's role of being the *via media*. On the other hand, the Radical Protestants, while insisting as strongly as Lutherans and Calvinists on the sole authority of the Scriptures, have often modified the view by emphasizing the right to private interpretation as well as the inner testimony of the Spirit.

The third major Protestant principle is the doctrine of the priesthood of every believer. Essentially, that means two things. First, it means that every person, whether clergy or laity, is competent to deal in the spirit with God with respect to sin and salvation. Indeed, every person must do so, in the final analysis. This does not mean, of course, that spiritual and moral influence are not possible, effective, or desirable; it does mean that every soul is responsible and capable before God. All external aids, including sacraments, clergy, Church and Scriptures, are possibly useful, perhaps God-given, but not essential. One corollary of this view is Luther's famous doctrine of vocation in which, among other things, he taught that all people are equal before God, whether male or female, clergy or laity, monk or farmer.

A second aspect of this doctrine of the priesthood of every believer has often been overlooked, but it is a significant aspect of Protestant theology. Simply put, it holds that every Christian is a priest before the altar of God in witness, prayer, and supplication on behalf of all people.

A priest by definition is one of his fellowmen whose privilege and obligation is to represent his people before God. Every believer, then, is obligated to be God's agent in attempting to bring all humanity to salvation. Every believer should lift up all others in prayers of sacrifice, intercession, and sanctification. It is the duty of each believer to be a priest on behalf of all believers as well as all sinners.

These three doctrines are the unifying essence of Protestantism. The next three chapters will delineate in more detail the distinctive characteristics of the four types of Protestants, describing their origins, leaders, and differences. Our primary interest is in discovering the contributions each has bequeathed to modern culture.

Chapter 23

Central Protestantism: Luther, Zwingli, and Calvin

The ferment of reform that had been boiling in the Western Church for more than a century finally burst to the surface during the first half of the sixteenth century. It occurred almost simultaneously in several places, especially in the German states, Switzerland, the Netherlands, and England. In the last chapter we have described the four primary types of Protestantism that were the product of that ferment. This chapter will describe the earliest outbreaks of the movement in the work of Martin Luther, Ulrich Zwingli, and John Calvin. We will first review the lives and works of these three seminal reformers; then we will compare and contrast the two forms of Protestantism that are the result of their experiences and convictions.

Luther's Road to Reform

Martin Luther has always been considered the prime mover of the Protestant Reformation, though he certainly did not initially intend for it to be that way. He began his career as a conservative, extremely serious-minded monk and hard-working scholar. His desire was to find a way to true righteousness for himself and for the whole Church. For fifteen years after he entered the monastery he sought valiantly to find relief from his own increasing burden of guilt and at the same time to contribute to the reform of the Church's false teachings and scandalous practices, as he and a multitude of others perceived them. But he wanted forgiveness and reform, not condemnation and revolution.

Luther was born in Eisleben, Saxony, on November 10, 1483, St. Martin's Day. His father was an ambitious and successful miner of copper who became prosperous through hard work and good investments in the smelting business. There were eight children in the family, among whom Martin was the second son. The father planned for his talented son to pursue a career in law and so enrolled him in preparatory schools in Mansfield, Magdeburg, and Eisenach. Then Martin studied at the University of Erfurt, from 1501 until 1505, when he attained the Master's degree. Soon afterwards he began the study of law at the same university, but in July of that year he suddenly entered the Augustinian monastery at Erfurt. The often-repeated explanation for the redirection of his life was a vow he made to Saint Anne that he would become a monk if he were spared during a frightening storm. He kept the vow, much to the displeasure of his father.

Luther applied himself to both severe self-discipline and intensive study while at the monastery. He was ordained to the priesthood in 1507 and went for further study at the new University of Wittenberg, where he earned the Bachelor of Theology degree. Returning to Erfurt, he continued his studies, receiving the *sententiarus,* a degree permitting him to lecture on Peter Lombard's *Sentences,* and, in 1512, the degree Doctor of Theology. During the winter of 1510-11 he made a memorable visit to Rome on behalf of his Augustinian Order, and by 1515 he had been appointed vicar over eleven monasteries. His primary responsibility, however, was as Professor at the University of Wittenberg, where he delivered lectures on the Psalms, Romans, Galatians, and Hebrews, all the while giving regular sermons at both the monastery and the university. As his responsibility and competence grew, so did his conviction of sin and terrifying anxiety as well as his concern for the moral state of the Church.

In September, 1517, Luther prepared a *Disputation against Scholastic Theology,* calling into question the validity of the whole system of Scholasticism. The work was typical of the academic method used to debate issues in morality and theology. His major point, anticipating the future, was to challenge the nominalist teaching that God's grace is infused into those who do good by virtue of their nature. He argued that the Scriptures teach that grace is a free gift of God that cannot be gained by merit and that natural man will not do good apart from the power of a prior gift of grace. With that already said, Luther was in no mood to allow the sale of meritorious indulgence to his parishioners by Johann Tetzel, the Dominican agent of the papacy who was traveling for that purpose throughout Germany.

The explosion occurred on October 31, 1517, when Luther posted another call for disputation that attacked and challenged the whole system of indulgences. This was, of course, his famous *Ninety-five Theses.* Within a few weeks, due to the newly invented printing press, his sharp words were spread throughout the Empire. He quickly became both a folk hero and an ecclesiastical outcast. The following April he was called before the chapter of the Augustinians at Heidelberg, where he debated his one-time friend, the able theologian Johann Maier of Eck, Professor at Ingolstadt. There he won the allegiance of Martin Bucer and Johannes Brenz, later to become the leaders of reform at Strasburg and Wurttemberg respectively. In October he was called to defend his views at Augsburg before Cardinal Tommaso de Vio, known as Cajetan from his birthplace. After a week, Luther quit the debate, appealing to the pope "to be better informed." The following year, 1519, he joined his colleague, Andreas Karlstadt, at Leipzig in a decisive debate again with Eck. There he was forced to acknowledge that he believed not only that the pope was in error but that a general council of the Church could be also. He claimed that the Council of Constance had been wrong in 1415 when it executed John Hus. Thus he was forced to the conclusion that all Christian faith and practice must ultimately be judged by Scripture alone.

Luther had therefore reached the essentials of subsequent Protestant theology by 1519, though he certainly was not fully aware of the consequences. He had rejected the saving power of good works in favor of God's grace alone, and he had concluded that the Scriptures alone are the final authority for faith and practice. It is no surprise that the following June Pope Leo X issued the famous bull, *Exsurge domine:* "Arise, O Lord, and judge thy cause . . . for a wild boar has entered into thy vineyard." Events followed rapidly one after another. In April, 1521, Luther was promised safe-conduct and required to appear before the Emperor Charles V and the imperial diet at Worms to answer a charge of heresy. In spite of the memory of a similar situation for John Hus a century earlier, Luther went to Worms and stood by his convictions. When asked to recant he declared the famous words: "Here I stand. God help me. I can do no other."

A bull of excommunication had already been published in Rome. Now under imperial ban, Luther was in grave danger of imprisonment and execution. However, his friend and supporter, the powerful Elector Frederick of Saxony, arranged for him to be hidden in a mountain fortress, the Wartburg, where he translated the Greek New Testament into German. That powerful document, based on the new Greek text published by Erasmus in 1516, was instrumental in the literary formation of the German language as well as in the support and spread of reformed ideas. When Luther learned that some of his friends at Wittenberg, led by Karlstadt, were upsetting the city and endangering the cause by excessive reform, he returned to the city and took charge. His powerful demand for restraint gained him permanent favor among the nobility and set the pattern for his future conservative social policy.

The remaining twenty-five years of life for the great reformer were spent in constant activity, filled with teaching, preaching, and writing.

Except for occasional journeys within Germany, he remained in Wittenberg. There he married a former nun, Katherine von Bora, who maintained a happy home for him and their five children. He guided the development of "evangelical" congregations throughout Germany, writing orders of worship, catechisms, masses, and various other treatises for the use of the churches. In addition, he published so vast a collection of commentaries and theological works that he finally became one of the most prolific authors in history. He reluctantly found it necessary to oppose the optimistic humanism of Erasmus, the wild apocalypticism of Thomas Muntzer, and the radical social revolution of the peasants. His theology developed and deepened, but there were no changes in the major principles after 1520. Finally, in poor health, he died during a visit to Eisleben on February 18, 1546.

Among the multitude of works that Luther composed, three treatises from the year 1520 have been regarded as so preeminent that they are usually referred to as the "primary works." The first, written in August, was *To the Christian Nobility of the German Nation.* It attempted to demolish three walls that protected the papacy: the superior power of the priesthood over the laity; the exclusive right of the papacy for the final interpretation of the Scriptures; and the claim that the pope alone can summon a reforming council. The treatise then proposed a program of major reform in social life, morality, and church practice that should be enacted by a council called by the secular authorities. Underlying it all was a popular appeal for human rights and patriotism against a foreign tyranny.

The second treatise, composed in October, was entitled *The Babylonian Captivity of the Church,* a clear reference to the recent scandalous schism of the Church as well as to the ancient exile of the Jews. The work is an unrelenting attack on the sacramental system. Luther argued that the Scriptures support only two sacraments, baptism and the Lord's Supper, both of which are signs of forgiveness based on faith. He rejected the efficacy of the other sacraments, insisting that the Eucharist should be given in both kinds to the laity and that it is a testimony of faith and not a repeated sacrifice. He even questioned the propriety of baptizing infants, since they have no faith for themselves, and he expressed doubts concerning the doctrine of transubstantiation. The treatise as a whole is a slashing, harshly-worded indictment of the essential practices of the medieval Church.

The third great treatise, *The Freedom of a Christian,* written in November, is of an entirely different character. Rather than being filled with vituperation, it is a joyful, peaceful work, full of piety and devotion. It holds that since Christians are sinners, redeemed by the gift of God's loving graciousness, they are free from legal obligation but bound by the inward motivation of love. Therefore, "a Christian is a perfectly free lord of all, subject to none; a Christian is a perfectly dutiful servant of all, subject to all." With that fundamental theme, Luther proceeded to establish Christian freedom without any pretensions of salvation by merit and at the same time to demonstrate Christian obligation to Christlike service and morality. It is a charter of theological liberty and ethics, and with it the Reformation, though not yet secure, was established.

Zwingli's Way to Reform

The father of the Swiss Reformation was Ulrich Zwingli, who jealously claimed that he developed his reformed ideas independently of Luther. "I object to being called Lutheran by papists," he wrote, "for I did not learn Christ's teaching from Luther but from the very word of God." The records shows that he was at least partially correct. He was originally influenced toward the reformed position by extensive humanistic training and by his own careful study of the Scriptures. However, it is also true that he read Luther's writings as early as 1521.

Zwingli was born on January 1, 1484, in the village of Wildhaus in eastern Switzerland, where his father was a prosperous farmer and local official. His uncle, the dean of Wesen, started him on the path of education by sending him while still a young lad to schools in Basel and Bern. While at Bern he came under the strong influence of the humanist Heinrich Wolflin, known as Lupulus. Then from 1500 to 1502 he attended the University of Vienna where he learned the classics from Conrad Celtis. Finally, he returned to Basel in 1502, where he graduated with the bachelor's degree in 1504 and the master's in 1506. During the formative years at Basel he was greatly influenced by the teachings of Thomas Wyttenbach, a humanist scholar who led him to reject the practice of indulgences and to accept the Scriptures alone as the ultimate authority for Christian faith and practice.

He became parish priest in the village of Glarus after leaving Basel and spent the next ten years there, becoming expert in Greek, learning Hebrew, and continuing his study of the classics, the Fathers, and the Bible. He expressed special delight with Erasmus' Greek text of the New Testament that had just been published in Basel. While at Glarus he also achieved recognition as a preacher and for his criticism of the employment of the Swiss as mercenary soldiers by France and the pope. Further, he moved in 1516 from Glarus to the pilgrim shrine of Einsiedeln where he increased his influence as a preacher and scholar.

In January, 1519, Zwingli began his career at the Great Minster in Zurich where he was people's priest and reforming leader. During the fall of that year he contacted the bubonic plague and came near to death. That experience coupled with his reading of Luther's works in 1521 caused him to add spiritual concern to his intellectual motivation for reform, and he began to lead the city toward a break with tradition. In 1522 he vigorously defended a group of citizens who unlawfully broke the Lenten fast on the grounds that the New Testament did not require such fasting. When the bishop of the diocese attempted to punish the innovators, Zwingli led the city council to a compromise decision, thus establishing civil control over religious affairs. By order of the council, public disputations were held in January and October of 1523 between Zwingli and his supporters on one side and the Romanists on the other. He prepared sixty-seven articles for the debate, advocating the sole authority of the Scriptures, salvation by faith alone, clerical marriage, lay communion in both kinds, and worship services in the vernacular instead of Latin. He also denied that the mass is a sacrifice and opposed the worth of merit for salvation, the intercession of saints, and the doctrine of purgatory. The council and a majority of the citizens enthusiastically agreed with him and began at once to institute the reforms required. Wisely, however, Zwingli counselled gradual change for the sake of good order.

An open break with Rome was in effect by 1525, the year Zwingli published his chief work, *The Commentary on True and False Religion*. His influence spread rapidly throughout Switzerland and within a short time most of the leading cities followed the example of Zurich. His teaching was also adopted in neighboring Constance, Mulhausen, and Strasburg, where a host of strong leaders were to give added strength in later years to the Reformed Tradition in place of Lutheranism.

Although in basic agreement, there were important differences between Luther and his followers on the one hand and the Zwinglians on the other. A major distinction was in the interpretation of the Lord's Supper. Luther insisted on a literal interpretation of Christ's words, "This is my body." He believed that Christ is present on a multitude of alters at once because of the *communicatio idiomatum* (communication of attributes), the ancient Christological doctrine that the divine nature, including ubiquity, is communicated to Christ's human nature. Therefore, when a believer partakes of the bread and wine of communion he is receiving the body and blood of Christ. Luther rejected the Scholastic doctrine of transubstantiation, but argued that a Christian must believe in the real presence. Zwingli just as strongly disagreed. Following the logic of the humanists rather than Luther's literal interpretation of the Scriptures, he held that a body can occupy only one place at a time and hence that since his ascension the body of Christ is in heaven, not on any earthly altar. He argued that the words of Christ must be understood symbolically. The real presence is in spirit only. Meeting for debate at Marburg in 1529, Luther and Zwingli could not agree and separated in anger. It was the beginning of a historically significant schism among the reformers that still remains unhealed.

Zwingli was a master at political maneuvering. He attempted to unite all of the cantons of the Swiss Confederation into a reformed league. However, several of the rural cantons and those adjacent to Italy remained staunchly Catholic. After an indecisive war between the camps in 1529, a new struggle ensued in 1531. Zurich and its allies were unprepared and a battle at nearby Kappel resulted in defeat and the death of Zwingli. Nevertheless, his cause was strong enough to continue in most of the cantons, later joined by the power of Geneva; but the Confederation has remained divided ever since, part Protestant and part Catholic.

Calvin and Calvinism

John Calvin (Jean Cauvin) was born on July 10, 1509, in Noyon, an ancient cathedral city of the French province of Picardy, 65 miles northeast of Paris. His prominent parents were Gerard and Jeanne Lafranc Cauvin. Thc father served as secretary to the bishop and attorney for the cathedral chapter. John was the fourth of five sons, two of whom died as children, and there were two daughters born later to the father's second wife. The oldest son, Charles, became a priest and was excommunicated in Noyon in 1537; the youngest, Antoine, stood by his famous brother as a reformer in Geneva, as did one of their half-sisters, Marie.

When John was only twelve years of age, his father secured ecclesiastical appointments for him from the cathedral canons of Noyon and from nearby village churches that would pay for his education, and the lad was soon enrolled for study at the Collège de la Marche of the University of Paris. There he came immediately under the tutelage of Mathurin Cordier, a humanist educator and Latin scholar who became his lifelong friend and mentor. Following that formative beginning, Calvin studied at the Collège de Montaigu for several years, graduating at 18 with the Master of Arts degree in 1528. The school was known for its strict discipline and Scholastic orthodoxy and it was harshly criticized by Erasmus and Rabelais, both of whom had studied, and, as they claimed, suffered there. However, the rigor and discipline were appealing to the young Calvin.

Gerard Cauvin quarreled with the authorities in Noyon in 1527 and consequently decided that his son should pursue a career in law rather than divinity. Obediently, John left Paris and went first to Orleans and then to Bourges, where he studied under outstanding jurists and humanists, completing a doctorate in law in 1532. Nevertheless, since his father had died in 1531, Calvin was free to follow his primary interest in classical scholarship. He returned to Paris and began the earnest study of Greek and Hebrew at the new Collège de France.

During the decade of formal education in Paris, Orleans, and Bourges, the youthful but serious John Calvin had already experienced the formation of his permanent character and spirit, a fact that he later attributed to the determinative will of God. He became a serious, learned, and polished scholar. He was well trained in both religious studies and law. He was enamoured by the liberating humanism that was ushering in a new age throughout western Europe. And, perhaps most significantly, he had become part of a community of French scholars and reformers, many in high places, who hoped to form a distinct type of evangelicalism by the merging of idealistic humanism and biblical moral teaching. Outstanding members of that circle were the elderly Jacques Lefèvre d'Etaples, a humanist and biblical scholar at the Sorbonne; Marguerite d'Angoulême, elder sister of King Francis I, who was a patron of the reforming causes; Guillaume Briçonnet, tolerant and reforming abbot at St. Germaine'-des-Près in Paris, who became Bishop of Meaux in 1516; Guillaume Farel, zealous student of Lefèvre, later to play a decisive role in the life of Calvin; and Nicholas Cop, a fellow student at the Collège de Montaigu who was to become, all too briefly, rector of the University of Paris.

The next four years were decisive in the life of Calvin. The events of those years not only set the course for his subsequent career but also, in so doing, made possible the broad influence of Calvinism in religion, economics, and politics that was to affect so profoundly the later history of the West.

In 1532, at the age of twenty-two, Calvin completed the doctorate in civil law. In the spring of that same year, he published his first book, a *Commentary on Seneca's Two books on Clemency*. The book did not receive the notice it deserved, but it was brilliantly written and it reveals Calvin's early devotion to both humanism and social morality. Calvin praised Seneca's attempt to inculcate Stoic humaneness into Nero's Roman tyranny, but he emphasized the necessity of a Christian foundation for an adequate ethic. Many scholars have suggested that Calvin's purpose was to evoke a humane toleration of religious dissent from Francis I, who was already engaged in persecuting Lutherans and other heretics.

On November 1, 1533, All Saints Day—sixteen years after Luther posted his ninety-five theses at Wittenberg—Nicholas Cop, Calvin's humanistic friend, delivered an explosive address at the Sorbonne, where he was being inaugurated as the new rector. If Calvin was not the real author of the oration, which is improbable though suggested by many, he certainly had a part in its preparation. It was an audacious call for toleration and reform, referring favorably to works by both Erasmus and Luther. The result was a command by the king for the immediate silencing and arrest of the "Lutherans," and both Cop and Calvin found it expedient to flee. Cop went to Basel and Calvin, in disguise, returned to his home in Noyon. During the following spring, Calvin enjoyed a long respite at Angoulême in the comfortable home of an old friend from Paris, Louis du Tillet. While there he was able to visit the dean of French humanists, Jacques Lefèvre, now one hundred years old, whom Calvin had never met but whose strong influence he had felt through many friends. In May, 1534, Calvin returned to Noyon, where he resigned the benefices that had supported him since his childhood. The act was a public signal that he had broken with the Church, casting his lot with humanism, scholarship, and reform.

Following further perilous travel in France, Calvin settled by January, 1535, in Basel, the great Swiss university city of freedom where Johannes Oecolampadious had labored to establish the evangelical cause and Erasmus had published the definitive text of the Greek New Testament. There Calvin brought to completion a work he had begun in Angoulême, entitled *Institutes of the Christian Religion.* It was published in March, 1536, and made him at once the recognized leader of French Protestantism. The *Institutes* was expanded several times, the last edition being published in 1559; and it has remained ever since the most significant single statement of Protestant theology.

The original edition of the *Institutes* contained only six chapters and was intended as a catechism from the evangelical point of view. Calvin acknowledged that he was not a creative theologian and that much of his work had its source in the thought of Luther and Bucer—a student of Zwingli. He intended to systematize and clarify the message of the Gospel for use in the educational mission of the churches. The first four chapters dealt with the Law, the Apostles' Creed, the Lord's Prayer, and the sacraments of baptism and the Lord's Supper. The fifth described the other five sacraments, rejecting their validity on the grounds that they are not taught in the Scriptures and because they had become the source of error and corruption in the Church. The sixth chapter discussed Christian liberty, including the relation of Church and state as well as the duties of Christian living. The whole work was prefaced by an open letter to Francis I, an eloquent appeal for tolerance and promoting a recognition of a need for reform.

The *Institutes* show even more clearly than Calvin's resignation from his ecclesiastical positions in Noyon that a radical change had occurred in his life between 1534 and 1536. In his *Commentary of the Psalms* of 1557 he referred to that change as a "*subita conversione*" (sudden conversion). No further explanation or description is available in his writings except that it involved a withdrawal from his stubborn addiction "to the superstitions of the Papacy," a withdrawal no doubt motivated by a zealous study of Scripture and by the moral idealism of humanism. He said simply that God "subdued my heart, too hardened for my age, to docility."

After the publication of the *Institutes* in 1536, Calvin left Basel for a visit of two months in Ferrara, Italy, where he accepted the hospitality of the French princess, Renée. The princess, now duchess of Ferrara, was a cousin of Francis I and his sister, Marguerite. Her husband, the duke, was the son of Lucrezia Borgia and thus the grandson of Pope Alexander VI. The duchess was sympathetic with the reformers but the duke was not. Calvin formed a friendship with Renée that made him her trusted spiritual advisor for life, but otherwise the duke saw to it that the evangelical spirit did not prosper in Ferrara. Calvin therefore soon made his way back to Noyon. On the final visit to his boyhood home he disposed of the remaining family property and, with his brother, Antoine, and sister, Marie, set out for Strasburg with the intention of settling there into a quiet life of scholarship. But again Providence intervened, with historic effect.

Because of intermittent war between Francis I and Charles V, a detour via Geneva was necessary. Intending to spend only one night in the city, Calvin met his old friend, Guillaume Farel, who was trying without great success to turn Geneva in the Protestant direction of Bern, Basel, and Zurich. He importuned Calvin in the name of God: "If you refuse to devote yourself with us to the work . . . . God will condemn you." Calvin later admitted that he was terrified and shaken by Farel's strong words, and both believed the occasion to be the work of Providence. In any case, Calvin remained at Geneva and joined Farel in the attempt to reform the rich and strategic city. He was initially known merely as "Ille Gallus," that Frenchman, and he began his ministry at the church of St. Pierre, giving lectures on Paul's Epistles under the academic title Professor of Sacred Letters. He had never been ordained.

Within a few months Calvin was the leading minister of Geneva. The city for a long time had been undergoing a struggle for independence from the House of Savoy, the dominant military power in the area south of the Rhone between France and Italy. Protestant Bern and Catholic Fribourg had joined in an attempt to free Geneva and to bring it into the Swiss Confederation. The plot came to fruition in 1525 when a citizen's movement (the Eidguenots) led by Besançon Hugues, forced the prince-bishop, an agent of Savoy and the Church, to flee. The Eidguenots and Hugues gave their names to the later Huguenots, French Protestants and refugees. Following independence, Geneva developed a highly efficient system of democratic government, composed in the main of the Council of Two Hundred, the legislative and judicial body, and the Little Council, the executive body. Calvin soon dominated the city, both its government and church, and set about the task of transforming Geneva into a model of theocracy. Soon, however, the pleasure-loving and wealthy citizens tired of his strictness and, in 1538, dismissed both him and Farel from the city.

Calvin moved to Strasburg, where he had intended to go before he arrived in Geneva. There he joined forces with Martin Bucer in developing a stronghold of the Reformation. Calvin served as pastor of an evangelical congregation, learned much from Bucer, and completed the second edition of his *Institutes*. He appeared to be settled and happy, even following the advice of Farel and Bucer by taking a wife. In August, 1540, he married Idelette de Bure, the widow of an Anabaptist, who remained his faithful companion until his death.

By 1541, however, the leaders of Geneva were imploring Calvin to return. Farel, now pastor at Neuchâtel, and Heinrich Bullinger, Zwingli's successor at Zurich, urged him to accept, especially because of his recognized leadership abilities and because of the strategic importance of Geneva for both the Swiss and evangelical causes. Never one to shirk a challenge, Calvin returned in September, 1541, and soon imposed his will on the character of the city in a way that became indelible. He remained there until his death in 1564.

This brief review of Calvin's life shows that he was a second-generation reformer. He was still a small boy when the Reformation began with the work of Luther, Melancthon, Zwingli, Bucer, and their numerous colleagues. He often confessed that he inherited the work of Luther and Bucer especially, though he seems to have been reluctant to admit a debt to Zwingli. Nevertheless, he clearly learned from all of them and, with an incisive mind, he added to their thought the vast store of teaching he had gained from long study of the classics, the Church Fathers, and the Scriptures. The result, developed by his successors, is known as Calvinism, which, though not exactly the same as his own teaching, has remained as his highly influential legacy to Western civilization. He was succeeded in Geneva by Theodore Beza. His teaching later became dominant in Scotland through the work of his student, John Knox. Many others carried his type of reform into France, Germany, Hungary, the Netherlands, and England. His influence also became one of the original and most powerful forces in the later formation of American culture.

A common but all-too-simple summary of distinctive Calvinistic teachings may be stated in the "five points of Calvinism." These were derived from the decisions of the Synod of Dort, a Calvinistic assembly in the Netherlands in 1618 that rejected the "Five Articles of the Remonstrants." The Remonstrants were followers of Jacobus Arminius, Professor of Divinity at the University of Leyden, who denied that God is the author of evil or that election is God's arbitrary decree without reference to foreseen merit. Holding a strict Calvinism, the Synod declared that an orthodox faith consists of belief in, among other things, the following:

1. Total depravity—that fallen human beings retain no basis for salvation apart from the gift of God's redeeming grace;
2. Unconditional election—that God has predestined some to salvation and some to reprobation, thereby revealing both grace and justice, though all deserve eternal condemnation;
3. Limited atonement—that the atoning death of Jesus Christ was intended and is effective only for those elected to salvation;
4. Irresistible grace—that God's gracious election cannot be finally refused by those who are chosen, since God is all-sovereign power;
5. Perseverance of the saints—that the elect cannot be finally lost because the power of God that saved them will surely keep them from falling away.

Lutheranism and Calvinism Compared

It is important to keep in mind that Luther and Calvin as well as their followers agreed on most matters of Christian faith and practice. Their agreements were much greater than their disagreements. For that matter, they held most elements of the faith in common with all other Christians, including not only the Radicals and the Anglicans but Roman

Catholics and Orthodox Christians as well. Even with Jews, they believed in the one God who seeks to redeem fallen mankind, and in the sacred authority of the Law and the Prophets. They joined their fellow Christians, whether Latin or Greek, in a common faith in the centrality of Jesus Christ and the saving efficacy of his death and resurrection. They confessed the Apostle's Creed and readily affirmed the dogmas of the first four councils of the ancient Church.

Nevertheless, there were differences between Luther and Calvin, and their differences are still visible and audible among their descendants. Lutheranism remains after more than four centuries, separate in some aspects of faith and practice from the Reformed followers of Zwingli and Calvin. Though they have accepted each other as fellow believers and often work and worship together, they remain in separate households of faith. Why is this true? What are the essential distinctions between these two forms of Protestantism that may be traced back even to the beginning? Let us observe a few of the major points of dissimilarity, possibly with some exaggeration for the sake of clarity.

First, the personal paths that led Luther and Calvin to separation from Rome were significantly different. Luther was a monk, a priest, and a professor of theology; Calvin was a lawyer, a classical humanist, and a dispassionate scholar. Luther was burdened by an increasing sense of guilt, depressed by anxiety, seeking assurance of forgiveness and salvation but unable to achieve it. He struggled for years with the inescapable question: *how* can the peace and security of salvation be found? Calvin, on the other hand, found in his study of classical literature as well as the Scriptures both the glory and the misery of the human condition. He discovered in Greek and Roman literature testimony to an inescapable fate that binds all humanity; and he saw in the Scriptures a revelation of God as omnipotent King who commands obedience. He heard the liberating Gospel of grace also, of course, but he saw that grace as given by the perfect will of God and made available through the work of Jesus Christ. He was convinced that saving grace does not depend upon human merit or even upon voluntary response; it is wholly from God's nature and will. His primary interest, therefore, was in another question: *why* does man need salvation and *why* does God give it?

Second, Luther and Calvin looked at the same God and saw him in different models. That was probably because of their distinctive approaches to him, as we have just observed. Luther began by thinking of God as an angry, demanding Father. His own father may have contributed to that conception. It was certainly supported by the medieval milieu in which he was nurtured and educated. However, when he was shaken by the joyful and liberating idea that God is essentially a kind and gracious Father, eager to forgive and redeem, he continued to think of God in personal terms. The family image was the same and only his understanding of the nature of the Father had changed. Now he thought of sin as more alienation than disobedience, and, as a result, salvation came to be conceived as a restored relationship to a loving Father.

Calvin, on the other hand, conceived of God as the glorious Sovereign who requires and commands obedience. He is absolute and eternal, knowing all things and controlling all things in complete perfection. Man's foreseen disobedience, made possible by the gift of freedom, may be overcome only by the gift of God's grace—God's redemptive and transforming power made available in creation by the work of Christ. All humanity deserves the fruit of disobedience, but it is God's inscrutable will that provides grace to save those who are chosen. Thus God's sovereignty is revealed in his command for obedience and his goodness is seen in his will to restore; but he is far too awesome to be approached with ease and familiarity.

A third difference between Luther and Calvin may be noted in their teaching concerning the relation between Church and state. Luther held to the doctrine of two realms. Church and state are both ordained by God and they contain the same people; but they have different functions and duties. Luther believed that the main duty of the Church is to teach and preach the Scripture as the Word of God and to nurture the people of God by ministry and the celebration of the sacraments. The state should promote and protect the Church, and the Church should guide and admonish the state; but they should respect each other's proper realms without undue interference. This doctrine of two realms has sometimes in Lutheran lands led to the Church's acquiescence in the face of political injustice. Calvin on the other hand, held to the goal of theocracy. He taught that the Church should guide the morality of the state and its people, and that the state should obey the teachings of the Church. No area of life is foreign to the concerns of the Church. That principle has led Calvinists to emphasize purity, sobriety, and industry in personal and social life. It may be suggested further that Calvinism, espousing this philosophy, has been the primary seedbed for an ethic of work and thrift, for capitalism, political democracy, and the social gospel.

Finally, Luther and Calvin developed different views of the Church. We have taken note of the debate concerning the Lord's Supper between Luther and Zwingli at Marburg in 1529. Luther insisted on a literal interpretation of Christ's words, "This is my body," whereas Zwingli argued just as firmly for a symbolic meaning. Luther was apparently motivated by a desire for assurance that participation in the sacrament would provide nourishment for the soul. Zwingli, on the other hand, interpreted the Scriptures, including the words of Jesus at the Supper, from the point of view of humanistic literary criticism. He could not accept the notion of the ubiquity of the body of Christ. Therefore, Zwingli and Luther separated in disagreement—Luther in angry rejection, Zwingli in sorrow. Later, Calvin took a middle ground. He agreed with Zwingli as to form but with Luther as to spirit. He believed in the real presence of Christ in the elements of the sacrament, but he held that presence to be spiritual. In the *Institutes of the Christian Religion* he wrote: "Christ, out of the substance of his flesh, breathes life into our souls, indeed, pours forth his life into us, though the real flesh of Christ does not enter us."

Both Luther and Calvin rejected the Roman practice of the mass and all the sacraments except baptism and the Lord's Supper. They condemned the papacy and most of the structures of the Church that had been developed during the Middle Ages. The churches that grew out of their teachings and influence have not remained static but have yielded to the needs of the cultures they serve. Together they have represented a central Protestant emphasis.

Chapter 24

The Radical Reformers

The Radical Reformation is a popular designation for a variety of individuals and groups that appeared on the fringes of central Protestantism during the second quarter of the sixteenth century. It was not a united movement but, as we shall see, there was enough similarity between the groups to warrant combining them for the purpose of description and discussion. They proposed to carry the reforms of the age to what they considered to be their logical and necessary conclusions, and that often included social and political revolution as well as the doctrinal and practical reform of the Church. However, they were a positive force with a program of their own; they were not merely reacting against Lutherans, Calvinists, and Romanists. They usually tended to be extremists, upsetting the stability of society on every hand. The result, of course, was suspicion, rejection, and persecution by Catholics and other Protestants alike. Even though they were relatively few, their influence has been far greater than their numbers.

Both opponents and sympathizers have always found difficulty in understanding and classifying these strange and stubborn radicals. One of the earliest names given to them was "Anabaptists," a term derived from the Greek word *anabaptismos,* "rebaptizers." The German equivalent is *Wiedertaüfer.* They were so called because they usually rejected infant baptism and therefore baptized those from other communions who joined their churches upon profession of faith. They denied that they were rebaptizing anyone since they held that infants had not been truly baptized in the first place. However, to call them Anabaptists was a serious charge because the old Roman law, newly invoked, held that it was a capital crime to rebaptize a Christian. Luther referred to them as the Schwärmer, "enthusiasts," because of their fanaticism and frequent claim to be following the inner direction of the Holy Spirit. They were radical in the sense that they would not accept a half-way reform but rather insisted on going to the *radix* (root) of biblical Christianity. In that sense they were primitives, intent on restoring the original Church.

The modern scholar who has done probably the finest work on the Radical Reformers is Professor George H. Williams. His book, *The*

Radical Reformation, is the definitive treatise on the subject. Williams classifies the radicals into three basic groups: the Anabaptists, whose modern heirs are the Mennonites; the Spiritualists, found today among the Schwenkfelders as well as other charismatic and Pentecostal groups; and the Evangelical Rationalists and Anti-Trinitarians, represented by Unitarians, Universalists, and other similar bodies.

Who were these unusual people, so few in number and yet so significant for future culture? What did they do and what happened to them? What did they teach, with such tenacity and at so great a cost to themselves? What is their permanent legacy to both Christian history and secular culture? These are the questions we shall investigate in this chapter.

Radical Beginnings

It is probably impossible to trace the ultimate sources of any historically significant idea. That is certainly the case with respect to the radicals of the Reformation. One of their major claims was that they intended to restore the Christian faith in its original simplicity and purity. Therefore they frequently attempted to rediscover fellow believers throughout the history of Christianity who were their antecedents, individuals and groups that had been carriers of the true faith even in spite of rejection, persecution, and martyrdom. They sought to follow what has been called the "trail of blood" back to Jesus and the Apostles.

In Chapter 22, above, we noted that the Radical Reformation had its roots, often unconsciously, in such groups as the Cathari, the Waldensians, the Joachimites, the Beguines and Beghards, the Brothers and Sisters of the Common Life, the Lollards, the Hussites, and many others like them. All of these emphasized the ideals of moral purity, simple living, and Christ-like service. Some of them also chose to live in separate, covenantal communities, eschewing especially the state with its taxes, oaths, and arms. However, they were not usually monastic or celibate. Many of them believed in some form of historical dispensationalism or millenialism, frequently expressed in terms of apocalyptic eschatology. Such persecuted minorities have historically found fortitude and hope not only in a fanatical conviction that they are the only true believers but also in an assurance that they will find victory and reward in the final utopia that God will bring to pass.

Thus there can be no reasonable question that the Radical Reformation was the continuation of the long history of idealistic dissent. Nevertheless, it was also a contemporary aspect of the sixteenth-century outbreak of reform led by Luther, Zwingli, Calvin, and their colleagues. The radicals were, as they have been called, "the left wing" of the Reformation.

The actual movement may be dated precisely as having begun during the Christmas season of 1521 when Andreas Bodenstein of Karlstadt, a fellow monk and ardent supporter of Luther, celebrated the Lord's Supper in a simple ceremony at the castle church, offering both bread and wine to the lay participants. Luther was absent from Wittenburg, hidden in the Wartburg where he was being protected by the Elector Frederick after his condemnation the previous April at the trial before the emperor at Worms. Karlstadt and several other monks began to challenge the celebration of the Mass and clerical celibacy as well as the use of icons, organs, and Gregorian chants. They led the city government to close the monasteries and confiscate their property. In addition, soon after Christmas a group of self-designated "prophets" from Zwickau came to Wittenburg and began to announce the imminent return of Christ and the end of the world. The people became agitated and soon the civil authorities, including the Elector, were concerned that the changes had gone too far for the sake of public order.

When Luther heard of the excesses, he returned to Wittenberg even though he had been forbidden to do so by Frederick. In eight days of powerful preaching, he condemned Karlstadt and the Zwickau prophets, insisting that they had gone beyond the teachings of the Scriptures by confusing essentials with externals. He thereby gained the support of the nobles and forced Karlstadt to leave the city. However, the rift between the conservative Lutherans and the radicals led by Karlstadt widened as the years passed. Karlstadt became pastor in the nearby town of Orlamünde where he persuaded a large following to adopt his radical teachings. Finally expelled from Saxony, he wandered with his wife throughout southern Germany, spreading his ideas, attacking both Catholics and Lutherans, and fomenting revolt among the peasants. He finally found refugc in Switzerland where he taught at Basel until his death by the plague in 1541.

Another early leader of the radicals was Thomas Müntzer a former priest from Zwickau who was much more extreme than Karlstadt. As early as 1520, he had begun to proclaim the superiority of dreams and visions over the Scriptures as revelations of God's will. Although initially a follower of Luther, he advocated a more thorough reformation of society that would eventually reestablish the true Apostolic Church that he believed had fallen because of the scholars and priests. In 1523 he became minister of the church in Allstedt, where he developed the first liturgy in the vernacular and otherwise sought to apply his increasingly radical ideas. His effort to replace the authority of the Scriptures with immediate revelations from the Holy Spirit and his teaching that the only valid baptism was not by water but by the Spirit led Luther to comment that he and his disciples were *Schwärmer* who had "swallowed the Holy Spirit, feathers and all." Müntzer finally became involved in the Peasants' War, preaching bloody revolution against all worldly authority. He was captured at Frankenhausen, where the peasant army was crushed, and, on May 27, 1525, he was tortured and beheaded.

Much has been written in the twentieth century concerning the relation between the great Peasants' War in 1524-25 and the Protestant Reformation. At the beginning of the century there was a spirited debate on the subject by two prominent German historians, Wilhelm Dilthey and Ernest Troeltsch. Dilthey argued that the Reformation was the religious aspect of the Renaissance, leading Christianity out of the otherworldliness and social controls of the Middle Ages into the modern period with its new emphasis on individualism, freedom, and progress. He was generally supported in his views by the famous sociologist, Max Weber, whose influential book, *Protestant Ethic and the Spirit of Capitalism,* credited Luther's doctrine of vocation and Calvin's encouagement of discipline, hard work, and investment, with the later growth of capitalism and wealth in northern Europe and North America.

Troeltsch, on the other hand, interpreted the social and economic aspects of the Reformation in a more complex manner. In his monumental work, *The Social Teachings of the Christian Churches,* he developed the useful distinction between the "church type" and the "sect type" of Christian culture. The former designates the condition in which one denomination dominates a nation or culture, as in Western Europe in the Middle Ages or wherever there is an established church. The latter refers to the various religious bodies that remain in a pluralistic and minority status, separate from the state and depending upon themselves for existence. By that definition, all "free churches" are sects, and in the United States, where an establishment is prohibited by constitutional provision, all church groups are necessarily sects, or divisions of the whole. On the basis of that distinction, Troeltsch claimed that the Lutherans and Calvinists (and later the Anglicans also) remained essentially medieval in outlook; but the Anabaptists and Spirituals, as he called the radicals, were more modern and progressive. These sect-type radicals were harbingers of individual freedom, human rights, representative government, and, indeed, of all the modern developments in science, economics, and politics.

Karl Marx and Friedrich Engels as well as twentieth-century Marxists have even made a hero of Thomas Müntzer. They have interpreted the Peasants' War as an important historical example of the class struggle. Discounting the religious aspects of the Reformation, they have read the history of the period as an early manifestation of the enslaved struggling to be free—the poor against the wealthy, the proletariat (peasants) against the bourgoise (clerics and nobles). Of course, Marxist analysis usually fails to take into account the predominant religious motivations involved in the social and religious struggles of the sixteenth century.

Our primary concern here is to recognize the Peasants' War as a tragic part of the beginnings of the Radical Reformation. Although a number of factors led to the revolt, there can be no doubt that the preaching of the radicals contributed to its sudden savagery. There had been several revolts by peasants in central Europe earlier in the sixteenth century. One of the most widespread was the *Bundschuh* (laced boot) movement in Switzerland and the Rhine Valley of 1513-1517. In February, 1525, the Swabian peasants met at Memmingen and drew up "Twelve Articles" demanding a redress of their social, economic, and religious grievances. After listing their rights, the peasants claimed to base their demands on the teachings of the Scriptures, and they named Luther as a theologian who would attest to the legitimacy of their position.

At first Luther sympathized with the peasants and wrote a tract, *An Admonition to Peace,* that advised compromise on the part of both peasants and lords for the sake of peace. However, when the peasants began to use force to achieve their aims, Luther strongly opposed them. In April, 1525, he issued what he called his "hard book," *Against the Robbing and Murdering Peasants,* accusing them of the sins of perjury, blasphemy, and rebellion, and savagely urging the princes to crush the revolt. Without needing Luther's advice, the princes, both Lutheran and Catholic, joined forces and put down the peasants with bloody ferocity. In the last battle, at Frankenhausen in Saxony, Thomas Müntzer, the religious leader of the peasants, was captured and killed, and more than 9,000 peasants were slaughtered. Luther has never been forgiven for his harsh attitude toward the peasants and support of the princes, but the radical aspects of the Lutheran reform were permanently crippled.

The Anabaptists

Just as Karlstadt and Müntzer, among others, finally opposed Luther because they thought his reforms did not go far enough, so did many of the followers of Zwingli in Switzerland. When Zwingli counseled gradual reform in Zurich, especially at the second disputation in 1523, some of his supporters urged immediate radical reform. Chief among these were Felix Manz, a scholarly priest, Conrad Grebel, a member of a prominent family in Zurich, and Balthasar Hubmaier, a well-educated priest at nearby Waldshut. They began by insisting that infant baptism is contrary to the teachings of the New Testament and that therefore, as Luther admitted, only adult believers should be baptized. Zwingli and the city council disagreed with them and the council ordered that all infants should be baptized within eight days of their birth. On January 21,1525, a small group of dissenters gathered in a house belonging to Manz's mother and Grebel baptized George Blaurock, a married ex-priest, who then baptized fifteen others. Thus began the "Anabaptist" movement in Switzerland. They preferred to be called simply "brothers and sisters" and are generally called the "Swiss Brethren."

Following the Zurich event, the Brethren began to hold preaching services and prayer meetings in private homes in the village of Zollikon, a suburb of Zurich. When a large number of people were won to their cause, the leaders baptized them, forming a community of believers who then celebrated the Lord's Supper in simple ceremonies. The following Easter, Hubmaier was baptized as a believer in Waldshut by one of the Zurich dissenters, Wilhelm Röubli. Soon several communities of the Brethren had been formed in both Switzerland and southern Germany. The Zurich city council condemned the movement and drowned Felix Manz in the Limmat River in a barbarous parody of baptism. Grebel escaped execution because he had already died from the plague. However, persecution scattered the radicals and in a short time they carried their message as far as Vienna, Moravia, upper Italy, and the Netherlands. Opposition from civil authorities combined with study of Scriptures caused the Brethren to refuse to swear oaths or to participate in military service. Hence in a relatively short time the radicals had developed their central convictions: believer's baptism, a "gathered" church of regenerated people, and insistence on the separation of church and state.

Hubmaier worked for some time in Augsburg, where he baptized Hans Denck, who in turn baptized Hans Hut. Together Denck and Hut established the movement in several German cities before their deaths, Hut by fire in 1527 and Denck of the plague soon afterwards. Hubmaier found temporary refuge in Moravia, where he was able to convert large numbers of Lutherans to the Anabaptist position. However, the Austrian authorities arrested him and burned him at the stake in Vienna on March 10,1528, drowning his wife in the Danube a few days later. Thus they followed in martyrdom the example set a year earlier by Michael Sattler and his wife.

Sattler, a former monk from Freiburg, was one of the most influential of the early Anabaptist leaders. Expelled from Zurich in 1525, he lived at Strasburg for a while where he was influenced by both Martin Bucer and Hans Denck. In 1527 he presided over a synod of Swiss Brethren at Schleitheim that produced under his leadership seven articles of faith, the so-called "Schleitheim Confession," which contain one of the best summaries of Anabaptist teaching with respect to believers' baptism, the Lord's Supper, the nature of the Church and its ministry, discipline, and Christian relations to the state. Unfortunately, soon after the synod Sattler was burned at the stake in Rottenburg and his wife was drowned. Yet the movement flourished in spite of the multiple martyrdoms. Among the leaders who arose were Pilgram Marpeck, Kaspar Schwenkfeld, Melchoir Hofmann, Jakob Hutter, and Menno Simons.

Marpeck was a layman, an engineer from the Tyrol, who worked for the Anabaptist cause in Strasburg, Ulm, and Augsburg until his death in 1556. He became a leading spokesman for a strict biblical faith, leaving voluminous writings which have recently received new notice. Schwenckfeld was a Silesian nobleman who first became a disciple of Luther and then joined the ranks of the dissenters. He grew increasingly radical in later life, leading a small group who emphasized the inner witness of the Spirit more than a literal interpretation of the Scriptures. His followers were later suppressed by the Jesuits in Swabia and Silesia and in 1720 they fled to America, settling in the tolerant colony of Pennsylvania, where they remain to this day.

Hofmann was also an early disciple of Luther who became a convert to the Anabaptist cause. At first he preached the evangelical faith in the Baltic countries but spent most of his active life working out a strange apocalyptic eschatology while in and out of Strasburg. He proclaimed himself to be the "apostle of the end" and announced that the final judgement would occur in 1533 with the establishment of Strasburg as the "new Jerusalem." He is a good example of the eschatological strain that frequently appeared among the outcast radicals. Jakob Hutter was a Tyrolean like Marpeck. Before his death at the stake in 1529 he joined the followers of Hans Hut in Germany who believed in the establishment of faithful communities of believers who would share all their lives and possessions in separate societies. The "Hutterites" thrived economically but were driven to Moravia and Hungary, and thence to the Ukraine. In the nineteenth century they were forced to leave the Russian Empire and they finally settled in South America, Canada, and the northern plains of the United States.

Perhaps the most enduring and successful of the original Anabaptist groups were the Mennonites. They sprang from the work of Menno Simons, a well-educated ex-priest from Friesland. He served as a priest for twelve years until 1536, although he had long questioned the Catholic teachings concerning infant baptism and transubstantiation. Finally he joined the Anabaptists and was ordained as a minister of that group in 1537. Hc was greatly disturbed by the distorted teachings of some of their leaders, such as Melchoir Hofmann, and by the unfortunate fate of their many followers. He therefore began an effort at rehabilitation and redirection, establishing stable congregations throughout the Netherlands and northern Germany until his death in 1561. His followers took the name ''Mennonites'' and have emphasized simple, service-oriented living and non-resistance to all forms of force. They have remained through the centuries as the most stable of the Anabaptist communities, both in Europe and America, exerting Christian influence far beyond their small numbers.

This brief survey of some of the leading Anabaptists indicates their variety of emphases and the usual tragic result of their radical beliefs. They were always a small minority and they suffered persecution by both mainline Protestants and Roman Catholics. Nevertheless they endured and maintained a faithful following who remain an important leaven in the modern world. Their teachings have been a formative factor in the creation of subsequent Christian denominations as well as social and political institutions and ideas.

Major Teachings of the Radicals

Those who represent the Radical Reformation were certainly Protestants in the general sense that they shared the fundamental principals that we have discussed in chapter 22, above, though sometimes with modifications. In fact, as we have also noted, they usually insisted on going much further in reforming the Church than the magisterial reformers were willing to go. In so doing they developed certain distinctive principles and beliefs that mark them as an identifiable and significant branch of the sixteenth century reformation. The remainder of this chapter is a brief account of those distinctives.

1. It is probably accurate to say that the first characteristic of the Radical Reformers is their rejection of infant baptism and insistence on baptism of believers only. In fact, they have often been referred to as antipedobaptists. They believed that baptism is a symbol of a prior saving faith in the death, burial, and resurrection of Jesus Christ and that the act itself has no sacramental power. Those who were baptized as in-

fants were not really baptized at all; therefore it is inaccurate to designate the group as "rebaptizers." The mode of baptism, whether by fusion or by immersion in water, is not of primary importance. It is the faith of the one being baptized that counts.

2. The true Church is the community of the faithful, composed of all of Christ's people. However, the visible Church is the local congregation of voluntary believers, all of whom are essentially equal before God. There may be various forms of organization, ministry, and worship; and associations of congregations may be formed throughout a nation or over the whole world for the effective work of God's people. The important principle to be maintained is volunteerism and congruity with the New Testament pattern. The true Church is a "gathered" congregation led by the Spirit of God; it is never coextensive with a nation.

3. The Church must be separate from the state. Christians should be the best of citizens but their first loyalty is to the revealed way and will of Christ. Therefore, true believers will not swear oaths nor take up the sword, as explicitly forbidden by Christ in the Sermon on the Mount and in other parts of the New Testament. (Not all of the radicals have held to this view, but most have practiced a strict policy of non-resistance.)

4. The Scriptures of the Old and New Testament are the source of God's revelation, but the indwelling and leadership of the Holy Spirit are equally important both for the interpretation of the Scriptures and for the nourishment and direction of daily life. This teaching makes essential a life of regular group worship as well as personal piety.

5. Believers are expected, even required, to live as expectant, serious, and disciplined followers of Christ. They are to share their care, service, and possessions. Those who fail to live by the standards of the community may be banned from fellowship and worship.

6. Human beings are endowed with free will so that they may either live in holiness and obedience or choose to disobey the will and commandments of God. No one is predestined by God to either good or evil, but all are responsible before God. Grace is offered to all and those who accept it are transformed into the image of Christ. Therefore, sin is not an inevitable condition of unbelief or unspirituality; it is rather the willful transgression of the moral law of God. (This position caused Lutherans and Calvinists to accuse the radical reformers of believing in salvation by good works, but the radicals replied that they believed that righteousness is the fruit of faith, not its cause.)

7. Many of the radicals, as we have observed, taught an apocalyptic eschatology and believed in the early end of the world and the imminent return of Christ. Often their experiences of persecution and banishment caused them to form utopian communities of the righteous who would endure pain and insist on righteousness while they awaited the victory and rewards of the final judgment.

Chapter 25

The English Reformation

The Reformation in England appears on the surface to have been "an act of state," to use the phrase of Sir Maurice Powicke, distinguished historian of Oxford. There can be no doubt that the political motivations of King Henry VIII and his successors played a major role in the separation of the Church of England from Rome. However, a closer study of English history during the fourteenth, fifteenth, and sixteenth centuries will reveal many social and religious factors in addition to the political ones that probably made inevitable the Reformation in England even if Henry had been happily married and the father of several sons by his first wife, Catherine of Aragon.

Behind the Break with Rome

One of the major preparatory factors that led to the relatively easy acceptance of Protestant ideas and practice by the people of England was the popular piety often designated simply as Lollardy. We took note of that movement in chapter 21 in relation to the reforming teachings of John Wyclif during the fourteenth century. The Lollards were poor priests and dedicated laymen who travelled throughout England, preaching and teaching the Gospel and distributing portions of the Scriptures in English so that the people could read and know the Bible for their own spiritual edification. The result was that a deep and private faith had become indigenous among the common people long before the overt changes that occurred with such apparent suddenness during the reigns of Henry VIII and his children. The records show that Lollard emphasis on private devotion, Bible study, and evangelical belief prospered in spite of official prohibition and persecution from the time of Wyclif until the outbreak of the Reformation itself. However, such piety, nurtured without clergy or sacraments and outside the scrutiny of the official Church, was not restricted to the unsophisticated. For example, as early as 1520 a group of Cambridge scholars gathered regularly at the White Horse Inn to discuss the new ideas that were filtering into the country from Germany and the Netherlands. They read about Luther and the devotional groups of the Netherlands, and though the Inn was called the "Little Germany," they preferred to be known simply as the

"Christian Brethren." Among them were such future Protestant leaders as Robert Barnes, Hugh Latimer, Miles Coverdale, Thomas Cranmer, Nicholas Ridley, Matthew Parker, and William Tyndale. Five of the group later became bishops and most of them suffered martyrdom for their faith.

Another deeply-rooted element of English life that prepared the ground for revolt against Rome was anti-clericalism. There was great resentment against the frequent arrogance and hypocrisy as well as the unbecoming opulence of the higher clergy. The laity were often offended and angered by the heavy financial demands of the Church and by the claim of absolute power over their souls. The spirit of the new age brought unprecedented questions, assumptions of human rights, rising expectations, and demands for greater justice. That spirit was fanned into flame by a widened acquaintance with the moral teachings of the Bible and by the encouragements concerning human nature and value reintroduced into Western culture by the Renaissance.

Cardinal Thomas Wolsey (1474-1530) displayed the kind of power and greed that caused many of the English, in both high and low estate, to despise the Church and clergy he represented. Wolsey came from humble origins but rose during the early reign of Henry VIII to hold positions in both state and church next to the king himself. A graduate of Oxford, he became a favorite of the King, who appointed him lord chancellor in 1515. The same year he was made a cardinal by Pope Leo X and, in 1518, papal legate to England. In addition, he became wealthy by holding numerous benefices through appointments to the offices of Archbishop of York, Bishop of Durham and Winchester, Deputy Bishop of Worcester, Salisbury, and Llandaff, and Abbot of St. Albans. He made his illegitimate son Dean of Wells and Arch-deacon of York and Richmond. He also appropriated the endowments of twenty-eight smaller religious houses and used them to found his own college at Oxford. He used public funds to build several palaces and manor houses, notably Hampton Court, and he strutted before the people in ostentatious style. No one caused greater revulsion toward the high clergy by the people of England than the great Cardinal Wolsey.

There were innumerable instances of popular anticlericalism throughout England before the Reformation but none was more notorious than the case of Richard Hunne in 1514. Hunne was a London merchant who became involved in a lawsuit with his rector over some burial clothes. His house was searched and Lollard writings were allegedly found there. He was forthwith imprisoned on the charge of heresy and later found hanging from a beam in his cell. The authorities claimed that he had committed suicide in remorse, but his friends believed he was murdered. A considerable public furor ensued and the case finally received the attention of Chancellor Wolsey, who of course found his authorities as "innocent as Abel." However, the notoriety of the injustice added flame to the rising fire of popular indignation against the powerful and self-serving higher clergy. The people were eager for reform.

A third factor, to which we have already alluded, that prepared the way for reform in England just as on the Continent was the growing power of humanism. The renewed study of the ancient classics was initiated in England during the late fifteenth century through various persons and agencies, most of them from Italy. They included artists and merchants as well as churchmen. Several prominent bishops had been students in Rome during the flowering of the Renaissance, and a number of Oxford dons had studied the classics in Florence. William Grocyn, for example, returned from Florence to Oxford where he taught three of the greatest humanists—John Colet, Thomas More, and Erasmus. The Bible-centered idealism that characterized humanism at the core led these intellectuals to question many aspects of Church doctrine and practice as well as to teach others to follow their reforming examples.

John Colet (1467-1519) was the son of a London merchant who studied at both Oxford and Cambridge before going to Italy for three years of further learning. While there he made contact with Marsiglio Ficino, the director of the new Platonic Academy in Florence, and probably also with Pico della Mirandola, whose *Oration on the Dignity of Man* is one of the most conspicuous of all Renaissance writings. Colet returned to England to lecture on Scripture at Oxford and then to spend the remainder of his life in London, where he became Dean at St. Paul's Cathedral. He was a driving force in the reform of the Church, the clergy, and theology. His friend and colleague, Thomas More (1478-1535), established himself as a leading humanist by the publication of *Utopia,* which argues for an ideal state in which religion and natural reason prevail. But More was also dedicated to the ideal of a united Christendom with the pope as its head. As a consequence, he refused to accept the supremacy of the king over the Church of England, and he who had hounded heretics into prison and martyrdom became himself a martyr for his refusal to accept the reforms of Henry VIII.

The humanism of pre-Reformation England was that of Colet, More, and Erasmus—morally idealistic, peaceful, and intellectual. It clearly saw the need for reform and most of its leaders supported the reform that came. However, this humanism maintained a moderate orthodoxy and preferred to conserve the past, not only in the classics of literature but also in the habits and forms of the Church. By that tendency, English humanism helped not only to sponsor the English Reformation but also contributed to its establishment as a *via media* between Rome and the Continental reformers.

Finally, a fourth element of English culture that made reform inevitable was the insularity and distinctive nationalism that had been characteristic of people and church in Britain since ancient times. There had been major invasions and infusions of foreign blood over the centuries, of course, including those by the Celts, the Saxons, the Danes, and the Norman French; but the English continued to think of themselves as a separate people, kept so by the mighty moat of the Channel. The French and the Spanish were their constant enemies and the Bishop of Rome was a foreigner whose very distance diminished his authority and power. Luther appealed to the nobles of the German states to declare their independence from the Roman pontiff, and, in like manner, Henry VIII could successfully appeal to most of his subjects to accept their king as their own sovereign over both state and Church.

The English Separation from Rome

These factors were smoldering just below the surface among all classes in England at the time the Reformation began on the Continent. They did not erupt into effective view, however, until separation from Rome became an ''act of state'' under the primary instigation of Henry VIII and two of his three children. The beginning was essentially a legal and official matter, without appreciable theological involvement. Henry's angry desire was to free the English crown and church from the power of the papacy, but he remained theologically an orthodox Catholic until his death. However, the political revolt soon became the occasion for the long-simmering religious and theological concerns to find overt expression and public application. The result was that England became both separated from Rome and a Protestant nation during the reign of the Tudors. On the Continent the religious aspects of the Reformation preceded the political, but in England the reverse was true.

Henry VIII (1491-1547) was the third child and second son of Henry VII and Elizabeth of York. His paternal grandfather was Owen Tudor, a Welsh nobleman, but his paternal grandmother was a member of the House of Lancaster, providing a basis for succession to the throne. Thus the marriage of Henry VII and Elizabeth of York contributed to the cessation of the devastating War of the Roses (1455-1485) between the

Yorks and the Lancasters. That war not only brought dread of civil war to the English people; it also diminished the power of the nobles and increased the power of the monarchy and Parliament. Therefore it was crucial that the Tudor line, begun by Henry VII, should continue with the reign of a strong king. It was believed that if Henry VII or Henry VIII died without a male heir the civil war would erupt again, bringing both national disaster and possible defeat by France or Spain.

Henry VIII became king when his father died in 1509. Although only eighteen, he had already demonstrated intellectual brilliance and personal strength, traits noted by Erasmus while visiting the court in 1499. He had earlier been destined for service in the Church but that prospect became moot upon the death, in 1502, of his older brother, Arthur, the first heir apparent to the throne. Arthur, named for the idealized King Arthur, had been married while still a boy to Catherine of Aragon, daughter of Ferdinand and Isabella of Spain. When it became likely that Henry would be the next king, he was betrothed to Catherine, his brother's widow, as part of a plan to ally England with the rising power of Spain against France. Nevertheless, Henry VII delayed the marriage of his son as long as he lived on the grounds it might be contrary to Scripture and canon law. One of the first acts of the new king after his succession in 1509 was to marry the Spanish princess to whom he had been already engaged for six years. Clearly, he wished to procure at least one legitimate male heir as quickly as possible.

Six children were born to the royal couple, but only one, Mary, survived infancy. Henry became increasingly convinced that the curse of God was upon them because they had violated the commandment forbidding marriage to a brother's widow (Lev. 20:21). He also found it unlikely that Catherine would give birth again. The only way he could have a male heir to perpetuate the Tudor line and thus to insure the peace of the kingdom was to replace Catherine with another wife. His advisors, especially Cardinal Wolsey, the chancellor and papal legate, thought that could best be accomplished by seeking an annulment from Pope Clement VII based on the claim that the marriage was illegal from the beginning. The Pope would not cooperate, however, because he was under the military control of Charles V, the Holy Roman Emperor, grandson and successor of Ferdinand and Isabella of Spain and the nephew of Catherine. Henry then sought advice from the great universities as to the canonical status of the question, but most of them, including Lutheran Wittenberg, supported the legitimacy of the marriage to Catherine.

In spite of the fact that he was loyal to the Church and had even been given the title "Defender of the Faith" by Pope Leo X for his erudite treatise, *Assertion of the Seven Sacraments,* against Luther in 1521, Henry now decided that the only solution to his problem was to establish a national church, separate from Rome, with the king as the supreme ruler of both state and church. In that way he would be able to divorce Catherine. He had already chosen as her successor Anne Boleyn, a woman of the court whose sister, Mary, was his mistress.

Henry initiated his plan in January, 1531, by charging the clergy with violating the statute of *Praemunire* which prohibited appeals to the pope. Wolsey had been summoned to trial on the same charge two years earlier but had died on the way to London. The clergy were required to pay an enormous fine and also forced, in convocations at York and Canterbury, to adopt a motion declaring: "Of the church and clergy of England, whose especial Protector, single and supreme Lord, and, as far as the law of Christ allows, even Supreme Head, we acknowledge his Majesty to be." Parliament proceeded, upon the king's orders, to adopt legislation enabling royal control over all church appointments, income, and practices. Henry then appointed Thomas Cranmer, a teacher at Cambridge and former member of the White Horse Inn group, the new Archbishop of Canterbury and Primate of England. In January, 1533, he secretly married Anne Boleyn, who was already pregnant; in May Cranmer annulled the marriage with Catherine and approved the marriage to Anne; on June 1, the new queen was crowned; and, on September 7, another daughter was born and given the name Elizabeth. Henry still did not have a male heir.

When Pope Clement VII in 1533 issued a bull of excommunication against Henry, the king secured the enactment of further restrictions against payments to Rome or obedience to the papacy. In 1534 Parliament passed the famous Act of Supremacy, which declared "that the king our sovereign Lord, his heirs and successors, kings of this realm, shall be taken, accepted, and reputed the only supreme head in earth of the Church of England, called *Anglicana Ecclesia*. . . . " When Bishop John Fisher of Rochester and Thomas More, the former chancellor, refused to accept the law, they were imprisoned and beheaded, More's bloody head being displayed on London Bridge. The new Pope Paul III made Fisher a cardinal before his death, an act that goaded Henry into saying, "Well, let the pope send him a hat when he will, but I will provide that whensoever it cometh, he shall wear it on his shoulders, for his head he shall have none to set it on."

The divorced queen, Catherine of Aragon, died in 1536, and a few months later Henry charged his new queen, Anne Boleyn, with adultery and had her beheaded. Twelve days later Henry married Jane Seymour, who finally bore him a son, christened Edward, in 1537. The mother died within a fortnight; however, at last there was a male heir to the throne, even though the child was sickly from the beginning and not expected to become a strong, long-lived monarch. He did have the advantage, however, of coming from the prominent Seymour family who would support the Protestant cause he would necessarily espouse.

Now that England was officially separate from papal control, Protestant ideas spread rapidly among the upper and middle classes. Thomas Cromwell, the king's chief minister, and Thomas Cranmer, the Archbishop, both promoted the Protestant cause. They even entered doctrinal discussions with the Lutherans of Wittenberg and planned English participation in the Schmalkaldic league, an alliance of Lutheran states in Germany against Catholic imperial forces. However, Henry remained orthodox in his theology, rejecting only the papacy. In 1536 he demonstrated his stand by writing and having adopted by Parliament the so-called Ten Articles as the official statement of faith of the English Church. Giving slight concession to Protestantism, the Articles affirmed the authority of the Bible, the three ancient creads, and the first four ecumenical councils of the Church. They defined three sacraments—baptism, penance, and the Lord's Supper—but did not reject the other four. They declared that justification is by faith alone but at the same time urged the necessity of good works. They supported the doctrine of the real presence of Christ in the bread and wine of the Supper, the invocation of the saints, the use of images in worship, and masses for the dead. As a whole, the Ten Articles were an early indication of the middle way between Rome and Protestantism that would later become the position of the Church of England. The issue was more clearly pronounced in 1539 when Parliament adopted, under the king's command, the Six Articles Act, known in history as "the bloody whip with six strings." The Act both affirmed orthodox faith and required its practice.

Since Jane Seymour had died soon after the birth of Edward, Henry agreed to marry the unattractive Anne of Cleves, sister-in-law of the Elector John Frederick of Saxony. Cromwell advised the marriage for both political and religious reasons, hoping thereby to cement relations with the Empire against France and at the same time to strengthen the Lutheran connection. However, upon marrying Anne, Henry declared her to be a "Flemish mare," rejected her, and paid her handsomely to withdraw while Cranmer annulled the marriage of seven months. The next month Henry took a fifth, Catherine Howard, who remained queen only a little more than a year before she met the same fate as Anne Boleyn. Finally, in 1543, Henry married Catherine Parr, who remained his wife until he died on January 28, 1547. He was survived also by two daughters, Mary and Elizabeth, and a son, Edward, who now became king as a sickly boy of nine.

The Establishment of the Church of England

King Edward VI was to reign for only six years but during that period great progress was made by the Protestant leaders in making the Church not only officially separate from Rome but also Protestant in faith and practice. The brother of Edward's mother, Edward Seymour, earl of Hertford, was appointed protector by the privy council. He led in the repeal of the Six Articles Act, encouraged the reading and teaching of the Bible, and carried further the confiscation of church properties. In 1549 Parliament passed the significant Act of Uniformity which required the use of a common liturgy in the churches. That liturgy was prescribed by the First Prayer Book of Edward VI and it remained predominantly Catholic in form and content. However, Seymour, now the Duke of Somerset, was overthrown as protector by the other members of the privy council, led by John Dudley, earl of Warwick, who soon became Duke of Northumberland.

As Protestant refugees from the Continent flooded the country, Warwick and the council permitted Cranmer to revise the Prayer Book so that, in 1552, the Second Prayer Book was issued. This one was much more Protestant, adopting practices in line with the Reformed Tradition of Zwingli and Calvin. Finally, in 1553, the young king approved a new statement of faith for the Church of England. This statement, the Forty-two Articles, had been composed by a council of theologians including the great Calvinist, John Knox, and it was unquestionably Protestant in content. Now the country was reformed both officially and theologically.

When it became obvious that the young king was dying, Northumberland and his colleagues of the privy council, supported by Archbishop Cranmer, arranged for the succession so as to exclude Mary, the Catholic daughter of Henry VIII and Catherine of Aragon. They planned to put Lady Jane Grey on the throne, since she was the Protestant granddaughter of Henry's sister, Mary, as well as the wife of Northumberland's eldest son. When Edward died, on July 6, 1553, the conspiracy worked, but only briefly. The sixteen-year-old Lady Jane was queen for less than two weeks when Mary, older sister of Edward and the legitimate heir, received popular support and, on July 18, was proclaimed queen. Northumberland and Lady Jane Grey were beheaded, Cranmer imprisoned, and the return to Rome began.

The Quenn has become known in history as "Bloody Mary" because of the increasing persecution of Protestants during her short reign. Hundreds of Protestants, both clergy and laymen, fled to Germany and Switzerland where they worked with fellow-Protestants to prepare for a subsequent return to England. One of their most important works was the translation known as the Geneva Bible in 1560. At least seventy-five prominent leaders, including John Rogers, Hugh Latimer, and Nicholas Ridley, were burned as heretics. Papal authority was restored and most of the laws enacted by Parliament under Henry VIII and Edward VI were repealed. The Queen's cousin, Cardinal Reginald Pole, who had been banished, now returned in triumph to become Mary's chancellor. Official Protestantism appeared to have been eradicated.

The popular demand for freedom from Rome and the reform of the Church remained, however, and it was soon coupled with the strong English feeling of nationalism. Mary was determined to marry Philip II, the son of Charles V, who was soon to become king of Spain. The marriage, so unpopular with the people because of their fear of Spanish control, took place on July 25, 1554, and the remainder of Mary's reign was filled with more severe persecution and increased unhappiness on her part. Philip soon returned to Spain, absenting himself from the Queen, who became convinced that she was childless because the curse of God was upon her as a result of her failure to cleanse England of Protestantism. Hundreds more, both men and women, were burned, all memorialized in the famous *Book of Martyrs* by John Foxe. Finally, Mary herself died in 1558, as did Cardinal Pole the same day. The reversal of the Reformation in England had not been successful in spite of all the bloodshed.

Surprisingly, one of the most glorious eras of English history began with the succession of Elizabeth, Protestant half-sister of Mary. The new queen was cautious and conservative by nature. She proceeded slowly to make the nation officially Protestant again, beginning by getting Parliament to pass a new Supremacy Act (1559) that made her the "Supreme Governor" of the Church of England. Papal power was permanently rejected, a new Prayer Book similar to Edward's Second Prayer Book was issued, and the Forty-two Articles were revised into the Thirty-nine Articles that have been the statement of faith of the Anglican Church ever since. Much of the old liturgy and practice of the Church was retained, but the main thrust of doctrine was Protestant. Elizabeth was able to maintain the claim to apostolic succession of the bishops by having Matthew Parker, her new Archbishop of Canterbury, consecrated by four bishops who had been consecrated under the old order—William Barlow, John Scory, Miles Coverdale, and John Hodgkin. Within five years Elizabeth was presiding over a national Church that was Catholic in form and Protestant in doctrine—the *via media.*

The consequences of the Elizabethean settlement, as it is called, and of her reign as a whole were to reverberate through the centuries that followed, affecting the history and culture of the whole world, especially in Britain and North America. It was the age of William Shakespeare, Sir Francis Drake, and Sir Walter Raleigh. Drake led in a decisive defeat of Spain's "Great Armada" in 1588, foiling the plans of Philip II to invade England and make the nation Catholic again. Thenceforth the power of England grew as she became the ruler of the seas and the center of a world-wide empire. Drake circumnavigated the globe, claiming unknown lands for the Virgin Queen, and Raleigh began the process of English settlement in North America.

Divisions in the Church of England

There has never been complete uniformity in the Church of England, despite strong attempts to make it so. The result has been the development and continuation of what have been called the high church tradition, the broad church tradition, and the low church tradition. The first is Anglo-Catholic, espoused by those who wish to retain as much as possible of the doctrine and practice of Rome while maintaining a distinctly national church without the sovereignty of the papacy. The last is clearly Protestant in theology and liturgy, though still marked by traditional forms. The broad church tradition has followed the middle way between Roman Catholicism and Protestantism, trying consciously to provide a bridge church with Catholic form and Protestant theology that might bear ecumenical fruit in the modern world.

In addition to these variations within the Anglican communion there have been significant departures on the right and the left. The Roman Church has maintained a tenacious foothold in England through the centuries, sometimes against legal restrictions, and there have been occasional defections back to the mother church even by clergymen of high standing. The most famous instance of return to Rome was that of John Henry Newman (1801-1890), an Anglican minister associated with the so-called "Oxford movement," which resulted in the conversion to Catholicism of several hundred clergy and laymen. Newman was rewarded for his conscientious conversion by being given a cardinal's hat by the pope. Nevertheless, large numbers were dissatisfied with the partial reform of the Church in England and finally found it necessary to withdraw on the left to create separate denominations of Christians. These Puritans, independents, and separatists were to become especially significant in the later establishment of North American religious pluralism and political toleration. Their social and political philosophy has left its mark throughout the world, especially during the nineteenth and twentieth centuries.

Many English churchmen who had fled during the Marian persecution or had been otherwise affected by Continental Protestantism arose to prominence early in the Elizabethan period. They insisted that the Scriptures were the only norm for faith and practice and they sought to carry the reform to its complete application. They especially condemned traditional clerical dress, kneeling for the reception of the Lord's Supper, using rings in marriage so as to suggest that the ceremony has a sacramental character, and making the sign of the cross at baptism. Such attempts to purify the Church of Catholic usage caused them to be designated "Puritans" as early as 1560. One of their strongest leaders was Thomas Cartwright (1535-1603), a professor of divinity at Cambridge who advocated a Presbyterian church polity modeled after Calvinistic practice and conforming strictly to biblical teaching. Although he desired to reform the Church of England from within, he was relieved of his position and income at the university and finally driven out of the country. He spent his last years wandering over the Continent, continuing to promote the Puritan cause.

Robert Browne (1550-1633) was a student under Cartwright at Cambridge. He became convinced of the Puritan presbyterianism advocated by his teacher, but when that appeared to fail he began to espouse separation from the established Church. Supported by a friend, Robert Harrison, he founded in 1581 an independent congregation of reformed believers in Norwich. The following year he published *A Treatise of Reformation without Tarying for anie (sic),* a famous work that proposed that a true church is a local, voluntary community of believers who covenant together to form a Christian body that is autonomous and organized according to its own decisions. Browne soon left Norwich and lived for a while in the Netherlands, but he finally returned to England, rejoined the established Church, and remained an Anglican clergyman until his death. Nevertheless, his work may be counted the beginning of the Congregationalism that was later to thrive in both England and New England.

The Puritans and separatists were effectively opposed by many of the learned Anglican clergy, notably by Richard Hooker (1533-1600), the author of the *Laws of Ecclesiastical Polity*. Hooker recognized that the non-conformists were orthodox in their basic theology but he held that they were wrong in their unnecessary opposition to the polity and worship of the established Church. He maintained that the Bible, the tradition of the Church, and tested reason are all legitimate guides for faith and practice. He agreed that in matters of faith the Scriptures are the ultimate authority; nevertheless, the Church should be free to adopt the forms, polity, and worship that are useful and appropriate. The question is not whether practices are "popish" in origin, he said, but whether they are good or bad in themselves. Hooker insisted that episcopal government is both scriptural and historically original, and he defended royal supremacy in the national Church.

Another form of the separatist movement arose during the reign of James I, who succeeded Elizabeth upon her death in 1603. This group later took the name Baptist. They began when a former clergyman of the establishment, John Smyth (c. 1570-1612) became pastor of a congregation of non-conformists in Gainsborough, near London. Another congregation was soon formed at Scrooby, in the house of William Brewster, led by the learned John Robinson, also a former Anglican clergyman. In 1608 the Gainsborough congregation fled to Amsterdam, and they were joined the next year by the Scrooby group led by Robinson and Brewster. Smyth came under the influence of Dutch Mennonites and adopted their belief in baptism of believers only, rejecting infant baptism. His group thus formed the first English-speaking Baptist church, though they were still in the Netherlands. Smyth soon died of tuberculosis and some of his followers affiliated with the Mennonites, but others in the congregation returned to England under the leadership of Thomas Helwys (1550-c. 1616) and thus formed the first permanent Baptist church in England. This group of Baptists had accepted the Arminian theology of the Mennonites and were designated "General Baptists" because of their rejection of a strict Calvinistic view of predestination. Another body of Baptists soon arose out of the Calvinistic Independents in England. They were known as "Particular Baptists," and they were the source of the majority of Baptists who have since become a major denomination of Christians in England, America, and throughout the world.

Finally, we should note here that another major denomination, the Methodists, came out of the Church of England more than a century later than the Congregationalists and Baptists. The Methodists owe their origin to John (1703-1791) and Charles (1707-1788) Wesley, sons of a poor Anglican clergyman at Epworth. Their friend and colleague from

Oxford, George Whitefield (1714-1770), also played a major role in their work. The Wesleys were ordained Anglican clergymen and remained so until their deaths, but, along with Whitefield, they did most of their work as itinerant preachers throughout England and in America. They became convinced while studying at Oxford of a greater need for warm, experiential religion, and they helped to promote a club to encourage personal devotion and Bible study. Their detractors referred to them as "the holy club" with a method of piety; hence the name Methodist.

While spending three years as missionaries to the Indians in the New colony of Georgia, the Wesleys came under the influence of the pietistic Moravians—descendants of the pre-Reformation Hussites—and John later visited the Moravian center at Herrnhut in Germany. Later he worked for a while with Moravians in London. By joining the Arminian theology of their father, the piety of the Moravians, the evangelistic preaching of Whitefield, and the opportunities accompanying the dawning industrial revolution in England, the Wesleys laid the foundation for one of the most vital Christian denominations to arise out of the English Reformation.

VIII.
NEW APPROACHES IN PHILOSOPHY

Chapter 26

Philosophic Rationalism

The foundations on which the scientific developments of the seventeenth and eighteenth centuries rested had their roots in antiquity, but they were closely associated with a philosophical flowering of that rootstock which produced two major developments popularly known as rationalism and empiricism.

The classification suggests differences between the two modes of thought which ought not to be given undue stress. There is a considerable amount of empiricism in those systems dubbed as ''rationalistic'' and an equal attention to reason in those called ''empirical.'' The schools, if they may be called schools, may be distinguished from each other primarily by differences in emphasis.

René Descartes may be regarded as the founder of modern rationalism on the Continent and has, indeed, been called, the ''father of modern philosophy.'' He was born at La Haye in Touraine in the year 1596, the son of a noble family. His father, a councillor of the Parliament of Brittany, saw to it that the boy was given an excellent education. From 1604 to 1612, he studied at the Jesuit college of La Flèche, where his curriculum included logic, scholastic philosophy, ancient languages, and mathematics. Of these, the last-named had the greatest effect on him, for he saw in it a source of clarity and certitude which he found lacking in other academic disciplines. He valued the study of language, which opened to him the door to the understanding of ancient literature, but concluded that to govern one's conduct by the examples found in that literature might cause one to ''fall into the extravagances of the knights=errant of Romance, and form projects beyond their power of performance.''Eloquence and poesy too, had strong appeal for him, but both, he thought, ''were gifts of the mind rather than fruits of study.'' Theology he honored, but he concluded that its revealed truths, which lead one to heaven ''are quite above our intelligence'' and require ''some extraordinary assistance from above.'' As for scholastic philosophy, ''it has been cultivated for many centuries by the best minds that have ever lived, and . . . nevertheless no single thing is to be found in it which is not subject of dispute, and in consequence which is not dubious.''

Finding himself at last free of his Jesuit tutors, he resolved to accept instruction only from what he could find in himself or in ''the great book of the world'' and devoted the rest of his youth to the collection of a variety of experiences. He went to Paris and, for a time, lived there the sort of life expected of a young gentleman of means. Then he spent some years in travel and voluntary military service, followed by another three years or so of residence in Paris. From 1629 to 1649, he wrote his principal works while living in Holland, where he had settled down to satisfy the need for the privacy demanded by his work. In 1649, he received an invitation from Queen Christina of Sweden, a scholarly monarch who wanted him to instruct her in philosophy. Unfortunately, Stockholm was bitterly cold in winter, and the Queen wanted her lessons at five o'clock in the morning. After a few months, he suffered a severe decline of health, and in February, 1650, he died.

Decsartes' Method

The ''book of the world'' to which Descartes had turned from his Jesuit studies did not provide him with the sort of knowledge he sought. The ''men of diverse temperaments and conditions,'' with whom he became acquainted in the course of his travels, had as many different opinions as the philosophers, and he prudently decided not to accept as certain anything which was guaranteed only ''by example and custom.'' On November 10, 1619, while he was on his way to return to military duty after attending the coronation of the Emperor, he found himself shut up by bad weather for a whole day in a stove-heated room in Germany. It was there that he conceived ''the foundations of a wonderful new science.'' On the following night he had three dreams which apparently confirmed him in his conviction that thenceforth he must rely on his own unaided reason to achieve the sort of intellectual certitude which, up to that time, he had found only in mathematics. Giving thanks to God for the revelation, he promised to make a pilgrimage to the shrine of the Blessed Virgin in Loreto.

Some ideas, like the rules which govern arithmetic, he observed, are apprehended clearly and distinctly and can then provide a basis for an orderly progression of thought to other truths. Intuition and deduction, then, ''are the most certain routes to knowledge.'' The business of intuition is to establish basic truths with such certainty that the conclusions drawn from them by valid reasoning can, with equal conviction, be accepted as true. Descartes formulated the method by which this process is to be carried out in the twenty-one rules laid out in his *Rules for the Direction of the Mind.* As in mathematics, he held, it is essential that all complicated and obscure propositions be reduced to those which are absolutely simple. When these latter are intuitively apprehended as certain, they can be used to ascend to further knowledge as far as the intermediate steps can be justified by intuitive cognition. Where a step cannot be so justified, one must refrain from proceeding further.

In his *Discourse on Method,* he stated four precepts which governed his thought. The first was to accept nothing as true which could not be clearly seen to be so beyond all doubt. The second was to divide all difficulties into as many parts as might be possible and necessary for the solution of the difficulties. The third was to follow an order of reasoning in which one ascends step by step from the simple to the complex. The fourth was "to make enumerations so complete and reviews so general" that one could be sure that nothing had been left out.

In order to establish the axioms on which such a system of thought must rest, it was necessary to follow a method recommended by the Pyrrhonic Skeptics of systematically doubting everything which can be doubted. If, then, something were to be found which is absolutely indubitable, it could be used as an axiom for the construction of the desired edifice of knowledge. Descartes was convinced that even one such basic truth would be sufficient for the establishment of a philosophy.

But where could such a truth be encountered? It could not be found in sense data, for they are notoriously deceptive. In his *Meditations on First Philosophy,* Descartes reflected that it seemed obvious enough on first glance that he was seated by a fire in his dressing gown holding a paper in his hand. But further consideration showed him that he had often dreamed the same sort of thing and that there was no clear way of distinguishing between dream and waking life. We cannot, in fact, be sure that we have bodies or, indeed, that physical objects exist at all outside our imagination.

But how about the very mathematical truths themselves, which provided the model for his method? Can we not be certain that three and two will always make five? It would seem so, but just suppose, Descartes suggested, that he has been created by an all-powerful god who, either because his goodness operates in a way we do not understand or, perhaps, because he is not good at all, but rather an evil genius, is dedicated to deceiving him. In such a case, he could never be sure of the truth of even the simplest proposition in arithmetic.

Is there, then, anything which cannot be doubted? Yes, Descartes concluded, echoing a reflection of St. Augustine centuries earlier. No one can doubt that he is doubting. I can, then, with complete confidence, assert, "Dubito." But to doubt is to think, and so I can begin my philosophy with the certain proposition "Cogito." But I could not think if I were not, and so I can say further, "Cogito ergo sum"—I think, therefore I am."

What am I then? I am a *res cogitans* a being which thinks. "What is a thing which thinks?" Descartes asked. "It is a thing which doubts, understands, affirms, denies, wills, refuses and which also imagines and feels." Such a thing is not a body. It is an ego—a mind.

Is it possible, given only this knowledge, to move beyond the thinking self? Descartes held that if he could establish other ideas as having the same sort of clarity and distinctness which he found in the *Cogito,* he would be justified in accepting them as true. A proposition is clear, he said, if it "is present and apparent to an attentive mind." It is distinct if it "is so precise and different from all other objects that it contains within itself nothing but what is clear." The data of the senses, of course, fail to demonstrate the existence of a material world when, judged by these rigorous criteria, and if God is a deceiver, even the truths of mathematics cannot pass muster. It became necessary, therefore, for Descartes to prove that God exists and that he is not deceptive.

To do this, he had recourse to logic. Starting with his own consciousness, the only source of data to which he could appeal, he found among his ideas, the conception of "a substance by which I myself and everything else, if anything else exists, have been created." He also thought it "manifest by natural light that there must be at least as much reality in the efficient and total cause as in the effect." I, as a finite and imperfect being, could not be responsible for a clear and distinct idea of infinitude and perfection, and without such an idea, I could not even know that I am finite and imperfect. It follows that the idea of a being possessing these attributes must have as its cause an existing being who is, in fact, infinite and perfect.

I am clearly aware that I am not the author of my own existence. If I were, I should have made myself perfect and capable of preserving myself. But such is clearly not the case. I recognize that I am deficient in nature, and even if I thought myself to be potentially the possessor of all the perfection I attribute to God, I could not be the cause of myself or my idea of perfection, for only "a being which is formal and actual" could produce the actual effect.

This line of reasoning is clearly cosmological in character, though the cosmos on which it rests is contained in the thinker's consciousness. To reinforce his proof, however, Descartes had recourse to a modification of the ontological argument of St. Anselm. The idea of God, he maintained, is the idea of a supremely perfect being, and to define such a being as lacking the attribute of existence would be to formulate a self-contradictory proposition. To exist belongs to the true nature of God, and we can, therefore, "with truth affirm of God that he exists."

It would be similarly self-contradictory to hold that God can be a deceiver, for fraud and deception can be clearly seen to spring from some defect, and a perfect being cannot be defective. This being the case, it must follow that error stems not from God, but from human failure to check the tendency of the will to make judgments which are not based on data having sufficient clarity and distinctness.

The Three Substances

God's reliability now guaranteed for Descartes what the senses alone were insufficient to establish. We have experiences which seem to us to come through our own senses and ultimately to be attributable to "extended substances" outside our own bodies. Some of our experiences do, to be sure, turn out to be delusory, but after we have used our God-given power to evaluate them, many are of such a nature as to produce an irresistible inclination to attribute them to corporeal objects. Such an inclination must come from God and so, since God cannot be a deceiver, must be accepted as providing proof for the existence of our own bodies and of other physical objects.

Descartes had now established, to his own satisfaction, the existence of mind, which has *thought* as its distinguishing attribute, and body, which is characterized by the attribute of *extension*. Each can be understood without reference to the other, and so his reflection had led him to a form of dualism—the theory that the world is composed of two sorts of substance. Substance, however, he defined as "an existent thing which requires nothing but itself to exist." Clearly, neither mind nor body meets this strict criterion, for both are dependent on God, who is, therefore, the only substance in the absolute sense. Mind and body may, however, properly be called substances in a subsidiary sense, for neither is dependent on the other.

The radical distinction between the two subsidiary substances permitted the development of a thoroughly mechanistic interpretation of the material world. The organic realm, no less than the inorganic, is governed by inexorable mechanical law. Animal bodies are no exception to the rule, and Descartes went so far as to maintain that the lower animals, contrary to appearance and popular belief, are no more than machines, without consciousness or purposiveness. The human body too is a machine but we know ourselves to be essentially mind, and so the explanation of our behavior must be more complicated than for that of members of other species. To account for that behavior, Descartes resorted to a theory of interaction. In some way the soul, or mind, comes into contact with the brain, probably in the pineal gland, and influences the otherwise mechanical activity of the body. Conversely, the body has its effects on the mind through the processes of sensation.

This sort of interactionistic theory did not entirely satisfy some of Descartes' followers. One of them, Arnold Geulinx, denied that the two substances directly affect each other and maintained instead that when one wills an action the willing is not the *cause* of the action, but only the *occasion* for it. Similarly, an external stimulus and the appropriate response is the *occasion* for the corresponding mental state. Actually, God is adjusting the mental and physical events in such a way as to give the appearance of a causal relation between them when in fact none exists. This doctrine, appropriately enough, came to be known as occasionalism.

Spinoza

Baruch (Benedictus or Benedict) de Spinoza was born in Amsterdam in 1632, a member of a Portuguese Jewish family which had fled from persecution in Spain and taken refuge in the Netherlands, a country at that time noted for its tolerance. Educated in the Hebrew Scriptures, the Talmud, and the writings of Maimonides, he intended to become a rabbi, but when doubts began to assail him, he studied Descartes and, at last, renounced Jewish orthodoxy. Ironically, his fellow Jews, themselves heirs of centuries of oppression, had no tolerance for his defection. At the age of twenty-four, Spinoza was expelled from the synagogue and forced to leave Amsterdam. He resided in several towns in the Netherlands and, at last, in 1669, settled at The Hague, where he earned his livelihood as a lens-grinder and became associated with the members of a little sect of Christians known as Collegiants. During his exile, he wrote extensively on a number of subjects. His treatment of the Jewish and Christian Scriptures paved the way for the subsequent development of what has come to be called the "higher criticism," and his *Treatise on Theology and Politics,* which was published anonymously in 1670 aroused such a storm that Roman Catholics and Protestants alike banned its sale. Called by some a "God-intoxicated man" because of his mysticism and saintly character, he was assailed by others as an atheist. On one occasion, he was accused of being a French spy, on no firmer basis of evidence than the conviction of his accusers that such a crime was precisely what might be expected of an atheist. He was offered a professorship at Heidelberg University, but turned it down because he feared that he would not be permitted to teach and write freely. His greatest work, the *Ethics* was not published until after his death of consumption in 1677.

Spinoza's philosophical method was, in essence, an extension of Descartes' for he shared the Frenchman's confidence in the power of human reason to achieve certainty about the nature of reality through methods analogous to those used in mathematics. He was even more precise in his method, however, than Descartes, and in his *Ethics* he developed the essentials of his philosophy in a form drawn directly from geometry. From definitions and axioms, he moved on to propositions, demonstrated in geometric fashion. These were accompanied by corollaries, which are necessitated by the propositions, and by scholia in which Spinoza gave a longer and less formal discussion of the matters under discussion.

God and Nature

Descartes had conceded that only one being, God, could, in the strictest sense, be described as substance. Spinoza, following the implications of that admission to its logical conclusion, denied that thought and extension can be called substance in any sense. What are they then? They are, he declared, attributes of the one eternal, self-subsistent substance, who can, with equal propriety, be called God, Substance, or Nature. The world, therefore, is not a separate product of God's creative activity. Looked at from one point of view, it is God, who, as the source of all reality, is *natura naturans* and, as the collection of existent things, is himself also *natura naturata.* It is with this idea of God that he thought philosophy must begin. "Whatever is is in God, and nothing can exist or be conceived without God."

God must exist, Spinoza maintained, for, in common with Anselm and Descartes, he held that the very definition of an infinite self-conceived substance entails its existence, so that if one claims to have a clear and distinct idea of substance while at the same time professing doubt concerning the existence of such a substance, "he is like one who says that he has a true idea and yet doubts whether it may not be false." The non-existence of God cannot be asserted without violating the law of contradiction.

God, he held, can be logically demonstrated to have an infinite number of attributes, each of which is infinite and eternal in its own kind. Of these, our minds know only two: thought and extension. Wherever one of these is manifest, the other must also be present, together with the infinity of other attributes inaccessible to our finite understanding. There is no question of interaction between body and mind, for thought and extension have nothing in common other than the fact that they are both aspects of the one ultimate reality. No interaction is necessary, however, for as they are simply facets of God's being, we are, when we apprehend mental or physical events, simply looking at two aspects of the one indivisible *Deus sive Natura,* who is thinking, extended, and possessed of an infinity of other qualities which only he can know. The relationship between mind and matter is, then, essentially one of psychophysical parallelism, in which the two attributes may be compared with two sides of a coin. If a penny is flipped into the air and falls to the ground, with the "heads" side up, we do not ask whether "heads" is up because "tails" is down or vice versa. We attribute the position of each to the total activity of the coin of which the two sides are facets.

God perceives reality not as we do, but *sub specie aeternitatis.* Time exists for us merely as a mode of thought, and so the whole chain of cause and effect, which involves temporal sequence, is, in effect, reducible to the sort of rational necessity found in logic and mathematics. This means, of course, that Spinoza's universe is devoid of any element of spontaneity. The system of Nature is completely deterministic, and everything is from eternity as it must be.

To be sure, Spinoza declared God to be free, but he is free only in the sense that there is nothing else to determine his actions. Freedom is thus definable as self-determination and everything that happens in the universe is what it is because "in the nature of things nothing contingent is granted but all things are determined by the necessity of divine nature for existing and working in a certain way." Spinoza rejected the idea of a God who works to achieve certain purposes. "I confess," he said, "that the view which subjects all things to the indifferent will of God and makes them depend on divine caprice, comes nearer the truth than the view of those who maintain that God does everything for the sake of the good. For these persons seem to place something outside of God which is independent of him, to which he looks as to a model while he is at work, or at which he aims as if at a mark. This is, indeed, nothing else than subjecting God to fate, and is a most absurd view of him whom we have shown to be the first and only free cause of the essence and existence of things."

Modes

As *natura naturata,* the attributes of God are expressed in *modes,* defined as "the affections or modifications of substance or that which is in another thing through which also it is conceived." Individual minds and bodies are finite temporal modes of the one substance under the attributes respectively of thought and extension. The infinite intellect consists of the totality of all ideas. Extension is expressed in motion and rest. The infinite intellect and the infinity of motion of rest make up the face of the universe. The relation of mode to attribute and of attribute to substance cannot be defined without plunging into a complex maze through which Spinoza himself threaded his way with some difficulty. It can be said, however, that it is in the world of modes that events which actually must be contingent on the ultimate rational structure of reality appear to involve the sort of causal sequence found in the laws of motion on the physical side and those of psychological association on the mental. In the Spinozist view of the world, self-contained sciences of physics and psychology can be justified without the necessity for positing any sort of causal relationship between physical and mental processes. Psycho-physical parallelism was, indeed, to be a postulate of some of the pioneer work in physiological psychology during the late nineteenth and early twentieth centuries.

For Spinoza, knowledge can be attained on three levels. The lowest has its origin in sensation and imagery, which have as their counterparts on the physical side, modifications of the body. Like Plato, Spinoza regarded information derived from this level alone as unreliable. The next higher level relies on reason. Here the mind can, in scientific fashion, contemplate ideas rather than particulars and perceive their necessary connections. The knowledge given by reason is adequate, true, and self-authenticating. Highest in the hierarchy is intuition, which "advances from an adequate idea of the objective essence of certain attributes of God to the adequate essence of things." Intuitive knowledge enables us to apprehend the scheme of nature and our place in it. Such an insight is, of course, a fuller knowledge of God than can be had on the lower levels, and in attaining it, we become "more perfect and blessed."

A human being as a finite mode of God is, looked at from one point of view, a physical object. From another point of view, he is a mind. Ontologically, there is no distinction between the two. The mind is the idea of the body and, as self-aware, is "the idea of the idea of the body" as well. From either standpoint, man is bound by inexorable necessity. Any freedom which he thinks he may have is as delusory as would be that of a stone flying through the air if it were to imagine its trajectory to be undetermined.

Ethics and Politics

His denial of personal freedom had a profound effect on Spinoza's treatment of ethics, the subject with which he was, perhaps, most concerned. If everything in the universe acts according to eternal and immutable law, terms such as "good," "evil," "wrong," "ought," and "ought not" clearly must have a different meaning from that ascribed to them by philosophers who hold that we are genuinely free to choose between two or more courses of action. There is no place in Spinoza's system for a distinct faculty such as will. A volition is nothing other than an idea.

The source of human conduct, then, is not free choice, but the fundamental passions of desire, joy, and sorrow. Underlying all these is the endeavor to preserve one's own being. Ethical terms derive their significance from our judgment of the extent to which a particular thing does or does not contribute to the satisfaction of our desires.

The terms "good" and "bad," Spinoza said, "indicate no positive quality in things regarded in themselves, but are merely modes of thinking, or notions which we form from the comparison of things one with another. Thus one and the same thing can be at the same time good, bad, and indifferent. For instance, music is good for him that is melancholy, bad for him that mourns; for him that is deaf, it is neither good nor bad."

In the last analysis then, everyday moral judgments, as seen by Spinoza, rest on a hedonic basis. We love and hope for that which causes pleasure. We hate and fear that which produces pain. Pleasurable emotions such as joy are good because they enhance our life-affirming sense of power. Painful ones like pity and sorrow are bad because they diminish that sense. Like Hobbes, Spinoza maintained that everyone has unlimited natural right to gain what is useful to him by any means possible. Spinoza, however, moderated that dictum by his insistence that one cannot discover what is truly useful to him except through the exercise of reason. Passion leads to slavery and knowledge to the only sort of freedom which had any meaning for Spinoza—the freedom which in its highest form comes from the intuitive knowledge of God. That knowledge is the goal of all rational striving and the source of the highest happiness or blessedness.

Again, in agreement with Hobbes, Spinoza recognized that the exercise of unlimited individual right would produce a state of conflict. To secure one's own well-being, then, it is essential for one to be willing to relinquish as much of one's natural right as may be necessary to secure a condition of peace. The results of such action by a group of individuals is the formation of a state, and with the advent of a state, justice and injustice become meaningful terms. In society, those attitudes which conduce to my own good are consonant with those which lead to the good of others, and the highest goal of each member of society, therefore, should be the achievement for himself and his fellows of the intellectual love of God.

Leibniz

Gottfried Wilhelm Leibniz was born in Leipzig in 1646. He was quite precocious and, while still a child, was reading and understanding difficult scholastic writings. Although he did not rebel against Scholasticism with the fervor of some of his contemporaries, he was highly receptive to the newer thought of the day. Throughout his life, he was, by temperament, given to compromise and synthesis, and one of his great ambitions was to bring together the warring Protestant states and to effect a reconciliation between Protestantism and Roman Catholicism that he thought might lead to a united Europe. His interests covered most of the fields of learning of his time. He studied philosophy at the University of Leipzig, mathematics at Jena, and jurisprudence at Altdorf, earning his doctorate in law at the age of twenty. He is given credit, along with Isaac Newton, for the discovery of the infinitesimal calculus. His results were, as a matter of fact, published three years before those of Newton, who claimed, however, that his discovery antedated that of Leibniz but that he had delayed giving his manuscript to the printers. Each of the philosophers suspected that the other had stolen the idea, and a long and bitter quarrel between English supporters of Newton and German supporters of Leibniz established an insuperable barrier to what might otherwise have become an amicable and fruitful association between the two men.

Leibniz had a distinguished career as a diplomat, councilor, and civil administrator, first in the service of the Elector of Mainz, and after that with the Duke of Hanover. Among his duties with the House of Hanover were those of family historian, archivist, and librarian. At one time, he was offered the post of librarian at the Vatican, but despite his ecumenical fervor, he declined to accept a position in which he might have been expected to convert to the Roman Church. He was made the first president of the Society of the Sciences in Berlin, the body which was later to become the Prussian Academy.

Pursuing several careers simultaneously, he nevertheless managed to produce several important works of philosophy in Latin, French, and German, among them, *New Essays in Human Understanding, Discourse on Metaphysics,* and *the Monadology*. Had it not been for his feud with Newton, he might have been invited to go to England when the Duke of Hanover ascended the English throne as George I. As matters stood, however, he remained in Germany, where his influence gradually declined to such an extent that his death, in 1716, was unnoticed by the learned world in which he had been such an outstanding figure.

The Problem of Substance

Leibniz was as much a rationalist as Descartes and Spinoza. Like them, he was convinced that the order of the universe is coherent and can be apprehended by the human intellect. Personally acquainted with Spinoza, he admired the ingenuity with which the older man solved the Cartesian problem of interaction by reducing the world to one substance. However, he thought that Spinoza's monism had led him into a pantheism which denied the distinctions that Leibniz wanted to retain between God and nature as well as between God and individual selves. He was not, however, disposed to go back to Descartes' dualism, and so, starting off on a new tack, he developed a theory which is monistic in the sense that it involves only one sort of substance, but pluralistic in the sense that it posits many substantial entities rather than one.

He justified his position by questioning the assumption that extension in space is the essential characteristic of the objects we think of as "physical." *Force,* or *energy,* he said, is the key to the understanding of the universe, and the ultimate constituents of all mental and physical reality are irreducible centers of force, which he called *monads,* a word used earlier by Giordano Bruno and derived from the Greek work *monas.*

"The monad, of which we would speak here," he wrote in the opening sentence of the *Monadology,* "is nothing other than a simple substance, out of which complex substances are built."

If that statement creates the image of an edifice made up of physical building blocks, it conveys the impression that was farthest from Leibniz's mind. The "simple substances" in question are not extended at all. They have no size, shape, or mass. Nor are they unextended points in a spatial continuum, for there is no such continuum outside the monads themselves. In short, they cannot be defined in material terms, for the sort of force which they represent is more akin to what we think of as *mind* than to the usual seventeenth-century conception of matter. Leibniz was, thus, not merely a rationalist, but a philosophical idealist—one who holds that reality is fundamentally of the nature of mind.

The monads are eternal. Leibniz referred to them as "uncreated," and short of a miracle, they cannot be destroyed. They are "fulgurated" by God, the Supreme Monad, who is pure activity—*actus purus.*

If the monads do not occupy different positions in a shared, ontologically real space, what distinguishes them from one another? Actually, if one were to try to think of them as exactly alike, there could not be a plurality of substances in Leibniz's view, for he stoutly affirmed the doctrine of the identity of indiscernibles, according to which, in order for two things to exist, they must in some way differ from one another. Leibniz affirmed the existence of an infinite number of monads and of logical necessity held that no two are exactly alike. They differ in that each one surveys the world from its own point of view.

To say that it "surveys the world" can be misleading, for there is no interaction or exchange of information among the monads. They are "windowless," and the entire history of every monad is contained within its own internal perceptions. However, those perceptions are implanted in such a way that everything that happens in the universe is in some degree, however small, represented in each monad. Leibniz was able, therefore, to posit an apparent continuity running throughout the whole of nature, even though its parts are discrete and discontinuous. There is a hierarchical gradation of differences of perceptions, from the confused and minimal perceptions of the "bare" or "naked" monads, which make up the most insensate things, to the supremely clear and all-embracing perceptions of God, the highest monad. The lower forms of living and non-living things are in a state resembling sleep. Animals are conscious. Men, in addition, have *apperception,* a "reflexive knowledge of the inner state."

Organic bodies differ from inorganic objects in that they have a central monad, in which the entire body is represented in greater degree than is the case with any of the monads which constitute the sort of thing that we would ordinarily, if incorrectly, think of as lifeless. It is in ruling "soul monads" that the identities of individual human beings as well as of animals are established.

The Preestablished Harmony

The relationship between a soul monad and the centers of force which constitute its body is essentially the same as that obtaining among monads generally. As they "have no windows," the coordination of their internal states requires an explanation which excludes interaction. Leibniz, whose pluralism ruled out psychophysical parallelism and who was opposed to occasionalism, solved the problem to his satisfaction through his doctrine of the pre-established harmony. God, he said, in establishing the universe, has decreed that the internal histories of all the monads shall be perfectly synchronized in such a way that everything that occurs in each of the monads is appropriately represented in all the rest. Thus, though there is no real interaction, the appearance of external causation is preserved. Actually, of course, causation is within to the monads themselves. Each of them is determined by its own nature in such a way that its whole history unfolds according to its appetence or desire. As these are mental processes, Leibniz's interpretation of causality is essentially teleological rather than mechanistic.

Although he would have had some difficulty in arriving at the notion of the preestablished harmony had he not had a prior conception of God, Leibniz saw no reason for not using the universal harmony as a new and powerful proof for God's existence. He was quite ready to accept the older proofs, including the ontological argument, but he had a higher regard for his own, claiming that "this hypothesis (which I dare to call demonstrated) is the only one which brings into relief the grandeur of God."

In arranging for this "harmony of many windowless substances, God, being all-good, all-knowing, and all-powerful, has created "the best of all possible worlds." This is not to say that there is no evil in the world or that at any stage in the development of the world it could not be improved. The judgment applies solely to the whole of the history of the universe, which is the only existent one among an infinity of possible worlds. God, who is omnipotent, could, in theory, have chosen to realize any of the possibilities. However, though he is in possession of all the power there is, he is nevertheless bound by his own goodness and his own logic. He cannot make contradictory propositions true, and, given the limitations which must exist in finite things, he must so arrange matters that the events which compose the history of the world are not merely *possible* in the abstract sense, but *compossible*. In Leibniz's words, "not all possible species are compossible in the universe, great as it is, and . . . this holds not only in regard to things which exist contemporaneously but also in regard to the whole series of things." Whereas our perception of facts produces synthetic propositions which appear to be of such a nature that their contradictories might have been true without disrupting the whole fabric of reality, even truths of fact are analytic in such a way that God can see in "the individual notion of Alexander," everything that could be predicated of him, even to the historical circumstances of his life and death. We may be confident, then, that however bad the world may seem, any other possible one would have been worse. Even the greatest crimes in history may, from Leibniz's standpoint, have been necessary for the working out of a greater good.

Such an insistence on the necessity of things was, of course, incompatible with indeterminism, but Leibniz was an ardent champion of another conception of human freedom. The soul monad of each human being, he held, being self-determined and capable of reason, can increasingly clarify its thinking and see more and more clearly the nature of reality. Although one's history is determined by the preestablished harmony, the causes of one's actions exist in one's own nature, and one is morally responsible for them. A bad man chooses to do bad things. To introduce any greater freedom than this into his system, Leibniz would have had to resort to occasionalism, which was repugnant to him. In all fairness, it should be pointed out that he saw no reason for positing any sort of freedom other than that which stems from the fact that the present of each monad is "big with its future." A world in which actions were capricious and predicated on nothing in the individual's nature would have seemed to him quite unintelligible.

In the last analysis, Leibniz was, then, as rationalistic and deterministic as Spinoza. In his insistence that reason rather than sense provides the higher and clearer sort of knowledge which reveals the nature of the world and that the seeds of this knowledge are innate in every human soul, he provided a powerful defense for the rationalistic faith that dominated Continental philosophy in the seventeenth century. His pluralism, however, did provide a better accommodation of that faith to belief in the individuality of human persons and the transcendence of God than Spinoza had been able to provide. Moreover, his contention that force or energy, rather than extension, is the basic concept with which science must concern itself was to prove prophetic in the light of developments in physics two centuries after his time and would ultimately rescue him from the obscurity into which he had fallen at the close of his life.

Chapter 27

Philosophic Empiricism

The rationalism of Descartes, Spinoza, and Leibniz was a natural reaction to the earlier Aristotelian revolution on the Continent, and had been shaped by combining, as it did, the Scholastic reverence for reason with the inquiring spirit of the new science. In England, where Platonism had remained strong and the dominant effect of the rediscovery of Aristotle had been to stimulate a centuries-long interest in the direct examination of nature, the philosophic mood of the seventeenth and eighteenth centuries was, not suprisingly, somewhat different. If Aristotle had to be confronted on the Continent, Plato too had to be challenged in England and the result of that challenge was dramatically evident in the work of three philosophers who progressively pushed an empirical approach to knowledge to its very limits.

John Locke, the first of the great British Empiricists, was born in 1632 at Wrington, in Somerset. After studying at Westminster School, he entered Oxford University, where he received the Bachelor's and Master's degrees. At Oxford, he, like Hobbes, was "perplexed with obscure terms and useless questions," stemming from the Scholastic nature of the instruction, but he stayed on at the University as a teacher. Under the influence of Sir Robert Boyle, he became interested in experimental science, and in 1674, he was awarded a medical degree and a license to practice. Shortly thereafter, he became acquainted with Lord Ashley, later to become Earl of Shaftsbury, one of the outstanding politicians of the day. The two men became friends, and Ashley took Locke into his employ as his personal physician and confidential adviser. Living in London with his patron, Locke made the acquaintance of a glittering array of prominent men and women. He also had an opportunity to learn something of the art of government. When Shaftesbury became a minister of state, Locke, in 1669, assisted him in the drafting of a constitution for the colony of Carolina.

Shaftesbury became involved in a move to keep James, second son of Charles I, from succession to the throne on the ground of his adherence to the Roman Catholic faith. In the resulting flurry of political disturbance, Shaftesbury lost office and fled to the Netherlands. James, who survived all the plotting and was crowned as James II, became suspicious of Locke, and, in 1683, Locke too found it expedient to seek refuge in Holland. In that same year, Shaftsbury died.

Locke became friendly with the Prince and Princess of Orange, and when, in 1688, James was overthrown and the royal couple were called to England to share the throne as William and Mary, Locke returned with them. His favored position at court gave him some scope for the expression of his political ideas concerning civil and religious liberty, education, economics, and the like.

In 1690, he published his two most famous works. *Two treatises of Civil Government* was written to justify the 1688 revolution, but it was to exercise its most powerful influence in later centuries in the shaping of Western political life. *An Essay Concerning Human Understanding* was the outgrowth of a conversation he had with some friends twenty years earlier in which the issues had become so hopelessly confused that Locke decided that before such subjects as morality and religion could be discussed, it would be necessary "to examine our own abilities and see what *objects* our understandings were, or were not, fitted to deal with."

His theological views aroused a storm of clerical criticism which did not unduly disturb him. An honestly religious man himself, he spent a good deal of time in the study of St. Paul's Epistles during his latter years, and before his death, in 1704, he declared that he was leaving the world "in perfect charity with all men and in sincere communion with the whole church of Christ, by whatever names Christ's followers call themselves."

Theory of Knowledge

For Locke, knowledge is "the perception of the connexion of and agreement, or disagreement and repugnancy of any of our ideas." An idea is something in the mind, rather than an objective reality outside it. Our ideas have their origins in experience and are of two sorts—sensation and reflection. Reflection, which occurs when the mind observes its own operation, is impossible without prior sensation, and so the mind initially had no content. It is a *tabula rasa*—a blank table upon which experience writes. We have innate predispositions, but no innate ideas.

In saying this, Locke was launching a direct attack against a theory accepted nor only by the Continental rationalists but, in England, by Locke's contemporaries, the Cambridge Platonists, notably Ralph Cudworth (1617-1688), Richard Price (1723-1791) and Benjamin Whichcote (1609-1683). In *The True Intellectual System of the Universe,* published in 1678, Cudworth sought to validate belief in God by an appeal to certain innately apprehended principles, holding that empiricism could only lead to atheism. Locke disputed that claim, holding that the existence of God could be proved without appeal to innate ideas. There are, he held, whole tribes of people who have no clear idea of God, or perhaps no idea of him at all, which could hardly be the case if the idea were innate. A rational being, surveying nature, must come to the conclusion that God exists, but the evidence for his existence, like that which shows the existence of anything else, is derived from experience.

Ideas are simple or complex. Simple ideas are received passively by the mind and may come through a single sense, as is true of color, sound, and taste, through more than one sense, as with space, figure, rest, and motion, or through reflection, as when the mind takes note of one of its operations. Some simple ideas, such as those of pleasure, pain, and duration, have their origin in both sensation and reflection. Complex ideas occur when the mind puts simple ideas together in any of three ways. It can join ideas to one another, bring them together and consider them as distinct but standing in relation to one another, or abstract them "from all other ideas that accompany them in their real existence [as when we separate the idea of *man* from John and Peter]; and thus all its general ideas are made."

Complex ideas are of three basic kinds: those referring to modes, substances, and relations. Modes are not thought of as existing independently, but are, rather, properties of substances. Simple modes involve the repetition of a single simple idea in different combinations. Thus, any number may be built up by the addition of units. Mixed modes are constructed from different kinds of simple ideas. Our ideas of substance involve the combination of ideas of qualities with a confused idea of something which supports these qualities. We call that substratum substance and so, are able to form ideas of God and of material and spiritual substance. Ideas of relations are gained by the comparison of one thing with another. The most significant relation apprehended by the mind is that of cause and effect, derived from sensation and reflection.

Although he held that knowledge cannot go beyond our ideas, Locke could not divorce himself sufficiently from metaphysical considerations to evade the question as to how ideas are related to the objects of the senses. The Galilean picture of a world of objects that have spatial attributes but are devoid of color, odor, and the other sense qualities seemed inescapable, but Locke had to attribute to objects, whatever they may be, certain qualities, a quality being defined as "the power to produce any idea in our mind."

Qualities are of two sorts, primary and secondary. Primary qualities really exist in physical objects in the way the mind apprehends them. In general, they may be said to be those which were ascribed to bodies by the physics of Locke's day—figure, number, motion, solidity, and the like. Secondary qualities such as those of redness or coldness, exist in the object only in its power to produce ideas in our minds which have no exact counterpart in the thing itself. In his distinction between the two kinds of qualities, Locke was undoubtedly influenced by Descartes, and he acknowledged his indebtedness to Newton.

Our knowledge is intuitive, demonstrative, or sensitive. Intuitive knowledge is immediate, direct, and as certain as is possible to imperfect human minds. We can have intuitive knowledge of certain mathematical ideas such as the difference between circularity and triangularity, but we can, additionally, know intuitively that we exist. Here again, Descartes the rationalist and Locke the empiricist were in agreement.

Demonstrative knowledge is the sort that results from using premises derived from ideas ideally having intuitive certainty to arrive at other ideas which are authenticated indirectly. In Locke's formulation, this is the process of establishing the agreement or disagreement of ideas by comparison with other ideas. This kind of demonstration is common in mathematics, but it can be used for other purposes too, notably to prove the existence of God.

It is, Locke held, intuitively certain that "bare nothing" cannot produce something, and we know that something exists. It is, then, "an evident demonstration *that from eternity there has been something;* since what was not for eternity had a beginning; and what had a beginning must be produced by something else." Moreover, whatever has its being from something else has all its powers from something else. What is eternal, then, must also be most powerful. It follows further that "there has been also *a knowing being from eternity,*" for it is "impossible that things wholly void of knowledge, and operating blindly, and without any perception should produce a knowing being, as it is impossible that a triangle should make itself three angles bigger than two right ones."

"Thus," Locke concluded, "from the consideration of ourselves, and what we infallibly find in our own constitutions, our reason leads us to the knowledge of this certain and evident truth—*That there is an eternal, most powerful, and most knowing* Being; which whether any one will please to call God, it matters not." Indeed, he affirmed, "we have a more certain knowledge of the existence of God than of anything our senses have not immediately discovered to us."

It is interesting that for the empiricist, as for the rationalist, sensitive knowledge "only passes under the name of knowledge." We cannot be sure that objects not now perceived by us exist. There is no necessary connection between the collection we call "man" perceived now and the later existence of the same collection. Therefore, "though it be highly probable that millions of men do now exist, yet, whilst I am alone, writing this, I have not that knowledge of it which we strictly call knowledge; though the great likelihood of it puts me past doubt."

Ethics and Politics

Locke made an earnest effort to develop his moral and political theories on empirical grounds, but his faith in the rational character of the universe was too great to permit him to lapse into an extreme form of empiricism which would lead to moral skepticism. His definitions of good and evil are, to be sure, merely hedonic. "Things are good or evil only in reference to pleasure or pain," he said. "That we call *good* which is apt to cause or increase pleasure and diminish pain in us; or else to procure or preserve us the possession of any other good or absence of any evil. And, on the contrary, we name that *evil* which is apt to produce any pain, or diminish any pleasure in us."

The choice of evil resides in our inability to assess "absent good" in the same way that we do present good. The more immediate pleasures exercise undue influence on us, and we choose a course of action which ultimately leads to unhappiness. Our experience aids us in the correction of this tendency, but we are also helped by the presence of laws that provide us with maxims of conduct which, if followed, conduce to our good. These laws are of three kinds: the divine law, the civil law, and the law of opinion or reputation.

Locke was convinced that our demonstrative knowledge of God's nature and understanding of ourselves as rational beings dependent on him, "if duly considered and pursued, afford such foundations of our duty and rules of actions, as might place morality amongst the sciences capable of demonstration: wherein I doubt not but from self-evident principles, by necessary consequences, as incontestable as those in mathematics, the measures of right and wrong might be made out to anyone that will apply himself with the same indifference and attention as he does to the others of those sciences." The sanctions by which God can enforce his laws include "rewards and punishments of infinite weight and duration in another life." The divine law, Locke declared, is "the only true touchstone of moral rectitude."

Ideally, of course, the other two kinds of law should conform to God's law. Civil law is established by the commonwealth and provides legal sanctions enforceable by the courts to reward conformity and punish nonconformity. The law of opinion or reputation is less formally promulgated. Its sanctions are provided by public opinion, which gives the name of virtue to some actions and vice to others. "Thus," locke said, "the measure of what is everywhere called and esteemed virtue and vice is this approbation or dislike, praise or blame, which, by a secret and tacit consent, establishes itself in the several societies, tribes, and clubs of man in the world: whereby several actions come to find credit or disgrace amongst them, according to the judgment, maxims, or fashion of that place."

Locke's assumption of the existence of eternal and immutable moral law, reflecting the whole ancient and medieval tradition of natural law, undergirds his political theory. Unlike Hobbes, he held that in a state of nature human beings are bound together by moral law. Even without a government, "reason, which is that law, teaches all mankind who will but consult it, that being all equal and independent, none ought to harm another in his life, health, liberty or possessions." Elsewhere, he prescribed a simpler catalogue of right: "life, liberty, and property." The state of nature, then, is a state of liberty, but not of license. It is, moreover, a state of equality, "wherein all the power and jurisdiction is reciprocal." This idea of equality is essential to Locke's theory. He was not, of course, speaking of equality in every respect. Experience shows us that men are unequal in height, weight, age, circumstances of birth, and a variety of other ways. What is important, however, is "the equality which all men are in respect of jurisdiction or domination one over another . . . the equality . . . being that equal right that every man hath to his natural freedom, without being subjected to the will or authority of any other man."

In view of the fact that men are "all free, equal, and independent," no one can properly be placed under the political power of anyone else without his consent. A community is formed when a number of individuals band together for their mutual comfort and security and agree that the body politic which they have formed shall be governed by the will of the majority. "And this is that," Locke said, "and that only, which did or could give beginning to any lawful government in the world."

A government is, of course, obligated to protect the natural rights of its citizens. The rights of life and liberty are limited only by the legitimate punitive authority of the state. The right to property presents a somewhat more complex problem. Originally, the earth and its resources given to man by God, "belong to mankind in common." Everyone, however, has one bit of "property" in his own person and his own labor. When he mixes his labor with something in nature and changes it, the object so changed becomes his private property. If he picks up acorns from under an oak or apples from a tree in the wood, they are his. There are, however, restrictions to the amount which may legitimately he appropriated in this manner. "As much as anyone can make use of to any advantage of life before it spoils," Locke said, "so much he may by his labor fix a property in. Whatever is beyond this, is more than his share, and belongs to others."

Land is acquired in the same way as other commodities. "As much land as a man tills, plants, improves, cultivates, and can use the product of, so much is his property." Here too, though, there is an important distinction. The appropriation of land by first occupancy and usufruct is justifiable on the assumption that it leaves enough for everyone else. Locke was not, in other words, defending the right of anyone to property the possession of which makes it impossible for others to exercise their right. The right to property is universal. Once property of any kind was acquired, he said, barter became inevitable, and this led to the discovery and use of money.

Unlike Hobbes, who advocated placing absolute power in the hands of the sovereign, Locke insisted that ultimate sovereignty always belongs to the people. The government holds power as a trust from the people, and, in a good government, the legislative and executive powers should be in different hands. Locke's own preference, based on the English model, was for a hereditary executive, a house of hereditary nobles, and an assembly chosen by the people.

A wisely run society, though it may make laws governing religious practices and ceremonies which might threaten the well-being of the commonwealth or its citizens, will have a high degree of tolerance for matters of religious belief, for "oppression raises ferments and makes men struggle to cast off an uneasy and tyrannical yoke." Church and state have different functions. "If each of them," Locke said, "would contain itself within its own bounds, the one attending to the worldly welfare of the Commonwealth, the other to the salvation of souls, 'tis impossible any discord should ever have happened between them."

The profound influence which Locke had on English political thought was to achieve its most dramatic expression among the American colonists, who would use his governmental theory as a justification for separation from the mother country. Locke himself gave them the charter for the rebellion, for he maintained that when a government has, in effect, been dissolved by external aggression or internal tyranny, the people may exercise their right of sovereignty and replace it. Thomas Jefferson was Lockian to the core when he penned the preamble to the

Declaration of Independence: "We hold these Truths to be self-evident, that all Men are created equal, that they are endowed by their Creator with certain unalienable Rights, that among these are Life, Liberty, and the pursuit of Happiness—That to secure these Rights, Governments are instituted among Men, deriving their just Powers from the Consent of the Governed."

That consent, he went on to say, was being withdrawn because of certain actions of the King, which Jefferson proceeded to enumerate—actions which in effect had dissolved the bond which gave George III his claim to executive authority over the colonies. Therefore, Jefferson declared, these colonies "are, and of Right ought to be, Free and Independent States." Some years later, the American constitution was also constructed on Lockian principles. It could,in fact, be claimed without too much exaggeration, that John Locke was pre-eminently the author of Anglo-American public philosophy.

George Berkeley

George Berkeley, a son of English parents, was born in Ireland in 1685. He entered Trinity College, Dublin, at the age of fifteen. After taking a B.A. degree, he became a fellow of the College and taught there for some years. He also received ordination as a clergyman of the Church of England. Before the age of thirty, he produced his most important philosophical works: *Essay towards a New Theory of Vision* (1709), *A Treatise Concerning the Principles of Human Knowledge* (1710), and *Three Dialogues between Hylas and Philonus* (1713). He traveled in France, Italy, and England. During a stay in London, he formed friendships with three of the foremost writers of the day, Joseph Addison, Richard Steele, and Jonathan Swift. There, he became interested in the American colonies and attempted to secure support in Parliament for the founding of a college in Bermuda for "the reformation of manners among the English in our western plantations and the propagation of the Gospel among the American savages." Newly married in 1728, he sailed with his young wife for America and settled down in Newport, Rhode Island, for three years, working on his ambitious project. Unfortunately, he never succeeded in raising the necessary funds for the establishment of the college, but he left his philosophical influence in America through an association with Jonathan Edwards, and, in a later century, his name was to be given to Berkeley, California, the seat of a greater educational institution than he could likely have envisioned for the New World. He returned to Ireland, and in 1734 was made Bishop of Cloyne, a position which he held for eighteen years. At the age of sixty-seven, he moved with his family to Oxford and lived there for a year before his death, in 1753. He was buried in Christ Church Chapel,Oxford.

Berkeley was concerned about the effect which the divorce of matter from mind in the Cartesian and Lockian systems had on religion. The result of making the object of science an insensible and inert material world, he observed, with considerable accuracy, had been to discredit mind, or soul, among "impious and profane persons." Materialism and mechanism had come, in consequence, to threaten the foundations of religion. Berkeley was sincerely interested in science and wanted to preserve a rationale for it, but not at the expense of the Christian faith.

His proposed solution of the problem was ingenious and direct. He had only to get rid of matter altogether. Then the category of soul, essential to religion, would have uncontested possession of the field, and science would still have its proper role in the observation and explanation of phenomena, without the necessity for positing an unintelligible substratum such as "matter."

He found justification for his assault on the material world in his critique of Locke's distinction between primary and secondary qualities. "They who assert that figure, motion, and the rest of the primary and original qualities do exist without the mind in unthinking substances," he pointed out, "do at the same time acknowledge that colours, sounds, heat, cold, and suchlike secondary qualities, do not; which they tell us are sensations, existing in the mind alone, that depend on and are occasioned by the different size, texture, and motion of the minute particles of matter." But, he went on, if one cannot, in thought, abstract the primary from the secondary qualities so as to conceive of extension and motion without some other sensible properties, "it plainly follows that *they* exist only in the mind." The "matter" posited by Locke is, thus, unintelligible, and therefore does not exist.

Berkeley can, perhaps be charged with an *argumentum ad ignorantiam* in his contention that because there is no evidence of substretive matter its existence can be denied. He would, though, undoubtedly have regarded such a criticism as nitpicking. Actually, he was applying Ockham's razor with great shrewdness and giving further strength to his argument by his demonstration that the term "matter" as applied to an unsensed bearer of qualities not only is unsupported by any proof, but is, in fact, a term so meaningless that those who use it cannot, when put to the test, say what they are talking about. He gave a clear and elegant demonstration of that thesis in his *Three Dialogues between Hylas and Philonous,* in which Philonous, representing Berkeley's position, forces his adversary to admit that the substance that Locke had described as ''something we know not'' can have nothing predicated of it other than qualities which can be shown to have their existence only in minds.

Hylas . . . I find it necessary to suppose a *material substratum,* without which [qualities] cannot be conceived to exist.

Philonus . . . *material substratum* call you it? Pray, by which of your senses came you acquainted with that being?

Hylas . . . It is not itself sensible; its modes and qualities only being perceived by the senses . . .

Philonous . . . It seems then you have only a relative *notion* of it, or that you conceive it not otherwise than by conceiving the relation it bears to sensible qualities?

Hylas . . . Right.

Philonous . . . Be pleased therefore to let me know wherein that relation consists.

Hylas . . . Is it not sufficiently expressed in the term *substratum* or *substance*?

Philonous . . . If so, the word *substratum* should import that it is spread under the sensible qualities or accidents?

Hylas . . . True.

Philonous . . . And consequently under extension.

Hylas . . . I own it . . .

Philonous. So that something distinct from, and exclusive of, extension is supposed to be the *substratum* of extension?

Hylas. Just so.

Philonous. Answer me, Hylas. Can a thing be spread without extension? Or is not the idea of extension necessarily included in *spreading? . . .*

Hylas. Aye, but, Philonous, you take me wrong. I do not mean that matter is *spread* in a gross literal sense under extension . . . you . . . take things in a strict literal sense. That is not fair, Philonous.

Philonous. I am not for imposing any sense on your words: you are at liberty to explain them as you please. Only, I beseech you, make me understand something by them. You tell me Matter supports or stands under accidents. How? Is it as your legs support your body?

Hylas. No; that is the literal sense.

Philonous . . . Pray let me know any sense, literal or not literal that you understand it in . . .

Hylas. I declare I know not what to say . . .

Philonous. It seems then you have no idea at all, neither relative nor positive of Matter; you know neither what it is in itself, nor what relation it bears accidents?

Hylas. I acknowledge it.

Philonous. And yet you asserted that you could not conceive how qualities or accidents should really exist, without conceiving at the same time a material support of them?

Hylas. I did.

Philonous. That is to say, when you conceive the *real* existence of qualities, you do withal conceive Something which you cannot conceive.

The Nature of Things

The world of objects remains intact in Berkeley's philosophy. In fact, their true nature can be all the better known to us, for they are precisely what they are perceived to be. Roses really are red, violets blue, and sugar sweet. An object, in short, is the sum total of all the properties which appear in it from any point of view from which it is experienced. "The only thing whose existence we deny, is that which philosophers call matter or corporeal substance. And in doing of this, there is no damage done to the rest of mankind, who, I dare say, will never miss it." Objects, then, exist only as clusters of perceptions or ideas, and they have their existence through being perceived. *Esse est percipi.*

Perception, however, entails a perceiver, and Berkeley accepted his awareness of his own being as a perceiver. *Esse est percipere.* He also had a *notion* of the existence of other selves, who are not, of course, perceived as they are but whose effects can be noted in the world of the senses. Most importantly, we can have a notion of "*an omnipresent eternal Mind,* which knows and comprehends all things, and exhibits them to our view in such a manner and according to such rules as he himself hath ordained, and are by us termed the *Laws of Nature.*" Objects, then, exist when we are not perceiving them so long as they are being perceived by God. The problem of conducting objects has been succinctly expressed by Ronald Knox:

> There was a young man who said, "God
> Must think it exceedingly odd
> If he finds that this tree
> Continues to be
> When there's no one about in the Quad."

The reply confirms Berkeley's solution:

> Dear Sir:
> Your astonishment's odd:
> *I* am always about in the Quad
> And that's why the tree
> Will continue to be,
> Since observed by
> yours faithfully,
> GOD

Not only are we left in undisturbed possession of the world of physical things. We are not even threatened in our pursuit of the physical sciences. Scientists must, Berkeley held, simply come to terms with the fact that the reality with which they are dealing is the sensible world itself and not an unimaginable world of abstractions like force, gravity, attraction, and the like. To be sure, words of this sort may legitimately be used as general terms denoting clusters of ideas derived from sensation, but they cannot legitimately refer to abstract ideas denoting real entities, for no such abstract ideas exist. The "notions" we have of ourselves, of other selves, and of God were, Berkeley thought, of quite a different character. The regularities of nature uncovered by scientific inquiry are attributable to the orderly pattern of things in the divine mind and to God's activity in coordinating the ideas of finite beings.

Just as Leibniz's rationalism had led him to idealism—the conviction that the world is fundamentally mental in nature—so had Berkeley's empiricism banished substrative matter from the scene. Indeed, Berkeley's mentalism was even more rigorous than Leibniz's monadogy, for, in effect, only the "soul monads" were left as carriers of the sense qualities. Berkeley's argument was a powerful one, and Samuel Johnson was unduly sanguine when he kicked a stone and proclaimed, "Thus I refute him." A Berkeleyan can kick stones to as good effect as a materialist. Berkeley was calmly convinced that he had refuted skepticism, atheism, and materialism. Actually, in pushing the implications of the empirical approach well beyond the boundaries set by Locke, he set the stage for the most devastatingly skeptical philosophy of the eighteenth century—that of David Hume.

David Hume

David Hume was a Scot, born in Edinburgh in 1711 to a family of rural gentlefolk. His father died when Hume was yet a boy, but his mother saw to his education. Expected by his family to become a lawyer, he abandoned his plans for a legal career because of his "insurmountable aversion to everything but the pursuits of philosophy and general learning." He studied at the University of Edinburgh but did not graduate. At the age of twenty-three, he went to France and lived frugally at La Flèche for three years on a small allowance from his family. During that period, he wrote *A Treatise of Human Nature,* hoping it would make his fortune for him. Unfortunately, he had difficulty in finding a publisher and when, at last, it was published, "it fell dead-born from the press, without reaching such distinction as even to excite a murmur from the zealots."

For ten years, Hume pursued a varied career, as paid companion to the Marquis of Annandale, then as private secretary to General James St. Clair, and, when the general became British Ambassador to Vienna and Turin, as a member of his entourage. He published *Essays Moral and Political* in 1741-42, and undertook a thoroughgoing revision of the *Treatise,* which received, in the process, the title by which it has been known since that time, *An Enquiry Concerning the Human Understanding.* This work, together with the *Enquiry Concerning the Principles of Morals,* the *Political Discourses,* and the posthumously published *Dialogues on Natural Religion,* made him a famous man

He was appointed librarian of the Advocates' Library at Edinburgh, but the curators objected to his choice of books, holding that they were "obscene." Hume, ridiculing their censorious attitude, resigned the post. A projected *History of England,* beginning with the Stuart kings, aroused a storm of criticism in England because of his assault on the Parliamentarians, whom he thought "full of fraud and of ardor," and his lack of enthusiasm for the Reformation, which he saw as a fight between "superstition" and "enthusiasm," with little to choose between them.

In the meantime, his works had become popular in France, and he was lionized when he went there in 1763 as secretary to the British Ambassador. He numbered Jean Jacques Rousseau among his many friends in the French world of letters. From 1767 to 1769, he served as Undersecretary of State, and found himself becoming as well-regarded in England as on the Continent. In 1769, prosperous and happy, he returned to Edinburgh, where he lived a quiet life, surrounded by admiring friends. He died in 1776.

Locke and Berkeley, though committed in moderate fashion to a theory of knowledge based on experience, had not taken the empirical method seriously enough to push it to its limits. Hume showed greater zeal in this enterprise than either of his two predecessors. All knowledge, he held, rests on what he called *perceptions.* These are of two kinds: *impressions* and *ideas.* They differ only in "their different degrees of force or vivacity." Impressions are sensations or passions or emotions as they make their initial appearance in consciousness. Thoughts, or ideas, are copies of impressions as they appear in memory or imagination. It follows then that all knowledge is ultimately dependent on impressions. Ideas, however, can employ the "faculty afforded us by the senses and experience.'' We can, thus, put together data acquired from a variety of experiences to produce new constructions of the imagination. In the last analysis, however, no ''supposed idea'' of philosophy can be validated unless it can be shown to be derived from some impression.

Ideas become associated with one another in such a way as to make it appear that certain ''uniform principles are at work.'' Those principles are *resemblance, contiguity,* and *cause and effect.* ''That these principles serve to connect ideas will not, I believe, be much doubted,'' Hume said. ''A picture naturally leads our thoughts to the original; the mention of one apartment in a building naturally introduces an enquiry or discourse concerning the others; and if we think of a wound, we can scarcely forbear reflecting on the pain which follows it.'' These *natural relations* are included in the broader category of ''philosophical relation,'' which are resemblance, identity, space and time (involving contiguity among other possible relations), quantity or number, degrees of quality, contrariety, and cause and effect. So called ''abstract ideas'' consist only of ''individual ideas along with a certain custom'' stemming from the fact that the word eliciting the idea has been applied to other individuals. Hume was, therefore, a thoroughgoing nominalist.

There is no idea of substance distinct from that of particular qualities in combination. Berkeley's ''notion'' of a spiritual substance had to be discarded along with the ''matter'' or ''body'' of Descartes and Locke. In perhaps the most daring of all Hume's iconoclastic attacks on metaphysics, he rejected the concept of the *self,* because it cannot be shown to be derived from any impression.

''For my part,'' he wrote in a passage which has become famous, ''when I enter most intimately into what I call *myself,* I always stumble on some particular perception or other, of heat or cold, light or shade, love or hatred, pain or pleasure. I never can catch *myself* at any time without a perception, and never can observe anything but the perception.'' Barring ''some metaphysicians'' who may lay claim to some sort of perception lacking in Hume and the rest of mankind, we are, he concluded, only a collection of impressions which rapidly succeed one another. ''The mind,'' he said, ''is a kind of theatre, where several perceptions successively make their appearance; pass, repass, glide away, and mingle in an infinite variety of postures and situations. There is properly no *simplicity* in it at one time, nor *identity* in different; whatever natural propension we may have to imagine that simplicity and identity. The comparison of the theatre must not mislead us. They are the successive perceptions only, that constitute the mind; nor have we the most distant notion of the place, where these scenes are represented, or of the materials, of which it is composed."

"Myself" now and "myself" in the past may not be identical at all. As a matter of convenience, we "feign" an identity "and run into the notion of a *soul,* and *self,* and *substance.*" In the same way, we "feign" the continuing identity of other objects which we really know only as collections of discrete impressions.

We cannot, of course, in Hume's view, have any impressions which could prove the existence of an external world, and he regarded the whole concept of causality as equally suspect. When we apprehend one event as the cause of another, we see first that the "cause" precedes the "effect," that it is contiguous to it, and that the sort of relation observed between them has been a constant one. All these observations rely on impressions. But in order to ascribe causality to the relationship, it is necessary to posit something else—a "necessary connexion" between the two, for which there can never be an empirical justification.

Religion and Ethics

Hume's skeptical treatment of causation carried over into his discussion of attempts to prove the existence of God in his *Dialogues on Natural Religion.* Of the causal arguments, the argument from design made the deepest impression on him, but it was not exempt from his destructive criticism. The argument rests, of course, on the recognition of an analogy between artifacts such as watches or houses and the universe seen as a sort of machine having similar order and arrangement. The manifest design, then, is held to demonstrate the necessary existence of a designer.

Even giving the idea of cause its full force, Hume held, any attempt to apply the notion of causation to the universe must fail, for the contiguity, priority, and constant conjunction necessary for a causal judgment can only exist between two perceptions, and we have no perception of anything antecedent to the universe which might have caused it. This criticism is, of course, as destructive of cosmological arguments as of the argument from design. Moreover, he held, the analogy between a mechanical artifact and the universe is imperfect. It may be more like a vegetative process than like a machine.

Religion, then, through not decried by Hume, had of necessity to rest on faith and could not be supported by philosophical proofs. It is equally clear that for him, there could have been no normative ethic based on revealed truths of religion. He was, moreover, convinced that moral judgments cannot be a product of reason. "Morals" he said, "excite passions and produce or prevent actions. Reason of itself is utterly impotent in this particular. The rules of morality, therefore, are not conclusions of our reason."

Morality, in his view, could be based on nothing other than feeling, and it follows that "when you pronounce any action or character to be vicious, you mean nothing, but that from the constitution of our nature you have a feeling or sentiment of blame from the contemplation of it. Vice and virtue . . . are not qualities in objects, but perceptions in the mind . . . though . . . [the realization of this fact] has little or no influence on practice. Nothing can be more real, or concern us more, than our own sentiments of pleasure and uneasiness; and if these be favorable to virtue and unfavorable to vice, no more can be requisite to the regulation of our conduct and behavior."

Justice arises in human experience with the establishment of a convention by which the members of a society attempt "to bestow stability on the possession of . . . goods, and leave every one in the peaceable enjoyment of what he may acquire by his fortune and industry." The convention is not in the nature of a promise, but is merely "a general sense of common interest similar to that felt by two men who pull on the oars of a boat, though neither is bound to the other by a promise." The laws of justice are the laws of society and nothing more. They would be unnecessary if everyone were solicitous for the welfare of his fellows or if nature supplies everything anyone could want or need. "Here then," Hume wrote, "is a proposition which, I think, may be regarded as certain, *that it is only from the selfishness and confined generosity of man, along with the scanty provision nature has made for his wants, that justice derives its origins.*"

It may, of course, be argued that these conditions show only why justice is needed. They do not provide an adequate explanation for its origin. Hume sought to remedy this deficiency by positing *sympathy* as the basis for the attachment of moral sentiment to justice and injustice. The sense of sympathy is a natural one, but in its social expression it is forwarded by the artifice of politicians, the processes of education, and public praise and blame. These same factors are, Hume said, sufficient to explain the development of that sentiment of morality which dictates the keeping of promises, as is, indeed, the case with other human virtues. Sympathy was held to be the source of morality in all the "artificial virtues" associated with justice. It is also of paramount importance in the "natural virtues," which enhance the well-being of the individual and "have no dependence on the artifice or contrivance of men." Sympathy is, "the chief source of moral distinctions."

Hume performed a real service to Western thought by carrying the empirical approach to its limit and showing that it ends in an extreme form of skepticism. As a critique of the thought of his day, his writings are masterful. He himself, however, confessed that his reflections seemed "strained and ridiculous" when applied to the conditions of everyday life. He did not succeed in providing a sufficient ground for any of the normative values on which individual and social life must rest, and his fame must rest chiefly on the skill with which he dug the hole from which subsequent thinkers have had to try to extricate themselves.

Chapter 28

The Kantian Revolution

The work of the empiricists and the rationalists set the stage for the flowering of the movement known in Germany as the *Aufklärung,* in France as *l'Illumination,* and in England as the Enlightenment. Though there is no universally accepted canon for the application of these terms, they are generally, if somewhat loosely, associated with a variety of eighteenth-century writers who confidently appropriated the fruits of the intellectual development of the preceding several centuries and asserted the power of the human mind to solve human problems on the basis of experience, reason, or intuition. The thinkers of the Enlightenment were, for the most part, unfettered by ecclesiastical or political restraints, and they did not confine themselves to ivory towers. It is likely that since the great days of Greece, there has never been a period in human history in which the writings of philosophers has had so much influence over the everyday lives of men, women, and children of all walks of life.

In Germany, the confident spirit of the age was reflected in the work of Christian Wolff (1679-1754), a professor at Halle, who, with restrained modesty, entitled his major work, *Reasonable Thoughts on God, the World, and the Soul of Man, also on All Things in General.* Basing his philosophy on the rationalism of Descartes, Spinoza, and Leibniz, he nevertheless held that sense experience will validate the claims of reason and can, thus, be a reliable source of knowledge. He attempted a sort of Aristotelian synthesis of all the sciences and wrote a number of textbooks which influenced the intellectual development of several generations of students in Germany.

Immanuel Kant

Immanuel Kant was born at Königsberg, East Prussia, on April 22, 1724. He was the grandson of a Scottish emigrant, and the family name was originally spelled "Cant." The boy's father was a master saddler, and both parents were influenced by the Pietist faith which was prominent in the religious life of the city. The influence of his home was strengthened by his early schooling at the Collegium Fredericianum, which was, at the time, under the direction of a Pietist. It was expected that young Kant would prepare for a career as a theologian, and, in fact, throughout his life he was greatly concerned with the questions of God, freedom, and immortality, but during his student days at the University of Königsberg, beginning in 1740, he became interested in mathematics and physics and abandoned the idea of a clerical vocation.

After his father's death, in 1746, he supported himself for some years as a private tutor, after which, on attaining his doctorate, he became a *Privatdozent* at the University, remaining in that position for fifteen years, during which period he attained some distinction as a lecturer and writer. His duties required him to teach physics, mathematics, logic, ethics, metaphysics, anthropology, physical geography, natural theology, and "philosophical encyclopedia." For several years he was also assistant librarian of the Royal Library.

In 1770 he was given the chair of logic and metaphysics and held that position until his retirement in 1797. His continuing association with the University enabled him to conform himself to the restricted routine for which he was to become famous. Though he was interested in geography and enjoyed talking with travelers, he was never in his life more than forty miles away from Königsberg. A confirmed bachelor, he arose every morning at five o'clock, regardless of the season. His manservant reported that in thirty years, he never failed to get up on time. He would study for two hours, lecture for two more, and then spend the rest of the morning at his desk.

He formed the habit of fixing his eyes on a church steeple, visible from his window, to put himself in the mood for writing. On one occasion, a neighbor allowed some trees to grow up in his garden until the Steeple was hidden from view. Before long, the word was out in Königsberg that Kant was not writing, and an *ad hoc* committee of alarmed citizens called on the philosopher to find out why not. It was the trees, he told his visitors. He could not write unless he could see his steeple. The committee called on the neighbor, who promptly cut down his trees, and the flow from Kant's pen was resumed.

He had dinner, his only regular meal of the day, at a restaurant promptly at one o'clock. After he became a tourist attraction, he often changed restaurants to thin down the crowds of strangers who came to watch him eat. A good conversationalist and reasonably gregarious, however, he frequently engaged in after-dinner talk until well on into the afternoon. At half past four, he took his daily exercise, walking eight times up and down the avenue on which he lived, with such regularity that, it was said, neighbors could set their watches by his progress. His evenings were spent in light reading, preparation for his next day's lectures, or the society of friends. His carefully planned regimen was in response to his concern over a naturally weak constitution and enabled him to escape serious illness for most of his life. He was a great reader on a variety of subjects and was, at the height of this fame, regarded as a sort of universal oracle.

In 1792, his religious views brought him into conflict with the previously sympathetic Prussian Government. The publication in Königsberg of the full text of his *Religion within the Limits of Reason Alone (Die Religion innerhalb der Grenzen der blossen Vernunft)* brought word from the court of King Friedrich Wilhelm II that it would be advisable for him to give his word not to write any more on religious subjects. Kant reluctantly made the pledge and kept it until the King's death in 1797. In that year he retired, and his health began to decline. On February 12, 1804, he died.

During his early years, Kant was a faithful advocate of what, to the displeasure of both Leibniz and Wolff, was called "the Leibniz-Wolffian philosophy." He studied Hume, however, and was awakened from his "dogmatic slumber." Both rationalism and empiricism had led to dead ends, and Kant thought Leibniz guilty of "intellectualizing appearances" and Locke of "sensualizing concepts." His task, as he saw it, was to explore the roles of sense and reason in evaluating experience and, having done this, to provide an antidote to the sterility of the scientific view of the world by making a place for value judgments. He addressed the first part of the enterprise in his *Critique of Pure Reason,* (1788) and the *Critique of Judgment* (1790), together with a number of somewhat smaller works.

Critique of Pure Reason

Kant had been convinced by his reading of Hume that reliance on sense alone can lead only to a radical skepticism, as destructive of science as of value. On the other hand, the rationalists seemed to him to be spinning elaborate fantasies which, professing to be pictures of the real world, rested on no firmer foundation than the speculative imagination. As this was done in the name of pure reason, it seemed appropriate to Kant to conduct an exhaustive examination of the limits of the faculty in order to determine what, if anything, could be accepted as reliable.

The *Critique of Pure Reason* is a ponderous book, liberally laced with terms devised by Kant or used by him in unconventional ways. A smaller and simpler work entitled *Prolegomena to Any Future Metaphysic* was published to provide a more succinct explanation of Kant's theory of knowledge.

The basic problem arises from the fact that everything we know, according to the empiricists' view, comes to us through experience. There is no way to arrive at a guarantee that such experience conforms in any way to a real world of objects outside experience. The book in one's hands is experienced as a combination of colors, touch experiences, and the like. What properties the *Ding an sich,* the thing in itself, may have, cannot be determined by reliance on the senses. Locke had laid the groundwork for an admission of that ignorance by his distinction between secondary and primary qualities. Berkeley, recognizing the danger, had solved the problem to his satisfaction by making the sense qualities the only objective reality. Hume, drawing out the implications of the Berkeleyan position, had been unable to find adequate grounds for subjective continuity, scientific knowledge, or value. Kant, while recognizing the cogency of Hume's argument, was seeking a way out of the destructive skepticism entailed by it.

The noumenal world, he admitted, the realm of the *Ding an sich,* is inaccessible to us. We can be sure that something exists that is responsible for our sensations, but we know nothing of its properties. How, then, is knowledge possible? Kant held that it must begin with experience, but he denied that the kind of universal and necessary knowledge which he thought to be the proper goal of science could arise from experience. That sort of knowledge must stem from judgments which are *synthetic* and *a priori.*

A judgment affirming a relation between a subject A and a predicate B is *analytic* if B is contained in A. It is *synthetic* if B, though connected with A, is not included in it. Thus, the judgment "All bodies are extended" is analytic, in Kant's view, whereas, in terms of the physics of his day, "All bodies are heavy" is synthetic. The predicate adds something to our knowledge of the subject which is not initially included in the concept named by the subject term.

A judgment is *a priori* if it is "a proposition which is thought together with its necessity; and if, besides, it is not derived from any proposition, except such as is itself considered as necessary, we have an absolutely *a priori* judgment." It is, therefore, necessary and universal and so, can be known to be true in advance of any experience which would illustrate its truth. An *a posteriori* judgment is one that does not meet these standards.

Now the trouble with empirically derived judgments is that while they are synthetic and thus add to our knowledge of subjects by the attribution to them of extraneous predicates, they are not *a priori.* The difficulty with *a priori* judgment, on the other hand, is that while they are necessary and certain, they are commonly thought of as analytic rather than synthetic. Thus, though important and necessary, they add nothing new to our concepts and so are too trivial to serve as a foundation for science. The possibility of fruitful scientific knowledge, therefore, rests on the existence of synthetic *a priori* judgments, and an important step in Kant's critical philosophy is his answer to the question as to how such judgments are possible.

All mathematical judgments, he said, are synthetic. In opposition to the generally held view that their apodictic certainty rests on the principle of contradiction, he maintained that a proposition such as $7 + 5 = 12$ is not analytic. We do not, he asserted, arrive at the number twelve by thinking the union of seven and five. That sum requires, for its realization, "an intuition" not included in the concept of the subject terms. "An arithmetical proposition is, therefore, always synthetical," he concluded, "which is seen more easily still by taking larger numbers, where we clearly perceive that, turn and twist our conceptions as we may, we could never, by means of the mere analysis of our concepts and without the help of intuition, arrive at the sum that is wanted." Similarly, Kant maintained that propositions in pure geometry and natural science (physics) are both synthetic and *a priori*. In intention, if not in accomplishment, metaphysics consists of synthetic *a priori* judgments.

Sensibility—the receptivity of the mind to sense data—provides us with the raw materials of knowledge, but the perceptual objects thus established must be conceived or thought before we claim to know them. "Percepts and concepts," Kant said, "constitute the elements of all our knowledge." He dealt with the percepts in the *Transcendental Aesthetic* and the concepts in the *Transcendental Analytic*. The two together constitute Kant's transcendental method—the examination of the formal properties of the mind's treatment of sense data.

The Transcendental Philosophy

Objects are given to the mind through the sensibility. "The effect produced by an object upon the faculty of representation," Kant said, "so far as we are affected by it, is called sensation. An intuition of an object by means of sensation is called empirical. The undefined object of such an empirical intuition is called a phenomenon." Sensations, themselves, however, cannot account for the fact that sensations are arranged in certain forms. They give us the *matter* of experience *a posteriori*. The *form*, however, must come from the mind *a priori* The *pure forms* of the sensibility—pure in the sense that there is nothing in them belonging to sensation—are space and time, and it is through these that perceptions are initially dealt with by the mind.

In placing space and time not in the noumenal world, the world of things in themselves, but rather in the mind itself, Kant was taking his "Copernican step" analogous to the replacing of the geocentric theory of planetary motion by the heliocentric one. "Space," he said "does not represent any quality of objects" apart form thc "subjective conditions of intuition." It is, rather, "the form of all phenomena of the external senses." Similarly, time is nothing which could exist apart from subjective experience. It is "the form of our internal sense, that is, of our intuition of ourselves, and of our internal state." Space, then, is the *a priori* condition of external phenomena, time, of all phenomena, internal or external. In Kant's view, then, the spatial and temporal "forms of intuition" can be isolated from the bare "impressions" described by Hume and given an *a priori* character as formal qualities of experience. It must be kept in mind that the pure forms of the sensibility tell us nothing about the world as it exists outside experience. They do, however, establish necessary conditions under which any phenomena must occur.

In order for knowledge to exist, however, it is necessary not only that objects be perceived as spatial and temporal. They must also be understood, and Kant undertook an examination of the way in which the intellect operates on the data furnished by the sensibility to provide that understanding. This is the subject of the Transcendental Analytic.

He began by establishing a table of theological forms taken by judgment. There are twelve such forms, divided into four groups:

I
Quantity
Universal
Particular
Singular

II
Quality
Affirmative
Negative
Infinite

III
Relation
Categorical
Hypothetical
Disjunctive

IV
Modality
Problematic
Assertoric
Apodictic

This gave Kant "a clue" for another table of "so many pure concepts of the understanding as there were in our table logical functions in all possible judgments." For the items of this table, he used the Aristotelian term "categories".

I
Of Quantity
Unity
Plurality
Totality

II
Of Quality
Reality
Negation
Limitation

III
Of Relation
Inherence and Subsistence
Causality and Dependence
Community

IV
Of Modality
Possibility—impossibility
Existence—nonexistence
Necessity—contingency

Real knowledge would be impossible without the transcendental deduction of the categories which the mind imposes on the data of the senses. But in order for an intelligible and connected world of experience to exist, there must be a unifying self-consciousness in which the experiencing and judging take place. Kant, avoiding an ontological pronouncement about the nature of the self, called this the "transcendental unity of apperception." Because it is the mind which prescribes laws for nature and because the mind acts in *a priori* fashion, it is possible for us to prescribe universal and necessary laws for nature. It must be remembered, however, that these laws can be applied only to experience and our intellectual treatment of it. They are not known as laws governing things in themselves. Nor can we know *a priori* the particular components of experience. The new data of consciousness come to us as they will, and we can be certain only that whatever colors, sounds, feelings, and the like may be presented to our minds, they must of necessity be organized under the auspices of the Transcendental Aesthetic and the Transcendental Analytic.

Phenomena and Noumena

Though knowing in the fullest sense is restricted to phenomenal reality, we can be certain that there is a noumenal world—the world of the *Ding an sich* which is responsible for the materials on which the mind works. Nor is the mind capable of restraining itself from attempting to push beyond the frontiers of experience. The concept of a noumenon is not self-contradictory and can properly exist as a limiting idea showing us the boundaries beyond which the imposition of the categories cannot be taken.

We have, however, a natural tendency to try to make sense of our experience as a whole, and so we are driven to think in terms of three "regulative" ideas which take us beyond the boundaries set for the application of *immanent* principles to experiences susceptible to the sort of treatment that gives us *a priori* synthetic knowledge. Those principles which transcend the limits are known as "transcendent" principles or *Ideas*. Reason *(Vernunft)* leads us, in the first place, to attempt "to represent all determinations as existing in a single subject, all powers, so far as possible, as derived from a single fundamental power, all change as belonging to the states of one and the same permanent being, and all *appearances* in space as completely different from the actions of thought." In this way, we form a concept of the *self,* or the *soul*.

In the same way, we try, through the exercise of pure reason, to form an idea of the "absolute totality" of the many items of our experience. Such a totality is never experienced, of course, but we are driven to posit it as a regulative principle, and so come up with the idea of the *world*.

Finally, we arrive, by a similar process, at the idea of *God,* as the ground of everything that exists. According to Kant, we have no rationally demonstrable ground for the assumption of the object of that idea. "It becomes evident," he said, "that the idea of such a being like all speculative ideas, seems only to formulate the command of reason that all connection in the world be viewed in accordance with the principles of a systematic unity—as if all such connection had its source in one single all-embracing being as the supreme and sufficient cause."

The regulative ideas are *transcendental* and give us a valid way of thinking about metaphysical questions. We fall into serious error, however, if we think of the objects of those ideas as *transcendent* entities, existing actually in such a way as to be susceptible to treatment under the pure forms of space and time or the categories of the understanding. A science of metaphysics analogous to the sciences through which we order our experience can lead only to intellectual barriers which can never be passed and which, therefore, serve to show us the limits of our knowledge. Kant illustrated the nature of these barriers by his discussion of four *antinomies* into which we fall when we attempt to reason the nature of the world posited by the regulative ideas. These are pairs of propositions similar to those used by the Pyrrhonic Skeptics to show that statements and their contradictions can be asserted or denied with equal force. Kant held that this is precisely the case with the theses and antitheses of his antinomies.

It can, he maintained, be demonstrated (1) that the world is spatially and temporally limited and that it is unlimited; (2) that physical bodies are infinitely divisible and that they are made up of simple parts and so are not infinitely divisible; (3) that freedom exists in the world and that freedom does not exist. (4) that there exists, either as a part of the world or as the cause of the world, an absolutely necessary being and that such a being does not exist.

Kant dealt effectively with the first two antinomies, of course, by his "Copernican step." If space and time are imposed on the world by the mind, we cannot say the the "world" in its entirety can be subjected to spatial and temporal categories. The thesis of the third antinomy would seem to find support in the phenomenal world, when every event can be placed in a causal chain which seems to exclude any notion of freedom. However, Kant said, we cannot say that the sequence of causality has any application to the noumenal world, and if we can find in human nature any reason for attributing freedom to man considered not as a collection of observable phenomena but as a spiritual being, we have a right to think of him as noumenally free. As for the fourth antinomy, it is possible, Kant held, to regard the chain of contingent events as being grounded in some being outside the chain, but efforts to use pure reason to prove the necessary existence of such a being are doomed to failure.

He explored the difficulty involved in such attempts in a critical analysis of three traditional proofs for the existence of God. The ontological argument, he maintained, is invalid because it shows at best that the *idea* of a supremely perfect being implies the *idea* of the existence of such a being. But between such an idea and the real existence of its object, there is an unbridgeable gulf. Echoing Gaunilon, Kant insisted that one may have the idea of the existence of a perfect hundred thalers in his pocketbook without thereby guaranteeing the existence of the sum. Existence is not a predicate which can be entailed by the enumeration of any set of hypothetical predicates. The denial of the existence of God is not, then, the denial of a single predicate, but of the subject together with all its predicates, and there is no contradiction in that sort of rejection, "for nothing is then left to be contradicted." Support of the ontological proof is, then, wasted effort. "A man might as well expect to become richer in knowledge by the aid of mere ideas as a merchant to increase his wealth by adding some noughts to his cash account."

The cosmological argument begins with the existence of the world, or some aspect of the world, and proceeds from that to the existence of an absolutely necessary being. The flaw here is that reasoning about causation is valid only within the framework of experience, whereas the cosmological argument seeks to take us beyond the sensible world, where the *a priori* categories of the mind have no force. We may arrive at the *idea* of God as a regulative idea of an ultimate ground of all contingency, but the cosmological argument falls back into the ontological because there is not way to bridge the gap between the idea of existence and existence itself.

For the physico-theological or teleological argument, Kant showed greater respect, for it may well be that our detection of order in the world suggests, by analogy with our experience with artifacts, an orderer responsible for all the order in the universe. But the argument does not lead to apodictic certainty, and at best it can do no more than point to the possible existence of a world-architect working with recalcitrant material. To try to use it to prove the existence of an omnipotent creator is to find ourselves back in the cosmological argument and, at last, in the ontological argument, which Kant had already demonstrated, to his own satisfaction, to be invalid.

By pure reason, then, neither the existence nor the nonexistence of God can be proved. Kant, however, was unwilling to remain in a state of agnosticism on such an important question. What he had been forced to eject from the front door found admission at the back in his *Critique of Practical Reason* and his *Fundamental Principles of the Metaphysic of Morals*.

Morality and Religion

In a theory of knowledge as austere as Kant's, it is clear that no basis for moral obligation could be found in an empirical study of human beings and the circumstances in which they are placed. He held, rather, that the metaphysic of morals is found *a priori* through a critical examination of pure practical reason. Moral philosophy must, he said, free itself entirely from any vestige of the empirical, which "is not only quite incapable of being an aid to the principle of morality, but is even highly prejudicial to the purity of morals. Pure and genuine moral law can be found only in pure philosophy, which is to say, in metaphysic. "Pure reason is practical of itself alone, and gives a universal law which we call the Moral Law."

Moral philosophy begins with the idea of the good will, the only thing that can be conceived that is good without qualification. "A good will," Kant said, "is good not because of what it performs or effects, not by its aptness for the attainment of some proposed end, but simply by virtue of its volition, that is, it is good in itself, and considered by itself is to be esteemed much higher than all that can be brought about by it in favor of any inclination, nay, even of the sum-total of all inclinations." The good will in rational beings is unique because they alone can act according to the conception of laws—which is to say, according to principles. As reason is the faculty by which actions are deduced from principles, the will may be defined as practical reason.

Nothing is *morally* good but the good will and so Kant's use of the adjective is in this context quite different from its employment in such expressions as "good apples," "good machines," or even "a good man in his field." All these uses of the term "good" imply that the object to which the term is applied is good *for* something. The apples are good because they are tasty and nutritious. The machine is good because it performs a useful function efficiently. The man is good at making better mousetraps. Kant's good will, however, is in one sense, "good for nothing" and he himself insisted that if it were totally impotent and could achieve nothing, "then like a jewel, it would still shine by its own light, as a thing which has whole value in itself."

The good will is one which acts out of a sense of duty, and duty involves an imperative. The moral imperative is not hypothetical. That is, it does not say, "If you would like such and such a result, then act in such and such a way." It is, rather, *categorical,* "an imperative which commands a certain conduct immediately, without having as its condition any other purpose to be attained by it." Kant gave three statements of the categorical imperative. The first—"*Act solely on that maxim whereby thou canst at the same time will that it should become a universal law*"—is an assertion that the fundamental principle of the moral law, whatever actions it may dictate, must be universal and necessary and not a matter of subjective or relative valuation. Consideration of the "law" as constituting a "law of nature" in the broader philosophical sense led Kant to a somewhat different statement of the same form of the imperative: "*Act as if the maxim of thy action were to become by thy will* a universal law of nature."

The second statement of the categorical imperative is, "*So act as to treat humanity, whether in thine own person or in that of any other, in every case as an end withal, never as a means only.*'' The word ''only'' is significant. Kant clearly did not mean to deny that there are ways in which human beings may be used as means. They may, for instance, be useful in the production and distribution of goods. They may not, however, be regarded as things. The second statement thus goes beyond the first in its explicit recognition of the intrinsic worth of every human being.

Kant strengthened the second maxim by urging that the will of every rational being is ''*a will which in all its maxims gives universal laws,*'' and so was led to the concept that all rational creatures constitute a *kingdom of ends,* in which everyone is at the same time sovereign and subject. The third statement of the imperative, then, implied in the first two, holds that everyone should ''always so act that the *will could regard itself at the same time as making universal law through its own maxim.*'' This formulation emphasizes Kant's insistence that the good will rather than being heteronomous—directed by something other than itself—is autonomous, or self-directed, in legislating moral law.

Moral judgments, in Kant's view, have an ultimate character which renders them clear to the most ordinary human beings. ''There is no one,'' he said, ''not even the most consummate villain, provided only that he is otherwise accustomed to the use of reason, who, when we set before him good maxims, of sympathy and general benevolence (even combined with great sacrifices of advantages and comfort), does not wish he might also possess these qualities.''

The will, Kant held, is concerned with the deduction of actions from principles, but the principles may in no case be deduced from actions. The motive is the significant thing rather than the effect, and any action that may be contemplated must be judged on the basis as to whether or not its formal character is of such a nature that its maxim could be willed to be universally binding.

Kant was generally insistent on the formal character of the moral law, as opposed to any sentiments which might dictate self-interested or benevolent conduct. Conduct is not moral, he argued, unless it is dictated solely by respect for the moral law. In citing applications of the categorical imperative, however, he could not wholly avoid considerations of sentiment or of the intrinsic desirability of certain consequences of projected acts. Kant was never wholly successful, in fact, in upholding the Spartan standard proclaimed in the *Critique of Practical Reason* that ''the moral law, which alone is purely objective (namely, in every respect), entirely excludes the influence of self-love on the supreme practical principle, and indefinitely checks the self-conceit that prescribes the subjective conditions of the former as laws.''He himself was not oblivious to the problem, and he dealt with it in some measure by elevating sentiments necessary for his system to a plane higher than mere feeling. Respect for the moral law, for instance, is a feeling "of such a peculiar kind that it seems to be at the disposal of reason only, and that pure practical reason." Even self-love and benevolence underwent something of a metamorphosis, for he justified his assertions that benevolent actions may be commanded by duty by arguing that the obligation to be benevolent results from the fact that in view of our need to get help from others in case of necessity, "we therefore make ourselves an end for others; and this maxim can never be obligatory except by having the specific character of a universal law, and consequently by means of a will that we should make others our ends. Hence, the happiness of others is an end that is also a duty." It is rather in Kant's favor than otherwise to suggest that in absorbing as much of an empirical and emotional character into his philosophy as was needed to make it work, he was rather like George Bernard Shaw, whose vegetarianism G. K. Chesterton once impugned with the remark, "Shaw cheats!" When asked how, he replied, "He takes liver extract and calls it 'those chemicals.' "

Be that as it may, the power of Kant's argument is unquestionable in its rejection of any reduction of moral law to non-moral sentiments, and he took full advantage of his restoration of moral value to philosophy to justify the belief in God, freedom, and immortality for which he could find no support in the empiricists' epistemology or the rationalists' metaphysics. Abandoning the attempt to provide "proofs" of apodictic certainty in noumenal areas, where such proofs could have no place in his philosophy, he contented himself with a strong justification for "postulates" which, in his view, could provide an intelligible framework for moral law.

The first of these is that the human will is free. Though no empirical data can support that contention, the fact that the moral law demands but does not compel obedience establishes a strong presumption in favor of freedom. No moral judgment may reasonably be made on objects in the natural world which are determined in their behavior. For a moral dictate to have meaning, an agent must have the option of disobeying or obeying it. "Thou oughtest," Kant affirmed, "Therefore thou canst."

This leads to the second moral postulate, that of immortality. We know that we ought to be perfect—that is, that the will should be absolutely good. In view of the fact that the moral law is rational, what it commands must be realizable. By the very nature of the will, however, there is no possible instant in time at which it could be said to be perfect in such a way that nothing more could be demanded of it. We may, thus, postulate an infinity of time in which to progress toward a goal which is itself infinite.

Finally, although the moral law as categorical commands us to do what ought to be done without counting the cost, we have a conception of the *summum bonum*—the highest good—as involving a union between goodness and happiness. It is repugnant to reason to postulate a universe in which a struggle to attain perfection would meet at every turn with utter misery. In the world of experience, however, this may well be the case, and we certainly find no evidence that goodness and happiness go hand in hand. We may postulate not only that an infinite time is necessary for the realization of the *summum bonum,* but that God must exist as its guarantor. ''The *summun bonum,*'' Kant wrote, ''is possible in the world only on the supposition of a Supreme Being having a causality corresponding to moral character. Now a being that is capable of acting on the conception of laws is an *intelligence* (a rational being), and the causality of such a being according to this conception of laws is his *will;* therefore, the supreme cause of nature, which must be presupposed as a condition of the *summum bonum* is a being which is the cause of nature by *intelligence and will* consequently its author, that is God.'' The moral law, then, leads to the religious view of the world for which Kant was able to find no support in traditional metaphysics.

Critique of Judgment

Having dealt with the function of determinate reason in giving us the categories of the understanding and of self-determinate reason as providing the postulate of freedom, Kant turned in the *Critique of Judgment* to a consideration of reason as applied to nature in providing the Idea of purpose, or the teleological Idea. Here he was confronted by another antimony. On the one hand, the creation of every material thing can be explained in terms of mechanical laws. On the other hand, there are some material things—organic bodies, for instance—which cannot be so explained and in which the activity of the parts seems to be determined by the idea of the whole.

Treating the propositions which constitute the antimony as regulative principles in the Kantian sense, we are at liberty to ascribe mechanical causes to those aspects of nature that invite such ascription and to look for purpose or final causes in the whole of nature or in those of its parts which appear not to be amenable to mechanical explanation. Sense experience can find no purpose in nature, to be sure, and we have no intuitive intellectual awareness of it, but what Kant calls ''reflective'' judgment compels us to think of the organic world as purposive. His observation is given some support by the almost universal tendency of scientists who profess to accept Darwinian natural selection as a sufficient explanation for the characteristics of animals and plants to refer to their biological functioning and behavior in teleological terms.

The sort of purpose we attribute to organic nature cannot, in Kant's view, be unconscious, for the very term contradicts the idea of purpose. The teleological idea as a workable postulate to help us to study nature must entail a willingness to think in terms of intelligent purpose. In Kant's highest vision, the moral Idea and the teleological Idea unite in his conception of the Supreme Cause.

IX.
EVOLUTION IN SCIENCE, PHILOSOPHY, AND RELIGION

Chapter 29

Reason, Revolution, and Romanticism

In England and France, the eighteenth century produced a ferment of thought which had far-reaching social and political consequences, along with profound changes in the ways in which human beings interpreted their relationship to nature. The respect for reason and for the political rights of human beings which had established a firm foothold in the English consciousness in John Locke's philosophy sprcad to the Continent and found militant expression in a French society still dominated by the repressive institutions of an absolute monarchy.

Locke's influence in other areas of thought was equally significant in the new philosophical climate. His work on the *Reasonableness of Christianity* contributed to the development of a mode of thought known as deism. Locke, in agreement with Lord Herbert of Cherbury (1583-1648), had held that certain truths of natural or rational theology, can be known by reason. Locke, of course, did not regard such knowledge as innate, but he judged it to be reliable and appealed to reason as the final arbiter of the revealed truths of Christianity. The deists adopted this Lockian standard in judging the claims made for religion based on revelation, and although most of the early English deists remained within the framework of the Christian Church, they held that what is really fundamental to Christianity is as old as creation and requires no revelation to authenticate it. From there, it was only a short step to the rejection of those parts of the Christian faith which cannot be supported by natural theology, and more orthodox churchmen became alarmed over the implications of the movement.

Joseph Butler (1692-1752), a bishop of the Church of England, while defending revealed religion in his *Analysis of Religion,* published in 1736, laid considerable stress on reason, particularly in its apprehensive function, in the development of his subtle and brilliantly conceived moral philosophy. Equating "conscience" with "moral reason, moral sense, or divine reason," he held that it is "a perception of the heart," as well as a function of the understanding. It is a "practical discerning power" which involves an apprehension of moral principles. One's duty is determined by conscience, "reasonable self-love," benevolence, and the specific propensities and motives that he called the "particular passions.'' A critic of deism, he may, nevertheless, be seen as representative of an age in which rational and empirical philosophical considerations were playing a major role in the evaluation of religious and ethical claims.

Some of the deists retained only the most tenuous association with Christianity, and an extreme wing of the movement, while maintaining that the existence of God as the architect and maker of the Newtonian universe could be proved by reason, was sufficiently influenced by the mechanistic features of that universe to regard the Creator as a sort of absentee landlord, who wound up the cosmos at the time of creation and then left it to run of its own accord.

The scientific optimism of the age continued unabated. Enormous strides were made in mathematics, physics, chemistry, and astronomy by men like Laplace, Herschel, Galvani, Volta, and Lavoisier, while Montesquieu, Adam Smith, and others were studying the social and economic forces which govern human societies, confident that they could be formulated as reliable laws.

Smith's *Wealth of Nations* is the principal source of the philosophy of economic individualism of the *laissez faire* variety. In it, he argued that the removal of economic restraints on commerce would produce the sort of competition which would promote the individual and general welfare. It seemed evident to Smith that ''the simple and obvious system of natural liberty establishes itself of its own accord.''

In France, the quest for the public good took a different form in the writings of François Marie Arouet (1694-1778), who became famous under the pen-name ''Voltaire''. Voltaire visited England and was delighted with Locke's political philosophy, Newton's universe, and the natural theology of the deists. On his return to France, he wrote *Lettres sur les Anglais,* which, after its publication in 1728, was distributed only long enough to be condemned by French censors and burned.

A deist who retained a lifelong belief in God, he found himself assailed as an atheist because of his implacable attacks on the organized church and the Roman Catholic clergy. His objection to the Church was not based on an objection to religion but rather to his conviction that it was being used by priests and lay rulers as a way exercising control over the populace. He himself had a vision of a pure religion that would repudiate superstition and proclaim an immutable and universal morality. In his play *Candide,* he assailed Leibniz's view of a God who is the author of the ''best of all possible worlds,'' but his own view, though less sophisticated, had something in common with that of Leibniz, proclaiming as it did that God, having to struggle with a recalcitrant matter in his creation of the world, did the best job possible.

He fought against governmental tyranny as vigorously as against ecclesiastical abuse. He was an unswerving champion of free elections, free parliamentary institutions, and a free press. His view of a proper organization of society, however, was not so much democratic as Aristotelian in its endorsement of a government in which a strong bourgeois middle class would keep the reins of power out of the hands of "lackeys, cobblers, and hired girls." Conservative as these views may seem now, they were considered so revolutionary in the France of Voltaire's day that he was, for most of his life, regarded as a thorn in the flesh or a monarchy which was already traveling the road which would lead it to destruction before the end of the century.

The seeds sown by the Continental rationalists and the British empiricists produced some results which were at odds with the major tenets of both schools. Descartes' suggestion that animals are machines and the empirical emphasis on sensations as the basis of thought led inexorably to the view that man as an animal is also a machine and that the sensations are nothing but physiological states. The view advanced earlier by Hobbes that thought is reducible to processes within the brain found renewed support in the writings of John Toland (1670-1721) and David Hartley (1704-1757), who, while not identifying conscious states with brain activity, held that the sequence of mental processes is dependent on that of vibrations occurring in the brain and so, on mechanical law. Joseph Priestley (1733-1804) was an out-and-out materialist. Curiously enough, however, he regarded his position as consistent with the propositions that God exists and that the soul is immortal. All that is necessary is to assert that both are material.

The new materialism found several important supporters in France. Julien Offrai de la Mettrie (1709-1751) wrote a widely-read book called *L'homme machine,* in which he maintained that man, like the lower animals in Descartes' scheme, is simply a machine and that no more complicated explanation is necessary to account for his behavior. Paul-Henri d'Holbach, (1723-1789), a German baron residing in France, advanced a completely atheistic, deterministic, and rather gross theory of materialism.

The emphasis on sense data in English empiricism was carried to an extreme by Etienne de Condillac (1715-1780), a French priest, who wrote a book called *Traité des sensations,* in which he attempted to reduce all the higher powers of the mind to sensation. If one could come into the world with no sensations at all, he held, he would have no mind. If then a single sense could be activated—smell, for instance—and he were presented with a rose, his mind would be the smell of the rose.

Confronted with another odor, he would become capable of comparison, and so, by degrees, all the so-called higher mental faculties, including judgment, reflection, reasoning, and abstraction could arise. If other senses were added, the whole of the experienced world of objects and all our reactions to it could be shown to be nothing more than sensation. Claude Adrien Helvetius (1715-1771) developed an ethical system based on sensationalism, and Denis Diderot (1713-1784), editor of the famous *Encyclopedia,* was a sometime materialist.

Rousseau

The *philosophes* who had such confidence in the power of the experience or reason of civilized man to solve the problems of the human race were not without their critics in the age of the Enlightenment. By far the most impressive of those critics, Jean Jacques Rousseau, was a native of Geneva. Not long after his birth, in 1712, his mother died, leaving the child in the care of his father, a watchmaker. A precocious little boy, he learned to read when he was little more than a baby. At the age of ten, he was put in charge of his uncle and shortly afterwards, sent to Bossey, near Geneva, to the home of a pastor. There he was, for the first time, given some formal schooling, but regarded it with little favor because he was expected to learn "all the insignificant trash that has obtained the name of education." After two years there, he returned to his aunt's home and never went to school again. He received some training as an apprentice engraver of watchcases, but, after a short time, left Geneva and wandered about Europe, reading, acquiring musical skills, and acquiring friends and patrons who enabled him to earn enough to keep himself alive and healthy.

In France, he made the acquaintance of a noblewoman, the Baronne de Warens, who took him under her wing, induced him to become a Roman Catholic, and, failing in her attempt to persuade him to further his formal education, helped him find employment. Despite his lack of schooling, he was a prodigious reader, and was able to make a living without having to work as a manual laborer. He copied music for a time, served as tutor to the children of the Grand Provost of Lyons, and became secretary to the French Ambassador to Venice, these activities being only a few of the variety of ways in which he eked out a somewhat meager existence.

He went to Paris, where letters of introduction from his employers in Lyons enabled him to meet a variety of prominent people. The contrasts between wealth and poverty, reverence and cynicism, and merriment and tragedy in the capital struck him with great force. Accepted by the upper strata of society, he remained shy, and found himself more comfortable, perhaps, with an ignorant young servant girl, Thérèse Levasseur, with whom he formed a liaison.

In 1750, the Academy of Dijon offered a prize for the best essay on the question, "Whether the restoration of the arts and sciences has the effect of purifying or corrupting morals?" Rousseau, whose observations of society had led to the conclusion that civilization was a corrupting influence, leaped at the chance to air his views and produced the prize-winning essay, entitled *Discourse on the Sciences and Arts*. With the publication of the work, he became famous, but his views made him a target for critics who pointed out the deficiencies of the work—deficiencies which Rousseau himself admitted, calling it "the weakest in reasoning of all the works I ever wrote."

A versatile man, with a sound knowledge of music and drama, he wrote an operetta, which was performed for the King at Fontainebleau, and a play, performed by the Comedie-Francaise. These were followed by other writings on social and political questions, and in 1761, he wrote his celebrated novel, *Julie ou la nouvelle Héloïse*. *Emile,* published the following year, was an exposition of his ideas on education and, while stressing the importance of religion, attacked some features of its institutions. In that year, too, Rousseau published *The Social Contract,* his most important work on political philosophy. In 1768, he married his faithful Thérèse, who by that time had given him five children, whom he had placed in an orphanage for their upbringing.

His health began to fail, and he was increasingly subject to feelings of persecution which were not altogether unjustified. By this time, he had come to be regarded as a danger to the state and an order went out for his arrest. He fled the country and, during the course of his exile, accepted an invitation from Hume to visit him. He spent sixteen months in England. At last, he was able to return to France, where he died in 1778. His autobiography, *Confessions,* was published after his death.

Man in his natural state, Rousseau maintained, is independent and good, in the sense that he is animated by "a natural sentiment *(amour de soi)* which inclines every animal to watch over his own preservation and which, directed in man by reason and pity, produces humanity and virtue." This view of the state of nature is in striking contrast to the savage picture painted by Hobbes, and, indeed, to Locke's theory, where the restraints on man are simply those prescribed by a recognition of "rights" which require government to secure them.

Whether a state of nature in which men are guided by proper sentiments ever existed in history or, indeed, ever will exist was not a matter of importance to Rousseau. It is a condition "of which it is nevertheless necessary to have true ideas, in order to form a proper judgment of our present state." The "noble savage," as envisioned by him is, then, a sort of ethical model, to be imitated as closely as possible, but never to be perfectly realizable in actual society.

What has degraded humanity, Rousseau maintained, is not some fatal flaw in its nature, but the development of civilization. The moral nature of human beings is more a matter of feelings that of intellect, and those feelings have been corrupted through the institutions of property, which has made men unequal. "Man is born free," Rousseau said, "and everywhere he is in chains." The difficulty begins, he thought, with the sort of contacts among men which lead to the development of "an artificial sentiment *(amour propre)* which is born in society and which leads every individual to make more of himself than every other." The sentiment is responsible for all the ignoble emotions which inspire the depredations human beings inflict upon one another. The problem, of course, is that men must live in societies. Rousseau thought it likely that they were originally forced to do so because of an increase in their number. The problem, then, is to develop the sort of society that will preserve the autonomy of every individual in the community while at the same time providing for the defense by the whole group of the person and property of each individual. This, he said, requires "the total alienation of each associate, together with all his rights, to the whole community."

The origins of all legitimate governments lie in the "social contract" theory, in which "each of us puts his person and all his power in common under the supreme direction of the general will, and, in our corporate capacity, we receive each member as an indivisible part of a whole." The term "general will" *volonté générale* is the key to the understanding of political legitimacy in Rousseau's philosophy. There is an implicit agreement of all the participants in a social contract to will the common good, which, clearly seen, would be recognized as the individual good of each citizen. Ideally, then, one is willing his own good when he wills the good of the society, and when everyone acts according to that ideal, the will of each individual and the general will are the same. Social cohesion and individual autonomy are thus brought into harmony. If the people are sovereign, as Rousseau believed, and the people make the laws, then each person who wills the good of the community, together with his fellows, is the author of the laws which govern him and so is free. Compulsion is necessary only when someone cuts himself off from the general will by violating the law.

The "general will" must be distinguished from the "will of all" *volonté de tous*. The latter refers to the will of special or private interests not necessarily directed toward the welfare of the entire community. The "will of all" cannot guarantee a just society even if the citizens favoring a proposal are in the majority. The distinction between the two may be made clearer by imagining an individual who decides to oppose a piece of legislation because in his best judgment it would not be in the best interest of the whole community. A majority of his fellows oppose his position, however, and pass the law in question. If he has reason to believe that the advocates of the victorious cause were motivated by a desire for personal gain and acted without regard for the common good, he may very well regard the action as one which infringes on his freedom. If, on the other hand, he can reasonably suppose that they are as devoted to the general will as he is, and if he has as much confidence in the judgment of the majority as Rousseau had, he can regard himself in a real sense as an author of the law. "When . . . the opinion that is contrary to my own prevails," he wrote, "this proves neither more nor less than that I was mistaken, and that what I thought to be the general will was not so." In voting, that is to say, I ought ideally not to ask whether or not I like a proposal. I ought rather to ask whether an enlightened citizenry would or would not regard it as in the general interest. If my view on the matter is rejected, I ought to be able to console myself that the winning decision was the one I would have made if I had been better informed concerning the *volonté générale*. Where that will holds sway, I can legitimately be required to obey the law—to be "forced to be free."

More democratic than Voltaire, Rousseau was a powerful spokesman for the rights of the laboring class as well as the *bourgeoisie*. There should be no privileged classes in a just society, and everyone should have the right to participate in the making of its decisions. Even representative government diminishes that right, and if Rousseau could have founded a commonwealth which would best embody his ideals, it would undoubtedly have been a smaller and simpler one than any of the great European states of the eighteenth century. He distrusted the art, the science, the literature, and the fashion which shape the minds of the citizens of the complex societies of the West. All these, together with a love of luxury, lower moral sensitivity, and commercial standards come to prevail over a love of virtue. Philosophy and science have their value, but unchecked diversity of opinion on questions which cannot be answered satisfactorily by the very requirements for proof set by those disciplines undermines the community of values and beliefs upon which a culture depends. When disciplines that should be pursued only by qualified persons become popular among the masses, skepticism becomes rampant, the fabric of society breaks down, and tyrants step in to impose by force the social unity which ought to be insured by patriotism. Rousseau realized, of course, that man could not go back to a state of nature, but he is under obligation to try to effect those reforms which will produce societies that promote natural virtue in the greatest degree possible. One key to the sort of reform he wanted to bring about may be found in his theory of education, which stressed the natural unfolding of a child's personality, preferably under private tutelage, through the elimination of the undesirable influences that would prevent the development of his best impulses.

Revolution and Reform

The writings of the French *philosophes* provided a powerful incentive to social and political change, accelerating the process set in motion by Locke. Most of the statesmen who shaped the institutions of the American Republic were as familiar with French as with English writers, and Thomas Jefferson in particular was an ardent lover of France.

It is, then, understandable that liberal Frenchmen like the Marquis de Lafayette saw in the American revolutionary cause an opportunity to put their sentiments to the test in the forming of a society based on the theories of the Enlightenment as a sort of rehearsal for the changes which they envisioned for their native country. The ideas expressed in the Declaration of Independence and in the Constitution of the United States are a sort of practical summation of the political philosophy of the British and French Enlightenment as applied to the formation of the institutions of a new nation specifically designed to conform to the dominant philosophical standards of the age. In the colonies the political institutions were already far more advanced along the road of constitutional development than were those of the Bourbon monarchy. Moreover, the War for American Independence was not, in the strictest sense, a revolution, for it involved no attempt to overthrow the British government, but rather an intent to separate from it. There was, then, little if any pitting of class against class, and the members of the political bodies set up to govern the Colonies during the war, as well as those which succeeded them after independence was attained, did not differ significantly from their counterparts in Parliament on most questions concerning political legitimacy. The struggle was, then, in the main, more jurisdictional than philosophical.

In France, the upheaval, when it came, was violent in the extreme. The earlier leaders of the French Revolution, to be sure, saw themselves as reformers and envisioned a parliamentary monarchy on the English pattern. The authors of the Declaration of 1789 were obviously influenced by Rousseau when he wrote, "Men are born and remain free and equal in rights. Social distinctions can only be founded on social utility." They even appealed to the *volonté-générale* by name when, in Article VI, they declared, "The law is the expression of the general will. All citizens have a right to take part, personally or by their representatives in its formation." These sentiments are a far cry from the later passions that led to the mass beheadings in the Place de la Concorde during the Reign of Terror. Despite their excesses, however, the leaders of the French Revolution never ceased to pay formal homage to the philosophical movement that had given rise to their expressed ideal of "liberty, equality, fraternity" and none of the many governments which France has had since that time has been totally unaffected by it. The homage paid to reason reached its height when the republican zealots enthroned reason as a goddess.

The ferment of the times continued to have pronounced effects on French political and social thought in the early part of the nineteenth century. August Comte (1798-1857), a child of the Revolution, despite his birth into a family of orthodox Catholics, wanted to revolutionize philosophic enquiry, the social sciences, and religion through the use of scientific methodology. Knowledge acquired by observation and experience, he held, is "positive" knowledge and is the result of a long process of historical evolution, in the course of which humanity passes through three stages: the theological, dominated by anthropomorphic gods, kings, and priests; the metaphysical, ruled by abstract powers, popular governments, and lawyers; and finally the positive, free from metaphysics and acknowledging only scientific laws.

Comte arranged the sciences in the order in which they arrived at the positive state, beginning with mathematics and proceeding through astronomy, physics, chemistry, and biology, to sociology, a science of which he may well be regarded as the father. The earlier are at the same time simpler and more universal than those which succeed them, and although each science presupposes those which went before it, the phenomena of each contain a new element that makes it impossible to reduce one to another.

Sociology, he thought, was ready to enter the positive stage already occupied by the earlier sciences and it culminates in moral concerns. Comte was above all a reformer, and in his later writings added ethics to his list of sciences as the seventh and greatest one. History, he maintained, is progressing toward an ideal society in which the leaders will be experts capable of regulating economic and social life on scientifically tested principles. Ultimately, religions based on an earlier and more primitive stage of human development will give way to a religion worshipping Humanity as the "Great Being" and honoring outstanding specimens of the human race on festive occasions throughout the year.

The Utilitarians

The English concern for morality characterized the work of the English utilitarians, who looked for much of their inspiration to the empiricists of their own country. If their conception of reality was somewhat circumscribed by the limitations of Hume's critique, it was nevertheless apparent to them that human beings do exist, that they experience pleasure and pain, and that they live in society. These truths they thought sufficient grounds for the establishing of a normative science of conduct.

The father of the movement was Jeremy Bentham, a precocious youth who became a brilliant if eccentric man. Born in London in 1748, he studied Latin at the age of four, went to Westminster School at eight, entered Queen's College in Oxford at twelve, took a bachelor's degree at fifteen, and, after a brief study of law at Lincoln's Inn, returned to Oxford and took a Master's degree at the age of eighteen. Deciding against the practice of law, he embarked upon an active career as a writer and reformer. Strongly influenced by Locke and Hume, he showed a preference for the more rigorously empirical and hedonistic elements of their philosophy over the theory of natural right, which played so important a part in Locke's philosophy.

In 1776, he published his first book, *Fragment on Government*. Unlike the American Declaration of Independence, published that same year, it made no initial appeal to the rights of man as a ground for social reform. In 1785, on a visit to his brother in Russia, he wrote *Defense of Usury,* in support of Adam Smith's *laissez faire* theory of political economy.

Later writings include his *Introduction to the Principles of Morals and Legislation* (1789). *A Plea for the Constitution* (1803), *Catechism of Parliamentary Reform* (1809) and *Deontology,* edited by J. Bowring and published after Bentham's death. He enjoyed a reputation as a radical for his incessant criticism of the established institutions of church and state and as a mild eccentric for views such as the one which led to his proposal that great men be stuffed after death and exhibited in public places. He, at any rate, achieved that very distinction when he died in 1832 and he can still be seen, sitting erect and uncompromising in a cabinet at the University of London.

Bentham set forth his commitment to hedonism in the first paragraph of his *Introduction to the Principles of Morals and Legislation:* "Nature has placed mankind under the governance of two sovereign masters, *pain* and *pleasure*. It is for them alone to point out what we ought to do, as well as to determine what we shall do. On the one hand the standard of right and wrong, on the other the chain of causes and effects, are fastened to their throne." The principle of utility, he said, acknowledges that domination and used it for "the foundation of that system, the object of which is to rear the fabric of felicity by the hands of reason and law."

The principle of utility is, according to Bentham, that act of mind, or that sentiment, which approves or disapproves acts according to whether they tend to promote or diminish pleasure in an individual or a community. Utility is that property in an object or in an act which tends to produce pleasure or prevent pain. The community is considered as a fictitious body the interests of which are those of its individual members.

An individual's interests are promoted when his sum total of pleasures is increased or his sum total of pains diminished. The same thing is true of the community with respect to its corporate pains and pleasures. Hedonic evaluation is merely quantitative, without any recognition of "higher" and "lower" sorts of pleasure. "The Deontologist," Bentham wrote, "is an arithmetician whose cyphers are pains and pleasures; his science is that of addition, subtraction, multiplication, and division."

By a sort of verbal *tour de force,* Bentham proceeded to connect the common language of morality with the principle which must, he maintained, be regarded as its only basis: "Of an action that is conformable to the principle of utility one may always say either that it is one that ought to be done, or at least that it is not one that ought not to be done. One may say also that it is right it should be done; at least that it is not wrong that it should be done. When thus interpreted, the words *ought* and *right* and *wrong* and others of that stamp have a meaning, when otherwise they have none."

Bentham was, in short, what is known as a psychological hedonist. If motives other than the desire to achieve pleasure or avoid pain are advanced as reasons for an action, he maintained, they will turn out on examination either to be empty verbalizations or to rely actually on the principle of utility.

There are, he said, four sanctions or sources of pleasure and pain: the physical, the political, the moral, and the religious. The physical sanction comes from non-conscious agencies when considered alone. It is, however, the basis of all the others in so far as earthly life is concerned. It is necessarily included in them, though it may, through the ordinary workings of nature, operate without them. The political sanction is exercised by persons in the community who have legal authority to dispense reward and punishment. The moral or popular sanction is vested in chance persons in one's community who spontaneously exercise it without reference to any legal authority, as in the case of social ostracism. The religious sanction embraces those pleasures and pains which are supposed to come directly from the hand of God, either in a present or a future life.

A serious question with reference to empirical and hedonistic systems of this sort arises from the necessity for providing a calculus whereby pain and pleasure may be measured. Bentham attempted to estimate the value of a pleasure or a pain, considered by itself, in terms of four factors: its intensity, its duration, its certainty or uncertainty, and its propinquity or remoteness. In considering the tendency of an act or event to produce pain or pleasure, two other circumstances are significant: its "fecundity" and its "purity", or the chance the resultant state has of being followed by the same kind of feelings and of not being followed by the opposite kind. Finally, in considering the value of a pleasure or pain with reference to a number of persons, the extent of the condition must be introduced as a sixth consideration.

No criteria for the value of any experience can be established other than an individual's own personal preference. "Every person," he said, "is not only the best, but the only proper judge of what, with reference to himself, is pleasure and what pain." This being the case, "prejudice apart, the game of push pin is of equal value with the arts and sciences of music and poetry."

There are, in the last analysis, no immoral motives, for pleasure is not only that which should be sought; it is the only thing which *can* be sought. "the object of every man's wish and of every man's endeavour from the beginning of his life to the end of it, is to increase his own felicity:—his felicity—as connected with pleasure and disconnected with pain."

If one can only seek pleasure, then clearly, the question as to whether one *ought* to seek it does not hold even academic interest. Bentham, in fact, showed a strong aversion toward the very word "ought" about which he said, "If the use of the word be admissible at all, it 'ought' to be banished from the vocabulary of morals." He displayed similar feelings about other words dear to the heart of moralists. "It is, in fact, very idle to talk about duties," he wrote; "the word itself has in it something disagreeable and repulsive; and talk about it as we may, the word will not become a rule of conduct. A man, a moralist, gets into an elbow chair and pours forth pompous dogmatisms about *duty* and *duties*. Why is he not listened to? Because every man is thinking about interests."

In view of the fact that the only conceivable motive anyone can have is the cultivation of his own pleasure, the calculus in which he engages in weighing his immediate inclinations against other considerations can never take into account the pleasures of others as constituting a part of his motive unless the promotion of those pleasures can be demonstrated to be that mode of conduct which will also give the agent the greatest amount of pleasure. If a conflict can exist between private and public happiness, therefore, altruistic conduct is in that instance rendered impossible.

Apparently seeing this difficulty, Bentham tried to restore a firm foundation to his social ethics by maintaining that empirical examination of the conditions of human life will show that the conduct most conducive to public happiness will always coincide with that most conducive to the happiness of the agent. Bentham, indeed, held that "the omnipresence of the self-regarding affection, and its intimate union with the social, are the bases of all genuine morality." This "intimate union" is based on the assumption that an individual's search for pleasure must, in order to be successful, involve beneficent activity. In terms of Bentham's philosophy, such altruistic conduct presumably could result only from one of two motives or from a combination of both of them. In the first place, one might examine the circumstances of a proposed action and conclude that the bread he casts upon the waters might be expected to return in the form of multiplied pleasures. In exercising "effective benevolence," a man "establishes a claim—a claim which will be felt to be irresistible—of other services to be rendered to himself in return." In the second place, one may be motivated by a feeling of benevolence, even when he cannot foresee any rewards. This fact is admitted by Bentham and can be explained only by assuming that the agent is acting benevolently simply because he enjoys it—that is, because he finds pleasure in the act itself. If one seldom or never is led to the conclusion that either of these motives dictates benevolent behavior on his part, it is difficult to see how Bentham's principle of utility can tell him that he ought to engage in it. The gulf between his egoistic hedonism and his ideal for society of the "greatest happiness of the greatest number" is not an easy one to bridge.

That ideal, however, was one which he pursued with the zeal of a crusader in his writings on social and legal matters. The "greatest happiness" principle requires a democracy, for a class of rulers enjoying privileges secured at the expense of others cannot be expected to serve the greatest good. "All government," to be sure, "is in itself one vast evil," for it exists only to inflict pain. It can be justified only on the ground that the evils to which it resorts are designed to prevent greater evils.

Bentham acknowledged the difficulty of arriving at a standard of measurement that would make a purely quantitative hedonic calculus possible. How is it possible to weigh pleasures and pains of different kinds in the same balance? It is, perhaps, a measure of the difficulty faced by an honest hedonist in providing a way in which his theories can be put into practice that he was obliged to reduce the calculus to monetary terms. "Money," he concluded, "is the instrument for measuring the quantity of pain or pleasure. Those who are not satisfied with the accuracy of this instrument must find out some other that shall be more accurate or bid adieu to politics and morals."

John Stuart Mill

Bentham had a friend named James Mill, a Scot who became a London journalist. An enthusiastic advocate of Benthamite utilitarianism, he attempted to give the system a sound foundation in psychology through his work entitled *Analysis of the Phenomena of the Human Mind.* The positions taken in the book were those at which Mill had arrived through his reading of Locke, Hume, and Hartley. The mind works mechanically. Sensations enter it and leave traces called simple ideas, which, in turn, become associated with one another to form complex ideas. As there are no innate or intuitive moral data, ethics must be based on a pleasure-pain calculus. Right education consists in teaching a child to choose the courses of action that will produce the greatest happiness for the greatest number.

James Mill had a son named John Stuart, born in 1806, and he made the boy the subject of an "educational experiment" designed to make him the ideal standard bearer for utilitarianism. At the age of three, the child began the study of Greek. By his eighth year, he had made the acquaintance of Heroditus, Aesop, Xenophon, Lucian, Isocrates, Diogenes Laertius, and Plato, as well as a substantial number of English authors. When he was eight years old, he began studying Latin, Euclid, and algebra and expanded his reading of classical writers. At about the age of twelve, he was studying Scholastic logic and reading Aristotle's

Organon in the original Greek. A year later, he began to learn political economy.

He saw a great deal of Jeremy Bentham and was profoundly influenced by the *Introduction to the Principles of Morals and Legislation.* That book, he said, "gave unity to my conceptions of things. I now had opinions, a creed, a doctrine, a philosophy; in one among the best senses of the word, a religion; the inculcation and diffusion of which could be made the principal outward purposes of a life."

At the age of sixteen, he founded a club called the Utilitarian Society and so gave formal sanction to a word which had occasionally been used to describe his father's and Bentham's philosophy. He was now, it seemed, on the threshold of a career which would follow faithfully the pattern set for him by his father. In his twentieth year, though, he fell into a "dull state of nerves," occasioned, he thought, by the narrowness of his studies, which placed great emphasis on analysis and almost none on feeling and emotion. He was thus, he observed, "left stranded at the commencement of my voyage, with a well equipped ship and a rudder, but no sail." Turning to English poets and essayists to supply the lacking ingredients in his education, he formed an appreciation of the necessity for the cultivation of the feelings which necessitated a recasting and broadening of the Benthamite principle of utility. His works include *System of Logic* (1843), *Principles of Political Economy* (1848), *On Liberty* (1859), *Considerations on Representative Government* (1861), *Utilitarianism* (1861), *Autobiography* and *Three Essays on Religion,* both published after his death in 1873.

Rejecting the idea of "natural" morality, Mill maintained that nature, considered as a physical system, can furnish no guide for human conduct in view of the many horrors which it perpetrates. In view of the fact that human beings, when uninstructed by society exhibit only the non-moral characteristics they share with the lower animals, Mill considered the moral as "artificial" or "acquired" in human experience. The motive for acquiring it, though, rests in the "natural" desire of men to attain satisfaction or avoid dissatisfaction in terms of hedonistic desires. Like Bentham, he insisted that "The creed which accepts as the foundation of morals, Utility, or the Greatest Happiness Principle, holds that actions are right in proportion as they tend to promote happiness, wrong as they tend to produce the reverse of happiness."

For Mill, though, the greatest happiness principle was not merely egoistic. The agent must seek not merely his own felicity but "the greatest amount of happiness altogether." In weighing his own interests against those of others, he must be "as strictly impartial as a disinterested and benevolent spectator.'' He even went so far as to maintain that ''In the golden rule of Jesus of Nazareth, we read the complete spirit of the ethics of utility. To do as you would be done by and to love your neighbor as yourself, constitutes the ideal perfection of utilitarian morality.''

He held that no non-hedonic sanctions are necessary for obedience to this principle. As a substitute, he suggested, first, ''external'' sanctions consisting of ''the hope of favor and the fear of displeasure, from our fellow-creatures or from the Ruler of the Universe, along with whatever we may have of sympathy or affection for them, or love and awe of Him, inclining us to do his will independently of selfish consequences.'' He postulated, second, an ''internal sanction,'' a feeling in our own mind; a pain, more or less intense, attendant on violation of moral duty, which in properly cultivated moral natures rises, in the more serious cases, into shirking from it as an impossibility.''

In the case of benevolence, the natural basis for the acquired moral imperative lies in ''the social feelings of mankind.'' We are given no real indication in Mill's appeal to feeling as to why one who feels no desire to promote the general happiness *ought* to do so. His own reasoning on this point is unconvincing. The desirability of an object, he held, is established by the fact that people desire it. No other proof is needful. Each person desires his own happiness. ''This, however, being a fact, we have not only all the proof which the case admits of, but all which it is possible to require, that happiness is a good: that each person's happiness is a good to that person, and the general happiness, therefore, a good to the aggregate of all persons.''

He can hardly have supposed, however, that an ''aggregate'' of persons can have any desires other than those of the individuals who compose it. If those individuals can be concerned, in the last analysis, only with their own happiness, a consistently utilitarian and altruistic position could be maintained only by showing that the happiness of the aggregate is consistent with the happiness of each and every individual. Otherwise, the individual with whose happiness the general welfare is not consistent has no reason for conduct of a non-self-regarding sort. Mill was unwilling to go as far as Bentham in asserting this necessary coincidence. This unwillingness led him to a genuine break with the Benthamite tradition. In practice, he held, virtue must itself be regarded as an end of conduct, and a man must, for the sake of his own highest well-being, practice the non-self-regarding virtues. Mill attempted to make this necessity contingent on the ''happiness'' principle by holding that virtue is not originally an end in itself, but becomes one through association with pleasure. "But through the association thus formed," he said, "it may be felt a good in itself, and desired as such with as great intensity as any other good . . . And consequently, the utilitarian standard . . . enjoins and requires the cultivation of the love of virtue up to the greatest strength possible, as being above all things important to the general happiness."

Having thus paid his respects to Benthamism, Mill wasted little time in trying to demonstrate that moral conduct is necessarily productive of pleasure and devoted rather large portions of his writings, notably certain sections of his essay on "Utility of Religion," to expressions of admiration for Christian morality and other codes of conduct which glorify self-sacrifice. The essay is liberally sprinkled with terms such as "high standard," "highest feelings and convictions," "high conception," "exalt the feelings," "ennoble the conduct," "actions which are blamable," and "qualities entitled to praise." In fact, while formally subscribing to the pleasure-pain principle, Mill in effect subverted the hedonic calculus by his recognition of a qualitative distinction between higher and lower pleasures. Men, having faculties "more elevated" than those of the lower animals, are not content even with greater quantities of the animal pleasures if they do not include gratification of the "higher faculties." It is true that he tried to validate this admitted qualitative superiority of some kinds of pleasure over others by suggesting a preference for the "higher" variety on the part of the majority of those who have experienced both. The inescapable impression left by his writings, however, is that it is not majority preference which is responsible for the distinction between higher and lower, but rather the distinction which is responsible for the preference of cultivated human beings for the more exalted pleasure. In no other way can his obvious feeling that one *ought* to prefer the higher be adequately explained. His view that "It is better to be a human being dissatisfied than a fool satisfied; better to be a Socrates dissatisfied than a fool satisfied" is not the mere recognition of a consensus, but a moral conviction.

In his discussion of justice, too, Mill introduced ideas not readily reducible to empirical data. Justice seems to have been for him, as for others, concerned with such matters as the protection of "rights," the awarding of good or ill "deserts," the keeping of "faith," and "impartiality" in the execution of all the duties implied in the concept of justice. Allied to impartiality is the notion of "equality," which Mill respected while considering it impracticable of application in any literal sense. To distinguish more explicitly the concept of justice from the remainder of the sphere of morality—about the whole of which the characteristics just cited could be predicated, Mill pointed out that "justice implies something which it is not only right to do and wrong not to do, but which some individual person can claim from us as his moral right."

Mill was reluctant to admit that this right is based on anything more than law, education, and opinion as expressions of "general utility", or that the sentiment of justice rests on anything higher than a hurt and the animal desire for retaliation. It may, however, be urged that although he successfully demonstrated that justice is useful, he failed to show that usefulness is justice. He himself implicitly acknowledged some fundamental moral principles in his championing of the individual against society, his insistence that one is not accountable to society for one's personal actions when they do not infringe on the rights of others, and his conception of government as simply a means to the protection of the rights and advancement of the welfare of individuals. In all these, the human person was recognized as having certain rights not absolutely granted by law or opinion.

The Rise of Romanticism

The rational and practical approach to problems of individual and social morality was not without its counterbalance. Rousseau is generally recognized as a precursor of romanticism because of his attack on an undue reliance on rational reflection, his glorification of a state of nature, and his insistence that feeling has its own claim as a source of knowledge. The groundwork of the movement, however, was actually laid by a number of German, French, and English philosophical, literary, and artistic figures. Kant's admission that things in themselves are unknowable by reason suited the temperament of many philosophers better than the claim of the Hegelians to provide a rational account of the whole of reality, although Hegel himself was not without influence on the romantic movement.

Like "Renaissance" and "Enlightenment", "romanticism" is not a term which lends itself to narrow or precise definition. It does not refer to a philosophical school, and, indeed, philosophies showing romantic coloration may run the gamut of metaphysical positions from idealism to materialism. Indeed, in all the areas of intellectual and artistic endeavor influenced by the romantic movement, there is a diversity of expression that is, perhaps, not surprising coming from men and women who were openly in revolt against the theories and practices which dominated the Enlightenment. Denying that sense experience and reflection can provide an adequate grasp of reality, the romantics called on imagination and feeling to give us a fuller understanding of ourselves and our world. The authority of the artist was for them greater than that of the man of science.

Romanticism was especially attractive to Europeans who were repelled by the increasingly mechanized world spawned by the industrial revolution. They turned away from the sterility of the intellect responsible, in their judgment, for the evils of that world and sought a deeper truth accessible to those faculties of intuition and feeling that had been scorned or ignored by the major figures of the Enlightenment.

Literary works giving a romantic treatment of nature, bygone days, far-away places, mystery, love, and death, became popular. Poets such as Wordsworth, John Keats, and Percy Bysshe Shelley challenged the claims of reason with their view that one best communes with reality through a childlike contemplation of the world, relying, in Wordsworth's case, at least, on a romanticized version of the Platonic notion that;

Our birth is but a sleep and a forgetting:
The soul that rises with us, our life's Star,
Hath had elsewhere its setting,
And cometh from afar;
Not in entire forgetfulness,
And not in utter nakedness,
But trailing clouds of glory do we come
From God, who is our home:
Heaven lies about us in our infancy!
Shades of the prison-house begin to close
Upon the growing Boy,
But he beholds the light, and whence it flows
He sees it in his joy;
The youth, who daily farther from the east
Must travel, still is Natures's Priest,
And by the vision splendid
Is on his way attended;
At length the Man perceives it die away,
And fade into the light of common day.

Romanticism in Philosophy

The outlook of the romantic poet was expressed with equal skill by a host of practioners of the other arts during the nineteenth century, and was not without its effect on speculative philosophy. Drawing on the essentially romantic rejection of the dominant role of reason implicit or explicit in the work of some of his German predecessors, Arthur Schopenhauer (1788-1860) stressed the will in his *The World as Will and Idea.* The sense data or "ideas" through which we suppose that we know the world really tell us nothing of the real entities which are the causes of the experiences. Reason has a limited utility in enabling us to deal with the complexity of everyday life, but its dangers are greater than the services it renders. It deceives us into making arbitrary distinctions where we should be noting similarities and reading identity into experiences which are really different. Moreover, it tempts us to try to apply concepts to moral and practical concerns that are better left to feeling and intuition.

Ultimately, the world is not a product of reason but of "will," a blind drive which expresses itself in complex fashion in the production of all the facets of our experience. A profound misanthrope, Schopenhauer regarded the will as the author of a senseless and depressing drama in which human beings experience a variety of evils ranging from boredom to agony—a fate which most of them richly deserve. The world, he said, is "a hell, which surpasses Dante's hell in that each man must be the devil to his neighbor."

Plunged into a senseless universe ruled by a malevolent power, one might conclude that life, which is nothing other than a futile striving of the will for a happiness that can never be achieved, is an unmitigated evil and that the only sensible course is suicide. Schopenhauer, however, declined to endorse so simple a way of trying to achieve the questionable salvation of annihilation. Mere termination of the individual's life does nothing to inactivate the will, which then simply manifests itself in some other form.

One can attack the will directly only through philosophy and art or through ethical action. The will as projected into human life is essentially self-centered and that self-centeredness may be attacked by the cultivation of attitudes that deny the self. Temporary surcease may be found in philosophy and art, which objectify and depersonalize the attention of their devotees. The cultivation of feelings of sympathy provides another partial solution to the problem. If the will is genuinely to be reduced to quiescence, though, something more drastic is called for, and Schopenhauer advocated, though he did not practice, a world-denying asceticism bearing some resemblance to the quest for Nirvana in Buddhism.

Friedrich Nietzsche

Nietzsche (1844-1900) does not fit neatly into any pigeonhole and, indeed, he made it clear in his wide-ranging writings that he was not to be identified with any philosophical school. His thought was shaped in large measure, however, by the romantic tradition, and, indeed, his work may with justice be considered as the culmination of nineteenth-century European romanticism.

Born in 1844, Nietzsche was the son of a Protestant minister and his wife. He attended the universities of Leipzig and Bonn and later became Professor of Classical Philology at the University of Basel. He served in the Prussian army as a medical orderly during the Franco-Prussian War but suffered severe damage to his health and returned to Basel. He became a close friend of Richard Wagner, whose position in the history of romantic music is not unlike that of Nietzsche in romantic philosophy. Radical differences in the outlook of the two men ultimately resulted in a break, however, and Nietzsche later expressed his disillusionment in a highly critical appraisal of the composer. In 1879, he resigned from the University of Basel on the ground of poor health and spent the rest of his active life in a number of places in Switzerland and Italy. Early in 1889, he became mentally ill and required constant care until his death in 1900.

Nietzsche was strongly affected by music and the visual arts, and in his first work, *The Birth of Tragedy,* published in 1872, he explored the relationship between the "Dionysian" and the "Apollonian" in the culture of the ancient Greeks. The Dionysian is the unrestrained, passionate element which finds its natural expression in music. The Apollonian is the principle of restraint and form most fully exemplified in sculpture. When the two were brought together in a proper fusion, Greek tragedy was the result, a supreme achievement which Nietzsche thought had been dealt a severe blow by the development of Socratic philosophy, with its emphasis on logic and morality. Nietzsche was not altogether an irrationalist, but for him, as for Schopenhauer, reason was an instrument of will—the will, as he put it, to power. Unlike Schopenhauer, however, Nietzsche did not endorse a world-denying pessimism. While holding the world to be "a monster of energy without beginning, without end," and denying all sorts of "eternal values, eternal forms, eternal souls," he nevertheless exalted the sort of Dionysian activity—using the term in his later writings to refer to a synthesis of the Dionysian and Apollonian elements of *The Birth of Tragedy*—that could produce a superior sort of human being, the *übermensch* or superman.

Nietzsche's writings are unsystematic, passionate, and abounding in paradox. He himself must bear some of the blame for the appalling interpretations put on his work by some of his more fanatical admirers, but the intemperate elements of his thought to which the Nazis appealed find eloquent counterbalances in his own writings. His conception of the superman was not that of an undisciplined brute. ''Dancing in chains'' is a figure of speech which suggests his ideal of the way in which power is to be used, and his taste was as often Mozartian as Wagnerian. A militant foe of Christianity and Judaism, he nevertheless admired Jesus and the ancient Hebrews. He loved a worthy opponent, living or dead, and proudly claimed, ''the most serious Christians have always been well disposed toward me.''

The Judaeo-Christian world view seemed to him, nevertheless, to have corrupted the Western world with a religion of meekness and pity, masking a resentment of the powerful—a ''slave morality'' in which a warped view of ''good'' is opposed to the life-affirming traits of character found in those holding to an aristocratic ethos characterized as ''evil'' by the weak. Opposed to this is the ''master morality'' in which the qualities seen as his *Beyond Good and Evil,* as in other works, notably his *Thus Spake Zarathustra,* Nietzsche urged a ''transvaluation of all values'' in which both sorts of morality would have their place but in which the illicit dominance of the slave morality would be at an end.

In 1881, while walking in the woods by the lake of Silvaplana in Switzerland, Nietzsche stopped by a pyramidal rock and found himself overcome by something having some psychological resemblance to an experience of religious revelation. All things, he suddenly concluded, must recur. Countless times in an infinite past and countless times in an infinite future, his life and every life is repeated again and again. He tried to explain this conviction by speculating that time is infinite and the number of centers of force is finite and that, therefore, ''in the great dice game of existence.'' every possible combination of those centers of force must be realized an infinite number of times. He insisted, however, that his concept was not merely mechanistic. It has profound significance for human life, and is, indeed, the ''highest formula of affirmation that is at all attainable.'' To rise above the ordinary, be able to affirm the values of one's life, and joyfully will to live it again and again is to bring one to ''the closest approximation of a world of *becoming* to one of being.''

Nietzsche's provocative writings covered almost every area of Western thought, and he has quite properly been recognized as one of the most readable of the great philosophers. Those who have devoted careful study to his work have generally found much of value in it, and his influence on twentieth-century philosophy, theology, literature, art, and music has been significant.

Chapter 30

Hegelianism and Western Culture

Kant's critical philosophy left an indelible mark on European thought, but there was a reaction among his successors against the barrier which he had erected to a penetration of the noumenal world by the intellect. Kant himself had, of course, suggested that although we cannot *know* anything beyond experience, we may nevertheless assert the existence of things in themselves and posit God, freedom, and immortality as moral postulates.

Johann Gottlieb Fichte (1762-1814) was an influential figure, not only in the development of romanticism, but as an important link in the chain which led from Kant to Hegel and the full flowering of idealism in Germany. Fichte respected Kant and had no desire to go back to the sort of metaphysics that his predecessor had been at pains to demolish in the *Critique of Pure Reason*. However, he thought that in saying that things in themselves *exist* and that they are the cause of sense data, Kant had given away too much. Existence and causation were, in the Kantian system, categories of the understanding which could not be applied to that which lies beyond experience.

Fichte disposed of the thing in itself by absorbing it into the mind. The objective world is a product of the ego, but the idea of an ego is not limited to that of individual selves. All such selves participate in a universal reason, and that reason is the absolute ego, or God. There is, then, nothing "unknowable" about the world as it is. To be is to be known by the absolute mind, which in its free activity differentiates itself into individual selves and the objective world. That world is "the sensualized material of our duty," an arena in which the ego can meet opposition, become conscious of itself, and achieve freedom.

Friedrich Wilhelm Schelling (1775-1854) carried idealism a step further in his development of the idea of everything as dependent on a universal mind, the Absolute, which unfolds itself in evolutionary fashion to achieve the goal of self-consciousness in man. He treated the universe as a living, organic whole, in which subject and object are one. We can know the nature of reality because, in our rationality and our freedom, we are part and parcel of it.

Hegel

Georg Wilhelm Friedrich Hegel was born in Stuttgart in 1770, the son of a minor official. Despite the fact that his family was not prosperous, he acquired an education in theology and philosophy at the University of Tübingen. During his five years there, he gained the friendships of Hölderlin and Schelling and took an active interest in the ideological issues involved in the French Revolution. After leaving the University, he served as a private tutor in Berne and Frankfurt for six years and worked on the development of his system.

In 1801, he became a member of the faculty of the University of Jena and published a book entitled *Difference between the Philosophical Systems of Fichte and Schelling.* In 1805, he was awarded a full professorship at the University, but after the Battle of Jena in 1806, the University was forced to close and Hegel found himself out of work. His first major book, *The Phenomenology of Mind,* was completed at midnight just before the battle.

From 1806 to 1808, he was editor of a newspaper in Bamberg. In 1808, he became director of the *Gymnasium* at Nürnberg and in 1811 he was married to Marie von Tucher. His *Science of Logic,* written during his residence at Nürnberg, won him invitations to join the faculties of several universities, and in 1816, he went to Heidelberg. In 1817, he published his ambitious *Encyclopedia of the Philosophical Sciences in Outline,* an exposition of his theory in its entirety, which won him an invitation to occupy the chair of philosophy at the University of Berlin. He went to Berlin in 1818 and for the rest of his life enjoyed widespread fame and the whole-hearted approval of the government of the Kingdom of Prussia. His success only served to confirm his conviction that he had arrived at the comprehensive and ultimate truth about the nature of reality, and he remained convinced of the rightness of his philosophy until his death from cholera in 1831 at the age of sixty-one. While at Berlin, he published his *Grundlinien der Philosophie des Rechts,* and after his death, his lectures on a variety of subjects were published by his students in a collection of his *Complete Works* in nineteen volumes.

Absolute Idealism

With Hegel, the transition from Kantian critical philosophy to a revised version of the sort of metaphysical system which Kant thought he had done away with once and for all was complete. Hegel denied any dichotomy whatsoever between thought and thing. What is rational is real, and what is real is rational. There is no unknown thing in itself on which the mind imposes its categories. Things are the sum of their categories, and the entire universe is in essence a logical system—an absolute mind not open to Hegel's characterization of Schelling's Absolute as "the night in which all cows are black," but an active dynamic subject responsible for the logical structure of the universe, the processes of nature, and the history of man.

Philosophy has as its object the acquisition of an understanding of the world, not in terms of the static categories of Aristotelian logic, but rather through the application of a sort of dynamic process of reason reminiscent of the tantalizing philosophy of Heraclitus. Objects, Hegel held, cannot be understood properly in abstraction. They must be considered concretely, which is to say, in all the complexity of their relations to everything else. Logic is the instrument through which we achieve this understanding, but since logic lies at the very heart of the universe, it cannot be for us "empty ratiocination." It must, rather, be "the apprehension of the present and the actual." The dynamic logic which is at the heart of reality and of our understanding of it is, he said, going back to an honored term in Greek philosophy, a *dialectic*.

The Hegelian dialectic, a structure of such formidable complexity that a condensed treatment can give only the barest notion of its nature, has a triadic character. It moves from a *thesis* to an *antithesis*, which is at the same time its complement and its opposite. The tension between the two results in a *synthesis*, and that, in turn, provides a new thesis which generates its own antithesis, and so on up the ladder until we reach the Absolute.

Theoretically, one should be able to begin at any point in the dialectic and from there deduce the whole system, but to illustrate the operation of it, we may conveniently begin with the thesis of the lowest level of the logic: being. Now nothing more general or more indeterminate can be said of anything than that "it is." Being is "the blank we begin with, not a featurelessness reached by abstraction, not the elimination of all character, but the original featurelessness which precedes all character and is the very first of all." As a featurelessness, however, being is, in a sense, "absolutely negative," which is to say, it is nothing—not-being. The very concept of being, then, generates its antithesis. Hegel, though admitting that the proposition that the two are the same "seems so paradoxical to the imagination or understanding that it is perhaps taken for joke," affirmed that this is the case. "It is as correct, however, to say that being and nothing are altogether different, as to assert their unity," he insisted. "The one is *not* what the other is."

What unites the two in one concept is becoming. Being passes into not-being and not-being into being. But becoming itself generates the idea of an indeterminate sort of being which has as its antithesis determinate being, and these two produce their synthesis, being for self. This, in turn, becomes the thesis for the next higher triad, quantity, quality, and measure, and measure provides a new concept of being which, when set over against essence, results in the synthesis, notion (*Begriff*). This in turn is sufficient to give the name "Logic" to the highest thesis in the Hegelian system. The whole structure is, of course, far subtler and more intricate than can be indicated by a skeletal summary, but Hegel was convinced that the entire framework of logic follows inevitably from the most abstract of the triads.

Logic itself, however, is still abstract. It is a system of thought without particular content, and so the logical Idea must itself externalize itself in its antithesis, Nature, the Idea "outside itself." The "outside" of course, must not be taken literally for, as in the other triads, synthesis and antithesis are one which at the same time are different. It is in his philosophy of Nature that Hegel examined the structure of the physical sciences, in itself a formidable task, but one which he thought essential to the realization of his project of providing an intelligible account of the whole of reality.

Logic and Nature are transcended (*aufgehoben* is the term Hegel used to describe the way in which synthesis is related to thesis and antithesis) by Mind, or Spirit (*Geist*). This is the highest stage of the dialectic, and this final triad defines the nature of the Absolute, which—or who—is the ground of all the processes of reality. Mind, like Logic and Nature, has an elaborate complex of triads under its auspices. Its highest triad consists of subjective mind, objective mind, and absolute mind. Subjective mind, in turn, is expressed as soul, consciousness, and spirit, with their concomitant sciences of anthropology, phenomenology, and psychology. It is, however, in his treatment of objective mind that Hegel produced some of his most influential writing, dealing, as it does, with important questions of ethics and politics.

Moral and Political Philosophy

In his *Philosophy of Right,* Hegel suggested that "ethical observance" is a synthesis of "abstract or formal right," and its antithesis, "morality." In this synthesis, the will realizes itself both externally and internally in "its absolutely universal existence."

"Abstract right" has a certain relation to the second and third expressions of the Kantian categorical imperative in that it stresses the dignity of the individual person and of the society of persons of which each individual is a part. It deals with man in his social relationships and provides him with a basic mandate for the conduct of those relationships: "Be a person and respect others as persons." A "person" is not merely an abstract subject, for "subject is only the possibility of personality," and personality is developed only by the recognition of certain factors of right in oneself through an expansion of the self in society.

How does the self become realized in society? According to Hegel, it is done under the auspices of the concepts of property, contract, and wrong, which represent aspects of the way in which the personality postulated by the concept of abstract right proceeds from the "abstractedness" of unrelated individuality to the "concreteness" of relationships with others.

In the possession of property, "freedom is that of the abstract will in general, or of a separate person who relates himself only to himself." Contract occurs when, by the mutual consent of two persons, property is transferred from one to the other. In this process, "a person by distinguishing himself from himself becomes related to another person, although the two have no fixed existence for each other except as owners." Wrong, or crime, is the condition of the will when it differs from and is in opposition to "its true and absolute self."

As abstract right is concerned with the implicit external relationships of human wills, so its antithesis, morality, is related to an equally important idealistic concept, that of spiritual autonomy as it tends to produce inner moral excellence. As in Kant's ethics, Hegel's emphasis on autonomy necessitated some considerations of the extent to which one's intention determines the morality of an action. So far as the moral worth of an individual is concerned, Hegel was as explicit as Kant in maintaining that since the moral will is inaccessible to outside forces and unassailable by them, "a man's worth is estimated by his inner act." Hegel's "will" like Kant's must recognize that "duty should be done for duty's sake," but Hegel acknowledged that "an act requires its own special content and definite end, and duty in the abstract contains no such end." The essence of duty, then, is "to do right, and to consider one's own well-being and the general well-being, the well-being of others."

The objectivity which Hegel found in his concept of abstract right and the subjectivity of morality are synthesized in the "ethical system" which is the idea of freedom. "It is," he said, "the living good, which has in self consciousness its knowing and willing, and through the action of self consciousness its actuality. Self consciousness, on the other hand, finds in the ethical system its absolute basis and motive. The ethical system is thus the conception of freedom developed into a present world, and also into the nature of self-consciousness."

Hegel considered the individual person to be of great importance for moral philosophy and was a staunch defender of "the right of individuals to their particularity." Self realization cannot properly be attained apart from organized society, which he examined in his development of the triad of the family, the civic community, and the state. The family involves three phases: marriage, the care of family property and goods, and the education of children and dissolution of the family. He discussed at some length that manner in which marriages have been and should be arranged, the importance of the marriage ceremony, the relation of marriage to concubinage, and the like. Despite its avowedly permanent nature, marriage was admitted to be dissoluble in practice because, "since it contains feeling, it is not absolute, but open to fluctuations." He held that such facts of nature should be recognized by the law, although divorce and separation should be made legally "as difficult as can be." His view of the family was patriarchal. One sex, he averred, "exhibits power and mastery." the other is "subjective and passive." These are facts of psychology, he thought, which determine the roles of men and women with reference to the internal affairs of the family and its relationships with the outer world. His views on the instruction of children were based in large measure on observation of juvenile capacities and traits of character considered with reference to the ends of education. He held that the instincts with which they are born cannot be relied upon to insure their development in the right direction if they are given complete liberty of self-expression.

As the family is naturally patriarchal, so the civic community is, by necessity, a result of agreement among persons more nearly equal in standing. Hegel's consideration of "the system of wants," the first of the three elements of this phase of his ethics, involved discussion of such mundane matters as physical desires, the training of laborers in appropriate skills, and the production and distribution of wealth. All these things are affected by accidental considerations. "The soil is more fertile in one place than in another, years differ in their yield; one man is diligent, while another is lazy." In "Labor" he pointed out that "human sweat and toil win for men the means for satisfying their wants." As for "Wealth," Hegel held that the "particular wealth" of the individual is based on capital and skill. Skill, in turn, depends on capital, accidental circumstances, and the differences among individuals in natural endowments and in opportunity for their development.

The state, the synthesis of the family and the civic community, is "the ethical whole." It is "the actualization of freedoms," and in it, "freedom attains its highest right over the individual, whose highest duty in turn is to be a member of the state. Since *freedom* is a term which has spiritual significance in Hegel's philosophy, the concept of the state has definite spiritual implications, for the state provides the necessary condition for the realization of freedom. It represents too the reality of "the Spirit which abides in the world and there realizes itself consciously." The state is, in its own nature, a spiritual whole and also the concrete embodiment of personal individuality and freedom. "In contrast with the spheres of private right and private good," Hegel wrote, "of the family and of the civic community, the state is on one of its sides an external necessity. It is thus a higher authority in regard to which the laws and interests of the family and community are subject and dependent. On the other side, however, the state is the indwelling end of these things and is strong in its union of the universal end with the particular interest of individuals. Thus, just so far as people have duties to fulfill towards it, they also have rights."

It is significant that for Hegel, the ethical finds its completion in religion. Like most thinkers who posit a ground for morality transcending mere social utility, he assigned a value to religion beyond mere form or feeling. It relates to an infinite whole in which morality is organically related to every other aspect of reality. The state is not simply a man-made structure dependent on social contract. It is "the march of God in the world," and the idea of the state must transcend any particular states or political institutions. Relations between two states are subject to transcendent judgment. "A third must therefore stand above and unite them," Hegel wrote. "Now this third is the Spirit, which gives itself reality in world history and constitutes itself absolute judge over states. Several states indeed might form an alliance and pass judgment upon others, or interstate relations may arise of the nature of the Holy Alliance. But these things are always relative and limited, as was the everlasting peace. The sole absolute judge, which always avails against the particular, is the self-caused self-existing Spirit, which presents itself as the universal and efficient leaven of world history."

The judgment of the Spirit is not, in Hegel's philosophy, embodied in any supra-national organization, nor can it be, for each state is sovereign and would have to will to obey an international tribunal order for such a scheme to work. In view of the fact that "welfare is the highest law governing the relations of one state to another," a state, in willing its own welfare, may come into conflict with another. If the disagreement cannot be settled by peaceful means, war is the inevitable result.

This fact did not unduly trouble Hegel. Like Heraclitus, who regarded war as "father of all and king of all," he saw the history of mankind, with all its conflicts as the unfolding of the Spirit through the dialectical process. A nation plays its role on the world stage, and when it becomes weak and is conquered by another, the victory of the stronger is simply a manifestation of movement to a higher plane. History is not created by the decision of great men except insofar as those decisions are instruments used by the Spirit for its own purpose. That purpose is the attainment of freedom, and the dialectic of history shows the way in which it is being progressively realized in the rise and fall of different civilizations. In the monarchies of the Orient, only the ruler was free. The classical cultures prized freedom for a limited citizenry. It was, however, the Germanic Christian peoples, who, according to Hegel, expanded the concept to include everyone. "The East," he said, "knew and to the present day knows, only that *One* is free; the Greek and Roman world that *some* are free; the German world knows that *all* are free." Hegel admired the Prussian constitutional monarchy of his day as a shining example of this Germanic achievement.

Art, Religion, and Philosophy

Subjective and objective mind in human experience lead to that knowledge of Absolute Mind which, in the light of Hegel's conviction that knower and known are one, amounts to self-knowledge by the Absolute through the human intellect. This knowledge too follows a dialectic process in its development.

The thesis of the main triad is provided by art, "a sensuous semblance of the Idea," in which the Absolute makes itself known through the beauty of sense objects. Like the state, art has developed in human history in accordance with a dialectical pattern, progressing from the symbolism of the Orient to the classicism of the Greeks, and finally to the romanticism of Christian European art. In the intuitive process responsible for art, the mind apprehends its inner nature in freedom.

Art leads inevitably to religion, which, like all antithetical developments is at the same time different from its thesis and one with it. Religion differs from art in that to a greater extent than art, it relies more on thought than on feeling. It is one with it in that it is essentially pictorial. Christianity, the highest of the religions, is the religion of the Spirit.

Philosophy synthesizes art and religion. Like religion, it "has no other object than God and is, therefore, essentially rational theology, as well as an enduring worship of God in the service of truth." The pictorial character of religion is, in philosophy, transformed into pure thought. For Hegel, the Father, the Son, and the Holy Ghost of the

Christian Trinity had their philosophical parallel in Logic, Nature, and Mind.

Art, religion, and philosophy all have their own histories. The march of philosophy is a progressive unfolding of the Absolute Idea in human thought. In Hegel's view, however, philosophy after him could exhibit no further dialectical development, for he was confident that his system was the ultimate synthesis of the long quest of the Mind to come to full consciousness of itself in human nature.

Hegel's philosophy, suggesting as it did that not only philosophy, but also statecraft, had reached its peak in the Germany of his day, enjoyed immense popularity for some years after his death. His followers, however, soon became divided into two camps. Conservative or "right wing" Hegelians interpreted the master's philosophy in terms of traditional Christianity. Liberal—"left wing" or "young"—Hegelians kept the idealistic flavor of the system, but interpreted it in more pantheistic fashion. His influence was felt not merely by professional philosophers, but among theologians, historians, and, indeed, scholars in nearly every field.

Hegelianism in Britain and America

In 1865, an Englishman, J. H. Stirling, published a work entitled *The Secret of Hegel* and set off a wave of Hegelian scholarship which, until well into the twentieth century, attracted some of the best minds in modern philosophy. Those Neo-Hegelians did not slavishly adopt a Hegelian dialectic, and their thought was frequently colored by Kantian views, but they were at one with Hegel in their attempts to order the whole of human experience in some sort of intelligible organic unity.

Thomas Hill Green (1836-1882), a distinguished Oxford scholar, was the first of the great British Neo-Hegelians. Green rejected the whole empirical tradition in favor of a German sort of absolute idealism. Like Hegel, he saw the conflict of ideas and cultures as materials to be reconciled by higher modes of thought. He deplored the tendency of many British thinkers to regard the spiritual as an outgrowth of the material order. Exactly the reverse is true, he maintained. The spiritual order, governed by a universal mind, is prior to the physical order, and the physical order is dependent upon it for its existence and for the formation of the particulars which make up the world, including the bodies of animals and men. There is nothing in the theory of evolution, he held, which is in conflict with this view. Bodies may have evolved in such a way as to enable mind to manifest itself in changing and progressive fashion, but there is no reason to suppose that minds have evolved out of bodily functions.

Specifically, human activity is not dependent on appetite or impulse, but on self-conscious motivation. Though the good a man can accomplish depends on the circumstances of his life, he is, for himself, an ideal object and can resolve to become better than he is. In the moral sense, then, he is a free agent, mirroring in himself the mind of God. The self-fulfillment which is demanded of an individual entails as well the effort to help other individuals to fulfill their own destiny.

Historically considered, moral codes and practices can be traced back to law and custom, but the laws and customs themselves require explanation in terms of a rational and transcendent source of moral ideals. The moral demands responsible for the beginnings of social institutions are not consciously and critically evaluated. As the reflective consciousness develops, the range of concern expands until the idea of a universal society of mankind emerges. Morality requires dedicated efforts to improve the lot of one's fellow men, but ultimately, morality aims at holiness—the commitment of the self to God. Indeed, the practical morality of the reformer itself has as its ultimate end the attainment by those who are helped by it of the saintliness which is the natural goal of human endeavor.

Probably the best known of the English Hegelians was Francis Herbert Bradley (1846-1924). Bradley was in complete agreement with Hegel that an attempt to understand the world as a collection of particulars is doomed to failure. To be sure, ultimate reality consists of nothing but sentient experience, and experience seems to confront us with specific things, related to one another in a variety of ways. Any attempt to base a philosophy on a plurality of phenomena, however, results in contradiction. Bradley's critical analysis of the philosophies which fall into unacceptable paradox earned him the sobriquet "the Zeno of modern philosophy."

One difficulty of pluralism is that it necessitates an explanation of relations. Two items cannot be considered at all unless they are related in some way, but if the fact of relation is admitted, formidable difficulties arise, for if A is related to B, a new relation must be posited to relate the relation to A and to B. "The links are united by a link," Bradley said, "and this bond of union is a link which also has two ends; and these require each a fresh link to connect them with the old." Any two terms then require an infinite series of relations between them, and this makes no sense. Any sort of relational philosophy is, Bradley thought, a "makeshift device" which serves a practical purpose and is, indeed, necessary, but it applies only to the realm of appearance and not to that of reality.

The reality which comprises all particulars in one intelligible whole is Bradley's Absolute. We cannot of course gain enough knowledge to know fully its nature, but our own nature enables us to understand it in some measure. Our immediate experience, for instance, hints at the sort of diversity in unity which on a grander scale is the life of the Absolute. "Sentient experience, in short, is reality, and what is not this is not real," he wrote in his *Appearance and Reality*. "There is no being or fact outside of that which is commonly called psychological existence. The Absolute is one system and its contents are nothing but sentient experience."

The Absolute is not personal in any limited sense. It is above all personality. It embraces all intellect, all feeling, and all phenomena. It is not itself in progress, but it is the ground of many histories with their internal purposes and finite progress. Philosophy is always incomplete, but a logic of judgments can give us an insight into the pattern of reality. Bradley preferred judgments to concepts or categories because judgments are more concrete reflections of the one reality. To judge that a sea-serpent exists, he said, is to "qualify the real world by the adjective of the sea-serpent."

Not surprisingly, Bradley was a self-realizationist in his ethical theory. In his *Ethical Studies,* he laid down his supreme moral injunction: "Realize yourself as an infinite whole." This can be done only by a conscious broadening of one's ends, recognizing that all finite ends are ultimately grounded in the Absolute, which swallows up all difference and all contradiction. The injunction means, then, "Realize yourself as the self-conscious member of an infinite whole by realizing that whole in yourself."

Considered in this fashion, the content of morality is afflicted by a certain vagueness which Bradley sought to correct by defining more specifically the boundaries of the intermediate whole of which selves are a part. These are the social institutions such as families, institutions, and states in terms of which one can realize one's larger self. One's specific duties are, then, prescribed by one's membership in such groups in Bradley's view, a position which he made quite clear in an essay in *Ethical Studies* entitled "My Station and Its Duties." The sort of moral conduct which he advocated was, in the main, the behavior expected by the society of which he is a member. An English child, for instance, will be not merely a member of a family, but a family having a certain position in an England of which it is a part. In Bradley's view, "a man's life with its moral duties is in the main filled up by his station in that system of wholes which the state is, and this, partly by its laws and institutions, and still more by its spirit, gives him the life which he does live and ought to live."

The extent to which this concept of ethics expressed the feelings of a highly stratified English society is suggested in W. S. Gilbert's libretto for the Gilbert and Sullivan opera *H.M.S. Pinafore,* which made its first appearance in 1878, two years after the publication of *Ethical Studies*. In a work the entire plot of which might be thought to hinge on "My Station and its Duties," Captain Corcoran, the commander of a British naval vessel, wants his daughter to marry Sir Joseph Porter, a First Lord of the Admiralty who has risen to that high post by doing the appropriate thing at the proper time at every stage of the ascent. Josephine, however, is enamoured of a common seaman, Ralph Rackstraw. Apprehended by her father in an attempt to elope with her lover, she gives an impassioned reply to her father's outraged objection that this "excellent crew, though foes they may thump any, are scarcely fit company, my daughter, for you." She sings, in company with Rackstraw:

> He humble, poor and lowly born,
> The meanest in the port division—
> The butt of epaulatted scorn—
> The mark of quarterdeck derision—
> Has dared to raise his wormy eyes
> Above the dust to which you'd mould him
> In Manhood's glorious form to rise.
> He is an Englishman—Behold him!

This attempt to expand the conception of Rackstraw's station strikes a responsive chord in the boatswain and the rest of the crew, who happily elaborate it.

> He is an Englishman!
> For he himself has said it,
> And its greatly to his credit,
> That he is an Englishman!
> For he might have been a Roosian,
> A French or Turk or Proosian,
> Or perhaps Itali-an!
> But in spite of all temptations
> To belong to other nations,
> He remains an Englishman!

The problem is not settled so easily, however, for the duties of station cannot be divorced from considerations of social position. Gilbert and Sullivan, mindful of this, achieved a happy ending only by arranging a discovery that Corcoran and Rackstraw were misplaced as babies, each taking the other's place. Corcoran thereupon becomes a common seaman and Rackstraw a captain. Since social usage permits a freer elevation through marriage for a woman than a man, Rackstraw is thus free to marry Josephine.

Bradley's Hegelianism cannot be fairly evaluated, of course, by taking such delightful buffoonery seriously, but it does provide an interesting example of the way philosophies in which all conflicts become swallowed up in an Absolute are often forced into an appeal to empirically based standards for ethics.

Other important British Neo-Hegelians were Bernard Bosanquet (1848-1923) and John Ellis McTaggart (1866-1925). Bosanquet contributed to the development of the coherence theory of truth—the contention that the criterion for the truth of a proposition lies not so much in its correspondence to a particular set of circumstances as in its coherence with a wider body of truths. McTaggart, while following the Hegelian logic and dialectic, denied the existence of an Absolute and advocated a spiritual pluralism.

In America, the idealistic philosophy of Josiah Royce (1855-1916) owed much of its content to British Hegelianism as well as to the direct influence of Hegel's own philosophy. Reality, in Royce's view, is ultimately one transcendent self—an all-knowing Logos—in which finite selves are included. Like other absolute idealists, he had some difficulty in formulating a ground for ethics which would be readily applicable to particular situations. His *Philosophy of Loyalty,* published in 1908, presented the formula "loyalty to loyalty" as the fundamental precept underlying all morality.

More strictly Hegelian were the members of the St. Louis School, so called because they were organized and had their meetings in that city. They adhered to the dialectical method and showed some interest in applying it to American history. In giving an account of the War Between the States, for example, they saw Sumter as thesis, Gettysburg as antithesis, and Appomatox as synthesis.

The Doctrine of Progress

The most widespread effect of Hegelian philosophy in the Western world was probably felt in the widespread acceptance during the nineteenth and early twentieth centuries of the doctrine of necessary and universal progress. The faith that the world is of such a nature that mankind must inevitably move onward and upward governed the outlook of many thoughtful of Europeans and Americans until it was dealt a serious and perhaps mortal blow by the wars of the twentieth century.

The philosophers of progress saw an ally in Charles Darwin, whose *Origin of Species* was interpreted as providing scientific support for their position. Herbert Spencer (1820-1903), however, was an evolutionist even before the publication of Darwin's work, advocating, as he did, the theory of Lamarck that characteristics acquired by members of a species in response to their environment can be passed on to their descendants. Philosophically, he was influenced by Schelling's view that life involves increasing differentiation. Spencer, an Englishman, had a grand design: to develop a philosophy that would explain the universe and all its processes, organic and inorganic, by the single unifying principle of evolution. To his mind, that principle was indissolubly linked with the idea of progress, and in the development of organisms from simplicity and homogeneity to complexity and heterogeneity, he saw a pattern which could, he believed, be applied to civilization. Social progress, he said, is not accidental, but necessary. "Instead of civilization being artificial, it is a part of nature; all of a piece with the development of the embryo or the unfolding of a flower. The modifications mankind have undergone, and are still undergoing, result from a law underlying the whole organic creation; and provided the human race continues, and the constitution of things remains the same, those modifications must end in completeness . . . so surely must man become perfect."

In his *First Principles,* the first volume of his *Synthetic Philosophy,* published in 1860, he expanded his conception of the evolutionary process, seen as a change from a condition of indefinite, incoherent homogeneity to one of definite, coherent heterogeneity, to include other features which he saw as being universally characteristic of matter and motion. Biology, sociology, psychology, and ethics were all encompassed by the law of evolution. Like Hegel, he had a vision of a unified system of thought which would embrace all knowledge, but knowledge, he said, can be had only of what is finite and limited. To think of finite things, though, we must relate them to one another and to an Absolute—a single reality underlying all phenomena. The Absolute, though its existence can be acknowledged by religion and science, is beyond all description and cannot, in the strict sense, be known. Religion attempts to give us some conception of it in the form of symbols, but cannot diminish the ultimate mystery. In our experience, the Absolute reveals itself under the forms of mind and matter.

In ethics, Spencer applied his evolutionary philosophy to an essentially hedonistic point of view. The good is defined in terms of the pleasurable, but a scientific study such as that advocated in his *Principles of Ethics* (1879) will show that the hedonic calculus properly conceived is not a short-term operation but rather one which aims at prolonging and enriching lives for the individual and for present and future society. The evolutionary process aims at a society in which justice and beneficence go hand in hand and in which a universal and reciprocal altruism will lead to a peaceful world in which the happiness of individuals will be assured.

The Rise of Marxism

By far the most visible effects of Hegelian thought in the modern world are those attributable to the inverted version of his philosophy developed by Karl Heinrich Marx (1818-1883), a native of Trier, in Germany, where his father was a Jewish lawyer who became a Lutheran. In 1835 he went to the University of Bonn, where he studied law, but he transferred to the University of Berlin after a year and took up the study of philosophy. He took a doctoral degree at the University of Jena. Hegelianism was a dominant philosophy in Berlin during his college days, and Marx was a member of a group of young Hegelians. It was not long, though, before he was subjected to other influences, especially the writings of Ludwig Feuerbach (1804-1872). Feuerbach had, in effect, stood Hegel on his head by making matter rather than mind the fundamental reality underlying all historical processes. Hegel's dialectic and Feuerbach's dynamic materialism were the twin sources of Marx's subsequent philosophy.

He lived for a time in Paris, where he met Friedrich Engels, the son of a German textile manufacturer. Their encounter was the beginning of a long friendship which later resulted in their collaboration in the writing of the *Communist Manifesto.* Marx was forced to leave Paris and later Germany for his part in revolutionary activities. In 1849, he went to London, where, with a wife and children to support, he lived in wretched poverty in a two-room apartment, working from nine to seven in the reading room of the British Museum and continuing his work at night. Subsisting on a small income from articles written for the *New York Daily Tribune* and a bit of help from Engels, he wrote prodigiously and finally published the first volume of *Capital* in 1867. The second and third volumes were published in 1885 and 1894, after his death.

His aim in *Capital,* he said, was "to lay bare the economic law of motion of modern society." That law, he thought, is dialectical materialism. Past, present, and future history is, he claimed, divisible into five historical eras: the primitive communal, the slave, the feudal, the capitalist, and the socialist and communist epochs. Past cultures have generated changes which by dialectical necessity have brought an end to the social orders which produced them and resulted in new ones. The central character of any society resides in its economic structure, and "man's ideas, views, and conceptions, in one word, man's consciousness, changes with every change in the conditions of his material existence, in his social relations, and in his social life."

In every age, the dominant ideas of a society have been those of its ruling class, which has exploited the masses for its own benefit. The European feudal system rested on a military aristocracy which determined all the cultural values of the age. When the economic system that made the aristocracy possible underwent changes which could not be accommodated in the framework of the old order, the Middle Ages came to an end. Burghers—men of the cities who had previously belonged to the exploited classes—acquired wealth and power and, in time, became a new and more efficient ruling class, which stripped away the veil of illusion of the feudal system in favor of "naked, shameless, direct, and brutal exploitation." The reign of the bourgeoisie has produced, Marx said, an inferior and vulgar culture in which "freedom" means only the liberty of the bourgeoisie to exploit the proletariat by paying them poor wages and selling them expensive goods.

It is precisely this process, he held, however, which contains the seeds of destruction which, by the very nature of capitalism, especially since the Industrial Revolution, cannot be eradicated from the system. The actual value of a product, Marx thought, is directly dependent on the amount of labor added to the materials which go into its manufacture. However, the capitalistic system is based on profit, and in order to make a profit, it is necessary to sell the product at a price higher than that value. The difference, which Marx called "surplus value," goes to the capitalist. This fact is not necessarily due to any moral deficiency in members of the owning class. It is simply a "scientifically" ascertainable necessity of the dialectical process in economic history.

Since the bourgeois owners are dependent upon the proletarian laborers for their markets and the laborers are not paid enough to buy all the products, Marx argued, capitalism, while useful and perhaps necessary for the development of an industrialized society, must inevitably produce a condition in which the rich become richer and the poor poorer until, at last, the wretchedness of the masses will produce a situation in which the proletariat must take over the means of production. In view of the fact that the bourgeoisie will not relinquish power without a struggle, such a drastic alteration of the structure of the society must be accomplished by revolution. Marx avoided the fanatical cant of much of the later communist literature, but he himself advocated revolutionary activity in order to hasten the dialectical process and "shorten and lessen the birth pangs."

When the revolutionaries seize power, they will establish the "dictatorship of the proletariat," and devote themselves to the "liquidation of the bourgeoisie." This term, which has acquired such sinister connotations in the subsequent history of Marxism, did not, in his thought, necessarily mean the wanton murder of capitalists. It referred rather to the elimination of the owning class as an economic and political force and the termination of exploitation—the paying to laborers of less than the actual value of their labor. This "dictatorship" is a temporary phase, in which the entire structure of values in human society will undergo progressive alteration to produce the sort of human being who will be fitted for the final stages of history—the "withering away of the state" and the emergence of the pure Communism of the "classless society." When this occurs, man will have been transformed and the dialectic of history will have come to an end. The means of production will be in the hands of all for the benefit of all, and everyone will contribute to the common good. "From everyone according to his abilities, to everyone according to his needs" will no longer be just a slogan; it will have become a reality. Crime, depravity, degraded social customs, and degenerate art will have withered away along with the state, for they will have been freed from the economic inequities which produced them.

Revolutionary Marxists exploited and enhanced a considerable amount of unrest in the West in the late nineteenth and early twentieth centuries, but it is an irony of history that their greatest victories were gained not in the most highly industrialized societies which, in Marx's theory should have been ripe for it, but in less well developed ones that he presumably would have regarded as ripe for capitalism. Needless to say, those countries which have embraced Communism have not been able to achieve the final goals which Marx envisioned for his revolution and, in many ways, have found it necessary to move away from them. It may be suggested that the failures which they have encountered, along with many successes, are due in no small measure to some fundamental flaws in the basic philosophy. Perhaps human beings are not wholly conditioned by their economic history, but are, rather, free creators of physical, intellectual, aesthetic, moral and religious values which derive their authenticity from a higher source than their material environment.

Chapter 31

The Rise of Religious Liberalism

Religious Liberalism may be defined as the type of religion that was developed in Western Europe and America during the eighteenth and nineteenth centuries in response to the challenge posed by modern science, philosophy, and changing social conditions. Its effect was primarily among Protestants and Jews. Historical circumstances generally prevented its spread among Orthodox Christians and Moslems as well as in the other religions of the world until the middle of the twentieth century and, as we shall observe in the next chapter, its influence was blunted among Roman Catholics until the second Vatican Council (1962-1965).

The character of liberalism is indicated by the fact that the term is derived from the Latin word *liber,* "free." Religious Liberalism sprang directly from the Enlightenment, which Kant defined as "man's release from his self-incurred tutelage." Thus it represents a reexamination of religious beliefs and practices free from the restrictions of custom and authority, no matter how ancient or revered, and it maintains a spirit of autonomy and toleration. Those who have constructed the theology of Liberalism have sought to interpret their traditional faith, whether Christian or Jewish, in the light of modern thought. They have attempted to restate the essentials of religious truth in such a way as to preserve both its truth and values while at the same time eliminating the forms of ancient and medieval expression and practice that they have considered outmoded and unacceptable for modern believers.

Many of the leaders and events we have discussed in previous chapters were the sources that made the rise of religious Liberalism inevitable. The breakup of Catholic unity in the West brought about by the various movements of the Reformation led eventually to freedom and modification in religious interpretation. It is remarkable that literally thousands were burned at the stake, hanged, drowned, beheaded, drawn and quartered, and otherwise tortured simply for theological dissidence during the sixteenth and seventeenth centuries; yet by the eighteenth century freedom of opinion and expression became more and more commonplace in Western Europe and there was widespread teaching and publication of ideas that were both heretical and atheistic by traditional standards. The work of scientists such as Copernicus, Galileo, and Newton made it necessary for theologians to revise their views of heaven and earth and to rethink their opinions not only about the place of the earth in relation to the sun and the stars but also about the centrality of mankind in so vast a universe. Copernicus and his successors opened up new worlds in the heavens; Columbus and his followers discovered new worlds on the earth; and Luther and his fellow reformers made possible new paths for the spirit. Together they made necessary a revision of ancient and medieval theological assumptions and dogmas, and that revision eventually became what is known as religious Liberalism.

The beginnings of the revision may be seen in the marriage of the new philosophy with religion as early as the middle of the seventeenth century in the work of Descartes, the "Father of Modern Philosophy," and Lord Herbert of Cherbury (1583-1648), the "Father of Deism." We have noted above, in chapters 27 and 28, how Descartes and the rationalists who followed him initiated a method of inquiry and construction that rejected all authority except that of tested reason. In like manner, John Locke and those who followed him in the development of empiricism insisted that all true knowledge, including that of religion, is derived from experience and is limited by the ways of human perception and conception. The rationalists and empiricists were accompanied and followed by a host of influential thinkers, especially in England, France, and Germany, who raised serious questions concerning the teachings of traditional religion and often suggested radical changes in its form and content. Among these in England were John Tillotson (1630-1694), Archbishop of Canterbury, along with John Toland (1670-1722) and Matthew Tindal (1655-1733), both teachers at Oxford. In France the most famous of the skeptical *philosophes* was Voltaire (1694-1778), whose tart writings disturbed and entertained Europe for half a century. And in Germany the new thought was promoted by Frederick the Great of Prussia (1712-1786), Hermann Samuel Reimarus (1694-1768), Professor at Hamburg, and Gotthold Ephraim Lessing (1729-1781), philosopher and literary critic. Finally, we should recall the "Copernican revolution" of Kant, who attempted to reconcile rationalism and empiricism by turning to the subject as knower rather than to the object as known, thereby demonstrating the necessary limits of knowledge and delineating the only possible basis for knowledge, belief, and value.

Leading Liberal Thinkers

It is customary and probably correct to designate Friedrich Daniel Ernst Schleiermacher (1768-1834) as the "Father of Modern Theology.'' A Prussian pastor, professor, and theologian, he challenged the increasingly skeptical and secular culture of Europe to distinguish between the essential truth of the Christian faith, which he believed to be of eternal value, and the outworn dogmatic forms in which it had been transmitted and received. He preached and taught among the sophisticated circles of Berlin, where religion was considered a relic of ancient ignorance and faith in the progressive powers of human culture was unbounded. Yet, Schleiermacher combined a stubborn devotion to Christian Pietism, which he had absorbed as a youthful student in Moravian schools, with Platonic Idealism (he translated Plato's dialogues into German) and the pervasive atmosphere of romanticism that dominated the literature, music, art, and spirit of the age.

Schleiermacher's first publication was *On Religion: Speeches Addressed to Its Cultured Despisers*. It was a ringing apology for the Christian faith that became immensely effective and popular. It is still in print and widely read. Soon afterward he published a second work of similar character, *The Soliloquies,* which was more personal and appealed for individual commitment and development under the guidelines of Christian faith and romantic naturalism. The success of these writings led the young preacher into an academic career, first at Halle and later at the new University of Berlin, where he lectured as a colleague of Hegel in a powerful counterpoint. His greatest contribution to the new Christian theology was his monumental *The Christian Faith,* in which he attempted to reconstruct theology on the foundation of experience rather than on a given propositional revelation mediated through the Scriptures or the traditions of the Church. He intended to remain genuinely Christian in his theology, and he emphasized the immediate, intuitive experience of God made possible by the redemptive work of Jesus of Nazareth. He spoke in the language of psychology and philosophy, and even of poetry, rather than in the traditional terms of dogmatic, creedal theology. Nevertheless, he wrote of the *Christian* faith, and his views of God and redemption were clearly Christo-centric and derived from the teachings of the New Testament.

Another leader of early Christian Liberalism was Albrecht Ritschl (1822-1889), who unintentionally founded a ''school'' of theology that dominated German Protestantism until World War I and exercised widespread influence in Britain and America as well. Like Schleiermacher, Ritschl was the son of a German Protestant minister and attended several German universities. He began his teaching career at Bonn in 1846 but spent most of his adult life in the theological faculty at Göttingen. His major publication, the fruit of his teaching career, was the three-volume work entitled *The Christian Doctrine of Justification and Reconciliation*. The very title itself indicated Ritschl's primary concern with the Christian view of redemption, both individual and social, and with the practical, moral, and effective power of that redemption.

Ritschl agreed with Schleiermacher that the faith must be expressed in terms consonant with modern thought. He also agreed that experience is both the basis and the goal of Christianity. However, he rejected the older theologian's emphasis on "Christian consciousness" and "feeling" because he perceived them to be dangerously subjective and potentially empty of practical, moral result. He was always primarily interested in history and practicality. For that reason he built his theology on the work and teachings of the historical Jesus found in the Gospels rather than on Schleiermacher's intuitive, mystical experience.

The key to Ritschl's theology was his concept of "value judgment." That phrase meant for him the commitment made by the faithful Christian to the biblical Jesus Christ, whose offer of forgiveness and reconciliation to God are accepted because he has the value of God to faith and thus should be obeyed in the world. Ritschl followed Kant as modified by the philosopher Lotze in rejecting metaphysics with its supposed analysis of a noumenal realm. He wished to live by faith as taught by Jesus, claiming to know only the phenomenal world of sensation and history. He was satisfied to be occupied with spreading the Kingdom of God in the world of mankind, emphasizing the moral and social aspects of the Gospel while allowing the mysteries to remain so.

A third prominent creator of Protestant Liberalism was Adolf von Harnack (1851-1930), an acknowledged disciple of "the Ritschlian school." He was born in Estonia, the son of a strict Lutheran professor of theology. He was educated at Erlangen and Leipzig to serve the Lutheran Church and began his brilliant teaching career at the latter. After holding professorships at Geissen and Marburg he began a distinguished service at Berlin in 1888 where he remained until his death during the difficult days following the defeat of imperial Germany.

Like his mentor, Ritschl, Harnack was primarily a historian, but even more so. He was a historian in the sense that he eschewed metaphysics in favor of a fundamental emphasis on the Jesus of the Gospels, and also in the sense that he sought to show that Christianity, like all religions, is a historical phenomenon that has been subject to historical forces and conditions and is thus subject to change in both form and expression. The normative essence of Christianity for him, therefore, was revealed in the life and teachings of Jesus of Nazareth; however, it has been affected throughout its long existence by various cultural forces, especially by Hellenism and the rationalist tradition flowing from that source, and the eternal essence should not be confused with any historical or cultural form or manifestation. Hence, according to Harnack, the task of the theologian and, indeed, of every Christian, is to know and be faithful to the Jesus of the Gospels, but it is also necessary to accommodate Christian truth to the knowledge and needs of the day.

Harnack's major works express these basic ideas clearly and in great detail. He was a prolific writer as well as an active churchman, publishing sixteen hundred books, monographs, and articles! His most significant works were the monumental seven-volume *History of Dogma;* a definitive study on *Marcion; The Mission and Expansion of Christianity;* and the unusually popular and controversial *What Is Christianity?* The first of these major writings used Hegelian categories to show the creative power exercised on primitive Christianity, the religion of Jesus, by its use of and adjustment to the Hellenistic culture of the ancient world. Harnack did not mean to denigrate the Hellenistic influence or any other historical formation. He was no simplistic "primitivist" wishing to return to the ideas and forms of first-century Palestinian Christianity. Rather, he wished to demonstrate that Christianity must be judged by its norm in the life and teachings of Jesus and at the same time must be expected to change its form in every age. His *History of Dogma* demonstrates both truths.

Harnack's standing as the archetypal liberal was perhaps best demonstrated by his famous *What is Christianity?* In that work he attempted to describe what he considered to be the quintessence of the Christian faith, taught by Jesus and normative for every historical expression. The true Gospel, he believed, may be expressed in three themes, each of which contains the whole: "Firstly, the kingdom of God and its coming. Secondly, God the Father and the infinite value of the human soul. Thirdly, the higher righteousness and the commandment of love" *(What Is Christianity?* p. 38).

A great many American students went to Germany during the late nineteenth and early twentieth centuries to study under the new theologians there, especially those in the Schleiermacher-Ritschl-Harnack tradition. Many others were influenced by reading the publications of the radical thinkers who were creating the new Liberalism. None of them was more significant than Walter Rauschenbusch (1861-1918), an American Baptist whose father was a professor at Rochester Theological Seminary. After graduating from the University of Rochester and the Rochester Seminary, young Rauschenbusch studied in Germany before serving for eleven years as pastor of a Baptist church near the slums of New York City, where he gained first-hand experience with the poverty, crime, and exploitation of the people in the area called "Hell's Kitchen."

In 1897 Walter Rauschenbusch began a relatively brief but influential career as Professor of Church History at the Rochester Seminary. Although he was by vocation and training a church historian, most of his work and writings were concerned with social issues, with the ethical aspects of the Gospel. He published three major books, all advocating a new interpretation and application of the Christian faith that would deal primarily with the moral problems brought about by modern life and the industrial age: *Christianity and the Social Crisis* (1907), *Christianizing the Social Order* (1912), and *A Theology for the Social Gospel* (1917). They were hard-hitting books that called on Christians to take seriously the moral teachings of Jesus that underlie his central theme of the Kingdom of God. Rauschenbusch's basic theology was not radically different from orthodox Protestantism, but his new emphasis on social issues became his interpretive principle that caused many to believe he had departed from the historic faith in some areas. He became known as "the father of the Social Gospel" movement, and his influence has resulted in many of the social and political reforms that have marked America since the great depression of the 1930's.

There were, of course, scores of other outstanding liberal theologians during the nineteenth and early twentieth centuries who contributed to the full development of Christian Liberalism. They did their work for the most part in Germany, Britain, America, and Scandinavia, though there were a few in other nations as well. Together they were the most notable Protestant scholars during the century and a half before the first World War. However, the four we have discussed so briefly—Schleiermacher, Ritschl, Harnack, and Rauschenbusch—are good representatives of the thinking of them all.

One especially significant aspect of liberal thought must be noted here because of its specific and lasting emphasis: the development of a new historical and literary criticism of the Scriptures and its particular concern with the historical Jesus. We have observed that one of the significant aspects of the Renaissance was the rise of a new critical interest in ancient literature, seen in the work of Lorenzo Valla of Florence and Erasmus of Rotterdam, among others. The central place given to the authority of Scripture by the Reformers also contributed to the development. The new approach appeared during the seventeenth century in the questions raised about the authority and accuracy of the Bible by such diverse figures as Thomas Hobbes, Benedict Spinoza, Richard Simon,

Richard Bentley, and Jean Astruc, the last a physician at the court of France.

The movement as such may be said to have begun with the unpublished work of Hermann Samuel Reimarus (1694-1768), a rationalist Professor of Oriental Languages at the University of Hamburg. Parts of his writings were published after his death by the German philosopher Lessing, librarian at Wolffenbüttel, who claimed they were anonymous fragments found in the library of the Duke of Brunswick. The materials, especially one entitled "On the Aim of Jesus and His Disciples," questioned the historical accuracy of the Gospels and raised doubts concerning the traditional understanding of the life and teachings of Jesus. An immediate storm of protest ensued from conservative churchmen, but many scholars followed the lead of Reimarus and began to write new interpretations of the Gospels in the light of modern scientific and philosophical views. One of the most famous was David Friedrich Strauss (1808-1874), a disciple of Hegel who was for three years a lecturer in philosophy at the University of Tübingen. In 1835 he published a two-volume work entitled *Life of Jesus, a Critical Treatment* which ruined his academic career but made him immediately known throughout Germany. In the book Strauss attempted to divest the Gospels of their mythological, pre-scientific forms and to show instead that Jesus should be understood as a mysterious, apocalyptic first-century teacher who remains largely inaccessible to historical investigation.

A flood of "lives of Jesus" followed that of Strauss, some more radical than others but all attempting to solve the problem of the historical Jesus and to describe the ancient figure in modern terms. Two basic questions for theology emerged: (1) how dependable are the Gospels, indeed the whole New Testament, as sources for a knowledge of the historical Jesus? (2) What is the essential relation in Christianity between faith and history? The long discussion among Protestant scholars, especially in Germany, reached its first summation in 1906 with the publication of Albert Schweitzer's classic, *The Quest of the Historical Jesus.* In that work Schweitzer reviewed the whole process from Strauss to his own time and pronounced the search a noble failure. He concluded: "The Jesus of Nazareth who came forward publicly as the Messiah, who preached the ethic of the Kingdom of God, who founded the Kingdom of Heaven on earth, and died to give His final work its final consecration, never had any existence. He is a figure designed by rationalism, endowed with life by liberalism, and clothed by modern theology in an historical garb. . . . The historical Jesus will be to our own time a stranger and an enigma. . . . He passes by our time and returns to his own'' *(The Quest of the Historical Jesus,* pp. 398-399). The new Liberalism began to be accused of being, among other faults, too subjective and of attempting to project nineteenth and twentieth century idealism backward into the times of the origin of Christianity, even into the person of Jesus himself. Some, especially Søren Kierkegaard, began to argue that faith does not depend upon historical accuracy, in any case.

Leading Principles of Liberalism

This brief survey of the rise of theological Liberalism may be profitably concluded with a list of some of the major principles that have characterized it, recognizing at the same time that by its very nature Liberalism involves variations of opinion.

1. One mark of liberal thought has been its acceptance of modern scientific discoveries and theories. It has not been hesitant to accept the astronomy of Copernicus and his successors, the physics of Newton and his followers, or the evolutionary hypotheses of Darwin and those who have accepted and modified his understanding of the development of all animals, including human beings. Liberals have tried to preserve the essential teachings and values of the Bible while at the same time admitting its historical conditioning and antiquarian world-view. This attempt has frequently led to a precarious walking of a tight-rope of faith between spiritual and moral values on the one side and the pitfalls of agnostic naturalism on the other.

2. Undergirding its openness to modern science is Liberalism's use of the method and authority of reason. This has meant the rejection of all traditional authorities, especially the historic teachings of the Church and the Scriptures, except where they are not contrary to reason. Liberalism has thereby questioned the ancient creedal formulations, sought their reinterpretation or revision, and thus found it necessary to reconstruct theology in terms more compatible with modern science, philosophy, and psychology. The miracles and apparent historical inaccuracies of the Bible have usually been dismissed out of hand. Special revelation has been rejected in favor of an appeal to the general truths of religion which are thought to be accessible to the universal processes of reason.

3. Christian Liberalism has been characterized by a fundamental belief in the natural, historical, and moral progress and the inevitable perfectibility of mankind. This view has its roots as far back as the idealistic philosophy of Socrates and Plato with its teaching that all human souls are eternal by nature, having fallen from a previous pristine state of goodness and truth, whence came the ideas innate in every human that can be elicited by the process of recollection. That ancient teaching be-

came a basic element of Neoplatonism, with its doctrine of emanation, and received its powerful and pregnant formulation in the vast system of Hegel (see chapter 30). According to this morally optimistic assessment, human beings are parts of a whole cosmic process of unfolding progress toward the fulfillment of the ideal. Though there are retrogressions along the way, the overcoming of all faults and the unity of all things are ultimately inevitable because of the nature of Being itself. This philosophy received visible expression in the joyful expectations of many Western Christians at the beginning of the twentieth century that the "Christian century" was dawning, bringing fulfillment to the promise of the inevitable establishment on earth of the Kingdom of God.

4. The liberal theology tended to dismiss all dogma as outmoded and divisive and thus to reduce Christianity to its social and moral essentials. As we have seen in the teachings of many of the nineteenth-century creators of Liberalism, there was a frequent rejection of metaphysics and a parallel disdain for all forms of other-worldliness in religion. Jesus was interpreted as a spiritual and ethical teacher among the first-century Jews, perhaps the greatest of all prophets and even superior to all teachers of history; but the dogmas of his deity and two natures, of his atoning death and supernatural resurrection, were discounted as outmoded and expendable. Some taught that the moral teachings of the Hebrew prophets and of Jesus, especially those summarized in the Sermon on the Mount, are the core of the Bible and that most of the remainder might be dismissed as irrelevant to modern times. The same process of reductionism and elimination also applied, of course, to such church practices as sacraments, intercessory prayer, asceticism and celibacy, and the whole structure of a hierarchical priesthood.

Another side of this reductionist attitude was its effect on the understanding and practice of Christian missions and the parallel relation to other religions. Missionary activity by Christians in other cultures and among believers in other religions began to be motivated less by a desire for a conversion and more by intentions to serve. Educational activities, medical facilities, civilizing influences, peace initiatives, and social services of many kinds began to occupy the efforts of the churches in foreign lands in place of the historic efforts to evangelize and to plant Western-type churches. There was a frequently expressed opinion that all religions are expressions of the general truths and moral aspirations of seeking humanity, with no one having a monopoly on truth or goodness.

5. A final mark of liberal Christianity that should be noted here is its ecumenical spirit and activity. The ecumenical movement is the rec-

ognition of a basic unity in faith and intention among all Christian bodies of the world and the resultant attempt to encourage toleration, cooperation, and organizational unity among them. It is an internal spirit within Christendom matching the more liberal and accepting attitude toward the other religions of the world. Just as Liberalism in theology was largely a development among Protestants in the nineteenth and early twentieth centuries, so the ecumenical movement was restricted for the most part to the mainline Protestant denominations. The Orthodox and Roman Churches were in most respects unaffected by the growing movement, and the Roman Church remained aloof and officially hostile until the Second Vatican Council (1962-65). Nevertheless, ecumenical attitudes and interest progressed during the nineteenth century until many positive results were accomplished by the beginning of the twentieth, culminating in the great international missionary conference at Edinburgh, Scotland, in 1910. Out of that meeting of leaders representing most of the Protestant denominations grew the Faith and Order and the Life and Work movements which, in turn, finally led to the establishment of the World Council of Churches in 1948. Since then the Orthodox Churches have joined the movement, and the Roman Church has abandoned its triumphalist isolation and begun to cooperate with its "separated brethren."

Reactions to Liberalism

The twentieth century has not been kind to the theology and growth of Christian Liberalism. The moral ambivalence of science and the intractibility of political and social problems in the world have raised serious questions concerning Liberalism's moral optimism and the messianic expectations of rationalistic science. A series of frightening calamities has occurred during the whole century, beginning with the First World War, followed by the great depression and then by the Second World War, leaving the entire world in a condition of unparalleled anxiety created by the inescapable threat of total extinction by the atomic power that human beings hold in their own hands. The anticipated "Christian century" has become the most violent and dangerous time in recorded history, and the greatest evils have arisen among the nations that were thought to be the most civilized, moral, and Christian. Optimism and confidence have become increasingly scarce, and Liberalism has appeared to be morally bankrupt and spiritually powerless.

The initial reaction to theological Liberalism came, as would be expected, from the defenders of traditional orthodoxy. We shall observe in the next chapter how the Roman Church firmly rejected the ideas of

Liberalism from the beginning and silenced the brave voices that dared challenge the new dogmas and the old traditions of the Church. Protestantism lacked the central organization and the authoritative power to deal so effectively with modernism, but there were many among all the denominations who did their best to defend the faith "once for all delivered" (Jude 3). Andrew D. White, one-time Ambassador to Czarist Russia and a founder of Cornell University, wrote a famous two-volume work, *A History of the Warfare of Science with Theology in Christendom* (1894), that thoroughly documents the long struggle. Conservative theologians were disturbed especially by the rising tide of biblical criticism and by the anthropological implications of the new Darwinism. The result was the formulation, during the first decades of the twentieth century of a theology generally designated as "Fundamentalism." The term was apparently derived from a series of pamphlets that were published under that title and given world-wide distribution.

Given the pluralism of most predominantly Protestant nations and the democratic toleration required in both politics and religion, many areas of theological belief were agreed to be variable and negotiable. Such matters as the nature of baptism and the organization of the churches vary without divisive challenge. However, Fundamentalism has been characterized by a number of positions that make it easily identifiable. These teachings are claimed to be essential and cannot be compromised, and these are the *sine qua non* "fundamentals." They usually include, first of all, a high view of the Bible that holds it to be divinely inspired, inerrant in all that it treats and the sole authority for all faith and practice. The defense of the Bible against all doubts is the first line of defense.

The rest of "the fundamentals" flow from the teachings of the Scriptures and are guaranteed by those sources. First, there is a *necessary doctrinal orthodoxy* that includes belief in the full deity of Christ; the historical and biological fact of the virgin birth of Jesus; the substitutionary, atoning death of Christ on the cross; the actual, bodily resurrection of Christ three days after his death and burial as well as the glorious resurrection of all believers at the end of history; and the premillenial return of Christ, culminating in the conquest of evil and a final judgment with rewards for the righteous and eternal punishment for the unredeemed. Acceptance of these doctrines is said to be necessary both because they are taught by the Bible and because salvation is by faith, which is defined as belief in revealed truth.

Other less rigidly held "fundamentals" usually consist of belief in the hopeless depravity of all mankind apart from the grace made available through Christ, the necessity of a rebirth of the soul by the power of God's grace through faith, and moral behavior according to a strict standard of legalistic ethics that emphasizes individual righteousness rather than social concern.

The struggle between Liberalism and Fundamentalism has continued throughout the twentieth century and shows no sign of abating. However, a new movement arose in European Protestantism at the end of the First World War that offered a third alternative. It has been called by various names but the most common one is Neo-Orthodoxy. Its first exponent was Karl Barth, a Swiss-born and German-educated pastor in a small town near Basel who, in 1918, having become disillusioned with the liberal theology in which he had been educated, found in the Bible "a strange new world." He soon published a revolutionary commentary on Paul's Letter to the Romans that made him instantly famous throughout war-devastated Europe.

Barth attacked the optimistic, man-centered theology then dominant in most of the Protestant churches, and he was soon joined by many colleagues in both Europe and America who began to develop a new theology that was Bible-centered and yet akin to both liberal and conservative views. The Neo-Orthodox theologians emphasized sin and judgment as well as grace and redemption. They did not reject modern science or the literary criticism of the Bible but they refused to accept the easy optimism of the old Liberalism. Their theology was Christocentric; at the same time it demanded social action by the professed followers of Christ. Neo-Orthodoxy lost some of its newness and appeal after the Second World War, but it remains a viable option for those who are dissatisfied with either the rigidity and obscurantism of traditional theology or the pale Liberalism that seemed to abandon much of the core of Christian teaching.

Chapter 32

Roman Catholicism and Modernity

The Roman Catholic Church was severely wounded by the Protestant Reformation. Many of the German states were lost to the Church along with parts of the Low Countries, Switzerland, Austria, Hungary, and Poland. England, Scotland and all of Scandinavia became entirely Protestant, and there were widespread disaffections in France as well. Reaction was necessary and inevitable. The various efforts toward reform "in head and members" that had borne such limited fruit during the fourteenth and fifteenth centuries now took on a new urgency. One of the chief results was the remarkable recovery that is often called by historians the Counter Reformation.

One of the earliest manifestations of the so-called Counter Reformation may be seen in the work of Ignatius of Loyola (1491-1551) who, in 1540, secured the approval of Pope Paul III to found the Society of Jesus in an effort both to improve discipline in the Church and to lead the struggle against heretics and pagans. Loyola was a Basque nobleman who spent his early years as a soldier until he was permanently crippled in the battle of Pamplona in 1521. During a lengthy convalescence from his wounds Loyola experienced mystical visions and dedicated himself to becoming henceforth a soldier of Christ. In 1534 he gathered a company of sworn followers in Paris and they became the core of what was to become the Society of Jesus, usually known as the Jesuits. Loyola himself spent the remainder of his life in a strong crusade for the reform and expansion of the Church. Obedience was the watchword of the order and missions became its world-wide task. Loyola wrote the *Spiritual Exercises,* a powerful work on personal devotion and strict loyalty that advocated absolute obedience to the teachings of the Church, with special concern for the defense of the papacy. The Jesuits have remained through subsequent history one of the strongest forces in the Church, giving particular emphasis to discipline, education, and missions. Francis Xavier, a member of the original company, is one of the greatest examples of successful Catholic missions in the newly opened Eastern world.

Perhaps the most significant aspect of the Counter Reformation was the work of the Council of Trent (1545-1563). There had been demands for a new council since the failure of the reforming councils of Constance and Florence in the fifteenth century and the brief Fifth Lateran Council early in the sixteenth century, just prior to the Reformation. However, the continuing struggles between the papacy and the Holy Roman Empire under Charles V caused the meeting to be delayed until it was finally convened by Pope Paul III in Trent, a little town in northern Italy but technically within the Empire. The council held twenty-five sessions, meeting intermittently during three periods: 1545-47, 1547-49 (at Bologna), and 1562-63. All were dominated by the papal-controlled Italian majority.

Although a few Protestants attended the early sessions, the council as a whole displayed a clear rejection of Protestant theology and a hardened reaffirmation of traditional teachings. The basic Protestant doctrine that justification is by faith alone, grounded on the imputed righteousness of Christ into the believer, was repudiated in favor of the scholastic definition that justification results from faith formed by the good works of an acquired or inherent righteousness. The authority of Scripture alone was denied, although the study of the Scriptures was emphasized and encouraged; rather, authority was professed to be in both the Scriptures and in the ''unwritten traditions'' handed down from the orthodox Fathers and the teachings of the Church which ''alone has the right to determine the true sense and interpretation of Scripture.'' The seven sacraments were confirmed, including the power of the Church to grant indulgences; and the doctrines of purgatory, transubstantiation, and masses for the dead, as well as the withholding of the cup from the laity and the liturgical use of Latin were all reaffirmed and required. On the other hand, the council enacted many reforms in the practices of the Church. Bishops were limited to one diocese and required to live within it. The establishment of a seminary for the better education of priests in every diocese without a university was enjoined, and priests were required henceforth to be faithful preachers of the Gospel and exemplary shepherds of souls. The religious orders were to be more closely supervised, and an index of prohibited books was approved. In sum, the council adopted a firmly negative position against Protestant doctrine but took important steps toward the practical reforms in the Church that had been demanded for centuries by the morally offended.

Just as the Roman Catholic Church refused to accept the proposed theological modifications demanded by the Reformers in the sixteenth century, so it also fought against the new ideas and discoveries that arose among scientists and philosophers in the seventeenth, eighteenth, and nineteenth centuries. Liberalism developed as a dominant force among

Protestants as they attempted to adjust their religious faith to modern discoveries, but the Roman Church held firmly to its ancient and medieval practices and theology.

The most famous example of the Church's extreme conservatism is the case of Galileo, noted in chapter 19, above. The theories of Copernicus had already been condemned as heresy, but when Galileo began to show that the ancient, Ptolemaic astronomy was demonstrably false and that the heavenly bodies, including the earth, do indeed revolve around the sun, he was ordered to stand trial before the Roman Inquisition. The heresy-hunting Cardinal Bellarmine, chief theologian of the Church, argued that "mathematical hypotheses" have nothing to do with physical reality and that Galileo could neither "hold nor defend" such dangerous doctrines. Supported by his observations through the recently invented telescope and his many experimental proofs, however, Galileo contended that "the Book of Nature is written in mathematical characters." In June, 1633, he was convicted of heresy and ordered to recant. He recited the prescribed formula with obvious reluctance and was required to live under house arrest for the remainder of his life. The Church continued successfully to oppose challenges to its dogmatic positions for the following three centuries.

Politics and Catholicism in France

The violence and rationalism of the French Revolution not only overthrew the autocratic and wealthy monarchy; it also wrecked the power of the Roman Catholic Church in France so thoroughly that it has never completely recovered. During the decade following 1789, the new leaders of France appropriated church lands for the state, pledged religious liberty, used French arms to make Rome a republic, and brought the pope to France as a prisoner. The Jacobin leaders even sought to wipe out Christianity in favor of a natural, rational religion. Nevertheless, during his brief reign, Napoleon, recognizing that a vast majority of the French people were at least nominal Catholics, attempted to restore some of the damage by making tentative peace with the papacy while taking care to retain control of the Church by the state. The result was a resurgence of Catholic strength in France during and following the Napoleonic period, a resurgence based on both increased clerical dependence on the papacy and on the rising tide of romanticism as the spirit of the age. That new loyalty to Rome was called Ultramontanism—"beyond the mountains"—a strengthening of Church ties to the Italian papacy for the remainder of the century.

The spirit of loyalty to Christianity, and to Catholicism in particular, on the basis of the ideals of romanticism was evident in the work of François René, Vicomte de Chateaubriand (1768-1848). In 1802 he published *Génie du Christianisme,* a popular and influential apology for the Christian faith in many ways similar to Schleiermacher's *Speeches on Religion,* which had been published in Germany just three years earlier. Chateaubriand opposed the rationalism of the eighteenth century and the French Revolution, choosing instead to defend Christianity on the grounds of aesthetics and history. He argued that the beauty and truth of Western civilization were derived from historic Christianity and that Roman Catholicism had been its channel and guardian. Adopting the spirit of romanticism, he claimed that the Catholic faith is the symbol and fulfillment of the greatest human aspiration.

The greatest exponent of Ultramontanism was Joseph Marie, Comte de Maistre (1753-1821). The excesses of the Revolution caused him to react against both intellectual rationalism and political liberalism. He began to support the Catholic Church as the custodian and guarantor of personal and social stability, and, in his powerful book of 1829, *Du Pape,* he defended both monarchy and papacy. He claimed, further, that since the pope is the universal sovereign he is supreme over all monarchs and his decisions are, indeed, infallible. De Maistre's teachings were primary sources of the soon-to-be promulgated dogma of papal infallibility (1870) as well as of the long-standing contest in Europe between clericalism and its political opponents.

Another French Catholic advocate of traditionalism was Hugues Félicité Robert de Lamennais (1782-1854), although later in life he became a leader of the liberal opposition. His *Essai sur l'indifférence en matière de religion* (1817) was immensely popular and led many to return to the Church. He believed that mankind suffers from an uncertainty and meaninglessness from which no escape can be found from within. Security and peace can come only from general reason or universal consent which cannot be produced by the individual search. That way leads to anxiety and anarchy. Rather, truth and peace may be found in the *sens commune* which is provided most perfectly in the Catholic Church with its dependable testimony and long tradition of truth and experience.

The Rise of Liberal Catholicism

Nevertheless, the acids of modernity that so thoroughly eroded orthodox Protestant theology in the nineteenth century to form Liberalism could not be prevented form seeping into Catholic thought also. That process may have begun in the work of Lamennais himself. In 1829 he published *Les progrès de la révolution et de la guerre contre l' église* in which he proposed an Ultramontanism different from that of De Maistre. He argued that the papacy should not be allied with the state and its kings or emperors but rather with the people, supporting their ideals of liberty, equality, and fraternity. He also published a newspaper, *L'Avenir,* which advocated the separation of church and state, freedom of thought, and freedom of the press. Lamennais was persuaded that if the people were free they would choose the Catholic Church which he, like Chateaubriand, believed to be the depository of truth and security.

Unfortunately for Lamennais and those who followed him, the bishops of France did not agree with his liberal optimism. His newspaper was prohibited. When he appealed to Rome, Pope Gregory XVI, a reactionary in his views of modern social and political ideas, responded with the encyclical *Mirari vos* (1832) which firmly condemned *L'Avenir,* calling its liberal teachings "absurd" and "perverse." It was the first major defeat for Roman Catholic Modernism, but there would soon be many others.

We should note that the struggle between the Church and modern thought, beginning with the Reformation and continuing with the rise of modern philosophy and science, was primarily political in France and Italy but fundamentally religious in Germany, England, and other parts of northern Europe. The liberal theology that developed in Germany (cf. chapter 31) was largely among Protestants, but it began to appear also in Catholic education. Two prominent examples may be seen in the work of J. A. Möhler (1796-1838), a Catholic Professor at Tübingen who was strongly influenced by Schleiermacher, and in that of Johann Joseph Ignaz von Döllinger (1799-1890), distinguished church historian at the University of Munich. Döllinger led in the unauthorized meeting of a Congress of Catholic Scholars in Munich in 1863. In an address to the Congress he denounced scholasticism and called for an unimpeded investigation of the history of dogma, free from the Holy Office and the Index. He was ultimately excommunicated but refused to promote a schism; however, his sympathizers separated from the Roman Church after the first Vatican Church promulgated the dogma of papal infallibility, the supreme triumph of Ultramontanism. The Old Catholic Church was formed in an attempt to restore the Church to its supposed prescholastic purity, and the group continues to exist in central Europe to this day.

Pope Gregory XVI, who had condemned Lamennais and his followers for their liberal ideas, was succeeded by Pius IX (1846-1878), during whose reign Ultramontanism reached its highest success but also, at the end, began a rapid decline. Three significant events occurred that signaled the triumph of papal power against the threat of modern thought. First, in 1854, Pius proclaimed the dogma of the immaculate conception of the Virgin Mary, a teaching that had no Scriptural basis but had been debated and ardently supported through many centuries of tradition. The dogma declared that the Virgin was protected from taint of original sin by a special miracle of God even when she was conceived in her mother's womb. With the papal bull of proclamation the dogma became a necessary article of faith and to question it is to "have suffered shipwreck concerning the faith."

Ten years later, Pope Pius IX issued an encyclical that included the infamous "Syllabus of Errors." That document listed the specific opinions of modern thought that the Church opposed, condemning them as errors that ought not to be accepted. These included not only atheism, rationalism, socialism, communism, and naturalism, but also Protestantism, secular education, the separation of church and state, and freedom of religion and the press. The list of errors concluded with the condemnation of belief "that the Roman pontiff can, and ought to, reconcile himself to, and agree with, progress, liberalism, and modern civilization." The Syllabus was not only a sweeping rejection of attempts to liberalize Catholic thought; it also caused severe shock and embarrassment to many thoughtful members of the Church.

However, Pius IX and his conservative supporters were not finished with their intent to defeat liberalism once and for all. The final blow came when the pope called a council to meet at the Vatican in 1870. The purpose was to carry on the work of Trent, which had defined church theology in opposition to Protestantism. Now the plan was to clarify the nature and authority of the Church. The Ultramontanists took charge of the council from the beginning and, on July 18, 1870, adopted the long-debated dogma of papal infallibility. There was strong opposition to the action, led by Ignaz Döllinger of Munich, but the final vote for the dogma, taken in St. Peter's under a severe thunderstorm, was 533 to 2. The claim now was "that the Roman Pontiff, when he speaks *ex cathedra* . . . is endowed with that infallibility, which the Divine Redeemer has willed that His Church—in defining doctrine concerning faith and moral—should be equipped . . . " Many interpreted the dogma to mean that no more ecumenical councils would ever be needed; the pope alone could define doctrine and govern the Church. Further, a major impediment was erected against future possibilities for reconciliation and reunion with the Orthodox or Protestants, since they would find it especially difficult to accept papal infallibility.

Nevertheless, apparent total victory against all forms of liberalism soon turned to bitter ashes. The unification of the many states of Italy had been progressing for more than a decade and, on September 20, 1870, Victor Emmanuel II, king of Sardinia, captured Rome and annexed the remaining papal states into the unified Kingdom of Italy. The Pope was left a sovereign over only the small acreage of Vatican City, declaring himself a "prisoner of the Vatican," where he remained without appreciable civil authority for the future. Ecclesiastical power had been won, but political authority was greatly eroded.

The Catholic Rejection of Modernism

It is apparently impossible to defeat a cultural movement or ideology with institutional power, much less with military force. For that reason, though liberalism in theology was overcome repeatedly by the Roman Church during most of the nineteenth century, the spirit of freedom, inquiry, and criticism continued to reappear. It arose with renewed vigor during the two decades following 1890, this time commonly designated "Modernism," only to be crushed again by papal action after the turn of the century.

The victorious Ultramontanist Pope Pius IX was followed by Leo XIII (1878-1903), who, although certainly not a liberal, appeared much more open to modern thought than his predecessor. He sought in many ways to accept the new democracies with their civil freedoms, and he was willing to condone modern scholarship and research. He even named the English Catholic convert John Henry Newman a Cardinal of the Church in spite of the fact that he was suspected of liberal tendencies because of his books, *Grammar of Assent* and *Essay on the Development of Christian Doctrine*. Such actions and attitudes brought new hope for freedom and change among scholars, especially in France, where liberal ideas had been strong and anti-clericalism rampant since the Revolution. The Abbé Louis Duchêsne (1843-1922) was Professor of Church History at the Catholic University of Paris for twenty years following 1877. He looked with favor on the scholarly development of science and history, influencing a large number of young students before his dismissal from the University. One of his disciples was Alfred Loisy (1857-1949), destined to become a major leader in the Modernist controversies as well as a renowned biblical scholar.

Loisy was a young priest whose bishop recognized his intellectual abilities and sent him to study in Paris where he fell under the influence of Duchêsne. He became a lecturer at the Institut Catholique in 1881 but at the same time began to attend the classes of the famous Ernest Renan at the Collège de France. Renan was an extremely liberal rationalist whose *Vie de Jesus* was in the Strauss tradition, interpreting the story of Jesus in the Gospels as a great romantic novel, controlled by modern thought. Loisy did not agree completely with Renan, of course, but became convinced that the essential truth of the Catholic faith can and must be adjusted to contemporary ideas. He applied that conviction to his biblical studies and, in 1890, defended his thesis on the canon of the Old Testament in which he questioned the traditional teachings of the Church concerning inspiration and interpretation. That book was followed by two other volumes that used the same critical methods with regard to the New Testament and the historicity of the book of Genesis.

Loisy's liberal works and the writings of others like him caused a heated controversy in the French Church with respect to biblical interpretation. The result was that Loisy was dismissed from his position at the Institut Catholique. Further, Pope Leo XIII issued an encyclical, *Providentissimus Deus,* which condemmed both rationalism and those who questioned the traditional conception of inspiration.

During the following five years Loisy served as chaplain at a school for girls in Paris where he was able to continue his biblical studies. He began the writing of a work entitled *L'Évangile et l'église* (*The Gospel and the Church),* which was finally published in 1903. He intended the book to be an effective reply to the famous work by Harnack, *What is Christianity?* that had recently appeared. Loisy carefully took up the major theses of Harnack's work and attempted to challenge each one by an analysis of its biblical and historical references and interpretation. In effect, however, Loisy called upon the Catholic Church to respond in its own way to modern thought as Harnack had done in Protestantism by reforming its views of the Bible, authority, and dogma. He received enthusiastic support from many Catholic intellectuals, but the Archbishop of Paris attacked him and condemned the book and its ideas.

Loisy was not by any means alone among Catholics in the advocacy of what is called Modernism, though he was the most famous leader as well as typical of the group. Three other representatives of the diverse movement were Edouard Le Roy in France, Hermann Schell in Germany, and George Tyrrell in England. There were many sympathizers in each country and also in Italy. They were not in any sense an organized group, but they shared a common interest in trying to engender openness in the Church toward the modern world.

The Modernists were finally rejected and effectively silenced. Loisy was excommunicated, Tyrell was condemned and dismissed from the Jesuits, and many of their writings were placed on the Index of prohibited books. The aged Leo XIII died in 1903 and was succeeded by Pius X (1903-1914) who set to work at once to crush the Modernist threat. Three decisive actions achieved the desired result: the decree *Lamentabili* and the encyclical *Pascendi gregis* were issued in 1907 and the anti-Modernist oath, *Motu Proprio Sacrarum antistitum,* was imposed upon all priests beginning in 1910. *Lamentabili* is a catalog of errors, modeled after the earlier "Syllabus of Errors." It condemns sixty-five Modernist errors concerning the Scriptures and the doctrines of the Church, holding that divine inspiration renders Scripture "immune from all errors." *Pascendi gregis* required that Scholastic philosophy be made the basis of theology, that Modernism be excluded from seminaries and universities, and that Vigilance Committees be instituted to guard against Modernist teaching and influence. The oath of *Motu,* which still applies to all candidates for the priesthood, enjoins submission to *Lamentabili* and the acceptance of orthodox doctrine.

By these actions and policies the Roman Church effectively crushed all attempts to introduce liberalism into its doctrines and practices. When the First World War brought an end to the nineteenth century and to the old political arrangements of Europe, the Church remained secure in its conservative bastion against modern thought. The succeeding popes were able to hold the line, culminating in the promulgation of the new dogma of the Assumption of the Blessed Virgin Mary by Pope Pius XII in 1950. Without the support of Scripture or a council, Pius proclaimed that "we . . . declare and define, as a dogma revealed by God, that the Immaculate Mother of God, ever-Virgin Mary, on the completion of the course of her earthly life, has been taken up, in body and soul, to the glory of heaven." The dogma ignores much modern science and cosmology.

Finally, the Church demonstrated its conscious spirit of triumphalism and intolerance toward other religious views by its complete refusal to participate at any level in the growing ecumenical movement. The Roman Church officially claimed to be the only true Church, having been founded by Christ himself upon the Apostles, with Peter and his successors, the bishops of Rome, the chief rulers. On that basis the popes regularly claimed that a reunion of all Christians is possible only through a return to the true Church by all who had departed form it, including especially the Orthodox and all Protestants. When Protestants, and later the Orthodox churches, began positive work toward cooperation and union, especially through the Faith and Order and the Life and Work movements after the First World War, the Roman Church was invited to attend the meetings and to participate. The answer in all cases was a polite but firm refusal. This occurred especially in the cases of the Lausanne Conference on Faith and Order in 1919 and the Stockholm meeting of Life and Work in 1925.

On July 8, 1927, the Holy Office in Rome issued a formal response to those who had inquired concerning participation in ecumenical meetings and movements: "May Catholics take part in or promote congresses, meetings, lectures, or societies which have the scope of uniting into a religious confederation all who in any sense whatever call themselves Christians?" The answer was an unconditional negative. In order to give further clarity to the question, Pope Pius XI issued an encyclical, *Mortalium animos,* on January 6, 1928, in which he forbade all participation in ecumenical affairs, which he called "panchristian." He listed reasons for the prohibition, chief among them being that such activity would suggest that the Catholic Church is not the only true Church of Christ. Again, on June 5, 1948, just before the formation of the World Council of Churches in Amsterdam, the Holy Office issued a *monitum* (admonition) which said in part,

> It has been learned that in various places, contrary to the prescriptions of the sacred canons, and without the leave of the Holy See, mixed congresses of Catholics and non-Catholics have been held, wherein matters of faith have been discussed. Let all remember, in accord with canon 1325 #3, that it is prohibited to take part in these congresses without the forementioned permission. This holds for the laity and clergy, both secular and religious. Much less is it permitted for Catholics to convoke or organize such congresses. The ordinaries, therefore, must urgently see to it that all observe these prescriptions strictly.

Finally, in order to make clear that the Church was not opposed to external considerations of unity, with the hope that non-Catholics might thereby see the light and return to the one, holy, catholic, and apostolic Church, the Holy Office again issued an Instruction, *Ecclesia catholica,* saying:

> The Catholic Church takes no actual part in "ecumenical" conventions and other assemblies of a similar character. Yet, as numerous pontifical statements show, she has, despite this fact, never ceased nor will she ever cease to pursue with deepest concern and promote with assiduous prayers to God every endeavor to bring about what was so close to the heart of Christ the Lord, viz., that all who believe in Him "may be made perfect in one" (Jn. 17:23).

Thus, until after the Second World War, the Roman Catholic Church turned away from every manifestation of liberalism, especially in terms of Modernist ecumenical activity. No compromise was acceptable.

The Second Vatican Council

When Pope John XXIII was elected in October, 1958, he was already elderly, having served the Church in numerous capacities for many years, finally as the Patriarch of Venice in his native northern Italy. It was generally believed that his choice was intended to provide stability to the Church on an intntnterim basis until the directions of the future could be charted. However, he became an instant surprise to everybody, not least the conservatives of the Roman Curia. He immediately and energetically served notice that he intended to "open the windows of the Vatican to let the fresh air come in." On January 25, 1959, he announced his intention to call an ecumenical council of the Church, and on October 11, 1962, the Second Vatican Council was convened. The Council met in several sessions until December, 1965, and it took many actions that were epoch-making in their radical significance. In those three years the Church reversed the position it had occupied for centuries and set a new course for the future.

Pope John, with disarming openness and love for all, gave the Council its spirit of *aggiornamento,* an Italian term for "bringing up to date." He called upon the council fathers to look forward, not backward. There would be no revocation of past dogmas or actions, but there would be new definitions and attitudes that would leave the past and bring the Church into a new day filled with hope, acceptance, and cooperation. Soon after calling the Council, the Pope said:

> We do not intend to set up a tribunal to judge the past. We do not want to prove who was right and who was wrong. Responsibility was divided. All we want to say is: "Let us come together. Let us make an end to our divisions."

In that spirit the Council for the first time accepted non-Catholic Christians—Protestant and Orthodox—as "separated brethren" with whom the Church was willing to cooperate with "respect and affection" in the joint Christian enterprise. These other "ecclesial communities" were recognized by the Catholic Church as churches, bearing the marks of the People of God. Pope John died in 1963, in the midst of the Council's meetings, but his work was carried to completion by his successor, Paul VI (1963-1978). As the Council closed, Paul travelled to Jerusalem and met with Athenagoras, Patriarch of Constantinople and spiritual leader of all the Orthodox churches. They exchanged kisses of peace, expressed regrets for past hostilities, and removed the bans of excommunication that had stood since 1054.

Sixteen documents were published by the Council, all with papal approval. They were of varying length and some were called constitutions while others were designated decrees or declarations. The distinction was apparently not of great significance, though some were clearly of greater historical import than others. Many have judged the *Dogmatic Constitution on the Church* ("Lumen Gentium") to be the most important single work of the Council. It proposes an entirely different ecclesiology from that of Trent and the centuries that have passed since then. Here the emphasis is upon the Church as the People of God rather than as a hierarchy or a visible, powerful institution. The laity is given a more central role and primary attention is given to spiritual development and relations. Further, the doctrine of the "collegiality of the bishops" is given strong expression. Without in any way revoking or even weakening the supremacy of the pope and the nineteenth-century dogma of papal infallibility, the constitution nonetheless modifies those doctrines by suggestion so that a balance is indicated concerning the power of the pope, the college of bishops, and an ecumenical council.

After affirming the ancient claim that the bishops are the ruling and pastoral successors of the Apostles, the Constitution says,

> Together with its head, the Roman Pontiff, and never without this head, the episcopal order is the subject of supreme and full power over the universal Church. . . . The supreme authority with which this college is empowered over the whole Church is exercised in a solemn way through an ecumenical council. A council is never ecumenical unless it is confirmed or at least accepted as such by the successor of Peter.

Then the document proceeds to limit the collegiality of all the bishops by stressing the final authority of the pope and specifying that the college acts only when called into being and presided over by the pope. The result is a practical arrangement of checks and balances, preserving the old system while in effect changing it.

Another affirmation of the Council is the *Constitution on Divine Revelation*. That document subtly modifies the old doctrine that there are two sources of revealed truth, Scripture and the tradition of the Church. That view, primarily Scholastic in origin, had been a fundamental element causing the Reformation. As we have seen earlier, Luther and the other Reformers rejected that teaching in favor of *sola Scriptura*. Now, however, the Council overwhelmingly compromised with Protestantism. It agreed that there is only one source of revelation, which is God himself. He makes himself and his will known to mankind through his Word, Jesus Christ. That word is transmitted through the witness of the Scriptures and the proclamation of the Gospel. "Sacred tradition and sacred Scripture form one sacred deposit of the word of God, which is committed to the Church." On that basis the Constitution gives new emphasis to Bible reading, Bible study, and Bible preaching in worship.

A third major document of Vatican II that shows perhaps more strikingly than any other the radical change in the attitude of the Catholic Church is the *Decree on Ecumenism*. Whereas, as we saw above, there had been hostility and prohibition concerning the modern ecumenical movement, now the reverse is true. The Council recognized the validity of other churches. It no longer demanded return to the fold as the only way to cooperation and spiritual unity. It warmly encouraged meetings, congresses, and dialogues at every possible level and opportunity. The result has been an amazing eagerness on the part of most Christians in other bodies to respond in new tolerance, understanding, and cooperation.

In addition to these three major documents, three others should be noted as especially revolutionary. The *Declaration on the Non-Christian Religions* acknowledges a commonality of experience and of problems among the great religions of mankind. It also has been received with enthusiasm because of its repudiation of the anti-Semitism that had for so long been a shameful blot on the hands of the Church. It specifically denies the ancient charge of deicide against the Jews because of the death of Jesus. *The Declaration on Religious Freedom* turned aside from the long, bloody years of persecution and political oppression, espousing instead a policy of freedom of conscience and religion, the right of differing forms of public worship, and immunity from coercion in matters of faith. It declares that "truth cannot impose itself except by virtue of its own truth." Finally, the *Pastoral Constitution on the Church in the Modern World,* reversing the proscriptions of the "Syllabus of Errors" of a century earlier, accepts and encourages the idea of human progress and promotes Christian social and political participation in the affairs of the world.

The full fruit of the Second Vatican Council cannot be seen until many years have seen it digested and applied. Many of its results were shocking to those who participated as well as to the clergy and laity who heard of them in stunned silence. There are multitudes of the faithful who have had difficulty adjusting their faith and worship to the new attitudes and methods. Nevertheless, it is obvious that the Church, led by Pope John XXIII, decided to abandon its stubborn rejection of all modern thought and rather to enter the contemporary world with a new spirit of tolerance, service, and redemptive love.

X.
THE WEST AND THE CONTEMPORARY WORLD

Chapter 33

A Century of Change

In 1881, a Polish-German-American physicist named Albert Abraham Michelson (1852-1931) made an experiment in the Berlin laboratory of the great Hermann von Helmholtz to attempt to determine the absolute motion of the earth through the lumeniferous ether, the medium supposed by nineteenth-century scientists to fill all space. To his complete surprise he was unable to detect any trace of an "ether wind," no matter in what direction he projected the beams of light that should have provided him with the information he sought.

The mind-boggling conclusion thus suggested—that the earth has no absolute motion that could, even in theory, be measured—was unacceptable to most scientists. A celebrated Austrian physicist, Ernst Mach (1836-1916), however, refused to join his colleagues in dismissing Michelson's data and announced promptly that science must dispense with the concept of an ether. Michelson himself regarded his experiment as a failure and wanted to try again with better equipment. In 1887, he and a chemist named Edward Williams Morley (1838-1923), made a second experiment in Morley's laboratory at Western Reserve University, using a highly sophisticated version of the interferometer invented by Michelson. Again, there was nothing whatsoever to indicate that the earth is not, as Ptolemy had held it to be, the stationary center of the universe. Subsequent experiments of even greater accuracy served only to confirm the initial Michelson-Morley findings, and scientists found themselves under the necessity of racking their brains for a theoretical solution of the difficulty which would not involve them in a geocentrism thought to have become anachronistic for a culture accustomed to thinking of the earth as an infinitesimal speck of dust in a cosmos of inconceivable immensity.

The New Science

In 1905, a twenty-six year old examiner for the Swiss patent office in Berne announced a theory which not only provided an explanation for the curious result of the Michelson-Morley experiment, but which was ultimately to enable its author to supersede the Newtonian picture of the universe by absorbing its formulas into a model at the same time grander and more baffling to the imagination. Its author, Albert Einstein (1879-1955), a son of German-Jewish parents, was a graduate of the polytechnic school at Zurich and, at the time of the publication of the 1905 work, he was studying for his doctorate in the University of Zurich while simultaneously attending to his duties at the patent office.

The outcome of the Michelson-Morley experiments was not the only factor involved in Einstein's interest in the behavior of light, but, in view of the widespread concern that the "failure" of the experiment had occasioned among scientists, his announcement of the theory, which came to be known as the special theory of relativity, was a timely one. It had as one of its principles the assertion that the velocity of light in a vacuum is a limiting one and cannot be exceeded by any physical object in linear motion. Another was that any physical object when its velocity is accelerated becomes shorter in the direction of its movement as the speed of light is approached. This had been suggested by George Francis Fitzgerald (1851-1901), an Irishman, and Hendrick Antoon Lorentz, (1853-1928), who, while continuing to hold to the concept of absolute motion, had provided a formula for the shrinkage that would explain precisely why no measurement could be made to determine the absolute speed or direction of that motion. Using v as the velocity of the object and c as the light, the length of the object at any velocity is:

$$\sqrt{1-\frac{v^2}{c^2}}$$

Einstein's theory incorporated this formula as a method of determining the length of objects moving relative to a framework from which the measurement is made. It maintained also that as such an object approaches the velocity of light, its inertial mass is increased and the length of its time intervals is increased in the following ratio:

$$\frac{1}{\sqrt{1-\frac{v^2}{c^2}}}.$$

In 1916, Einstein announced his general theory of relativity, broadening the special theory to include not only uniform motion but accelerated motion as well. This more comprehensive account was centered on a truly revolutionary concept—the idea that gravity and inertia are one and the same thing. Fused into one, the two theories meant that there are no optical or mechanical experiments that any observer could perform to determine whether he is at rest or whether he is in uniform or accelerated motion.

While relativity theory was being developed, equally startling changes were being made in the scientific view concerning the composition of matter. Up until the middle of the nineteenth century, the dominant conception of the smallest units of which material objects are made was not too different from that held by the atomists of antiquity. They were thought to be irreducibly small solid particles, influencing one another only in ways described by classical mechanics. Then it was discovered that the traditional picture could not provide an adequate explanation for the behavior of matter as that behavior was revealed by the improved instruments of nineteenth-century science. It came to be realized first that the "field" in which the atom moved had to be explored and then that the "atoms" were not in the strictest sense atoms at all, but highly complex structures of electrically charged particles. The model of the atom suggested by Ernest Rutherford in 1911 was presented to several generations of students in classrooms all over the Western world, and the image of a cluster of little balls constituting a nucleus and orbited by other little balls representing electrons became firmly fixed in the public mind.

With further advances in the study of the internal structure of the atom, it became increasingly evident that the atom had to be described as a highly complex structure composed of a number of different forms of energy, and by the third quarter of the twentieth century, advances in what had come to be known as quantum mechanics—the consideration of phenomena too small in scale to be dealt with by classical mechanics—had contributed as much as relativity theory to a picture of the physical world very different from that which had prevailed at the beginning of the century. Among the major pioneer contributors to this new approach to the submicroscopic nature of matter were Max Planck (1858-1947), Neils Bohr (1885-1962), Erwin Schrodinger (1887-1961), Max Born (1882-1970), and Werner Heisenberg (1901-1976).

Widespread philosophical interest was aroused by Heisenberg's "principle of indeterminacy," which proposes that exact information about both the velocity and the position of a quantum of energy is unattainable. "The knowledge of the position of a particle is complementary to the knowledge of its velocity of momentum," he wrote. "If we know the one with high accuracy we cannot know the other with high accuracy." At the subatomic level, Heisenberg suggested, the laws of probability must replace the notion of absolute necessity. The idea of real indeterminacy offended some scientists, including Albert Einstein, who attributed the Heisenberg observations to no more than inability to make accurate measurements and affirmed stoutly that "God does not play dice." Other physicists, however, were content with the statistical reliability to be found in observations of larger masses and found no serious threat to the "predictability" so valued by scientists in the apparent "freedom" of the smallest units of which the physical world is built.

Although at some points, relativity theory and quantum mechanics were difficult to fit together, at others, they complemented each other quite well. The reduction of matter to energy confirmed one consequence of Einstein's calculations, according to which mass and energy are interchangeable in amounts defined by the formula $e = mc^2$, where e stands for energy, m mass, and c the velocity of light. Together, these two principal developments in the physical sciences and the remarkable flood of development that flowed from them as the twentieth century drew toward its close had profound influences on the ways in which philosophers thought about the world. Gone were the absolute verities of time and space that had provided a stable framework for the Newtonian cosmos and had seemed intuitively self-evident to Kant as *a priori* forms of the sensibility. Whether the new conception of the cosmos was interpreted in material terms or as necessary ways of thinking about a universe having its real existence in minds, a door had been opened into a cosmological wonderland rich in paradox, in which nature might require description involving a multiplicity of dimensions, space and time were welded together in an indissoluble union, the whole of the material world might be curved back on itself in non-Euclidian fashion to form a finite but not bounded universe reminiscent of the Eleatic philosophy, two remotely separated events could not meaningfully be said to occur simultaneously, matter and energy were interchangeable, the behavior of subatomic particles was unpredictable, and gravitation was no longer a force but rather a sort of structural warp in a space-time continuum.

If the lay mind was incapable of grasping the mathematics of the new science, the sense of wonder it engendered began to pervade the popular culture, where it produced ways of thinking about reality that a century earlier would have been grounds for certifying anyone holding such views as a lunatic. Popularizers of science and writers of science fiction eagerly appropriated the new discoveries which increasingly powerful tools of research made possible in overwhelming numbers, and by the third quarter of the twentieth century, it was far from uncommon for after-dinner conversations to contain casual references to hypercubes, black holes, quarks, and the big bang.

While the physical scientists were fashioning radical changes in our thinking about the universe, another science was asking questions about the nature of human beings, implications as far reaching as those resulting from the theory of evolution. Speculations about the human mind were nothing new, but psychology as an experimental science was not really established on a firm footing until 1879, when Wilhelm Wundt (1832-1920) developed the first laboratory for psychological research at the University of Leipzig.

Wundt had a number of talented students who enthusiastically promoted the spread of the new science. One of them, an Englishman, Edward Bradford Titchener (1867-1927), came to America and taught at Cornell University. Together with William James, who had in some degree anticipated Wundt by developing a small laboratory for the purpose of demonstration, Titchener may be regarded as a founder of American psychology.

It is not suprising that the pioneers in the field, struck by the success of the older physical and biological sciences, attempted to imitate their methods of investigation as faithfully as the subject matter of their discipline would permit. But just what was the subject matter to be? Several "schools" of thought were developed, but in general the early researchers shared the conviction that their studies dealt with the mind, however it might be defined, and that access to the mind could be had through an examination of conscious processes.

This assumption was challenged by John B. Watson (1878-1958), the founder of behaviorism. A native of Greenville, South Carolina, Watson studied at Furman University and at the University of Chicago, where he taught for a while. He later held positions as Professor of Experimental and Comparative Psychology at Johns Hopkins University and as Lecturer at the New School for Social Research in New York City.

Watson argued that introspection, the examination of one's own states of consciousness in a scientific way,is impossible. In view of the fact that the definition of psychology as a study of mind is a dependent on precisely that activity, the discipline had to be redefined to leave out all reference to mind and to consciousness. Watson occasionally got so carried away with his argument as to make it evident that he was denying the existence of either. Certainly he laid the groundwork for the position of behaviorists in general that if they do exist, they have no effect on what he regarded as the legitimate object of psychological investigation of behavior.

Other investigators, notably Ivan Pavlov (1849-1936) in Russia, had conducted animal studies which, if they could be considered psychological studies at all, had necessarily relied on reports of behavior in view of the obvious inability of infrahuman subjects to give introspect reports of what they were experiencing. Watson, choosing to ignore any difference on this score that might be claimed to exist between mice and men, proclaimed that behavior, including verbal responses of subjects, is not to be thought of as indicative of some sort of mental state but as the whole of the subject matter with which psychology is concerned. A stimulus is presented to an organism, and it responds with some sort of behavior. A second stimulus, not normally eliciting that response is presented in conjunction with the first, and the process is repeated a certain number of times. Finally the second stimulus is presented by itself. If the behavior initially elicited by the first stimulus is the result, a conditioned response is said to have occurred. The conditioned response, in varying degrees of complexity, is the basis of behaviorial psychology.

As a method, of course, it had great utility, and even for investigators interested in states of consciousness, it provided valuable data concerning the behavioral correlates of those states. But Watson and his followers, among whom two of the most notable were J. F. Dashiell (1888-1975) and B. F. Skinner (born 1904), failed to keep to Watson's original professed resolve simply to study behavior as behavior and arbitrarily call that psychology. Rejecting all forms of metaphysics that might entail the existence of something called mind, they were left with an implicit materialism, which they refused to recognize as being itself a metaphysical position. They denied all purposiveness in behavior. There is no clear place for imagination, and thinking itself is no more than "incipient verbalization" or, even more narrowly, sub-vocal movement in the larynx. The implications become increasingly clear in the work of the latter-day behaviorist B. F. Skinner, who denied that Hitler's depredations were a result of any feelings he might have had and who, in his most widely read books, *Walden Two* and *Beyond Freedom and Dignity,* could come up with no value structure for which he could make a more persuasive claim than that it was a product of his own conditioning and that he was conditioned to propagate it. For the many advocates behaviorism could claim during its heyday, human beings had been successfully reduced to the level of Descartes' unconscious lower animals—that is, to the level of machines.

While American psychology, under the auspices of behaviorism, was emulating the older physics by making itself as mechanistic as possible, physics was becoming less and less so, and a new generation of psychologists were looking for a new model. By the fourth decade of the century, the rigid behavioristic doctrine was being replaced by sophisticated variants, and few psychologists would call themselves behaviorists today. Its methods are, however, still widely and usefully employed, and its materialistic world view survives in more subtle form in much of the literature in the fields of psychology and the social sciences, as well as in certain philosophical theories which treat consciousness not merely as intimately associated with brain states but as identical with them.

Meanwhile in Europe, another approach to psychology was developing. Sigmund Freud (1856-1939) was a native of Freiberg in Moravia but spent most of his life in Vienna, where he became a clinical neurologist. The germ of the theory on which his fame rests was planted in his mind in 1884, when Josef Breuer, a Viennese physician, told him of a case in which a patient appeared to have been cured of hysterical symptoms by being hypnotized and induced to recall, with all the associated emotional experiences, the situation in which the hysteria had its origin. Freud found support for his interest in the method the following year when he studied under the celebrated neurologist J. M. Charcot in Paris. He published several works on the subject and collaborated with Breuer on a book, called *Studien über Hysterie,* based on the case that had originally launched him on his investigations.

In 1894, be abandoned hypnosis as a method of recall in favor of a technique of having the patient discuss his symptoms while fully conscious. This led at last to the final step in the development of the psychoanalytic method, the use of free association. Freud saw profound significance in the submerged memories he could dredge up from the depths of his patients' minds by letting them relax and talk freely, and he became convinced that his research provided a key to the understanding of "normal" people as well as of those suffering from psychoneuroses.

For Freud, consciousness is no more than a thin layer of mental activity lying like the exposed tip of an iceberg atop the vast bulk of psychological activity that constitutes the unconscious. Specifically, in the mature development of his theory, the human personality is divided into three parts: the "id", the innate source of psychic energy, operating on a hedonistic basis; the "ego," the "executive of the personality," through which the individual seeks through contact with the outer world to serve the id; and the "superego," the learned value structure of the personality, which places restraints on the ego and may come into conflict with the drives of the id. This conflict may result in feelings of guilt which, if sufficiently severe, may result in mental illness. Acting through the "censor" the person "represses" objectionable desires by pushing them deep into the unconscious. In dreams, with censorship partially relaxed, the repressed wishes assume disguised forms and make their way into the dreamer's consciousness. The symbolism of dreams is, therefore, an important part of psychoanalytic theory.

Freud laid much stress on the ''libido'' or sexual drive. Infantile sexuality was seen as the major source of psychological conflicts, and Freud dipped into the literature of antiquity for terms like ''Oedipus complex'' to describe the conditions resulting from a child's earliest sexual attitudes. His work, though highly controversial, had enormous influence in the twentieth century on medical science, philosophy, religion, and the arts. The cause of psychoanalysis was advanced by a number of talented younger colleagues of Freud, who in some instances modified the theory. Of these, the most notable was Carl G. Jung (1875-1961), a Swiss psychologist and psychiatrist. Initially regarded as heir-apparent to Freud's mantle, Jung broke with the master over Freud's contention that sexual conflict was the source not only of psychoneuroses, but, in ''sublimated'' form, of the greater part of human creative activity. For Jung, motivation was more broadly conceived, and more recent conflicts of varying sorts were as important as those occurring in early childhood in providing material for understanding neuroses.

Jung saw the human psyche as composed of the ''ego'', the ''personal unconscious,'' and the ''collective unconscious,'' the last named being the most interesting as well as the most controversial aspect of his system. A ''storehouse of latent memory traces from man's ancestral past,'' the collective unconscious is treated as a sort of universal repository of ''archetypes'' on which the individual may draw as sources of power. Jung's description of such archetypes as ''the child,'' ''the earth mother,'' and the like, contributed to a renewed interest in mythology and had some influence on literature in the West.

Neuroses, he held, develop when imbalances in the personality occur in the attempt to achieve selfhood through the spiritual process of ''individuation.'' Like Aristotle, Jung was teleological in his approach to human development, and unlike Freud, who regarded religion as illusion, Jung saw it as indispensable of the attainment of healthy selfhood. ''Among all my patients in the second half of life—that is to say, over thirty-five—there has not been one,'' he said, ''whose problem in the last resort was not that of finding a religious outlook on life.''

The Advance of Technology

The rapid advances of theoretical science were accompanied by and in no small measure facilitated by an explosion in technology, well under way in the nineteenth century but accelerating in the twentieth to such an extent that within the space of fewer than a hundred years the material conditions under which citizens of Western nations lived underwent more changes than in the preceding three millennia. The successes of applied science are what most present-day people have in mind when they speak of "progress" and during the early years of the century,it was generally assumed that such progress is beneficent. It is only since the Second World War that the optimistic view of modern technology has been generally challenged by a more apocalyptic assessment as the tremendous strides made in a number of fields of research and application have seemingly outrun the ethical capacity of the human race to use them for the public good and opened up the very real possibility that they may provide the instruments by which humanity will annihilate itself through war or through the destruction of the environmental systems that make human life possible.

In addition to the opportunitics and hazards it posed for its future exploitation, the technological revolution had significant effects, some obvious and some subtle, in the ways in which men and women living in the late nineteenth and twentieth centuries thought about themselves and their environment. Ingenuity in devising effective means for achieving desired material ends soared to heights undreamed of in earlier centuries, and philosophers began to develop sophisticated theories reflecting the popular concern.

Pragmatism

This tendency was particularly evident in America, where confidence in technology and respect for material achievement seemed higher than anywhere else in the world. The doctrine of practicality achieved its best and clearest American statements in the philosophies of Charles Peirce, William James, and John Dewey.

In 1878, Peirce (1839-1914) had an article published in *Popular Science Monthly* entitled "How to Make Our Ideas Clear." In it, he stated the "pragmatic maxim" succinctly: "In order to ascertain the meaning of an intellectual conception one should consider what practical consequences might conceivably result by necessity from the truth of that conception; and the sum of those consequences will constitute the entire meaning of the conception." Pierce was a philosopher of considerable breadth and worthy of attention for his contributions in a number of areas of thought, but he is best known as the founder of pragmatism.

William James (1842-1910), a cultivated New Yorker and brother of the novelist Henry James, achieved distinction as a physician, a pioneer psychologist, and a philosopher. A brilliant writer of highly readable books, he elevated pragmatism to a status of preeminence among philosophical systems bearing a distinctive American stamp. It is, he said, "a method," a method of establishing truth opposed to the dogmatism which he saw as inseparable from rationalism. Pragmatism, he said, "has no dogmas and no doctrines save its method." Its fundamental purpose is the clarification of ideas—the providing of a test for determining the meaningfulness of concepts. Philosophical positions have no meanings apart from the practical consequences that might flow from the adoption of one or another of them. An intelligible proposition must have "cash value," the potential for producing results. Truth is expediency. It is that which works for human purposes. It is not something existing in static fashion which we discover by contemplation. Something created in action, in dealing with the raw experience, is our only source of knowledge. It was this uncompromising emphasis on experience that causes James to characterize his philosophy as a "radical empiricism" though in the breadth of its method of applying the pragmatic formula, he saw a kinship with nominalism, utilitarianism, and positivism.

In *The Will to Believe,* published in 1897, James explored the problem of freedom as it relates to the selection of positions that will determine what an individual holds to be true. Neither the determinist's view nor that of the indeterminist can be vigorously proved, he held. This fact caused him no distress, for if, indeed, such proof were possible, James's whole system would seem to be in danger. Our problem here, as elsewhere, is to determine which of the two theories "works." On that score, so far as James was concerned, there is practically no contest. If we choose to consider the will not to be free, we cannot meaningfully make a "judgment of regret," for if what happened had inevitably to happen, it makes no sense to regret it. We do, however, make such judgments and must face the question of whether to take them seriously. The whole moral life, with its implication that we make genuine choices for which we are really responsible is bound up with the idea that the will is not determined. So although freedom cannot be proved in any way that would satisfy the rationalist, it makes sense to "will to believe" in it. Such a belief "works" and is therefore "true." The will to believe is similarly important in settling other questions of moment. It may lead to the creation of new truths which would not have existed if the will had not been exercised, or it may lead us to belief in truths not forced on us by reason that nevertheless meet the pragmatic criterion.

That James, despite his pragmatic theory of truth, was convinced of the truth of a great number of propositions about reality is evident to any reader of his works. He was accurate in his description of the role of the will in making belief in such truths possible. When a hypothesis is presented for approval or disapproval, it must meet certain requirements if the will is to be invoked to solve the question. The will requires a genuine option for its exercise. That option must be "alive" and not dead. That is, the alternatives under consideration must be ones which could actually be believed by a person under a given set of circumstances. It must be "forced", the sort of option that cannot be avoided by a reservation of judgment. Finally, it must be "momentous" in terms of the effect that the choice made will have on one's life.

In applying his method, James argued for the "cash value" of pluralism, the belief that the universe presents us with diversity and novelty. He similarly supported a theism in terms of which God was seen as a personal and moral being with whom communion is possible in ways explored in James's *Varieties of Religious Experience,* published in 1897. Eschewing optimism and pessimism, he announced himself a meliorist, holding that the world confronts us with a picture of good in which it is possible and morally obligatory to reduce the quality of evil and increase the quantity of good.

John Dewey, the third of the great American pragmatists, was a native of Burlington, Vermont, and had a distinguished teaching career at several midwestern universities and finally at Columbia University. He was, for a time, director of the school of education at the University of Chicago, and, while there, experimented with the educational theories that made him perhaps the most influential single figure in American educational theory.

Dewey preferred to call his philosophy "instrumentalism" or "experimentalism," defining it as "an attempt to constitute a precise logical theory of concepts, of judgments and inferences in their various forms, by considering primarily how thought functions in the experimental determination of future consequence."

As much as any philosopher of his day, he sought to base his thinking on science, rejecting entirely the concept of truth as something eternal to be discovered in favor of a view that thought and action are inseparably bound together, just as rational reflection and experimentation are indissoluble in scientific endeavor. Learning involves doing. Human beings are organisms being shaped by and at the same time shaping their environment. We think by confronting and solving problems, and the complexity of the problems of the modern world has been greatly increased by the rapid advance of science and technology. "With tremendous increase in the control of nature," he said, "in our ability to utilize nature for human use and satisfaction, we find the actual realization of ends, the enjoyment of values, growing unassured and precarious."

The ends and values that motivate our actions are not absolute and fixed. They vary from individual to individual and situation to situation. What is constant is the desirability of growth, and in society the conditions that promote growth are best assured through democracy and education.

True to his conception of the union of thought and action, Dewey was vigorous in his efforts to gain acceptance for his philosophy and his educational methods. A far more pedestrian writer than William James, he nevertheless articulated some aspects of American experience so successfully that his influence on twentieth-century American thought is still widely felt.

Twentieth Century Realism

The term "realism" in British philosophy developed a somewhat different connotation from that which it had in the Middle Ages. To be sure, it does entail the reality of universals, and a form of Platonic realism was stoutly upheld in the seventeenth and eighteenth centuries by the Cambridge Platonists, notably Ralph Cudworth (1617-1688), Richard Price (1723-1791), and Benjamin Whichcote (1609-1683). For these thinkers, sense experience provided a way of knowing particulars, but the mind can also know universals in the divine mind which have, as Cudworth put it, "not only an eternal, but also a necessary existence, so that they. . . . can never possibly perish or cease to be, but are absolutely undestroyable." The strong empirical element so characteristic of British thought, however, was evident in the thought of the Scottish realists Thomas Reid (1710-1796) and Dugald Stewart (1753-1828), who, though they were just as convinced as the Cambridge Platonists that universals like "right" and "wrong" have, in Stewart's words, "a distinction necessary and essential, and independent of the will of any being whatever," laid equal stress on the reality of particulars.

In the early years of the twentieth century, there was a resurgence of realism in Great Britain, led by G. E. Moore (1873-1958) and Bertrand Russell (1872-1970).

Moore, a student, fellow, and professor at Cambridge, also lectured at Princeton University, Columbia University, and Smith College. He became widely respected in philosophical circles for his *Principia Ethica* (1903), *Ethics*(1912), *Philosophical Studies* (1902), and *Some Main Problems of Philosophy* (1953). Although his early essay "The Refutation of Idealism" was responsible for the birth of twentieth-century English realism, he owed his interest in philosophy to Russell, an older student at Cambridge when Moore was an undergraduate. Russell, however, readily acknowledged the leading role his young friend played in the reaction against Bradleyan idealism which led to the movement. Russell described the feeling of emancipation that resulted from affirming the reality of what is confirmed by common sense, of permitting oneself to acknowledge "that grass is green, that the sun and stars would exist if no one was aware of them, and also that there is a pluralistic timeless world of Platonic ideas."

Where philosophy contradicts common sense, Moore held, philosophy is wrong. He ran into some complicated problems, however, in determining the relation between sense data, or "sensibles" and existent physical objects. Some sensibles—dreams, hallucinations, and images of the imagination, for instance—presumably do not exist in the absence of a percipient. Others do. Moore recognized the difficulty the realist would face in saying that sensibles are *in* objects, but, if it is true that we preceive nothing but the sensibles directly and the sensibles are not in the object, then we can know the object only indirectly. After reflecting on the matter from a number of different points of view, he confessed that he was "puzzled about the matter."

Being, he said, is a property of anything belonging in the universe, which is the sum total of all things, past, present, and future. The existent entities that compose it are of three sorts: particulars, which are individual objects; facts, such as "that lions exist" or "the existence of lions;" and universals, which are the objects of abstract thought—numbers and the like. All can exist whether or not anyone is thinking of them. "Being," "existence", and "reality" are equivalent terms.

Moore made an important contribution to moral philosophy in critical evaluation of the meaning of the term "good." Philosophers have been led astray, he thought, in their attempt to reduce goodness to something else, the hedonists to pleasure, the metaphysicians to some suprasensible reality, and even Kant to the commands of an autonomous will. All these philosophers, Moore thought, miss the mark in their failure to recognize that goodness is indefinable and insusceptible to reduction to more elementary terms. They thus commit what Moore called the "naturalistic fallacy." The term "good" has, he held, a meaning quite different from that of any of those words with which it it equated in the philosophers' efforts to define it. It is an ultimate.

Moore's ethic, though not hedonistic, was, in a sense, utilitarian, in that he held that the goodness of an action is determined by its consequences as intended by the agent. One ought, he believed, to perform those actions that it is reasonable to suppose will result in the maximum amount of good and the minimum amount of evil. Moral prohibitions are based on the probability that certain sorts of actions will produce undesirable effects, and the prohibitions should be obeyed because of that possibility. Those things that are good—human associations, the appreciation of beauty, and the like—are evident to common sense.

Moore's friend and fellow realist Bertrand Russell was born in Monmouthshire in 1872. His grandfather was Lord John Russell, who later became Earl Russell, and John Stuart Mill was his godfather. Orphaned at the age of three, he was brought up by his grandmother and educated by governesses and private tutors. Despite the fact that the courts had given him into his grandmother's care to thwart his father's desire that he be brought up as an agnostic, he went a step farther and became an atheist at the age of eighteen, abandoning at the same time belief in free will and immortality. In 1980, he entered Trinity College, Cambridge, and while an undergraduate there, studied mathematics for three years and philosophy during the fourth. He admired Bradley at that time and was himself Hegelian in his thinking. He was an attaché at the British Embassy in Paris in 1894, and the following year, he studied economics and social democracy in Berlin. In 1898, with his young friend G. E. Moore, he abandoned Hegelianism for realism. He wrote several books of his own during the early years of the twentieth century, and in 1910, 1912, and 1913 the three volumes of his important work in collaboration with Alfred North Whitehead, *Principia Mathematica,* were published. Whitehead (1861-1947), himself a distinguished English mathematician and philosopher, later became a pioneer in twentieth-century process philosophy and theology.

In the First World War, Russell acquired a reputation as a radical pacifist and was subjected to a number of legal penalties including a six-months prison term. He succeeded to the earldom in 1931. For the rest of his life, his unconventional views on morals and his espousal of radical causes made him a controversial figure in his native country and in America, where he lived for many years, but he was awarded the Order of Merit in 1949 and the Nobel Prize for Literature in 1950. He died in 1970. In addition to his work with Whitehead, he was author of a number of widely-read books, among them, *The Problems of Philosophy* (1912), *Our Knowledge of the External World* (1914, 1926), *Why I an Not a Christian* (1927), *An Inquiry into Meaning and Truth* (1940), *My Philosophical Development* (1959), and *Logic and Knowledge, Essays 1901-1950* (1956).

Russell's realism, in its first manifestation after his break with Bradleyan idealism, was of a more or less Platonic or medieval variety. Physical things are real, as are space and time, but so are mathematical entities and universals. He modified his position several times, but in spite of the complexities he introduced into his system, he never abandoned his conviction that philosophy must come to grips with questions concerning the nature of reality and that facts are not dependent on the processes by which they are known. Although his contributions to analytical philosophy were so significant that he is considered as a pioneer in twentieth-century linguistic analysis, the study of language was for him not an end in itself but rather the refining of an instrument by which philosophers could attempt to understand and describe the world. In the *Principia Mathematica,* he and Whitehead sought to develop a precise logical language to refer with scientific precision to things as they are. Mathematics itself was ingeniously reduced to logic, and Russell set himself the further task of demonstrating that philosophy itself is nothing but logic. The realism developed on the basis of this conviction he called "Logical Atomism."

He was a confirmed pluralist. "The things in the world," he said, "have various properties and stand in various relations to each other. That they have these properties and relations are *facts* . . . " Facts have components and so can be analyzed.

Some words, such as *red* or *green,* are simple predicates and cannot be analyzed into components. Others are "proper names" referring to particular things. Propositions are arrangements of words that express facts. Propositions that express atomic facts are atomic propositions. When two or more propositions are joined together by words such as "and," "or," "if . . . then . . . ," one has a molecular proposition. All *facts* however, are atomic, and so the truth of molecular propositions can be determined only by determining the truth or falsity of their component parts and relating their truth values according to the indication given by the words that connect them. Thus the molecular proposition "p and q" is true if p is true and q is true. The proposition "p or q", however, is true if either of the atomic propositions is true and false only if both are false. The connectives denote *truth functions.* When specific terms are substituted for the letters, atomic and molecular propositions say something about the nature of the world, and, in a linguistic structure as refined as the one which Russell had as his ideal, the statements in which propositions are couched are supposed to be very accurate indeed.

Russell propounded a "theory of descriptions," which made a sharp distinction between names and descriptions. "Sir Walter Scott" is a name. "The author of *Waverley*" is a description. Descriptions, Russell held, refer to things which may or may not exist, and it is, therefore, meaningful to assert existence or non-existence of them. A name, however, cannot be used properly in a proposition unless there is something which it names, and so an assertion such as "Sir Walter Scott exists" is redundant. The device which enabled Russell to avoid ascribing a sort of shadowy existence to "golden mountains" and the like is the propositional function—an expression containing one or more variables to which values may be assigned which would convert the expression into a proposition. "The golden mountain does not exist" is expressed as "The propositional function '*x* is golden and a mountain' is false for all values of *x*." "The author of *Waverley* exists" is translated as "There is a term *c* such that '*x*' wrote *Waverley* is always equivalent to 'x is c.' " Existence was thus reduced by Russell to "a case of a propositional function being true of at least one value of the variable." Moore protested against the treatment of existence as nothing more than a logical function. Ordinary language, he pointed out, certainly permits the ascription of existence to individuals. Russell, though, was convinced that ordinary language is logically faulty and that "the logician, as such, does not know of the existence of Socrates or of anything else." Existence is not a *property* of individual objects.

This does not mean, of course, that such objects do not exist. The reason existence cannot be predicated of them is that it cannot conceivably be denied of them and so adds nothing to any description given them. Russell remained a realist of sorts all his life, although his treatment of the relationship between subjects and objects underwent many changes and involved some unresolved ambiguities.

Logical Positivism

Ludwig Wittgenstein, (1889-1951), an Austrian living in England, where he was at one time a student of Russell, wrote a book in 1919 entitled *Tractatus Logico-Philosophicus* devoted to an attempt to clarify language. In it he said that "whatever can be said at all can be said clearly." The work was well received by a group of scholars in Vienna who, though interested in philosophy, were scornful of metaphysics. Preoccupied with mathematics and science, they ruthlessly pruned the subject matter of philosophy to deny meaning to any language that could not be verified by one of those disciplines. They came to be known as the Vienna Circle and their philosophy as logical positivism or logical empiricism. The movement attracted men of competence in a number of academic fields, some of the best known logical positivists being Moritz Schlick (1882-1936), Rudolph Carnap (1891-1970), Herbert Feigl (b. 1902), and Kurt Gödel (1906-1978). Though born on the Continent, the school attained its greatest popularity in England and America, its best known English apologist being A. J. Ayer (b. 1910).

The position of the logical positivists underwent a number of changes, and, indeed, it was not monolithic from the outset. There were certain principles, though, on which all the members of the Vienna Circle and their followers agreed. They all rejected metaphysics, and they all subscribed to some version of what was called the "verification principle."

According to this principle, a sentence is cognitively meaningful if and only if it is one of two things. It may, on the one hand, be a synthetic statement that is empirically verifiable directly or indirectly. Carnap gave as an example of a directly verifiable one, "Now I see a red square on a blue ground," and of an indirectly verifiable one, "this key is made of iron." It may on the other hand, be an analytic proposition, the truth or falsity of which can be determined by an analysis of the language used to determine whether it is a tautology and therefore true or a contradiction and therefore false. If a statement does not belong to one or the other of these categories, the logical positivists held, it is neither true or false. It is, they said, meaningless, for the meaning of a proposition lies in the method by which it is verifiable.

In view of the fact that the method of verification for any proposition must be empirical or logically analytic, it follows that even the laws of science, applying as they do to an infinite number of instances, cannot be verified in the strictest sense, and Carnap treated them as hypotheses that may be "confirmed" in greater or less degree. As for value judgement in the fields of aesthetics, ethics, religion, and metaphysics, they are all expressive, emotive, or directive, and none of them has cognitive meaning.

The goal of the logical positivists was, in Carnap's words, "to exhibit *an exact method of philosophy,*" and they envisioned philosophy as a sort of handmaiden of science, but a difficulty in formulating their position became evident to critics. There appears to be no way in which a statement can be formed to affirm the correctness of their own position that will meet their criteria for meaningfulness. This somewhat embarrassing circumstance, together with the narrow scope for thought provided by a point of view that made it impossible to talk intelligently about values, led to the next stage in the development of modern linguistic philosophy.

Ordinary Language Philosophy

In 1929, Wittgenstein returned from Vienna to England and, at Cambridge, began what amounted to a new career in philosophy. Still convinced that the substance of philosophy lay in the study of language, he nevertheless abandoned many of the views expressed in the *Tractatus* that had endeared him to the Vienna Circle. Over the years that followed, he jotted down his ideas in a disconnected series of comments which were published after his death under the title *Philosophical Investigations*. In these remarks there emerged a view of language as a heterogeneous group of expressions comprising a number of different sorts of games or tools and not simply as a medium for expressing facts.

Words, he said, have many different functions, and those functions are related only by "family resemblances" and not by some property that they all have in common. The meaning of a term lies in its use in a particular situation. Unlike Russell, who had the goal of constructing an ideal language, the later Wittgenstein saw the main function of philosophy as being the study of ordinary language. In relieving us of the "mental cramp" occasioned by linguistic confusion, philosophy serves a therapeutic function. Wittgenstein shunned metaphysics and claimed to have no philosophical opinions. He did, however, claim to be the author of a new method. His development of two quite different approaches at two different periods of his life and the enormous impact of both approaches on two distinct groups of linguistic philosophers testify to his unique place in the history of twentieth-century thought.

At Cambridge, Norman Malcom, Morris Lazerowitz, and John Wisdom, among others, became advocates of the new method, stressing the therapeutic value of the examination of language while refraining from commitment to absolute answers in philosophy. In time the new method invaded Oxford and attracted a number of scholars there, among them Gilbert Ryle, John Austin, S. E. Toulmin, and H. H.Price, who invested it with an aura of classical studies more typical of Oxford than of Cambridge, where Wittgenstein, whose formal education had been in engineering and mathematics, had found himself in company with others whose principal interest lay along scientific lines. It was at Oxford that "ordinary language philosophy" became recognized as a full-blown challenge to the more restrictive system of the logical positivists. Its advocates were a heterogeneous group, but they were united in their regard for the broader options in the study of language sanctioned by G. E. Moore and the Wittgenstein of the *Philosophical Investigations*. As the influence of the Vienna Circle declined, the analysis of ordinary language became the major preoccupation of professional philosophers in England and America. For the most part, the new linguistic philosophers have had as little regard for metaphysics as did the logical positivists, but a number of them have felt free to discuss the sort of language used in aesthetics, ethics, and religion, even if they have more often than not shown reluctance to pursue the more troublesome question as to the nature of the categories of reality designated by the terms being considered.

Existentialism

For many thoughtful Europeans, the Nazi terror and the Second World War provided conclusive evidence of the bankruptcy of the dominant modes of thought in the West. Their failure, as the critics saw it, lay in the transference of attention from the individual self to an extraneous system of one sort or another. It was in this context that existentialism came to the fore in post-war Continental Europe.

It was by no means a new mode of thought. Foreshadowed by men like Pico della Mirandola, it had been eloquently argued in nineteenth century Denmark by Søren Kierkegaard (1813-1855) in the form of an essentially romantic and highly personal brand of Protestant Christianity in which existential elements were dominant. Kierkegaard denied that anything more than abstract knowledge can be achieved through objective investigation or rational speculation. Truth is attained only when an individual makes a free and unconditioned "leap over the abyss." A commitment to Christianity so established leads to personal knowledge of God through the mediation of Jesus Christ. It was Kierkegaard who first used the term *existence* with the meaning it has come to have in modern existentialist philosophy.

The modern German development of the movement was charted in the period between the two world wars by Martin Heidegger (1899-1976) and Karl Jaspers (1883-1969). Drawing on German romanticism, their writing exalted feeling over reason, decision over reflection, freedom over order, and a sense of tragedy over facile optimism.

Heidegger, a professor of philosophy at Marburg and Freiburg, held that human existence is given importance by the knowledge that one is finite and transient. The awareness of impending death produces anguish, which, in turn, results in a confrontation with nothingness. Nothingness in this sense, however, is not mere non-existence, but the primordial ground of being itself. His identification of nothingness with ultimate being involved Heidegger in a concern with ontology that led to a complex analysis of being in its various ramifications. He distinguished *das Sein,* absolute or pure being, from *das Seiende,* concrete being, and both of these from *Dasein,* "being there." *Dasein* is peculiar to human beings. One who recognizes his relation to being has *existence,* a continuing decision to affirm being self-consciously in the shadow of nothingness. One's essence is not a prior something determining the mode of one's being. It is what one chooses it to be, and in choosing, one achieves self-transcendence with relation to the world, other selves, and the future.

Karl Jaspers (1883-1969), who began his professional career as a psychologist and pathologist and only later turned to philosophy, brought to his studies a broadly based academic competence. He recognized the usefulness and authenticity of approaches to knowledge other than those of the existentialist while acknowledging the limitations of all philosophical method. The search for world-orientation through the sciences is, he thought, helpful so long as we never lose sight of the limitations of scientific method.

What Jaspers called the "elucidation of existence" requires the exercise of the absolute freedom and responsibility that existentialists generally regard as necessary for the attainment of essence. Here Jaspers was concerned not with the individual in abstract isolation but with free persons in their interrelationships. Metaphysics, the search for "the one being," involves the use of speculative philosophy to go beyond both science and existential thought in imaginative models of reality. In spite of the scope of his philosophy, unusual for an existentialist, Jaspers agreed with Heidegger in his conception of anguish and his essentially tragic orientation toward death.

In France, existentialism showed two very different faces in the philosophies of Gabriel Marcel (1889-1973) and Jean Paul Sartre (1905-1980).

Marcel, a playwright and literary critic, had much in common with Kierkegaard, in that he found the ultimate resolution of the questions he confronted in Christianity—in his case, the Christianity of the Roman Catholic Church, to which he became a convert at the age of thirty-nine. The critical attitude of the Vatican toward other expressions of existential philosophy led Marcel to deny being an existentialist, but the nature of his thought has made it impossible for him to escape identification with the movement.

Marcel made an important contribution to the understanding of the radical difference between an "I" and an "it" by his insistence that the question of what one is oneself is not a *problem* of the sort that can be solved by examining an object, analyzing it into its parts, acquiring information about it, and then reasoning one's way through to a solution. It is, rather, a *mystery,* which can never be solved within the framework of "objective" thinking. According to Marcel, objects—stones, trees, chairs, and the like—cannot "be in a situation," by which he appears to have meant that they lack subjectivity and are incapable of entering into ethical relationships with others. For him, the essence of human relations is to be found in the quality of fidelity, which is the key to the affirmation of being in a human individual.

Jean Paul Sartre, a writer and teacher of philosophy, belonged to the atheistic faction of the movement. The absence of God, which he regarded as self-evident, was not for him a matter for satisfaction, and he had little regard for those humanists who see in atheism a welcome liberation from divine control. He thought it, rather, a source of existential anguish. So obvious to him, however, was the necessity for denying a theistically grounded reality that he virtually excommunicated existentialists of different persuasions, defining existentialism as "nothing but an attempt to draw all the consequences from a consistent atheistic position."

Sartre held that atheism makes it impossible for one to consider the nature of a human being in the same way that one would consider that of an artifact—that is, as an object the character and purpose of which is conceived in the mind of its maker before it actually exists. We find ourselves plunged into existence with no access to any given "human nature," either in divine mind or in a realm of antecedent ideas. If atheism is to be taken seriously, he maintained, existence must be regarded as preceding essence. Human beings first exist, and they must define themselves without recourse to any standard outside themselves.

Such a view would seem at first glance to provide grounds for no more than an arbitrary subjectivism and to be fatal to any sort of normative ethic. It must have been tempting to Sartre to voice the sentiment recorded by Dostoievsky in *The Brothers Karamazov* that "if God is dead, everything is permitted." Avoid it he did, though. A stone, he said, has only *l' en soi,* being-in-itself. A human being also has *le pour soi,* being-for-itself, a quality not to be confused with essence, but one, nevertheless, which confers upon its possessor special dignity as a conscious self, standing before a future and freely creating oneself. On this basis, Sartre made a daring leap forward and declared human beings to be accountable and responsible for what they make of themselves. Then, appropriating at least a shadow of the Kantian imperative, he held that in choosing any course of action authentically, one is, in effect, choosing for all humanity. We are condemned to freedom, and our knowledge of our unlimited responsibility for choosing our own actions and willing them for others is the source of our forlornness, anguish, and despair.

Sartre's long shadow tended to dominate French thought in the years following the Second World War, though a certain intemperance in his own definition of ethical and political goals kept him involved in controversy. His work and that of other Continental existentialists was influential in providing an escape form the sterilty of much modern Western philosophy. Existential thought proved to be especially adaptable to literary expression and was evident in a number of novels and plays exploring the absurdity of events and the burden of human freedom. Theologians too were influenced not only by the writers who chose theism but by others who, in rejecting it, still found themselves impelled to affirm the dignity of an "I" and the sanctity of a "thou."

Chapter 34

Conflicting Ideologies in War and Peace

The impact of the shifting currents of thought we have been discussing was not confined to Europe and America. Western energy had for several centuries made itself felt over the face of the globe in an ever expanding network of trade, combined with an active colonialism that enabled nations more highly developed in technology, commerce, and military power to establish lucrative beachheads in areas rich in natural resources. The last resistance to contacts with the West on the part of a major culture of the East crumbled in 1853, when aggressive American diplomacy, backed by a show of naval strength, persuaded the Japanese Empire to open its doors to trade after centuries of isolation.

The rapid acceleration of technological progress in the twentieth century, making communication and travel ever more rapid and efficient, brought the widely divergent cultures of the world into a proximity to one another that was at the same time instructive and abrasive. The impressive accomplishments of Europeans and Americans in producing goods and services could not fail to excite admiration and sometimes envy in societies that had moved at a slower pace, and the worldview responsible for those accomplishments began to infiltrate in varying degrees the thinking of the inhabitants of those societies. The influences, of course, were not strictly one-directional, for interest in other ways of life and thought was never lacking in Europe and America, but in general, it could be said that the promise, or threat, of the Westernization of the world did not seem something which could be easily discounted.

Two world wars only stepped up the pace of the process. Japan, after being brought to its knees in 1945, improved on the technology that had enabled it to challenge the Western industrialized nations in the first place, and with an astonishing burst of creative energy, became one of the leading economic powers in the world. In somewhat lesser degree, other countries in the Orient followed suit.

The Challenge of Marxism

The history of the Soviet Union provided a different example of Western influence. The Russia of the Czars, astride Europe and Asia, was an empire composed of diverse peoples, some of whom, especially those in the western part of the vast land mass, had developed the beginnings of a modern industrial establishment while others still followed ways of life that had remained virtually unchanged for centuries. With the overthrow of the Czarist state and the subsequent triumph of the Bolsheviks, a new society came into being, pledged by its leaders to the creation of the first state based on the principles set down by Karl Marx.

Marx had envisioned the revolutions that would establish the dictatorship of the proletariat as occurring in countries thoroughly prepared for them by the development of mature capitalistic societies like those of Western Europe. Now V. I. Lenin and his colleagues faced the task of imposing Marxist idealogy on a polyglot collection of cultures, many of which had not moved beyond tribalism or feudalism. In order to prepare such a populace ideologically to fit the dialectic laid out in *Das Kapital* and the *Communist Manifesto,* it would be necessary to exercise rigid controls over every aspect of life in the new Union of Soviet Socialist Republics. Lenin was by no means averse to such controls. A successful revolution, he thought, must be firmly guided by people who knew what they were doing.

The successes of the enterprise cannot be denied. A totalitarian regime somehow coalesced diverse populations who retained many of their cultural differences around a central idea imported from Germany with such ruthless efficiency that the Soviet Union achieved a degree of modernization sufficient to enable it to play a major role in the defeat of Germany in the Second World War and subsequently to assert its position as a "superpower."

The rapid rise of the nation still popularly called "Russia" was not greeted with universal gratification outside its borders. The doctrinal dedication of the Bolshevik leaders to a program of world revolution sent a wave of alarm through the governments of nations more committed to ideas of monarchy or democracy or free enterprise than to a utopian vision of a classless society, to be achieved by dictatorial methods. An expeditionary force sent by the Western nations in an attempt to put down the revolution in its early stages had been unsuccessful, and there seemed to be nothing that could be done effectively to challenge the spread of Marxism other than to provide evidence that the economic and social systems of the West could produce results that would refute the dialectic.

Over the years between the two great wars, Western Europe and America faced a number of crises that would have gratified Marx. Most notable of these was the Great Depression of the nineteen-thirties. Marxists active in the West confidently predicted that matters were coming to a head and that revolution was imminent. That they were proved wrong testifies to the resiliency of Western institutions.

A major strength of the West was the growing democritization of political life in Europe. The First World War had swept away many of the monarchial governments on the Continent, and those that remained in power did so by virtue of their accommodation to the idea of constitutional restraints and decentralization of power. Though experiments in democracy were sometimes chaotic and short lived among peoples unaccustomed to the perils of political freedom, the nations that had a longer tradition of self government had within their borders a reservoir of well-informed citizens able through the electoral process to bring governments to power which were willing and able to effect political and economic changes designed to alleviate human misery, avert fiscal collapse, and discourage revolutionary movements. The United States, Canada, some of the nations of Central and Northern Europe, and the self-governing countries of the British Commonwealth had a considerable measure of success in achieving those ends, and France, despite a less stable constitutional system, declined to take the Marxist road.

The Rise and Fall of Fascism

Other nations, less steeped in democratic traditions, did not fare so well in their efforts to meet their post-war problems. The Italian monarchy, lacking the strength to control the chaotic politics of that country, let a dictator, Benito Mussolini, come to power in 1922 on the strength of his promises to ward off communism while at the same time making things work. The ideology that he imposed on the people of Italy was known as Fascism from the Italian word "fascismo," derived in turn from the Latin word "fasces," denoting the bundle of rods fastened together with an axe carried by the lictors in ancient Rome.

Originally, the movement had no aims except the Machiavellian goal of the acquisition of power. Just before taking over the government, Mussolini said, "Our program is simple: we wish to govern Italy." As the ideology developed once its advocates were in control of the government, it was opposed both to Marxism and to the democratic liberalism of the Anglo-Saxon and French tradition. It was nationalistic, irrational, authoritarian, militaristic, hierarchical, and contemptuous of the notion of individual rights. "To believe, to obey, to fight" was one of the principal slogans in Fascist Italy. While rejecting the Marxist doctrine of public ownership of the instruments of production and distribution, the Fascists instituted a rigid control of the economy, avoiding stirring up the hostility of landowners and businessmen by protecting their profits and suppressing free trade unions.

In 1933, Germany's attempt at post-war democracy, the fragile Weimar Republic, broke down under a barrage of economic disasters and a skillful appeal to deep-seated passions by Adolf Hitler, a former army corporal who burned with resentment over the treatment accorded Germany by the victorious Allies under the treaty imposed on the Central Powers at Versailles after the First World War. Though this humiliation provided Hitler with a convenient set of grievances to be exploited in his rise to power, he was driven by a much more complex set of motives than the mere desire to redress a wrong. The forces working on him were, as it happened, precisely those which directly or indirectly exercised a powerful influence on a substantial segment of the German people, and he had a remarkable ability to articulate those feelings and bring them to the fore in his followers. If the authority exercised by Mussolini was that of the political chieftan, that of Hitler was, as Jung suggested, the mystical influence of the medicine man.

The instrument for his march to power was the Nationalsozialistische Deutsche Arbeiter Partei (NSDAP). Hitler was its father and nurtured it from its birth in 1919 to the day in 1933 when the ailing President of the Weimar Republic, Marshal Paul Von Hindenburg, appointed him Chancellor. Hindenburg's death a little more than a year later gave Hitler the opportunity to abolish the office of president altogether. He kept the title of chancellor but assumed that of *Reichsführer* as well. From that time until his death in 1945, he was absolute ruler of Germany.

In popular terminology, the name of the party became shortened to "Nazi." The Nazi ideology resembled that of Mussolini's Fascism in its militant nationalism, its aversion to Communism and Western liberalism, and its totalitarian character. Hitler added to the basic doctrine a number of features that would, he thought, made it a more suitable vehicle for the expression of the German spirit. Some of these were drawn from the myths of Wagnerian music-drama and the literary tradition of romanticism, particularly in its darker aspects. The rule of reason was replaced by the reign of feeling. "I think with my blood," Hitler boasted. The conception of blood, in his sense of the term, was central to Nazism. Germans and, to some extent, other persons of "Nordic" or "Aryan" ancestry were, in his eyes the "master race" envisioned by Nietzsche. That Nietzsche would have regarded Hitler's version of his thought as distressingly vulgar is almost certain, but Nazi apologists appropriated it to their own ends in claiming the right of the Nordic superman to go "beyond good and evil" in asserting his will to power.

There were other German writers who exercised a powerful influence on Hitler's thought. Oswald Spengler (1880-1936), the author of a massive work entitled *The Decline of the West,* had marshaled an impressive array of evidences to support his thesis that each "culture" has its own distinctive character and in living out its destiny goes through its springtime, summer, fall, and winter, degenerating at last into a "civilization" and dying under the onslaught of internal disintegration and external assault. Spengler examined three such cultures, the classical, the "Magian" and the "Faustian," the latter being the culture of the West, characterized by dynamic striving. Hitler saw himself as the founder of a new order which would endure for a thousand years.

Every dictator needs a good enemy for purposes of propaganda. Hitler enlarged on this Platonic dictum to point out shrewdly in his *Mein Kampf* that if one is to appeal effectively to the masses, it is best to find some one enemy to whom all the machinations of a variety of opponents can be attributed. He found such an enemy in the Jews. They were held to be responsible for the downfall of Germany in the First World War, for monopolistic capitalism in the West, for Communism in Russia, and, in short, for all the obstacles to the fulfillment of the Nazi vision of a new world order ruled by "the highest human species given by the grace of the Almighty to this earth." The extermination of the hated race and the development of a superior Aryan breed became, in his mind, a necessary step toward world domination. The death camps at Auschwitz and Buchenwald and the indoctrination in fanaticism of the *Hitlerjugend* were, in the dialectic of National Socialism, logical and carefully planned methods of carrying out his program.

Paranoia often makes its nightmares come true. Hitler's success in convincing the German people that they were surrounded by enemies at last so roused the democracies of Europe that the Third Reich became recognized as a greater menace than the Kaiser's government had been a generation earlier. England and France held their fire when Hitler annexed his native Austria, but the invasion of Poland marked the beginning of the Second World War. That invasion had been made possible by a cynical agreement with the Marxist government of the Soviet Union. Germany's violation of that agreement would later contribute to its downfall.

The pact with the Communists and the subsequent assault on a Catholic county, Poland, angered one of the European states that had been friendly to Hitler's government. Spain, between 1936 and 1939, had suffered the trauma of a bloody civil war in the course of which it had come under control of General Francisco Franco Bahamonde, who had established a totalitarian rule along broadly fascist lines. The instrument used in the process was the Falange Espãnola Tradicionalista, a party dedicated to a state-controlled economy characterized as "national-syndicalist." Spain maintained a status of nonbelligerency during the Second World War, though Germany's invasion of Russia in 1941 regained for her enough favor in Franco's eyes for him to send a division of volunteers to fight with German troops in the Ukraine. Efforts by the Falangists to cultivate influence throughout the Hispanic world through the formulation of a "Council of Hispanity" in 1940 had little of the hoped-for effect in Latin America, where only Argentina showed favor to fascist totalitarianism generally. After the War, Spain found itself shunned by most of the countries engaged in the formation of the United Nations. Franco intensified an effort to change his public image that had been begun during the latter stages of the war when the Falangist government was declared to be an "organic democracy." He secured his own survival and that of his regime by showing some adaptability to changing conditions and by promising the ultimate restoration of the monarchy. In 1955, Spain was admitted to the United Nations, and in 1969, Franco named Prince Juan Carlos as the future king. On Franco's death in 1975, Spain became a constitutional monarchy.

Some ten years earlier, Hitler and Mussolini, who had pursued a less cautious course, had died violently in the chaotic days immediately preceding the unconditional surrender of the Axis powers. With the death of Franco and the end of the Spanish dictatorship, fascism ceased to be a live ideological option in Europe. Japan, the Axis ally in the Orient, was not a totalitarian state in the European sense, but an empire with an ambitious military government eager for a dominant position in the Pacific. Its defeat had shifted the balance of military power in that area but left the Emperor on the throne, subject to constitutional restraints imposed by the occupation forces.

The Post-War World

The end of the War provided opportunities for an expansion of the power and influence of the Marxist government of the Soviet Union. Between 1945 and 1949, an East-West split developed in Europe, with the Soviet Union, Bulgaria, Czechoslovakia, Hungary, Poland, Rumania, and the German Democratic Republic in one camp and the countries that looked to the United States for friendship and cooperation in the other. The "iron curtain" of which Winston Churchill spoke in 1946 became a symbol of the ideological differences dividing the nations of the world, a symbol given even more concrete form when East Berlin was cut off from the remainder of the city in 1961 by the erection of the Berlin Wall.

China had been one of the Allied powers during the War and had participated in the formation of the United Nations. Internal disturbances soon forced a crisis in the country, however, and in 1949, the republican government was forced to move to Taiwan (Formosa), some ninety miles off the coast of the mainland. The great land mass of China came under control of the Communist revolutionaries led by Mao Tsetung. Although the exiled Kuomintang in Taiwan claimed to be the only legitimate government of China, the new People's Republic gradually achieved recognition from most of the nations of the world. The United States continued to recognize the government in exile, and in 1950, the People's Republic allied itself with the Communist forces in the Korean War and played a decisive part in forcing a stalemate with Korean and American forces, aided by some units from other countries. Korea was divided north and south, and the stage was set for further confrontations in the Orient between two ideologies having their origins in the West. In 1972 and 1973, however, the United States, on Chinese invitation, began official contacts with the Chinese People's Republic and in 1976 recognized the Communist regime as the sole legal government of China.

A major confrontation in the East occurred in Vietnam, once a French colony and occupied by Japan in the Second World War. France was defeated in an attempt to reestablish control over the country, and it was divided into two parts, with the Communists controlling the north and their opponents the south. The United States ultimately became involved in the enduring war, but was unsuccessful in effecting the survival of the Saigon government in the south, which fell to the northern forces in 1975. All of Vietnam was now committed to the Marxist ideology. Neighboring Laos fell to the Communist Pathet Lao and became a "People's Democratic Republic" in that same year. Cambodia, which had become heavily involved in the Vietnam conflict, was taken over by the revolutionary Khmer Rouge in 1975. The new regime instituted an unreasoning and bloody reign of terror and was, in turn, overthrown by Cambodian rebels and an invading Vietnamese army, which captured the capital, Phnom Penh, in 1979.

By this time, the supposed monolithic unity of the Marxist nations had been shown to be fictitious, and Russia and China were at odds on a number of questions, including the Cambodian civil war, in which Russia backed the Vietnamese-supported forces and China the Khmer Rouge. This lack of Communist solidarity had earlier been made manifest not so much in disagreements between the two largest Marxist countries as in the independent course followed by the government of Yugoslavia, the nationalistic spirit shown by several other Communistic states in their application of Marxist principles, and open, if unsuccessful, rebellions in Hungary and Czechoslovakia, suppressed only by Soviet military power.

In their conviction that their ideology was the wave of the future, though, the leaders of the Marxist world were in agreement. The emerging nations of what has been called the "Third World," many of them newly freed from colonial influence, provided a tempting target for revolutionary activity guided by Marxists. Those countries, widely scattered over the face of the globe, became political and, in some instances, military battlegrounds. The dialectic could not, in the underdeveloped nations, follow the pattern predicted by Marx, who had envisioned revolution as a method by which the instruments of production in a highly developed capitalistic society would become the property of the people collectively. It was now being regarded as an instrument for providing conditions under which backward societies could quickly become industrialized.

Marxist doctrine had one glaring weakness that limited its appeal in countries where religion played an important role in the life of the people. Marx, regarding all religious institutions as instruments of oppression, had seen their eradication as a goal of Communism, and the espousal of atheism had become a sort of test for party membership in the established Marxist States, even though their governments had been obliged to make accommodations with churches that stubbornly declined to wither away. In some of the underdeveloped countries, notably those of Latin America, a substantial number of the clergy of the dominant Roman Catholic Church became convinced that Western capitalism could not serve as an effective instrument for overcoming the adverse political, economic and social effects of years of "colonial exploitation," which they saw as the principal cause of the intractable cycle of poverty afflicting the majority of the people of the region. They began to develop a body of thought known as "liberation theology," based in part on Vatican pronouncements about social justice and in part on economic and political theories that included a free adaptation of certain aspects of Marxist thought. The movement, although eyed with some unease by the Vatican, produced a variety of clerical and lay expressions and became highly influential throughout Central and South America. It also colored the thinking of Roman Catholic and Protestant theologians in the United States, especially those actively concerned with minority problems. Concurrently with these developments, the broader problem of Christian-Marxist dialogue was addressed by a number of thinkers of both persuasions in other parts of the world.

The tendency to interpret the ideological conflicts of the second half of the twentieth century as simply a problem of "East against West" or "Communism verses democracy" did not do justice to the enormous complexity of the concerns embodied in the actual struggles waged around the world to achieve a variety of ethnic, political, and religious ends. Religious and secular questions became inextricably entangled in the process. In Northern Ireland, Christians were divided into hostile Roman Catholic and Protestant camps as a result of the seemingly unsolvable political problems stemming from the division of the country. An intermittent warfare between Israel and the Arab states of the region assumed in many minds the character of a Jewish-Moslem conflict. In Iran and Iraq, hostilities over questions of sovereignty and territory were bound up with the age-old conflict between Sunni and Shiite Moslems. In India, disputes between Hindus and Sikhs resulted in political conflict and widespread bloodshed. These and other similar hostilities were inevitably detrimental to efforts being made by many people to bring about better understanding among the adherents of the different religions of the world.

It is evident that in the twentieth century traditional causes of international conflict—dynastic ambitions, territorial claims, and trade disputes—were being replaced or modified in unusual degree by emotionally charged ideological concerns. The domestic affairs of nations showed something of the same tendency. The very nature of totalitarian societies, of course, required the imposition of efficient indoctrination on their citizens and control of their actions. In countries where individual liberty was more highly valued, ideological commitment was a matter of personal choice. Terms like "conservative" and "liberal" were used to designate constellations of political beliefs and the people who held them, while epithets like "reactionary" and "radical" were often applied to the same beliefs and the same people by their opponents. While a substantial number of citizens of the Western democracies made an effort to evaluate individual issues on their merits, others found it more convenient to accept or reject particular proposals on the basis of whether they were endorsed or opposed by the political parties or other organized groups to which they belonged. In America, as in other countries, the lines between religious and political convictions often were not clearly drawn.

Reflections on the Future

In a world of such ideological complexity, haunted on the one hand by a sense of existential meaninglessness and on the other by fears of atomic destruction and environmental disaster, clarity of thought is perhaps more essential than at any other time in history. It is imperative, of course, that wise decisions be made on the specific issues that will determine whether the human race will destroy everything it has built or whether it will enter a new era of achievement like those which have in the past brilliantly illuminated the human experience. Those decisions, however, can be made only if the basic ways of thinking that underly them are sound. Since the great days of Greece, the cultivation of the sort of discipline that enables human beings to rise above ideological passions and specialized interests and to think clearly and comprehensively about the great questions of meaning and value has been the province of philosophy.

In recent years, however, the fragmenting of the philosophic enterprise has contributed to a loss of much of its traditional synthetic function and, correspondingly, of its public influence. The loss of the influential role it once played in the individual and corporate life of Western men and women is not one that should be contemplated with equanimity, for by the very nature of the organization of learning in the West, philosophy has had the task of interpreting and coordinating the data provided by the special fields of inquiry.

If that synthetic function is to be restored, the "nothing but" ways of looking at the world which have dominated much modern thought must be subjected to rigorous examination. It is by no means self-evident, for instance, that conscious processes are nothing but brain states, that moral insights are nothing but emotional prejudices, or that politics is nothing but the exercise of power. Since the time of Socrates, the most significant advances in human thought have been made in ages in which there was a willingness to question sophisticated orthodoxies and look at the world with some measure of naiveté.

Such an enterprise may not be amiss in an age in which many systems that served our ancestors well seem to have run their course and the theoretical foundations on which Western civilization rests are in danger of dissolution. But the intellectual life of creative ages of the past had another feature that must not be overlooked. In instance after instance, the freshness of vision attained by the best thinkers of such periods was made possible by a rediscovery—or at least a reconsideration—of older modes of thought. When long-buried ideas are brought into play to challenge and modify the dogmas of a given age, the resultant ferment can have a more salutary effect than can be had with unadulterated innovation. A constructively naive look at the world does not proceed from the emptiness of the infant mind, but rather from the sort of child-like attitude which can make use of past and present ideas alike without being dominated by a closed system of inflexible notions.

What does such a procedure entail in our own day? It is unlikely to lead immediately to the creation of towering new metaphysical systems like those of Plato and Hegel. The more modest systems of the future may be regarded more as useful models to enable us better to picture certain aspects of the universe than as strait jackets for thought. With this understanding, we must be prepared to rid ourselves of the aversion to ontology and metaphysics characteristic of much current philosophy, for implicitly those disciplincs provide the assumptions on which we evaluate our experience. A good metaphysic kicked out through the front door will almost invariably be replaced by a bad one sneaked in through the back. We should cultivate a healthy skepticism about all systems that can, in effect, by expressed by the words "Reality is . . . ," followed by a single substantive predicate or a larger but arbitrarily limited set of such predicates. We should especially have a profound distrust of the concealed metaphysical assumptions that enable their proponents to define with absolute assurance what can be known not to exist. A proposition of non-existence is always shaky unless it is a denial of the existence of something that would by its nature entail a logical contradiction. Thus, one can say with certainty, "There are no rectangular circles in this room," but cannot with equal certainty deny the presence of angels. One can, of course, say something like "There is nothing in this room which I recognize as being an angel," but that is simply to make an affirmative statement about my own mental processes. It should be even more evident that statements that angels—or ghosts or leprechauns—do not exist anywhere in the universe must be left to those who have greater faith in their own omniscience than our philosopher of the future ought to have.

A reappraisal of the uses of the word "real" might be useful. If, in its substantive form, "the real," it simply means "everything that is," the term serves little useful purpose. If it is used in a Platonic sense to mean something like "eternal," "unchanging," or "ideal," there are words which better make a distinction which rests on the acceptance of a particular world view. If "real" refers to a quality of a thing as distinguished from the absence of that quality in something imagined, it becomes impossible to attribute any sort of reality to imagined things.

The word "real" may, perhaps, best be used to differentiate between a genuine member of some definable class and something which has some but not all of the definitive characteristics of objects belonging to that class. When the dipsomaniac is told that his pink elephant is not real, his informant ought to mean no more than that it is not an elephant that can be subjected to public examination and pass muster as a genuine "*Elephas Maximus*" or *Loxodonta Africana*. It is, however, a real *hallucinated* elephant, that is to say, an object having four legs, a trunk, and a variety of other perceived elephantine qualities but lacking extension in public space. If it is true that the imagined pachyderm is not Jumbo from the circus, it is equally the case that if Jumbo should wander into the field of vision of our alcoholic friend and initially be mistaken for one of his familiar companions, it might prove to be a serious error to treat him as a real *hallucinated* elephant. "Real", in this more useful sense has no independent significance but rather derives its meaning from its association with another term. It is, then, better employed as an adjective—or in its adverbial form, "really"—than as a noun, "the real" although "reality" may on occasion be useful enough to designate everything that is, or even in popular usage to distinguish certain sorts of experience from others.

A related term that calls for reexamination is "objective." Objectivity is much admired by modern thinkers, and some philosophers have tried to manipulate language in such a way as to make it almost impossible to formulate a healthy skepticism. For instance, one is asked to believe that one can "know" another's pain in the same way that one can know one's own—the contention being based, it seems, on the curious notion that "pain" and "pain behavior" are equivalent terms.

This appears to be a philosophic *cul de sac*. It is true that one, as subject, can think reflexively about oneself as object. Moreover, one can have experiences that one attributes to the presence of other selves and external objects and can assume that other persons have experiences similar to his own, but the egocentric predicament still presents an impregnable defense against rational attack. The assumption that an external world exists must ultimately rest on something more akin to faith than to pure reason.

But faith of that sort can take us a long way when it rests on the best use of faculties on which we have to rely for the sort of decisions we must make when judgment cannot properly be suspended. The necessity of deciding in such cases may well be a primary source for the notion of an objective environment. After all, the distinction between the dream world and what we call the "real" world has not seemed as obvious in some cultures as in our own.

In the last analysis, of course, all experience is subjective. We attribute varying degrees of objectivity to the things we experience on the basis of two characteristics. The first of these may be called, for lack of a better name, "thereness." The other is confirmability by the reports of others.

Now every experience, of course, involves a measure of "thereness." Some experiences force themselves upon us, and others are more subject to voluntary control. Some are sharply defined and stable, whereas others are more amorphous. Some are consistent with the context in which they appear. Others lack such consistency. The degrees of involuntariness, definition, stability, and consistency present in each experience are determinants of the extent to which we initially ascribe objectivity to its content. When the fourth of these characteristics is lacking, we are disposed, even if the other three are richly present, to wonder whether we are victims of illusion, hallucination, or dream. In any case, but especially in those instances in which the data of direct experience are lacking or are marked by imprecision or incongruity, the criterion of confirmability comes into play. Confirmation is ordinarily a subtle process, consisting largely in the sort of clues provided by shared observations and activities, but in doubtful cases, more direct assurance may be sought. "Did you hear that?" is a common question, and in cases which are fortunately rarer, the alcoholic may ask plaintively, "Don't you see that bat coming out of the wall?" The class of things marked by a strong flavor of thereness and a high degree of confirmability constitutes for us the "real world" of popular parlance as opposed to the "imaginary world" of private experience.

The distinction is, of course, a practical one, and there are no absolute guarantees of its metaphysical authenticity. All efforts to gain public verification for one's private perceptions are dependent upon the very private perceptions by which one apprehends the public verification. And, indeed, there are cases which the "thereness" is so overwhelming that sensible persons feel impelled to treat the objects of their experience as having independent existence, even though they may lack confirmation by others who might be expected to have similar observations.

A prime problem for thinking human beings is the determination of the sorts of things to which a reasonably high degree of objectivity should be ascribed. If "thereness" and confirmability were frankly admitted to be the criteria for such ascription it is not unreasonable to suppose that an increasing number of scholars might once again feel at home in areas of investigation from which they have been driven by the spirits of the age.

Those criteria, applied on the one hand to sense experience and on the other to logical and mathematical law are the foundations on which experimental science rests. They are, implicitly, the standards to which the logical positivists appealed in making their distinction between the cognitive and the emotive. One of the most important philosophical tasks for our day must be the decision as to whether they are applicable only to empirical and logically analytical judgments or whether they can legitimately be applied in such a way as to permit significant truth claims of other kinds. A philosophy capable of doing justice to the Western tradition of meaning and value must, it seems, acknowledge that they can be applied in at least three other areas of investigation: the aesthetic, the moral, and the religious.

Judgments made in these fields certainly seem to have a cognitive status not wholly unlike that of empirical and logical propositions. If one says, "The Alba Madonna is a beautiful painting," that statement, contrary to the contention of the emotivists, does not seem to be equivalent to "I like the Alba Madonna." This is true for several reasons.

In the first place, the assertion that the Alba Madonna is beautiful, unlike the observation that one likes it, refers not to oneself, but to the painting as perceived. It has, therefore, a *prima facie* objective character. The two statements are certainly not identical in meaning if, as seems evident, it is possible to say with complete intelligibility, "the Alba Madonna is beautiful, but I don't like it," or conversely, "The Alba Madonna isn't beautiful, but I like it." I may, to be sure, say, "I like it because it is beautiful," but then the specification of that reason turns attention back to an alleged property of the painting as perceived which had as much "thereness" for the perceiver as the flesh tones of the figures on the mathematical properties of the design. The glib aphorism, "Beauty is in the eye of the beholder," raises a host of metaphysical questions, but even if it were held to be true, it would be no more so than to say that "color is in the eye of the beholder" or "tone is in the ear of the auditor" or "geometric axioms are in the brain of the mathematician."

It can, then, reasonably be maintained that the popular modern view, which is by no means limited to logical positivists, is either too skeptical or not skeptical enough. It cannot plausibly be urged that we are obliged to be gullible about sense data while at the same time denying "thereness" to aesthetic properties. Nor is it fair to argue the subjective position on the ground that not all persons perceive the aesthetic properties of the painting. It is equally true that there are those who do not perceive the colors. We do not discredit color on those grounds, nor do we deny objectivity to mathematics because there are aborigines whose system of numbers is limited to "One, two, three, many."

This reflection leads to another of considerable importance. Throughout the history of thought, propositions of an aesthetic nature have been treated not merely as matters of personal taste but as being subject to normative judgement. At this point, the relativist will, of course, insist that the standards of judgement differ from culture to culture and person to person. Two observations may be made in this regard.

The first is that attention to the admitted differences ought not to obscure the similarities that make agreement possible when attention is focused on certain aspects of art or nature which elicit responses involving an aesthetic vocabulary that expresses concepts shared by a variety of cultures. Moreover, our recognition of aesthetic diversity should be accompanied by a recognition of the fact that similar divergences exist in every other field of human experience. Even the most exact of the physical sciences harbor disputes at their more esoteric levels no less divisive than the disagreements among art critics.

Secondly, and perhaps even more significantly, the very possibility of disagreement itself provides a presumption of objectivity. We may *differ* in our subjective attitudes. We do not normally *disagree* about them. If John says, "I like spinach, Susan is not disagreeing with him when she says, "But I don't."She is merely contributing the second part of a conjunctive proposition. She could challenge his statement only by saying, "No you don't," and although propositions of that sort sometimes enliven family arguments, they cannot be based on any direct observation of the state of mind of the person who made the original statement. That state, in other words, is not something thought of as being in the public domain. Clearly a discussion by two critics about a painting or a musical composition is not merely intended as an expression of their psychological differences or as a dispute over their sincerity.

Artistic criticism, however, cannot be practical at all without the assumption that the aesthetic aspects of experience have not only "thereness" but confirmability as well. The purpose of argument about the merits of a particular work of art is to call attention to features of the work which conform or fail to conform to normative standards assumed to be publicly accessible to properly qualified observers.

All the foregoing considerations are similarly applicable to matters of ethics. "Oughtness" in the moral sense cannot successfully be reduced to "isness." A killing cannot be fully described by the most exhaustive cataloguing of the empirically ascertainable qualities of the act—the force of the blow, the trajectory of the knife, the dimensions of the wound and the like. Nor can its ethical implications be reduced to its aesthetic properties. As Augustine pointed out, we are at liberty to admire the skill with which the murderer strikes the fatal blow. The moral quality of an act must be included in an enumeration of its properties and, indeed, belongs to that class of attributes most significant for the formation of personal, political, and legal judgments. Here again, the very fact that disputation is not only possible but inevitable establishes a presumption of the objective character of moral discourse.

Finally, it must be maintained that religious data satisfy the requirements for objectivity. The testimony of prophets, saints, mystics, and ordinary men and women throughout the history of mankind furnish ample evidence of the "thereness" experienced in religious encounters. The existence of religious communities and, just as importantly, the wide areas of agreement concerning the nature of religious experience among members of diverse faiths, testify to its confirmability. An arbitrary rejection of religious claims on the ground that one's personal experiences of the numinous are less than compelling is as little warranted as the refusal of a color blind individual to acknowledge the existence of red and green or the denial by a mathematical ignoramus of the legitimate claim of arithmetic to public acceptance.

These areas of experience provide the materials on which judgments of meaning and value are based in human culture, and the perverse insistence of some influential shapers of modern thought that one, two, or three of them are inauthentic is at least one source of our present ills. To take them seriously does not, of course, automatically underwrite any particular philosophical or theological system, but it does make possible a better understanding of the nature and scope of the data on which any intelligent attempt to understand ourselves, our environment, and the values by which we live must be grounded. That those values are real and enduring is an article of faith that has found frequent and eloquent expression in Western thought since its powerful expression in Sophocles' *Antigone* more than two millenia ago.

> No ordinance of man shall override
> The settled laws of Nature and of God;
> Not written they in pages of a book
> Nor were they framed today or yesterday.
> Whence they are we cannot say, but this we know,
> That they from all eternity have been,
> And through all eternity shall endure.

Index